Cyberlaw

Management and Entrepreneurship

Aspen College Series

Cyberlaw

Management and Entrepreneurship

Margo E. K. Reder
Jonathan J. Darrow
Sean P. Melvin
Kabrina K. Chang

Wolters Kluwer

To contact Customer Service, e-mail customer.service@wolterskluwer.com, call 1-800-234-1660, fax 1-800-901-9075, or mail correspondence to:

Wolters Kluwer
Attn: Order Department
PO Box 990
Frederick, MD 21705

Printed in the United States of America.

1 2 3 4 5 6 7 8 9 0

ISBN 9781454850458

Library of Congress Cataloging-in-Publication Data

Cyberlaw: management and entrepreneurship / Margo E. K. Reder, Jonathan J. Darrow, Sean P. Melvin, Kabrina K. Chang.
    pages cm. — (Aspen college series)
  Includes bibliographical references and index.
  ISBN 978-1-4548-5045-8 (alk. paper)
  1. Internet—Law and legislation—United States. 2. Electronic commerce—Law and legislation—United States. 3. New business enterprises—Management. I. Reder, Margo E. K., author.
  KF390.5.C6C935 2015
  346.7307—dc23
                                    2015022628

About Wolters Kluwer Law & Business

Wolters Kluwer Law & Business is a leading global provider of intelligent information and digital solutions for legal and business professionals in key specialty areas, and respected educational resources for professors and law students. Wolters Kluwer Law & Business connects legal and business professionals as well as those in the education market with timely, specialized authoritative content and information-enabled solutions to support success through productivity, accuracy and mobility.

Serving customers worldwide, Wolters Kluwer Law & Business products include those under the Aspen Publishers, CCH, Kluwer Law International, Loislaw, ftwilliam.com and MediRegs family of products.

CCH products have been a trusted resource since 1913, and are highly regarded resources for legal, securities, antitrust and trade regulation, government contracting, banking, pension, payroll, employment and labor, and healthcare reimbursement and compliance professionals.

Aspen Publishers products provide essential information to attorneys, business professionals and law students. Written by preeminent authorities, the product line offers analytical and practical information in a range of specialty practice areas from securities law and intellectual property to mergers and acquisitions and pension/benefits. Aspen's trusted legal education resources provide professors and students with high-quality, up-to-date and effective resources for successful instruction and study in all areas of the law.

Kluwer Law International products provide the global business community with reliable international legal information in English. Legal practitioners, corporate counsel and business executives around the world rely on Kluwer Law journals, looseleafs, books, and electronic products for comprehensive information in many areas of international legal practice.

Loislaw is a comprehensive online legal research product providing legal content to law firm practitioners of various specializations. Loislaw provides attorneys with the ability to quickly and efficiently find the necessary legal information they need, when and where they need it, by facilitating access to primary law as well as state-specific law, records, forms and treatises.

ftwilliam.com offers employee benefits professionals the highest quality plan documents (retirement, welfare and non-qualified) and government forms (5500/PBGC, 1099 and IRS) software at highly competitive prices.

MediRegs products provide integrated health care compliance content and software solutions for professionals in healthcare, higher education and life sciences, including professionals in accounting, law and consulting.

Wolters Kluwer Law & Business, a division of Wolters Kluwer, is headquartered in New York. Wolters Kluwer is a market-leading global information services company focused on professionals.

Summary of Contents

part one

Business Formation, Business Models, and Business Cycles   1

part two

Intellectual Property: Business Assets in the Information Age   117

part three

Transactional Law: Creating Wealth and Managing Risk   299

part four

Regulatory, Compliance, and Liability Issues 425

Contents

Part I   Business Formation, Business Models, and Business Cycles

Chapter 1   Introduction to Cyberlaw: Management and Entrepreneurship   3

Chapter 2   Inventions, Innovations, and Business Models: Developing and Implementing the Ideas and Technology Fundamental to Startups   23

Chapter 5   Copyright   161

Part III	**Transactional Law: Creating Wealth and Managing Risk**

Chapter 9   **The Employment Relationship**   **365**

Chapter 10   Social Media: Risk and Liability   399

Part IV   Regulatory, Compliance, and Liability Issues

Chapter 11   Dispute Resolution: Jurisdiction, Litigation, and ADR   427

Preface

We are pleased to present a new edition of *Cyberlaw: Management and Entrepreneurship*—the fourth edition overall and the first with Wolters Kluwer—the first, and still leading, text on this subject. Written in response to the Internet's remarkable, unprecedented, and myriad impacts on business law, the text continues to evolve as the Internet has developed into the default platform for new businesses, new business models, and more. This edition hones its focus further, most notably becoming the first text to address business and cyberlaw issues from the perspective of entrepreneurial, Internet-based startups.

The text takes a cohesive approach, addressing business and cyberlaw, entrepreneurship, and management issues in the order in which these challenges arise in typical Internet-based startups. This approach not only creates internal consistency, but also fosters students' appreciation for the connectedness between and among the topics, thus deepening their meaningful comprehension of the subject.

Cyberlaw covers one of today's most dynamic aspects of business: the legal challenges associated with entrepreneurial Internet-based startups. Characterized by high concentrations of intellectual property assets and talented, mobile, and international employees, the situations these Internet-based startups face are typically further complicated by being founded on difficult to value inventions for which even assigning ownership can be a challenge. These businesses are built out before a formalized entity is created or ownership clearly defined. They may make money from the start, or they may never make money—yet they may still have billion-dollar valuations . . . .

The text moves on from these initial issues to cover the topics that arise as these startups continue to build out. The authors address all the complex issues facing these Internet-based startups as they become operational, including entity formation, financing, contracts and licensing, human resource and employment, social media use, dispute resolution, regulatory and compliance, data privacy and management, and finally data security and crime.

By taking this lifecycle approach, *Cyberlaw* assures that students receive broad exposure to every business law topic encountered by typical startups. Achieving this familiarity enables students to create a platform from which they can develop further competencies in cyberbusiness and entrepreneurship and the means with which to effectively translate and adapt their academic and theoretical experience to the needs of their professional work environments.

Additional key features complementing the text's notable approach and substantive content include international sections or cases, an ethical component, and a Managers' Checklist in each chapter. Another core feature is a reference in each chapter to a thread case, focused on Twitter's management of the main substantive topic or issue addressed in the chapter. This thread case makes the topic vivid for students, enhancing their appreciation and understanding of how the individual issues relate to startups and how the topics interrelate. The focus on companies of interest to students makes the material interesting, current, and relatable. The text is further augmented with PowerPoint slides for use in the classroom that provide a complementary narrative to the text material. Also available is an Instructors' Manual, containing materials the authors have found useful in presenting the materials effectively.

Cyberlaw: Management and Entrepreneurship is an ideal choice for Business Law electives focusing on the Internet and the web in relation to startups and entrepreneurship. The comprehensive coverage, cohesive format, and many enriching features ensures this text will continue to be the leading and foundational text for business cyberlaw and entrepreneurship electives. We welcome instructors and students to this text and to the fascinating, engaging, and challenging material within.

—Margo E. K. Reder, Jonathan J. Darrow, Sean P. Melvin, and Kabrina K. Chang

Acknowledgments

I am super excited that this project came together. This edition was only made possible because David Herzig took a bet on us. Susan Boulanger helped guide the process, and for this I am immensely grateful. Such a work can only be created through the dedication of wonderful colleagues, and thanks to my co-authors Jon, Sean, and Kabrina for signing on and producing this marvelous work. Boston College has consistently supported this work. Through the visionary efforts of then-Department Chair, Prof. Christine Neylon O'Brien, we developed a curriculum for this material, which has yielded incredible results. Department Chair Prof. Stephanie M. Greene continued the support and, in fact, expanded on this original mandate, all while demonstrating support and vital leadership. Thank you all. **—M.E.K.R.**

I gratefully acknowledge Avis Bohlen, Stefan Gruber, and Beth Newton of Harvard Law School for their able research assistance; Bill Slawski for generously sharing his knowledge of Google's patents; and the staff of the Harvard Law Library, especially Mindy Kent, for assistance in obtaining difficult-to-find research materials. The intellectual property chapters substantially benefitted and were transformed thanks to the insightful comments and suggestions of Dean P. Alderucci, Patrick J. Myers, Michael Risch, Ethan Schiffres, and Kenneth R. Shurtz. I am especially indebted to Stephen M. Darrow, who provided detailed comments for all four intellectual property chapters, and to Stephen D. Lichtenstein and Gerald R. Ferrera whose mentorship and support over the years has enabled me to develop as a legal writer. Finally, my contribution to this text would not have occurred at all if not for Christine Neylon O'Brien, who first inspired me to begin a career in law teaching and scholarship. **—J.J.D.**

Thanks are owed to Sean J. Melvin for his case research work on this book. **—S.P.M.**

Many thanks to Research Assistant Extraordinaire Julia Molinaro for her hard work, creative and intelligent research, and ability to read my mind. **—K.K.C.**

Margo E. K. Reder is a Lecturer in Law and Researcher at Boston College, Carroll School of Management, currently on leave working in the private industry. The recipient of numerous honors and awards for excellence in research and writing, Professor Reder teaches undergraduates, as well as electives in the M.B.A. program covering e-commerce, entrepreneurship, technology, and intellectual property. Professor Reder consults with startups and judges Business Law competitions. A top-ranked author, Professor Reder has co-authored five previous texts and over 25 law review articles and is a member of the Academy of Legal Studies in Business. As a law student, Professor Reder received top honors and was a member of the Board of Editors. Professor Reder is admitted to practice in the Commonwealth of Massachusetts, United States District Court for the District of Massachusetts, the United States Court of Appeals for the First Circuit, and the United States Supreme Court.

Dr. Jonathan J. Darrow recently completed a postdoctoral fellowship in the Program on Regulation, Therapeutics, and Law (PORTAL) at Harvard Medical School/Brigham & Women's Hospital. He holds a BS in biological sciences from Cornell, a JD from Duke, an MBA from Boston College, and an SJD (a dissertation-based doctorate, the law discipline's highest degree) from Harvard, where he also completed the LLM program. After admission to the bar, Dr. Darrow practiced law in the Silicon Valley offices of Cooley Godward and later worked on patent litigation matters at Wiley Rein & Fielding in Washington, DC. He is admitted to practice before the U.S. Patent & Trademark Office, has served on the business law faculties of Boston College, Plymouth State, and Bentley, has clerked for the Honorable Evan J. Wallach of the U.S. Court of Appeals for the Federal Circuit, and has testified before the Massachusetts legislature on the ownership of email. His scholarship on technology and intellectual property has appeared in numerous publications, including the *New England Journal of Medicine,* the *Stanford Technology Law Review,* the *Minnesota Law Review,* and the *Harvard Journal of Law & Technology,* among many others. He is a co-author of two major textbooks: *Cyberlaw: Text and Cases* (the predecessor to this text) and *The Legal and Ethical Environment of Business.* Dr. Darrow previously explored the relationship between innovation policy and global health during stints at both the World Trade Organization and World Health Organization in Geneva, Switzerland.

Sean P. Melvin is an associate professor of business law at Elizabethtown College (PA), where he served as department chair for eight years, won the Delta Mu

Delta Outstanding Teacher of the Year award, and received several Faculty Merit awards for teaching and scholarship. Before his academic career, Professor Melvin was a corporate lawyer in a large Philadelphia-based law firm and went on to become vice president and general counsel at a publicly traded technology company. He is the author of seven books (including four textbooks), has contributed scholarly and professional articles and case studies to dozens of publications, and is a member of the Academy of Legal Studies in Business (ALSB). His article "Case Study of a Coffee War" was selected as Best International Case Study at the eighty-sixth annual ALSB conference.

Kabrina Krebel Chang is a Clinical Associate Professor of Law and Ethics at Boston University's School of Management, where she has received numerous awards for teaching and service to the undergraduate program. Professor Chang teaches business ethics, business law, and employment law in the undergraduate program and business law in the MBA program. Her research focuses primarily on employment matters, looking at legal off-duty conduct, in particular, participation in social media, and how that impacts employment and management decisions. She is the author of several articles on the management implications of legal off-duty conduct, including participation in social media and use of medical marijuana, and, most recently, on a business's obligations toward victims of domestic abuse. Before her academic career, Professor Chang was a trial lawyer in private practice.

Cyberlaw

Management and Entrepreneurship

Part one

Business Formation, Business Models, and Business Cycles

With the development of the Internet . . . we are in the middle of the most transforming technological event since the capture of fire . . . .
—**John Perry Barlow, co-founder Electronic Frontier Foundation; retired rancher and Grateful Dead lyricist**

Introduction to Cyberlaw

Management and Entrepreneurship

Learning Outcomes

After you have read this chapter, you should be able to:

● Understand the history of the Internet and the web, which are different technologies, and gain an appreciation for the cooperation, collaboration and vision it took to build out this network, and how uniform, patent-free standards are key to this universal accessibility.

● Understand how the Internet and web transcend geographic and political boundaries, and why this matters to businesses.

● Understand how the current legal and regulatory environment applies to physical businesses, and therefore is of limited applicability to new businesses and models, which often have to operate with little guidance.

● Understand how each chapter presents the historical and legal background of each topic and establishes its relevance to entrepreneurial networked startups.

Overview

This text covers business, law and technology, and all topics within this discipline as they apply to managing entrepreneurial startups. The authors present the material in parallel progression to the timing that information age entrepreneurial startups need to address these challenges. Each topic is discovered and mastered through the presentation of current cases, laws, and text readings and practical assignments. We start with the technology that made such businesses possible—the Internet and web, and then the innovations and inventions that have been built out on those platforms. We then turn to business formation models, management, and exit strategies. We next cover a unit entirely devoted to the main business assets of new economy businesses: intellectual property. The four chapters covering trademarks, copyrights, patents and trade secrets, explore the cases, laws and strategies involved in protecting as well as leveraging these increasingly important business assets. We next cover a unit on the operational and transactional challenges of startup businesses, including contracts and licensing, employment, jurisdiction and dispute resolution. The final unit concerns regulatory and compliance issues, including data management and privacy, and end with data security and crime, all topics that matter ever more for businesses. The text, now in its fourth edition, enables students to recognize the impact of the Internet and web, and further, how to manage business transactions in a highly uncertain and dynamic legal environment.

In this chapter students read about the Internet and web, how these technologies were imagined and built out, and then read short excerpts of representative topics and cases from each of the chapters as a means to quickly explore the text and course. At the conclusion of this chapter students will become acquainted with this fascinating intersection of technology, business and law, and understand why this subject matter is relevant and useful in the legal environment of business and especially for startups, how this area of law is currently developing and why this matters.

Overview of the Internet and World Wide Web

It is difficult to overstate the impact of the **Internet** and **World Wide Web** on our lives—everything from ways of transacting business, to our culture and even our friendships. As a reference point, try to guess how many times—just today—you have already been online? This is how we: contact friends, find restaurants, review products, get music, order tickets, find jobs, check the weather, our calendar, and navigate to the next event. Everything, it seems, is mediated through these technologies. Every service, production, application is Internet-enabled. We live in an era of pervasive and embedded computing, and it provides a seamless interface between our personal, work and in-between interactions.

As with all inventions the knowledge and skills are cumulative, the stage having been set with previous inventions such as the telegraph, telephone, radio and computer. Other inventions facilitated these breakthrough technologies including: digitization, processing chips and compression technology. The Internet and web combine to represent a revolutionary communications system capable of global reach and instantaneous distribution, thereby fostering collaboration, communication and interaction without regard to cost, time or space. This stunning development inverts traditional paradigms of power and modes of control with regard to content. Suddenly each of us has the publishing power of a national newspaper or broadcast network. The Internet's open architecture, model of self-governance, and its lack of alignment with any political entity, combine to make it possibly the most democratic platform ever for communication.

History of the Internet

Starting in the 1950s, governments and businesses identified the need to process large quantities of data, then done manually with rudimentary analog calculators, one task at a time. Researchers developed supercomputers for such work and added remote connection capabilities to enable time-sharing. By 1958, the then Soviet Union's satellite launch further motivated the United States to close the technology achievement gap that existed with its Cold War rival. The U.S. established the **Advanced Research Projects Agency (ARPA)** within the Department of Defense. It was tasked with formulating and executing advanced R&D projects to capitalize on the country's military potential as a means to promote national security. One of the ARPA team members, M.I.T. Professor J.C.R. Licklider, envisioned a way to solve research problems and described how a computer could be like an automated library with a common database that users could simultaneously access. He imagined that a large number of distributed computers connected to a network would be a more powerful resource than any one computer could ever be, and called this conception the "galactic network."

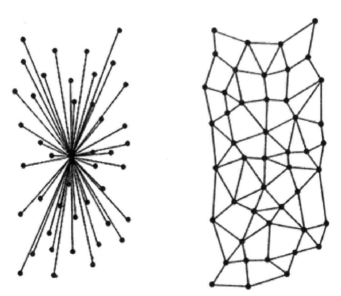

These diagrams represent centralized (left) and distributed (right) communications networks, as conceptualized by Paul Baran, a researcher at RAND Corporation.

As this concept was built out by ARPA, which then became known as **DARPA (Defense Advanced Research Projects Agency)**, a number of design options existed. To effectively address concerns of vulnerability, along with command and control problems associated with centralized assets, the team identified the need for a survivable network. Paul Baran, then working for DARPA was tasked with creating the technical underpinnings for a distributed communications system that could survive an attack and therefore be less vulnerable to disruption. For this, he articulated a concept of parallelism in a network of nodes in which data could travel along any path, and to the extent one part of the network was down, data could travel along another path. This mesh network without a centralized hub therefore achieved redundancy and survivability. This design structure was more robust than either a centralized or completely decentralized network structure. Another design feature of the Internet too is the packet-switching of data. In this method of transmission, data is grouped into optimized blocks, sorted into efficient paths, and then reassembled at the end point.

The three major organizations working in this area of communications and computers—DARPA; the National Physical Laboratory in Britain, and **RAND Corporation** (Research and Development Corporation, a nonprofit R&D facility benefitting U.S. defense forces)—joined together in 1967 to create common standards for this proposed network of computers. They sent out Request for Proposals seeking help on building the first network, called the ARPANET. By 1969, the earliest iteration of the Internet as we know it was up and running, though its uses were more academic than military. The original network consisted of four nodes connecting computers at four locations: U.C.L.A., U.C.-Santa Barbara, Stanford Research Institute and the University of Utah. Soon thereafter, computers at M.I.T., Harvard, Systems Development Corporation, and the offices of DARPA contractor Bolt, Baranek and Newman were joined to the ARPANET.

Coordinating the build-out of this network required collaboration and, most fundamentally, open standards. Proprietary technology was rejected as antithetical to an open royalty-free platform. This open standard of transmission and global addressing protocols ensure that every computer linked into the network recognizes and operates with the same technical standards and therefore complete functionality, no matter the hardware manufacturer, no matter the country. This any-to-any connectivity is a defining feature of the Internet. To coordinate this network across so many research universities and countries, participants developed a Network Working Group along with a protocol for submitting comments on ideas, problems and solutions. Starting with the first **Request for Comment** in 1969, the network is governed by this culture of open governance and common standards.

While this describes the forerunner to the Internet, it is notable that there were a number of Internet-like networks early on that separately co-existed. In 1973, Vinton Cerf and Robert Kahn addressed this lack of interoperability and envisioned a way for all computers to interact with every computer network. Towards this end, while working at DARPA, they collaborated on developing a common transmission standard (TCP/IP). By 1974, in Request for Comment 675, this transmission standard was recommended for all computer networks and so eventually each network agreed to follow this common protocol and joined to form what we now know as the Internet. They articulated the specifications that allow for universal end-to-end connectivity, directing how digital communications are packeted, transmitted, routed and received.

With a universal set of rules for exchanging digital information, the conventions were in place that set the stage for the modern Internet. The Internet was essentially "turned on" in 1973, and starting in 1988, the Internet was expanded beyond elite academic, scientific, engineering and government uses, paving the way for personal and commercial uses of this network. With just two pieces of hardware, a computing device, and a modem to connect to the network, each of us is now a world citizen. Since its inception, we have witnessed a million-fold scaling of this technology without it completely collapsing, a testament to the many founders of the Internet, who made it able to withstand myriad attacks.

Development of the World Wide Web

Though many consider the Internet and the web to be the same, they are two separate inventions. The web, in fact, may be the original killer app of the Internet. The web uses the Internet's platform and mechanics to communicate between computers. **Tim Berners-Lee**, then a researcher at the **European Organization for Nuclear Research (CERN)** recognized that the developing Internet featured dazzling amounts of information, but no easy method of retrieval. The idea behind his invention is that each resource needs an independent addressing system and once found, users should be able to go in any direction between that resource and others linked to it as they research. As users access one resource, they ought to be able to access others that are referenced in the original, and thereby go resource-to-resource, rather than go back to the original starting point each time before accessing subsequent resources. And strikingly, Mr. Berners-Lee insisted that the system be royalty-free, because fees for each click would clearly inhibit large-scale research. Mr. Berners-Lee created the call and response system, known as **HTTP (hypertext transfer protocol)**; the software coding for creating links, known as **HTML (hypertext markup language)**, the domain addressing system (the .com, the .edu, for example), the resource addressing system known as **URLs (uniform resource locators)**, all to work with browsers (the navigational tool), and servers (that serve the response to requests for resources).

The fact that the Internet and the web are open platforms and royalty-free, available for all software applications, and run on any hardware in any country, has had an inestimable impact on their development. This has yielded tremendous benefits for each of us. In order to sense the importance of this open access, royalty-free design, ask yourself a few questions: first, what if you had one Internet for work, and then another for shopping, and still a different one for travel, but none accessible except from one manufacturer's computer? Second, what if you were in a different country and were unable to access the U.S. Internet? Third, what if you had to pay even a nominal amount every time you clicked on a link (a royalty payment to Mr. Berners-Lee—imagine the effects for him!), and for us and how it would radically change the dissemination of information? Fourth, how would you even book a plane ticket? and more. . . .

The Interaction of Technology, Business, and Law

The effect of these technologies is nothing short of an information revolution where there is now almost universal access to both free information and free tools to disseminate information—the product of an open, transparent deliberation and collaboration. The level of connectivity and interactivity is revolutionary. The Internet and World Wide Web each have academic pedigrees in which the values of open functionality, collaboration and accessibility trumped the values of profit-taking, privacy, security or control.

The range of information now freely and easily accessible worldwide has made it possible to update old business models as well as new and different business models. For example, while we shopped exclusively at physical stores before the Internet, we can now shop in the physical stores, or through their own sites, or even reach their sites through consolidating sites such as Amazon or Wayfair. And businesses now can exist only in, and because of, the Internet. Consider Wiki-pedia for a moment. It is a not-for-profit entity with just under 100 employees, and a cadre of motivated, interested volunteer contributors who work together but do not know each other. Even as they collaborate, they work asynchronously and oftentimes anonymously. Wikipedia is an iconic 'only-because-of the-Internet company,' and it is not hyperbole to state that its effect on the entire world is astounding.

This text focuses on the cycle that managers must prepare for: the development of technology, business adoption and diffusion of the technology and the inevitable subsequent legal issues and challenges. Technology and business move quicker than the law. Here are two examples of legal responses to new Internet-enabled technologies. First, technology now allows users to share music files. Businesses are formed to leverage this technology. It all seems to be an amazing, fun and exciting time until only later on, when legal questions arise with respect to whether these users and businesses are possibly liable for copyright infringement. And as it turns out, the short answer is 'yes,' there is a law covering this type of copyright infringement, though there are a number of nuances to the facts. For example, in general sites are not liable, but users may be. Sites have started using behavioral advertising, generated by monitoring and measuring user inter-actions with their site. They use data analytics to evaluate the information gath-ered as a means to increase the effectiveness of the user experience and correspondingly, their revenue. Again, later on, after sites began this practice, users objected, and questions arose with respect to whether this was legal. As it turns out, the response is not so involved because for the most part, there is no law covering this practice. The federal government has taken a 'light-touch,' 'wait-and-see' approach in this area of data privacy, relying instead on industry self-regulation and market-based solutions. But it gets better: state laws are more protective of users. Such practices may violate a state's law, and further, such uses surely violate the E.U. Data Privacy legal scheme.

These cases beg the question of how businesses are to make decisions and viably operate concerning the legality of many of their new business practices, and thus the legal status of their operations is unclear and untested. Operating in this legal vacuum means moving first and answering questions and challenges later. The legal environment for Internet-related issues is just maturing, and precedent is finally being established.

The importance of the U.S. system of laws on business and technology applications made possible by the Internet and web is likewise unclear. With its peer-to-peer architecture, distributed nodes and no central point of control, no one can 'turn off' the Internet. Its structure, as it turns out, is anathema to any one government or organization's desire to control or manage it. Some countries have attempted to control political speech on the Internet; still other countries have tried to control gambling. The Internet resists such control precisely because of its open architecture and unique governance structure.

Sample Case Studies

Chapter 2: Inventions, Innovations, and Business Models

In this chapter we cover topics of high concern to start-ups—the people who start the startups—and all the associated questions: is it an innovation? Or an invention? Is there anything to patent or copyright or trademark? Should it be kept as a trade secret? What are the processes and technologies needed and who owns those? Do they need to buy that company too? Who is an owner of the startup? Who is a co-founder?

Typical Chapter 2 Challenge. Snapchat, the 'it' startup of the moment, is a photo and video messaging app started by Evan Spiegel and Bobby Murphy for one of Spiegel's classes at Stanford University where he was a design major. The point of this app is to share a fun moment with friends that disappears. Quite the opposite of social media juggernauts Facebook and Twitter in which nothing disappears and users are left to manage, or lose control of their ability to erase, the past, Snapchat is meant to put the fun back in communicating through fleeting, ephemeral content that automatically disappears after 10 seconds. Frank Reginald Brown IV claims to have invented the idea for disappearing messages, designing the logo and thinking of the app's original name, "Picaboo." They changed the name from that to Future Freshmen, to Toyopa group, then to Snapchat.

Brown asserts that he approached Spiegel and they agreed to work together. They needed to find someone to write the code and they found Murphy. Murphy and Spiegel worked on the technical side of the project, and Brown was to work on the marketing and administrative side. Meanwhile, he started paperwork on filing a patent for the software. Brown claims there was a falling out and the other two locked him out by changing the passwords to the code and site. Spiegel now claims 60 percent of the company and Murphy owns the remaining 40 percent.

Snapchat has not earned any income yet, and yet reportedly turned down a $3 billion offer to purchase from Facebook, as well as a $4 billion offer from Google.

Questions:

If Brown's allegations are true, that he had the original idea—and nothing more—should he be considered a co-founder? Should he be cut a share of the ownership? How can a business be worth so much if it does not earn any money? Is this a typical scenario? Does Stanford possibly have an ownership interest in this company since it was founded during their undergraduate education? How can parties better protect present and future interests?

Chapter 3: Forming, Financing, and Managing a New Venture

In this chapter we cover topics related to financing startups such as debt and equity, dilution of ownership, valuation challenges, change in control, exit and dissolution of the business. Further, this chapter covers creating a sustainable business model, forming a business entity, officers and directors, fiduciary duties owed to the business and shareholder rights. The range of startups and new business models made possible by the Internet are so varied and abundant, and so this material is particularly timely.

Typical Chapter 3 Challenge. Currently the Securities and Exchange Commission has developed proposed rules that would allow businesses to raise capital through crowdfunded offerings. This was made possible by the JOBS Act (Jumpstart Our Business Startups Act, signed into law April 2012), allowing businesses to raise up to $1 million annually through crowdfunded sources. There are investing limits based on investors' reported annual incomes or net worth. Transactions are supposed to be conducted through registered brokers, or a new entity called a funding portal.

Questions:

How does this new funding method increase the possibility of success for the startup? Identify some risks for the businesses in agreeing to take this money.

Chapter 4: Trademarks

In this chapter we cover the topics of trademarks, trademark laws, including discussion of domain names, trade dress, keywords, aspects of packaging and design, and more. Branding and brand management have become increasingly important since users rely much more on Internet search and keywords to identify desired goods and services.

Typical Chapter 4 Challenge. Apple pioneered the co-development model with its App Store, created in 2008, a year and a half after the introduction of the first iPhone, a device that was equal parts phone and computer. With its substantial operating system and just over a dozen built-in apps, it was the platform for the mobile revolution. Apple already had the iTunes checkout system to build from and so Apple created a first—and branded it the "App Store." The App Store has been phenomenally successful, and since then a number of competitors launched similar services. Ominously, they have used the same trade name: "app store." Apple applied for a trademark on the term "App Store," which was tentatively approved in 2011. During this time, the term "app" became a popular buzzword.

Apple asserts that Amazon's 2011 launch of its own marketplace for the Android software market and calling it "Appstore" infringed rights in Apple's trademark "app store." Amazon countered that the term 'app store' had become so generic that using it would not mislead customers.

Questions:

If you were developing a type of app store for your devices, what would you name it? What if anything did Apple do wrong? Do you think Amazon's naming strategy was ethical? How should Apple respond to Amazon's challenge?

Chapter 5: Copyright

In this chapter we cover the topics of copyrights and copyright laws, including the broad scope of copyright, the bundle of exclusive rights, infringement, as well as limitations on copyrights and especially the fair use defense. The Digital Millennium Copyright Act is covered as well, with focus on the anti-circumvention and safe harbor sections. Managing copyrighted content is one of the most challenging tasks in this practice area due to the ubiquity of sharing content on the Internet.

Typical Chapter 5 Challenge. A group of music publishers that own the music and lyrics of many popular songs, including hits by Lady Gaga, Kanye West, Britney Spears and others, are being covered and featured online. Among the most popular videos on YouTube are cover versions of songs, often by amateurs or semi-professionals who have built an online following. The publisher-copyright owners are upset, asserting that without a proper license from them, these videos infringe the publishers' copyrights, and further, they are not paying publishers and songwriters the royalties earned from ad revenue.

Questions:

Should the music publishers file suit against the actual cover artists? Or just YouTube? Articulate how it is that the original artists actually benefit from these cover artists. Is there some way to better align the interests of YouTube, the cover artists, and the music publishers? How can YouTube avoid this legal issue in the future?

Chapter 6: Patents

In this chapter we cover the topics of patents and patent laws, including discussion of the qualifications for a patent, the bundle of exclusive rights, software patents, design patents, non-practicing entities (also pejoratively called trolls), patenting challenges and strategies, as well as the Bayh-Dole Act incenting commercialization of federally-funded inventions.

Typical Chapter 6 Challenge. U.S. patent 5,412,730 (the '730 patent) was filed in 1992, and in 1995 it was granted to inventor Michael Jones. Thereafter, he assigned the patent to his employer. At a later point in time, TQP Development purchased this patent. TQP did not invent this technology and has earned over $45 million in licensing fees from this one patent. TQP asserts that the patent covers the common Internet encryption security system used by retailers like Newegg. Newegg was using a version of this patent without a license from TQP, so TQP filed suit. Newegg defended the charges of infringement asserting that the patent was not valid, that everything about it had already been anticipated, so that the patent should not have been issued in the first place. A top cryptographer provided additional testimony supporting this point. The Eastern District Court of Texas ruled in favor of TQP, a jurisdiction that has an astonishing win rate for patent holders. Damages are set at $2.3 million. TQP has similar lawsuits pending against Google, LinkedIn, and Sony.

Questions:

How can one jurisdiction in Texas become the epicenter for plaintiffs' patent lawsuits? Should Newegg appeal the jury's decision? How do companies quantify this litigation risk? If Newegg was right, that the patent was wrongly issued because the software was not a new invention, how could it have been patented? How can companies plan for these issues, and defend against such patent claims? Do you think it matters that TQP was asserting rights in this patent when it was not even the inventor?

Chapter 7: Trade Secrets

In this chapter we cover the topics of secret business information that yields a competitive advantage, including discussion of the qualifications of a trade secret. We cover state and federal trade secret laws, as well as the steps businesses take to maintain secrecy, including operational and technological measures and agreements with employees to maintain secrecy. Trade secrets are ever more valuable as patenting is not always possible or desirable, and so maintenance of secrets is critical in this era of increased job mobility.

Typical Chapter 7 Challenge. In one recent trade secret case, an executive employee departed his company to take a job with a similar type of company. He was one of only seven people who were privy to the trade secret, which gave this company a huge competitive edge. His old company filed a request for an injunction against him starting a new job at a competitor, and the company won as the judge agreed that the employee would inevitably disclose the trade secret in the course of employment at the new job. He gave up his old job, but then he lost the new opportunity. The law in this practice area is governed by state law, and not every state recognizes this theory of inevitable disclosure.

Questions:

This is an incredibly bad outcome for this employee. Where can he possibly use the skillset he's developed over his career? This case makes us ask: what is it we may take from a job as we depart? As between the employer and the employee, which party is favored in states that recognize this theory? Do you think this rule incents innovation? Do you think this rule has an effect on employee salaries?

Chapter 8: Contracts and Licensing

In this chapter we cover a range of contracts as they represent the means by which deals are executed, assets are leveraged, and wealth is created. Agreements covered in this chapter include formation, performance and discharge issues, partnering agreements with other businesses (such as supply chain, and materials and technology transfer agreements), and with users (such as Apple's software development program). Furthermore, since courts construe licenses for the use of goods and services to be contracts, we address in this chapter site and software agreements, along with a range of software licenses, such as for proprietary software, open source software, as well as for free and open source software.

Typical Chapter 8 Challenge. In a recent case, a couple decided to purchase mobile phones through AT&T. The advertisement they relied on provided that customers were to receive free phones and then they had to agree to a two-year phone plan. AT&T gave them a written agreement, plus made it available online. AT&T's agreement stated they had a right to unilaterally change the terms of the agreement at any time and without notice to users. After the users signed up for the deal, AT&T charged to their first bill sales taxes of $30.22 for each phone that was advertised as free. The family filed suit and AT&T argued that in the agreement, the family agreed not to sue, and to arbitrate the dispute instead. Further, that they were not allowed to join in one large class action lawsuit against the company; instead each person injured had to litigate the same issue on their own. AT&T lost in California; and it won in a Supreme Court 5-4 decision.

Questions:

We "agree'" to such terms all day long, but what is the effect of the Supreme Court's decision on businesses? On users? Try to articulate why California favored the users, and what its rationale could be.

Chapter 9: The Employment Relationship in the Internet and Technology Sectors

In this chapter we cover the relevant employment issues in the Internet and tech sectors, in which human capital is the star and the talent economy is borderless. Issues are addressed from pre-employment screening, to during and after the term of employment, as well as the duties employees and employers owe to each other. Employment status is a salient issue in many startups and discussion includes internships, independent contractors, temps and permatemps. Ownership of creative works is also covered as software and other business assets can potentially be owned by the business or by the worker. Third-party labor helps startups grow faster and so off-shoring, outsourcing and foreign workers with visa issues are covered as well. Finally the agreements between businesses and workers, such as invention assignment, non-compete, equity stock ownership plans, and so forth, are covered.

Typical Chapter 9 Challenge. During the recent tech boom, Apple, Google, Intel, Adobe and other businesses had agreements to not hire each other's employees. For example, here is one email from Apple. "Eric [Schmidt, of Google] I am told that Google's new cell phone software group is relentlessly recruiting in our [business]. If this is indeed true, can you put a stop to it? Thanks, Steve [Jobs]." A document from Adobe allegedly shows the company warning not to recruit workers from Apple, Bell Canada, EMC, SAP, and others.

Questions:

How does this impact the hiring environment? How does this impact salaries? Recruiters? Can you articulate any circumstance in which some restraints would be legitimate?

Chapter 10: Social Media and Speech

Entirely new to this edition is a chapter devoted to social media and speech. In this chapter we cover a range of social media topics that impact businesses such as discrimination in hiring, liability for employees' posts, employees' posts that negatively impact the internal work environment, posts by workers in highly regulated industries such as the financial, or healthcare sectors, allegations of false advertising, data privacy violations, IP infringement, defamation, and more.

Typical Chapter 10 Challenge. There have been a number of instances in which individuals tweet or post about work and non-work issues. Yet, because the Internet and social media have become the go-to place for sharing, the reaction to controversial postings means that just one post by one person can go viral in just hours. Cases are currently being decided on whether these posts should cost employees their jobs.

For example, recently the InterActiveCorp Communications Director tweeted this: "Going to Africa. Hope I don't get AIDS. Just kidding. I'm white!" The response came quickly. Millions soon attacked her with hatred, threatening to rape, shoot, kill and torture her. They found her Facebook and Instagram accounts and began threatening the same perils to those whose photos she posted as friends and family. The incident became a trending topic on Twitter and a large forum thread on Reddit. Within twelve hours she was fired from her job, as soon as she landed in Africa.

Questions:

How do businesses proactively avoid such risks? What about the other posters? Should they lose their jobs too?

Chapter 11: Dispute Resolution: Jurisdiction, Litigation, and ADR

In this chapter we cover topics related to resolution of legal claims through litigation or ADR, and concerns on managing these risks. Legal exposure has grown exponentially since the Internet is ubiquitous and transcends geopolitical boundaries, yet each jurisdiction retains sovereignty over matters arising within its territory. Therefore, where the case is heard and which country's law to apply becomes more important than ever. These cases expose the tangle of values that each country expresses.

Typical Chapter 11 Challenge. In one recent case, a French Twitter account holder in France tweeted about some matter that, as it turns out, violated that country's hate speech laws, a criminal offense. The tweet did not violate U.S. law. Twitter's Terms of Service provides that any legal action related to the business is "governed by the laws of the State of California without regard to or application of its conflict of law provision or your state or country of residence. . . . All claims . . . will be brought solely in the federal or state courts located in . . . California . . ." The French prosecutor issued an Order requiring information about the identity of the posters. Twitter had to respond to this French Order.

Questions:

What should Twitter do?

Chapter 12: Government Regulation

In this chapter we cover topics of related to regulation of the Internet, as well as new business models and practices that have developed for which there is no precedent and therefore no regulatory scheme. As to the Internet regulation, we cover topics related to net neutrality, network, spectrum management, data surveillance and tower dumps, states' taxation of online transactions, businesses' movement of IP to low-tax jurisdictions. New issues that have emerged as businesses' practices of making 'in-app' purchases easy and so, for example, children have bought millions of dollars of goods and services online without authorization, and questions of whether governments should regulate this or just let the user and business sort it out. Another example of an emerging sector is the shared economy in which peer-to-peer transactions take place, such as when users arrange for transportation using the Lyft ridesharing app, or when users book accommodations through Airbnb. Shared economy businesses lead to a more efficient market and pose especially vexing issues because there is no regulatory scheme, and such services seem great. That is, until they aren't. The question arises now whether local, state or federal legislators should develop regulations for this nascent sharing economy, or adopt a "light-touch," "wait-and-see" approach.

Typical Chapter 12 Challenge. Uber is just one of a number of ridesharing apps that let smartphone users summon a taxi or car service. Drivers likewise have the app, and the software connects the driver with the passenger with the ride priced by distance plus time. Users rave about this service. Uber is strictly a software app, and the business does not employ or supervise the drivers, nor does Uber own the vehicles. There are minimal requirements to be a driver. As such, there are no taxi medallions, no training, etc.; the service entirely evades regulatory schemes in every city. At this time, traditional taxi services are challenging such startups contending that they are illegal. Cities have mixed reactions. One city has proposed rules forbidding car services from using a GPS device as a meter. Another rule proposes to forbid drivers from accepting rides made less than 30 minutes in advance. Uber contends that such proposals are meant to shut them down and to impede innovation.

Questions:

How should these new services respond to criticism and mixed reception? Since they are still in startup mode and are not yet profitable (though venture capital firms are investing in these businesses), how can they stay in business and spend the time and money that it takes to deal with such challenges? When creating new markets, do you think there is a penalty for being the first to market?

Chapter 13: Data Privacy and Management

In this chapter we cover a topic that speaks to the complex bargain users have made: the "cost of a free Internet is our user information." We cover federal privacy laws, state privacy laws, privacy at work and in public places. We learn how this is accomplished by businesses who gather users' session-level data, engage in behavioral advertising and study user engagement and interactions. Plus, we consider an emerging concept known as the right of publicity, which has potential to recalibrate users' rights to control their online data. The United Nations voted recently to adopt a resolution that states, "the same rights that people have offline must also be protected online, including the right to privacy." This evolving concept of privacy is examined in this chapter.

Typical Chapter 13 Challenge. A couple's home was photographed by Google's Street View team, who drive with cameras on top of their car and photograph objects and places in public space. The cars are using public ways and there are no allegations of a physical trespass to their property. However, the couple has clearly marked their property as "private" and they did not allow Google to take these images and put them on the web for the world to view. If they want Google to remove the images, they have to go through a number of procedures (get a verification form, a sworn statement, copy of a driver's license, etc.). The couple filed a lawsuit instead.

Questions:

What will be gained by the lawsuit? Why is the default set to include all street view images, and why do people have to affirmatively opt-out of Google's system? How would you (from the viewpoint of a user) develop a privacy policy on this type of data?

Chapter 14: Security and Computer Crime

In this chapter we cover the topics that highlight the most strategic and vulnerable points of the Internet, such as the lack of security and how it sets the stage for crime. The Internet was meant to be a tool of open communication, and therefore, its inherent open design is at odds with proprietary information. It is exceedingly difficult to secure the Internet against criminal activity. The material covers crimes for which the Internet is a tool as well as a target. The chapter also covers the many technical challenges to prosecuting cybercrime, including intent, age, jurisdiction, and more. As we build our lives around networks, the challenges will multiply.

Typical Chapter 14 Challenge. A couple found the car of their dreams on Craigslist and arranged a meeting with the seller to have a look at the car. When they arrived, they were hit, thrown in the car, and brought to their bank where they were forced to withdraw thousands. They were picked up by another person in a van, brought to a remote spot and thrown out of the car, fortunately alive, though victims of a Craigslist robbery.

Questions:

How much of this is Craigslist's fault? Do you think Craigslist has vicarious responsibility? How should Craigslist respond to this criminal activity, which is not directly attributable to the site, but is facilitated by the site?

Conclusion

Each chapter presents the historical and legal background of each topic and establishes its relevance to entrepreneurial networked startups. The cases are carefully selected and, with few exceptions, represent the most current thinking in that practice area. Older cases are presented only to the extent they represent important and defining cases. The original case decisions are typically five times the length of the book version, and we take care when excerpting cases to present the most cogent language of the case in order to share with readers only the most important insights each case offers. Cases conclude with target questions meant to emphasize managerial decision-making and leadership. The authors provide a short reference to Twitter in each chapter, and this threaded feature offers students further insights into how this representative business has dealt with such a problem in this practice area. The continuity provided by these insights throughout the text and course is highly valuable to students, and enhances comprehension on the challenge of doing business in a new economy business. Further, the text contains questions and observations throughout as well as ethical considerations, an especially relevant feature in an area where the gap is quite large between business practices, the legal environment and regulatory oversight. Chapter questions are meant to gauge mastery of the topic, and each chapter concludes with resources for further exploration of that topic.

Summary

This chapter provides students with necessary background on the development of both the Internet and the web. It is notable that it was a product of a challenge-response that existed during that historical moment. Work went forward only at the pace that technological development allowed. Progress was the result of politically and technically neutral agreements. It is neither owned nor controlled by any government. Any regulations that exist are layered on by cities, states and nations. The short description of each chapter is meant to show the course progression as well as the breadth of the legal issues created by this intriguing interaction between technology, business and law. The end result has fundamentally transformed our existence—the way we work, play, think, read and interact.

Key Terms

ARPA Advanced Research Projects Agency, an agency within the U.S. Department of Defense that was tasked with developing and building out the Internet, originally known as the ARPANET.

DARPA Defense Advanced Research Projects Agency, a U.S.-government-sponsored organization within the Department of Defense responsible for developing emerging technologies for use by the military.

RAND Research AND Development Corporation, a nonprofit global policy research organization for basic and applied research and analysis.

request for comment Sponsored by the Internet Engineering Task Force, it is a collaborative platform for discussing and agreeing upon the technical development and standards-setting necessary for the Internet to function.

CERN European Organization for Nuclear Research is an organization sponsored by 21 nations for basic and applied research.

Internet The global system of interconnected computers that communicate through modems employing a standard communications protocol.

World Wide Web A system based on a number of protocols that allow resources to be linked, enabling users to request and access each resource.

HTTP Hypertext transfer protocol, the coding protocol developed in order to exchange or transfer online resources.

HTML Hypertext markup language, the coding protocol for creating live links for which users can click to reach online resources.

URL Uniform resource locator, a resource-addressing system that assigns a unique identifying syntax string of characters to each specific online resource.

Tim Berners-Lee Formerly, a contractor at CERN, he invented the web and its associated protocols, HTTP, HTML, and URL.

Manager's Checklist

1. The Internet and web are constantly evolving technologies; keep informed on updated standards and protocols.

2. The Internet is an open architecture system and therefore inherently insecure; make data security a priority for critical assets and infrastructure.

3. Sites are available in every country and some content may not be in compliance with local laws; be prepared to respond to this challenge.

4. Since the legal environment does not cover all business strategies, especially those relating to new technologies, make every effort to conduct reasoned decision-making.

5. Consider engaging a government relations specialist and joining an industry trade group to keep apprised of the legal environment as well as to impact the legal environment.

Ethical Consideration

The governments of many countries (though not the U.S.) require all Internet service providers (ISPs) to apply for a government license, and once granted, the ISPs must comply with all government regulations, or risk being shut down. Say you were managing one of the ISPs in the U.S—how would you respond to any suggestion or legislation that embraces such a licensing scheme?

Questions and Case Problems

1. Say you created a new software program that is ideal for a particular application, and in fact, revolutionizes that field. Describe the different impacts on your wealth, as well as public adoption of that program if: (a) you patented this program; or if (b) you decide to just let everyone download it freely and with no licensing restrictions.

2. Currently there are just a few ISPs (like Comcast, Verizon, AT&T). They wish to control aspects of the cable and fiber optic networks that they've built out over the years. In the future, they may, for example, give preferential rates and speed to a partner like Disney's content, while slowing down and charging more for competitors' content. Articulate what the government can or should do.

3. The Pirate Bay became a popular file-sharing site. Its founders were sentenced to one year in jail after a court concluded the operators profited and therefore were liable for their users' conduct based on the many ads placed next to the content on the site. Say you manage eBay or Google, describe how this legal decision concerns you.

4. Recently a number of websites were compromised and taken down in an Internet attack that lasted five days. Months later, independent experts as well as government investigators are still unclear who is responsible for the attacks. Computers implicated in the attacks were identified and found in several different countries. Experts refer to the Internet as a "wilderness of mirrors." Can you identify any points in the Internet system and architecture that can effectively point to verifiable information about identity, and how to prevent other such attacks in the future?

5. Recently, a college football fan, an alumnus of that school, brought her two-year-old to a game. The gate attendant refused to allow in any of the prepared food she brought for the child, and so she posted a photo and comment on Facebook about this incident that was not flattering. While seemingly a common incident, describe how you would decide whether the school should respond, and further, describe how the Internet recalibrates power structures between large organizations and individuals.

Additional Resources

Internet Assigned Numbers Authority. http://www.Internetassignednumbersauthority.org/.
Internet Corporation for Assigned Names and Numbers. https://www.icann.org/.
Internet Engineering Task Force. https://www.ietf.org/.
Internet Society. http://www.Internetsociety.org/.
World Wide Web Consortium. http://www.w3.org/.

" Timing, perseverance and ten years of really hard work will eventually make you look like an overnight success.

—Biz Stone, Twitter co-founder, angel investor and startup advisor

Inventions, Innovations and Business Models

Developing and Implementing the Ideas and Technology Fundamental to Startups

Learning Outcomes

After you have read this chapter you should be able to:

● Understand the process and stages of inventing and innovating.
● Know how to identify resources that help in this process.
● Understand the market and non-market catalysts that impact this process.
● Recognize the difference between ideas for inventions and ownership of the invention, and also who is, and is not, a founder.
● Understand how business models are the architecture of value creation and how the Internet tolerates a range of business models.

Overview

You have a great idea. You observe a market inefficiency—in other words, you recognize this as a great moment and opportunity for your innovation or invention. Now what do you do? How do you build it out? Who will help you? Might these helpers actually have title to your invention? This chapter explores the environment of inventing, how the Internet and web have transformed the possibilities for entrepreneurial startups. Digital and networked technologies make it possible for startups to easily and inexpensively open borders and markets, to build out ideas for goods and services. The Internet and web, combined with free and open source software, low-cost cloud storage and business services from companies such as Amazon, have accelerated the pace. This chapter focuses on research and development and the stages of inventing, along with catalysts or impediments that impact this process. Then we turn to issues of ownership of inventions (and in some cases, this is *not* the individual who had the idea initially), and then as a business is built out, who is a founder. Inventorship, foundership and ownership disputes involve legal questions. To most businesses in the startup phase, these are not yet important or relevant issues, but they become critical in the next phase of scaling up to a business. Finally, this chapter covers the range of business models that are possible for startups.

The Environment of Innovations and Inventions

This chapter explores how Internet and web technologies transform business models. The materials detail the confluence of technology with imagination, innovation, and invention, and the process of translating this alchemy into commercially viable technologies as platforms for networked businesses. Innovation drives economic growth and leads to job growth through: 1) giving businesses the first-mover advantage in marketing new goods and services, 2) leading to a virtuous cycle of expansionary effects which increases employment and 3) leads to higher productivity, higher wages, and lower prices, further expanding the overall level of economic activity.

We invent or innovate in order to create something—a product or service that performs better than what presently exists. We think we can do better, be more efficient, and therefore add value and contribute. Innovation and invention policy is a mature discipline in some nations and is emerging in the United States as businesses, universities and governments consider the mix of factors that spur creation of industries, sectors, and jobs, including research, education, government incentives, immigration, and even tax and intellectual property regulation. Innovations and inventions are the building blocks for businesses' technological and intellectual property portfolios and thereby become the asset and revenue base for digital and networked businesses.

The Internet and web transformed conventional paradigms of business models, most notably creating new ways of doing business. They also altered the balance of power between individuals and large commercial or government entities. Individuals in many respects now have the same publishing and distribution power as large complex organizations. When the web developed, it revolutionized the Internet from a purely technological infrastructure for academics into a popular network, instantly becoming the instrument by which individual users interact with diverse global communities and share ideas, information, and now goods and services. Opened to commercial entities in the early 1990s, the Internet and the web are now the central platforms for business transactions. It is a place where a thirteen-year-old can make a killer iPhone app, or a sixteen-year-old's YouTube video goes viral and turns into a business opportunity, rivaling the work and success of a global company; and a place where "toddler-age" companies (such as, at the time, Facebook, Snapchat, Uber, and so forth) with no as-yet known way to earn revenue, have billion-dollar valuations.

Notably, too, the legacy business-to-consumer hierarchy "push" model of developing goods and services based on what consumers want or need is rapidly being displaced by interactive, collaborative business-with-consumer models (such as Airbnb, Yelp, and so forth), including the emerging sharing economy.

This chapter covers a number of topics, including the process of developing innovations and inventions, the disruption this creates, the role of research and development, catalysts as well as impediments to this process, inventorship status, foundership status, and finally, commercialization and creation of business models.

Innovations and Inventions

The process of innovation is fraught with difficulties even as opportunity-driven individuals dream of molding and shaping their abstract ideas into finished form, ready for market. Who can imagine a day without Wikipedia, without Google, without a mobile phone? This section explores this process and how and why it starts, along with the incentives that have the potential to accelerate the process, and impediments that slow the process. This chapter addresses the technology innovation phenomena: technology as the harbinger of a new business model. We explore R&D, innovations and inventions, how to incent more, who owns what, what does this produce, how do companies adapt to new technologies and interpret new conditions that create new prospects, how companies reshape their business models to absorb these changes, and finally, why some companies disappear while others survive.

Why Invent? Innovate?

If you could improve a recipe, your favorite site, your dorm room layout, what would you do differently, and better? These are the questions. If you could invent a better way to travel, a way to live forever, and so forth, what could you possibly dream up? Innovation is most fundamentally about seeing an inefficiency or limitation and responding with a different and better process. The inefficiency could be a lack of opportunity, inequality of information, or access, and so forth. The return is a competitive advantage. This innovation process starts with observing the problem or inefficiency and asking why, and then by imagining an improved system, design, or outcome. It is about raising new questions by looking at problems from an original perspective. It is a challenge-response to what should be or what could be. It may also be a matter of exploiting a *competitor's* weakness or limitation. For example, as Facebook faces a continuing firestorm of criticism over its seeming disinterest in data privacy, and constantly changing data control interfaces and terms, a number of rival social networking sites that feature a greater choice on privacy settings are starting to attract the attention of investors. The issues are creating a market opportunity for startups to capitalize on and capture disaffected Facebook users.

Another example of why people innovate and invent, and what their motivations could be, is how web search evolved. The web went live in 1989, and by 1995 there were at least 10 million webpages. It became, in a sense, too big for the existing search engines to navigate. One well-known site at that time listed search results in alphabetical order. Larry Page, then a computer science graduate student, was casting around for a thesis-worthy topic. Working with a leader in the human-computer interaction field, Page became interested in the challenge of effectively finding information on this emerging web platform. He asked why search was so difficult, and asked fundamentally, what really mattered to users when they were looking for resources. His theory was that there should be an internal organization scheme to measure the quality and relevance of each site. His premise was that each link represented, in essence, a citation to that source. Citations are indicia of quality. Here is why his insights are so spectacular. His theory about what made a link relevant was the number and quality of other links that linked *back* to that page. Crawling the web to discover the sum of the links back to a page is the essence of Page's insight. The resulting invention became Google's search algorithm.

Page teamed up with another graduate student, Sergey Brin, who applied his mathematics expertise to this aspect of the problem. At that time, there were 10 million documents on the web to crawl through and rank. This so-called PageRank system rewarded links that came from the most cited and relevant sources, and punished those that did not. Their work counts the number of links into a site as well as the number of links into each of the linking sites. His new way of looking at this problem of how to find resources on the web yielded revolutionary results. The rest is history: the PageRank system invention (US patent number 6,285,999) is an outstanding invention in the field of large-scale data mining and is the technology that makes Google search the most relevant source for queries.

Defining Innovation and Inventions

In describing what is an **innovation**, how it differs from an **invention**, and the ecosystem from idea to commercialization, it is useful to provide readers with a brief background on each of these process components. These are the building blocks for creating wealth and value in market economies. Generating ideas is the start of this process.

Innovation

Although there is no one established definition, an innovation is considered to be a creative technological breakthrough from conventional procedures or thought that goes beyond marginal improvements of existing products and services: they advance the state of the art. There are roughly two types of innovations: (1) innovations that support goods and services that presently exist; and (2) innovations that change the way the goods and services model works presently.

Invention

Inventions can be defined as ingenious expressions of ideas that offer a uniquely better solution to a problem. It is a practical implementation of an idea in the form of a new composition, matter, device, or process that extends the boundaries of knowledge, experience, and culture that results in something new to the marketplace. Inventions may be entirely new discoveries or developments or incremental additions to existing formats. There is some overlap, too, with innovations. In some respects, invention's distinction from innovation may be just a matter of degree. As an example of the first type of invention, consider playing online video games using a console like Microsoft's wildly popular Xbox system. Microsoft's research showed that users generally liked the experience but that the controller (or joystick or trackball) was not optimal. With its Project Natal complete, they invented a device that allows games to be controlled by gamers' bodies for a controller-free gaming experience. As an example of the second type of invention, 3M teamed with Littmann Stethoscopes to invent, then develop, an electronic stethoscope. The technology is dazzling. It features sound-amplifying technology, captures heartbeat data, and lets users transmit in real-time to computers. The data can be attached to electronic medical records and shared simultaneously. Most critically, it is a formulation plus a complete means for solving the problem.

Innovations and inventions are sometimes incremental, and at the extreme, they can be paradigm-shifting inventions. (An example of incremental innovation: first, wired Internet access, then wireless Internet access. An example of a complete game-changing invention: first, access to music through CDs, then access to music through p2p Internet file-sharing software.) No matter the magnitude, each innovation or invention necessarily introduces disruption to established business practices and business models. The task for the innovators and inventors is to keep and maintain their competitive advantage; the test for competitors is how to interpret this disruption and respond.

Stages of Innovation and Invention

Collectively known as **research and development (R&D)**, this is creative work undertaken on a systematic basis to increase knowledge and devise new applications. These stages describe the typical path to commercialization of innovations and inventions. These steps may occur out of order, or an entirely new methodology may be developed. Cambridge University Emeritus Professor Alfred North Whitehead wrote of this formulation that "the greatest invention of the 19th century was the invention of the method of invention." In this way, research and development led directly to discovery, patenting, development, production, distribution, diffusion, and adoption.

Multiple discovery is the well-known phenomenon of inventions occurring simultaneously to different people in different places: calculus (Liebniz and Newton); the light bulb (Brush, Davy, Edison, Swan, and maybe others), and so forth.

Technological improvements are, to an extent, evolutionary, based on the range of tools and collaboration available and the merging of ideas at a given time.

- *Basic/Pure Research:* creative research and work on fundamental principles to increase knowledge. This is theoretical, or empirical work, with no end result other than increased knowledge.
- *Applied Research:* this stage is directed towards research to prove feasibility. It is for a more targeted purpose, typical of what most companies produce in research. This is research that is driven by client or other commercial needs. (It may be time to look for outside funding, along with partners, and start to become concerned with logistical or staff support.)
- *Experimental/Commercial Development:* sometimes referred to as **translational research** in which developments are translated into practical applications. This is the time for technical as well as commercial evaluation of the technology's limits and potential. This includes working on designs, prototypes, pilot facilities, trial production, beta testing, and data collection. Currently there is an emphasis on speed over quality, and releasing minimally viable products (MVP) or prototypes, rather than a later release of a more developed, finely detailed product. Also known as the fast, inexpensive, restrained and elegant (FIRE) design and build-out strategy. At this phase it becomes necessary to consider legal protections for the technology. (During this pre-commercialization stage, entrepreneurs may consider licensing their technology.)
- *Demonstration:* a presentation or display to show the knowledge or the product in an operational environment. The rationale for its development is offered, as are the distinguishing characteristics of this product from the existing ones. (Companies at this stage ensure partners in their supply chain are adequately performing and readying for the commercialization stage.)
- *Product Launch:* the actual technology is completed; the model is ready enough for roll-out, with associated manufacturing, marketing, and distribution. This could be a solo venture or accomplished through partnering or other strategic relationships.
- *Diffusion of Innovations and Adoption:* the results from the launch of goods or services. Diffusion is the measure by which new technologies spread among users over time. Adoption is the selection and use of this innovation or invention by users. Adoption rate, as measured by the monthly gain in unique users, is a key metric of success for startups.

Early adopters are prized by entrepreneurs as they are typically younger, savvier, and more articulate opinion leaders. Through the efforts of early adopters, there is viral speed to diffusion and adoption. These phenomena were described early on and known as Metcalfe's Law, named after networking and Internet pioneer Bob Metcalfe. He identified the importance of many, in that the more people you can reach, the more reasons you find to reach them, so that each new connection adds far more value than the one preceding it. There is a sort of magnetic principle involved to networks: the more users, the stronger the pull.

Categories of Innovation and Invention

A method to describe the possible categories of innovations and inventions is helpful when considering the types of workers with specialties and how each can impact the goal to continue to improve and add value to goods and services.

- *Process:* improvement to procedures anywhere in the supply chain, from manufacturing to distribution;
- *Product:* improvements to the actual product in terms of quality, utility, or user experience;
- *Cultural:* characterized by a shift in thinking, changes in attitudes, and behaviors, making different approaches possible;
- *Marketing:* a repositioning of markets, products, and packaging to impact the overall user experience that results in improvements.

Effect of Innovation and Invention

No business sector is more aware than the tech industry of the theories of economist Joseph Schumpeter. He famously wrote about business cycles, noting that the catalyst for capitalism is "creative destruction"—the forces of innovation and invention unleashed on markets, causing businesses to rise and fall, and in the end drive the economy toward greater productivity, and thereby make the economy stronger and wealthier in the long term.

No matter the source of this R&D, whether it was made in-house, bought through outsourcing, bolted on through a supply chain, or how much the innovations or inventions improve the world, the net result is that they unleash a disruptive force on business. Innovations and inventions upend established channels of purchasing, distribution, communications, and sales, persistently improving and refining methods, and thereby increasing productivity. Back to the revolutionary patented PageRank search algorithm. The patent has since expired on this invention, and search has moved quite far from this original iteration, described in their 1997 provisional patent disclosure. As the world has gone mobile, users are bypassing the "traditional" Google search experience and instead target exactly the app for a certain utility, Flixster for films, Kayak for flights, and so forth. This same disruptive innovation that Google produced for desktop search is now occurring in the context of mobile search.

The creative destruction process in the job market causes structural changes to the workforce, eliminating jobs and workers whose work can be done more cheaply by computers or off-shore by less expensive workers. These are the costs of productivity and efficiency growth for U.S. businesses.

The disruptions are typically found in these categories, as the innovations and inventions bring new efficiencies and opportunities in these areas:

- Products and equipment
- Markets, marketing, and advertising
- Sources of labor and raw materials

- Methods of organization or management
- Methods of transportation
- Methods of communication
- Financial instruments
- Legal strategies

Incentives to Innovate and Invent: Market and Nonmarket Catalysts

This is currently an area of keen interest among businesses, governments, and nongovernment organizations (NGOs) such as the OECD, World Bank, and the World Economic Forum. The theory is that incentives can accelerate the process since businesses usually do not completely capture all the return from inventing, and some stimulus is beneficial. In the United States, leaders cite Bureau of Labor Statistics data on job growth in high-tech sectors. On average, there are 40 high-tech companies per 1,000 private-sector firms nationally. Yet high-tech jobs have clustered, so much so that there are now areas with the highest concentration of high-tech companies, tech-oriented jobs, and employees with secondary degrees. For example, San Jose averages nearly 120 high-tech companies per 1,000 private-sector firms. In another example, Boston is partnering with area universities, city planners, architects, and developers to create an Innovation District. The question is how to duplicate this vibrancy, openness, and momentum in top-tier innovation areas such as Silicon Valley and Greater Boston, known for their powerful array of overlapping networks.

Market/Private Business Catalysts

These are policies that businesses can implement to incent innovation and invention. The overall effect is to build relationships by creating new connections, and this generates a multiplier effect. A number of "innovation factories" like Xerox PARC, RAND and Bell Labs, were financed by private companies whose profit margins were sufficient enough to support this work. This includes targeting local universities (EMC recently announced an alliance with M.I.T.'s Media Lab; Johnson & Johnson hosts 30 startups in a 40,000 square foot lab incubator facility, for example, opening satellite offices near these areas, holding office hours in coffee shops, participating in university business plan competitions, mentoring fledgling entrepreneurs, serving on their boards, investing in their ideas, and more. Thomson Reuters introduced an annual report on the "Top 100 Global Innovators," studying patenting activity, success rates, globalization and influence of a range of companies and industries worldwide.

One notable catalyst has been the contest format. Netflix famously set up a contest, offering a $1 million prize to anyone who could significantly (>10 percent) improve its movie recommendation system.

Businesses should consider internal operations as well. What does the hierarchy, the chain of command, and reporting structure promote? Does the business value minimizing conflict over creativity? How to manage conformity and risk? It is quite possible that there are ways to group workers and work projects to foster creativity and intelligent risk-taking while optimizing outcomes. Google is known for its "20 percent time," enabling engineers to work on projects that were not in their job descriptions, leading to results even when there is no formal budgeting for these projects. Even in the 1950s, 3M had a 15 percent set-aside for engineers who developed masking tape and Post-its on an informal, ad hoc basis.

Nonmarket/Government Catalysts

Perhaps of equal importance are government policies that impact business decisions, planning, and behavior. The President appointed its first Chief Technology Officer, charged with developing metrics to measure the role of innovation in the economy. Policies are typically implemented through laws, and currently include:

- Antitrust oversight (to maintain competitive markets, as information products tend towards monopoly power)
- Tax policy (including corporate tax rate adjustments, tax credits, deductions, reductions, exemptions, and tax holidays)
- Education benefits (these may be in the form of student loan policies)
- Immigration (this could be in the form of temporary work or start-up visas and this is covered primarily in the Employment chapter)
- Grants (these could be in the form of federal or state grants funded through specific agencies; for example, the Department of Energy offered grants for energy-saving ideas and inventions)
- Loans (these are currently available through the Small Business Innovation Research, and Small Business Technology Transfer programs within the Small Business Administration)
- Promoting ownership in technology funded by the US government and developed in research universities (widely known as the Bayh-Dole Act, this has been a significant spur to inventions and is covered primarily in the Patents chapter). The US government currently spends $126 billion per year on R&D
- Health care policy (often a disproportionate burden for small companies, healthcare reform is ongoing)
- Zoning policy (cities are creating innovation districts, clustering industries, supporting subsidized housing for entrepreneurs, and more)

Government support is vital to promoting growth, and even incubating ideas that are built out by the private sector. The long-term importance of government-supported research and policies has consistently yielded outstanding results, from the original build out of the Internet, to the more recent fiscal, tax, and immigration policies today. Recently the World Bank published *The Impact of Government Support on Firm R&D Investments: A Meta-Analysis*

(July 2013), a Policy Research Working Paper (6532) concerning government support of innovation.

Impediments to Incentives

International Paradox

The international paradox describes the global platforms that many Internet companies have built out, such as Google or Facebook, that are so attractive to users and advertisers—but their services operate at a loss in the poorest parts of the world where there are not enough advertisers to cover operations. Although there are 3 billion Internet users worldwide, less than half have incomes high enough to interest advertisers. Costs associated with engineering, servers to produce enough bandwidth, and storage capacity are becoming cost-prohibitive in less affluent areas, and therefore act as a disincentive for further innovation and invention in those areas.

Galapagos Syndrome

Named for Charles Darwin's invaluable work in the Galapagos Islands studying plants that genetically developed in isolation, the Galapagos syndrome describes a product that evolves in isolation from world markets. For example, Japanese-manufactured smartphones are generations ahead in features. Detail-oriented consumers in Japan prefer to buy products loaded with features usable only through reference to detailed instruction manuals. Japan cannot build on this competitive advantage, however, because the rest of the world cannot support its advanced network or technology interface that underlie these phones, and instead prefer simpler, more intuitive interfaces. This divide between Japanese consumers and the rest of the world acts as a disincentive for, in this example, Japanese export of its technology.

Innovators' Dilemma

Businesses arrive at a point where there are difficult choices to make, since they are so invested in their present goods or services and marketing channels that they are reluctant to risk on a bet on re-tooling for different goods or services. Amazon was at that point with its Kindle. Should it continue with its original screen technology? Or should it mimic the iPad's touchscreen technology? This is called a "strategic inflection point." Do they choose to stay the course and continue to invest in its established model, the predictable revenue producer (as IBM did with mainframes, and therefore was too slow to market on the PC trend), or do they risk it all with a new direction that has no proven revenue, and which necessitates a huge investment in order to retool? The innovators' dilemma can stall innovation and invention, where incentives to switch appear to be too low in relation to the assumed risk. This dilemma is more pronounced in less-developed, less resource-rich regions, which can "leap" over legacy systems. There, diffusion of inventions occurs more rapidly, since there exists no pre-existing systems to consider. For example, Israel built electronic tolling into its new highway system in 2000 (never needing to consider what to do about switching from a manual toll-collector-in-a-booth system), while the US is still making the transition to electronic-only tolling systems.

Institutional Resistance

When businesses focus on short-term performance benchmarks, quarterly earnings, and operations, they are probably not cultivating an environment that is conducive to breakthroughs in new directions, goods nor services. This is the opposite of a culture that rewards and promotes innovations and inventions for turning bright ideas into commercially useful goods and services in a timely fashion without interference from destructive internal competition. What happened to ten years' worth of R&D at Microsoft in tablet PCs and E-books? They never made it to market. IBM did the earliest work in the new field of relational database computing, yet Oracle is now the market leader in this field. Just after the iPad was introduced, Dell issued an advance announcement of a competing product, and Microsoft announced a personnel shake-up in its tablet division. Companies must evaluate their systems for innovation and diffusing new technologies to the market.

Incentives to innovation and invention are powerful mechanisms to spur growth and productivity. When the right mix of work, people, goals, and opportunities is in place, businesses can capitalize on this as they measure, experiment, share and replicate their results and commercialize the technology. Ensuring availability of quality people is crucial as well. Innovation areas can expect to reap high employee satisfaction, a ready supply of highly qualified and motivated labor sector, and other associated benefits within communities. As a measure of the success of innovation areas, investors and companies focus on stay rates, that is, the rate at which university graduates settle in the geographic area of their university to start up a business. The national average is 45 percent. In a notable disparity, Massachusetts, with its renowned academic universities, has a stay rate of just 29 percent, while California's is 69 percent. Clearly, policies on innovation and invention matter.

Disruptive Effects of Innovations and Inventions

As a reference point, consider for a moment the computer industry. Computing dates back to ancient civilizations, though the modern computing industry roughly dates from 1935, when Bell Laboratory researcher George Stibitz developed the first modern digital computer. The industry has gone through many phases, each characterized by a challenge for which no solution presently existed. Such problems centered on scientific, math, and defense-related needs, such as decrypting enemy codes, U.S. census needs for computing the number of U.S. residents, and so forth.

Each innovation created better tools, as well as obsolescence. Ask yourself (or your parents) what happened to their first home desktop computer. Well, it is now mobile. During the early phase of the "PC Revolution," computers became ever larger, more powerful, and capable of amazing feats—that today seem quaint as well as inefficient. Computers needed to accommodate new programs and demands. Over time, new changes disrupted the present thinking. For example, before the Internet, users bought software programs in a box. But because of the Internet, users began to download the programs. This change reverberated throughout the industry and changed the idea and format of stores such as Best Buy. Second, the Internet made cloud computing possible. In a cloud computing world, the programs, the documents—nearly everything—moves off the desktop and resides on remote servers. Suddenly there is no longer a need for powerful personal home computers or processors. And because every device is now smaller, more powerful, and faster, there is no dedicated device such as a "home or desktop computer." Mobile computing is the standard now.

Consider the original cohort of domestic retail digital computer makers circa 1936-1976: Atanasoff-Berry, Remington Rand, IBM, Burroughs, Sperry, MOS Technology, Micro Instrumentation and Telemetry Systems, and Apple. (Notably the ENIAC was a U.S. Army-sponsored project.) How many of these names do you recognize? How many have survived, or re-tooled? Apple is the only company in this original group still actively engaged in the computer hardware manufacturing sector. Which of these companies is currently making smartphones? This cohort includes: Apple, Google (since it bought Motorola), (manufacturer of Blackberry), HTC, LG, and Samsung, for the most part. Why couldn't (or why didn't) most of the computer makers transition to smartphone manufacturing? The disruptive effect of innovations and inventions means that products change, different skill sets are needed, and markets evolve. Will Research in Motion's (RIM) once-vaunted gold-standard-in-mobile Blackberry survive? Or will it land in the hall of fallen giants (with pagers, the Sony Walkman, the Palm Pilot, the Polaroid instant camera, the Atari game console, Hewlett-Packard's TouchPad tablet, and more)? Companies invent, pivot, or die.

Legal Claims to Innovations and Inventions by Inventors, Founders, and/or Owners of the Business

Inventors

Inventors work with abstract concepts—mere ideas—and through determination, create a practical application of that work. Note that there is no legally protectable property interest associated with just an idea, and the only legally protectable interest is in the actual invention, which may be patented or maintained as a trade secret. Oftentimes, inventing is done in conjunction with others and then a myriad of questions arise. Which person(s) working on a project is/are the actual inventor(s)? What if one person articulated the concept, but another person developed the actual working prototype, with some help from a third person? Who owns the invention if no one signs anything? What if that third person formed the company and assigned rights in the invention over to this company?

Inventions often have many parents. As the ideas take shape through experiments and refinements, re-writes and beta-testing, market testing and more, the team of people morphs—some people remain, others drop out, others are asked to leave. The typical scenario is a couple of people who have a great idea and devise a genius solution. They add a bunch of great people who all jump into the project and base the entire start on a verbal agreement fueled by optimism and trust. They realize they need a coder for software, a marketing person, and someone who can organize the whole operation. Then things unravel. Each participant, even those people who earlier left the project, may have enough work involvement to assert claims of inventorship, or ownership, in the technology that resulted from the project. It is highly problematic to measure participation and contribution. Should the appropriation theory, "first in time, first in right" govern? The risk of being late to market may be too high. To the extent that the work was done while they were employed elsewhere on another company's work time, or on an ad-hoc basis out of that office not on work time, matters are further complicated. Funding from external sources, including grants, means that there are additional parties who have potential legal claims to the technology.

Inventorship rights between two competing claims is decided by identifying which party conceived the invention and held intellectual domination over it, in contrast to someone who merely assists in reducing it to practice. (Only later on will they figure out that they need financial and legal expertise.) For example, just read Nick Bilton's *Hatching Twitter*, or watch *The Social Network*, to get confirmation that legal questions surrounding the title of inventor are quite complicated. Legal claims to inventions and company ownership is a murky and opaque area fraught with uncertainty and competing claims.

Founders

A founder of a business is a special kind of entrepreneur. Founders, who might also be inventors, find a commercially viable application for the invention and start a business based centrally around the invention. Founders pull together the initial invention with enough expertise to launch the business. It is critically important to clarify who has title to the invention at this point: does the startup? Or does the inventor still own the invention? Of course, the founders will want to ensure the invention is assigned to the new entity.

For example, take three founders. One point of view is that they should receive equal recognition and ownership share (1/3 each). Another point of view is that they should receive recognition based on fairness, *i.e.,* a share/ownership split commensurate to the value of their contribution—perhaps one contributed money, another contributed coding, and the third contributed business and marketing expertise. Founders start up the entity, though at a certain point, too, founders may be just that, and simply be unable to manage a scaling business enterprise. The needs of a growing business change rapidly. Businesses can outgrow the founder's skill set and competence, especially if the hoped-for occurs and the business scales up to an ongoing sustainable business entity. Working with an ongoing entity is entirely different from starting one up. Even Twitter, with legendary growth, continues to experience growing pains. Twitter's Board (which includes some of its venture capital backers) pushed aside Jack Dorsey, who had the original idea and formed the business, and the Board gave the job to Evan Williams, also one of the early founders of Twitter.

In a '*it's deja vu all over again*' moment, Jack Dorsey was subsequently involved in another startup, Square, the online payment app. A Washington University Professor, Robert Morley, claims to be the sole inventor of the Square card reader, and co-invented with James McKelvey the corresponding magnetic stripe decoding algorithms of the Square app. Morley created a prototype, as well as tested and demonstrated it. Morley received a patent for this invention (U.S. Patent No. 8,584,946). After this success, Dorsey, Morley and McKelvey formed a joint venture to enter the mobile payments industry. Dorsey and McKelvey later incorporated a company, Square, to leverage this technology, but excluded Morley from being an officer or shareholder of this corporation. Morley was angry, and assigned the patent to another business, REM, Holdings 3 LLC, instead of to Square. This lawsuit is ongoing (case No. 4:14-cv-00172, filed Jan. 30, 2014 (Fed. Dist. Ct. E.D. Miss.)). A variation of this foundership/ownership of the business litigation is ongoing too. See the *Snapchat* case (Chapter 1).

Equity Owners of the Business

These are the shareholders of the business, and they can also comprise the inventors and the founders. As the business grows and they seek outside funding, founders' shares diminish in percentage since investors are added and the original share 1/3 each split changes as shares are re-allocated (see Chapter 3 for complete coverage of this). To clarify this and more, inventors and founders should initially create two documents: a **Memorandum of Understanding** (MoU) and a **Contribution Agreement**. The MoU is analogous to a letter of intent; it is not as formal as a contract, but it sets out parties' expectations. Contribution Agreements formalize arrangements as to any technology a party is contributing to the startup. The contributing party grants the startup all rights in the technology and warrants that the property is free and clear of any encumbrances (limitations on use or competing claims of ownership). The party also agrees to make the technology and the know-how for that technology available for uses under the terms and conditions of the agreement. Know-how is privately maintained knowledge experts have regarding technology they developed. The startup typically offers shares of stock in the company in return for contributions. In some cases, there are carve-outs to Contribution Agreements, meaning that certain technology or know-how will not be company property and continue to be owned and controlled by the individual who initially controlled it and is, therefore, specifically excluded from the startup.

The first case concerns workers at one company who invented a product, and then left to form their own company, amid question of ownership, and more. This is an area that overlays with the Employment chapter. Employers have historically attempted to capture all innovations and inventions from employees. This right historically evolved as a shop right, an automatic license for employers to use inventions worked on within the scope of employment using employer resources. Employees have limited and non-assignable rights in these inventions.

Several states have attempted to recognize inventors' rights to the extent they do not conflict with legitimate employer claims. For example, California enacted California Labor Code Section 2870, which shifts the balance between employees and employers. This section provides:

> (a) Any provision in an employment agreement which provides that an employee shall assign, or offer to assign, any of his or her rights in an invention to his or her employer shall not apply to an invention that the employee developed entirely on his or her own time without using the employer's equipment, supplies, facilities, or trade secret information except for those inventions that either:
>
> 1. Relate at the time of conception or reduction to practice of the invention to the employer's business, or actual or demonstrably anticipated research or development of the employer; or
>
> 2. Result from any work performed by the employee for the employer.
>
> (b) To the extent a provision in an employment agreement purports to require an employee to assign an invention otherwise excluded from being required to be assigned under subdivision (a), the provision is against the public policy of this state and is unenforceable.

The line of demarcation between work time and non-work time has grown more blurred now that the tools for creating inventions are computers, software, smartphones, and networks, and the hours of work are less rigid than they used to be. Employers try to control this risk by requiring employees to sign Inventor Assignment Agreements. While the following case is older, it is an outstanding example of the range of issues that need resolution in these legal challenges.

Iconix, Inc. v. Tokuda,
457 F. Supp. 2d 969 (N.D. Cal. 2006)

Facts: Plaintiff Iconix provides email identity services that proactively combat email fraud phishing schemes. Defendants Lance Tokuda and Jia Shen began working at Iconix in December 2004. Tokuda was Vice President of Engineering and Chief Technology Officer. Among other things, he supervised the development of Iconix's new intellectual property and ideas. Shen was Manager of Client Development at Iconix and his responsibility included overseeing software development. Both signed contracts entitled "Proprietary Information and Inventions Assignment Agreement."

In the fall of 2005, Iconix was actively generating, developing, and evaluating ideas for increasing traffic to its site. This included new features that would entice users to download its email identity product. Iconix was particularly interested in penetrating social network sites and needed to develop marketing tools for this purpose. At this time, Tokuda and other engineers discussed the idea of creating a feature that would rotate through users' pictures. Users would download the email product and then be able to use the picture feature. Iconix began testing this feature in early 2006.

Back in December 2005, Tokuda gave notice to Iconix. His last workday was January 23, 2006. Iconix discovered that in October 2005, while still an officer of Iconix, Tokuda secretly registered the domain name rockmyspace.com, and had covertly developed a slideshow feature for his personal benefit, and also secretly formed his own company, Netpickle, for the purpose of exploiting his slideshow feature. Tokuda also solicited Iconix employees for his new venture. By February 2006, rockmyspace had already exceeded 1.1 million registered users. Iconix fired Shen when it learned that he was one of the employees solicited by Tokuda.

Iconix sent Defendants a cease-and-desist letter on all activity that uses software or derivative works owned by Iconix. Iconix also requested the return of the slideshow program and source code, asserting that Iconix was the rightful owner. Defendants refused to comply. Plaintiff filed suit in court seeking a preliminary injunction against Defendants on theories of breach of fiduciary duty, breach of contract, and copyright infringement.

Judicial Opinion. Judge Saundra Brown Armstrong:

1. PAROL EVIDENCE

Plaintiff objects to the following two paragraphs and has filed a Motion to Strike these from the evidence. Iconix objects to the introduction of the evidentiary Declarations of Tokuda and Shen.

Specifically, the Tokuda Declaration states:

> [Iconix's CEO] Mr. Picazo came to me with the Iconix Proprietary Information and Inventions Assignment Agreement and wanted me to sign it. I had signed similar agreements before, but this one bothered me. I felt it required me to disclose every idea I had whether it was related to Iconix or not, including ideas I had away from work. That was impractical since I have been doing start-ups for most of my entire career, and I often have multiple ideas in a day. I expressed my concern to Mr. Picazo and he said that he had used this form with his previous companies. He told me not to worry, that the agreement was a formality. Mr. Picazo said that he would never use the agreement against me and that even he had signed it. Based on what he said, I signed the agreement.

The Shen Declaration states:

> When we first received our Proprietary Agreements in March/April 2005, I had concerns. They seemed overbroad. Lance [Tokuda] and I both asked for a revision before we signed. Months later, I was asked to sign a new, supposedly modified Proprietary

Agreement in haste. Mr. Picazo said he really needed me to sign it, and it was urgent that I do so. I was told that the agreement was a mere formality and was needed to complete my HR file. In response to my concerns, Mr. Picazo said that these things "would never be used" and "not to worry." I signed it in good faith based on Mr. Picazo's representations.

Plaintiff asserts that under California law, such statements are inadmissible to contradict the terms of the Agreement. The Rule generally prohibits any extrinsic evidence, whether oral or written, to vary, alter or add to the terms of a written instrument. This applies to any type of contract, and its purpose is to make sure that the parties' final understanding, deliberately expressed in writing, shall not be changed. The Agreements here provide:

> The terms . . . may not be contradicted. This Agreement shall constitute the complete and exclusive statement of its terms . . . This Agreement may not be amended or waived except by a writing. . . .

Tokuda's and Shen's claims that the Agreement "would never be used" against them are inconsistent with the Agreement's explicit statement. Therefore, these paragraphs in the Defendants' Declarations are barred by the parol evidence rule. The Court SUSTAINS Plaintiffs objections and STRIKES these paragraphs.

2. PRELIMINARY INJUNCTION

A party seeking a preliminary injunction must show either (1) a combination of probable success on the merits and the possibility of irreparable injury, or (2) that serious questions are raised and the balance of hardships tips sharply in favor of the moving party [Plaintiff]. [The Court then considers Plaintiffs three claims to determine if any have a probability of success, which would be grounds for issuing a preliminary injunction.]

A. BREACH OF FIDUCIARY DUTY

i. Evidence of a Fiduciary Duty. Plaintiff argues that Tokuda owed a fiduciary duty to Plaintiff and its shareholders, which he breached.

Under California law, an officer who participates in management of the corporation, exercising some discretionary authority, is a fiduciary of the corporation. Conversely, a "nominal" officer with no management authority is not a fiduciary. Tokuda and Shen argue that Tokuda "had no discretionary authority" and had to seek . . . approval for everything, including contracts, hiring, and budget." Plaintiff offers evidence of Tokuda's discretionary power. First, Tokuda was the only person to interview Jia Shen before he was hired. Second, Tokuda hired the Romanian engineering team, Gemini, and signed an amendment to their agreement which bound Iconix for over a million dollars without consulting anyone else.

On balance, Plaintiff makes a convincing argument that Tokuda was an officer of Plaintiff, with some discretionary authority, who thus owned a fiduciary duty to Plaintiff.

As an officer with a fiduciary duty, Tokuda was required to exercise:

> the most scrupulous observance of his duty, not only affirmatively to protect the interests of the corporation committed to his charge, but also to refrain from doing anything that would work injury to the corporation, or to deprive it of profit or advantage which his skill and ability might properly bring to it. . . .

ii. Evidence that Tokuda Breached his Fiduciary Duty.

Plaintiff specifically argues that Tokuda breached his fiduciary duty to Plaintiff by violating the corporate opportunity doctrine, which:

> prohibits a fiduciary from acquiring, in opposition to the corporation, property in which the corporation has an interest or tangible expectancy. . . . [A] corporate opportunity exists when a proposed activity is reasonably incident to the corporation's present or prospective business and is one in which the corporation has the capacity to engage.

With regard to the slideshow software and the corporate opportunity doctrine, Plaintiff asserts that it had the capacity to engage in this activity, that this was an area that Iconix was seeking to exploit. Plaintiff also asserts that the target market was the same for the products. Tokuda and Shen do not challenge Plaintiffs arguments that it had the capacity to engage in the proposed activity. Instead they argue that Tokuda had no duty to disclose rockmyspace to Plaintiff because Plaintiff was in the business of "branded email," and anything not directly tied to achieving email downloads was outside the scope of Iconix's business.

But [evidence shows that] the slideshow feature was listed as a top priority for Plaintiffs medium term plan in the January 10, 2005, Product Plan Review document (Exhibit G).

Shen, in his Deposition, stated as follows:

> **Q:** What triggered the idea [for the rockmyspace site with the slideshow feature]?
> **A:** We had been doing a lot of work related to social networks.
> **Q:** And when you say "we," who are you talking about?
> **A:** Me and the people at Iconix.

Shen explained that the initial idea for rockmyspace was to "do something viral for myspace," and acknowledged that at this same time, Iconix was also looking to "do something viral for myspace."

Finally Plaintiff cites to an instant messaging transcript in which Tokuda states, "Yeah, we actually lucked out with Iconix being so bad it was an easy call to leave versus trying to save them with our best ideas." In his Supplemental Declaration, Tokuda seeks to clarify this statement, explaining that he had (a) presented his best ideas and features to Iconix management and (b) lobbied strongly in favor of those ideas for many months. Tokuda explains that these ideas were rejected, so it was "an easy call to leave Iconix." Tokuda claims that he would have had to convince Iconix to change focus and adopt his ideas—something that Tokuda claims "was not going to happen."

On balance, Plaintiff presents convincing evidence of a breach of fiduciary duty based on the corporate opportunity doctrine. Tokuda acquired the rockmyspace website "in opposition to" Plaintiff; this site is at least "reasonably incident" to Plaintiffs present and prospective business and is an activity in which Plaintiff had a capacity to engage. Further, it appears that Tokuda failed "to refrain from doing anything that would . . . deprive [the corporation] of profit or advantage which his skill and ability might properly bring to it."

B. BREACH OF CONTRACT

Plaintiff argues that Tokuda and Shen breached their Agreements by failing to disclose, assign, and transfer the work they developed for implementing an animated slideshow tool and the website that they developed, launched, and operated while in Plaintiffs employ.

Tokuda and Shen both signed Proprietary Agreements that state:

> I agree to assign and transfer to the Company, without further consideration, my entire right, title and interest... free and clear . . . in and to all Inventions. Such assignment and transfer shall be continuous during my employment. The Company may, in its sole discretion, agree to provide consideration for certain Inventions through a written agreement. In all other cases, no consideration shall be paid. The Inventions shall be the sole property of the Company, whether or not copyrightable or patentable or in a commercial state of development. In addition, I agree to maintain adequate and current written records on the development of all Inventions, which shall also remain the sole property of the Company.
>
> *Inventions.* "Inventions" collectively means any and all ideas, concepts, inventions, discoveries, developments, know-how, structures, designs, formulas, algorithms, methods, products, processes, systems-and-technologies in any stage of development that are conceived, developed or reduced to practice by me alone or with others; any and all patents, patents pending, copyrights, moral rights, trademarks and any other intellectual property rights therein; and any and all improvements, modifications, derivative works from, other rights in and claims related to any of the foregoing.
>
> *Disclosure.* I agree to disclose promptly to the Company all Inventions and relevant records.

Plaintiff argues that all of the work that Tokuda and Shen did relating to the rockmyspace site while employed by Iconix falls under the Proprietary Agreement. Plaintiff argues that the exception in California Labor Code section 2870 does not apply. Section 2870 provides an exception to the assignment of inventions, and would apply only if Tokuda and Shen developed rockmyspace (1) entirely on their own time; (2) entirely without use of Iconix's equipment, supplies, or facilities; and (3) rockmyspace was not related to Iconix's business, or actual or demonstrably anticipated research or development, or result from any work that Tokuda and Shen performed for Iconix.

Plaintiff asserts that there is overwhelming evidence that Defendants used Company equipment and resources to develop and operate rockmyspace. Iconix's Director of Information Technology testified that examination of Shen's computer revealed that the computer contained the "source code for the site and the related application used by the site including the customizable slideshow application." They also found logs of instant messaging conversations, a database of users, a presentation for investors, all of which took place during business hours. In defense of this, Tokuda argues that the Proprietary Agreement stands for the proposition that if Plaintiff determined that it did not wish to pursue its broadly coined definition of "Invention," no "assignment" under the Agreement was necessary.

However, this construction is not supported by the language of the Proprietary Agreement. The Agreement requests disclosure in order to determine whether an idea is an "Invention" subject to this Agreement. The clear terms of the Agreement indicate that Tokuda and Shen did not have the discretion to retain any ideas. They had to disclose not only all Inventions but also "any idea" that they did not believe to be an Invention so that Plaintiff could determine whether or not the idea qualified as an Invention.

Defendants next argue that the rockmyspace slide-show and site cannot be claimed under the Proprietary Agreement given the circumstances surrounding their limited use of Plaintiffs equipment: (1) Shen used his Iconix computer on vacation to program, and (2) Iconix computers were used to handle minor operational issues, and he took the computer on vacation only because Iconix asked him to bring it along. They further argued that "using Iconix computers for personal purposes was allowed and Iconix never said it would [claim] title to such things."

Defendants' arguments are unavailing. Regardless of whether use of Iconix computers for personal purposes was considered *acceptable,* the Proprietary Agreements clearly require that Tokuda and Shen *assign and transfer* all inventions to Plaintiffs, unless those inventions were developed entirely on the employee's own time, without using the employer's equipment, supplies, facilities, or trade secret information. Even then, as discussed above, the Proprietary Agreements provide an exception to this exception, requiring assignment and transfer of those inventions that either: (1) relate at the time of conception or reduction to practice of the invention to the employer's business, or actual and demonstrably anticipated research or development of the employer, or (2) result from any work performed by the employee for the employer. To the extent that Tokuda and Shen believed that the rockmyspace slideshow and site were not Inventions, they still had to disclose those ideas to Plaintiff.

In response to Plaintiffs arguments that Tokuda and Shen work on the site during business hours, Defendants concede that they sometimes worked on maintenance of the site between the hours of 9 a.m. and 5 p.m. They argue, however, that given that the two often worked 14- to 16-hour days for Iconix or worked throughout the night, the idea that something was done on "work time" simply because it happened between 9 and 5 is artificial. Even so, Tokuda and Shen fail to convincingly rebut Plaintiffs allegations that they worked on rockmyspace during work hours. As noted above, the exception to the assignment and transfer provision provided in that California law applies only to "an Invention that the employee developed *entirely* on his or her own time." On balance, Plaintiff provides convincing evidence that the California labor law does not apply to excuse Tokuda and Shen's failure to assign and transfer rockmyspace to Iconix and they breached the terms of their Proprietary Agreements.

C. COPYRIGHT INFRINGEMENT

[The court found that Plaintiff raised sufficient questions as to infringing uses by Defendants.]

CONCLUSION

1. All Defendants, their officers, directors, employees, and all persons in active concert and participation with any of them are prohibited from making use of, transferring, distributing or reproducing any implementations of technology, including software code, created by any person while that person was an employee of Iconix.
2. All Defendants . . . are prohibited from infringing Plaintiff's copyrights . . . in any software code developed by Defendants.
3. Within 10 days of service of this Order, Defendants are required to deliver to Plaintiff, and to erase, any and all copies of software that would infringe Iconix's copyrights . . . in any software code . . . except that Defendants' counsel shall be permitted to retain one copy of any such software code to be used for litigation, and not operational, purposes only.
4. Defendants are prohibited from using, selling, licensing or transferring the domain name rockmyspace.com.
5. Within 20 days of service of this Order, each Defendant shall file with the Court . . . a sworn affidavit detailing the manner in which that Defendant has complied with this Order.

IT IS SO ORDERED.

Case Questions

1. There was commentary after this case that the Proprietary Agreements Defendants signed were overly broad. Describe how.
2. For Tokuda, Iconix was too confining, too slow, too lacking in an entrepreneurial culture, and the company failed to grasp the relevance of his work. Recommend how you would restructure that work environment and/or his compensation to incent and reward such employees in ways that would make them stay even if they were frustrated at times.
3. The concept of fiduciary duty seems out of place in the Information Age. Identify how it can be one of the most crucial legal theories in suits against directors and officers.

The next case began when one company, Novartis, tried to advance its drug pipeline through collaborating with a world-class research hospital, and its team of doctors and researchers, some of whom started the Gatekeeper company. Even these sophisticated parties needed a court to sort out exactly which parties owned the invention.

Dana Farber Cancer Inst. v. Gatekeeper Pharms., Inc.,
No. 10-11613-DPW (D. Mass. Oct. 12, 2012)

Facts: Dana-Farber Cancer Institute brought this declaratory judgment action against Gatekeeper Pharmaceuticals to establish the rights and responsibilities of each party in connection with a newly discovered compound, WZ-4-002, which has the potential to be an effective treatment for a subset of non-small-cell lung cancers that are resistant to two other existing drug treatments. The focus of this case is whether third-party defendants affiliated with the Novartis pharmaceutical group were entitled to license WZ-4-002 under the Collaborative Research Agreement between Novartis and Dana-Farber.

Dana-Farber is a cancer-research organization that employed the scientists who discovered WZ-4-002. It receives funding from a variety of sources, including Novartis. Dana-Farber and Novartis entered into their agreement that provided that in exchange for funding from Novartis, Dana-Farber agreed to give Novartis first priority to license Program Intellectual Property. This was defined as rights to any funded Invention conceived or reduced to practice . . . .Pursuant to the Research Agreement, Novartis has donated between $7.9 to 9.8 million annually. A Steering Committee, comprised of two Dana-Farber and two Novartis members, decides how to distribute the Novartis funding. Drs. Eck and Gray applied for and received Novartis funding for their separate work, though they collaborated on some aspects of kinase inhibitors. Dr. Zhou, who was a post-doctoral research assistant for Dr. Gray, did not receive any funding. Dr. Janne did not receive

Novartis funding, but instead funded his research through grants from the National Institute of Health.

Dr. Janne discovered the T790M mutation of the EGFR kinase in 2005. Dr. Eck immediately became interested, and directed his research assistant to study that mutation. Drs. Eck and Gray, Novartis-funded researchers, decided to try an make a particular irreversible inhibitor, and so Dr. Zhou (Gray's assistant) created a library of all known irreversible kinase inhibitors, and created some crystal structures to aid them. As part of this project, Dr. Zhou also created WZ-4-002. According to his notebook, Dr. Zhou first synthesized WZ-4-002 on May 31, 2007. Then in the summer of 2008, Dr. Janne approached Dr. Gray to ask if he could use his library of inhibitors to see if they were effective against the EGFR T790M mutation, and he reported early success with the WZ-4-002 inhibitor.

In October 2008 Drs. Gray, Zhou, Janne, and Eck filed a Dana-Farber Invention Disclosure Form disclosing the effectiveness of the WZ-4-002 compound on the T790M mutation of the EGFR kinase. In the section disclosing the source of funding that supported the work leading to the invention, only two grants were listed, and neither was from Novartis. Drs. Janne and Gray assigned their rights to the invention to Dana-Farber. Two months before submitting the patent application, Drs. Gray and Janne founded Gatekeeper and began negotiations with Dana-Farber for license rights to commercialize WZ-4-002. [Dr. Eck did not join Gatekeeper in party because the other founders were concerned about a conflict between his Consulting Agreement with Novartis in the area of kinase oncogenes.]

Dana-Farber entered into an Option Agreement with Gatekeeper to use the compound. Dana-Farber also conducted an internal inquiry to determine whether the compound fell under its Research Agreement with Novartis, such that Novartis might have first priority to a license. On the basis of representations made by Dr. Gray, Dana-Farber determined that the compound did not implicate the Research Agreement. Novartis learned of the compound's discovery, and made a claim to Dana-Farber that it was covered under the Research Agreement—and therefore had first priority for licensing the '419 patent. Right at that point, Gatekeeper gave Dana-Farber notice that it raised the necessary funds to exercise the option for the '419 patent. Dana-Farber next concluded that the compound was subject to the Novartis agreement; it notified Gatekeeper, and then Gatekeeper's financial backer withdrew their funding.

Faced with conflicting claims of priority, Dana-Farber filed this action. Novartis filed a motion for summary judgment on the grounds that it was entitled to license the '419 patent pursuant to the Research Agreement.

Cancer can result from unchecked cellular growth when protein kinases, such as epidermal growth factor receptor (EGFR) are over-activated. Kinase inhibitors stunt over-activation, effectively shutting off the biochemical reactions that cause cellular proliferation. In this way, kinase inhibitors can be effective at treating certain cancers. In 2008 Dana-Farber researchers discovered an irreversible kinase inhibitor, WZ-4-002, that was effective at inhibiting the EGFR kinase with the T790M mutation.

Judicial Opinion. Judge Woodlock:

1. ENTITLEMENT UNDER THE RESEARCH AGREEMENT

Under the Research Agreement, Novartis could claim licensing priority over the '419 patent if it was invented, discovered or developed in whole or in party by an Institute Program participant, and was conceived or reduced to practice as part of a research project under the direction of an Institute scientist based upon a grant proposal that was submitted to and which was accepted by the Steering Committee . . . for funding pursuant to the Research Agreement. Thus, Novartis must show that: (1) the '419 patent was developed at least in part by an Institute Program Participant . . . ; (2) it was conceived or reduced to practice; and (3) it was done so using grant funds obtained from Novartis under the Research Agreement. The first element is not in dispute to the extent that the parties recognize that Dana-Farber scientists 'engaged in scientific activities' under the Research Agreement . . . were involved in the discovery of all the compounds here.

However, there is some disagreement over the meaning of 'in part.' Novartis argues that 'in part' is quite broad, encompassing ideas that are passed between researchers, information that they share, and sources of inspiration for further independent work. It claims that elements of the '419 patent were discovered 'in part' using funding from Novartis because (a) the 'original seed' of applying irreversible inhibitors to kinases to inhibit cellular proliferation came from Dr. Eck's Novartis-funded work with Jak3; (b) Dr. Eck discovered that the T790M mutant of the EGFR kinase worked by increasing the kinase's affinity for ATP rather than changing its shape; and (c) it was only after Dr. Eck share his ideas with Drs. Gray and Zhou that they began working on WZ-4-002. Gatekeeper, on the other hand, mostly ignores Novartis's implied definition of 'in part' and focuses solely on the direct line of steps from Dr. Zhou's creation of WZ-4-002 to Dr. Janne's discovery that WZ-4-002 inhibits the T790M mutant. As will become apparent below, I am of the view that Novartis's implied understanding it too broad, and that Gatekeeper's apparent assumption more accurately captures the meaning of 'in part.'

i. Conceived or Reduced to Practice

To say that an invention must be 'conceived or reduced to practice' is to invoke terms of art in patent law. In interpreting a contract . . . within a certain industry . . . courts are to apply the technical meaning of the term. As a term of art, 'conception' requires that the inventor have a specific, settled idea such that 'one skilled in the art could understand the invention.' The inventor must be able to describe his invention with particularity. [W]ith chemical compounds conception does not occur unless one has a mental picture of the structure of the chemical, or is able to define it by its method of preparation . . . or whatever characteristics sufficiently distinguish it. Conception also requires a definite and permanent idea of the complete and operative invention as it is thereafter to be applied in practice. [S]imple . . . understanding of the structure of a compound does not satisfy the requirements of conception in the absence of an understanding of either applications in practice, or experimentation to determine the compound's chemical properties. Given the difficulty . . . conception and reduction to practice generally occur simultaneously for chemical compounds. To show that an idea has been reduced to practice, the inventor must prove that he constructed an embodiment or performed a process that meets all the limitations of the claim, and that he determined that the invention would work for its intended purpose.

Here, although WZ-4-002 was first synthesized on May 31, 2007, it was neither conceived nor reduced to practice on that date because its inventor had not discovered its effects on the T790M mutation of the EGFR kinase. Instead, it was only truly conceived and reduced to practice when it was found to be effective at inhibiting the EGFR kinase with the T790M mutation during Dr. Janne's, Dr. Gray's, and Dr. Eck's research in the summer of 2008. It is undisputed that Dr. Janne's lab was the source of the discovery, through testing, that WZ-4-002 was effective as applied to the T790M mutation.

ii. Sources of Funding for WZ-4-002

Under the terms of the Research Agreement, Novartis is entitled to a license of WZ-4-002 only if it was conceived or reduced to practice as part of a Funded Research Project, that is, a research project based upon a grant proposal that was submitted to and . . . accepted by the Steering Committee. Since WZ-4-002 was only created on May 31, 2007, and it was not until the summer of 2008 that it was discovered to be an effective inhibitor of the T790M mutation of EGFR kinase, Novartis must show that the scientists involved were working on a research project funded by Novartis in the summer of 2008.

Novartis strings together a number of different projects over a four-year period in an effort to create a chain or Novartis-funded researchers. However, the relevant time period for the discovery of WZ-4-002's effectiveness against the T790M mutation is somewhere between May 31, 2007, and the end of 2008. Dr. discovered [important properties regarding] the T790M mutation. He therefore suggested that Drs. Janne and Gray [act upon this]. Dr. Gray refused, so Dr. Janne and Dr. Eck did it themselves. Dr. Janne borrowed from Dr. Zhou's library of inhibitors to test . . . and discovered the compound's effectiveness in either September or October 2008. It was then that WZ-4-002 was reduced to practice, and therefore it is within this time period that I must look to see whether the reduction to practice occurred under a Funded Research Project.

The only Novartis grants during this time period provided to scientists arguably involved in the reduction of the WZ-4-002 to practice are (1) Dr. Gray's grant for 2007-2008. [The] grant application does not mention an irreversible covalent bond targeting the T790M mutation at all. [His stated method] is an entirely different method of attacking the kinase, and therefore Dr. Gray's grant application cannot be the source of funding under which WZ-4-002 was reduced to practice. [The other possibility] Dr. Eck's 2007-2008 grant . . . also does not cover WZ-4-002. The goal of the grant application was to determine the three-dimensional structure of . . . proteins [and] [n]one of these aims or goals involve EGFR, or the T790M mutation.

Therefore, Novartis cannot show under the Research Agreement that it was the source of funding for the discovery of WZ-4-002's efficacy in inhibiting the T790M mutant of the EGFR kinase.

Case Questions

1. Describe how Dana Farber can avoid this confusion in future cases.
2. How can Novartis better protect its rights in the future?
3. Dana Farber has a very permissive policy with regard to outside professional pursuits within the same field of work, and so the doctors were able to form a company to leverage their invention, though they still were employed by Dana Farber. Do you recommend changing this policy? Yes/no, and why?

University Inventions for which U.S. Government Research Funds Were Used:

Research by universities, utilizing university resources, and additional government grants and funding, is known as sponsored research. The terms of sponsorship normally create obligations with respect to ownership, and mandate disclosure of inventions, technical data, and so forth. There are potentially three layers of ownership claims in such cases: the workers, the university, and the sponsoring government or private company. Universities own the ideas and technologies invented by their faculty and staff, including those of graduate students who are paid to perform this work. The government has a permissive ownership program, though it reserves the right to march-in and claim rights if the technology does not become fully leveraged by the research team.

This next case is the most recent Supreme Court decision construing the Bayh-Dole Act, and it is crucial to understand the chain of ownership in this invention.

Board of Trustees of Leland Stanford Jr. Univ. v. Roche Molecular Sys., Inc.,

563 U.S. __, 131 S. Ct. 2188 (2011)

Facts: Dr. Mark Holodniy, a post-doctoral research fellow, worked at Stanford University's Department of Infectious diseases studying HIV. When Dr. Holodniy joined Stanford, he signed a Copyright and Patent Agreement ("CPA") stipulating that he "agree[d] to assign" to Stanford "right, title and interest in" inventions resulting from his employment in the department. At some point during his employment at Stanford, research came to a standstill because Stanford needed more knowledge for it to continue. Cetus, a small California-based company formed by former Stanford researchers, was developing a new technique called polymerase chain reaction ("PCR") for quantifying blood-borne levels of HIV. In order to further Stanford's research, Dr. Holodniy's supervisor made arrangements for him conduct research in a cross collaboration with Cetus. As a condition of researching at Cetus, Dr. Holodniy had to sign Cetus' Visitor's Confidentiality Agreement ("VCA") stating that he "will assign and do[es] hereby assign" to Cetus his "right, title and interest in . . . inventions [made] as a consequence of his access" to Cetus' facilities and knowledge.

While working at Cetus, Holodniy co-created with Cetus employees a PCR-based method of measuring the amount of HIV in a patient's blood. He then returned to Stanford and tested the procedure. Stanford subsequently obtained written assignments of rights from Holodniy and other Stanford employees involved in the refinement of the PCR process, and the University proceeded to secure three patents for this new process.

Another research firm, Roche Molecular Systems, later acquired Cetus' PCR-related assets including all rights Cetus had obtained through its agreement with Dr. Holodniy. Roche then commercialized the process Holodniy developed while at Cetus, and began to market HIV test kits that are now used globally. This litigation arose when the Board of Trustees of Stanford sued Roche, claiming that these test kits infringed the patents Stanford had secured. Stanford based its argument on the Bayh-Dole Act, which was created to streamline patent policy with regard to federally funded research and to prompt small businesses, universities, and similar nonprofit organizations to reduce inventions to practice and commercialize them in order to confer benefits on the public. Congress sought to accomplish these aims under the Act by assuring those that it funded that they may keep title to intellectual property they own. However, it is important to note that, under the Act, the government retains "march-in rights" which gives it the power to grant licenses itself to other parties if contractors fail to commercialize the invention.

Stanford argued that the Bayh-Dole Act was triggered because this research was funded by the federal government via the National Institutes of Health. Stanford contended that because of its status as a federally funded contractor of this research under the Bayh-Dole Act, title to Holodniy's invention automatically vested in Stanford. Therefore, Holodniy owned no rights to assign. Roche, on the other hand, argued that it had acquired these rights through Holodniy's VCA agreement with Cetus and that these rights were not extinguished by the Bayh-Dole Act, rendering it a co-owner of Holodniy's invention and depriving Stanford of proper standing to file suit against it.

In this essentially inconsistent assignment case, the District Court ruled in favor of Stanford, holding that the Bayh-Dole Act superseded Holodniy's agreement with Cetus. The Court of Appeals for the Federal Circuit disagreed, holding that the Act did not automatically extinguish Holodniy's right to the title of his invention and that while the language of Dr. Holodniy's CPA with Stanford contained a promise to assign future rights to Stanford, the VCA assigned his present rights to Cetus immediately, trumping Stanford's claim as a matter of contract law. The Court ruled, therefore, that rights passed to Roche when it acquired Cetus' PCR-related assets. The Supreme Court granted certiorari and Chief Justice Roberts delivered the opinion of the Court.

Opinion, Chief Justice Roberts: Since 1790, the patent law has operated on the premise that rights in an invention belong to the inventor. The question here is whether the University and Small Business Patent Procedures Act of 1980—commonly referred to as the Bayh–Dole Act—displaces that norm and automatically vests title to federally funded inventions in federal contractors. We hold that it does not.

* * * * *

In 1980, Congress passed the Bayh–Dole Act to "promote the utilization of inventions arising from federally supported research," "promote collaboration between commercial concerns and nonprofit organizations," and "ensure that the Government obtains sufficient rights in federally supported inventions." To achieve these aims, the Act allocates rights in federally funded "subject invention[s]" between the Federal Government and federal contractors ("any person, small business firm, or nonprofit organization that is a party to a funding agreement"). The Act defines "subject invention" as "any invention of the contractor conceived or first actually reduced to practice in the performance of work under a funding agreement."

The Bayh–Dole Act provides that contractors may "elect to retain title to any subject invention." To be able to retain title, a contractor must fulfill a number of obligations imposed by the statute. *** The "Federal Government may receive title" to a subject invention if a contractor fails to comply with any of these obligations.

The Government has several rights in federally funded subject inventions under the Bayh–Dole Act. The agency that granted the federal funds receives from the contractor "a nonexclusive, nontransferrable, irrevocable, paid-up license to practice . . . [the] subject invention."

* * * * *

Congress has the authority "[t]o promote the Progress of Science and useful Arts, by securing . . . to Authors and Inventors the exclusive Right to their respective Writings and Discoveries." *** Although much in intellectual property law has changed in the 220 years since the first Patent Act, the basic idea that inventors have the right to patent their inventions has not. Under the law in its current form, "[w]hoever invents or discovers any new and useful process, machine, manufacture, or composition of matter . . . may obtain a patent therefor." *** In most cases, a patent may be issued only to an applying inventor, or—because an inventor's interest in his invention is "assignable in law by an instrument in writing"—an inventor's assignee.

Our precedents confirm the general rule that rights in an invention belong to the inventor.

* * * * *

It is equally well established that an inventor can assign his rights in an invention to a third party. *** Thus, although others may acquire an interest in an invention, any such interest—as a general rule—must trace back to the inventor.

In accordance with these principles, we have recognized that unless there is an agreement to the contrary, an employer does not have rights in an invention "which is the original conception of the employee alone." Such an invention "remains the property of him who conceived it." In most circumstances, an inventor must expressly grant his rights in an invention to his employer if the employer is to obtain those rights.

Stanford . . . contend[s] that the Bayh–Dole Act reorders the normal priority of rights in an invention when the invention is conceived or first reduced to practice with the support of federal funds. In their view, the Act moves inventors from the front of the line to the back by vesting title to federally funded inventions in the inventor's employer—the federal contractor.

Congress has in the past divested inventors of their rights in inventions by providing unambiguously that inventions created pursuant to specified federal contracts become the property of the United States. *** Such language is notably absent from the Bayh–Dole Act. Nowhere in the Act is title expressly vested in contractors or anyone else; nowhere in the Act are inventors expressly deprived of their interest in federally funded inventions. Instead, the Act provides that contractors may "elect to retain title to any subject invention."

* * *

The Bayh–Dole Act's provision stating that contractors may "elect to *retain* title" confirms that the Act does not *vest* title. *** You cannot retain something unless you already have it. *** The Bayh–Dole Act does not confer title to federally funded inventions on contractors or authorize contractors to unilaterally take title to those inventions; it simply assures contractors that they may keep title to whatever it is they already have. Such a provision makes sense in a statute specifying the respective rights and responsibilities of federal contractors and the Government.

The Bayh–Dole Act states that it "take[s] precedence over any other Act which would require a disposition of rights in subject inventions . . . that is inconsistent with" the Act. *** But because the Bayh–Dole Act . . . applies only to "subject inventions"—"inventions of the contractor"—it does not displace an inventor's antecedent title to his invention. Only when an invention belongs to the contractor does the Bayh–Dole Act come into play. The Act's disposition of rights—like much of the rest of the Bayh–Dole Act—serves to clarify the order of priority of rights between the Federal Government and a federal contractor in a federally funded invention that already belongs to the contractor. Nothing more.

* * * * *

[O]ur construction of the Bayh–Dole Act is reflected in the common practice among parties operating under the Act. Contractors generally institute policies to obtain assignments from their employees. Agencies that grant funds to federal contractors typically expect those contractors to obtain assignments. So it is with the NIH. In guidance documents made available to contractors, NIH has made clear that "[b]y law, an inventor has initial ownership of an invention" and that contractors should therefore "have in place employee agreements requiring an inventor to 'assign' or give ownership of an invention to the organization upon acceptance of Federal funds." Such guidance would be unnecessary if Stanford's reading of the statute were correct.

Stanford contends that reading the Bayh–Dole Act as not vesting title to federally funded inventions in federal contractors "fundamentally undermin[es]" the Act's framework and severely threatens its continued "successful application." We do not agree. As just noted, universities typically enter into agreements with their employees requiring the assignment to the university of rights in inventions. With an effective assignment, those inventions—if federally funded—become "subject inventions" under the Act, and the statute as a practical matter works pretty much the way Stanford says it should. The only significant difference is that it does so without violence to the basic principle of patent law that inventors own their inventions.

Concurring, Justice Sotomayor: I agree with the Court's resolution of this case and with its reasoning *** Like the dissent, however, I understand the majority opinion to permit consideration of these arguments in a future case.

Dissenting, Justice Breyer and Justice Ginsburg: * * * I would return this case to the Federal Circuit for further argument *** The importance of assuring this community "benefit" [of invention] is reflected in legal rules that may deny or limit the award of patent rights where the public has already paid to produce an invention, lest the public bear the potential costs of patent protection where there is no offsetting need for such protection to elicit that invention. Why should the public have to pay twice for the same invention?

* * * * *

[T]he [Bayh–Dole] Act's provisions reflect a related effort to assure that rights to inventions arising out of research for which the public has paid are distributed and used in ways that further specific important public interests. I agree with the majority that the Act does not simply take the individual inventors' rights and grant them to the Government. Rather, it assumes that the federal funds' recipient, say a university or small business, will possess those rights. The Act leaves those rights in the hands of that recipient, not because it seeks to make the public pay twice for the same invention, but for a special public policy reason. In doing so, it seeks to encourage those institutions *to commercialize* inventions that otherwise might not realize their potentially beneficial public use *** Given this basic statutory objective, I cannot so easily accept the majority's conclusion—that the individual inventor can lawfully assign an invention (produced by public funds) to a third party, thereby taking that invention out from under the Bayh–Dole Act's restrictions, conditions, and allocation rules.

Case Questions

1. Who owns an invention initially? The individual inventor employed by an organization, or the organization?
2. Can you develop a rationale for why universities and other research teams would maintain a permissive licensing arrangement with its researchers, even knowing the outcome of this case?
3. Say Congress wants to revisit the language of the Bayh-Dole Act after this decision. How should the statute be re-written so as to avoid such an outcome as this in the future?

Inventions of University Students

The rules governing ownership rights to the work of *undergraduate* students generally are that the university has no rights to the invention. The resolution of cases is less clear however, if, for example, the work is created by students where significant use was made of university funds or facilities. This may be subject to a department review and finalized by a university committee.

Here is an example of an invention made on campus by undergraduates resulting in a rather unclear situation. Four students in a freshman design class at Rensselaer Polytechnic Institute created a neat building solution for a class project challenging them to solve a social problem. Two years later, two of the students met off-campus, refined their original design, and attempted to commercialize their earlier work. The university's licensing managers quickly got involved and began asking questions. When had the students conceived the design? Were their design sessions held on or off campus? What equipment had they used for building their prototypes? The university ultimately decided that it owned the idea but that the two students owned the design, and it required the students to license the technology from the university. (The general split for royalties at universities is approximately one-third to inventors, two-thirds to the Department/Lab/Research Center. Because this case involved a studio design course, the university re-allocated the royally split to three-quarters to inventors, one-quarter to the university.) With the tools for developing new ideas broadly available to everyone thanks to the Internet and free and open source software, university technology licensing offices have become intensely interested in student work.

Open Letter from Aaron Greenspan, president and CEO of Think Computer Corporation to Mark Zuckerberg, founder of Facebook: "Remember that web site you signed up for at Harvard two days before we met in January, 2004, called houseSYSTEM—the one I made with the Universal Face Book that pre-dated your site by four months?"

Another famous invention from a college campus involves Facebook's intricate and shadowy struggle with a number of undergraduate students claiming rights to the idea, the site, the technology, and even part ownership of the company itself. (The university had no legal claims to the invention since it was not accomplished with any significant university resources.) Just one of the many lawsuits against Facebook, this next case was brought by three former classmates asserting ownership of the original social networking idea, and copyright to the software.

The Facebook, Inc., v. ConnectU,
Order Granting Plaintiffs' Confidential Motion to Enforce the Settlement Agreement, No. C-07-01389-JW (N.D. Cal. June 25, 2008)

Facts: Then college sophomores Divya Narendra, Cameron Winklevoss, and Tyler Winklevoss first conceived of an idea, a dating site to connect students at Harvard and other universities in December 2002, and tentatively name it "Harvard Connection" (later changing the name to "ConnectU"). Lacking the programming expertise for this, they enlisted Sanjay Mavinkurve, then a senior, to write its code. When he left, the founders enlisted Victor Gao, then a junior. Gao subsequently left the team too, and in November 2003, the founders enlisted defendant Mark Zuckerberg to complete the portion of the site devoted to student-alumni networking. (Zuckerberg had caught the attention of Plaintiffs because in September 2003, he had created a site called "facemash," a Harvard version of "am I hot-or-not." It was met with intense criticism; he was accused of hacking into the university's computer system to copy and incorporate dorm ID images, violating copyright, and personal data privacy of students, and placed on academic probation.)

The four worked over a period of three months, meeting a few times and exchanging a number of emails. The Plaintiffs told Defendant what they were trying to accomplish, and Defendant agreed to finish their site. There was no formal contract, nor was pay discussed. Apparently Defendant put in about 10 hours of computer programming time. According to Defendant, the work scope was not clearly conveyed, and way more needed to be done than Plaintiffs thought. Defendant testified that he thought he was little more than an occasional contributor, and that he fell out of contact with Plaintiffs and barely completed any of the work Plaintiffs asked for due to his more important computer science projects. The two sides met for a ConnectU planning session January 14, 2004, and Defendant expressed doubts about the viability of the project. He did not inform them of his own projects. Meanwhile, three days prior to this, Defendant had registered the domain name, thefacebook.com for himself, unbeknownst to Plaintiffs. With the help of classmates Eduardo Saverin, Dustin Moskovitz, Chris Hughes and Andrew McCollum, on February 4th, Defendant's site went live.

On February 8th, Plaintiffs learned that Defendant launched his site. Thefacebook site was designed in a way that it could be introduced at other schools. It had a similar look and layout to what Harvard Connection was trying for; yet at this point Plaintiff's site was not ready to launch because the coding was incomplete. On February 10th, Plaintiffs sent a letter to Defendant claiming that he used their ideas to build a competing site. The Facebook quickly went viral and by June 2004, it was available on 30 campuses and 150,000 students were registered.

Plaintiffs petitioned the university's disciplinary board asserting that the theft of their intellectual property violated college regulations when Defendant stalled them while incorporating their ideas into his own project that became Facebook. The board ruled in Defendant's favor, as the board considered the dispute to fall outside the scope of the college's authority. Harvard Connection, by then re-named ConnectU, went live in May 2004, but by then it was overshadowed by Facebook and Plaintiffs' site failed to gain traction.

Plaintiffs filed suit in federal district court in Massachusetts alleging that Defendants stole their idea, their site's source code, and business plan when he worked for them as an unpaid programmer. Further that he breached the agreement to provide source code and that his intentional delay was tortious, done simply to gain a competitive advantage. They requested that Facebook's assets be transferred to them. Defendant countersued in federal district court in California, accusing ConnectU of unfair business practices. The California court ordered the parties into mediation.

In the Massachusetts litigation, even though discovery had not been com-pleted, the parties agreed to suspend proceedings in anticipation of California mediation. This dispute resolution process resulted in an Agreement being produced wherein the parties agreed that the California federal district court shall have jurisdiction to enforce the Agreement, and therefore the Massachusetts litigation ceased.

The parties agreed to a settlement, but while discovery was ongoing, Con-nectU reportedly found instant messages on Facebook's computers amounting to a "smoking gun" of evidence substantiating their allegations, and so ConnectU tried backing out of the settlement. Facebook filed this lawsuit seeking enforce-ment of the original settlement agreement, which is an enforceable contract.

Judicial Opinion. Judge Ware:
In the course of this series of lawsuits, the parties engaged in private mediation. They agreed to resolve all of their disputes and to dismiss the pending lawsuits, and that there may be "more formal documents but these terms are binding." In the Agreement, the parties stipulate that the federal court has jurisdiction to enforce it. Based on a belief that a court order is necessary to enforce the Set-tlement Agreement, Facebook filed the present motion in this Court. The question for decision is whether the Settlement Agreement contains sufficiently definite and essential terms that it may be enforced.

ConnectU contend that Facebook's motion should be denied because (1) the agreement is missing material terms... and...(3) Facebook committed fraud in the procurement of the Agreement. [NOTE: valuing Facebook was difficult because at that time, it was a private company with no known business model, nor was there a comparable business for which to gauge approximate value.]

THE MATERIAL TERMS

California has a strong policy in favor of enforcing settlement agreements. [Here] the Agreement clearly states the consideration for the performance required and how it must be paid. In exchange for a specified amount of cash and stock in Facebook, ConnectU founders . . . have no further claims against Facebook. Second, the Agreement clearly defines the structure of the transaction. Subsequent negotiations might have proposed a different structure for the transaction or other additional terms, but those proposals were, apparently, rejected. Third, the principals of each company all signed the Agreement. One ConnectU stockholder did not. A share exchange transaction only needs to be approved by majority vote. Therefore, the lack of this signature is not an impediment to enforcing the Agreement.

WHETHER THE AGREEMENT WAS PROCURED BY FRAUD?

A contract is not enforceable if it was induced by fraud. To prove fraud in the inducement of a contract, a party must establish the elements of common law fraud. ConnectU contend that they were defrauded during settlement negotiations because Facebook did not disclose a valuation of Facebook common stock that had been made by the Board of Directors. (This valuation of company stock was for $15 billion, which would have given the ConnectU founders a much larger settlement than they received, which was based on a Facebook valuation of $3.75 billion.) As the Agreement does not attribute a specific value to the Facebook shares, there is no admissible evidence of any such representation while negotiating a settlement. The Court finds ConnectU has failed to establish that Facebook made misrepresentations during negotiations. On or before June 30, 2008, the parties are directed to submit a proposed form of judgment consistent with this Order.

[Note: The parties reached a settlement for Facebook to pay $65 million to ConnectU reportedly, most of it in the form of Facebook stock, plus $20 million in cash.]

There are three postscripts to this case:

Postscript 1: Aaron Greenspan's HouseSYSTEM. Another aggrieved inventor. Greenspan apparently had the original idea for this type of site and *his work preceded both projects.* His Web portal launched August 1, 2003, rich in features that he designed as an improvement to the official university site. It was also more useful than the printed and bound "Face Book" that every incoming freshman received (a nearly one-hundred-year old tradition). By September 2003, Greenspan referred to his invention as a "Universal Face Book," and occasionally, as "the facebook." He met with Zuckerberg in early January 2004, at which time Zuckerberg, Hughes, Moskovitz, and Eduardo Severin were already users of Greenspan's HouseSYSTEM. They talked about their projects, and at one point Greenspan suggested the two integrate their systems, but they eventually decided to work on their own site projects separately. Right after this meeting, on January 11, 2004, Zuckerberg registered the domain name thefacebook.com.

Postscript 2: *Chang v. Winklevoss,* 2011 Mass. Super. LEXIS 60 (Mass. Super. Ct., Apr. 28, 2011). Another aggrieved participant, Wayne Chang was well-known for his i2hub file-sharing program that relied on high-speed connections available at universities; his work caught the attention of the ConnectU founders in late 2004. At that time, Facebook had launched and ConnectU languished, but they had filed the original lawsuit. The founders approached Chang about going into business together. In Chang's complaint, he asserts that he signed a Memorandum of Understanding (this is a statement of intent describing the parties' goals, though not generally construed as a contract). He was given a 15 percent stake in the new venture and in return he was to provide integration of ConnectU and i2hub assets. In addition he helped build new technologies including a textbook resale site called Jungalu, and an aggregator site called Social Butterfly that pulled data from other social networking sites. He claimed that the ConnectU founders abruptly severed ties in April 2005 after everything was built out, in contravention of the terms in the Memorandum, and therefore he was entitled to part of the proceeds from the multi-million-dollar *ConnectU v. Facebook* settlement. The Judge refused to grant ConnectU's motion to dismiss these claims.

Postscript 3: *Ceglia v. Zuckerberg,* Case No. 10-CV-00569A(F) (Fed. Dist. Ct. W.D.N.Y, Jan. 10, 2012). Paul Ceglia filed a complaint claiming that he owns a majority stake in Facebook based on a 2003 agreement he signed with Zuckerberg to perform site design and coding work. The agreement outlines a series of events that conflicts with other of Zuckerberg's statements as to the idea and creation of the Facebook site. Though there is conflicting evidence on some claims for coding work, in 2012, federal agents arrested Ceglia, charging him with fabricating evidence specifically as to the Facebook claims.

Case Questions

1. Who do you think should be known as the one who came up with the original idea for social networking? And which do you think is more important from a business perspective: the idea or the execution of the idea?
2. Given that the judge ordered a $65 million cash-stock award to the ConnectU founder, and ConnectU's legal bill is reportedly $13 million, the ConnectU founders are in arbitration with the law firm now over the bill. Recommend an alternative verdict and award in this case.
3. Can you identify strategies to best protect against getting beaten to market by a competitor who is a former employee?

The rules governing ownership rights to the inventions of *graduate* students (such as in the *Board of Trustees* case, above) generally are that the university has legal rights, since these students are in an employment relationship with the university. With the exception of students' theses, universities claim all intellectual property developed, using significant university facilities, equipment or funds—or even if their research was funded externally by the government, since such agreements are administered by the university. As an example of this, recall that the algorithm for Google search was claimed by Stanford since it was developed by graduate students who used significant university resources, and even as it was the subject of a government research grant. When the inventors founded a business, Google, Inc., Stanford negotiated a license agreement with the newly-formed company for allowing exclusive use of the technology that they invented. Universities require all employees to execute invention assignment and disclosure agreements agreeing to assign title to the invention, and further, to disclose all inventions created during the course of employment.

Business Models for Startups Made Possible by the Internet and Other Disruptive Innovations

"'Check this! @Newsweek was just sold for $1. To show you how media has changed, the asking price for my @Twitter account's $65 billion. Cash.' 2.29 p.m. Aug 4th via web."—http://twitter.com/ConanOBrien

This section considers how the Internet changed business models and considers which models the Internet can tolerate. We consider a number of scenarios, including: How can businesses start up (like Facebook), reaching only for users initially while ignoring the need to make money? How can businesses start up (like Wikipedia) and survive by relying only on donations to cover expenses? How can businesses charge for content (like newspapers) when users have become used to free content? Can businesses compete with free? And what about the emerging sharing economy?

A **business model** can be defined as a series of activities designed to yield a new product or service that will give company a competitive advantage as well as a sustainable financial return, a plan that creates value with levers to impact return on equity to shareholders.

More broadly, business models are defined as "a business model describes the rationale of how an organization creates, delivers and captures value" and yields comparative advantages. *Business Model Generation* p.12 (2010). This can be in the form of added economic value or even social value. This is achieved through a number of initiatives in areas that include product development, marketing, delivery. Developing a business model is the core to a successful business strategy.

How the Internet Changed the Possibilities for Business Models

It is useful to consider traditional business models using two examples: a traditional car-manufacturing company, and a legacy network TV show. In the manufacturing scenario, there are enormous fixed costs: large factory spaces, complicated supply chains for raw materials and finished parts, and byzantine distribution chains for the finished product; plus there are a myriad of government regulatory standards (safety, pay, immigration compliance, and so forth) at both the federal *and* state levels. Cars are designed and built "on spec," meaning that they are dreamed up by a small internal work team, built out, and sold before actually knowing whether they these are the cars consumers want to buy. There is an element of betting to this model. Much is the same with network TV shows: they are created, produced and distributed, like cars, and networks present this content to viewers without choice as to time, or format (22 minutes, with 3 commercial breaks). It's an asymmetrical, top-down "push" model. Think about how the Internet became a point of departure from this historical business-to-consumer model, and how, therefore, the Internet creates new possibilities for business models.

It is almost as if the process is reversed because of the Internet. The Internet flattens, and to an extent, flips, this hierarchy, with users more able to take control of content and manipulate it in new inventive ways. The effect has radically transformed business models.

1. The classic legacy business model is known as a "**push model**." It is built on a hierarchical structure and predicated on control. Producers or suppliers initiate transactions and push goods through channels. There are physical limits at every phase, including limits to output, distribution, inventory and so forth. The traditional business model is defined by the need for large spaces to accomplish the work, along with a large number of workers at the work site simultaneously. It is a model of command and control in essence. Networks tell us when we can watch a show; movie studios use the "windowing" system and control movie releases, and so forth.

2. The Internet changed possibilities and created some new paradigms. For example, in this era, the Internet can support a range of different business models because the conditions, the goods, and the services are quite different. These models are more in the form of a "**pull model**." Here customers initiate transactions and pull goods through the distribution channels. There are many other fundamental differences to the goods and services online as well. For digital goods, there are no limits on output, distribution, inventory, or time; work can be done remotely and asynchronously; marginal costs related to transmission and distribution of these goods are at, or near, zero. Also, there is an ethos of cooperation and a comfort level for self-organizing in ways that are similar to the original Internet build-out, perhaps stemming from its origins as an open academic communications platform.

The Internet offers an architecture of openness and encourages collaboration as well as participation. This is made possible by the external technical environment, especially because of lightweight platforms, simplicity of the software, mashable products, open APIs, and feeds. Also, there are efficiencies and cost savings because many of the goods and services are intangible. The Internet makes such jobs tradable anywhere—there are no borders to the Internet. The Internet made communication and distribution free, and sharing easy, allowing for global participation in digital work outside the confines of formal corporate cultures. This has made possible daring business strategies of pursuing users and growth first, leaving the worrying about monetizing for later, all because of network effects: the value of a site increases with the number of users. Furthermore, the Internet was built on an ethos of cooperative, collaborative and free. This is exemplified by the phenomenon of cooperative free labor capacity on the Internet, with Mozilla's Firefox browser as an example—the self-organizing teams of people to create valuable resources outside of traditional corporate culture. Firefox competes against proprietary browsers like Google's Chrome, Microsoft's Internet Explorer and Apple's Safari, for which each company spent enormous resources. The Internet leveled the field as to distribution and access. How will companies be able to compete?

Businesses have to be more transparent, too, because their users are online communicating about them. For example, Appleinsider covers Apple, Inc. Such user communities may serve users even better than the company does. In this environment, businesses need a structure, a model that allows them to collaborate and communicate with their users. It is no longer a hierarchy—customers may also be business partners in the form of app developers. Users want what they want, when they want it, and how they want it. They do not want to buy an expensive CD when they want only two of the songs it contains. They will go to any number of sites to access that content for free—even if it is not the best recording, or they may go to a paid site if it works easily and well enough—or they may opt to not even own music anymore and just stream songs they want. So it becomes reasonable for this class of goods and services to have different models that feature some aspect of free use or tiered access. The Internet has empowered individuals at the expense of large organizations and governments. In a Web 2.0 world, businesses have to adjust their models because Internet users have access to the same tools for collaboration and building knowledge as businesses.

To be sure, there are common aspects to traditional and new business models. No matter what, there are still costs for capital, production, labor, operating and non-operating expenses. In the final analysis, while business models may differ, the ends are the same: namely, to maintain a commercial advantage in the form of a competitive barrier with resilient, scalable, differentiated and global goods and services.

Business Models facilitated by the Internet

Free

So-called because there is no defined cost to users. Sites give away their services or content to users for free, generating revenue from third parties to cover expenses. This is Google's business model for its search engine. Google and all other companies that use this model analyze users' behavioral data for some period of time in order to improve relevancy for their advertisers, as well as to enhance the user experience on its site. It is said that users pay for free with their privacy. For more on this issue, consult the Privacy chapter.

Freemium

This model is a tiered service: free access to some content, and paid access to a similar, though premium-level user experience, such as enhanced content, coverage, speed, capacity or services. It is often employed when a site's ad revenue is not high enough to cover all costs. The *Wall Street Journal* employs the freemium model. Low barriers for membership and payment for full-site access and services are signatures of this model. Research shows that users will pay for sites they have an affinity for and find the paid content has added value. The challenge is figuring out what content to charge for, and at what price.

Subscription

Users pay a set periodic fee to maintain access to that service. Instead of a one-time sale, it amounts to a recurring sale that is meant to build brand loyalty and generate steady, predictable revenue. The subscription, or license, could be for timed access to a service, for a single copy, or for unlimited use. This is the model used by Netflix, for example. Apple and other hardware makers are utilizing subscription models for some apps.

Auction

In this business model, users bid against each other for goods or services. This is particularly useful for unique goods that trade infrequently and do not have an easily established value. Think of a postcard with a photo of a long-gone summer camp that you would not pay a penny for, though someone who was a camper there would gladly pay a relative for the opportunity to own this memento. Famously a central feature of eBay and Priceline, sites earn revenue from listing fees and/or commissions based on the transaction's value.

Co-development and Open Innovation

These are models based on collective intelligence and cooperation, such as the Mozilla Firefox build-out. In a co-development model, businesses share work responsibilities with consumers/users/non-employees, who are actively engaged in product development with a company they do not work for. In a straight, open innovation model, businesses provide only the building blocks, the platform and tools for participation (like M.I.T.'s sourcemap, Wikipedia, Linux, SourceForge, etc.). Another active area currently is cooperative build-outs of digital payment systems. Though its status as a legitimate currency is disputed, Bitcoin uses p2p cooperation to operate a digital payments system without a single administrator or a central government banking authority. It is challenging to develop a sustainable open innovation business model (though at this time Bitcoin purchasers are charged fees, but no such fee schedules exist with other open innovation models). Research shows that the open innovation model mostly succeeds for carefully designed discrete tasks with incentives crafted to attract effective participants (like in the Netflix prize example).

Donation

This model is also free to users. Sites or software are supported not by ads, but rather by voluntary donations. Wikipedia is perhaps the most prominent of the donor-funded sites, and it is entirely a work of collaboration among remote, asynchronous non-aligned users who share their expertise while donating their time.

Pay-What-You-Want (PWYW)

The name is self-explanatory; the social impact is quite remarkable. This model essentially asks users to consider the value of the product or service and personally assess worth, rather than be told its worth, and using this model, consumers avoid "buyers' remorse." Producers may set a minimum price in this model. Radiohead released their album *In Rainbows* using this payment scheme. Analysis showed that 38 percent of downloaders chose to pay something, and 62 percent did not. The average price paid was $6 globally. US downloaders paid just over $8. The worldwide average was $2.26. Twelve percent were willing to pay in the range of the typical costs of an album on iTunes. Panera experimented with this in one of its restaurants as, "take what you need, leave your fair share." Panera co-founder Ron Shaich quipped, "It's a test of human nature. The real question is whether the community can sustain it."

Sharing/p2p

In this emerging model, users manage their transactions using businesses' software apps that connect individual users through easy, intuitive templates covering communications, logistics, insurance, and payments between users. The software business receives a transaction fee for transactions processed through its app. Uber and Airbnb are classic examples of this model. Though each is presently valued in the billions, neither owns any physical assets like taxis or hotels. Airbnb is the go-to site that turns users into hoteliers for hosting other users, even though the company does not own one hotel room, and Uber is the go-to site connecting drivers to riders though the company does not own any taxi medallions. Is Airbnb merely a software app? Or are hosts running hotels, and therefore, subject to city and state safety codes, nondiscrimination mandates, and hotel taxes? Is Uber merely a software app? Or are drivers running taxi services, and therefore, subject to city and state safety codes, nondiscrimination mandates, and the regulatory control of the medallion system? The sharing model has generated a huge amount of controversy in these instances, for these are entirely new classifications for goods and services. Innovations and inventions that break through established classifications and thereby establish new categories of goods and services are on the front lines of navigating the inevitable regulatory snarl.

The next three cases showcase the surprising challenges of pioneering a new category of goods and services. As it turns, out, there are typically outsize rewards for such disruptive innovators. These category creators experience higher growth rates and receive much higher valuations than companies that produce merely incremental innovations.

Airbnb, Inc. v. Schneiderman,
No. 5393-13 (Sup. Ct. N.Y. May 13, 2014)

Facts: Petitioner Airbnb provides a site connecting individuals who offer accommodations (hosts) to individuals who wish to book accommodations (guests). If the parties agree on the price and terms, they complete the transaction on the site, and Airbnb receives a 6-12% commission, plus a value added tax, if applicable, which is added to guest payments.

Airbnb's business model prompted scrutiny under two different New York state laws. First, New York law makes it illegal to rent out one's own apartment to someone else for less than 30 days, unless the actual renter is physically present during this time. Very occasional renting of one's apartment is exempted.

Second, New York law provides that city hotel rooms are subject to a 14.75% tax (comprised of a city hotel room occupancy tax, and a state sales tax). Hotels are defined as buildings regularly used for the lodging of guests. Hotel operator is defined as anyone operating a hotel in the city, and therefore must collect the taxes.

The Office of the New York State Attorney General asserts that even the most cursory review of Airbnb listings on any given day would produce 19,000+ listings, for just New York City. Further, the City's Department of Finance figures show that only a small minority of these Hosts filed Certificates of Registration. The record indicates that there are Hosts regularly using their apartments to provide lodging, and who may not be complying with the state and local tax requirements, and thus are illegal hosts, as well as evading taxes.

The Attorney General's Office sent a subpoena to Airbnb commanding it to produce the following data for 225,000 New Yorkers:

1. "An Excel spreadsheet identifying all Hosts that rent accommodation(s) in New York State including: (a) name, physical and email address, and other contact information; (b) website user name; (c) address of the accommodation(s) rented, including unit or apartment number; (d) the dates, duration of guest stay, and the rates charged for the rental; (e) method of payment to Host including account information; and (f) total gross revenue per Host generated.
2. For each Host . . . documents sufficient to identify all tax-related communications your website has had with the Host."

Airbnb challenged this order, asserting that the subpoena should be quashed as: (i) there is no reasonable, articulable basis to warrant such investigation and the subpoena constitutes an unfounded 'fishing expedition' . . . and (iii) the subpoena is overbroad and burdensome; and (iv) the subpoena seeks confidential, private information from petitioner's users.

Judicial Opinion. Judge Connolly: The law requires that some factual basis be demonstrated to support a subpoena. [T]he agency asserting its subpoena power must show ' . . . some basis for inquisitorial action' [citations omitted].

Factual Basis Upon a motion contesting a subpoena, the Attorney General need only show that the records and book which he seeks bear a reasonable relation to the subject-matter under investigation and to the public purpose to be achieved. He does not, it is true, have arbitrary and unbridled discretion as to the scope of his investigation, but, unless the subpoena calls for documents which are utterly irrelevant to any proper inquiry or its futility to uncover anything that is inevitable or obvious, the courts will be slow to strike it down. Based upon the facts as alleged in the record before the Court, petitioner's assertions that a factual predicate has not been established are without merit as there is evidence that a substantial number of Hosts may be in violation of the . . . Dwelling Law and/or New York State and/or New York City tax provisions.

Breadth of the Subpoena A general factual predicate for the issuance of the subpoena has been established. The subpoena, however, broadly requests information for 'all Hosts that rent accommodation(s) in New York State.' The subpoena . . . is not limited to New York City Hosts . . . nor is it limited to rentals of less than thirty days. Further, with respect to the [city hotel tax] such subpoena is again not limited to New York City Hosts, nor does it take into account the exception. Finally . . . the state tax law applies . . . where a building is considered a 'hotel' and is 'regularly used and kept open as such for the lodging of guests.' The subpoena at issue, however, does not provide any limitation with respect to petitioner's Hosts (*i.e.*, exempting such Hosts that have used [Airbnb] only once).

While petitioner bears the burden of demonstrating that the subpoena is overbroad . . . a plain reading of the subpoena in light [of the laws] meets such burden. Based on the foregoing, the subpoena at issue, as drafted seeks materials that are irrelevant to the inquiry at hand and accordingly, must be quashed.

Unduly Burdensome Petitioner has failed to demonstrate that the subpoena is unduly burdensome. Respondent seeks . . . the Host's name, address of accommodation, dates of stay, rates, method of payment and total revenue from the rental. Petitioner . . . with . . . hundreds of thousands of separate (presumably) electronic records, has failed to establish . . . that such information is not collected by petitioner nor readily accessible by petitioner. Petitioner's conclusory assertions that it will be difficult to provide, *inter alia*, the names, addresses and

STATE OF NEW YORK
OFFICE OF THE ATTORNEY GENERAL

ERIC T. SCHNEIDERMAN
ATTORNEY GENERAL

DIVISION OF ECONOMIC JUSTICE
INTERNET BUREAU

May 20, 2014

Via Electronic Mail
Belinda Johnson, Esq.
General Counsel
Airbnb, Inc.
888 Brannan Street, 4th Floor
San Francisco, CA

     Re: Agreement Regarding Compliance with Subpoena

Dear Ms. Johnson:

This letter confirms an agreement (the "Agreement") reached between the Office of the Attorney General of the State of New York ("NYAG") and Airbnb, Inc. ("Airbnb") regarding the subpoena served upon Airbnb in the course of an NYAG investigation.

(1) NYAG issued a subpoena on Wednesday, May 14, 2014, and NYAG and Airbnb hereby agree that compliance with the terms of this Agreement shall be considered compliance with the May 14 subpoena.

(2) Airbnb shall provide to NYAG a data set that is consistent, in its composition, with the data set requested by the May 14 subpoena. The data set shall be anonymized, however, by redacting for users: (a) name, e-mail address, telephone numbers, and any social media account information; (b) Website user name, HostID, ListingID; (c) unit/apartment number(s); (d) social security number or tax identification number(s); and (e) any specific payment or payout instrument account numbers, codes, security questions/answers or password information that would enable access to an account. User names will be replaced by unique identifiers. Unit/apartment number(s) will also be replaced by unique identifiers. The data set shall also indicate if a listing is currently inactive and became inactive after October 1, 2013. The information required by this paragraph shall be produced beginning twenty-one (21) days after execution of this agreement and continuing on a rolling basis until Airbnb certifies that all such information has been produced. Production shall take no longer than thirty (30) days unless extended by NYAG in writing.

(3) For a period of twelve (12) months from completion of production of anonymized data, Airbnb shall further comply with the subpoena by producing the (a) name, e-mail address,

telephone numbers, and social media account information; (b) Website user name, HostID, Listing ID; (c) unit/apartment number(s); and (d) tax identification number(s) for individual users about whom anonymized data is produced pursuant to paragraph 2 above, and who are then the subjects of an investigation or potential enforcement action by NYAG or the New York City Office of Special Enforcement. Airbnb shall produce the information required by this paragraph only if Airbnb receives written notice under the authority of NYAG or the City of New York's Office of Special Enforcement (served by U.S. Mail to 888 Brannan Street, 4th Floor, San Francisco, CA 94013 [and any physical office for business that Airbnb has or may establish in the City of New York] and by email to Attn: General Counsel at legal@airbnb.com, with a copy to Roberta Kaplan at Paul Weiss, 1285 Avenue of the Americas, New York, NY 10019-6064). Airbnb shall produce the unredacted documents as provided in this paragraph within ten (10) days of receipt or such other period as is extended in writing.

(4) Within twenty-one (21) days after execution of this agreement and for twelve (12) months thereafter, Airbnb shall require all Hosts that list new properties located in New York State to view and click through Exhibit A before they are allowed to list property through Airbnb's platform. Exhibit A shall also be sent to all Hosts that currently list properties located in New York State in an email that does not include other content, other than a short explanation of the reason existing Hosts are receiving it. Prior to the expiration of twelve (12) months from execution of this agreement, Airbnb will meet with NYAG and/or the City of New York's Office of Special Enforcement in good faith to discuss means of providing a summary of New York Law to Hosts listing property in New York State.

(5) NYAG agrees that, to the extent it is permitted by law, it will keep confidential and not share the anonymized data set produced pursuant to paragraph 2 with any third party or other agency, except and only to the extent it is permitted by law without the consent of Airbnb to share such data with the New York City Office of Special Enforcement, the New York City Department of Finance, the New York State Department of Taxation and Finance, prosecutorial or law enforcement agencies, or except in connection with an investigation of an individual or filed enforcement action as permitted by law or by an agreed upon protective order entered by the court. This confidentiality requirement does not apply to the results of any analysis of the data set conducted by NYAG. Nothing in this paragraph shall be deemed to be consent by Airbnb to the transfer of any data by NYAG to any third party. In the event of a FOIL request or other challenge to this provision of the agreement, NYAG agrees to provide advance written notice to Airbnb (email to Attn: General Counsel legal@airbnb.com) in sufficient time to permit Airbnb to seek protective or other relief at its sole expense.

(6) Cooperation. Airbnb agrees to cooperate with NYAG to effect and accomplish the terms of this Agreement. Airbnb will not take any steps to knowingly undermine this Agreement, and shall not take any action or make any statement denying, directly or indirectly, the propriety of this Agreement.

(7) Future Enforcement. Nothing in this letter negates, impinges upon, or waives any enforcement or subpoena right that NYAG or any other law enforcement agency may have against Airbnb or any Host, and does not negate, impinge upon or constitute a waiver of any objection, defense or other right Airbnb may have.

(8) <u>Miscellaneous</u>. This Agreement shall not be deemed or construed to be any approval by NYAG of any of the practices, procedures or conduct of Airbnb or its users, including without limitation, rental activity or the payment of applicable taxes.

This Agreement constitutes the entire agreement between NYAG and Airbnb and supersedes any prior communication, understanding, agreement, whether written or oral, concerning the subject matter of this Agreement.

This Agreement shall be governed by the laws of the State of New York, and any action arising under this Agreement shall be heard by the courts in the State of New York.

Sincerely,

Clark Russell

Clark Russell
Deputy Bureau Chief
Internet Bureau

AGREED TO BY AIRBNB, INC.:

Belinda Johnson

By: Belinda Johnson
Position: General Counsel
Date: 5-20-14

contact information of its Hosts and the address of the Accommodations being rented, as well as any tax communications, if any, that it has provided its Hosts, is insufficient to demonstrate that the subpoena is unduly burdensome.

Confidentiality Petitioner also contends that the subpoena seeks "confidential, private information" from petitioner's users. Initially, petitioner has failed to demonstrate that the requested information is confidential, particularly where petitioner's privacy policy provides that petitioner will disclose any information in its sole discretion that it believes is necessary to respond to, inter alia, subpoenas.

Based on the foregoing, it is hereby

ORDERED that the Court grants petitioner's instant application to quash the subpoena as overbroad and denies respondent's cross-motion to compel.

SO ORDERED.

[Post-script. The parties entered into an agreement the following week regarding the scope of information requested by the Attorney General.]

Case Questions

1. The subpoena in this case was judged to be overbroad, so the AG will have to re-draft his request. Describe the information he actually needs to establish his case.
2. Why is it a matter of concern for the state's Attorney General if people use Airbnb to rent out their spare rooms or homes?
3. Say the average rate of an Airbnb stay in New York City is $100 per night, and the average stay is three nights: how much hotel tax revenue is New York failing to capture? If you were representing hotels, how would you respond to this new category of overnight accommodations?

Boston Cab Dispatch, Inc. v. Uber Techs., Inc.,
2014 U.S. Dist. LEXIS 42063 (D. Mass. Mar. 27, 2014)

Facts: This dispute arose after Uber entered the market for private transportation services in Boston. The crux of the plaintiffs' complaint is that Uber has gained an unfair advantage over traditional taxicab dispatch services and license-holders because it avoids the costs and burdens of complying with the extensive regulations designed to ensure that passengers have access to fairly prices and safe transportation options throughout the city, and yet reaps the benefits of others' compliance with the regulations.

Plaintiff Boston Cab is an approved taxi dispatch service as defined by Rule 403. Its members consist of the owners of Boston licenses, defined as medallions. By statute, the Massachusetts legislature empowered the Police Commissioner to regulate the taxi business in Boston and fix fare rates. The taxi industry is heavily regulated. There are copious regulations and inspections for medallions. For example, drivers must be pre-screened for drugs, alcohol, infractions and comply with further driver requirements, including a ban on mobile phone use. Taxis must be fully functioning and modified in certain respects, including a taxi-meter to calculate fares based only on mileage, offer multiple payment options, comply with a nondiscrimination mandate as to passengers and neighborhoods, a two-way radio (which they must pay a weekly fee for), and an administrative process to resolve disputes. The City of Boston capped the number of medallions at 1,825.

Uber is a software app connecting drivers to passengers, using location-based technology on smartphones, and it completes the transaction based on stored credit card information, calculating fares dynamically, based on distance and/or time to destination, and occasionally based on surging demand or other extraordinary conditions. Uber is simply a software utility. It does not own one vehicle; nor does it own a radio association, or medallions, and it does not employ the drivers. In its terms, Uber states that, "Uber is a request tool not a transportation carrier." Further, "The company does not provide transportation services, and the company is not a transportation carrier."

There are four categories of Uber-affiliated vehicles: Uber Black Car sedans, Uber SUVs, Uber Taxis, and UberX. The categories vary in price range and passenger capacity. Uber determines the fares for each category of vehicle. For example, as to Uber Taxis, which are comprised of Boston taxi cab drivers who are subject to Rule 403, the fare is calculated first with the flat rate Rule 403 system, then Uber adds a $1.00 'fee' and a 20% 'gratuity' (and only 10% of this is going to drivers). The final charge therefore, exceeds the maximum rate applicable to taxis under Rule 403. Uber requires drivers to use their smartphones. Uber-affiliated cars are not periodically inspected, there are no partitions, no taximeter, no radio to send a signal in the event of an emergency, no driver criminal background checks, and insurance premiums on cars are often lower than applicable to taxis. Drivers are subject to a five-star rating system, which they start with and drop below if there are negative passenger reviews. Uber continues to use drivers with lower ratings. Uber in its terms states that it is not responsible for third party transportation providers; the company will not be a party to disputes, and so forth.

Boston Cab alleges numerous federal and state violations. Uber filed a motion to dismiss the complaint in its entirety. That motion was referred to Magistrate Judge Marianne Bowler for a Report and Recommendation (R&R), and she produced a 96-page R&R, and this court reviews the motion and the Magistrate's R&R.

Judicial Opinion. Judge Gorton: Count III of plaintiffs' complaint alleges that Uber has engaged in a series of false representations that constitute unfair and deceptive acts in commerce. Chapter 93A proscribes those engaged in trade or commerce from employing 'unfair methods of competition and unfair or deceptive acts or practices.' In the context of disputes among businesses, where both parties are sophisticated commercial players, the 'objectionable conduct must attain a level of rascality that would raise an eyebrow to the rough and tumble of the world of commerce.' [Citations omitted.] Count III alleges the following four misrepresentations of the defendant Uber give rise to a claim under Chapter 93A:

a) that it is affiliated with medallion owners and radio associations;
b) that it only collects a $1 fee and pays the full 20% 'gratuity' to taxi drivers;
c) that its service is lawful under Boston Taxi Rules; and
d) that its vehicles do not need to be licensed and regulated as taxis in Boston.

Alleged misrepresentations (a) and (b) fail to meet the pleading requirements for the reasons stated above. [Moreover] the unfair practice . . . must be shown to have caused the loss of money or property. [P]laintiffs have not pled a cognizable injury caused by misrepresentation. With respect to alleged misrepresentations (c) and (d), Uber correctly notes that, elsewhere in her R&R, the magistrate judge explained that "the complaint does not identify a representation in which Uber states explicitly or conveys by necessary implication that "Uber assigned taxis are operating lawfully . . . "." The Court agrees with the magistrate judge that Uber has not made such explicit representations and also notes that plaintiffs have alleged no facts to support their allegations with respect to either (c) or (d). Conclusory allegations such as these, unsupported by facts, will not survive a motion to dismiss.

Count IV of the complaint alleges that Uber unfairly competes with plaintiffs, in violation of Chapter 93A, by 1) "operating" its service without incurring the expense of compliance with Massachusetts law and Boston ordinances and 2) diverting revenues for credit card processing that the plaintiffs are contractually obligated to pay its credit card processor. The magistrate judge recommended dismissing the second part of the claim but allowing the first to survive. The Court agrees that plaintiffs have sufficiently stated such a claim.

The Court finds Uber's objection to the magistrate judge's reasoning unconvincing. Uber claimed in its memoranda in support of its motion to dismiss that it could not be held liable under Chapter 93A because it does not own any cars, medallions, or radio associations and does not employ drivers. The magistrate judge correctly found that Uber's argument was based on an unduly narrow conception of the term 'operating.' The Court agrees with the magistrate judge that there is sufficient evidence that Uber exercises control over (or is 'in charge of') vehicles-for-hire that compete with plaintiffs in the private transportation business.

The Court . . . disagrees with Uber that plaintiffs have failed to state a claim against Uber because any unlawful conduct is attributable only to drivers and not Uber in light of the fact that Uber sets policies that those drivers follow, such as the use of mobile telephones.

ORDER

In accordance with the foregoing,

1) Defendant's objections to . . . the R&R . . . are, with respect to Count . . . III, SUSTAINED . . . , and

2) Magistrate Judge Bowler's R&R . . . pertaining to defendant's motion to dismiss for failure to state a claim . . . is, with respect to Count . . . IV, ACCEPTED AND ADOPTED, but is with respect to Count . . . III, REJECTED.

Case Questions

1. What is left to be litigated after this decision? And what would you decide as to that claim?
2. Being a category creator means being the first, and only company initially, to face such regulatory scrutiny. What do you recommend for the CEO to stay ahead of this challenge?
3. Uber is facing a number of legal challenges throughout the U.S., and internationally. How does this impact this one company? How does this impact Uber's competitors?

This next case is also a ruling on the Uber software app. Note the difference in approach, and outcome.

Pennsylvania Public Utility Comm'n v. Uber Techs., Inc.,

Petition before the Pennsylvania Public Utility Hearing Commission and Emergency Order, P-2014-2426846 (July 1, 2014)

Facts: The Administrative Law Judges conducted a hearing on the Petition of the Pennsylvania Public Utility Commission's Bureau of Investigation and Enforcement (I&E) for interim emergency relief filed against Uber Technologies, Inc. The complaint alleges that Uber drivers use their personal vehicles to respond to ride requests.

I&E avers that Uber, through its app, is acting as a broker of transportation in Pennsylvania without proper Commission authority. I&E avers that pursuant to 66 Pa.C.S. § 2505(a), brokers of transportation in the Commonwealth of Pennsylvania must obtain a brokerage license issued by the Commission prior to engaging in business, and that Uber does not hold a license, and must also be issued a certificate of public convenience to operate as a motor carrier of passengers. Further, Uber engages non-professional drivers, who are not certified motor carriers, using their personal vehicles for commercial transportation in violation of 66 Pa.C.S. § 2505(a). I&E further averred that by letter dated July 6, 2012, Uber was directed to cease and desist from acting as a broker of transportation without the authority to provide the service.

I&E further avers that on March 13, 2014, Uber announced the launch of the UberX service in Pittsburgh, and that drivers do not have proper Commission authority to transport passengers for compensation within Pennsylvania, thereby violating 66 Pa.C.S. § 1101. The Petition seeks an Order from the Commission directing Uber to immediately cease and desist from operating its ride-sharing passenger transportation service until it receives the requisite authority to do so.

The purpose of an interim emergency order is to grant or deny injunctive relief during the pendency of a proceeding. I&E asserts that the need for relief is immediate and ongoing as it has attempted to stop Uber from unlawfully brokering transportation service using non-certified drivers, without success, and that the injury to public safety would be irreparable if relief is not granted. I&E argues that Uber has unilaterally deprived the Commission of its obligation to ensure driver integrity, vehicle safety and the maintenance of sufficient insurance coverage.

In its answer, Uber avers that it is not a taxi broker, but instead, is a software company that licenses a smartphone application. Uber asserts, in Pennsylvania, it licensed its smartphone app to Gegen LLC., and by granting the requested relief, the Commission would be ordering a software company to stop operating, without a comprehensive review of whether any activities violate state law. Such relief, Uber asserts, would be injurious to the public interest by depriving the public access to an innovative, economic and reliable service that is not available from traditional transportation providers.

Judicial Opinion. Presiding Officers, Administrative Law Judges Mary D. Long and Jeffrey A. Watson: The issue the Commission must resolve in this emergency proceeding is whether I&E has established the requisite need to order that Uber immediately cease and desist from utilizing its digital platform to facilitate transportation for compensation to passengers using non-certified drives in their personal vehicles within the Commonwealth of Pennsylvania.

I&E witness Officer Bowser testified that he is charged with enforcing the Public Utility Code and . . . enforce the public safety provisions. As Uber drivers are not certificated . . . the Commission is unable to exercise any oversight over the drivers or vehicles, and the failure to provide such oversight can also have a detrimental impact on the public safety.

Emergency relief is governed by 52 Pa.Code §§ 3.1-3.12. The provision defines an emergency as follows: "a situation which presents a clear and present danger to life or property of which is uncontested and requires action prior to the next scheduled public meeting." To be granted an interim emergency order, the party seeking relief must prove by a preponderance of the evidence that the facts and circumstances meet all four of the requirements set forth in § 3.6(b):

1. The petitioner's right to relief is clear.
2. The need for relief is immediate.
3. The injury would be irreparable if relief is not granted.
4. The relief requested is not injurious to the public interest.

[As to 1:] I&E has established that its right to relief is clear. That is, the Petition raises a substantial legal question and I&E adduced sufficient evidence to conclude that it has a reasonable expectation of success on the merits of a proceeding on the underlying complaint.

[As to 2:] I&E avers it has attempted, on numerous occasions, to stop Uber from unlawfully brokering transportation service using non-certificated drivers, without success, and that Uber continues to broker transportation. We therefore conclude that I&E has established by a preponderance of the evidence that its need for relief is immediate.

[As to 3:] [T]he Commission has a fundamental duty to ensure driver integrity and vehicle safety for the service provided by each carrier. Uber has unilaterally deprived the Commission of its obligations [in these respects]. It is well settled that a violation of law constitutes irreparable harm per se . . . [and therefore] the harm would be irreparable if the relief requested is not granted.

[As to 4:] It is not in the public interest for the Commission to ignore its statutory mandate. It is therefore not in the public interest to permit Uber to continue to provide the contested service, pending a full and complete hearing . . . [and therefore] the relief requested is not injurious to the public interest.

In conclusion, I&E has demonstrated by a preponderance of the evidence that it is entitled to interim emergency relief.

IT IS ORDERED:

That Uber Technologies, Inc., shall immediately cease and desist from utilizing its digital platform to facilitate transportation to passengers utilizing non-certificated drivers in their personal vehicles until such times as it secures appropriate authority from the Commission.

Case Questions

1. What did this judge decide?
2. What are the jurisdictional and time limits of this decision?
3. Say you are CEO of Uber. How do you respond to your Board of Directors after this decision, knowing that there are a number of other, similar lawsuits still pending?

Summary

What happened to buggy whip factories? Eastman Kodak? Polaroid, bookstores, music stores, movie theaters? What will happen to the once-vaunted Blackberry? In fact, what is happening to every industry? Creative churn and disruption is replete throughout our industrial and commercial history. With respect to the Internet and the Web, consider all types of content, films, broadcast TV, cable TV, paper books, paper newspapers, songs, and so forth. How do they adapt to survive, in the digital era? Which companies will adapt and thrive, which will retreat? What will happen to cable TV? Media has been especially anxious about the rapid transformation to a digital, networked, broadband, large-bandwidth p2p environment. These industries would be happier if time stood still and they made money based on their legacy models. These are just a few of the examples of business models that are failing to adapt. The real issues are not about demand for their content, which is robust, but instead the issues are more about control, distribution, derivative works, and access. Just consider at this moment: somewhere between the content creators (author, screenwriter, and so forth) and users, there is a multi-billion-dollar market. What would you recommend to these industries?

Robust economic and social developments are made possible by innovations and inventions. Managing this process, anticipating trends and fostering these goals in market and nonmarket economies is crucial, yet there are costs to it. It unleashes a wave of creative destruction and disruptions to status quo. Further, legal recognition of status as to who is a founder, inventor, and/or owner of the technology is critical to understand during the scale-up from invention stage, to becoming an ongoing business entity.

The net impact though creates a culture of possibility, replete with questions, experimentation, and results. What will the Internet and Web be like in the future? What is next is always on our minds—what will be built out on mobile platforms, how will the Internet of things develop, what will the immersive web be like? These are just some examples of the inventions and innovations that managers will need to evaluate for market-worthiness and readiness, while clearing rights to ownership, and more.

Key Terms

business model A series of activities designed to yield a new product or service that will give company a competitive advantage, as well as a sustainable financial return; a plan that creates value with levers to impact return on equity to shareholders.

innovation A technological, creative breakthrough from conventional procedures or thought, that go beyond marginal improvements in existing products and services that advance the state of the art.

invention Ingenious ideas that offer a uniquely better solution to a problem; a practical implementation of an idea in the form of a new composition, matter, device, or process that extends the boundaries of knowledge, experience, and culture, which results in something new.

research and development Creative work undertaken on a systematic basis to increase knowledge and devise new applications.

basic research Creative, theoretical or empirical research and work on fundamental principles to increase knowledge.

applied research Targeted research to prove feasibility.

experimental development Research that is translated into practical application and tested for technical limits and commercial potential.

translational research Research that is translated into practical application and tested for technical limits and commercial potential.

demonstration Presentation or display to show the knowledge or the product in an operational environment.

product launch Actual technology is completed; the model is ready enough for roll-out, with associated manufacturing, marketing, and distribution.

diffusion or adoption of innovation Measure by which new technologies spread among users over time.

international paradox A phenomenon where diffusion in low-income areas is not occurring and is limited to the extent that revenue does not cover expenses in the least affluent areas.

galapagos syndrome A phenomenon where goods and services evolve in isolation from world markets and this limits diffusion beyond the original market.

innovators' dilemma An impediment to innovation when incentives to switch appear to be too low in relation to the assumed risk of a new direction)

memorandum of understanding Letter of intent, not as formal as a contract, setting forth the parties' expectations.

contribution agreement Formal agreement between parties as to technology that is being contributed to the start-up.

Manager's Checklist

1. Projects clearly need to be managed, from inception to commercial roll-out.

2. Keep a unified workforce and align incentives of all team members to avoid attrition and lost opportunities in order to maximize the prospects the innovation or invention makes possible.

3. Consider how to make the best use of all employees to maximize their effort and participation in the organization.

4. Managers should consult with legal counsel to ensure that the organization is placed to capture all employee work for which it is entitled.

5. Managers must keep track of former employees who left to work for a competitor or set up their own business, to ensure that sensitive business information (including inventions and innovations) are not being used by these competitors.

Ethical Consideration

Inventing is an area fraught with uncertainty in terms of contribution to work and return on that work. There are instances where contributions are not properly attributed and/or apportioned. How would you create a system during build out for ensuring recognition of key contributions and a process for clarifying who is an inventor?

Questions and Case Problems

1. For apps to be featured on the iPhone, developers must build it with Apple's Software Development Kit, and then apply for approval. Apple rejected Google's Voice iPhone App, and further stated that it would not accept any applications that incorporated Google Voice functionality, reasoning that this app duplicates its phone's core features. It also rejected Google's location-based app Google Latitude. *If you were developing a collaborative platform with the main goal being to maximize innovation, do you think the best model is this collaborative model, or is the open innovation model better? What if your main goal is to make money?*

2. Inventor Michael Powell approached Home Depot with an ingenious invention: a saw guard, that when installed on the stores' radial saws, kept employees' hands safe from horrible accidents. The company liked it, and Powell asked for $2,000 per unit to be installed in 2,000 stores. The company balked at this and, instead, secretly dispatched a team to re-create the saw guard. Powell filed suit, and prevailed. The jury found damages in the amount of: $15 million for theft of the idea; $3 million in punitive damages; $1 million in interest owed since the theft; and $2.8 million in attorneys' fees. *Powell v. Home Depot Stores*, 2010 U.S. Dist. LEXIS 5806 (S.D. Fla. Jan. 26, 2010). *What do you recommend for independent inventors after this case?*

3. Tomita Technologies, founded by former Sony engineer Seijiro Tomita, has a 3D (stereoscopic) patent, useful for displaying images users can see in 3D without having to wear 3D glasses. Tomita showed a prototype of the technology to seven Nintendo officers while the patent was still pending. Nintendo had a number of other meetings with other 3D companies, and ultimately created its own technology it called 3DS. Tomita charged that Nintendo's 3DS technology used key aspects of its patent. In 2013, a jury found in favor of Tomita, and Judge Jed Rakoff ruled that Nintendo must pay to Tomita, 1.82 percent of the wholesale price of each Nintendo 3DS unit sold (*Tomita Tech. v. Nintendo Co.*, 2013 U.S. Dist. LEXIS 174162 (S.D.N.Y. Dec 13, 2013; 2013 U.S. Dist. LEXIS 116486 (S.D.N.Y. Aug. 14, 2013)). Describe the dynamic in this business transaction between the small startup and the large business entity, and recommendations for each side on such transactions in the future.

4. Target Corp. wanted to upgrade its online presence, and so it debuted a subscription service for users to receive shipments of specified items at regular intervals. This service took off and its online traffic grew at double-digit rates during holidays. Mobile sales have climbed 100 percent year-over-year. They've begun other online initiatives too. However, Inventor Holdings, LLC claims it owns the patents on the method to provide subscription purchase agreements to consumers, and this patent holding company has

sued Target. The lawsuit is ongoing (case No. 1:14-cv-00784-UNA, filed Del. Dist. Ct., June 19, 2014). What do you recommend for Target, and other innovators who expand their business opportunities?

5. Think about a good or service, or a site that is in the news—one that is really in trouble, financially, or is rapidly losing market share, etc. *Using what you learned from this chapter, describe your approach to solving this; that is, describe how you could generate solutions.*

Additional Resources

Massachusetts Institute of Technology. *Production in the Innovation Economy.* February 2013.

The Brookings Institution. The Rise of Innovation Districts: A New Geography of Innovation in America. Metropolitan Policy Program, The Brookings Institution. May 2014.

Kauffman Foundation for Entrepreneurship. http://www.kauffman.org.

Thomson Reuters. 2013 Top 100 Global Innovators. October 2013.

United States Bureau of Labor Statistics. http://www.bls.gov.

Entrepreneurship and the U.S. Economy. http://www.bls.gov/bdm/entrepreneurship/entrepreneurship.htm

United States Small Business Administration. Starting and Managing a Business. http://www.sba.gov/category/navigation-structure/starting-managing-business.

The World Bank. The Impact of Government Support on Firm R&D Investments, A Meta-Analysis. The World Bank Entrepreneurship and Innovation Unit. July 2013.

 Money is like gasoline during a road trip. You don't want to run out of gas on your trip, but you're not doing a tour of gas stations.

—Tim O'Reilly, Digital Media Entrepreneur and founder/ CEO of O'Reilly Media

3

Forming, Financing, and Managing a New Venture

Learning Objectives

After you have read this chapter, you should be able to:

- Identify the factors that an entrepreneur or intrapreneur should consider when selecting a business entity for their venture.
- Explain and distinguish the various methods of raising capital to finance a business venture.
- Provide examples of equity instruments and debt instruments.
- Recognize the regulatory impact of securities laws on fundraising and describe exemptions.
- Articulate the structure of a corporation and explain the roles of officers, directors, and shareholders.

Overview: New Venture Planning

Whether the founders of a new venture are entrepreneurs or intrapreneurs, they should address a series of planning issues to avoid any misunderstanding that may interfere with the success of the venture. All new ventures start with an idea, but in the early stages of developing the idea the founders will likely not have thought out details. However, once the idea begins to mature to the point where the parties believe that it would be a profitable venture, they must begin formal planning for forming a business entity, financing the venture, and operating the business.

For example, suppose that Franz is an entrepreneur who is using his background in logistics consulting to advance an idea for a new software package that will save companies time and money by providing increased efficiency in the their international shipping and logistics efforts. He teams up with Josef, a computer programmer, to work on designing the program and developing the software. Although they have funded their start-up efforts primarily with their own money, they realize that they will need more money for research and development to bring their product to market. Of course, they are also interested in attracting investments related to expanding their venture and market share.

At the outset, they will have to make decisions on how to effectively bring the venture from idea to reality. The first set of questions relates to formation: What type of business form should they use? Is one better than the other? What kind of risk are they taking? Should they incorporate now or wait until the product is ready? Where should they form the entity? The second set of questions relates to financing: What are their options for raising capital? What are the potential sources for financing and what do the principals give up? Should they solicit outside investors or use a bank loan? Can shares be diluted by additional investors? What is the role of venture capital in a start-up? Third, the principals will have to decide on ownership and management concerns: Who will own what percent of the venture? Who will run the day-to-day operations of the business and how will business decisions be handled by the principals? What happens if a key principal dies, is incapacitated, or declares bankruptcy?

These decisions can be difficult and typically require the advice of counsel to fully understand the impact of the choices. In some cases, the founders may have different concerns and different financial circumstances that drive their decision-making. In any case, effective planning allows the entrepreneurs to focus on developing their product and service.

Formation of a Business Entity

One of the primary decisions that the owners of a business venture must make is what form of business entity will best suit the current and future needs of the parties. Business entities (also known as business organizations) are legally recognized forms of associations that have various advantages and limits for operating the business on a day-to-day basis. Owners of the business, called **principals**, typically have a variety of choices based on their circumstances and nature of the business. Although a business entity choice is not set in stone (i.e., the entity may be converted to another business entity in the future), the ramifications of the initial choice are still very important and a change later may come with increased costs.

Factors in Choosing a Start Up Business Entity

There are four major factors used in planning a business entity that center on liability, operations, raising capital, and tax consequences.

- *Liability of principals*: The inherent risks of operating a business may incur liability typically as a result of a breach of contract (e.g., a lease agreement) or a tort (e.g., negligence that results in an injury to a third party). However, if the business venture is without any income or assets, the question becomes to what extent are the principals personally liable for the debt owed by the business venture. For example, in our Franz-Josef hypothetical (earlier), suppose that they decide to sign a two-year lease for luxury office space in order to impress their potential investors. After a year, the fundraising does not go as planned and they decide to abandon the venture and the office space. Since the assets of the business are not sufficient to pay the remaining lease payments, their landlord will likely be looking at the *personal* assets of Franz and Josef to satisfy the debt. Personal assets include personal bank accounts, stocks, and real estate.

- *Management and operation:* The principals should decide early what the role of each party will be. One of the initial considerations will be whether a principal will be drawing a salary or other compensation/benefits from the entity and how that will be calculated in any profits or losses. Another important (albeit difficult) conversation among principals is an agreement on what happens if a principal leaves the entity (voluntarily or involuntarily), dies, files for bankruptcy, or is incapacitated to the point where the principal can no longer work for the entity. In the Franz-Josef venture discussed earlier, both principals are key components to the business venture and the separation of a principal from the entity may result in the termination of the venture. Management and operational issues are typically addressed during the choice of entity discussion and are memorialized in an agreement (e.g., Operating Agreement of an LLC) and other internal rules (e.g., bylaws of a corporation). These choices and agreements are discussed in more detail later in this chapter.

- *Capitalization*: Perhaps one of the most important factors for the principals to understand is how their choice of entity will impact their ability to raise money for the business. Although traditional financing remains the bedrock for many business entities, the Internet now allows principals to have access to capital from private investors by using such methods such as *crowdfunding* and *angel investors*. The various forms of capitalization and their attendant advantages and disadvantages are discussed in detail in the next section.

- *Tax consequences*: While many entrepreneurs and intraprenuers may be reluctant to delve into the tax code because they believe it to be an accounting function, a basic understanding of how a business entity is taxed is important in selecting an appropriate entity. Because the financial situation of the principals will inevitably vary, their tax implications and goals may vary as well. Fundamentally, entities that are classified "pass- through" are those where the profits are taxed at the individual principal's individual tax rate. Non pass-through entities typically pay corporate tax based on the business's overall income. Because the tax laws contain so many deductions and tax credits for business owners, there is no universal answer to whether the principals would or would not benefit from a pass-through entity. Rather, the decision has to be made on a case-by-case basis with the help of a tax professional.

Comparing Business Entities

Entrepreneurs and intrapreneurs typically have six different alternatives when choosing a business entity: sole proprietorship, general partnership, limited partnership, corporation, limited liability company (LLC), and limited liability partnership (LLP). In order to maximize both flexibility in operations and limit their liability protection, principals must carefully consider the important factors in choosing an entity, compare advantages and disadvantages, and decide on a location for the entity's recognition by state authorities.

Sole Proprietorships

This is a most common form of start-up business organization primarily because it is so easy to form and maintain. An individual simply owns and manages the business with complete control and personal responsibility for all transactions and liabilities. This personal liability is usually tempered through the purchase of a business insurance policy. Owners receive all income to keep or reinvest in the business. They have unlimited liability for losses the business or employees incur. Business and personal assets of the sole proprietor are always at risk. The entity itself is not taxed because sole proprietors report business income or losses on their individual tax return.

General Partnerships

A general partnership is owned by a group of two or more partners. Typically, partners draft an agreement detailing each partner's capital contribution along with their rights and duties. The agreement specifies the division of responsibility for management, profits and losses, and salaries. General partners report profits and losses on personal tax returns. Liability is an issue however, as general partners are jointly and severally liable for all acts done by other partners or employees in the scope of the **partnership**. Partners are bound contractually under the Partnership Agreement and also by fiduciary duties (discussed later). Death, departure of a partner, and incapacity are problematic as these events may trigger dissolution of the partnership unless agreed otherwise in the partnership agreement.

Limited Partnerships

This entity reflects a two-tier structure and exists by virtue of a state statute that recognizes one or more principals as managing the business enterprise, while other principals participate only in terms of contributing capital or property. A limited partnership has at least one general partner (managing principal) and at least one limited partner (investing principal). In the absence of an agreement, the state law based on the Revised Uniform Limited Partnership Act (RULPA) governs a limited partnership. Although the RULPA does not formally require a partnership agreement, the vast majority of limited partnerships have one. The agreement details the rights, obligations, and relationships between partners. These partnerships typically use the designation LP at the end of their business name to signify the limited partnership as their form of entity. Each general partner in a limited partnership is personally liable for all of the partnership's debts and liabilities, just as if the general partners were in a general partnership. However, limited partners do not have the same automatic personal liability of a general partner. Rather, the limited partner's liability is limited to whatever the limited partner contributed to the partnership. Limited partnerships are pass-through entities just like general partnerships. The same rules apply for taxation as in a general partnership. That is, profits or losses are reported in the principal's personal tax return and tax is paid in accordance with the individual partner's individual tax rate. The general partner is responsible for filing an information return with taxing authorities, but limited partnerships do not pay corporate taxes.

Joint Ventures

While not considered an actual business entity, joint ventures are essentially general partnerships for a limited period of time or a single project. It is typically based on a mutually beneficial project. The parties typically draft a joint venture agreement detailing respective rights and responsibilities. Parties to a joint venture do not ordinarily have a relationship of trust, and to this extent there is no fiduciary duty between the parties. For example, in our running hypothetical with Franz and Josef, suppose that they are approached by Blackwell for the purposes of developing a specific software program for Blackwell's shipping business using specialized trade knowledge contributed by each party. The parties agree to a joint venture instead of a partnership because the relationship is based on a single project and the obligations will terminate once the project is completed.

Limited Liability Company (LLC)

A limited liability company is an entity whose primary characteristics are that it offers its principals the same amount of liability protection afforded to principals of a corporate form of entity, and it offers pass-through tax treatment for its principals without the restrictions on ownership and scope required for other pass-through entities (such as an S corporation, discussed later). LLC members are insulated from personal liability for any business debt or liability if the venture fails.

LLCs are frequently governed by agreement of the parties in the form of an **operating agreement**. If the parties do not execute an operating agreement, the state LLC statute sets out default rules. Operating agreements, similar to partnership agreements, cover much of the internal rules for the actual operation of the entity. One of the primary benefits of an LLC is that it affords its members a great deal of flexibility in terms of the rights and responsibilities of each member.

Another attractive advantage of an LLC is the various tax treatment alternatives. Although many LLCs are typically treated as a pass-through entity, the LLC's members may also elect to be taxed as a corporation if they consider the corporate tax structure more favorable.

Limited Liability Partnership (LLP)

Most states recognize limited liability partnerships through their partnership statutes. Recall that the chief danger of being a general partner is the amount of potential liability for acts of other general partners or the debts and liabilities of the partnership itself. LLP statutes provide general partnerships with the right to convert their entity and gain the protective shield ordinarily only afforded to limited partners or corporate shareholders. Although the origins of LLP laws were rooted in protection of professional service firm partnerships (law, accounting, etc.), the use of LLPs is much more widespread now as some family businesses have also used the LLP form as a way to handle issues unique to the transition from one generation to another in a family business. Of all of the business entities that we have discussed thus far, the LLP has the greatest variance of liability protection under state law. While the general idea behind being an LLP is that all partners have liability protection for debts and liabilities of the partnership, some states impose conditions on these limits. In cases except where a partner has engaged in some misconduct or tortious conduct (such as negligence), the LLP acts only to shield the personal of assets of other partners—never the partner who committed the misconduct or negligence.

Some states provide liability shields for LLP partners only when the liability arises from some negligence by another partner, but not for other types of liabilities such as those resulting from a breach of contract.

Corporations

A corporation is a fictitious legal entity that exists as an independent "person" separate from its principals. Although this corporate person is a legally created fiction, it is a well-established and deeply seated principal of American law. In a business context it is also important to note that a corporation, like an individual person, may file suit or be sued, or may form a contract or breach a contract. In contrast to sole proprietorships and partnerships, the obligations of corporations are separate and distinct from the personal obligations of their principals. Corporations are created through a state law filing, and formation is governed through *state statutes*. State statutes vary in their corporate formation and governance rules, but each state has a specific law, often called the Business Corporation Law or something similar, that covers such matters as the structure of the corporation, oversight of the activity of the corporation's managers, rights of the principals in the case of the sale of assets or ownership interests, annual reporting requirements, and other issues that affect the internal rules of the business venture. Over half of the states have adopted all or substantial portions of a model act known as the Revised Model Business Corporation Act (RMBCA).

Perhaps the most attractive feature of a corporation is its limited liability for the personal assets of its owners and, with certain exceptions, for its officers and directors. In general, shareholders, directors, and officers of a corporation are insulated from personal liability in case the corporation has significant debt or suffers some liability. This protection is often referred to as the **corporate veil**.

Another advantage of this form of business is that it is relatively easy to raise money, attract talent, and pursue strategic business opportunities. However, reporting and compliance requirements are more burdensome and expensive than other forms of entity.

Generally we think of corporations as large public entities, but the vast majority of the United States' economy is comprised of small businesses with fewer than 500 employees. According to *Forbes*, there are more than 25 million small businesses in the U.S., which account for between 60-80 percent of all jobs.[1]

Tax impact: "C" Corporation versus "S" Corporation

If a corporation does make an "S" election during its tax year, it is called a "C" corporation referring to its tax status. "C" corporations pay taxes both at the corporate level and again when any profits are distributed as dividends to shareholders. "S" election is essentially a tax choice that allows shareholders to treat the earnings and profits as distributions and have them pass through directly to their personal tax returns and pay taxes at the shareholder's individual rate.

The primary reason that some corporations do *not* choose an S election is because the tax code only allows certain types of corporations to have that status and pass through tax treatment. However, only C corporations are entitled to certain tax deductions (e.g., amounts used to pay for employee benefits). Small business entities that qualify for S corporation status sometimes opt to be a C corporation if it reduces their overall tax liability.

In order to qualify as an S corporation, the enterprise must meet the following criteria:

- *Limited classification.* S corporations must be a domestic corporation with no nonresident or alien shareholders.
- *Single class of stock.* An enterprise cannot be an S corporation if it has more than a single class of stock (except a differentiation of voting and nonvoting stock, explained later in this chapter).

---

1. http://www.forbes.com/sites/rebeccabagley/2012/05/15/small-businesses-big-impact/

- *No corporate shareholders.* An enterprise cannot be an S corporation if any of its shareholders is a corporation, a partnership, or a discretionary trust.
- *Limited scope of business.* Banks and insurance companies may not elect to be an S corporation.
- *Limited number and type of shareholders.* An enterprise cannot be an S corporation if it has more than 100 shareholders. Only individuals, estates, and certain trusts may be shareholders.
- *80 percent subsidiaries.* An enterprise cannot be an S corporation if it owns more than 80 percent of the stock of a subsidiary corporation.
- *Unanimous consent.* All shareholders must consent to S corporation status.

Summary Table	Comparison of Entities			
	Liability	**Management**	**Capitalization**	**Tax**
Sole prop	Proprietor has full personal liability for debts of business	One person	Typically self-funded	No corporate tax
Partnerships	GP: Joint and several liability LP: Limited to investment in venture	GP: Management responsibility LP: No day-to-day involvement	Self-funded, debt, or equity (sell partnership shares)	No corporate tax
C-Corp	Corporate veil protection	Officers and Directors	Debt or equity (i.e., shares)	Corporate tax on income
S-Corp	Corporate veil protection	Officers and Directors	Debt or equity (i.e., shares)	No corporate tax; Distributions to shareholders taxed
LLC	Corporate veil protection	Managing member or Managed by all members	Debt or equity (limited)	Choice of status between "C" corp and "S" corp
LLP	Corporate veil protection, but only for negligence of *other* partners	Managing partner or Managed by all partners	Debt or equity (limited)	No corporate tax

Capitalizing a New Venture

Methods of capitalizing a new business venture vary widely. In most cases, the initial capital to fund the entity and start up costs comes from the principals' personal resources. Additional funding that is needed to commence operations and formally launch the product and service is raised during a preliminary fundraising stage called a **seed round**. Once the business has launched its product or service, the principals may decide to seek additional funding to expand the venture or shore up the entity's financial condition. In the Franz-Josef hypothetical discussed earlier, the principals will typically fund certain start up costs from personal funds that are invested into the corporation to cover initial costs of equipment and work space. Once the concept has gone from idea to viable business opportunity, Franz and Josef would now be planning to raise funds to operate and expand their business in a seed round. Since they will likely be seeking capital from third parties (including relatives and friends), they must be conscious of the regulatory scheme in planning their seed round. They may also use the seed round opportunity to plan for future and potentially more complex stages of fundraising.

Sources and Categories of Capital

Fundamentally, businesses raise money by using one of two methods: 1) selling ownership, called **equity**, to investors who are hoping for a return on their investment based on the profitability of the business; or 2) borrowing money that must be paid back, called **debt**, either from a private source (such as a relative), a commercial source (such as a bank), or by issuing more sophisticated public debt instruments such as bonds.

Businesses that raise equity from investors or issue debt to investors are subject to an array of state and federal securities laws. This also includes money raised from friends and relatives in most circumstances. Federal and state statutes typically cover specific types of securities such as notes, stocks, transferable shares, and bonds. Securities law also defines a security very broadly through application of the *Howey*[2] test. Under the modern version of this test, a security is defined as any investment transaction where the parties have a common expectation of profits primarily through the efforts of another.

In the case below, a seminal case in cyberlaw, a federal appeals court decides whether a plan to buy and sell stock in a virtual company constitutes a securities transaction under the *Howey* test.

Securities and Exchange Commission v. SG Ltd.,
265 F.3d 42 (1st Cir. 2001)

Facts SG's Ltd operated a website called "StockGeneration", which offered users the opportunity to purchase shares in eleven different virtual companies listed on the website's virtual stock exchange. SG arbitrarily set the purchase and sale prices of each of these hypothetical companies in biweekly rounds, and guaranteed that investors could buy or sell any quantity of shares at posted prices. SG placed no upper limit on the amount of funds that an investor could invest in its virtual offerings.

---

2. Based on the U.S. Supreme Court case *SEC v. Howey*, 328 U.S. 293 (1946)

At least 800 United States citizens made cash purchases of virtual shares of the hypothetical companies listed on SG's virtual stock exchange. In the fall of 1999, more than $4,700,000 in participants' funds was deposited into an off-shore bank account in the name of SG Trading Ltd. The following spring, more than $2,700,000 was deposited into another bank account in the name of SG Ltd.

The SEC investigated one such virtual enterprise referred to by SG as the "privileged company." SG advised potential purchasers to pay "particular attention" to shares in the privileged company and boasted that investing in those shares was a "game without any risk." To this end, its website contained representations that the privileged company's shares would appreciate at an average rate of return of 10% monthly. SG also represented that the share price was supported by the owners of SG so that risk was non-existent.

The SEC filed a complaint against SG alleging that its virtual security games were actually investment contracts under the *Howey* test. SG defended that the website was a fantasy investment game created for the personal entertainment of Internet users and not within the jurisdictional reach of securities laws.

The district court ruled that the SG transactions were not subject to federal securities laws and the SEC appealed.

Judicial Opinion . . .

ADMINISTERING THE TRIPARTITE TEST

What remains is to analyze whether purchases of the privileged company's shares constitute investment contracts. We turn to that task, taking the three Howey criteria in sequence.

A. INVESTMENT OF MONEY.

The first component of the Howey test focuses on the investment of money. The determining factor is whether an investor "chose to give up a specific consideration in return for a separable financial interest with the characteristics of a security." We conclude that the SEC's complaint sufficiently alleges the existence of this factor.

To be sure, SG disputes the point. It argues that the individuals who purchased shares in the privileged company were not so much investing money in return for rights in the virtual shares as paying for an entertainment commodity (the opportunity to play the StockGeneration game) . . .

SG [represented] that participants could "firmly expect a 10% profit monthly" on purchases of the privileged company's shares. That representation plainly supports the SEC's legal claim that participants who invested substantial amounts of money in exchange for virtual shares in the privileged company likely did so in anticipation of investment gains. . . .

B. COMMON ENTERPRISE

The second component of the Howey test involves the existence of a common enterprise. . . .

The case at bar requires us to take a position on the common enterprise component of the Howey test. We hold that a showing of horizontal commonality—the pooling of assets from multiple investors in such a manner that all share in the profits and risks of the enterprise—satisfies the test. This holding flows naturally from the facts of Howey, in which the promoter commingled fruit from the investors' groves and allocated net profits based upon the production from each tract . . .

SG's virtual shares bear striking factual similarities to the financial instruments classified as investment contracts in Infinity Group. SG's flat 10% guaranteed return applied to all privileged company shares, expected returns were dependent upon the number of shares held, the economic assurances were based on the promoter's ability to keep the ball rolling, the investment was proclaimed to be free from risk, and participants were promised that their principal would be repaid in full upon demand. Like the Third Circuit, we think that these facts suffice to make out horizontal commonality.

In all events, SG's promise to pay referral fees to existing participants who induced others to patronize the virtual exchange provides an alternative basis for finding horizontal commonality. The SEC argues convincingly that this shows the existence of a pyramid scheme sufficient to satisfy the horizontal commonality standard . . .

C. EXPECTATION OF PROFITS SOLELY FROM THE EFFORTS OF OTHERS

The final component of the Howey test [is] the expectation of profits solely from the efforts of others . . . The Supreme Court has recognized an expectation of profits in two situations, namely, (1) capital appreciation from the original investment, and (2) participation in earnings resulting from the use of investors' funds. These situations are to be contrasted with transactions in which an individual purchases a commodity for personal use or consumption. The SEC posits that SG's guarantees created a reasonable expectancy of profit from investments in the privileged company, whereas SG maintains that participants paid money not to make money, but, rather, to acquire an entertainment commodity for personal consumption. . . .

[In this case] SG made . . . representations on its website that played upon greed and fueled expectations of profit. For example, SG flatly guaranteed that investments in the shares of the privileged company would be profitable, yielding monthly returns of 10% and annual returns of 215%. In our view, these profit-related guarantees constitute a not-very-subtle form of economic inducement . . .

We turn now to the question of whether the expected profits can be said to result solely from the efforts of others. The courts of appeals have been unanimous in declining to give literal meaning to the word "solely" in this context, instead holding the requirement satisfied as long as "the efforts made by those other than the investor are the undeniably significant ones, those essential managerial efforts which affect the failure or success of the enterprise.

We need not reach the issue of whether a lesser degree of control by a promoter or third party suffices to give rise to an investment contract because SG's alleged scheme meets the literal definition of "solely." According to the SEC's allegations, SG represented to its customers the lack of investor effort required to make guaranteed profits on purchases of the privileged company's shares, noting, for example, that "playing with [the] privileged shares practically requires no time at all." SG was responsible for all the important efforts that undergirded the 10% guaranteed monthly return. As the sole proprietor of the StockGeneration website, SG enjoyed direct operational control over all aspects of the virtual stock exchange. And SG's marketing efforts generated direct capital investment and commissions on the transactions (which it pledged to earmark to support the privileged company's shares).

CONCLUSION

We need go no further. Giving due weight to the economic realities of the situation, we hold that the SEC has alleged a set of facts which, if proven, satisfy the three-part *Howey* test and support its assertion that the opportunity to invest in the shares of the privileged company, described on SG's website, constituted an invitation to enter into an investment contract within the jurisdictional reach of federal securities law. Accordingly, we reverse the order of dismissal and remand the case for further proceedings consistent with this opinion.

REVERSED AND REMANDED.

Case Questions

1. What was SG's defense in this case? Why did they claim their website was not subject to securities law?
2. According to the court, how does SG meet the "horizontal commonality" requirement?
3. Could SG adjust their business model so that it would not be construed as an investment opportunity? How?

Self-funding and Credit

Perhaps the most common source of initial start-up capital is the personal assets and credit of the venture's founders. Because the business does not have a credit record or any assets to secure a loan, certain start-up costs such a filing fees, equipment, legal and accounting costs, are necessary as a first step to move from the idea stage to the development stage. Some business ventures will have very low start-up costs, but others may require a significant investment by the founders. Future investors also may be wary to invest in a venture when the founding principals have not committed any personal resources to the venture. In any case, the founding principals should agree on whether the self-funding is a loan to be paid back by the venture in a certain period of time (debt), or is an investment to purchase ownership (equity), or some combination of both. Once any cash or property is committed to a venture (either pre- or post-formation), it is important to memorialize the agreements through a promissory note or pre-incorporation agreement.

Crowdfunding

The media attention generated by crowdfunding investments has made it a permanent part of fundraising lexicon. One industry analyst quoted in *Forbes* magazine estimated that more than 1 million campaigns globally have raised more than $5 billion in one year. Fundamentally, crowdfunding is asking both friends and strangers to invest or donate a defined amount of money for a specific cause. From an entrepreneurial standpoint, crowdfunding is a way to raise money by asking individuals who are interested in investing to fund a certain business venture. Because the investments can be very small, it has the potential to tap into a larger investor community and generate significant sums of money for business ventures in relatively short order. This type of fundraising is done via the Internet through crowdfunding firms such as Kickstarter or Peerbackers. Crowdfunding may be used to raise money either through debt or equity and the crowdfunding firm typically charges a percentage fee for their services. Crowd-funding sites range from those that work only for charitable donations to those that focus on funding entrepreneurs and innovation. Exhibit 3.1 lists the top ten crowdfunding companies in terms of Internet traffic.

Crowdfunding gained a significant boost after the passage of the Jumpstart Our Business Startups (JOBS) Act of 2012. The law required the SEC to carve out a niche in securities laws that permitted crowdfunding as a fundraising tool for small business. In 2013, the SEC adopted rules that attempt to balance concerns about protecting relatively unsophisticated investors from fraud with helping to grow the economy by making more capital available from the investing public. The rule restricts companies from raising more than $1 million per year through crowdfunding sources. Investors also have similar caps based on their own resources. Exhibit 3.2 sets out investor limits in a crowdfunding context.

Companies also are now subject to certain disclosure requirements about the principals, use of funds, and financial conditions. These disclosures are discussed in more detail in the section "Regulation of Securities," later in this chapter.

Exhibit 3.1 Top 10 Crowdfunding Sites Based on Traffic

Name	Campaigns	Fee
1. Kickstarter	Creative projects such as design, film, publishing, music, gaming, and technology.	3-5%
2. indiegogo	Originally focused on film, now accepts all types of campaigns.	9%
3. YouCaring.com	Personal and charitable.	5%
4. Causes	Non-profits and charities.	4.75%
5. Giveforward	Personal fundraising only.	5%
6. RocketHub	Projects related to science, education, business and social good projects. Also partnered with A&E cable network.	5%
7. Peerbackers	Entrepreneurs and innovators.	5%
8. SoMoLend	Peer-to-peer platform to facilitate business or personal loans.	Variable
9. Crowdrise	Personal and creative fundraising.	5-6%
10. Fundly	Personal or charitable fundraising.	4.9%

Sources: Crowdfunding.com and Entreprenuer.com

Exhibit 3.2 Investor Limits on Crowdfunding

Investor's annual income/net worth	Maximum investment	Comments
At least $100,000/$100,000	10% of annual income or 10% of net worth (whichever is greater).	No more than $100,000 of investment in a 12-month period.
Less than $100,000/$100,000	$2000 or 5% of annual income (whichever is greater).	Maximums are calculated over a 12-month period.

Angel Investors

Angel investors generally are high-net-worth individuals willing to invest personal money in early-stage companies, or even earlier than this, sometimes based just on the idea of a talented individual. Angels bridge the funding gap between the families or friends type of investors and venture capital investors. Angels provide quick infusions of capital to founders—usually up to $500,000—without too many terms or conditions (such as control over the board), in exchange for an ownership stake, usually preferred stock. Angels generally fund the building of the good or service (in complement to later-stage venture capital investors who fund the building of the company infrastructure and systems). Even though they may understand that the idea is experimental, they are looking towards the future for solid returns, evidence of a plan for how and what the money is to be used for, and some sort of business plan. They also want a well-defined exit strategy including what companies are potential suitors, and what other like-positioned companies have produced for returns. Angels are usually acting alone and at the earliest start-up stage and they typically do not maintain extensive oversight in company operations and do not always serve on the board of directors like venture capital investors do. To the extent a start-up does not need millions of dollars or extensive board oversight, angel investors are ideal matches for such ventures.

Venture Capital

Venture capital is comprised of pooled investments of a group investors' capital that is managed by venture capital firms seeking new high-growth companies operating with a competitive advantage in established sectors, or perhaps even those who are creating entirely new market sectors. Investments are usually in the range of $8-10 million with a focus on companies that can most efficiently be brought to profitability and a mature operational phase in order to be sold, or go public. Notable companies financed by venture capital are: Apple, Amazon, Cisco, Facebook, Federal Express, Google, Yahoo, and Twitter.

Venture capital investors (VCs) typically receive a management fee of 2 percent of the invested capital plus 20 percent of the profits from a successful exit. Most terms in the investment agreements are triggered only when there are grave problems. For example, VCs always stipulate they are the first to get their money back upon sale or liquidation—so that they will get paid before even the founders, who may end up with nothing. In another typical clause, they may rewrite the stock agreements to provide that the founders' stock vests over a period of up to five years, effectively prohibiting founders from cashing out and leaving the company right away.

The rights VCs usually expect in agreements with founders include:

- The right to elect members to the board of directors
- The right to receive financial reports
- The right to have stock registered for a public offering
- The right to maintain their percentage share ownership even with subsequent investors

As founders need more money than angels can supply, along with expertise and experience, VCs become involved. The cost to founders for this oversight, skill, and cash infusion is that they must cede a degree of control in the start up.

Initial Public Offerings (IPOs) and Private Placement

When a privately held corporation's needs for capital exceed the amount that can typically be raised through private investors, the company may choose to "go public" through an Initial Public Offering (IPO). Many companies that go public do so as part of a plan created by venture capitalists that invested significant funds to develop a business to the point where the venture is the best position to pursue an IPO strategy. The IPO process is a very complex and time-consuming one involving specialized legal counsel, investment bankers, and financial underwriters. Companies that pursue an IPO convert a private corporation into a company that sells its voting common shares to outside investors through public markets such as the New York Stock Exchange. Once public, a company and its principals are subject to a wide array of statutes and regulations involving their corporate governance and disclosures. Government regulation of corporations is discussed in more detail in Chapter 12.

Privately held business entities may also sell equity to the public on a more limited basis through a **private placement**. Using private placements allows for selling of equity to the general public without the full burden of securities laws because qualified private placements are exempt from certain securities regulations. However, private placements still have multiple disclosure requirements and anti-fraud provisions to protect investors. Private placements are discussed in more detail later in this chapter in the context of securities regulation.

Debt Instruments

Companies also raise capital through issuing debt instruments (e.g., promissory notes) to holders who expect a fixed rate of return through payback of principal and interest. Bank loans and family loans fall into this category. This may be attractive for some investors because debt holders typically are entitled to payments that are senior in priority to investors holding stock. Senior in priority means that those investors are paid first if the business must liquidate its assets. Of course, the downside of a debt investment is that the investor does not share in the success of a venture. The rate of return for a debt instrument is the same for business ventures that are highly profitable and those that are not profitable. Some corporations will issue debt to public investment markets in the form of bonds (secured by a specific asset) or debentures (secured by a corporation's general credit). In the past decade, even smaller companies have taken advantage of low rates on bond debt through issuance of micro bonds that are typically between $500,000 and $1 million.

Pre-Fundraising Issues

Once the venture has been formed and is developed enough to be considered a viable entity and the principals have generally agreed on what source(s) of capital would be most advantageous, it is important for them to agree on how the ownership will be structured, what percentage of the venture will be owned by what principal, and how the corporation will be controlled and managed until the investor fundraising begins.

Concept Summary: Sources of Capital

SELF-FUNDING/CREDIT

Founding principals' personal assets.

EQUITY (OWNERSHIP IN THE COMPANY)

Crowdfunding
Internet-based fundraising from a larger pool of smaller investors.

Angel Investors
High-net worth individual investors seeking higher return on investment than standard investments.

Venture Capital
Pool of money managed by venture capital firm for investing considerable funds into ventures that show promise of significant growth.

Initial Public Offering
Converting private company to public company for purposes of selling its stock through public markets.

DEBT (BUSINESS PAYS BACK PRINCIPAL WITH INTEREST)

Promissory Notes
Instrument used by banks or family members to evidence debt.

Bonds and Debentures
Issued to public markets in return for low interest rates and operational flexibility.

Structuring Ownership

One of the most difficult questions that the principals of a new venture must answer is how to split the initial ownership among them. The founders will typically act as the venture's initial board of directors who will allocate and issue the shares. While there is no specific formula, principals will usually decide the percentage of ownership based on a combination of factors including:

- Cash contributions to the venture from the principal's personal assets
- Equipment or property contributions by a principal
- Level of talent needed to develop the venture
- Amount of hours worked to bring the idea to fruition ("sweat equity")
- Connection to potential investors
- Anticipated hours needed to develop venture for fundraising rounds

In addition to the existing ownership split, the principals must also anticipate if any additional principals will need to be brought on before the fundraising phase begins. A board of directors will typically handle this challenge by authorizing a certain number of shares, but only issuing a certain percentage of its shares to its initial founders. This reserves the outstanding shares for future key employees and investors. It is important to understand that issuing additional stock after the initial round may result in dilution of ownership and have an impact on control of the business (dilution is covered in more detail later).

Common Stock versus Preferred Stock

The most common type of equity used is **common stock**. Common stock entitles the holder to payments based on profitability of the venture, known as dividends, based on the decision of the board of directors. Common stock owners also have the right to be compensated for their stock in the event the company is sold or liquidated (unless the company is worthless, such as in a bankruptcy). In most cases, a new venture will issue its pre-fundraising stock as common stock. **Preferred stock** is a similar equity instrument that is used primarily for investors. The major advantage of preferred stock is that holders have preference rights over common stockholders in receiving dividends, compensation for sale of the company, and recovering their investments in case of liquidation.

Dilution

If the company ends up having to sell more shares than it initially issued, the result is that the existing shareholders' equity is now diluted to the point where they own less of the company. There are two primary reasons to issue more shares after the initial allocation: talent and investment. A start up venture will typically have some type of missing element (perhaps a financial expert) as they develop the venture and the initial principals will want the flexibility to issue shares quickly as an incentive to acquire the talent. Companies interested in investment must be willing to sell equity to investors which will naturally dilute the existing shareholders overall percentage of ownership. Although dilution isn't always bad because it potentially gives the original handlers a smaller percentage slice of a bigger economic pie, there are ways to help reduce the impact of dilution. Dilution should be a part of every venture's pre-fundraising plan. In some cases, it makes sense from the outset to reserve approximately 20 percent of the authorized shares for future equity issuance. There may also be certain agreements among the shareholders that would limit the total dilution amounts and minimize any impact of dilution on the control of a corporation. Dilution is one aspect of a pre-fundraising agreement among the shareholders. Other important provisions are covered in the next section.

Shareholders Agreements

Agreements among shareholders resulting from discussions about ownership, fundraising, and control should always be memorialized in a **shareholders agreement**. Many legal disputes among founders are centered upon a misunderstanding or different versions of agreements between the parties. Unfortunately, these misunderstanding can sour relationships between the parties just at a time when the venture needs them to work together and disputes may spawn expensive and contentious litigation. Shareholders agreements concerning ownership and structure (which may or may not be part of a larger agreement) typically cover: 1) vesting, 2) restrictions on transfer, 3) right of first refusal, 4) buy-sell agreements, and 5) voting agreements. Some agreements also address dilution (discussed earlier).

Vesting

The concept of **vesting** is to ensure that the founders have an incentive to stay and build the company for a certain period of time. A vesting provision provides investors and key employees with some degree of assurance that a shareholder is interested in the venture's future beyond its initial fundraising and development. In a typical vesting plan, the parties agree that a principal's right to ownership "vests" (i.e., full ownership rights are triggered) according to a vesting schedule. Many vesting schedules contemplate a one year minimum, known as a cliff, before the principal's ownership vests to 25 percent of the total amount issued to that principal. Thereafter, the principal's ownership rights vest at approximately 2 percent per month for an additional three years. It is important to understand that if a principal leaves the venture before 100 percent of the stock is vested, the company has the right to repurchase unvested shares of founder stock at the original purchase price.

Limits on Transferring Stock

Shareholders agreements at this stage will also limit any transfer of any of the issued stock (vested or unvested) to third parties. Fundamentally, the restrictions help the shareholders maintain control over the venture. Consider the dilemma of the remaining shareholders if one were permitted to transfer controlling shares of stock to a third party who would be objectionable to shareholders or future investors. The most common restriction on the transfer of stock is through a **right of first refusal**. This ensures that any shareholder who wishes to sell to a third party must first offer it to the company on the terms and conditions being offered by a legitimate third party purchaser. If the company does not exercise its right, the departing shareholder is free to complete the sale transaction with the third party. In some cases, the non-selling shareholders want to assure that they have the liquidity (i.e., cash) to exercise their right to purchase the stock in certain instances. This is typically done through a **buy-sell agreement** whereby the parties agree to certain transfers at a set price. The company may also fund the buy-sell agreement through the purchase life insurance on a key shareholder. For example, suppose that a key founder dies with a significant percentage of stock. The company then uses the proceeds of the key person life insurance to purchase the stock from the estate of the deceased shareholder according to a valuation formula set out in the buy-sell provision. The principals are able to continue operations and control, purchase the stock, and the heirs of the deceased shareholder are the beneficiary of the full value of the stock without having to locate a third-party buyer.

Voting Agreements

Voting agreements are also an important provision because it ensures the composition of the board of directors is in accord with the founding shareholders wishes. They normally require each party to cast their shareholder vote for a designated individual to serve as a director. Some voting agreements also include "drag-along" rights that require a shareholder to agree to sell the venture if the majority of shareholders (in terms of percentage) agree to the sale terms.

Purdum v. Wolfe is a cautionary tale of the dangers of not having a clear agreement among the founding principals as the business venture is developed.

Purdum v. Wolfe,
No. C-13-04816 DMR (N.D. Cal. 2014)

Facts Purdum and his partners, Armenta, and Maher (collectively "Purdum") joined forces with Wolfe to develop a business for designing, manufacturing, and selling high-end men's shorts through a men's athletic apparel company called Olivers Apparel ("Olivers"). Over the course of several months, the parties developed the idea further with advice from friends knowledgeable about the fashion industry. At some point, the parties agreed that they would each become equity holders in the venture. The parties reached a "hand-shake" agreement whereby they agreed to go into business together to form Olivers. The parties also agreed to run a crowdfunding campaign on Kickstarter, an online funding platform, to raise capital for the new venture.

All four individuals met in June, 2013 and agreed to a partnership structure which would be non-binding and in place only through the Kickstarter campaign to raise investor money whereby Wolfe would hold a 50 percent equity stake while Purdum and his partners would each hold a 16.66 percent stake and that an LLC Operating Agreement would be in place by the end of July. On July 31, 2013, although the parties had not entered into an operating agreement, Wolfe submitted Olivers' Articles of Organization of a Limited Liability Company to the California Secretary of State. The Articles of Organization stated that the LLC would be managed by "one manager," who was not identified on the form, and listed Purdum's business address as Olivers' address. Wolfe signed the document as "Organizer." On August 13, the parties signed a brief document which set out certain obligations and contributions for each party. The document was titled "Operating Agreement Parameters" but it did not specify use of funds from an upcoming crowdfunding campaign. They agreed that these parameters would be part of a more comprehensive Operating Agreement in the future.

The parties had still not signed an Operating Agreement when they launched Olivers' Kickstarter campaign in late August. The Kickstarter site featured a short video created by a production company assembled and hired by Wolfe. The video features each of the four founders and represents to investors that the founders had experience running a tailored men's wear company. The campaign was an enormous success, and in thirty days, Olivers raised $271,043 from 3,307 individuals.

Following the unexpected success of the Kickstarter campaign, negotiations on the final Operating Agreement became contentious and the partnership between Purdum and Wolfe soured. Purdum ultimately sent Wolfe an ultimatum involving two choices: (1) Wolfe gets 100% of Olivers' stock, pays Purdum 60% of the Kickstarter funds, and relinquishes any intellectual property rights of Olivers to date; or (2) Wolfe turns over day-to-day operations and control of Olivers to Purdum, keeps a 5 percent equity stake, and receives 40 percent of the Kickstarter funds.

Wolfe's attorney sent Purdum a response that indicated that Wolfe considered Purdum's ultimatum as a repudiation of all previous agreements between the parties and that Olivers was a single member limited liability company founded and owned exclusively by Wolfe. The response also indicated that all intellectual property and trade secrets created on behalf of Olivers was the sole and exclusive property of Olivers.

Purdum discovered that Wolfe had changed the passwords to the Kickstarter page, all of Olivers' social media pages, and Olivers' bank accounts containing the Kickstarter funds. However, Wolfe did not disclose these changes to the approximately 3,300 Kickstarter investors. Instead, he continued to communicate with investors on the Kickstarter page using the names of the original founders.

Purdum filed a motion for a preliminary injunction seeking to prevent Wolfe from selling any shorts manufactured without Purdum's assistance and a court order requiring Wolfe to turn over the passwords to Olivers' social media and bank accounts so that Purdum may again have the ability to rightfully control the company that they co-founded and partially own.

Judicial Opinion

Legal Standard "A preliminary injunction is an extraordinary remedy never awarded as of right." *Alliance for the Wild Rockies v. Cottrell,* 632 F.3d 1127, 1131 (9th Cir. 2011). A plaintiff seeking a preliminary injunction must show (1) a likelihood of suffering irreparable harm in the absence of a preliminary injunction, (2) a likelihood of success on the merits, (3) that the balance of equities tips in the movant's favor, and (4) that an injunction would serve the public interest.

Likelihood of Success on the Merits . . .
[Purdum] points to the evidence of an agreement between the parties, including the meeting notes and the August 13, 2013 Operating Agreement Parameters document, that set forth the parties' equity stakes, voting rights, and expected time commitments to Olivers. They argue that Wolfe breached the Operating

Agreement Parameters when he unilaterally terminated Purdum from Olivers by changing all of the passwords for Olivers' social media sites and Kickstarter page and taking sole control of Olivers' bank account.

Wolfe does not dispute that there was an agreement between the parties, as memorialized in the Operating Agreement Parameters document. However, he argues that [Purdum] will be unable to prevail on their contract claims for two reasons. First, [Purdum] must show that they performed their obligations under the parties' agreement. According to Wolfe, this will be difficult as the September 6, 2013 email shows that [Purdum was] "unwilling to perform the terms of the Agreement," as they stated they would either stop all work on Olivers or Wolfe would relinquish his stake in the company. Wolfe emphasizes that the Operating Agreement required Purdum to each devote one year of work to Olivers at the rate of twenty hours per week before beginning to accrue equity in the company, and appears to base his argument that they "expressly refused to perform" under the agreement on the fact that one of the two options was for Plaintiffs to stop working on Olivers altogether. Second, Wolfe argues that [Purdum has] not shown evidence of a breach by Wolfe. Specifically, he argues that [Purdum]'s September 6 email was an anticipatory breach of the parties' agreement, and that his actions in locking [Purdum] out of Olivers were a lawful reaction to [the] breach.

Ultimately, whether Wolfe's actions constituted a breach of the parties' agreement or a reaction to [Purdum]'s anticipatory breach is a disputed question of fact that lies at the heart of [Purdum]'s breach of contract claim. The court "is not bound to decide doubtful and difficult questions of law or disputed questions of fact" in deciding a motion for preliminary injunction. As the record before the court is limited, the court declines to resolve this factual dispute, and accordingly finds that Plaintiffs have failed to demonstrate a likelihood of success on the merits on this claim.

. . .

Likelihood of Irreparable Harm Even if [Purdum] had shown a probability of prevailing on any their claims, the court finds that they have failed to show a likelihood of irreparable harm in the absence of a preliminary injunction. [Purdum] argued that the "irreparable injury stems from Wolfe's current manufacture and sale of shorts without the manufacturing expertise of the [Purdum]." According to [Purdum], Wolfe's manufacture of shorts without [Purdum]'s expertise hurts [Purdum]'s reputation, because when a customer receives a "shoddily manufactured" [pair of] shorts from Wolfe, the customer will believe the product was made by [Purdum] as they are unaware that [Purdum was] removed from Olivers. However, [Purdum has] not presented any evidence of "shoddy manufacturing" by Wolfe, and thus [Purdum]'s theory of irreparable harm is purely speculative.

CONCLUSION

For the foregoing reasons, Purdum's motion for preliminary injunction is denied.

Case Questions

1. What was the impact of the "Operating Agreement Parameters" document in this case?
2. How could the parties have made their agreement more clear to avoid litigation? Suggest some language that may have been appropriate in the final Operating Agreement.
3. *Ethical Consideration:* Although Wolfe marketed the company in Kickstarter as one of four founders with experience in the industry, the reality ended up being quite different. Was it ethical to make those representations and continue to represent that there were four principals instead of just one? Why do you think Wolfe failed to notify their Kickstarter investments?

Franz-Josef Hypothetical

In our Franz-Josef example, suppose that Franz has contributed $10,000 in capital from his personal resources to cover start-up costs such as office space, legal and accounting fees, and equipment necessary to develop the software. Josef is not in a financial position to contribute cash, but he contributes some equipment such as laptops and specialized software to help develop the venture. Each puts in significant time into the venture while also working full-time at other jobs until the entity can be developed to the point of generating enough income to pay salaries. After meeting with counsel and discussing their contributions, they decide initially to authorize 50,000 shares of common stock with 6,000 shares issued to Franz and 4,000 shares issued to Josef. In order to plan for the future, they also issue 10,000 shares in reserve for a future key employee and/or preliminary investors. They also understand that future investors may be looking for assurances through a vesting plan and agree to a schedule whereby each of them will vest 25 percent of their total shares only after the first year of operations. After the first year, they will vest 2 percent per month until they reach 100 percent. Because they are both key shareholders of the venture and have expertise necessary to develop the business, they also enter into a shareholders' agreement with a right-of-first refusal, a buy-sell provision, and a voting agreement to ensure control of the entity.

Raising Capital in Rounds

Raising capital should be thought of as a process rather than an event. Typically, fundraising occurs in rounds (e.g., a few rounds of preliminary financing, followed by subsequent stages of financing). Each stage is marked by certain defining characteristics, in terms of the sources and uses of funds, dilution of share ownership and control, as well as challenges for the founders, managers, and investors.

Pre-seed Financing

The money usually comes from the founders' savings or perhaps a retirement or severance plan. The money is used to fund translation of the idea into some sort of prototype product or site.

Seed Financing

The money may still be from a personal network of spouse and family, but may also start to use exemption financing through a private placement memorandum. This is the first benchmark and is used to develop the goods or services, including filings for intellectual property ownership, market surveys, and engaging key personnel talent.

Series A Round

This occurs when the start up is ready to launch and it needs more marketing, staff, and management resources. The company is functioning with at least a prototype or a beta-tested site. There may be some revenue at this point. This is usually the first time when a larger number of outside investors are brought in either as angel investors or through private placement. There is a significant amount of paperwork and due diligence investigatory work to be done. It becomes another to-do item for management to manage this infusion of money. Investors are making decisions in the entity as well, supervising development, recruitment, and management performance. At this point, management creates or overhauls internal reporting systems, and the board of directors is typically expanded to include investors and key talent. This can be a challenging period of transformation for the founders effect a tremendous change on the culture of the entity. Some firms use crowdfunding sources at this stage, but some prefer to develop the venture further to increase the possibility of a larger offering.

Series B (and Subsequent Rounds)

Also called second-stage financing, the company seeking this type of financing must demonstrate evidence of sales, management, and marketing. Investors at this stage may also include venture capital firms or private funds (including hedge funds and other private placement funds under Regulation D). The marketing and sales demands may exceed the capacity of the original founders, and this is when there is high potential for dilution of the founders' ownership interest.

Pre-IPO or Bridge Financing

This occurs at least two years ahead of a planned IPO. Since the process of becoming a public company requires time and significant capital from previous investors, some sort of bridge financing (i.e., a bridge between the private company and the public company) is necessary. Companies must be able to demonstrate increasing sales, consistent growth, highly developed marketing, and a track record of earnings.

Regulation of Securities

Transactions involving securities are subject to an array of federal and state laws that require important disclosures by the business entity (e.g., information about officers' experience in the industry) and set out procedures and processes for raising capital from the general public. Securities laws are in place primarily to protect investors from fraud through transparency of the entity and its principals. Even the distribution of a business plan to a third party investor may trigger securities laws and both entrepreneurs and intrapreneurs must be aware of the legal fundamentals in securities law. Although securities law is primarily regulated through federal statutes, each state has similar disclosure and anti-fraud laws that are typically known as "blue-sky laws."

Federal securities laws are enforced by the Securities and Exchange Commission (SEC) which is a federal administrative agency. The SEC's powers also include rulemaking and adjudication of federal securities laws. The SEC is categorized as an independent agency because although its five commissioners are appointed by the President (subject to approval by the Senate), they are not cabinet officers subordinate to the President's direct control. Additionally, commissioners may only be removed for misconduct. Note that no SEC commissioner has ever been removed since Congress created the commission in 1934. The SEC maintains an important public database, called EDGAR, which serves as a national clearinghouse for public corporation disclosures and filings.

Securities Offerings

The original issuance (or re-issuance) of securities offered to the general public is regulated by the Securities Act of 1933 (the "'33 Act"). The '33 Act requires a business issuing securities to register the transaction with the SEC and to make certain disclosures concerning the business's financial condition and governance of the venture. The '33 Act also provides defrauded investors with remedies against issuers that violate securities laws.

'33 Act Exemptions

Although the primary objective underlying the '33 Act is to protect the investment community through disclosure and transparency, the process of issuing a security that is in compliance with securities can be extremely burdensome and costly for many businesses. To encourage the movement of capital, Congress has carved out several **exemptions** to a full blown registration requirement. The exemptions are aimed primarily at small and mid-sized businesses seeking capital from a limited number of investors over a limited timeframe. Indeed, most businesses that seek capital from groups of third party investors offer securities (such as common stock) on an exemption basis. The basic framework for exemptions recognizes that certain investors are sufficiently sophisticated so as to be able to make their own judgment regarding risk. It is important to note that even exempt securities have disclosure, transparency, and filing requirements depending on the exemption provision. A group of exemptions under **Regulation D** apply to offers that are limited in amount and scope. It exempts securities offerings by companies raising capital using three tiers based on the amount of the offering: $500,000, $1 million, or up to $5 million in a single 12-month period.

The amount of formal registration and disclosure requirements correlate to the amount of the offering. Another common exemption is known as a **private placement**. A private placement offering may only be offered to investors who meet a personal net worth and/or income requirement threshold, called *accredited investors*, where the offerings are up to $5 million in a 12-month period. Disclosures are made through a private placement memorandum. These memorandums contain, among other things, disclosures related to risk factors, use of proceeds, dilution, financial data, biographies of the management team, legal matters such as pending lawsuits, and management's analysis of the financial conditions that may impact the business.

Crowdfunding Exemption

In 2013, the SEC fashioned special rules for investing through crowdfunding. They also created a new SEC registered intermediary category called a "funding portal" (similar to a broker dealer registrant). These rules include limits on the amounts raised by a business venture and restrictions on the amount invested by individual investors (discussed earlier). The SEC crowdfunding rules also impose disclosure requirements on companies that fundraise through crowdfunding. These disclosures include:

- Biographical information on directors, officers and shareholders owning 20 percent or more of the company
- Specific description of how the company intends to spend the proceeds
- Description of the financial condition of the company
- In larger campaigns, the company must provide financial statements of the company accompanied by a copy of the company's tax returns
- Background checks on all principals with 10 percent or greater ownership and disclosure of pertinent details revealed through the background check

The Financing of Twitter

Twitter, one of the most popular social networks ever created, actually sprung from another tech company called Odeo whose podcasting business had been eclipsed by Apple's dominant position in the podcast space. Odeo investors were skeptical of Twitter's business model and the founding principals ended up buying back all of the Odeo stock and continuing to develop the Twitter business venture. Twitter was launched in 2006 and funded primarily through seed rounds to private investors. The company went public in 2013 with their stock climbing nearly 70 percent in its opening day on the market. Their fundraising tactics were not without controversy and just before its IPO, Twitter was hit with a $124 million lawsuit. The suit was filed by two financial firms that alleged that Twitter executives fraudulently engaged them to organize a private sale of its shares before the IPO, but then cancelled the sale at the last minute. The financial firms alleged that Twitter had no intention of actually going through with the sale, but rather intended to stoke investor interest and create an artificial private market in order to boost its IPO potential. The lawsuit alleges that Twitter executives were worried about the problems that afflicted the disastrous IPO of Facebook. However, in 2014, a federal judge ruled that the financial firms had not shown any indication that Twitter committed fraud and dismissed the case. The case, *Precedeo Capital Group v. Twitter*, was heard by the U.S. District Court (S.D.N.Y.) (No. 13-Civ. 7678).

Trading Securities: Securities Exchange Act of 1934

After a security has been properly issued under the '33 Act, federal laws continue to regulate the sale of the securities *between* investors under the Securities Exchange Act of 1934 (the "'34 Act"). Much of the '34 Act regulates professionals involved in stock trading, such as brokers, dealers, and brokerage firms. It compels all sellers of securities offered on a national market exchange to be registered with the SEC and requires disclosures and transparency when selling a security to the investing public. This includes information about the financial condition of the company, how the corporation is governed, and disclosures of increased or decreased risk that occur in between filings. Section 10(b) is the antifraud provision in the '34 Act and is best known for its use by the SEC to prosecute insider-trading cases.

Corporate Management, Control, and Fiduciary Duties

Fundamentally, corporations are structured around an allocation of power based on three categories: *shareholders, directors,* and *officers.* Shareholders are the owners of the corporation and act principally through electing and removing directors and approving or withholding approval of major corporate decisions. **Directors** are responsible for oversight and management of the corporation's course of direction. **Officers** carry out the directors' set course of direction through management of the day-to-day operations of the business. Although this allocation of power is based primarily on the Revised Model Business Corporation Act, many states allow a corporation to alter the structure as necessary to meet the needs of the entity. Very large corporations and very small corporations often manage their operations using a modified form of this structure. For example, in some cases a corporation has only one or two shareholders, each of whom acts as director and an officer. The structure is essentially useless, so they may opt to adopt a slightly different structure through the bylaws and/or an agreement among the shareholders as to the rights and responsibilities of each shareholder.

Board of Directors

Directors are meant to act on behalf of shareholders and oversee management. Directors are elected or appointed according to the provisions in the corporation's by-laws, and ultimately voted on by the shareholders during a general meeting. They serve for a defined term and are responsible for supervision of the overall affairs of a company, leaving day-to-day management issues to the officers, though the directors are the highest authority within a corporation. To the extent the corporation is a start up or other relatively small entity, the directors will also be the shareholders and officers, thus there is no real division of, or checks on, power. Major functions of board members include:

- Planning (philosophy, strategy, capital allocation)
- Organization (appraise management, succession planning, committee appointments)
- Operations (review results in comparison to philosophy, approve capital expenditures, acquisitions, divestitures, new strategies)
- Audit and Oversight (to assure compliance with government regulations, conflict-of-interest issues, and to keep adequately informed).
- Compensation (review and approval of CEO and outside director compensation)

Inside Directors

These are directors that have a dual role, serving as members of the board as well as having management responsibilities. While their knowledge is highly valuable in board decisions, it comes with a bias towards an entrenched way of doing things.

Venture Capital Investors in Management

Venture capital investors are in the business of investing and as part of the bargain for accepting venture funding, start ups must agree to management participation and control through board representation. This board-level oversight continues so long as the original core management team is achieving goals in a timely fashion; to the extent objectives are not met, venture capital investors reserve rights to more substantial participation in day-to-day operations.

Outside Directors

These directors have no other affiliation with the company other than serving on its board. They are asked to serve, in most instances, because they have some special knowledge or expertise, along with bringing a fresh perspective that benefits the business.

Officers

The corporation's officers are appointed by, and may be removed by, the board of directors. The officers carry out the day-to-day operations of the corporation and execute the strategy and mandates set out by the board of directors. As a practical matter, officers work closely with the directors in setting the course of a corporation's path, but major changes in the corporation may not be taken through officer action alone. Although some states still require the traditional officer roles to be filled (president, vice president, secretary, and treasurer), the current trend is to allow the names and responsibilities of the officers to be set by the bylaws or through action of the board of directors. Officers have both express and implied authority. Express authority comes from the bylaws or by a board of directors' resolution, which gives specific authority to a particular officer. For example, the board of directors may pass a resolution authorizing the treasurer of a corporation to open up a bank account or to start a money market account for surplus cash on hand. Officers may also have inherent authority, based on their position, to act on behalf of the corporation. Note that certain corporate officers have *implied authority* to be an agent of the corporation. This is an important concept in corporate law because it helps define the powers of corporate officers.

President

Traditionally, the president has the implied power to bind the corporation in ordinary business operation transactions and the oversight of non-officer employees.

Vice President

Depending on the size and scope of the corporation, the vice president may have some limited implied authority. For example, a vice president for marketing would likely have implied authority to bind the corporation to a vendor of advertising. The implied authority of a vice president may also have additional powers to bind the corporation in ordinary business transactions if such authority is a routine practice in a certain industry.

Treasurer

Aside from the routine tasks of collecting the accounts receivable and paying the accounts payable, the treasurer has little or no other implied authority.

Secretary

The secretary has the implied authority to certify the records and resolutions of the company. When the board of directors passes a resolution, it is the secretary who affixes his signature to it, which confirms that the document is genuine. Third parties in a particular transaction may rely on this certification.

Fiduciary Duties of Directors and Officers

Directors and officers are charged with acting on behalf of the corporate entity that is owned by the shareholders. Directors and officers therefore owe a fiduciary duty to shareholders. These duties are independent of and in addition to the contractual relationship directors and officers have with the corporation. A fiduciary is one in a trusted relationship who has undertaken to act on behalf of the other, giving rise to a legal duty to act with a high degree of honesty and diligence. High-profile cases involving claims of excessive pay, insufficient over-sight or disclosure, take-over deals that went bust, corporate scandals along with bankruptcies, and other similar developments are subjecting corporations to increased public and legal scrutiny. At the core of the relationship between the corporation and its directors and officers are these fiduciary duties.

Duty of Loyalty

Officers and directors owe a **duty of loyalty** to shareholders. Significant share-holders that have some degree of control over corporate decisions also owe a duty of loyalty to other shareholders. The duty of loyalty is principally a duty intended to prevent a conflict of interest that would result in oppression of minority share-holders. The duty of loyalty is primarily focused on providing protection to shareholders in cases where a transaction occurs where the possibility of self-dealing is present. Self-dealing in this context is where an officer, director, or controlling shareholder has some personal financial stake in a transaction that the corporation is engaged in and the officer, director, or shareholder helps to influence the advancement of the transaction.

The duty of loyalty also requires disclosure and good faith when an insider (i.e., director, officer, or controlling shareholder) learns of a potentially lucrative business opportunity that could enrich her individually, but is related to the corporation's business. Known as the corporate opportunity doctrine, an insider may not usurp for herself a business opportunity that belongs to the corporation or would benefit the corporation in some direct way.

Duty of Care

Fundamentally, officers and directors must exercise the degree of skill, diligence, and care that a reasonably prudent person would exercise under the same circum-stances. Most states define the duty of care through a three-part test. First, the officer and director must always act in good faith. Second, they must also act with the care that an objectively prudent person in a like position would exercise under similar circumstances. Third, they must carry out their duties in a manner that is reasonably calculated to advance the best interests of the corporation. This duty applies to all directors and officers without regard to the size of the corporation or whether the directors are paid or unpaid. Courts have held that a director breaches her duty of care when she has failed to fulfill her role in oversight. This may occur in several ways: 1) negligence (e.g., director doesn't read reports or financial records), 2) lack of diligence (e.g., failure to question any suspicious activity by the corporation or its officers, 3) rubber stamp (e.g., failure to investigate a transaction proposed by the officers).

Business Judgment Rule

At first glance, the duty of care looks onerous. When a corporation engages in a certain transaction or in a certain course of conduct that generates losses, some shareholders may inevitably believe it was the fault of the directors' lack of care. The business judgment rule protects officers and directors from liability for decisions that may have been unwise, but did not breach the duty of care. This rule insulates directors from liability when, based on reasonable information at the time, the transaction or course of action turns out badly from the standpoint of the corporation. Directors and officers often seek protection of this rule when an individual shareholder or group of shareholders files a lawsuit against them. Every state has adopted the rule (either by including it in their statutes or recognizing its applicability in common law) as a defense to a breach of the duty of care claim against a director. Fundamentally, directors must have acted in *good faith* to insulate themselves from liability for breach of care.

In some cases, directors and officers of a corporation are one in the same. In the following case, a court considers these duties in the context of an individual who was both a director and an officer of the corporation.

Thomas Weisel Partners, LLC v. BNP Paribas and Praveen Chakravarty
2010 U.S. Dist. LEXIS 32332 (N.D. Cal. 2010)

Facts Thomas Weisel Partners LLC (TWP) is an investment bank headquartered in San Francisco, California. In 2005, TWP formed two other entities. First, it formed Discovery Research, headquartered in Mumbai, India, to provide low-cost research on stocks for TWP's clients. Second, it formed Thomas Weisel International Private Ltd. (TWIPL) as a holding company for its Indian assets, including Discovery Research. Chakravarty joined TWP as a research associate in 2003. In 2005, he was transferred to Mumbai and became an officer of TWP in 2007. He was also elected as a Director on the boards of both Discovery Research and TWIPL. Chakravarty had managerial responsibility for the research analysts working for Discovery Research.

Plaintiffs state that he informed TWP by email on November 7, 2007, that he "would be unable to continue at TWP." TWP terminated his employment for cause that same day, as did Discovery Research and TWIPL. Chakravarty, it turns out, received an offer of employment in the same field from BNP Paribas Securities on November 1, 2007, and began officially working at that company in December 2007. Furthermore, Chakravarty had initially reached out the Pierre Rousseau, BNP Paribas's Global Head of Equity Brokerage, much earlier, in September 2007. He wanted to set up a meeting to discuss BNPs potential entry into India and stated, "We have an existing operation that may be of interest." They first spoke by telephone, and Rousseau told Chakravarty that he was recruiting people for a new operation in India and asked Chakravarty whether the Discovery Research "platform will be for sale." Chakravarty replied that he could "make that happen." On October 11, 2007, the two met with another BNP executive, Jonathan Harris; Chakravarty also introduced them to six of the Discovery Research analysts. On October 15th, Harris sent an email to Chakravarty's TWP email account, describing next steps. Harris wanted him to identify core team members and strategized on how to engineer a plan to resign en masse from Discovery Research. Harris imagined that Discovery Research would have to just close up due to the scope of such a move. Then PNB would swoop in and offer to take over operations to save them office shutdown costs. Harris further asked for lists of all employees and their current compensation, bonuses, seniority, job descriptions, education, and background. That same day, Chakravarty replied with spreadsheets containing all the requested information, plus proposed salaries at BNP Paribas, and he highlighted which of the Discovery employees would move with him.

Harris emailed his colleagues at BNP and told them that during "my visit to India last week, we found a very interesting and cost-effective possible solution to building equity research capabilities in India." He attached the Chakravarty spreadsheet and a memo regarding the opportunity "to acquire the team, and possibly total operation, of Discovery Research." They set up meetings at a business center to interview the 12 core analysts. Afterwards, Chakravarty emailed his proposed compensation and benefits package, and in it set up tentative timelines for effectuating the new venture, including resignation dates and start dates. At least 18 analysts resigned between October 31 and November 6, 2007, the date when Chakravarty also resigned. At no point prior to his departure did Chakravarty inform his supervisor that he was facilitating BNP's recruitment of Discovery Research employees. He did present some evidence that he approached his supervisor to inform him that BNP might be interested in a joint venture. TWP did not pursue any opportunities in this regard. BNP ultimately hired over 20 Discovery Research employees for its new India operation and appointed Chakravarty the CEO. Unable to continue operating the Mumbai office after the loss of these employees, plaintiffs closed the office on December 6, 2007. Plaintiffs filed this lawsuit for, inter alia, breach of fiduciary duty against Chakravarty, seeking over $24 million in damages. Plaintiffs allege he occupied a position of trust and confidence with TWP by virtue of his employment with TWP, and as an officer and director. As such, plaintiffs contend, Chakravarty owed TWP fiduciary duties of loyalty and confidentiality, which he breached by facilitating a raid on Discovery Research's employees by BNP prior to Chakravarty's departure from plaintiffs employ.

Judicial Opinion To establish a cause of action for breach of fiduciary duty, a plaintiff must demonstrate the existence of a fiduciary relationship, breach of duty and damages.

I. Existence of Fiduciary Duty Corporate officers and directors stand in a fiduciary relation to the corporation and its stockholders and are not permitted to use their position of trust and confidence to further their private interests. A rule established by public policy "demands of a corporate officer or directors, the most scrupulous observance of his duty." A company's fiduciaries are not limited solely to those individuals who exercise "top-level control"; rather, an officer who participates in management of the corporation, exercising some discretionary authority is a fiduciary of the corporation as a matter of law. A fiduciary of a subsidiary also owes a fiduciary duty to the subsidiary's parent corporation. The undisputed record indicates that Chakravarty was an appointed Director on TWIPL's Board and was an officer as "Head of Research." Evidence demonstrates that he was a member of the Discovery Research management team. He argues in opposition that the titles bestowed upon him were meaningless, and that, therefore, plaintiffs have failed to establish that he owed a fiduciary duty to TWP as a matter of law. The court holds that Chakravarty owed a fiduciary duty to TWIPL and the parent company TWP [because] even if [the titles] were a sham and entirely devoid of meaning, Chakravarty was an officer who participated in management of the corporation, exercising some discretionary authority.

II. Breach of Fiduciary Duty A fiduciary breaches his duty as a matter of law when the evidence shows a consistent course of conduct by him designed to obtain for a competitor those of plaintiffs employees whom the competitor could afford to employ and would find useful. [Chakravarty defended his actions on four grounds.] He claims the salary information he passed on was not confidential because he obtained it from the analysts themselves who granted him permission to provide it to BNP. Even if this is true, he was only privy to that information by reason of the position of trust that he inhabited with TWP. Second, he asserts Discovery Research was about to be shut down and employees were disgruntled and looking for other work. An individual's fiduciary duty toward his employer continues until either corporation cease to exist or the fiduciary resigns. Third, he contends that the two businesses were not direct competitors and therefore there can be no breach of duty.

Chakravarty cites no authority for this proposition; no matter the resolution of this, there is absolutely no dispute that Discovery Research and BNP were competitors in the same labor market for skilled financial analysts. Otherwise they were not having had any interest in acquiring these employees. Fourth, he avers that his conduct does not amount to a breach because he never solicited employees and did not encourage or coerce employees to leave for BNP. He solicited employees by conveying their interest to BNP and by setting up interviews, reviewing contracts — in short, he engaged in a consistent course of conduct designed to benefit a competitor. He did not inform Discovery Research of any business opportunity involving BNP until one day before he resigned and so plaintiffs failure to act on this opportunity is not probative. The actions taken by Chakravarty to facilitate the en masses defection of 26 employees falls squarely within a breach of fiduciary duty to TWIPL and TWP.

. . .

CONCLUSION

Plaintiffs' motion for partial summary judgment for breach of fiduciary duty against defendants granted.

Case Questions

1. Identify Defendant's best legal theory going forward at trial.
2. What other theories might Plaintiffs be able to develop at trial in this case?
3. This case was litigated in California, half a world away from the office in this case; the costs of litigating this case are staggering in relation to the purpose of the operation in India—save money on research. Identify more economical ways of doing business and resolving disputes.

Summary

Entrepreneurs and managers increase their chances of success if they bring their venture from idea to reality through careful planning and attention to the legal impact of forming, financing, and managing a new business. By discussing their expectations, objectives, and financial realities early in the venture launch process, the principals avoid disputes and capitalize on financing options that will help them enjoy the fruits of their labor and creativity.

Key Terms

principal Generic term for individual with ownership in a business entity.

sole proprietor Single-person form of business entity in which the principal/ proprietor is the alter-ego of the business.

partnership Multiple-person business entity which uses flow-through taxation and offers limited partners limited liability while holding general partners jointly and severally liable for liabilities of the partnership.

limited liability company Multiple-person business entity that gives more flexibility than other entities and provides liability protection for its principals.

limited liability partnership Multiple-person business entity that provides the benefits of partnership taxation with more liability protection for the partners.

corporation Single or multiple-person entity which exists as an independent "person" separate from its principals.

seed round Preliminary fundraising stage for capitalizing a business venture.

equity Ownership interest in a business entity.

debt Money used by a business entity which must be paid back (e.g., a commercial loan).

crowdfunding Raising capital through an offering to potential investors using a web-based platform such as Kickstarter.

angel investor High-net-worth investor willing to risk investing in early-stage companies in exchange for a relatively high rate of return.

venture capital Typically a pool of investors that is managed by a venture capital firm seeking to invest in high-growth companies.

initial public offering Seeking investment by selling equity on publicly traded markets such as the NYSE.

common stock Equity interest that entitles the holder to payments based on profitability of the business based on the discretion of the board of directors.

preferred stock Equity interest that entitles the holder to payments based on profitability and provides for preference rights over common stockholders in recovering their investments in the case of liquidation.

shareholders agreement Agreement among the principals of a corporation with respect to ownership, fundraising, and control.

vesting Minimum time period required to earn ownership interests from a business entity.

right of first refusal Restriction on transferring stock that requires the seller to offer the stock to existing shareholders first.

buy-sell agreement Device typically used to be sure that resources exist to fund a buyout of a departing shareholder.

voting agreement Provision of a shareholders' agreement used to ensure that the composition of the board is in accordance with founding shareholder wishes.

exemption Carve-outs from the '33 Act registration requirements.

Regulation D Section of '33 Act that provides registration exemptions for relatively small offerings.

private placement Registration exemption that requires investors to meet certain net worth and income criteria in order to invest.

director Individual elected by shareholders of a company to oversee finances and manage the corporation's course of direction.

officer Individual appointed by the board of directors to manage day-to-day operations of the business.

fiduciary duty Duty owed by directors and officers to carry out the best interests of the corporation.

Manager's Checklist

1. Entrepreneurs and managers must make decisions early on regarding the form of business organization with a complete understanding of the impacts on ownership, control, fundraising, and taxation.

2. Early stage planning must include long-range views of fundraising and entrepreneurs/managers should consider the various advantages and disadvantages of sources of capital available to them at various stages of development.

3. Raising capital from the public typically triggers securities law requirements. Managers and entrepreneurs should be knowledgeable about the basics of offering securities for sale and exemptions for small- and mid-sized businesses.

4. Entrepreneurs and managers will inevitably be serving as officers and directors of their business venture and therefore must have a working knowledge of the fiduciary duties imposed upon them by law.

Questions and Case Problems

1. Shareholders of Palm, Inc. filed suit against the Palm board of directors arguing that they did not make the best deal when it approved the $1.4 billion in cash for its acquisition by Hewlett-Packard Co. (This meant an offering price of approximately $5.70 for every Palm share.) *How might a court construe this claim?*

2. American International Group (AIG) filed a lawsuit against its former CEO, asserting that he breached his fiduciary duty to the company when he and others misappropriated a special block of AIG shares worth $20 billion. These were transferred to Starr International Co., an AIG affiliate used as a special deferred compensation vehicle for certain AIG employees. AIG later suffered material losses that were not due directly to this transaction, but investors want this money back to pay out AIG shareholders. *What is the outcome?*

3. H. Ross Perot became the single largest shareholder and a director of General Motors as a result of GM's acquisition of Perot's highly successful company Electronic Data Systems (EDS). A rift grew between Perot and GM's other directors, and after appointing a subcommittee of directors to study possible alternatives, GM's directors offered to purchase back Perot's stock at a significant premium over market value. In exchange for the payment, Perot agreed to leave his director's seat, not compete with any GM subsidiary (particularly EDS), and cease any criticism of GM's directors. A group of GM shareholders sued the directors under a theory that the directors had breached their fiduciary duty by wasting corporate assets in buying Perot's silence. The directors asserted the business judgment rule as a defense. *Who should prevail and why? What fiduciary duty is at issue?*

4. Chapman was the sole shareholder, officer, and director of Region Associates (Region). In 2001 Goldman obtained a judgment against Region in the amount of $209,320 as a result of Goldman's lawsuit against Region (but not Chapman individually). Goldman attempted to collect the judgment from Region but was unsuccessful because Region was without any substantial assets. After exhausting all efforts to collect the judgment from Region, Goldman filed suit asking the court to allow him to pierce Region's corporate veil and collect the judgment from Chapman's personal assets. *Who should prevail and why? Did Chapman use the law to perpetrate an injustice?*

Additional Resources

Crowdfunding Academy. www.crowdfundingacademy.com.

Security and Exchange Commission. Exemptions. www.sec.gov/answers/regd.htm.

IPO page. www.sec.gov/answers/ipo.htm.

Small Business Advocate. Capitalizing your Business. www.smallbusinessadvocate.com/small-business-articles/capitalizing-your-company-20.

Socialnomics. History of Twitter. www.socialnomics.net/2013/01/23/the-history-of-twitter.

two

Part II

Intellectual Property: Business
Assets in the Information Age

 [I]f someone is operating a web site under another brand owner's trademark, such as a site called "cocacola.com" or "levis.com," consumers bear a significant risk of being deceived and defrauded, or at a minimum, confused. The costs associated with these risks are increasingly burdensome as more people begin selling pharmaceuticals, financial services, and even groceries over the Internet.

—Senate Report 106-140, 106th Congress (1999)

4

Trademarks

Learning Outcomes

After you have read this chapter, you should be able to:

- Explain what a trademark is and give examples.
- Explain what is meant by trademark infringement and trademark dilution.
- Identify the major problem areas related to trademark use on the Internet.
- Explain what a domain name is and how domain name disputes are resolved.

Overview

As you take out your smart phone and go online, you will notice trademarks everywhere. Your phone is likely identified by a trademark, such as "HTC" or "Samsung." Or perhaps your phone's shape and design allow you to immediately identify it as an Apple iPhone. A product's distinctive shape or design can also be a trademark. As your smart phone boots up, you might hear a trademarked start-up sound. And as you prepare to select an application, you may see a distinct configuration of familiar icons arranged in a particular manner. That distinct visual display may also be a trademark. What do each of these words, letters, sounds, and designs have in common? They each are recognizable and distinct, allowing consumers to quickly associate a given product with the maker or source of that product.

You probably already have an intuitive grasp of why trademarks are important. Do you buy textbooks from Amazon.com or listen to music using Spotify, or do you prefer other websites? Your choice probably depends on the qualities you

Exhibit 4.1   **SMS Display Configuration Trademark of Apple, Inc.**

Reg. No. 3470983. Owner: Apple, Inc.

associate with each site, such as scope of offerings, ease of use, and price. Trademarks allow you to associate the qualities of a given product or service with a unique signifier, which can guide your online activities and purchasing decisions. More generally, trademarks serve to distinguish products and help buyers locate the products and services they want quickly and easily.

Intellectual Property (IP)

Trademarks constitute just one of the four principal types of **intellectual property** (**IP**). The others are copyrights, patents, and trade secrets:

- *Trademarks* serve as indications of source and distinguish the various goods and services in the marketplace.
- *Copyrights* prevent others from copying creative or artistic works, such as movies, books, software, photographs, or downloadable songs.
- *Patents* prevent others from making, using, or selling inventions such as software or business methods.
- *Trade secrets* help firms prevent others from using proprietary, secret information, such as manufacturing processes or marketing plans.

Note that there is some overlap between the different types of intellectual property. Software, for example, may be simultaneously protected as a copyrighted work and as a patented invention. Software might also be protected as a trade secret. Similarly, an image such as Mickey Mouse may be simultaneously protected by both copyright and trademark law. Copyrights, patents, and trade secrets will be explored in Chapters 5, 6, and 7.

Intellectual Property Symbols

Products or services protected by intellectual property rights may have one of the symbols shown in Exhibit 4.2 associated with them, depending on the type of intellectual property.

Comparing Intellectual Property to Ordinary Property

The term "intellectual property" can be somewhat misleading. Although intellectual property is an asset and can have a significant impact on the ability of a business to raise venture capital, it is distinct from ordinary property in several ways.

First, intellectual property is a "negative right" in that it allows the owner only to prevent others from doing something. Many people are surprised to find that intellectual property law generally does *not* confer an affirmative right on the owner to use the owner's own property. For example, if you obtain a patent on an improvement of a business method, and the underlying business method is already patented by someone else, the holder of the underlying business method patent can prevent you from putting your improvement into practice. Similarly, the owner of a trademark does not necessarily have the right to use its mark in a domain name if the particular domain name is being used for legitimate purposes by someone else (domain names will be discussed below).

Second, unlike ordinary property, control over intellectual property is generally limited in duration. The basic terms of protection for each type of intellectual property are summarized in Exhibit 4.3.

Third, the ideas that constitute the essence of intellectual property can be used by many people at the same time without diminishing the ability of others to use the ideas, which is not possible with ordinary property. For example, only one person can use a given computer at a given time, but an essentially unlimited

---

Exhibit 4.2 Intellectual Property Symbols

Type of Intellectual Property	Symbol(s)
Trademarks	®, TM, SM
Copyright	©, Copr., ℗
Patents	Pat.
Trade Secrets	(no symbols)

Exhibit 4.3	Intellectual Property Duration in the United States

Right	Duration
Trademarks	10-year initial term, renewable for unlimited additional 10-year terms

Copyright	70 year minimum:
	1. Individual author: Remainder of the author's life plus 70 years
	2. "Works made for hire" (e.g., works made by an employee for a corporation), either:
	   • 95 years from date of publication; or
	   • 120 years from date of creation,
	whichever is shorter

Patents	20 years, nonrenewable (utility patents; plant patents) 14 years, nonrenewable (design patents)
Trade Secrets	Perpetual: • For as long as trade secret remains secret • Loss of trade secret rights can occur if a third party independently develops and patents secret

number of people can download a given ebook (protected by intellectual property) and read it simultaneously. Because of this quality, intellectual property is said to be **nonrival**.

For these reasons, intellectual property is often characterized not as property but as a government-sanctioned monopoly of limited duration. However, the more common term *intellectual property* will be used in this text.

What Is a Trademark?

Trademarks are sometimes informally referred to as "brands." Formally, a trademark is defined by the federal **Lanham Act**[1] of 1946 to include "any word, name, symbol or device" used to distinguish the goods or services of one company from those of another.[2] A key aspect of this definition is the requirement that a trademark be **distinctive**. That is, consumers viewing (or hearing) the trademark must be able to distinguish it from other trademarks. So long as this requirement is met, almost anything that is distinctive can serve as a trademark. Sounds, shapes, colors, scents, and flavors have all received protection under U.S. trademark law. For example, Apple has registered the three-dimensional oval-shape of its electronic connectors as a trademark, and T-Mobile has registered

---

1. The Lanham Act of 1946, also known as the Trademark Act, is the name of the principal federal legislation governing trademarks.
2. 15 U.S.C. § 1127.

| Exhibit 4.4 | Apple's Oval-Shape Design Trademark Reg. No. 4512283 Apple, Inc. |

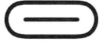

its specific shade of magenta in connection with its wireless plans, phones, and tablets. See Exhibit 4.4.

Types of Marks

The Lanham Act defines several types of marks. **Trademarks** are used to distinguish goods, and may be indicated with the symbols ™ or ®. **Service marks** are used to distinguish services, and may be indicated with the symbol ℠ or ®. For example, "Wikipedia" is a registered service mark. The symbols ™ and ℠ are generally used when an entity is claiming intellectual property rights in a mark but where the mark has not yet been registered by the United States Patent & Trademark Office (USPTO). For example, the symbols ™ or ℠ might be used while a trademark application is pending. Their use is not governed by federal law, although state law or the law of foreign jurisdictions may apply. Once the mark is registered with the USPTO, the mark holder may use the symbol ®.[3]

Under the Lanham Act, nonprofit entities that sell neither products nor services may also obtain trademarks. The Electronic Frontier Foundation, a nonprofit organization that advocates public access to Internet resources, has registered its name as a trademark. In addition, **collective marks** can be granted for use by members of an association or organization, such as the Boy Scouts of America. A **certification mark** can be granted where the mark owner intends to permit third parties to use its mark in connection with quality certification of that third party's product or service. For example, VeriSign permits third parties to display its "Norton Secured" mark to customers completing online transactions to indicate a certain level of security.

Trademarks, service marks, collective marks, and certification marks may be collectively referred to as "marks." Because all are treated in a similar manner under the Lanham Act, it is common to see the words "mark" and "trademark" used interchangeably, and this text will follow that convention. Keep in mind that the principles of trademarks discussed in the text and cases also apply to the other types of marks.

The Distinctiveness Continuum

As already noted, the Lanham Act allows businesses to secure protection in many types of distinctive marks. However, not all marks are equally able to distinctively

---

3. 15 U.S.C. §1111.

identify a product or service. Marks are therefore grouped into four categories based on eligibility for trademark protection: (1) generic, (2) descriptive, (3) suggestive, and (4) arbitrary or fanciful.[4]

Generic

A **generic** term is simply the word for a given product or service and can never be registered as a trademark. For example, the following words have been held to be generic terms and are therefore unavailable as trademarks: "e-ticket," "net bank" (Internet-based banking), "lawyers.com," and "the computer store."

Descriptive

A **descriptive** mark, as the name implies, describes a product or its qualities but is not the generic term for it. "Virtual fashion" as a mark for online fashion retailing, "iBooks" as a mark for books sold over the Internet, and "Instant Messenger" as a mark for America Online's (AOL) real time communications service have been found to be descriptive.

A descriptive mark may be registered as a trademark only if it has acquired *secondary meaning*, that is, if consumers have come to recognize the mark as denoting a particular company rather than being merely descriptive. For example, the term "App Store" describes a venue for purchasing software applications. Without more, "App Store" might not be registrable as a trademark. However, if many consumers recognize the name as denoting a particular company (e.g., Apple), a court might find that the mark had acquired secondary meaning, and it could then receive trademark protection.[5] As you might suspect, a mark that begins as a merely descriptive mark can become registrable over time via effective marketing and advertising.

Suggestive

A **suggestive** mark hints at the qualities of a product, but does not describe it directly. For example, "Netflix" suggests online movies, "PayPal" suggests a simple payment system, and "Facebook" suggests a collection of profile pictures. Suggestive marks are considered **inherently distinctive** and may therefore be registered without the need to show secondary meaning.

Arbitrary or Fanciful

An **arbitrary** mark is one used in a way that is unrelated to the product or service represented. "Yahoo!," "Uber" (ride sharing), and "Monster.com" (job board) would likely be considered arbitrary marks, as would "Apple." A **fanciful** mark is one that is coined or created and that at the time of creation would not be found

---

4. See *Abercrombie & Fitch Co. v. Hunting World, Inc.*, 537 F.2d 4 (2d Cir. 1976).
5. *Apple, Inc. v. Amazon.com, Inc.*, No. C 111-1327 PJH, 2011 WL 263891 (N.D. Cal. July 6, 2011).

in a dictionary. For example, "Spotify," "Hulu," and "Mozilla" are fanciful marks. Fanciful and arbitrary marks are grouped together because they are generally considered equally distinctive. Both types of marks are considered to be inherently distinctive and are therefore registrable without the need to show secondary meaning.

As you might suspect, there is no clear division between categories. It is therefore helpful to conceive of trademark categories as residing on a continuum from least to greatest distinctiveness, as illustrated in Exhibit 4.5. When selecting a trademark to represent a product or service, businesses should be aware that more distinctive trademarks are easier to register and receive greater protection under the Lanham Act.

Trade Dress and Websites

In the physical world, trademarks are commonly placed on products but are physically separable from them, as when a "Levi's" label is sewn into a pair of jeans or when a "Ford" symbol is placed on an automobile. In contrast to these separable and physically distinct labels, **trade dress** consists of a product's design, packaging, or overall look and feel.

Although trade dress is not as discrete as a traditional mark, it may nevertheless serve to distinguish products in the marketplace and therefore can be protected under the Lanham Act as a trademark. For example, you may be able to identify the electrical connectors associated with Apple products by their distinct shape, even absent any identifying marks. As noted above, the shape

Exhibit 4.5 **The Trademark Distinctiveness Continuum**

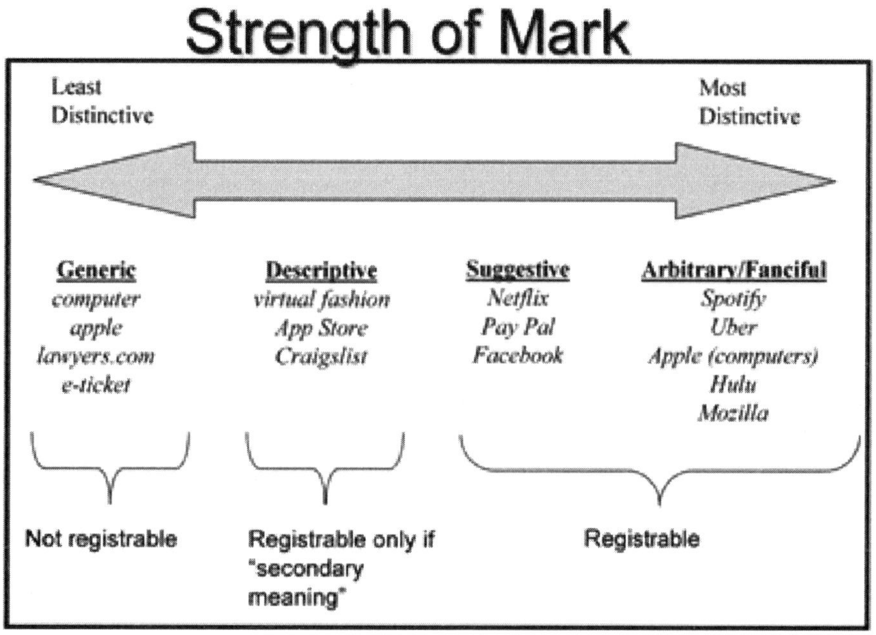

| Exhibit 4.6 | Trade Dress and the Trademark Continuum |

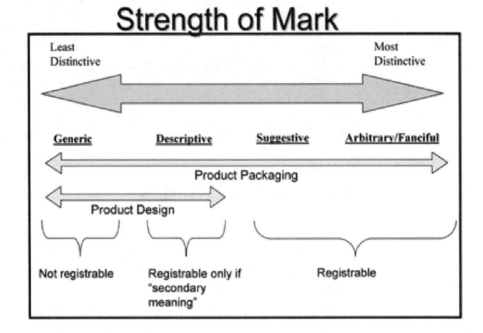

of these connectors was registered as a trademark in 2014. This is an example of registrable trade dress (Exhibit 4.4). In *Two Pesos v. Taco Cabana*, the Supreme Court provided another example of trade dress, holding that the distinctive festive decor of a Mexican restaurant could be protected under the Lanham Act.[6] In *Wal-Mart v. Samara Brothers*, the Court added that distinctive clothing design could be protected as trade dress.[7]

Product Design and Product Packaging

Trade dress may be divided into two main categories: (1) product design and (2) product packaging. On the trademark continuum, **product packaging** may fall anywhere along the distinctiveness spectrum, though in practice it may be more difficult to categorize trade dress than it is to characterize a word mark (Exhibit 4.6). Product packaging may be inherently distinctive and therefore not require a showing of secondary meaning. In contrast, **product design** always requires a showing of secondary meaning. It is therefore more difficult to register product design than product packaging (Exhibit 4.6). Why is product design accorded less favorable treatment than product packaging? According to the Supreme Court, copying of a product by competitors can have beneficial effects in the marketplace. Moreover, product design usually serves purposes other than source identification.

---

6. 505 U.S. 763 (1992).
7. 529 U.S. 205 (2000).

| Exhibit 4.7 | Trade Dress and Secondary Meaning |

Type of Trade Dress	Secondary Meaning Required?	Ease of Registration
Product Design	always	more difficult
Product Packaging	sometimes	easier

In cyberspace, product packaging and product design do not exist in the same sense, raising the question of whether websites should be classified as product design or product packaging, or whether they should constitute protected trade dress at all. Although several cases have concluded that the look and feel of websites can constitute protected trade dress, plaintiffs have not always been successful in preventing imitation. In *SG Services v. God's Girls*,[8] for example, the court found website design to be more analogous to product design than to product packaging, making it more difficult for the plaintiff to succeed in its trade dress infringement claim. The following case highlights another challenge that plaintiffs may face in protecting their website content.

Parker Waichmann, LLP v. Gilman Law, LLP,

2013 WL 3863928 (E.D.N.Y. July 24, 2013)

Seybert, U.S. District Judge

Facts Plaintiff, a personal injury law firm, arranged for the design, coding, production, and maintenance of the website, YOURLAWYER.COM, to market its services over the internet . . . . Plaintiff employed [Robert] Laraia to assist in programming and designing certain pages of YOURLAWYER.COM . . . . Defendant Gilman, also a personal injury firm, hired Laraia to assist it in preparing its own website. The Complaint asserts that Gilman was "well aware" of YOURLAWYER .COM, "was desirous to copy it, and hired Laraia in furtherance of that goal." . . . Plaintiff asserts that Gilman's website "copied" certain features of YOUR LAWYER.COM, "includ[ing], but . . . not limited to":

A. A blue header bar listing topics in white type. . . .
B. Directly above (A) on the left is the firm name and logo . . . .
C. Directly below (A) is an element of scrolling images and news headlines with back, pause and forward buttons.
D. Directly below (C) is a shaded box containing links to current drugs, products and legal issues. . . .

---

8. *SG Servs. Inc. v. God's Girls Inc.*, No. CV 06-989 AHM 2007 WL 2315437 (C.D. Cal. May 9, 2007).

E. A blue footer bar of approximately ten lines repeating the element (B).
F. A brightly colored side banner form allowing visitors to input: (i) their personal information; (ii) the date of their incident; (iii) the name of the drug, device or accident description; and (iv) a description of their case, with a larger white text heading that states:
"FREE CASE REVIEW NO COST ● NO OBLIGATION" . . . .

Trade Dress Infringement To state a valid claim for trade dress infringement, a plaintiff must allege that: (1) the trade dress is distinctive in that it identifies the source of the product; (2) there is a likelihood of confusion between the parties' goods; and (3) the trade dress is not functional—i.e., "essential to the use or purpose of the article" or "affect[ing] the cost or quality of the article." . . . Trade dress traditionally included only a product's packaging (and later a product's design) and the application of trade dress law to websites is a somewhat novel concept. While there is sparse case law on the topic, a few district courts in other circuits have recognized that a website's "look and feel" can constitute a protectable trade dress.

The Court's Decision Laraia argues that the Complaint fails to adequately define the allegedly protected "look and feel" of YOURLAWYER.COM. The Court agrees. The few courts to address this issue have held that "a mere cataloguing of a website's features does not give defendants adequate notice of a plaintiff's trade dress claim," especially, when, like Plaintiff here, the list of features comprising the trade dress is not complete ("include, but are not limited to"). Rather, to survive a motion to dismiss, a complaint must synthesize how these features combine to create the website's protectable "look and feel." Plaintiff has not done that here: the Complaint merely lists a few, but not all, of the features of YOUR-LAWYER.COM that it believes constitute its trade dress. The Complaint makes no attempt to synthesize those elements or even remotely address the other three elements of a claim for trade dress infringement. Instead, the Complaint alleges that the trade dress "serves to identify [Plaintiff]" and is "widely recognized," that it is "distinctive" and "not merely functional," and that Gilman's similar website is "likely to cause consumer confusion." These allegations are conclusory and fail to plausibly suggest that the combination of blue headers, pause and forward buttons, and brightly colored boxes are synonymous with Plaintiff's firm[9] or would cause consumers to mistake Gilman's website for YOURLAWYER.COM.[10]

9. [footnote 3 in court's opinion] The Court seriously questions whether this defect is curable, as Plaintiff's allegation that the "look and feel" of YOURLAWYER.COM "serves to identify [Plaintiff] as the source of its services" is belied by the fact that Plaintiff has "hundreds of websites" that do not contain the features of YOURLAWYER.COM described in the Complaint as constituting protectable trade dress . . . .
10. [footnote 4 in court's opinion] The Court also questions, without deciding here, whether it is appropriate to ever give websites trade dress protection, because, unlike a product on a shelf, in order to access a website, a user must either know the URL or type a query into a search engine (and, thus, select a website without first seeing its "look and feel"). Thus, given the affirmative steps that need to be taken to access a website, it is unclear how a consumer could ever find his or her way to one website and be misled into thinking it is another website simply because some of the websites' features are allegedly similar. Plaintiff has failed to plead facts plausibly suggesting such consumer confusion here.

Accordingly, [the Defendant's] motion to dismiss the trade dress claim is GRANTED.

Case Questions

1. According to the court, what three elements must a plaintiff allege to state a valid claim for trade dress infringement?
2. Can the look and feel of a website constitute protected trade dress under the Lanham Act? If so, why didn't plaintiff prevail in this case? If not, why not?
3. *Ethical Consideration:* Suppose a business is careful to design its website in a way that will not lead to consumer confusion or violate the Lanham Act in any manner. So long as a business complies with the law, is there anything troubling about a business that tries to recreate the look and feel of a successful competitor's website to the greatest extent that the law will allow? Is such imitation unethical, or is it the essence of free market competition?

How Does a Symbol Become a Trademark?

Federal Law and Registration with the USPTO

The Lanham Act of 1946 governs trademarks at the federal level and provides for the registration of trademarks with the **United States Patent & Trademark Office** (**USPTO**), a government agency located just outside of Washington, D.C. The USPTO maintains a helpful website at www.uspto.gov, where users can search for existing trademarks and apply online to register a new trademark. In order to register a trademark, the applicant must actually use the mark in commerce and pay a fee of several hundred dollars.

Scandalous or disparaging marks may not be registered. For example, in 2014 the federal registration for "Redskins" as a service mark associated with the Washington, D.C., professional football team was determined by the USPTO's Trademark Trial and Appeal Board to be disparaging of Native Americans. Because intellectual property confers only negative rights, however, the cancellation of federal registration does not mean that the team must change its name or alter its *use* of the mark, but it could limit the ability to *prevent others* from using the mark. For example, only registered marks can be recorded with U.S. Customs to block importation of infringing or counterfeit goods, such as T-shirts, that bear any of the Redskins' former marks.

Domain Names as Trademarks

Domain names may be registered as trademarks. For example, "Amazon.com" and "IBM.com" have both been registered with the USPTO. More commonly, however, a trademark is used in a domain name, but is not identical with it. For example, "Instagram" is a registered trademark used in the domain name

Instagram.com, but "Instagram.com" is not itself registered. However, the determination that a word or phrase cannot be a trademark does not preclude its use in a domain name. For example, although "Obama Bin Laden" was rejected as a trademark, it nevertheless appeared for a time in the domain name Obamabinladen.com. The process of obtaining a domain name is a distinct process from the registration of trademarks and will be discussed below.

Unregistered Trademarks

Even if a mark is not registered with the USPTO, it still receives protection under the Lanham Act similar to that of a registered mark. Nevertheless, businesses will generally want to register their marks because registration:

- Enables the trademark owner to use the ® symbol
- Establishes a clear date of trademark ownership, helping the business to prevail against others who adopt the same or similar mark after that date
- Allows a business to record the registration with U.S. Customs and Border Protection to prevent importation of infringing foreign goods
- Facilitates international enforcement of trademark rights under relevant treaties

State Law

State trademark laws exist alongside the federal Lanham Act. This concurrent regulation by both state and federal laws contrasts with the regulation of patents and copyrights, which are governed almost exclusively by federal law. Because the websites of online businesses are accessible without regard to state borders, however, the Lanham Act has particular relevance to cyberlaw trademark issues. This chapter will focus exclusively on federal trademark law and will not discuss state law.

Keeping a Trademark

An initial trademark registration lasts for 10 years (provided a Declaration of Use is filed, and fee paid, between years five and six) and can be renewed for an unlimited number of 10-year periods. Marks can be lost through (1) nonrenewal, (2) abandonment, or (3) genericide.

Abandonment occurs when a mark owner stops using the mark and does not intend to resume using it. A mark is presumed to be abandoned when the mark owner has failed to use the mark in commerce for three years.

Genericide occurs when a mark becomes commonly used to denote a product or service rather than a particular manufacturer or provider of that product or service. The mark is then said to have become generic. Former trademarks that have become generic terms include aspirin, trampoline, cellophane, shredded wheat, thermos, and dry ice. From a trademark owner's perspective, genericide is ironic: The trademark owner has been so successful in making its mark well-known that it loses protection in the mark. However, the policy rationale supporting genericide reflects consumer interests in free speech and effective communication by both consumers and manufacturers. For example, if the trademark "Thermos" had not been held by a federal appeals court to be a generic term,[11] what word other than "thermos" would today's competing manufacturers use to describe their products?

While trademarked terms can become generic through genericide, the reverse is not true. That is, a generic term can never become a trademark, except as applied arbitrarily to an unrelated product or service. Thus, the term "Apple" could never become a trademark for apples, but is a highly distinctive trademark as applied to computers and other electronics. More generally, it should be recognized that a term may be generic in one market and descriptive or suggestive in another.

Why Protect Trademarks?

Imagine you have recently become concerned about animal welfare and want to find out what you can do to end animal homelessness and prevent cruelty to animals. A friend tells you there is an organization called People for the Ethical Treatment of Animals, or "PETA." Excited to learn more, you go online and carefully type "peta.org" into your web browser's Uniform Resource Locater (URL) bar. To your surprise and dismay, a website entitled "People Eating Tasty Animals" appears, containing links to organizations related to meat and fur products, hunting, and animal research. In the landmark case of *PETA v. Doughney*,[12] the Fourth Circuit held that such a use of the PETA trademark in the domain name registered by the defendant violated the Lanham Act. Check the site peta.org and you will find that it is now the website of People for the Ethical Treatment of Animals.

Trademarks serve two principal purposes. First, as in *PETA v. Doughney*, they reduce consumer confusion and lower search costs. Second, they help to ensure that the trademark owner, rather than a competitor, will reap the reputation-related rewards associated with desirable products or services. Both of these goals are promoted via the likelihood of confusion standard. In addition, the likelihood of dilution standard prevents third parties from free riding on the goodwill of others' famous trademarks.

Trademark Infringement Standard: Likelihood of Confusion

The **likelihood of confusion** standard is the touchstone of a trademark infringement action. Under the Lanham Act, a trademark violation occurs when a party

---

11. See *King-Seeley Thermos Co. v. Aladdin Indus.*, 321 F.2d 577 (2d Cir. 1963).
12. 263 F.3d 359 (4th Cir. 2001).

other than the trademark owner uses a similar or identical mark that is likely to cause consumer confusion as to the origin, sponsorship, or approval of the defendant's product or services.

Whether a given use of a mark is likely to confuse consumers will be determined based on a number of factors, which vary from one federal appellate court to another. In general, however, confusion is more likely to be found when:

- The marks are more similar to one another (or identical)
- The two parties' goods or services compete in the same market (Thus, Toyota may use the mark "Lexus" despite the similarity to the mark of the information database "Lexis" because automobiles and information databases do not compete with each other)
- There is evidence that consumers have in fact been confused
- The mark is at the more distinctive end of the continuum
- The defendant intended to divert sales from the trademark owner
- The consumers are unsophisticated (i.e., less discriminating, knowledgeable, or careful when making purchase decisions)

The likelihood of confusion standard enables trademark owners to police the market to ensure that services in the market remain distinguishable from one another. From the consumer's perspective, the likelihood of confusion standard helps to prevent consumers from mistakenly buying the wrong products. From the perspective of trademark owners, the standard helps to prevent both diversion of customers and free riding by competitors on the reputations of mark owners.

Trademark Dilution

Trademark **dilution** can be thought of as an extension of the ordinary trademark infringement standard to cases where there is no likelihood of confusion. Under the **Federal Trademark Dilution Act of 1995 (FTDA)**, a trademark owner who is unable to prove that consumers are likely to be confused may still prevail in court if the defendant's use of the mark is likely to cause dilution. In 2006, the FTDA was amended to clarify that dilution may take the form of either blurring or tarnishment.

Dilution by Blurring

Dilution by **blurring** occurs when the defendant's use of the mark "impairs the distinctiveness of the famous mark."[13] As with the likelihood of confusion standard, a trademark owner is more likely to succeed in a dilution action the more similar the marks and the stronger the plaintiff's mark on the trademark continuum. The legislative history to the FTDA offered the following as examples of trademark uses that would likely constitute unlawful dilution: Dupont shoes, Buick aspirin, and Kodak pianos. In the online environment, the use of

---

13. 15 U.S.C. § 1125(c)(2)(B).

"PerfumeBay" in connection with the selling of perfumes over the Internet was found to create a likelihood of dilution with respect to the famous eBay[14] mark, and Facebook was able to prevent the unauthorized use of "Teachbook"[15] for a social networking site targeted at teachers.

Dilution by Tarnishment

Dilution by **tarnishment** occurs when the defendant's use of the mark "harms the reputation of [a] famous mark."[16] Tarnishment may occur when a third party associates a mark with products of poor quality or uses it in an unsavory context. On the Internet, claims of dilution by tarnishment are commonly brought when the defendant is using the same mark or a confusingly similar mark in connection with pornography. For example, Hasbro is the owner of the trademark "Candy Land," which it uses in connection with its child-friendly board game. When another company began using the name "candyland" to identify a sexually explicit Internet site located at candyland.com, Hasbro brought a successful dilution action resulting in an injunction.[17] Another court enjoined the use of "Adults 'R' Us" in connection with a the sale of sexual devices and clothing, finding that such usage tarnished the famous "Toys 'R' Us" mark.[18]

Trademark Infringement Versus Trademark Dilution

Trademark infringement claims can be brought concurrently with trademark dilution claims, and trademark owners frequently include both types of claims in their complaint. However, there are important differences between the two types of claims.

First, dilution claims can only be brought by owners whose marks are "famous," defined by the statute to include only those marks "widely recognized by the general consuming public of the United States."[19] The category of marks that qualify as "famous" for purposes of the dilution standard is narrower than the category of marks that would be considered strong and distinctive under the likelihood of confusion test.

Second, a trademark owner can prevail on a dilution claim "regardless of the presence or absence of actual or likely confusion, competition, or of actual economic injury."[20] Thus, a trademark owner may prevail in a dilution action even if the defendant is using its mark in a different market and does not operate a business that competes with the mark owner. The dilution standard thus prevents free riding on famous marks while protecting the singular association of that mark with a given source of goods or services.

---

14. *PerfumeBay.com v. eBay*, 506 F.3d 1165 (9th Cir. 2007).
15. *Facebook, Inc. v. Teachbook.com LLC*, 819 F. Supp. 2d 764 (N.D. Ill. 2011).
16. 15 U.S.C. § 1125(c)(2)(C).
17. *Hasbro, Inc. v. Internet Entertainment Group*, 40 U.S.P.Q.2d 1479 (W.D. Wash. 1996).
18. *Toys "R" Us, Inc. v. Akkaoui*, 40 U.S.P.Q.2d 1836 (N.D. Cal. 1996).
19. 15 U.S.C. § 1125(c).
20. *Id.*

Exhibit 4.8	Comparing Trademark Infringement and Trademark Dilution			
Type of Claim	**US Law**	**Marks Covered**	**Legal Standard**	**Competition**
Infringement	Lanham Act (1946)	all marks	likelihood of confusion	increases likelihood of infringement
Dilution	FTDA (1995)	only "famous" marks	(1) blurring, or (2) tarnishment	not required

The differences between trademark infringement claims and trademark dilution claims are summarized in Exhibit 4.8.

Online Trademark Infringement

Trademark disputes can arise in a number of ways on the Internet, such as linking to the content of a trademark owner's site without authorization or framing that content in a confusing manner. Third parties may use others' trademarks as metatags to draw traffic to their site or to trigger pop-up or banner advertisements. Search engines may use trademarks in order to trigger pay-per-click advertisements. Perhaps the most obvious yet enduring problems relating to trademarks on the Internet, however, involve the use of trademarks in domain names. Each of these issues will be explored below.

Linking and Deep Linking

A familiar feature of the Internet is the ability of users to find desired content by clicking on hyperlinks that lead to other sites. This process of **linking** usually raises no trademark issues. In a few early cases, however, trademark owners complained that third-parties were **deep linking** to a subsidiary page of the trademark owner's site rather than to its homepage. Although this practice might lead Internet users directly to the material they seek, it can bypass homepage advertising and, it was argued, potentially confuse consumers regarding the sponsorship of the content. In the leading case of *Ticketmaster Corp. v. Tickets.Com*,[21] the court found that deep linking was unlikely to constitute a trademark violation so long as consumers were not confused regarding whose website they were visiting.

Although linking and deep linking are unlikely to create trademark liability, businesses should nevertheless exercise caution. Whenever there is a possibility

---

21. 54 U.S.P.Q.2d 1344 (C.D. Cal. 2000).

that users might mistakenly believe that the destination site is affiliated with the linking site, a disclaimer could be used. In *Ticketmaster Corp.*, for example, the defendant made it clear to users that they were leaving the defendant's website and navigating to the trademark owner's site by stating that "the link above will take you directly to the other company's website." Businesses should also be aware that linking and deep linking may raise copyright, contract, or other legal issues.

Framing and In-line Linking

Framing occurs when one website presents the content of another website as an integrated portion of the first website, rather than by linking to it in the traditional manner. Because the material from the second website appears within the context of the first, this type of linking is sometimes described as **in-line linking**. For example, a website might present the news stories of another website within its own border, potentially creating confusion as to the source of the stories. Businesses should avoid practices that might confuse consumers regarding from which website content originates. Framing and in-line linking can also raise copyright issues, as will be seen in the chapter on Copyright.

Metatags

Google and other search engines are a primary means for users to locate desired content online. When a user types a search string into the search engine, a list of relevant results appears. Because it is of obvious value to a company to appear at the top of search results, online businesses engage in **search engine optimization** in order to ensure that this occurs. One method of optimizing results is via the use of **metatags**, invisible text embedded within websites which can nevertheless be read by search engines. The trademark issue arises when websites seek to optimize placement in search engine results pages by using others' trademarks as metatags without permission. In the landmark case of *Brookfield Communications v. West Coast Entertainment*,[22] the Ninth Circuit held that such use could constitute trademark infringement. Although search engines today rely on a number of factors other than metatags when ranking search results, businesses should be aware that the use of trademark terms as metatags can give rise to liability.

Initial Interest Confusion

Brookfield is also important because it established that **initial interest confusion** could be actionable in an online context. Initial interest confusion has been described as "a 'bait and switch' tactic that permits a competitor to lure consumers" at an early phase of the decision-making process.[23] It differs from the ordinary likelihood of confusion standard in that any initial confusion is dispelled by the

22. 174 F.3d 1036 (9th Cir. 1999).
23. *Vail Associates, Inc. v. Vend-Tel-Co.*, 516 F.3d 853 (10th Cir. 2008).

Exhibit 4.9	Search Results: Organic Results and Pay-Per-Click Advertising

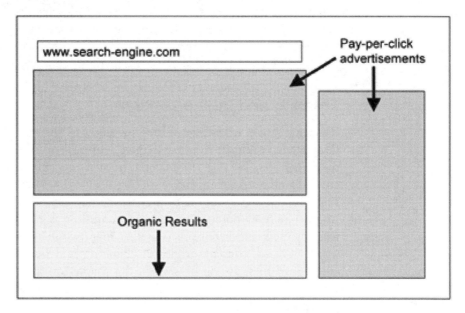

time of sale. In *Brookfield*, the defendant West Coast Video had used terms similar to the plaintiffs "MovieBuff" trademark in West Coast's metatags. Although the court acknowledged that consumers would not be confused as to whose website they were visiting, it noted that West Coast would improperly benefit by diverting customers. Although initial interest confusion remains a viable cause of action, it has been criticized by some as an unwarranted expansion of the likelihood of confusion standard.

Pay-Per-Click Advertising

If you have used a search engine recently, you have probably noticed that not all the results look alike. For example, Google sometimes displays a narrow column of results at the top and right-hand side of the screen entitled "Ads." On mobile phones, a similar lightly shaded section of links may appear at the top of the search results. See Exhibit 4.9. These sections of search results constitute **pay-per-click advertising**, meaning that businesses can pay the search engine in order to achieve more prominent placement on these sections of the results page.

Organic Results

In contrast to these paid results sections, search engines also provide **organic results**, sometimes called unpaid or "natural" results. Organic results are composed of links to target websites that the search engine displays as a result of a user's search query and should not be influenced by payments made by the target website owners to the search engine. The Federal Trade Commission, which has the ability to bring civil suits against entities for unfair business practices, has indicated that paying for placement in organic results may violate the law.

Keying

Selling generic terms such as "bicycle racing" or "toothpaste" generally will not implicate trademark law. The trademark issue arises when a search engine sells trademarked terms to entities other than the trademark holder in order to trigger pay-per-click advertisements. For example, a search engine might sell the term "1800Contacts," a service mark owned by contact lens retailer 1-800 Contacts, Inc., to its competitor Lens.com so that advertisements for Lens.com appear whenever a person types "1800Contacts" into the search engine. When this occurs, the advertisement is said to be **keyed** to the trademarked term.[24]

The "Use in Commerce" Requirement

The Lanham Act imposes liability only on defendants who use a mark in commerce. Because a defendant's purchase of key words from a search engine is not directly apparent to Internet users, some early cases found that this invisible use of a trademark did not constitute use in commerce. Following a landmark 2009 decision,[25] the judicial consensus is that the use of key words to steer customers to websites where purchases may be made can meet the use in commerce requirement.

Liability for Keying

Trademark owners must still prove that the use of key words to trigger pay-per-click advertisements is likely to cause confusion, which may be a difficult showing to make. A number of lawsuits brought in recent years to **enjoin** (prevent) the selling of trademarks as key terms in pay-per-click advertising have been unsuccessful. In the case involving 1-800 Contacts, for example, the court found that consumers were unlikely to be confused when the link was clearly labeled as an advertisement and bore a name ("Lens.com") that was different from the search term ("1800Contacts").

In another case,[26] Super Duck Tours sought to compete with incumbent Boston Duck Tours in the provision of sightseeing tours of Boston, Massachusetts, in amphibious vehicles designed to travel both on land and in water, commonly known as "ducks." The court found that use of the phrase "boston duck tours" to trigger pay-per-click advertisements for Super Duck Tours was unlikely

24. *1-800 Contacts, Inc. v. Lens.com, Inc.*, 722 F.3d 1229 (10th Cir. 2013).
25. *Rescuecom Corp. v. Google Inc.*, 562 F.3d 123 (2d Cir. 2009).
26. *Boston Duck Tours, LP v. Super Duck Tours, LLC*, 527 F. Supp. 2d 205 (D. Mass. 2007).

Google

An Advertising Behemoth. Google is by far the most popular search engine in the United States, capturing about two thirds of the market (Bing and Yahoo! are a distant second and third, respectively). Despite its size and popularity, it might be wondered how a free search engine can be leveraged to create a profitable business. And Google is indeed profitable, reporting more than $59 billion in annual revenue and $13 billion in annual profits in a recent year. The answer is advertising.

AdWords. Through Google's AdWords program, businesses can create advertisements that will appear in the Ads section of the Google results page. When a user types a search string into the Google search box, an algorithm is used to examine the entered text and advertisements deemed most relevant to that search are displayed as advertisements. If a user clicks on an advertisement, Google charges the advertiser a fee. Unlike the ranking of organic results, ranking of advertisements depends in part on how much the advertiser is willing to pay per click. Advertisers bid to establish a "cost-per-click," which could be as much as $0.50 or more per click. The more an advertiser bids, the higher on the page the advertisement is likely to appear and therefore the more likely it is to be noticed by users. Advertisers are willing to pay such high costs per click in the hope of reaching customers at the exact moment when they are searching for related products or services. Related Google programs allow advertisements, including video ads, to appear on independent websites, thus providing both an additional venue for advertisers and an opportunity for the hosting websites to share advertising revenue with Google.

Click Fraud. One challenge advertisers have faced with the AdWords program is known as **click fraud**. Click fraud occurs when competitors or others intentionally click on a link for a purpose other than an interest in viewing the result. For example, competitors wishing to raise the advertiser's costs and thereby put it at a competitive disadvantage might repeatedly click on a link, thereby inflating the amount that the advertiser must pay to Google. Recognizing this problem, Google actively monitors clicks to detect click fraud.

to cause confusion, noting that "Super" and "Boston" were substantially dissimilar based on sight, sound and meaning.

Internationally, the European Court of Justice and the Australian High Court have issued decisions similarly favorable to the sale of trademarked key words by search engines, helping to legitimize this advertising practice around the globe.

The Rise of Internet Advertising

Online advertising has grown dramatically, in 2013 becoming the biggest single medium of advertising by revenue—more than television, newspapers, or radio. Mobile advertising has increased especially sharply, from virtually nothing in 2009 to $7.1 billion in 2013. These trends have been driven in large part by key word selling, with approximately 93 percent of Google's revenues deriving from advertising (including both trademark and non-trademark key word sales).

Managing Pay-Per-Click Advertising

Businesses seeking to advertise via a search engine key word program can reduce the risk of trademark liability by purchasing only terms that are not trademarked. If a business does purchase a trademarked term, it can reduce the likelihood that consumers will erroneously believe there is a sponsorship or affiliation with the trademark owner by refraining from including the trademarked term in the advertisement itself.

From the trademark owner's perspective, pay-per-click advertising means that a business must pay search engines and bid against competitors in order to engage in pay-per-click advertising based on the use of its own mark! Of course, a link to the trademark owner's website may appear in the organic results without any payment. Trademark owners wishing to use the courts to prevent competitors from using their trademarks as search engine key words should be prepared to provide evidence of a likelihood of confusion.

Secondary Trademark Liability on the Internet

Where a competitor uses another's trademark in a manner that creates a likelihood of confusion, that competitor may be liable to the trademark owner for direct infringement. In addition, indirect or **secondary liability** may be imposed on third parties who encourage infringement or who have an ability to control the primary infringer's activities. Secondary liability comprises two main types: contributory liability and vicarious liability. A party may be guilty of **contributory liability** if it (1) intentionally induces the primary infringer to commit infringement or (2) continues to provide a product or service to a buyer knowing that the buyer is engaging in trademark infringement.[27] Where a defendant provides a service rather than a product to a primary infringer, the likelihood of a finding of contributory infringement increases the greater the degree of control exercised over the primary infringer. **Vicarious liability** may be found where a defendant exercises control over the infringing product or service. From these definitions, it should be apparent that vicarious and contributory liability overlap somewhat, and plaintiffs often include claims for both.

Secondary Liability and Web 2.0 Businesses

The potential for secondary liability is especially present with **Web 2.0** service providers, which may host millions of items uploaded by individual users. The term "Web 2.0," which is not a legal term, has been used to refer to online activities involving large numbers of users that both produce and consume content. Twitter, YouTube, Tumblr, and Wikipedia are examples of Web 2.0 service providers. Another example is eBay, a giant online marketplace that facilitates transactions between millions of individual buyers and sellers.

---

27. *Inwood Labs., Inc. v. Ives Labs., Inc.*, 456 U.S. 844 (1982).

In 2004, the famous jewelry store Tiffany brought suit against eBay, alleging that hundreds of thousands of items sold on eBay infringed Tiffany's rights under the Lanham Act. Even though eBay was not itself the origin of the allegedly infringing goods, Tiffany argued that eBay should be contributorily liable for the infringement of eBay users. The court had to decide whether eBay had intentionally induced the infringement or continued to supply its services to primary infringers with knowledge of their infringing activities.

Tiffany (NJ) Inc. v. eBay, Inc.
600 F.3d 93 (2d Cir. 2010)

Sack, Circuit Judge

The Parties eBay is the proprietor of www.ebay.com, an Internet-based marketplace that allows those who register with it to purchase goods from and sell goods to one another. . . . In its auction and listing services, it provides the venue for the sale of goods and support for the transactions, but it does not itself sell the items listed for sale on the site, nor does it ever take physical possession of them. . . . eBay has been enormously successful. More than six million new listings are posted on its site daily. At any given time it contains some 100 million listings. eBay generates revenue by charging sellers to use its listing services. . . . For any completed sale, it charges a "final value fee" that ranges from 5.25% to 10% of the final sale price of the item. . . . For nearly a decade, including the period at issue, eBay has also maintained and administered the Verified Rights Owner ('VeRO') Program—a "notice-and-takedown" system allowing owners of intellectual property rights, including Tiffany, to report to eBay any listing offering potentially infringing items, so that eBay could remove such reported listings. . . .

Tiffany is a world-famous purveyor of, among other things, branded jewelry. . . . Sometime before 2004, Tiffany became aware that counterfeit Tiffany merchandise was being sold on eBay's site. Prior to and during the course of this litigation, Tiffany conducted two surveys known as "Buying Programs," one in 2004 and another in 2005, in an attempt to assess the extent of this practice. Under those programs, Tiffany bought various items on eBay and then inspected and evaluated them to determine how many were counterfeit. Tiffany found that 73.1% of the purported Tiffany goods purchased in the 2004 Buying Program and 75.5% of those purchased in the 2005 Buying Program were counterfeit. The district court concluded, however, that the Buying Programs were "methodologically flawed and of questionable value". . . .

The Issue The [issue] that the parties have properly focused our attention on is whether eBay is liable for contributory trademark infringement—i.e., for culpably facilitating the infringing conduct of the counterfeiting vendors. . . .

The *Inwood* Test The Supreme Court most recently dealt with the subject [of contributory trademark infringement] in *Inwood Laboratories, Inc. v. Ives Laboratories, Inc.*, 456 U.S. 844 (1982). There, the plaintiff, Ives, asserted that several drug manufacturers had induced pharmacists to mislabel a drug the defendants produced to pass it off as Ives'. According to the Court, "if a manufacturer or distributor intentionally induces another to infringe a trademark, or if it continues to supply its product to one whom it knows or has reason to know is engaging in trademark infringement, the manufacturer or distributor is contributorially responsible for any harm done as a result of the deceit."

Infringement Analysis Tiffany does not argue that eBay induced the sale of counterfeit Tiffany goods on its website . . . . It argues instead, under the second part of the *Inwood* test, that eBay continued to supply its services to the sellers of counterfeit Tiffany goods while knowing or having reason to know that such sellers were infringing Tiffany's mark. . . . The [district] court found that eBay's practice was promptly to remove the challenged listing from its website, warn sellers and buyers, cancel fees it earned from that listing, and direct buyers not to consummate the sale of the disputed item. . . . [In addition,] repeat offenders were suspended from the eBay site. . . . The [district] court therefore declined to hold eBay contributorially liable . . . . We agree.

Dilution Federal law allows the owner of a "famous mark" to enjoin a person from using "a mark or trade name in commerce that is likely to cause dilution by blurring or dilution by tarnishment of the famous mark." 15 U.S.C. § 1125(c)(1). . . . The district court rejected Tiffany's dilution by blurring [and dilution by tarnishment] claim on the ground that eBay never used the TIFFANY marks in an effort to create an association with its own product, but instead, used the marks directly to advertise and identify the availability of authentic Tiffany merchandise on the eBay website. . . . We agree. There is no second mark or product at issue here to blur with or to tarnish "Tiffany."

Case Questions

1. Why wasn't eBay held liable for the infringing sales made by users? [Hint: Describe how the elements of the *Inwood* test apply to eBay's actions.]
2. Can online providers of services (as opposed to suppliers of products) ever be held liable for contributory trademark infringement? What steps might a business take to reduce liability exposure? (Hint: What steps did eBay take?)
3. *Ethical Consideration:* As an online service provider, to whom do you owe the greater duty? To your customers who wish to knowingly (i.e., without confusion) buy cheaper, imitation products? Or to unrelated businesses whose valuable intellectual property is being flagrantly violated on your site? Would you take precautions beyond what the law requires to reduce infringing sales?

Secondary Liability on the Internet: A Difficult Case to Make

As seen in *eBay*, it may be difficult to succeed on the basis of a contributory trademark liability claim in the Internet context. Suits brought against Google and other search engines for contributory liability based on the key word purchases of its customers have generally also been unsuccessful.

Claims for vicarious trademark infringement involving online businesses may be equally challenging to win. In *Perfect 10, Inc. v. Visa*,[28] plaintiff Perfect 10 alleged that Visa was vicariously infringing its trademarks by continuing to process credit card payments of individuals who subscribed to websites that infringed Perfect 10's trademarks. Perfect 10 operated a subscription website featuring images of nude models, which images appeared without authorization on the alleged primary infringer's websites. Although Visa had been notified of the activities occurring at the offending websites, it continued to process payments associated with these sites. The Ninth Circuit held that Visa did not exercise direct control over the websites and could therefore not be held vicariously liable.

Nevertheless, the potential for secondary liability remains, and businesses must be careful not to induce or contribute to infringement by individual users. Aware of the potential for secondary liability, Twitter, a popular social networking site that allows users to display short online status reports, has adopted a policy under which trademark violations that create consumer confusion may result in account suspension.

Conversely, trademark owners who believe that online service providers are inducing or benefiting from the infringing activity of users may wish to include as defendants the alleged secondary infringer in addition to the direct infringer and pursue claims for secondary liability in the lawsuit despite the apparent obstacles to success.

Domain Names

Domain names present special problems for businesses that may not be adequately addressed under the Lanham Act. Difficulties arise in part because there is imperfect overlap between domain names and trademarks. While a domain name may contain a trademark within it, and while it is possible to trademark a domain name, each is governed by different rules that are administered by different organizations. When disputes over domain names arise, plaintiffs may seek to resolve them in either of two parallel adjudicative systems.

The Structure of a Domain Name

An Internet address includes a **top-level domain** (**TLD**), a second-level domain, and possibly third- or lower-level domains. See Exhibit 4.10. The TLD is the

---

28. 494 F.3d 788 (9th Cir. 2007).

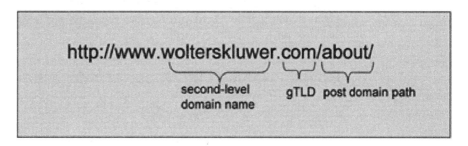

Exhibit 4.10 **Domain Name Components**

portion of the domain name furthest to the right. (The portion of the address appearing to the right of the TLD, if any, is called the "post domain path.") For example, common TLDs include .com, .org, .edu, .net, and .gov. These are called generic TLDs, or gTLDs, because they are not associated with any particular country. In addition to gTLDs, more than 240 country-code TLDs (ccTLDs) exist, such as .uk (United Kingdom), .mx (Mexico), and .us (United States). A listing of gTLDs and ccTLDs can be found on the website of the Internet Assigned Numbers Authority (IANA), www.iana.org. IANA is operated by the Internet Corporation for Assigned Names and Numbers (ICANN), a nonprofit organization established in 1998 that is not directly affiliated with the USPTO.

The Dramatic Expansion of Domain Names.

In 2013, the number of gTLDs began to dramatically expand under a new ICANN program that allows such gTLDs as .fishing, .career and .Paris, as well gTLDs bearing non-Latin characters such as ‎.شبكة‎, ‎.中信‎, and ‎.संगठन‎. Because the creation of each new gTLD involves the potential for trademark infringement, ICANN has established the Trademark Clearinghouse to help trademark owners protect their rights.

Second-level domains appear to the left of the TLD and frequently include the name of the organization associated with the website. For example, "tamu" is the second-level domain in www.tamu.edu, the website of Texas A&M University.

Registering a Domain Name

While trademarks are registered with the USPTO, domain name registration is a separate and independent process. Domain names may be registered for a small annual fee through any of the hundreds of registrars accredited by ICANN. When an application for a domain name registration is received, applicants must represent that, to their knowledge, the domain name would not violate the trademark rights of others, but registrars do not actively inquire into trademark issues. So long as the identical domain name has not already been registered by another party, the registrar will process the request. For new gTLDs, trademark owners are given at least 30 days to pre-register domains containing their marks during a "sunrise period," before public access to the gTLD is made available.

Domain Names and Opportunistic Behavior

The ease with which domain names can be acquired led to a virtual land grab on domain names in the early days of the Internet that reemerged with the launch of the new gTLDs. By registering key domain names before others appreciate their value, individuals can acquire Internet "real estate" that can be later sold for a profit. This type of opportunistic behavior is known as **cybersquatting**.

Trademark Cybersquatting:

Panavision v. Toeppen In the landmark case of *Panavision v. Toeppen*, the tension between domain name registration and trademark rights came to a head. In 1995, an individual named Dennis Toeppen registered a number of domain names based on well-known trademarks, including panavision.com, deltaairlines.com, eddiebauer.com, and yankeestadium.com. At the time of Toeppen's domain name registration, businesses were only beginning to utilize the Internet, and Toeppen realized that businesses might pay substantial amounts in order to acquire a preferred domain name. He offered to give up the domain name panavision.com if Panavision, a well-known manufacturer of film and television camera equipment and owner of the trademark "Panavision," would pay him $13,000. Instead, Panavision brought suit. In finding for Panavision, the court concluded that Toeppen's conduct diluted Panavision's marks in violation of the FTDA and prevented Panavision from using its marks within an important new business medium. The court enjoined Toeppen from further use of the Panavision mark in a domain name.

Non-trademark Cybersquatting

Panavision was ultimately successful because it was the owner a valid trademark that Toeppen had used as part of a domain name. Some cybersquatters, however, register domain names that are unrelated to any trademarks. These cybersquatters have been able to command thousands or even millions of dollars for domain names such as Wiki.com and Bhutan.com.

TypoSquatting

As trademark owners prevailed against cybersquatters and as the most obvious domain names were claimed, cybersquatters turned to **typosquatting**— the speculative purchase of an Internet domain name that incorporates an intentional misspelling ("typo") of a trademark. As with cases involving ordinary cybersquatters, suits against typosquatters have often resulted in victory for the trademark owner. In one leading case, the Third Circuit upheld an award of $10,000 for each of five infringing domain names plus attorney fees and costs totaling an additional $39,000.[29]

Not all typosquatting cases have been successful. In one case,[30] the Internet Movie Database (IMDb) initiated arbitration proceedings to have the domain name "indb.com" transferred to it. IMDb maintains a popular website at imdb.com that contains movie reviews and other movie-related information. Although "indb.com" differed by only one letter from "imdb.com," complainant IMDb was unsuccessful. The arbitration panel reasoned that any likelihood of confusion was outweighed by the needs of other registrants given the scarcity of potential four-letter domain names.

Some trademark owners have attempted to address cybersquatting by pre-emptively registering multiple domain names that typosquatters or others might find desirable. For example, if you type "wallmart.com" into your computer's URL bar you will be redirected to WalMart's official website at walmart.com.

The Economics of Cybersquatting

From an economic perspective, cybersquatting (including typosquatting) is wasteful. Because every dollar gained by a cybersquatting seller is necessarily offset by an equivalent loss to the buyer, society gains little from the practice. Moreover, cybersquatting involves costs. Cybersquatters expend effort in selecting and registering names and negotiating with potential buyers, while potential buyers incur the costs of locating and communicating with cybersquatters, hiring counsel, and negotiating with sellers. If a lawsuit ensues, both parties may incur substantial litigation costs. Finally, the public incurs costs to the extent that cybersquatting makes it more difficult to find information. In *Panavision*, for example, visitors seeking to obtain information about camera equipment at panavision.com found themselves viewing aerial pictures of Pana, Illinois that had been posted by Toeppen.

From the perspective of individual cybersquatters, however, the potential for profit can be alluring. In one case, a cybersquatter registered six domain names including the "Harley" mark such as "2003harley.com" and "2003harleydavidson.com" and attempted to sell them for $300,000 on eBay.[31] The envisioned profits, however, did not materialize. In an ensuing proceeding, an arbitrator transferred the domain names to Harley Davidson.

The AntiCyberSquatting Consumer Protection Act (ACPA)

Responding to the problems of cybersquatting, Congress enacted the AntiCyberSquatting Consumer Protection Act of 1999 (ACPA). The ACPA creates civil

---

29. *Shields v. Zuccarini*, 254 F.3d 476 (3d Cir. 2001).
30. *IMDb, Inc. v. Seventh Summit Ventures*, Nat'l Arbitration Forum Claim No. 0503000436735 (Apr. 25, 2005).
31. *H-D Michigan, Inc. v. Morris*, Nat'l Arbitration Forum Claim No. FA0212000137094 (Jan. 29, 2003).

liability for cybersquatters who (1) register a domain name identical with or confusingly similar to a trademark and (2) have a bad faith intent to profit from the mark. Those found liable under the ACPA are subject to statutory damages of $1,000 to $100,000 per domain, with the exact amount determined at the discretion of the court. In 2013, a court awarded Pinterest, an online bulletin board service, $7.2 million in damages after an individual registered 100 confusingly-similar domains, including "pimterest.com" and "pinterost.com."[32]

Note that the ACPA does not prohibit non-trademark cybersquatting. Similarly, because the ACPA only applies where a defendant has acted in bad faith, the statute does not address the case where two parties have legitimate claims to a domain name, such as where a mark is used by multiple entities in different noncompeting industries (e.g., Delta Dental and Delta Airlines) or where a mark is used by different entities in different states or countries.

What Constitutes "Bad Faith"

The ACPA lists nine factors that courts may consider when determining whether the domain name registrant possessed the requisite "bad faith intent to profit."[33] Although no one factor or group of factors is outcome determinative, a bad faith intent to profit is more likely to be found where the defendant:

- Offers to sell the domain name to the trademark owner for a fee
- Provides false contact information when registering the domain name
- Registers multiple domain names that are identical or confusingly similar to the marks of others
- Does not have any particular reason to use the domain name, other than the fact that it is similar to another's trademark
- Does not use the domain name for the bona fide sale of goods or services
- Attempts to divert customers from the trademark owner's website in a way that creates confusion as to sponsorship or affiliation
- Registers a domain name similar or identical to a mark that is on the more distinctive end of the trademark continuum

Using Domain Names for Critical Commentary: Gripe Sites

Gripe sites, sometimes known as "suck sites," are websites whose domain names include the trademark of another and that often contain critical commentary of the trademark owner, usually in the form "[trademark]sucks.com." Examples might include uhaul-sucks.com, guinness-sucks.com, or harvardsucks.org.

Litigation involving suck sites has forced courts to balance the rights of trademark owners and interests in reducing consumer confusion against rights to free speech. Noncommercial sites containing only non-defamatory criticism

---

32. *Pinterest, Inc. v. Qian Jin*, No. C 12-04586 RS, 2013 WL 5460821 (N.D. Cal. Sept. 30, 2013).
33. See 15 U.S.C. § 1125(d)(l) (B)(i).

Exhibit 4.11   Critical Images on Products Offered for Sale by Smith

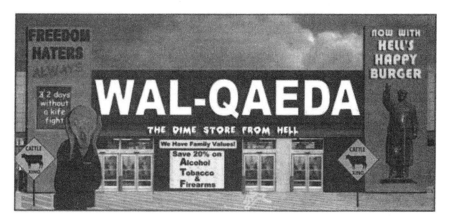

usually survive challenges under the ACPA. For example, where a dissatisfied homebuyer established a gripe site at trendmakerhome.com but neither sought to sell the domain name nor included any advertising on the site, the owner of the "TrendMaker Homes" mark and trendmakerhomes.com website could not enjoin the use.[34]

However, suck sites may be more vulnerable where the domain name registrant seeks to profit and where the content of the site does not clearly indicate a lack of affiliation with the trademark owner. For example, even where a domain

---

34. *TMI Inc. v. Maxwell*, 368 F.3d 433 5th Cir. (Apr. 21, 2004).

Exhibit 4.12   **Comparing UDRP with Federal Court Enforcement**

Venue	Organizing Body	Governing Rules	Possible Remedies	Advantages
UDRP	WIPO/ICANN	UDRP contract	cancellation and transfer	cost, speed, broad jurisdiction
Federal Court	US Gov't	US Law	cancellation, transfer, damages, and attorney fees	potential to recover damages and fees

name registrant uses the site to express genuine criticism, an ACPA violation may be found if the registrant seeks or accepts payment from the trademark owner in order to discontinue the critical use of the site.

Offering goods for sale on a gripe site does not necessarily give rise to infringement, however. In *Smith v. Wal-Mart Stores, Inc.*,[35] Smith offered for sale products imprinted with graphical concepts critical of WalMart (see Exhibit 4.11) using the domain names walocaust.com and walqaeda.com. The court allowed Smith to retain his domain names and continue offering his items for sale, concluding that his designs were successful parodies that were not likely to cause confusion. The court noted that revenues from sales of Smith's items did not cover the costs of maintaining his websites.

Uniform Dispute Resolution Policy (UDRP)

Trademark disputes brought in federal court under the ACPA can be expensive and time-consuming. In order to provide a less expensive and more streamlined remedy, the World Intellectual Property Organization (WIPO) developed an arbitration proceeding known as the Uniform Domain-Name Dispute Resolution Policy (UDRP).

Trademark owners may choose to pursue a UDRP proceeding or file a suit in federal court. In addition to their cost and time advantages, UDRP proceedings may be attractive to aggrieved parties because they can be brought against defendants located anywhere in the world. In contrast, plaintiffs filing in federal court must establish jurisdiction over the defendant, which may be more difficult when defendants are located overseas. Plaintiffs may nevertheless prefer federal courts as these courts are able to award damages and attorney fees in addition to ordering the cancellation or transfer of a domain name. In contrast, UDRP panels are only able to cancel or transfer domain names. Julia Roberts, Morgan Freeman, Tom Cruise, Scarlett Johansson, and Lance Armstrong have all brought successful WIPO arbitration proceedings against cybersquatters.

35. No. 1:06-cv-526-TCB (N.D. Ga. Mar. 20, 2008).

UDRP panels do not apply the ACPA or other trademark laws of the United States. When a party seeks to become a domain name registrar, it must agree to follow the UDRP, which operates as a contract between ICANN and the registrar. The registrar must agree that it will in turn require domain name registrants to agree to the UDRP. Thus, arbitration panels applying the UDRP are enforcing the policies agreed to by all involved. Nevertheless, the rules embodied in UDRP are generally consistent with those of the ACPA.

In the following case, a UDRP panel had to decide whether to transfer the domain "quebec.com" to the government of Quebec, Canada, from a company that had used the site for 15 years for commercial purposes.

Government of Quebec v. Anything.Com
Case No. D2013-2181 (May 16, 2014) [WIPO Administrative Panel Decision]

Meijboom, Brown & Landry, Panelists

Parties Complainant is the Government of Quebec, represented by a Minister. Complainant is the registered owner of [three trademarks for QUEBEC, filed between 1968 and 1983].

Respondent is a company domiciled in [the] Cayman Islands. Respondent claims that it acquired the Disputed Domain Name [of quebec.com] on July 10, 1998.

Applicable UDRP Rules In order to succeed in its claim, Complainant must demonstrate that all of the elements enumerated in paragraph 4(a) of the [UDRP] Policy have been satisfied:

   (i) the Disputed Domain Name is identical or confusingly similar to a trademark or service mark in which Complainant has rights; and
   (ii) Respondent has no rights or legitimate interests in the Disputed Domain Name; and
   (iii) the Disputed Domain Name has been registered and is being used in bad faith.

Complainant's Rights in the Mark Respondent submitted that this first element has not been satisfied because Complainant has made an admission that it has no trademark rights to the word "Quebec." The reason why this is said to be so is that Complainant applied for a trademark to be issued by the United States Patent and Trademark Office ("USPTO") for each of BONJOUR QUEBEC, BONJOUR QUEBEC.COM and QUEBEC ORIGINAL and in the course of that application had given a disclaimer acknowledging that it made no claim to the exclusive right to use "Quebec" and "Quebec.com" respectively, apart from the marks for which it was applying. . . . Had the trademark on which Complainant relied been the US trademarks BONJOUR QUEBEC, BONJOUR QUEBEC.COM or QUEBEC ORIGINAL, Respondent's argument would clearly have had some substance. However, Complainant's case is based not on those trademarks, but on the Canadian trademarks set out earlier in this Decision. Those trademarks are clearly valid, do not contain any disclaimer[,] and establish Complainant's trademark rights.

Identical or Confusingly Similar   The next question that arises is whether the Disputed Domain Name is confusingly similar to the Canadian trademarks. . . . [T]he question thus becomes one of whether Internet users would assume that the Disputed Domain Name was invoking the province of or the city of Quebec. . . . [I]t is possible that some observers, before seeing Respondent's website, may wonder if the Disputed Domain Name itself relates to the provincial government and they may to that extent be confused.

Respondent's Rights or Legitimate Interests   [P]aragraph 4(c) of the Policy . . . describes various ways by which a respondent may show that it has rights or legitimate interests in the domain name, namely:

> "Any of the following circumstances, in particular but without limitation, if found by the panel to be proved based on its evaluation of all evidence presented, shall demonstrate your rights or legitimate interests to the domain name for purposes of paragraph 4(a)(ii):
>
> (i) before any notice to you of the dispute, your use of, or demonstrable preparations to use, the domain name or a name corresponding to the domain name in connection with a bona fide offering of goods or services; or
>
> (ii) you (as an individual, business, or other organization) have been commonly known by the domain name, even if you have acquired no trademark or service mark rights; or
>
> (iii) you are making legitimate noncommercial or fair use of the domain name, without intent for commercial gain to misleadingly divert consumers or to tarnish the trademark or service mark at issue." . . .

[T]here is no evidence that Respondent has a registered trademark for QUEBEC or that it is or has been commonly known by the Disputed Domain Name and it has not been alleged that Respondent is making a legitimate noncommercial or fair use of the Disputed Domain Name. Moreover, Respondent is not affiliated with Complainant and has not been authorized by the Complainant to use its trademark in a domain name or anywhere else. . . . [However,] Respondent has adopted a geographic indicator as its domain name and has sought to put it to good use in providing links to various information and commercial sites offering goods and services in or related to Quebec.

Respondent's current website carried links to information services such as maps, directions and driving instructions and also links to sites offering hotel and flight bookings, other travel related businesses and a few other services such as immigration visas. . . .

If Respondent were pretending to be Complainant itself, if its website purported to offer governmental services, if it laid some claim to speak on behalf of the region or to be an authoritative voice on governmental or municipal matters, or if it sought to mislead Internet users as to the true nature of the site, the outcome may well have been different. But one can examine Respondent's website closely and yet not find any such matters.

Accordingly, the Panel finds that the use to which Respondent is putting the Disputed Domain Name is the legitimate one of using a word for its value as a word, analogous to the use of a generic, descriptive or common dictionary word and not as an attempt to transgress by using it as a trademark.

In particular, the Panel does not accept the argument of Complainant that Respondent registered the Disputed Domain Name with the intention of diverting Internet users looking for the Government of Quebec, by creating confusion regarding and tarnishing the image of Complainant's official marks. . . . the Panel finds that Complainant has not made out its case that Respondent does not have a right or legitimate interest in the Disputed Domain Name

Registered and Used in Bad Faith Paragraph 4(b) of the [UDRP] sets out a series of circumstances that are to be taken as evidence of the registration and use of a domain name in bad faith, namely:

(1) "circumstances indicating that Respondent has registered or has acquired the disputed domain name primarily for the purpose of selling, renting, or otherwise transferring the disputed domain name registration to Complainant . . . , for valuable consideration in excess of Respondent's documented out-of-pocket costs directly related to the disputed domain name; or

(2) Respondent has registered the disputed domain name in order to prevent Complainant from reflecting the mark in a corresponding domain name, provided that Respondent has engaged in a pattern of such conduct; or

(3) Respondent has registered the disputed domain name primarily for the purpose of disrupting the business of a competitor; or

(4) by using the disputed domain name, Respondent has intentionally attempted to attract, for commercial gain, Internet users to its website or other online location, by creating a likelihood of confusion with Complainant's mark as to the source, sponsorship, affiliation, or endorsement of its website or location or of a product or service on its website or location." . . .

[T]here is no evidence bringing the case within sub-paragraph [1], that relating to an intention to sell or rent the Disputed Domain Name. . . .

It is also difficult to conclude that there has been a breach of paragraph 4(b)(ii) as Respondent has not prevented Complainant from reflecting its QUEBEC trademarks in a corresponding domain name; there are numerous domain names available consisting solely of the word "Quebec," alone and in combination with other words. . . .

Likewise, the facts of the case do not bring it easily within sub-paragraph 4(b)(iii) of the Policy. Again, the fact that Respondent registered and used the Disputed Domain Name for an apparently legitimate purpose and retained it for 15 years, continuing to do the same thing with it during that period does not fit comfortably with the notion of Respondent wanting to disrupt Complainant's business. . . .

[As to paragraph (4)(b)(iv),] it is difficult to conclude that Respondent had the intention to create confusion with the Canadian marks as to Respondent's website . . . . Its website makes no suggestion that it is the Government of Quebec, that it is modeling itself on the government, that it has any authority in governmental affairs . . . . [I]n the present case, there is nothing either expressly or by inference to suggest that Internet users would think that by typing into their browsers, they would find the governmental services of the Province of Quebec, rather than goods, services or information about Quebec, which was clearly Respondent's intention, judging from the available evidence. . . .

For these reasons, the Panel finds that the Disputed Domain Name was not registered or used in bad faith.

CONCLUSION

For the foregoing reasons, the Complaint is denied.

Case Questions

1. Why don't Meijboom, Brown and Landry, the panelists and authors of the decision you just read, cite the Anticybersquatting Consumer Protection Act?
2. The complaint was lodged in 2013, even though Respondent had been using the site since 1998. Why might the government of Quebec have waited so long to file a complaint? Do you think this long time delay influenced the panel's decision?
3. *Ethical Consideration:* The Respondent used the site Quebec.com to offer services related to Quebec such as maps, directions and links to sites offering hotel and flight bookings, a use which the panel found "legitimate." Is it ethical, do you think, for a private party to register a geographic domain name associated with a local, regional or country government? Why or why not?

Cybersquatting Today

The fact that the panel declined to transfer the domain name quebec.com in *Government of Quebec v. Anything.com* demonstrates that not all cybersquatting is actionable. In fact, the market for domain names remains vibrant and is likely to become more so as new TLDs are added. Online exchanges such as eBay remain a popular medium of exchange for cybersquatters, where thousands of domain names may be for sale at any given time.

Typosquatting remains an equally popular and potentially lucrative technique. One study found that misspelled domains may be visited as much as 68.2 million times every day and that more than half of these sites contain pay-per-click advertisements that may be generating as much as $500 million per year in advertising revenue.

Cognizant of potential secondary liability concerns associated with trademark rights and cybersquatting, some businesses have proactively sought to reduce risk. Facebook, for example, has taken a number of steps to prevent cybersquatting on its personalized domain names, which might take the form "www.facebook.com/ [username]." In an effort to avoid trademark issues and reduce the possibility of opportunistic behavior, Facebook prohibited the transfer of usernames, stated it would remove or reclaim usernames used for squatting, and implemented a procedure by which trademark owners could assert their rights.

Summary

Intellectual property, or "IP," consists of trademarks, copyrights, patents, and trade secrets. A trademark is a distinct word, name, symbol, or device that distinguishes goods and services in the marketplace. Under the federal Lanham Act of 1946, the look and feel of websites may be protected as trade dress, while domain names or terms within domain names may be registered as trademarks so long as they are not likely to cause confusion with existing marks. The likelihood of confusion standard is the touchstone of a trademark infringement action, and use of a mark that will confuse customers as to origin, sponsorship, or approval is unlawful. Even where businesses do not compete and no confusion is likely, an unauthorized use of a famous mark may nevertheless violate the Federal Trademark Dilution Act of 1995 if it is likely to cause blurring or tarnishment of the famous mark.

Trademark infringement and dilution can occur in many ways in the online environment, such as by inline linking, framing, metatagging, purchasing another's trademark as part of search engine advertising, or registering a domain name. The Anticybersquatting Consumer Protection Act (ACPA) restricts the activities of cybersquatters who register domain names and then attempt to sell them to trademark owners in bad faith. Trademark owners involved with domain name disputes may vindicate trademark rights through either of two parallel routes. Bringing suit in federal district court can result in an award of damages and attorneys fees, while resolving disputes under the World Intellectual Property Organization's (WIPO) Uniform Dispute Resolution Policy (UDRP) arbitration proceedings may be faster, less expensive, and present fewer jurisdictional challenges.

Key Terms

intellectual property (IP) A "negative right" that allows the owner to prevent others from doing something. Categories of IP include patents, copyrights, trademarks, and trade secrets.

nonrival A quality of the ideas underlying IP that allows multiple individuals to use the IP at the same time without diminishing the ability of others to use those ideas.

Lanham act The principal federal trademark law.

distinctive A characteristic by which consumers viewing (or hearing) the trademark are be able to distinguish it from other trademarks.

trademarks Any word, name, symbol, or device used to distinguish the goods or services of one company from those of another.

service marks Marks used to distinguish services rather than products.

collective marks Marks used by members of an association or organization, such as the Boy Scouts of America.

certification marks Marks used to certify the quality of third party products or services.

generic The word used to describe a type of product or service that can never be registered as a trademark.

descriptive The word used to describe the mark for a product or its qualities but is not the generic term for it.

suggestive The word for a mark that hints at the qualities of a product, but does not describe it directly.

inherently distinctive The quality of mark that is suggestive, arbitrary, or fanciful and therefore can be registered without the need to show secondary meaning.

arbitrary The word describing a mark used in a way that is unrelated to the product or service represented.

fanciful mark The word describing a mark that is coined or created and that at the time of creation would not be found in a dictionary.

trade dress A product's design, packaging, or overall look and feel.

product packaging The container or packaging within which a product is sold.

product design The design or configuration of the product itself, as distinct from its packaging.

United States Patent & Trademark Office (USPTO) A government agency located just outside of Washington, D.C., that registers federal trademarks.

abandonment Condition of a mark when the owner stops using the mark and does not intend to resume using it.

genericide Condition of a mark that becomes commonly used to denote a product or service rather than a particular manufacturer or provider of that product or service, causing loss of trademark rights.

likelihood of confusion The touchstone of a trademark infringement action; exists when consumers are likely to be unsure of the origin, sponsorship, or approval of the defendant's product or services.

dilution An extension of the ordinary trademark infringement standard to cases where there is no likelihood of confusion; includes blurring and tarnishment.

Federal Trademark Dilution Act of 1995 (FTDA) A federal law that provides a right of action for trademark dilution even in the absence of confusion.

blurring Use of a famous mark that impairs its distinctiveness.

tarnishment Use of a famous mark that harms its reputation.

deep linking Linking to a subsidiary page of the trademark owner's site rather than to its homepage.

framing Content from a website presented as integrated within the context of another website.

in-line linking Material from one website appearing within the context of another website.

search engine optimization Techniques used by website owners to try to ensure that their website appears at the top of Internet search results.

metatags Invisible text embedded within websites that can be read by search engines.

initial interest confusion A "bait and switch" tactic that permits a competitor to lure consumers at an early phase of the decision-making process.

pay-per-click advertising A tactic in which businesses pay search engines to achieve more prominent placement on certain sections of the search results page.

organic results Unpaid or "natural" Internet search results.

keyed An advertisement linked to a search term because the search engine has been paid to include it in a pay-per-click advertising agreement.

enjoin A legal process to prohibit certain conduct.

click fraud Competitors or others intentionally click on a link for a purpose other than an interest in viewing the result.

secondary liability Liability imposed on third parties who encourage direct infringement or who have an ability to control the primary infringer's activities

contributory liability A type of secondary liability that results when a party (1) intentionally induces the primary infringer to commit infringement or (2) continues to provide a product or service to a buyer knowing that the buyer is engaging in trademark infringement.

vicarious liability A type of secondary liability where a defendant exercises control over the infringing product or service.

Web 2.0 A term used to refer to online activities involving large numbers of users that both produce and consume content.

top-level domain (TLD) The portion of the domain name furthest to the right (e.g., ".com").

cybersquatting Registering domain names before others appreciate their value to later sell them for a profit.

typosquatting The speculative purchase of an Internet domain name intentionally incorporating a frequently made misspelling ("typo") of a trademark.

Manager's Checklist

1. When selecting a trademark, first conduct a preliminary trademark search at www.uspto.gov.

2. Consider the availability of domain names when selecting and registering a trademark.

3. Work with your lawyer to select, register, and maintain both trademarks and domain names. Timely renewal and payment of fees is necessary to avoid loss of rights.

4. Consider preemptive registration of multiple similar domain names to avoid later conflicts with cybersquatters or typosquatters.

5. Avoid using others' trademarks on your website or "borrowing" elements of third-party websites in a manner that could give rise to trade dress liability.

Questions and Case Problems

1. In 1993, William Jefferson Clinton began his term as the 42nd President of the United States. In 2009, Clinton through his counsel initiated arbitration proceedings against Web of Deception, an entity that had registered the domain names "williamclinton.com," "williamjclinton.com," and "president-billclinton.com." Visitors to these sites are redirected to the website for the Republican National Committee. Web of Deception has also registered a number of domain names that include names such as Obama and McCain. Web of Deception has not requested or accepted any payment from Clinton and does not otherwise seek financial profit from the site. *Who should prevail and why?*[36]

2. There are currently over 250 country code top level domain names (ccTLDs) in addition to more than 20 of the more familiar TLDs such as .com, .org, and

---

36. See *William J. Clinton v. Web of Deception*, Nat'l Arbitration Forum Claim No. FA0904001256123 (June 1, 2009).

.net. Recently, ICANN has begun to dramatically expand the number of domain names to include, for example, city names (for example: www.secondleveldomain.chicago). *What are the advantages and disadvantages of such additional domain names? From the perspective of existing businesses, what are the relevant trademark issues to consider?*

3. As discussed in the text, Google and other search engines rely on advertising revenue as a central aspect of their business models. Key words entered by consumers into the search engine are used to more effectively match advertisements with the consumers most likely to find those advertisements helpful. In the United States, Google uses both trademarked and non-trademarked terms as key words in its search algorithm, and sells these key words to both trademark owners and others to affect placement of pay-per-click advertisements. *Should search engines be allowed to sell trademarked key words to affect the placement of pay-per-click advertisements (as distinct from the organic results)? Why or why not?*

4. Plaintiff, Kraft Foods Holdings, Inc. ("Kraft"), is the manufacturer and distributor of Velveeta brand cheese products and has owned the Velveeta trademark since 1923. Defendant Stuart Helm calls himself "King Velveeda" and operates a website at http://www.cheesygraphics.com that contains sexually explicit photographs, drawings, and other material and provides noncheese merchandise or services for sale to the public. Mr. Helm's website also contains illustrations of drug use and paraphernalia. One of the items Helm designed and sells on this site is a comic book called "Velveeda SINGLES and Seconds." Helm's website and its use of the name brought on a lawsuit from Kraft claiming Helm was tarnishing the Velveeta trademark in violation of the Lanham Act. *Prepare a statement arguing that Kraft should prevail in court.*[37]

5. *Ethical Consideration:* Should dissatisfied consumers have the right to establish gripe sites that use the trademark of the offending company in the domain name? How likely is it that consumers will be confused as to the "origin, sponsorship, or approval" of the gripe site by the offending company? Whether or not you think that confusion is likely, should a gripe site be considered to tarnish the targeted company's trademark and thereby violate the Federal Trademark Dilution Act? Why or why not?

Additional Resources

Arnot, Jordan A. *Navigating Cybersquatting Enforcement in the Expanding Internet*, 13 J. MARSHALL REV. INTELL. PROP. L. 321 (2014).

Chen, Wei-ehr. *Optimizing Online Trademark Protections Given the Proliferation of Generic Top Level Domains*, 38 J. CORP. L. 585 (2013).

---

37. See *Kraft Foods Holdings, Inc. v. Helm*, 205 F. Supp. 2d 942 (N.D. Ill. 2002).

Darrow, Jonathan J., and Gerald R. Ferrera, *The Search Engine Advertising Market: Lucrative Space or Trademark Liability?*, 17 TEX. INTELL. PROP. L.J. 223 (2009).

Internet Corporation for Assigned Names and Numbers. www.icann.org.

National Arbitration Forum. www.adrforum.com/ (click on "Domain Name Disputes").

United States Patent & Trademark Office. www.uspto.gov.

World Intellectual Property Organization. Search WIPO Cases and WIPO Panel Decisions, http://arbiter.wipo.int/domains/search/index.html.

 The enactment of copyright legislation by Congress under the terms of the Constitution is not based upon any natural right that the author has in his writings . . . but upon the ground that the welfare of the public will be served . . . by securing to authors for limited periods the exclusive rights to their writings.

—House of Representatives Report No. 2222, 60th Congress (1909)

5

Copyright

Learning Outcomes

After you have read this chapter, you should be able to:

● Explain what a copyright is and how it differs from a trademark.
● Explain the potential secondary liability that online businesses may face as a result of infringing activity by users of their online services.
● Explain the factors that determine whether a given instance of copying constitutes "fair use."
● Understand the major provisions of the Digital Millennium Copyright Act.

Overview

Of the four main types of intellectual property—trademarks, copyrights, patents, and trade secrets—copyrights are perhaps the most important, ubiquitous, and far-reaching in the online context. In fact, the Internet has been described as a "giant photocopier" because it is particularly well suited to the rapid distribution of virtually unlimited numbers of perfect digital copies around the globe.

Almost any activity related to the Internet has the potential to implicate copyright law. The mere act of turning on a computer can cause a software program to be copied from the hard drive to the computer's random access memory (RAM). Forwarding an email message may cause multiple copies of that message to be reproduced, particularly if the message is addressed to multiple recipients. Downloading smartphone applications and watching online videos cause those applications and videos to be reproduced or displayed on users' electronic devices.

Given the ease of copying, it is important that businesses understand how to avoid infringing the rights of others. Conversely, businesses will also want to know how their own creative works can be protected from infringement.

Obtaining a Copyright

Unlike trademarks, copyrights are governed almost exclusively by federal law. Section 102 of the federal **Copyright Act of 1976**, the principal federal enactment of copyright law, provides that copyright extends to the eight subject matter categories listed in Exhibit 5.1.

The Copyright Act of 1976 has been amended many times, and the text of the current law can generally be found online. For example, because the Copyright Act is codified in Title 17 of the United States Code, Section 102 can be found by searching online using the search string: "17 USC 102."

The Broad Scope of Copyright

A great deal of online content falls within the generous ambit of "literary works," including ebooks, software, and website content. Note that the term "literary" does not imply any particular level of qualitative merit or artistic skill. Ordinary email messages, text messages (provided they are of sufficient length) and blog postings, for example, will almost always qualify for copyright protection. The vast number of videos, songs, and images available online are similarly eligible for protection, irrespective of subjective notions of quality. Thus, for example, finding "clip art" or other images on the Web and using them in an online business likely implicates the rights of others, and permission may be required.

Due to these broad categories and the very flexible requirements for obtaining a copyright, a vast amount of information on the Internet is protected. Section 102 of the Copyright Act defines the broad scope of copyright:

> Copyright protection subsists . . . in original works of authorship fixed in any tangible medium of expression, now known or later developed, from which they can be perceived, reproduced, or otherwise communicated, either directly or with the aid of a machine or device.

Requirements for Copyright

In addition to falling within one or more of the subject matter categories, a work must meet two principal requirements for copyright protection: The work must be (1) original (i.e., not copied) and (2) fixed in a tangible medium of expression. Note that there is no need for either government registration or the placing of a copyright notice ("©") on the work. As with trademarks, however, there are

| Exhibit 5.1 | Copyrightable Subject Matter |

Section 102 Subject Matter Category	Examples
1. Literary works	books, blog postings, text messages of sufficient length
2. Musical works	the notes embodied in, e.g., sheet music
3. Dramatic works	plays, musicals, and operas
4. Pantomimes* & choreography	
5. Pictorial, graphic, or sculptural works	digital photographs
6. Motion pictures	movies, homemade videos
7. Sound recordings	a song fixed in a CD or in an MP3 file
8. Architectural works	

*A pantomime is a type of dramatic work told with movements rather than speech.

| Exhibit 5.2 | Requirements for Copyright |

Element	Required?
Appropriate subject matter	Yes
Originality	Yes
Fixation	Yes
Registration	No (but beneficial)
Notice	No (but beneficial)

advantages to both registration and notice. The elements of originality, fixation, registration, and notice are summarized in Exhibit 5.2 and will be discussed below.

Originality

Authors may claim copyright only in original works that they create. An "original" work is one created by the author, rather than copied from a pre-existing work. For example, if one were to scour the Web and find an image that did not have an easily identifiable author, the finder would not be able to claim a copyright in that image because the finder did not create it.

On the other hand, an author may claim copyright in the works she creates even if they are similar or identical to preexisting works, so long as the author created the work independently and did not copy.[1] Thus, if a business were to independently design a website that was similar or identical to a preexisting website, the business would not infringe the copyright of the earlier website. (In practice, however, an identical or substantially similar website may tend to show that the defendant did in fact copy the earlier work.) Note that the originality requirement of copyright law differs from trademark law, where an identical or confusingly similar mark may infringe the rights of another mark owner, even if both marks were independently created.

Fixation

Copyright protection is only available for works "fixed in any tangible medium of expression." In the analog world of bricks and mortar, a work might commonly be "fixed" by printing it on paper (e.g., a book), embodying it in a vinyl record (e.g., a song), or recording it on videotape (e.g., a movie). Note that any tangible medium will suffice, so long as the work "can be perceived, reproduced, or otherwise communicated, *either directly or with the aid of a machine or device.* A book, for example, can be perceived directly, while a song on a vinyl record can be perceived only with the aid of a record player ("a machine or device"). Although the Internet may seem less tangible than a book, digital works stored on hard drives and perceivable via the use of a computer are considered fixed and are therefore eligible for copyright protection.

Registration

Recall that trademarks can be registered with the U.S. Patent & Trademark Office (USPTO), an agency of the U.S. Department of Commerce located just outside Washington, D.C. Similarly, copyrightable works may be registered with the U.S. Copyright Office, housed within the Library of Congress in Washington, D.C. The registration of a single copyrightable work can be completed online for a modest fee of $35, which is far less than the cost of an initial trademark registration. The Copyright Office maintains a helpful website, including a listing of forms and current fees, at www.copyright.gov.

Although works may be registered with the Copyright Office, registration is not required. Under Section 102 of the Copyright Act, copyright protection "subsists" from the moment of creation. This means that the instant a work is fixed in a tangible medium of expression, that work is protected by federal copyright law without the need for any action on the part of the author. For example, the moment an email is written or a blog entry is made available on the Web, it is copyrighted. Given the automatic nature of copyright, it is easy to see that the volume of works protected by copyright is enormous!

1. *Sheldon v. Metro-Goldwyn Pictures Corp.*, 81 F.2d 49, 54 (2d Cir. 1936) ("[I]f by some magic a man who had never known it were to compose anew Keats's Ode on a Grecian Urn, he would be an 'author,' and . . . others might not copy that poem. . . .").

Nevertheless, registering a copyright confers significant benefits:

- An infringement action cannot be filed in federal court until a work is registered. (It is generally permissible, however, to register a work after infringement for the purpose of filing suit.)
- If a work is registered prior to infringement, the copyright owner may collect statutory damages (up to $150,000 per infringed work) and attorney fees.
- A copyright registration can be recorded with the U.S. Customs Service to assist in preventing the importation of infringing articles into the United States.

Notice

Copyright notice is not required for works published after 1989. Nevertheless, placing a notice of copyright on a work can inform others that the work is copyrighted and thereby prevent infringers from defending a copyright lawsuit on the basis of innocent infringement. Notice must include three elements:

- The copyright sign or abbreviation (either "©" or "Copr.") or the word "Copyright"
- The date of first publication
- The copyright owner's name

For example, copyright notice for a book might read: "© 2012 Wolters Kluwer" or "Copyright 1923 Jane Smith" or something similar. You will notice that many web pages contain copyright notices, usually placed at the very bottom of the screen.

Why Copyright?

This chapter's opening quotation, excerpted from a House Report to the 1909 Copyright Act, suggested two possible rationales for the existence of copyright: a natural rights rationale and a utilitarian or welfare rationale. The **natural rights** rationale emphasizes a person's inherent connection with the fruits of that person's creative labor and views it as unfair to allow others to copy the creator's works without compensation. Under the natural rights approach, copyright is viewed as necessary because the unauthorized use of another's work is morally wrong. In contrast, the **utilitarian** rationale views copyright primarily as a means to promote overall public welfare through the stimulation and dissemination of creative works. Under the utilitarian view, copyright is necessary to the extent that authors will create fewer works if they are unable to recoup the costs of creation and distribution.

The United States Approach: Promoting Welfare

Although there is ongoing debate regarding the proper justification for copyright, several observations suggest that the traditional view in the United States may tend toward the utilitarian approach. The quoted 1909 House Report, for example, explicitly endorsed the utilitarian rationale and rejected the natural rights rationale, noting that the goal of copyright is to serve the public welfare. The Supreme Court has twice quoted the 1909 House language and elsewhere stated directly that the public benefits of copyright are the copyright law's primary justification.[2] Most significantly, the ability of Congress to enact copyright (and patent) legislation derives from the Constitution's **Intellectual Property Clause,** which reflects a utilitarian approach:

> The Congress shall have Power . . . To promote the Progress of Science and useful Arts, by securing for limited Times to Authors and Inventors the exclusive Right to their respective Writings and Discoveries.[3]

Justifying Copyright and the Internet

Whether one embraces a natural rights view or a utilitarian view of intellectual property has fundamental implications for the application of copyright law on the Internet. Although there is agreement that the Internet has dramatically lowered the cost of copying and distribution, there is disagreement as to the appropriate response to this phenomenon. Proponents of the natural rights theory may argue that the ease of copying and distribution requires longer (or even perpetual) copyright terms, stricter copyright enforcement, and more effective restrictions on the ability of the public to use the works of creators. Proponents of the utilitarian theory, on the other hand, may argue that near zero copying and distribution costs create the potential for tremendous public benefit and that this benefit could be enhanced by shorter copyright terms, more flexible copyright enforcement, and the expanded ability of the public to use and modify existing works.

Exclusive Rights

Copyright, as the word implies, provides rights owners the ability to exclude others from making copies of a given work. However, the reproduction (copying) right is only one of several rights available to copyright owners. Section 106 of the Copyright Act of 1976 provides that copyright owners have the following six exclusive rights:

1. Reproduction (copying)
2. Preparation of derivative works (e.g., making a book into a movie)
3. Distribution of copies to the public (e.g., selling or renting)

---

2. *Fox Film Corp. v. Doyal*, 286 U.S. 123, 127 (1932) ("The sole interest of the United States and the primary object in conferring the monopoly lie in the general benefits derived by the public from the labors of authors.").
3. U.S. Const. art. I, § 8, cl. 8.

Exhibit 5.3 Synthesis of Section 106 Rights and Section 102 Works

§ 102 Works \ § 106 Rights	Reproduce	Prepare derivative works	Distribute	Publicly perform	Publicly display	Publicly perform (digital)
1. Literary works						***
2. Musical works						***
3. Dramatic works						***
4. Pantomimes & choreography						***
5. Pictorial, graphic, or sculptural works						
6. Motion pictures					*	***
7. Sound recordings						
8. Architectural works		**				

* = Public display right pertains to individual images of motion picture
** = Third parties may photograph buildings if viewable from a public place
*** = Digital performance rights are subsumed under the ordinary performance right for categories 1-4 and 6, but set forth separately for category 7 because sound recordings do not enjoy the ordinary performance right

4. Public performance
5. Public display
6. Public performance of sound recordings by means of a digital audio transmission (e.g., broadcasting music over the Internet)

Recall that Section 102 of the Copyright Act sets forth eight categories of works. Although the first three Section 106 rights apply to all works, the remaining three do not. Exhibit 5.3 summarizes which rights apply to which works (shading indicates that a right applies).

The solid shading in the first three columns indicates that copyright owners of all types of works hold the exclusive rights to reproduce, prepare derivative works, and distribute copies of the original work. It should also be easy to remember that pictorial, graphic, sculptural, and architectural works cannot be "performed," and so are not associated with the performance right, but can be displayed. You will notice that the rectangles corresponding to the two types of performance rights in each of categories 5 and 8 are not shaded. Similarly, a motion picture can be shown ("performed") but only individual images can be displayed. Sound recordings are unusual in that they do not benefit from the general public display or public performance right, but do benefit from a *digital* public performance right. Music copyrights are a particularly complicated area of intellectual property law and are treated separately below.

Courts have frequently been called upon to apply, in the Internet context, the various exclusive rights to reproduce, prepare derivative works, distribute, display, and perform.

Reproduction Right and the Internet

As you might expect given the ease, quality, and speed of copying on the Internet, the reproduction right is a frequent subject of litigation. Although not delineated as such in the statute, it may be helpful to think of the reproduction right as potentially being violated in two main ways. First, a party might engage in **piracy**, the copying of a work with little or no pretense that the copying is lawful. Second, a party may have a reason to believe that copying is lawful, such as the doctrine of fair use, but that assessment may turn out to be wrong. (Fair use and other limitations to the exclusive rights are discussed below.) Although many of the case examples in this text fall within the second category, it is likely that the volume of copyright infringements that constitute piracy is far larger than those whose illegality is more uncertain.

Suits Against Napster and Other File-Sharing Services

A very common violation of the reproduction right on the Internet involves the copying of music, such as uploading, downloading, or otherwise transferring music electronically from one party to another. In the late 1990s and early 2000s, file-sharing software made by companies such as Napster, Limewire, and Grokster enabled widely dispersed parties who did not know each other to "share" music over the Internet. Early lawsuits brought by copyright owners against such file-sharing services were often successful and led to the dramatic redesign or disappearance of those services.

Suits Against Individuals

Nevertheless, new forms of file-sharing services continued to emerge, and around 2003 the music industry began to pursue suits not only against the file-sharing services but also against more than 30,000 ordinary consumers. While most of these suits settled before trial for a few thousand dollars, a few resulted in judgments. In one of these, *Sony BMG Music Entertainment v. Tenenbaum*,[4] a jury found that an undergraduate named Joel Tenenbaum had illegally downloaded 30 songs and awarded damages to the copyright owner of $675,000! We will revisit the calculation of this astonishing damage award when we consider the remedies available to copyright owners below.

In 2008, an association of record labels known as the **Recording Industry Association of America** (**RIAA**) indicated that it planned to end its mass litigation strategy against end users. Although illegal file-sharing continues to occur, the market has evolved substantially. Leading music and video sites such as Spotify and Netflix now generally obtain licenses that provide the right to use copyrighted works.

---

4. *Sony BMG Music Entm't v. Tenenbaum*, 721 F. Supp. 2d 85 (D. Mass. 2010).

Derivative Works Right and the Internet

Copyright owners have the exclusive right to prepare **derivative works**, which are defined by the Copyright Act to include adaptations or transformations of the original work. For example, the owner of a book copyright could prevent others from translating the book into another language, making a movie based on the book, writing an abridgment of the book, or writing sequels to the book.

An example of the derivative work right in the Internet context is provided by *Pearson Education, Inc. v. Ishayev*,[5] in which defendants sold unauthorized digital copies of solution manuals to copyrighted textbooks. Although copyrights in the solution manuals were not registered, the court found the manuals to be derivative works of the textbooks, the copyrights of which had been registered. The court nevertheless denied the plaintiffs' motion for summary judgment because although the defendants had sent buyers hyperlinks to the infringing works, there remained a genuine issue of fact as to whether the defendants had uploaded (copied) the infringing works.

Distribution Right and the Internet

Traditionally, the distribution of a work via sale or rental would necessarily take place after reproduction of the work. For example, Party A might manufacture illegal copies of software on compact discs and then transfer the compact discs to Party B for distribution to the public. This scenario is illustrated in Exhibit 5.4.

In Exhibit 5.4, only Party A has violated the reproduction right while Party B has not. Without the distribution right the copyright owner might find it difficult to prevent Party B from selling copies of the infringing software to the public, thereby undercutting the market for the copyright owner's authorized sales.

Exhibit 5.4   **Comparing Reproduction and Distribution Rights**

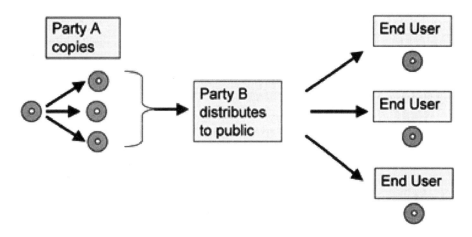

---

5. *Pearson Educ., Inc. v. Ishayev*, 963 F. Supp. 2d 239 (S.D.N.Y. 2013).

The availability of both a reproduction and a distribution right helps to ensure that copyright owners have legal recourse even if the source of the illegal copies is overseas or cannot be found.

Internet File Sharing: Inadvertent Distribution?

On the Internet, distributing a work to other computers would seem to always require the simultaneous creation of copies of the work on the recipients' computers. It is therefore common for plaintiffs to allege violation of the reproduction right whenever the distribution right is asserted. This has been the case, for example, in many of the lawsuits brought by the music industry against users of music file-sharing programs. In *Warner Bros. Records, Inc. v. Walker*,[6] an Allegheny College student used a peer-to-peer file-sharing program known as Ares to download 19 copyrighted songs from other Ares users. The court found this to constitute a violation of the reproduction right. However, the court also found the defendant to have violated the distribution right because the Ares program, like many file-sharing programs, contained a shared folder feature where users could place music files so that they could be downloaded by other Ares users over the Internet. The court noted that placement of the copyrighted music files by the defendant in this shared folder, in conjunction with proof that they had been downloaded from this folder by others, constituted a violation of the distribution right even though the defendant was unaware at the time that his actions made the music available for others to download.

Public Performance/Display Rights and the Internet

The last two rights that will be discussed in this section are the public performance and public display rights. (Sound recordings and the digital public performance right are treated in a separate section below). Performing a work on the Internet is most likely to occur through the streaming of videos or music. An example of the latter is Pandora, an Internet radio station that serves 200 million users and streams more than 1,000,000 different songs (and pays copyright owners for the privilege of doing so). Displaying a work on the Internet typically occurs when a copyrighted work is made available for viewing, such as by including an image on a website.

Definition of "Public"

Only *public* performances and displays are within the copyright owner's exclusive rights. Thus, transmitting a copyrighted image via Instagram, an online photo-sharing service, to a single recipient would be unlikely to constitute a violation of the display right, although it would still implicate the reproduction right.

---

6. *Warner Bros. Records, Inc. v. Walker*, 704 F. Supp. 2d 460 (W.D. Pa. 2010).

Performing or displaying a work publicly is defined by the Copyright Act as:

1. to perform or display it at a place open to the public or at any place where a substantial number of persons outside of a normal circle of a family and its social acquaintances is gathered; or
2. to transmit or otherwise communicate a performance or display of the work to a place specified by clause (1) or to the public, by means of any device or process, whether the members of the public capable of receiving the performance or display receive it in the same place or in separate places and at the same time or at different times.

Telephone Ringtones: Cellco Partnership v. ASCAP

The second paragraph of the definition of a public performance was tested in *Cellco Partnership v. ASCAP*,[7] which involved the downloading of ringtones by Verizon Wireless customers. The **American Society of Composers, Authors, and Publishers** (**ASCAP**) is one of three major performing rights societies in the United States and licenses public performance rights on behalf of copyright owners of musical works. Verizon was already paying music publishers, who owned the reproduction rights to the musical works, $0.24 each time a customer downloaded a ringtone. ASCAP, however, asserted that Verizon must also pay for the public performance rights, based on its transmission of ringtones to customers' phones that would be audible each time a customer received an incoming call. This scenario where two different parties control the reproduction and public performance rights of a given work, illustrated in Exhibit 5.5, is possible because the Copyright Act allows copyright owners to license or assign (transfer) separately the exclusive rights to a given work. Thus, copyright owners can assign their reproduction rights to one party and their public performance rights to another.

The court held that there was no violation of the public performance right, and that Verizon therefore did not owe ASCAP compensation. Among other considerations, the court noted that when Verizon initially transmitted the ringtone file to the customer, the ringtone was not contemporaneously perceivable by either the customer or the public, and that it therefore did not constitute transmission of a "performance." Moreover, any later performance of the ringtone as an announcement of an incoming call was initiated by the incoming caller, not Verizon. Finally, individual Verizon customers were not liable even if the phone rang in public, owing to a specific exemption in the Copyright Act.

In 2014, the Supreme Court had to determine whether a "public performance" occurred when a company provided remote equipment that enabled subscribers to view almost-live, over-the-air broadcast television programming on Internet-connected devices at the locations of their choosing.

---

7. 663 F. Supp. 2d 363 (S.D.N.Y. 2009).

Exhibit 5.5   **Schematic Representation of *Cellco Partnership v. ASCAP***

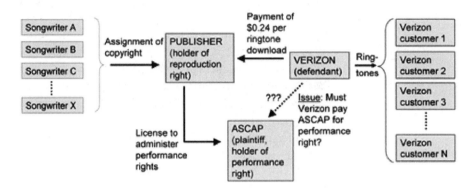

American Broadcasting Cos., Inc. v. Aereo, Inc.

134 S. Ct. 2498 (2014)

Justice Breyer, J.

Facts The Copyright Act of 1976 gives a copyright owner the "exclusive right" to "perform the copyrighted work publicly." 17 U.S.C. § 106(4). The Act's Transmit Clause defines that exclusive right as including the right to:

> transmit or otherwise communicate a performance . . . of the [copyrighted] work . . . to the public, by means of any device or process, whether the members of the public capable of receiving the performance . . . receive it in the same place or in separate places and at the same time or at different times.

We must decide whether respondent Aereo, Inc., infringes this exclusive right . . . .

For a monthly fee, Aereo offers subscribers broadcast television programming over the Internet, virtually as the programming is being broadcast . . . . Aereo's system is made up of servers, transcoders, and thousands of dime-sized antennas housed in a central warehouse. It works roughly as follows: First, when a subscriber wants to watch a show that is currently being broadcast, he visits Aereo's website and selects, from a list of the local programming, the show he wishes to see.

Second, one of Aereo's servers selects an antenna, which it dedicates to the use of that subscriber (and that subscriber alone) for the duration of the selected show. A server then tunes the antenna to the over-the-air broadcast carrying the show. The antenna begins to receive the broadcast, and an Aereo transcoder translates the signals received into data that can be transmitted over the Internet.

Third, rather than directly sending the data to the subscriber, a server saves the data in a subscriber-specific folder on Aereo's hard drive. In other words,

Aereo's system creates a subscriber-specific copy—that is, a "personal" copy—of the subscriber's program of choice.

Fourth, once several seconds of programming have been saved, Aereo's server begins to stream the saved copy of the show to the subscriber over the Internet. (The subscriber may instead direct Aereo to stream the program at a later time, but that aspect of Aereo's service is not before us.) The subscriber can watch the streamed program on the screen of his personal computer, tablet, smart phone, Internet-connected television, or other Internet-connected devices. . . .

Petitioners are television producers, marketers, distributors, and broadcasters who own the copyrights in many of the programs that Aereo's system streams to its subscribers. They brought suit against Aereo for copyright infringement in Federal District Court. They sought a preliminary injunction, arguing that Aereo was infringing their right to "perform" their works "publicly." . . .

Analysis [A]n Aereo subscriber receives broadcast television signals with an antenna dedicated to him alone. Aereo's system makes from those signals a personal copy of the selected program. It streams the content of the copy to the same subscriber and to no one else. One and only one subscriber has the ability to see and hear each Aereo transmission . . . .

[The Transmit] Clause suggests that an entity may transmit a performance through multiple, discrete transmissions [("*in the same place or in separate places and at the same time or at different times*")]. That is because one can "transmit" or "communicate" something through a *set* of actions. Thus one can transmit a message to one's friends, irrespective of whether one sends separate identical e-mails to each friend or a single e-mail to all at once. So can an elected official communicate an idea, slogan, or speech to her constituents, regardless of whether she communicates that idea, slogan, or speech during individual phone calls to each constituent or in a public square. . . .

We do not see how the fact that Aereo transmits via personal copies of programs could make a difference . . . . [W]hether Aereo transmits from the same or separate copies, it performs the same work; it shows the same images and makes audible the same sounds. Therefore, when Aereo streams the same television program to multiple subscribers, it "transmit[s] . . . a performance" to all of them. Moreover, the subscribers to whom Aereo transmits television programs constitute "the public." . . .

[T]o the extent commercial actors or other interested entities may be concerned with the relationship between the development and use of [new] technologies and the Copyright Act, they are of course free to seek action from Congress.

Justice Scalia (Joined by Justices Thomas and Alito), Dissenting The defendant may be held directly liable only if the defendant *itself* "trespassed on the exclusive domain of the copyright owner." Most of the time that issue will come down to who selects the copyrighted content: the defendant or its customers. . . . The key point is that [Aereo's] subscribers call all the shots:

Aereo's automated system does not relay any program, copyrighted or not, until a subscriber selects the program and tells Aereo to relay it. . . .

We came within one vote of declaring the VCR contraband 30 years ago in [*Sony Corp. of America v. Universal City Studios, Inc.*, 464 U.S. 417 (1984)]. The dissent in that case was driven in part by the plaintiffs' prediction that VCR technology would wreak all manner of havoc in the television and movie industries. The Networks make similarly dire predictions about Aereo. We are told that nothing less than "the very existence of broadcast television as we know it" is at stake. . . . I conclude, as the Court concluded in *Sony*: "It may well be that Congress will take a fresh look at this new technology, just as it so often has examined other innovations in the past. But it is not our job to apply laws that have not yet been written. Applying the copyright statute, as it now reads, to the facts as they have been developed in this case, the judgment of the Court of Appeals [that no injunction should issue against Aereo] must be [affirmed]."

Case Questions

1. If an individual installs an antenna and uses it to receive an over-the-air broadcast television program, is the public performance right implicated?
2. Given that each of Aereo's subscribers could lawfully receive free over-the-air broadcast programming without the help of Aereo, why does the majority consider Aereo's actions to constitute "public performances"?
3. *Ethical Consideration:* The dissent compares the *Aereo* technology to VCR technology, noting that the Court in 1984 held—by a narrow margin—that the predecessor to the VCR did not violate the copyright laws. Should the *Aereo* Court have fashioned a rule more favorable to the development of new technology, or is it more important to protect copyright owners' rights?

Limitations to the Exclusive Rights

Although copyright owners enjoy a broad range of rights, these rights are limited in a number of ways. The Constitution's Intellectual Property Clause specifies that copyrights shall last only for limited times, after which they expire and become part of the public domain. Moreover, even while the copyright is in force, the copyright owner's exclusive rights are subject to limitations such as the fair use doctrine and the first sale doctrine. Several of the more important limitations to the exclusive rights are presented below.

Duration

The Constitution's Intellectual Property Clause provides that copyrights may last only "for limited times." Congress has broad discretion, however, to specify the precise duration of copyright. Since the first U.S. Copyright Act in 1790, the copyright term has increased substantially, particularly in the last half century. Exhibit 5.6 illustrates the dramatic growth in copyright duration. It has been

| **Exhibit 5.6** | **United States Copyright Duration (1790-2015)*** |

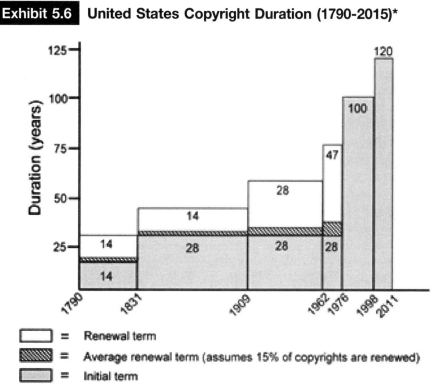

= Renewal term

= Average renewal term (assumes 15% of copyrights are renewed)

= Initial term

*To promote readability, Exhibit 5.6 deliberately ignores several important nuances of copyright duration, such as the date from which the term begins to run, and reflects the fixed work-for-hire durations rather than the variable terms that are based on the life of the author.

suggested that the continued lengthening occurs in part because it is easier and more lucrative for copyright owners to collectively advocate for expansion of rights than it is for users of copyrighted works to advocate for reduction of those rights.[8]

The Copyright Act of 1790 provided for an initial copyright term of 14 years, renewable for another 14 years. The initial term was extended to 28 years in 1831, and the renewal term was extended to 28 years in 1909. In 1962 the renewal term was extended to 47 years. Because studies indicate that only about 15 percent of works have historically been renewed, the average duration of copyrighted works under the renewal regime is much shorter than these renewal terms suggest, as reflected in Exhibit 5.6.

With the Copyright Act of 1976, Congress discarded the fixed term for ordinary copyrights and replaced it with a variable term that lasted for the life of the author plus 50 years. At the same time, Congress provided a different term for works made for hire.

A **work made for hire** is one prepared by an employee within the scope of employment. Because works made for hire are considered to be authored not by the employee but by the employer, which is often a corporation, duration is not

8. William M. Landis & Richard A. Posner, *The Political Economy of Intellectual Property Law*. AEI-Bookings Joint Center for Regulatory Studies (2004).

Exhibit 5.7	Current Copyright Duration

Type of Work	Duration
Ordinary Works	Life of the author + 70 years
Works Made for Hire (e.g., employee-created works, owned by corporations)	Earlier of: • 95 years from publication • 120 years from creation

based upon the "life" of the employer. Instead, Congress provided for a fixed term that expires the earlier of 75 years from date of first publication or 100 years from the date of creation. In 1998, under pressure from copyright owners such as the Walt Disney Company whose copyright on Mickey Mouse was about to expire, Congress enacted the **Sonny Bono Copyright Term Extension Act** (**CTEA**), extending copyright terms by 20 years. Current copyright duration is summarized in Exhibit 5.7.

The CTEA did not merely extend the copyright terms of works that would be created after 1998, but also applied the 20-year extension retroactively to existing works whose copyrights had not yet expired. Some viewed the CTEA, and particularly its retroactive character, as an unwise and even unconstitutional exercise of power by Congress. However, in 2003 the Supreme Court upheld the extension in *Eldred v. Ashcroft*.[9]

Public Domain

Once a copyright on a work expires, that work is said to have fallen into the **public domain** and may be used freely by anyone. The public domain also includes any work of the United States government, such as judicial opinions or statutes.[10]

Public Domain and the Internet

A number of Internet sites have emerged to promote access to public domain works. The website of Project Gutenberg makes available for free download digital copies of more than 45,000 books, such as *Pride and Prejudice*, *The Adventures of Huckleberry Finn*, and *The Iliad*, the copyrights for most of which have expired. The Mutopia Project provides more than 1800 pieces of sheet music for free download and performance, including works by Bach, Beethoven, and Mozart. PublicDomainFlicks.com hosts more than 450 full-length movies from 1914 to 1963 for immediate download.

---

9. 537 U.S. 186 (2003).
10. 17 U.S.C. § 105.

Determining Public Domain Status

Although a number of websites have emerged to offer works believed to be in the public domain, Internet users should exercise caution. Websites generally do not guarantee the public domain status of works residing on their sites, and penalties for copyright infringement can be assessed even where a defendant has a good faith belief that a work is in the public domain.

Determining public domain status can be a challenging undertaking. Due to the CTEA and previous copyright laws, only works published prior to January 1, 1923 can be presumed to be in the public domain. The Copyright Office publishes a document entitled "Circular 22: How to Investigate the Copyright Status of a Work," available at http://www.copyright.gov, that provides further information.

Fair Use

Even during the time a copyright remains in force, all six of the exclusive rights enumerated in Section 106 are limited by the doctrine of **fair use.** Section 107 of the Copyright Act provides four factors that help courts determine whether a given use is fair and therefore not an infringement: (1) the purpose and character of the use, (2) the nature of the copyrighted work, (3) the amount and substantiality of the portion used, and (4) the effect of the use upon the potential market for or value of the copyrighted work. Applying these four factors, a finding of fair use is more likely if:

- The use is nonprofit or transformative (factor 1)
- The work is factual rather than creative (factor 2)
- Only a small portion of the work is used (factor 3)
- The use will not detract from the copyright owner's revenues (factor 4)

For example, if a defendant "shares" music with friends, this would not constitute fair use because the use is not transformative (the music has not been altered or given new expression), musical works are creative works, entire works are being copied, and friends will be less likely to purchase music they have already obtained for free.

Fair Use: A Flexible Standard

Although Section 107 provides a list of activities that may be more likely to constitute fair use, including "criticism, comment, news reporting, teaching . . . , scholarship, or research," there are no hard and fast rules. Nonprofit activities are not necessarily fair uses. For example, if a professor were to post a scanned copy of an entire textbook on a course website so that students did not need to buy copies, this would almost certainly constitute infringement. On the other hand, the incidental displaying of copyrighted works in the background of online episodes of "The Daily Show with Jon Stewart" likely constitutes fair use even though it relates to for-profit programming. Moreover, a finding of fair use does not require that any particular number of the four factors support the fair use determination. Instead, courts must weigh the factors together to make an overall determination and may consider other factors when relevant. As you might suspect, in some circumstances it is difficult even for copyright experts to determine in advance whether a given use is fair, and disputes must often be resolved through litigation or settlement.

In the following case, the Fourth Circuit had to determine whether an anti-plagiarism service provided by a company called iParadigms violated students' copyrights in their class papers and essays or whether such use was protected by the fair use doctrine.

A.V. v. iParadigms
562 F.3d 630 (4th Cir. 2009)

Traxler, Circuit Judge

Facts Plaintiffs brought this copyright infringement action against defendant iParadigms, LLC, based on its use of essays and other papers written by plaintiffs for submission to their high school teachers through an online plagiarism detection service operated by iParadigms. . . . Defendant iParadigms owns and operates "Turnitin Plagiarism Detection Service," an online technology system designed to evaluate the originality of written works in order to prevent plagiarism. According to iParadigms, Turnitin offers high school and college educators an automated means of verifying that written works submitted by students are originals and not the products of plagiarism. When a school subscribes to iParadigms' service, it typically requires its students to submit their written assignments via a web-based system available at *www.turnitin.com* or via an integration between Turnitin and a school's course management system. In order to submit papers online, students must be enrolled in an active class and must enter the class ID number and class enrollment password supplied by the assigning professor.

After a student submits a writing assignment, Turnitin performs a digital comparison of the student's work with content available on the Internet, including student papers previously submitted to Turnitin, and commercial databases of journal articles and periodicals. For each work submitted, Turnitin creates an "Originality Report" suggesting a percentage of the work, if any, that appears not to be original. The assigning professor may, based on the results of the Originality Report, further explore any potential issues. . . .

When they initiated the lawsuit, the four plaintiffs were minor high school students. . . . According to the complaint, [the students'] schools required students to submit their written assignments via Turnitin.com to receive credit; failure to do so would result in a grade of "zero" for the assignment under the policy of both schools. . . . Plaintiffs filed a complaint alleging that iParadigms infringed their copyright interests in their works by archiving them in the Turnitin database without their permission. . . .

[Fair Use] The ownership rights created by the Copyright Act . . . are not absolute. . . . [T]he copyright owner's monopoly . . . is limited and subject to a list of statutory exceptions, including the exception for fair use provided in 17 U.S.C. § 107.

Section 107 provides that "the fair use of a copyrighted work . . . for purposes such as criticism, comment, news reporting, teaching (including multiple copies for classroom use), scholarship, or research, is not an infringement of copyright." Congress provided four nonexclusive factors for courts to consider in making a "fair use" determination:

1. the purpose and character of the use, including whether such use is of a commercial nature or is for nonprofit educational purposes;
2. the nature of the copyrighted work;
3. the amount and substantiality of the portion used in relation to the copy-righted work as a whole; and
4. the effect of the use upon the potential market for or value of the copyrighted work.

17 U.S.C. § 107. Section 107 contemplates that the question of whether a given use of copyrighted material is "fair" requires a case-by-case analysis in which the statutory factors are not treated in isolation but are weighed together, in light of the purposes of copyright.

First Factor [Purpose and Character of the Use] A use of the copyrighted material that has a commercial purpose tends to weigh against a finding of fair use. . . . [However, Courts must also] examine whether and to what extent the new work is transformative. . . . [T]he more transformative the new work, the less will be the significance of other factors, like commercialism, that may weigh against a finding of fair use. A "transformative" use is one that employ[s] the quoted matter in a different manner or for a different purpose from the original, thus transforming it. . . . The [district] court concluded that "iParadigms, through Turnitin, uses the papers for an entirely different purpose, namely, to prevent plagiarism and protect the students' written works from plagiarism . . . by archiv-ing the students' works as digital code." Although the district court recognized that iParadigms intends to profit from its use of the student works, the court found that iParadigms' use of plaintiffs' works was "highly transformative," and "pro-vides a substantial public benefit through the network of educational institutions using Turnitin." . . . iParadigms' use of plaintiffs' works had an entirely different function and purpose than the original works. . . . The district court, in our view, correctly determined that the archiving of plaintiffs' papers was transformative and favored a finding of "fair use."

Second Factor [Nature of the Copyrighted Work] In considering the nature of the copyrighted work, the Supreme Court has instructed that "fair use is more likely to be found in factual works than in fictional works," whereas "a use is less likely to be deemed fair when the copyrighted work is a creative product." . . . The district court noted that, if anything, iParadigms' use of the students' works fostered the development of original and creative works "by detecting any efforts at plagiarism by other students." . . . [T]he district court . . . concluded that even if the plaintiffs' works [of fiction and poetry] were highly creative in nature, iParadigms' use of the plaintiffs' works was not related to the creative core of the works. . . . [W]e find no fault in the district court's [determination that this factor favors neither party].

Third Factor [Amount and Substantiality of the Portion Used] The third fair use factor requires us to consider "the amount and substantiality of the portion used in relation to the copyrighted work as a whole." 17 U.S.C. § 107(3). Generally speaking, as the amount of the copyrighted material that is used increases, the likelihood that the use will constitute a 'fair use' decreases. . . . Although copying an entire work weighs against finding a fair use . . . it does not *preclude* a finding of fair use; therefore, the extent of permissible copying varies with the purpose and character of the use. The district court found that this factor, like the second factor, did not favor either party. The court concluded that although iParadigms uses substantially the whole of plaintiffs' works, iParadigms' "use of the original works is limited in purpose and scope" as a digitized record for electronic "comparison purposes only." Having already concluded that such use of plaintiffs' works was transformative, the district court concluded that iParadigms' use of the entirety of plaintiffs' works did not preclude a finding of fair use. . . . We find no error in the district court's analysis.

Fourth Factor [Market Effect] Finally, § 107 directs us to examine the market of the copyrighted work to determine "the effect of the use upon the potential market for or value of the copyrighted work." 17 U.S.C. § 107(4). The Supreme Court described this factor as the "single most important element of fair use." . . . Our task is to determine whether the defendants' use of plaintiffs' works would materially impair the marketability of the work[s] and whether it would act as a market substitute for them. . . . The district court concluded that iParadigms' Turnitin system did not serve as a market substitute or even harm the market value of the works, highlighting the deposition testimony of the plaintiffs—each of whom denied that iParadigms' impinged on the marketability of their works or interfered with their use of the works. The district court also noted that, although the pleadings alleged iParadigms' use would adversely impact plaintiffs' ability to market their works to other high school students seeking to purchase completed term papers or essays, each plaintiff indicated that such transactions were dishonest and that he or she would not sell their original works for submission by other students.

CONCLUSION

In sum, we conclude, viewing the evidence in the light most favorable to the plaintiffs, that iParadigms' use of the student works was "fair use" under the Copyright Act and that iParadigms was therefore entitled to summary judgment on the copyright infringement claim. [Affirmed.]

Case Questions

1. What examples of activities that might constitute fair use does the Section 107 of the Copyright Act provide? Note that these examples are not necessarily fair uses. Instead, fair use must be determined by weighing the four fair use factors. List the four factors described in Section 107.
2. Summarize the court's evaluation of each of the four fair use factors. How many factors favored iParadigms? How many favored the students? How did the court balance the factors?
3. *Ethical Consideration:* Do you think that companies such as iParadigms are performing a valuable service or profiting from the invasion of individual privacy? If you were a decision-maker at a high school or university, would you require students to use an anti-plagiarism service such as Turnitin? Why or why not?

Google

The Google Book Project

In 2004, Google officially announced a program that would eventually become Google Books, an ambitious endeavor to digitize every book in every language that could be located anywhere the world. By 2009, the Google Book Project enabled Internet users in 124 countries to search scanned copies of books in over 100 languages. In order to enable the scanning to occur, libraries at major research universities such as Harvard, Stanford, the University of Virginia, and the University of Wisconsin-Madison agreed to provide access to their holdings, as did the New York Public Library and university libraries in several foreign countries. These libraries sought to participate in order to fulfill their missions of making knowledge easily available to scholars and the public. Digitization also facilitated these libraries' preservation efforts. As part of the Google-university agreements, Google provided participating libraries with a digital copy of any book they contributed.

Soon, however, questions emerged regarding the lawfulness of Google's actions under the Copyright Act. A necessary step in the creation of the Google Book Project database was the scanning (i.e., copying) of entire books. In addition, works were displayed to users of the Google Book Project, implicating another exclusive right under the Copyright Act. In 2005, the Author's Guild and the Association of American Publishers filed two separate lawsuits asking the court to enjoin Google from further infringement and to award statutory damages, costs, and attorney fees.

The Google Book Project included three types of works. First, approximately two million (~16 percent) of the books scanned were in the public domain and therefore did not raise serious copyright questions. Google made entire books available for works in this category. Another 9 percent were under copyright and still in publication. For these books, Google worked with copyright owners through its Book Search Partner Program to make as much of those books available as the copyright owners would allow. Because these books were scanned and displayed with the copyright owner's authorization, they similarly raised no copyright problems. The lawsuits, however, were directed at the remaining 75 percent of the scanned books which were still under copyright but no longer in print. Many of these works were **orphan works**—works still under copyright for which the copyright owner cannot be easily identified or located. Orphan works occur in part due to the very long term of copyrights, during which time authors may pass away and publishers may cease to exist. Google provided only "snippets" of these books. Exhibit 5.8 summarizes the three categories of works within the Google Book Project.

Exhibit 5.8   Google Book Project: Types of Works

Category	Google Book Project Provided Users:
Public Domain	Digital copies of whole works
In Copyright, In Print	As much as copyright owners allowed
In Copyright, No Longer in Print	Snippets only

For the third category of works—those still under copyright but no longer in print—Google's project relied heavily on the doctrine of fair use. Favoring Google, it might have been argued that its book search engine was transformative in that the purpose of the Google Book Search was to help users find desired material rather than to provide them with full text versions of the book, because only snippets were provided (see Exhibit 5.9). It might further have been argued that, as with the plagiarism detection system of *iParadigms,* the copying of entire works by Google was incidental to the search functionality. Moreover, books no longer in print do not have a current market that can be adversely affected. Finally, Google would remove any book upon the request of the author to "opt out" of the Google Book Project. On the other hand, Google was copying whole works, some of them highly creative, and displaying at least parts of them to a potential audience of hundreds of millions of people, as part of its for-profit business.

In 2013, a federal court held that Google's actions constituted fair use, noting that the copying associated with Google Books was "highly transformative" in that it transformed expressive text into a comprehensive word index that helped readers, scholars, researchers, and others find books, and that as a result Google Books enhanced rather than diminished sales.[11]

---

11. *Authors Guild, Inc. v. Google, Inc.*, 954 F. Supp.2d 282 (S.D.N.Y. 2013).

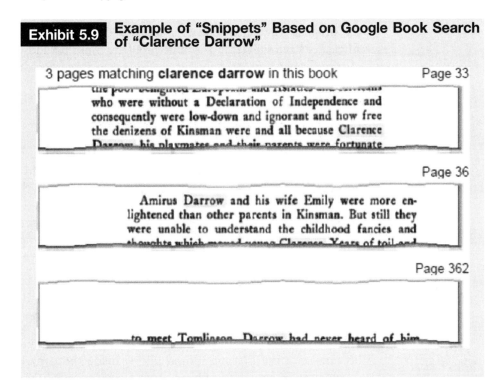

Exhibit 5.9 Example of "Snippets" Based on Google Book Search of "Clarence Darrow"

First Sale Doctrine

Another important exception to the exclusive rights of the copyright owner is the first sale doctrine. Under the **first sale doctrine**,[12] the owner of a particular copy of a copyrighted work may resell or otherwise dispose of that copy without the permission of the copyright owner. For example, you may resell or give away a physical (but not necessarily digital) copy of this book at the end of the semester without the permission of the copyright owner. Unlike the fair use doctrine, which limits all of the exclusive rights, the first sale doctrine limits only the exclusive right of distribution. Moreover, it only applies where the copy in question was lawfully made. Thus, selling or even giving away a flash drive containing an unlawful copy of a copyrighted software program would not be protected under the first sale doctrine.

Proposed Digital First Sale Doctrine

Advocates of a **digital first sale doctrine** have suggested that the first sale doctrine be expanded to cover the sale of digital works over the Internet. This is a tempting proposition, as it is much easier to transfer a digital copy of a work to a buyer than it is to mail the buyer a traditional physical embodiment of that work. However, the transmission of an electronic work does not actually entail a transfer. Instead, an additional copy of the work must be created on the recipient's computer, while

---

12. 17 U.S.C. § 109(a).

the original copy simultaneously remains on the sender's computer. Although advocates have suggested that this problem could be addressed through the use of *transfer-and-delete* technology, the digital first sale doctrine has so far not been enacted into law.

Digital Licensees and the First Sale Doctrine

Another barrier to a digital first sale doctrine arises from the efforts of manufacturers of software or other digital works, who have sought to avoid the first sale doctrine by characterizing transactions as licenses rather than sales. Because the first sale doctrine allows only *owners* of copies to resell—and licensees are not owners—this technique helps prevent customers from reselling on the secondary market. While the legitimacy of using contract law to supersede the statutorily prescribed first sale doctrine has been questioned, courts have often found these licenses valid and enforceable.

International Aspects of the First Sale Doctrine

Outside the U.S., the first sale doctrine is known as the **exhaustion doctrine**, because once the first authorized sale is made the copyright owner's exclusive distribution rights are considered to be exhausted (used up). What happens if the initial sale takes place abroad? In 2013 the Supreme Court held that a Cornell University student named Supap Kirtsaeng, who asked friends and family in Thailand to ship to him over 600 copies of foreign editions of English-language textbooks, could lawfully resell those books in the U.S.[13] Critically, the copies sent had been lawfully made abroad. Had they been pirated copies, importation into the United States would have constituted copyright infringement. The Supreme Court found that importation of these lawfully made copies was permissible even though the copyright page of one of the books stated: "This book is authorized for sale in Europe, Asia, Africa, and the Middle East only and may be not exported out of these territories." The rule announced in *Kirtsaeng* may help to speed the already accelerating transition to digital media, to which the first sale doctrine, so far, does not apply.

Idea-Expression Dichotomy

Copyright protects only "expressions" of ideas and not the ideas themselves. For example, the idea of a computer game where shapes sequentially fall from the top of the screen and must be fit by the player into available spaces below is an unprotectable idea. However, when a defendant developed a Tetris-like game called "Mino" for use on Apple's iPhone, it was held that the defendant had copied not merely the idea of the game, but also the style, shape, design, and movement of the pieces, and therefore had infringed the copyright in Tetris.[14]

---

13. *Kirtsaeng v. John Wiley & Sons, Inc.*, 133 S. Ct. 1351 (2013).
14. *Tetris Holding, LLC v. Xio Interactive, Inc.*, 863 F. Supp. 2d 394 (D.N.J. 2012).

Exhibit 5.10	Direct Infringement: Plaintiff's Prima Facie Case and Defendant's Rebuttal

First, Plaintiff must Prove:	Then, Defendant may Offer a Defense:
1) Plaintiff owns copyright	1) Fair use or other exceptions in Sections 107-122
2) Violation of one or more exclusive rights	2) Other defenses such as: • Independent creation • Authorization from the copyright owner • Running of the statute of limitations • Invalidity of the copyright • Public domain status of the work

Other Limitations to the Exclusive Rights

Unlike the Lanham Act, the Copyright Act includes a number of lengthy and detailed provisions that limit the exclusive rights of copyright owners. These limitations, including fair use and the first sale doctrine just discussed, are set forth in Sections 107-122. In brief, these limitations relate to, among other things:

- Section 107: fair use
- Section 108: exceptions for libraries
- Section 109: first sale doctrine
- Section 110: exceptions for nonprofit classroom education
- Section 114: exceptions for sound recordings
- Section 115: exceptions for musical works
- Section 116: exceptions for jukeboxes
- Section 117: exceptions for software, including the making of backup copies
- Section 120: exceptions for architectural works
- Section 121: exceptions for the creation of Braille versions or other formats for the blind or disabled

Infringement and Defenses

To succeed in an infringement action, a plaintiff must (1) demonstrate ownership of a valid copyright and (2) provide evidence that the defendant has violated at least one of the copyright owner's exclusive rights. In the case of the reproduction right, the copying need not be exact to constitute a violation. Copying which is "substantially similar" will be sufficient. Once the court has received evidence of ownership and violation of an exclusive right, the plaintiff has met its *prima facie* (initial) burden and will prevail unless the defendant can successfully rebut the prima facie case. At this point, the defendant can still avoid liability by presenting a defense, such as by establishing that the copying was a fair use, that the defendant independently created the work, or that the copying occurred with the authorization of the copyright owner. The respective burdens of the plaintiff and defendant in a copyright infringement action are set forth in Exhibit 5.10.

Remedies

Copyright owners who prevail in an infringement action may be able to obtain **damages** (monetary payment) from the defendant. A court may also **enjoin** (prohibit) the defendant from committing further infringement. Under certain circumstances copyright infringers may be subject to criminal prosecution by the government and face fines or imprisonment.

Damages

A court may order a defendant to pay the copyright owner **actual damages**, which can include (1) lost profits the copyright owner would have earned had copyright infringement not occurred and (2) profits of the infringer that are attributable to the infringement. The court in its discretion may also award *attorney fees* and *court costs* to the prevailing party.

Statutory Damages

Sometimes it may be difficult to establish actual damages. The Copyright Act therefore allows copyright owners to collect **statutory damages** in lieu of actual damages. Statutory damages are defined by Section 504 as not less than $750 and not more than $30,000 per infringed work. The court has broad discretion to order damages of any amount within this range, according to the circumstances. In addition, damages may be reduced to $200 where the infringer was not aware of and had no reason to believe that his acts constituted an infringement and may be raised to $150,000 where the infringement was willful. Note that these amounts are *per infringed work*. Thus, for example, willfully downloading 10 songs from the Internet could result in minimum statutory damages of $7,500 (10 x $750) and potentially as much as $1.5 million! Recall that statutory damages are generally available only if the work was registered with the Copyright Office prior to infringement.

Statutory Damages: *Sony BMG v. Tenenbaum*

The statutory damages provisions explain the very large damages requested by plaintiffs and sometimes awarded by courts or juries. In *Sony BMG Music Entertainment v. Tenenbaum*, discussed earlier in this chapter, the jury arrived at the figure of $675,000 by multiplying the 30 songs illegally downloaded by

$22,500, well within the statutory range of damages for willful infringement. The trial judge described the amount of the jury verdict as "unprecedented and oppressive" and reduced the award to $2,250 per work in a process known as *remittitur* (reduction of an excessive jury award). In a 2013 appeal, however, the First Circuit reinstated the jury's verdict.[15] While it may seem that such a large damage award is unconstitutionally excessive under the Due Process Clause, appellate courts have rejected this argument, noting that Congress has broad discretion in setting statutory damages in order to secure adherence to the copyright laws.

Domain Name Registration and Willfulness

Defendants facing a charge of copyright infringement for material posted on a website should be aware that willfulness will be presumed if the defendant provided false contact information to a domain name registrar in connection with the infringement.

Injunctions

Held just during court duration.

A court may, in addition to awarding damages, enjoin the defendant from further infringing conduct. A **permanent injunction** may be issued by the court after a trial. Because litigation can sometimes last several years, however, the court may also issue a **preliminary injunction** at an earlier stage of the litigation if it appears that the plaintiff will likely prevail and certain other conditions are met.

Criminal Liability

Injunctions and damages may result after a private business or individual brings a successful copyright infringement claim. In addition to private enforcement of copyright law, the government may in some cases also prosecute individuals for criminal copyright infringement. If the defendant is convicted, substantial fines and imprisonment can result. Under the **No Electronic Theft Act of 1997 (NET Act)**, criminal penalties can be imposed for willful infringement: *no profit is necessary.*

> if the infringement was committed . . . by the reproduction or distribution, including by electronic means, during any 180-day period, of 1 or more copies or phonorecords of 1 or more copyrighted works, which have a total retail value of more than $1,000. . . .[16]

Prison sentences for first offenses can be as long as five years and can be combined with fines of up to $250,000. Note that the NET Act imposes criminal penalties even where the defendant does not profit from the infringement. The NET Act thereby expands criminal liability to include not only large-scale for-profit activities of organized crime groups but also activities such as file sharing by college students, so long as the requirements of the statute are met.

---

15. *Sony BMG Music Entm't v. Tenenbaum*, 719 F.3d 67 (1st Cir. 2013).
16. 17 U.S.C. § 506; *see also* 18 U.S.C. § 2319 (imprisonment) and 18 U.S.C. § 3571 (fines).

Special Aspects of Online Copyright

Websites

Various elements of websites are subject to copyright protection. Textual material, individual images, and pictures contained on a website may all be separately subject to copyright protection as literary, pictorial, or graphic works. Even where individual elements of a website are in the public domain, the overall selection and arrangement of those elements may be subject to copyright protection. For example, in *Mortgage Market Guide, LLC v. Freedman Report, LLC*,[17] plaintiff Mortgage Market Guide (MMG) had registered a copyright for one of its web pages that presented financial information related to mortgage based securities. The court noted that although the bond prices, trend lines, moving averages, and charts included on the web page were in the public domain, the particular selection and arrangement of the various elements on the website constituted copyrightable expression. The defendant, a competitor of MMG that had copied MMG's web page, was permanently enjoined from further infringement.

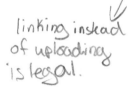
The way the website is unique therefore its protected.

Linking and Deep Linking

Linking to another's website generally will not create liability for copyright infringement. After all, that other party likely created its website intending that Internet users view its content. Similarly, **deep linking** to a subsidiary page of another website is unlikely to create copyright liability in most cases. Nevertheless businesses can reduce risk by seeking permission before linking, by informing users when a link will take them to an unrelated website, and by not linking to sites that contain infringing content.

linking instead of uploading is legal.

In-line Linking, Framing, and Embedding

In-line linking, framing and *embedding* refer to similar processes by which a web page incorporates content from another computer, such as where a YouTube video is embedded in a blog post. In a landmark decision, the Ninth Circuit held that Google's practice of in-line linking and framing copyrighted photographs as part of its image search engine did not violate the copyright owner's right of exclusive public display because the images were transmitted from third party servers rather than from Google servers.[18] A similar result was reached in 2012 with respect to embedded videos.[19]

Creative Commons

The Copyright Act sets forth the maximum extent of a copyright owner's exclusive rights. Copyright owners, however, may sometimes prefer *not* to assert

---

17. No. 06-CV-140-FLW, 2008 WL 2991570 (D.N.J. July 28, 2008).
18. *Perfect 10, Inc. v. Amazon.com, Inc.*, 508 F.3d 1146 (9th Cir. 2007).
19. *Flava Works, Inc. v. Gunter*, 689 F.3d 754 (7th Cir. 2012).

| Exhibit 5.11 | Creative Commons, Conditions for Licensing |

<table>
<tr><td>⊙</td><td>Attribution</td><td>Others may copy, display, distribute, modify, and perform the copyrighted work but must give credit (attribution) to the creator</td></tr>
<tr><td>↻</td><td>Share Alike</td><td>Others may make and distribute derivative works, but only under a license identical to the license governing the copyrighted work</td></tr>
<tr><td>🚫$</td><td>Noncommercial</td><td>Others may copy, display, modify, and perform the work only for non-commercial purposes</td></tr>
<tr><td>=</td><td>No Derivative Works</td><td>Others may copy, distribute, display and perform the work, but may not create derivative works based upon it</td></tr>
</table>

their rights to the maximum extent, and instead may be happy to allow others to use their works under certain conditions. To this end, a nonprofit organization known as **Creative Commons** has developed a way for creators to mark their works to let others know what uses are permitted by the copyright owner. Wikipedia content, for example, is licensed under the Creative Commons Attribution-ShareAlike license. Flickr, and online photo-sharing site, has incorporated Creative Commons licensing options into its user interface, and more than 300 million Flickr images have been licensed under the Creative Commons system. Exhibit 5.11 sets forth the conditions that authors may choose to include in their Creative Commons licenses, as well as the associated symbols.

Music: Two Works, Two Copyrights

The Composition Copyright

Copyright protection for music is especially complicated because there are not one but two types of copyrights that may apply simultaneously to a given song. The musical notes and lyrics created by a composer or songwriter are protected by a **composition copyright**. Like all copyrightable works, these notes and lyrics must be fixed in some tangible medium of expression, for example, by writing them down in the form of sheet music. Section 102 denotes this category of work as a "musical work."

Exhibit 5.12   **Synthesis of § 106 Rights and § 102 Works—Music**

§ 102 Works ↓ \ § 106 Rights →	Reproduce	Prepare derivative works	Distribute	Publicly perform	Publicly display	Publicly perform (digital)
Musical works (the notes & lyrics fixed in, *e.g.*, sheet music)						***
Sound recordings (*e.g.*, songs on a CD)						

*** Digital performance rights are subsumed under the ordinary performance right musical works, but set forth separately for sound recordings because sound recordings do not enjoy the ordinary performance right

The Sound Recording Copyright

It is possible that a musical work will never be performed and recorded by a singer or musician and so only a single copyright, the composition copyright, will exist. If, however, the composition is performed by a musician or group of musicians and this performance is fixed in a CD, digital music file, or other tangible medium of expression by a recording studio, the resulting sound recording will be protected by a separate **sound recording copyright**. The tangible medium of expression in which a sound recording is fixed is known as a "phonorecord" rather than a "copy," and notice of copyright is therefore designated with a "℗" rather than a "©."

Different Rights Associated with Each Music Copyright

You will notice that the two types of music copyrights are associated with different sets of exclusive rights. In particular, the owner of the composition copyright enjoys all of the exclusive rights under Section 106, while the sound recording copyright does not carry with it the right to exclude public performances or displays. The two categories of creative works and corresponding exclusive rights from Exhibit 5.3 have been selected and juxtaposed in Exhibit 5.12 for your convenience.

Copying sheet music would implicate only the composition copyright because only the musical work is being reproduced. Publicly performing a sound recording, on the other hand, would implicate both the composition copyright and the sound recording copyright, because both works are being publicly performed. However, because the owner of a sound recording copyright does not enjoy the right to exclusive public performance (unless it is by means of a "digital audio transmission"), those wishing to publicly perform a sound recording need only obtain a license from the musical work copyright owner.

| Exhibit 5.13 | Music Copyrights and Public Performance |

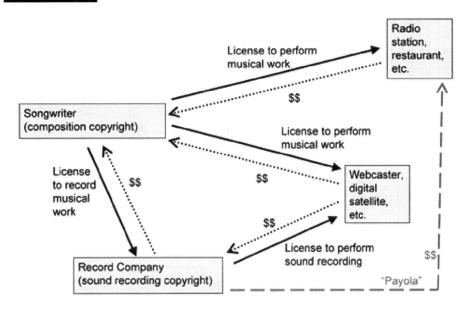

In practice, the differential rights enjoyed by owners of the two different copyrights mean that radio stations, restaurants, shopping malls, or others who wish to publicly perform a sound recording must pay license fees only to the composition copyright owner. The sound recording copyright owner, who does not enjoy rights to exclusive public performance, receives compensation instead through the sale of the sound recording embodied in the form of CDs, digital downloads, or other media. In contrast, those who stream digital music over the Internet, known as **webcasting**, must pay license fees to both the composition copyright owner and the sound recording copyright owner, because both hold the rights to exclusive *digital* performance. This complicated scenario is illustrated in Exhibit 5.13 (intermediaries, such as ASCAP, have been omitted for clarity).

Webcasting and Record Company Revenues

One might wonder why those engaged in online webcasting, which is essentially a type of digital radio station, are treated less favorably than traditional over-the-air radio broadcasts. Some have suggested that the answer lies in the formidable lobbying power of the traditional broadcasting industry, which effectively resisted the creation of a performance right in sound recordings. The incipient webcasting industry, by contrast, was unable to achieve similarly favorable treatment.

Another explanation was embraced by Congress, which pointed to the new and unique threat webcasting posed to the market for sound recordings. Before the advent of the Internet, the playing of songs by radio stations served as a form of advertising for record companies, who could expect to sell more CDs the more a song was played on the radio. In fact, it was once common practice for record companies to contribute **payola** (money) to radio stations to play songs, reversing the expected direction of payment so that it ran from the owner of the copyright to the user of the sound recording! See Exhibit 5.13.

Unlike traditional over-the-air radio broadcasting, however, webcasting threatened to reduce CD sales rather than stimulate them. First, if online listeners were able to record the digital transmissions, they could potentially create perfect digital copies of the music. By contrast, recording a song played over the airwaves on a cassette tape produced a lower quality recording. Second, webcasting created the possibility that listeners could choose to listen to particular songs at particular times. Such "interactive services" threatened to reduce CD sales because listeners who could call up any song at any time through a webcaster were assumed to be less likely to buy a CD.

Digital Performance Right in Sound Recordings Act of 1995

As a result of fears that webcasting would adversely affect the market for owners of sound recordings, Congress passed the **Digital Performance Right in Sound Recordings Act** (**DPRA**) in 1995. The DPRA gave sound recording copyright owners the exclusive right to publicly perform the sound recording by means of a digital audio transmission. This relatively new digital public performance right is reflected in the last column in Exhibits 5.3 and 5.12 and is what underlies the different treatment of traditional radio stations and webcasters illustrated in Exhibit 5.13. Webcasting now generates over $450 million in royalties each year.

Secondary Copyright Liability

Just as online businesses may be held secondarily liable for the trademark infringement of their customers, business must also take care to avoid secondary copyright infringement. **Secondary liability** refers to the imposition of liability on one party based on the direct infringement of another party. For example, in the landmark case of *Fonovisa, Inc. v. Cherry Auction, Inc.*, the Ninth Circuit held the owners of a flea market secondarily liable for sales of counterfeit music recordings made by individual vendors who had rented booths at the flea market.[20]

Types of Secondary Copyright Liability

As with secondary trademark liability, secondary copyright liability can take one of two principal forms. *Contributory liability* arises where one has knowledge of another party's infringing activities and materially contributes to them. *Vicarious liability* occurs when one profits from another's infringement while declining to exercise a right to control or prevent the infringement. In addition a third type of secondary liability known as *inducement liability* occurs where one party

---

20. 76 F.3d 259 (9th Cir. 1996).

Exhibit 5.14 Contributory, Vicarious, and Inducement Liability

Type of Secondary Liability	Elements Needed to Establish Liability
Contributory Liability	• Knowledge of infringing conduct • Material contribution
Vicarious Liability	• Right and ability to control • Financial benefit
Inducement Liability	• Distribution of device (e.g., software) • Affirmative steps taken to foster infringement

---

distributes a device and intentionally encourages others to use it for infringing purposes.[21] For example, the Ninth Circuit has held that maintaining a BitTorrent site, where third parties are encouraged to upload "torrent files" that facilitate the unauthorized downloading of copyrighted movies, gives rise to inducement liability.[22] The three types of secondary liability are summarized in Exhibit 5.14.

Secondary Liability and Transaction Costs

From the perspective of copyright owners, secondary liability is critically important because it avoids the adverse publicity associated with suing end users and greatly reduces copyright owners' enforcement costs. For example, when the Recording Industry Association of America (RIAA) brought suit against tens of thousands of direct infringers for the illegal downloading of music in the middle of the last decade, not only did it risk alienating music fans and the larger public, but it was also forced to incur substantial attorney and administrative costs unlikely to be justified by monies received from judgments and settlements.

In contrast, secondary liability allows copyright owners to stem the direct copyright infringement of thousands or millions of end users via a single suit. Because lawsuits involve significant attorney fees and other transaction costs, secondary liability can therefore dramatically reduce the costs of enforcing owners' rights. Viacom, Paramount Pictures, and other copyright owners chose this approach when they sued YouTube for $1 billion for the enormous volumes of allegedly infringing videos posted and viewed by YouTube users.

Exhibit 5.15 illustrates how secondary liability can greatly reduce the volume of litigation needed to enforce a copyright.

Website Design and Secondary Liability

Even businesses that do not host user content or otherwise engage in Web 2.0 technologies must take care to avoid secondary liability. For example, many

---

21. 545 U.S. 913 (2005).
22. *Columbia Pictures Indus., Inc. v. Fung*, 10 F.3d 1020 (9th Cir. 2013).

| Exhibit 5.15 | **Direct Versus Secondary Liability** |

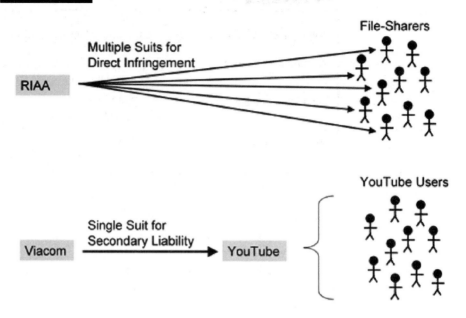

traditional "offline" companies have hired contractors to design and build websites in order to increase visibility and drive business. In *Corbis Corp. v. Starr*,[23] defendant Nick Starr, who operated a janitorial maintenance company, hired an Internet services firm to redesign and host its website. When plaintiff Corbis discovered that its copyrighted images had been included by the Internet services firm in Starr's website without its permission, it filed suit. Although Starr quickly instructed the Internet services firm to remove the infringing images, which it did, Corbis pursued claims against both companies alleging direct and vicarious infringement. Not only did the court find the Internet services firm liable for direct infringement, but it also found Starr liable for vicarious infringement. Starr financially benefited from the infringement because the redesigned website was intended to attract new customers. Moreover, Starr had the right and ability to approve or reject the use of the images.

Website Design: Who Owns the Copyright?

A business that hires an independent contractor to design its website should seek to include within the written contract a provision that assigns all resulting website copyrights to the business. Without such a provision, the copyright may remain with the independent contractor and the business could later be surprised to find that its competitors have been provided with similar websites by the same contractor.

---

23. No. 3:07 CV3741, 2009 WL 2901308 (N.D. Ohio Sept. 2, 2009).

Google

In the previous discussion of the Google Book Project, you learned that a number of libraries entered into agreements that provided Google with access to their holdings. You might be wondering whether the libraries' participation exposed them to the risk of suit for secondary copyright infringement. The answer is that it did. Without access to the libraries' books it would have been impossible for Google to scan them. This provision of required inputs might have constituted "material contribution." Moreover, these libraries knew that Google was intending to reproduce and display at least portions of the books without the author's permission, received free digital copies of the scanned books from Google in return for their cooperation, and had the right to refrain from entering into contracts with Google. These facts could have been marshaled to support either a vicarious or a contributory liability claim. The libraries took one of two approaches to the copyright dimension of the Google Book Project. A group of libraries including Oxford, Princeton, the New York Public Library, and University Complutense (Spain) took a conservative approach and provided Google with permission to scan only those works in their collections that were in the public domain, thereby side-stepping the issue of secondary liability altogether. Another group of libraries, including Cornell, Stanford, the University of California, and the University of Texas-Austin, believing Google's use to be fair, provided access to both public domain works and those that were still in copyright. Google, aware of the libraries' concerns regarding secondary liability, included **indemnification clauses** in its contracts—that is, promises to reimburse the libraries for any copyright liability they incurred as a result of their participation in the Google Book Project.

The Digital Millennium Copyright Act (DMCA)

A Changed Technological Environment

The ability to rapidly and inexpensively distribute perfect copies of digital works is one of the greatest contributions of the Internet, but also means that any person with a computer and an Internet connection can engage in copyright infringement on an unprecedented scale. Before the emergence of the Internet, it was much more time consuming and costly to photocopy books or make analog tapes of music or video, and any copies made would be of a lower quality than the original. Large scale, high quality counterfeiting was effectively limited to those with sophisticated copying equipment and distribution networks. Today, the Internet has dramatically expanded the ability of ordinary individuals—parents, college students, and even children—to commit copyright infringement that would have been difficult or impossible in the past.

Congressional Response: The DMCA

In 1998, the **Digital Millennium Copyright Act (DMCA)** was enacted in response to the dramatic growth in online communication and commerce. The provisions of the DMCA reflect a balancing of two interests. On the one hand, Congress sought to more effectively secure the exclusive rights of copyright owners through anticircumvention provisions. At the same time, Congress provided safe harbors from liability for online service providers, in order to promote the full development and utilization of Internet businesses and technologies. The DMCA enacts into United States law principles established internationally in two 1996 World Intellectual Properly Organization (WIPO) treaties: the WIPO Copyright Treaty and the WIPO Performances and Phonograms Treaty.

Anticircumvention Provisions

The increased threat of copying heralded by the Internet led copyright owners to develop **digital rights management** (**DRM**) systems for controlling certain uses of their copyrighted works. DRM technology may involve encryption or other technological means to limit the ability of users to access, copy, or otherwise use a copyrighted work. For example, a DVD may include technology that makes it difficult to copy the DVD or play it in a DVD player manufactured for use in another country. The DMCA's **anticircumvention** provisions support these privately developed DRM measures by making it illegal to circumvent (get around) them by hacking or similar means.

Antitrafficking Provisions

Most ordinary individuals would be unable to circumvent DRM technology without the aid of software or devices that enable such circumvention. In order to reinforce the anticircumvention provisions, the DMCA's **antitrafficking** provisions make it illegal to manufacture or distribute such devices. For example, movie studios such as Universal, Paramount, and Disney utilize DRM technology known as the Content Scramble System (CSS) to prevent the unauthorized reproduction of DVDs. Software known as DeCSS can be used to defeat CSS, thereby allowing individuals to illegally copy DVDs. The anticircumvention provisions of the DMCA prohibit individual owners of DVDs from using DeCSS to access the DVD content without authorization, while the antitrafficking provisions prohibit the manufacturing or distribution of DeCSS itself.

In the landmark case of *Universal City Studios v. Corley*, the Court of Appeals for the Second Circuit enjoined the defendant both from posting DeCSS on its website and also from knowingly linking to other websites that contained copies of DeCSS.[24] Thus, although linking generally may be unlikely to result in copyright liability, there are circumstances under which linking can constitute an actionable offense under the DMCA. Exhibit 5.16 illustrates how the antitrafficking and anticircumvention provisions might apply to the different activities in *Corley*.

---

24. 273 F.3d 429 (2d Cir. 2001).

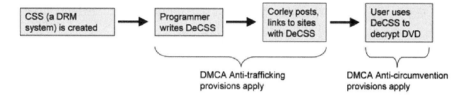

Exhibit 5.16 DMCA Antitrafficking and Anticircumvention Provisions

The Section 512 Safe Harbors

Businesses can help to develop the vast potential of the Internet via the introduction of useful and innovative online services. Prior to the passage of the DMCA, however, several lawsuits against bulletin board operators and others revealed uncertainties over the extent of copyright liability faced by businesses operating online. For example, in *Playboy Enterprises v. Frena*,[25] the court found that a computer bulletin board operator had committed copyright infringement based on infringing images present on his subscription bulletin board system, even though the images had been uploaded by users and the operator had removed them as soon as he became aware of the matter.

Because businesses may be reluctant to invest in new business models where copyright liability is uncertain, Congress provided online service providers (OSPs) a series of safe harbors from copyright infringement liability in the DMCA. A **safe harbor** is a provision in the law that provides protection from liability for certain activities so long as the required conditions are met.

Activities Protected Under the DMCA Safe Harbors

Section 512 of the DMCA provides protection from liability for four types of online activities: (1) routing and transmission; (2) caching; (3) hosting of content uploaded by users; and (4) providing information location tools (e.g., search engines). These four protected activities are discussed below.

Routing and Transmission. Under the routing and transmission safe harbor, OSPs will be protected from liability for serving as passive conduits of the communications of others. Entities protected under this exemption might be analogized to telephone companies, which will not be held liable if telephone customers use their phone lines to transmit infringing content. For example, in *Ellison v. Robertson,* the Ninth Circuit found that America Online (AOL) qualified for the DMCA's routing and transmission safe harbor when it served as a conduit for a newsgroup through which infringing materials were exchanged.[26]

25. 839 F. Supp. 1552 (M.D. Fla. 1993).
26. 357 F.3d 1072 (9th Cir. 2004).

Caching. Caching refers to the intermediate and temporary storage of recently accessed digital content. For example, Google accesses the web pages of others and stores them in its cache (temporary computer memory) as part of the process of providing Internet search results. Since 1998, Google's search engine has provided links to view not only pages in their current form from their original sources, but also a link labeled "Cached" (visible by clicking the green arrow below the search result) that users may select to view the older cached version of pages that are copied and stored by Google. The display by Google of cached pages has been held to fall within the DMCA safe harbor.[27]

Hosting of Content Uploaded by Users. Perhaps the most important and most frequently litigated safe harbor under the DMCA relates to the hosting of content uploaded by users. This safe harbor provides an exemption from copyright infringement liability for Web 2.0 OSPs. You may recall from the previous chapter that the term Web 2.0 has been used to refer to services such as those provided by Facebook, eBay, YouTube, and others that involve the exchange of content between large numbers of users. The DMCA provides that online providers of Web 2.0 services will not be liable for the copyright infringement of their users, so long as certain conditions are met. For example, in *Hendrickson v. Amazon.com*[28] Amazon was found to qualify for this DMCA safe harbor after the owner of the copyrighted movie "Manson" sued for copyright infringement based on the unauthorized sale of a copy of Manson by a third party using Amazon's website.

Providing Information Location Tools. The final safe harbor provided under the DMCA shelters information location tools such as search engines or Internet directories from copyright infringement liability. Despite the exemption, a number of suits have been brought against Google based on its various search tools. Although those suits have frequently been unsuccessful, they serve as a reminder that the Section 512 safe harbors may reduce risk and uncertainty but cannot eliminate the possibility of suit.

Qualifying for the Safe Harbors

In order to qualify for any of the four safe harbors-routing and transmission, caching, hosting of third party content, and providing information location tools—online service providers must meet the detailed requirements of Section 512. To complicate matters, the requirements differ for each safe harbor. In general, however, the activities of an OSP will fall within the protections of the DMCA safe harbors only if the OSP:

- **Qualifies as an Online Service Provider (OSP).** An OSP is broadly defined by the statute to include virtually any entity engaged in the

27. *Field v. Google, Inc.*, 412 F. Supp. 2d 1106 (D. Nev. 2006).
28. 298 F. Supp. 2d 914 (C.D. Cal. 2003).

provision of online services or network access. Court decisions have established that YouTube, eBay, Amazon, and Google constitute OSPs under one or more of the DMCA safe harbors.

- **Adopts a Termination Policy for Repeat Infringers.** OSPs must adopt a policy by which the accounts of users who repeatedly engage in copyright infringement will be terminated and must inform account holders of this policy.

- **Does Not Interfere with "Standard Technical Measures."** OSPs must accommodate and not interfere with **standard technical measures**— technological measures used by copyright owners to identify copyrighted works and protect them from infringement. For example, in 2012 a Web 2.0 photo-sharing service known as Photobucket successfully availed itself of the DMCA safe harbor after an artist discovered unauthorized versions of her artwork on its site. Although Photobucket provided image editing tools that could allegedly be used to remove **digital watermarks**—a type of standard technical measure that can be embedded in digital works and used to trace the origin of the work—the court held that provision of the editing tools did not constitute "interference" because they were used to remove watermarks, if at all, by users and not by Photobucket.[29]

In addition to these requirements, OSPs seeking to benefit from the content hosting and information location tool safe harbors must:

- **Not Have Knowledge of Infringing Activity.** OSPs seeking to benefit from the content hosting and information location tool safe harbors must not be aware of infringement, or must remove infringing content expeditiously once infringing activity becomes known. This requirement incorporates one of the elements of contributory liability.

- **Not Receive a Direct Financial Benefit.** OSPs seeking to benefit from the content hosting and information location tool safe harbors must not receive a financial benefit directly attributable to the infringing activity where the OSP has the right and ability to control the activity. This requirement incorporates the elements of vicarious liability.

In the case below, the Second Circuit had to decide whether YouTube qualified for this safe harbor, or whether it had failed to act as required under the statute and would be liable for as much as $1 billion based on the infringing videos posted by its users.

---

29. *Wolk v. Kodak Imaging Network, Inc.*, 840 F. Supp. 2d 724 (S.D.N.Y. 2012).

Viacom Int'l Inc. v. YouTube, Inc.
676 F.3d 19 (2d Cir. 2012)

Cabranes, Circuit Judge

Facts YouTube [is] a consumer media company that allows people to watch, upload, and share personal video clips at www.YouTube.com. . . . By March 2010 . . . site traffic on YouTube had soared to more than 1 billion daily video views, with more than 24 hours of new video uploaded to the site every minute. The basic function of the YouTube website permits users to upload and view video clips free of charge . . . . During the upload process, YouTube makes one or more exact copies of the video in its original file format. YouTube also makes one or more additional copies of the video in "Flash" format, a process known as "transcoding." . . .

Plaintiff Viacom, an American media conglomerate, and various Viacom affiliates filed suit against YouTube on March 13, 2007, alleging direct and secondary copyright infringement based on the public performance, display, and reproduction of their audiovisual works on the YouTube website . . . .

Background [The DMCA] established a series of four "safe harbors" that allow qualifying service providers to limit their liability for claims of copyright infringement based on (a) "transitory digital network communications," (b) "system caching," (c) "information residing on systems or networks at [the] direction of users," and (d) "information location tools."

The § 512(c) safe harbor [i.e., storage of content at the direction of a user] will apply only if the service provider:

> (A) (i) does not have actual knowledge [of infringement];
> > (ii) . . . is not aware of facts or circumstances from which infringing activity is apparent; or
> > (iii) upon obtaining such knowledge or awareness, acts expeditiously to remove, . . . the material; [and]

> (B) does not receive a financial benefit directly attributable to the infringing activity, in a case in which the service provider has the right and ability to control such activity; . . .

Knowledge or Awareness . . . [K]nowledge or awareness alone does not disqualify the service provider; rather, the provider that gains knowledge or awareness of infringing activity retains safe-harbor protection if it "acts expeditiously to remove . . . the material." . . . Viacom cites evidence that YouTube employees conducted website surveys and estimated that 75–80% of all YouTube streams contained copyrighted material. . . . Th[is] approximation suggest[s] that the defendants were conscious that significant quantities of material on the YouTube website were infringing. But such estimates are insufficient, standing alone, to create a triable issue of fact as to whether YouTube actually knew, or was aware of facts or circumstances that would indicate, the existence of particular instances of infringement.

Beyond the survey results, the plaintiffs rely upon internal YouTube communications that do refer to particular clips or groups of clips . . . . For instance, YouTube founder Jawed Karim prepared a report in March 2006 which stated that, "[a]s of today[,] episodes and clips of the following well-known shows can still be found [on YouTube]: Family Guy, South Park, MTV Cribs, Daily Show, Reno 911, [and] Dave Chapelle [sic]." . . . [I]n a July 4, 2005 e-mail exchange, YouTube founder Chad Hurley sent an e-mail to his co-founders with the subject line "budlight commercials," and stated, "we need to reject these too." Steve Chen [another founder] responded, "can we please leave these in a bit longer? another week or two can't hurt." . . .

Upon a review of the record, we are persuaded that the plaintiffs may have raised a material issue of fact regarding YouTube's knowledge or awareness of specific instances of infringement. . . . We hasten to note, however, that although the foregoing e-mails were annexed as exhibits to the summary judgment papers, it is unclear whether the clips referenced therein are among the current clips-in-suit. We vacate the order granting summary judgment and instruct the District Court to determine on remand whether any specific infringements of which YouTube had knowledge or awareness correspond to the clips-in-suit in these actions.

Control and Benefit Apart from the foregoing knowledge provisions, the § 512(c) safe harbor provides that an eligible service provider must "not receive a financial benefit directly attributable to the infringing activity, in a case in which the service provider has the right and ability to control such activity." . . . [T]he "right and ability to control" infringing activity under § 512(c)(1)(B) "requires something more than the ability to remove or block access to materials posted on a service provider's website." . . . We think it prudent to remand to the District Court to consider in the first instance whether the plaintiffs have adduced sufficient evidence to allow a reasonable jury to conclude that YouTube had the right and ability to control the infringing activity and received a financial benefit directly attributable to that activity

By Reason of Storage at the Direction of a User The § 512(c) safe harbor is only available when the infringement occurs "by reason of the storage at the direction of a user . . . [and] extends to software functions performed for the purpose of facilitating access to user-stored material. [YouTube's software functions include] [t]ranscoding, [which] involves making copies of a video in a different encoding scheme in order to render the video viewable over the Internet to most users. [YouTube's] playback process involves delivering copies of YouTube videos to a user's browser cache in response to a user request. The District Court correctly found that to exclude these automated functions from the safe harbor would eviscerate the protection afforded to service providers by § 512(c). A similar analysis applies to the "related videos" function, by which a YouTube computer algorithm identifies and displays thumbnails of clips that are related to the video selected by the user. . . . The record makes clear that the related videos algorithm is fully automated and operates solely in response to user input without the active involvement of YouTube employees.

The final software function at issue here—third-party syndication—is the closest case. In or around March 2007, YouTube transcoded a select number of videos into a format compatible with mobile devices and "syndicated" or licensed the videos to Verizon Wireless and other companies. The plaintiffs argue—with some force—that business transactions do not occur at the "direction of a user" within the meaning of § 512(c)(1) when they involve the manual selection of copyrighted material for licensing to a third party. The parties do not dispute, however, that none of the clips-in-suit were among the approximately 2,000 videos provided to Verizon Wireless. . . . [W]e remand for fact-finding on the question of whether any of the clips-in-suit were in fact syndicated to any other third party.

CONCLUSION

[W]e vacate the order denying summary judgment to the plaintiffs and remand . . . .

Case Questions

1. If a service provider is aware of infringing activities, does this mean it will be excluded from the DMCA § 512(c) safe harbor?
2. The court cites evidence that YouTube founder Steve Chen was aware that Bud Light commercials had been posted to YouTube and deliberately sought to leave them on the site for "another week or two." Does this mean that YouTube will be excluded from the safe harbor?
3. *Ethical Consideration:* What duty should OSPs such as YouTube that host content uploaded by others owe to copyright holders? Should such OSPs be required to "police" their websites to detect and prevent copyright infringement?

Summary

A great deal of online content is protected under the Copyright Act, including web pages, music, movies, and software. Indeed, because notice and registration are not required in order to secure copyright protection, it is prudent to assume that any content a business did not itself create is subject to the exclusive rights of others, unless the business has a particular reason to believe otherwise. These exclusive rights include the right to reproduce, prepare derivative works, distribute, publicly display, and publicly perform a copyrighted work. The broad reach of the exclusive rights is tempered by the limited duration of copyrights, the ability of the public to make fair use of copyrighted works without the permission of the copyright owner, and the ability to resell particular copies of works under the first sale doctrine. These and numerous other complex and detailed exceptions to the exclusive rights are provided in Sections 107-122 of the Copyright Act. A nonprofit organization known as Creative Commons offers a simple licensing scheme that copyright owners may use to give permission to others to use their copyrighted works.

The Internet has dramatically expanded the ability of the public to copy and distribute copyrighted works. Congress responded by enacting the Digital Millennium Copyright Act (DMCA), which prohibits the circumvention of technological measures that copyright owners use to prevent unauthorized access to copyrighted works. In addition, the DMCA's antitrafficking provisions prohibit the manufacture or distribution of devices designed to facilitate unauthorized access to or use of copyrighted works. In order to reduce uncertainty and promote the development of online businesses, the DMCA includes four safe harbor provisions that protect businesses from liability for certain online activities, such as passive routing and transmission, system caching, hosting of third party content, and providing information location services. In order to benefit from these safe harbors, OSPs must meet the detailed requirements of Section 512, which generally require good faith efforts to cooperate with copyright owners to reduce third party infringement.

Key Terms

Copyright Act of 1976 The principal federal enactment of copyright law.

natural rights The natural rights justification of intellectual property emphasizes a person's inherent connection with the fruits of that person's creative labor and views it as unfair to allow others to copy the creator's works without compensation.

utilitarian The utilitarian justification of intellectual property views copyright primarily as a means to promote overall public welfare through the stimulation and dissemination of creative works.

Intellectual Property Clause The provision within the U.S. Constitution that provides the basis for federal patent and copyright laws.

piracy The act of copying of a work with little or no pretense that the copying is lawful.

Recording Industry Association of America (RIAA) An association of record labels that opposes the unauthorized sharing of its members' music.

derivative works Works of expression derived from other works, such as adaptations or translations.

American Society of Composers, Authors, and Publishers (ASCAP) One of three major performing rights societies in the United States that licenses public performance rights on behalf of the copyright owners of musical works.

work made for hire A work prepared by an employee within the scope of employment.

Sonny Bono Copyright Term Extension Act (CTEA) A 1998 law that extended the copyright term by 20 years.

public domain Works for which a copyright have expired are said to have fallen into the public domain and may be used freely by anyone.

fair use A provision in the copyright law that permits unauthorized copying when the use is "fair," as determined by a flexible four-factor test.

orphan works Works still under copyright for which the copyright owner cannot be easily identified or located.

first sale doctrine An exception to the exclusive rights of a patent or copyright owner, by which the owner of a particular copy of a copyrighted work or patented invention may resell or otherwise dispose of that copy or invention without the permission of the copyright or patent owner.

digital first sale doctrine A proposed expansion of the first sale doctrine that would allow the doctrine to apply to digital works.

exhaustion doctrine The term used outside the United States to refer to the first sale doctrine.

prima facie An initial showing made by one litigant that shifts the burden of moving forward to the other litigant.

damages An award, typically monetary, paid to compensate for loss or injury.

enjoin To prohibit.

actual damages Either (1) lost profits the copyright owner would have earned had copyright infringement not occurred or (2) profits of the infringer that are attributable to the infringement.

statutory damages Damages provided in the copyright act of $750 to not more than $30,000 per infringed work.

remittitur Reduction by a judge of an excessive jury award.

injunction, permanent An order of a court prohibiting a party from engaging in some action, after a final judgment.

injunction, preliminary An order of a court prohibiting a party from engaging in some action, prior to a final judgment.

No Electronic Theft (NET) Act A federal law that authorizes criminal penalties for willful copyright infringement.

deep linking Linking to a subsidiary page of the trademark owner's site rather than to its homepage.

Creative Commons A nonprofit organization that has developed a way for creators to mark their works to let others know what uses are permitted by the copyright owner.

composition copyright (music) The copyright covering the musical notes and lyrics created by a composer or songwriter.

sound recording copyright (music) The copyright covering the recorded performance of a musical composition (as distinct from the composition itself).

webcasting The streaming of digital music over the Internet.

payola Money that was once paid by record companies to radio stations to play the record companies' songs.

Digital Performance Right in Sound Recordings Act (DPRA) A 1995 law that gave sound recording copyright owners the exclusive right to publicly perform the sound recording by means of a digital audio transmission.

secondary liability The imposition of liability on one party based on the direct infringement of another party.

indemnification clauses Promises by one party to reimburse another party for liability costs.

Digital Millennium Copyright Act (DMCA) A 1998 law that created safe harbors from liability for online service providers, while also prohibiting the circumvention of digital rights management systems and also the trafficking in circumvention devices.

anticircumvention provisions Provisions of the DMCA that make it illegal to circumvent (get around) digital rights management systems by hacking or similar means.

digital rights management (DRM) Encryption or other technological means to limit the ability of users to access, copy, or otherwise use a copyrighted work.

antitrafficking provisions Provisions of the DMCA that make it illegal to manufacture or distribute devices that enable the circumvention of digital rights management systems.

safe harbors A provision in the law that provides protection from liability for certain activities so long as the required conditions are met.

caching The intermediate and temporary storage of recently accessed digital content.

standard technical measures Technological measures used by copyright owners to identify copyrighted works and protect them from infringement.

digital watermarks A type of standard technical measure that can be embedded in digital works and used to trace the origin of the work.

Manager's Checklist

1. Place a copyright notice (e.g. "© 2011 ABC Corp.") on any works, such as a web page, to inform others that the work is copyrighted; or, use a Creative Commons license to let others know what uses you are authorizing.

2. Register your works, including websites, with the Copyright Office in order to secure benefits such as the ability to obtain statutory damages.

3. Create your own works; don't copy other websites or incorporate the copyrighted works of others without permission.

4. Do not link to websites that contain infringing content.

5. Work with your attorney to ensure compliance with the requirements of Section 512 to ensure protection within the DMCA safe harbor.

Questions and Case Problems

1. It is common practice for recipients of email messages to sometimes forward those messages to others. *Does such forwarding constitute copyright infringement?* In your answer, be sure to specify which, if any, of the exclusive rights may have been violated by the act of forwarding and whether the doctrine of fair use applies. *What remedies, if any, might a successful plaintiff be able to obtain?*

2. Amazon's Kindle is an electronic book reader that allows users to download and read in electronic format any of more than 1,700,000 books and other titles. A special text-to-speech feature allows users to hear the books read aloud by the Kindle in an electronic voice. Suppose you are an author whose books are available for download to the Kindle. *Can you think of any reasons why you might oppose the text-to-speech feature? What markets for your work, if any, might be adversely affected? If you wanted to prevent Amazon from including the text-to-speech feature, what arguments can you make that the feature violates copyright law?*

3. Plaintiff Leslie Kelly, a professional photographer who has copyrighted many of his images of the American West, licenses those images to other websites. The defendant is Arriba Soft Corp., an Internet search engine that displays its results in the form of small pictures. Arriba copied 35 of Kelly's images to its database without Kelly's permission and used them on its website so users could click on those small picture "thumbnails" to view a large version of the picture. When Kelly discovered this, he brought suit against the defendant for copyright infringement. *What critical factors are analyzed in determining whether use in a particular case is a fair use? Decide if Arriba Soft's use of the pictures is a fair use.*[30]

4. If you have ever read the small print accompanying a purchase of a box of software, you may have noticed that purchase transactions are often characterized as "licenses" rather than "sales." If they are sales, then the first sale doctrine allows the buyer to resell the software to third parties. As noted in the text, courts have often upheld such contract terms, finding the transaction to constitute a license. But not always. In *Vernor v. Autodesk*,[31] a district court

---

30. *Kelly v. Arriba Soft Corp.*, 336 F.3d 811 (9th Cir. 2003).
31. 555 F. Supp. 2d 1164 (W.D. Wash. 2008), *rev'd*, 621 F.3d 1102 (9th Cir. 2010).

held that when Autodesk, Inc. transferred a physical copy of its AutoCAD software to a transferee, the purported license was actually a sale. As a result, Vernor (a transferee) could resell his copies on eBay. The court described as a "critical factor" in its decision the fact that Autodesk did not require the transferee to return the software. *If you were Autodesk, why might you not want copies of AutoCAD resold on eBay? Would you require transferees to return the software in order to ensure the transfer was characterized as a license?*

5. ***Ethical Consideration:*** Recall that the Google Book Project required the cooperation of a number of university and other libraries to contribute the books that would be scanned by Google. If you were a university library and Google asked for access to your holdings, would you agree to help facilitate the copying of copyrighted works, in addition to the copying of those in the public domain? Is it ethical to do so? *Are there any reasons it may be unethical to decline to assist Google?*

Additional Resources

Creative Commons. http://creativecommons.org.

Brown, Elizabeth. *Bridging the Gap: Improving Intellectual Property Protection for the Look and Feel of Websites*, NYU Journal of IP & Entertainment Law (2014).

Darrow, Jonathan J., and Gerald R. Ferrera. *Who Owns a Decedent's E-Mails? Inheritable Probate Assets or Property of the Network?*, 10 NYU Journal of Legislation & Public Policy 281 (2007).

Harvard University, Berkman Center for Internet and Society. http://cyber.law.harvard.edu.

Herman, Bill D. The Fight Over Digital Rights: The Politics of Copyright and Technology (Cambridge University Press 2014).

United States Copyright Office. http://www.copyright.gov.

World Intellectual Property Organization (WIPO). http://www.wipo.int.

 I now believe it's possible that the current rules governing business method and software patents could end up harming all of us—including Amazon.com and its many shareholders. . . .

—Jeff Bezos, CEO of Amazon.com (2000)

 [I]t is a fact, as far as I am informed, that England was, until we copied her, the only country on earth which ever, by a general law, gave a legal right to the exclusive use of an idea. In some other countries it is sometimes done, in a great case, and by a special and personal act, but, generally speaking, other nations have thought that these monopolies produce more embarrassment than advantage to society; and it may be observed that the nations which refuse monopolies of invention, are as fruitful as England in new and useful devices.

—Thomas Jefferson (1813)

Patents

6

Learning Outcomes

After you have read this chapter, you should be able to:

● Explain what a patent is and how it differs from a copyright.
● Explain the five major requirements for patentability.
● Describe the different types of patents.
● Provide examples of Internet-related technologies or business methods that may be protected by patents.

Overview

The dramatic growth of the Internet over the last two decades has been accompanied by an equally dramatic increase in the number of Internet-related patents. Although not a statutorily defined category, Internet patents provide exclusive rights to the hardware, software, and business methods that enable the Internet to function. For example, patents have been issued on methods of conducting online auctions, connecting people in online social networks, ranking search results, responding automatically to email messages, and gaming via the use of avatars.

Software companies and other online businesses have amassed large portfolios of patents which they acquired in the hope of achieving or maintaining an advantageous market position. For example, International Business Machines (IBM), which owns more U.S. patents than any other organization, obtained an average of more than 6,000 patents per year between 2011 and 2013. Also topping the list is Samsung, which increased its annual patent acquisitions from 97 in 1996 to

4,652 in 2013. To put these impressive figures in perspective, renowned innovators such as 3M and Apple obtained 509 patents and 1775 patents in 2013, respectively. Although patents have long been sought after by the most innovative companies, the race to acquire Internet-related patents has been especially intense since the landmark 1998 opinion of *State Street v. Signature Corp.* opened the floodgates to an important and controversial category of patents known as business method patents, which allow companies to obtain exclusive rights to methods of doing business (often by automating processes with the use of a computer). Business method patents will be explored below.

During the last five years, both Congress and the Supreme Court have been particularly active in considering some of the pressing issues in patent law in the context of a rapidly changing business environment. In this chapter you will explore the basic features of patents, study examples of how patents are being asserted in the online context, and examine several of the Supreme Court's recent pronouncements in the field of patents.

What is a Patent?

A **patent** is a government-granted, temporary *right to exclude*, awarded in return for an individual's public disclosure of a new and useful invention. In the United States, patents are granted by the U.S. Patent & Trademark Office (USPTO) and last for a nonrenewable term of 20 years. (Two less common types of patents, discussed later in the chapter, are plant patents and design patents, which last for terms of 20 years and 14 years, respectively.)

Exclusive Rights: Independent Invention Is Not an Excuse

Patent owners enjoy the temporary right to exclude others from engaging in any of the following activities with respect to their inventions:

- Making
- Using
- Selling (or offering to sell)
- Importing into the United States

Although the patent term is much shorter than the copyright term, the exclusive rights of the patent owner are broader than those of the copyright owner. For example, while copyrights are limited by a generous fair use doctrine, patents are not subject to any comparably broad exception. Similarly, while independent creation of a copyrighted work is a defense to a copyright infringement action, independent invention is *not* a defense to a patent infringement action. The right to exclude others from making a patented invention can be used to block even those who later independently invent the same invention without knowledge of the earlier patent.

The fact that independent invention is not a valid defense to a patent infringement action means that online businesses must be aware of others' patent rights even if they do not copy other companies' business methods or technologies. For example, in 2002 Friendster launched its pioneering social networking website and became an early leader in a phenomenon that accelerated throughout the decade. Although it was eventually eclipsed in popularity by Facebook, Friendster nevertheless succeeded in obtaining a number of patents between 2006 and 2009, including one entitled "System, Method and Apparatus for Connecting Users in an Online Computer System Based on Their Relationships Within Social Networks."[1] Even if Facebook did not copy Friendster in designing and implementing its online business, it nevertheless faced liability risk for infringing one or more of these patents by independently inventing the same patented subject matter. Facing strong competition, Friendster repositioned itself as a social gaming site in 2011 and Facebook strengthened its strategic position by acquiring seven of Friendster's patents and eleven of its patent applications.

Patents Confer "Negative Rights"

It is a common misconception that patents provide patent owners with the affirmative right to make or practice an invention. In fact, patents confer only "negative rights" to *exclude others* from making, using, selling, offering to sell, or importing an invention.

To illustrate, suppose Inventor 1 invents and patents a pencil. Inventor 2, seeking to improve the pencil, adds a rubber eraser to the tip of the pencil and patents the combination of a pencil with a rubber tip. Inventor 1 cannot make the pencil with the rubber tip because Inventor 2 has a patent on this combination. Note also, however, that Inventor 2 cannot make his own invention of a pencil with the rubber tip because Inventor 1's patent on the pencil itself precludes him from doing so. In this scenario, illustrated in Exhibit 6.1, the improvement patent ("Pencil/Eraser Patent") would be known as a **blocking patent** because it blocks the first inventor from making the improved version (pencil with a rubber tip) of that inventor's own invention.

Licensing and Cross-Licensing

Because virtually all inventions build to some extent on earlier inventions, blocking patents are quite common. Of course, patent owners are not required to use their patents to prevent others from making, using, or selling their inventions. In some cases, the patent owner may instead wish to **license** (allow) another party to practice the invention, usually in return for **royalties** (money) or some other form of compensation.

Licensing is particularly important in the software and information technology industries, where large firms may hold hundreds or even thousands of patents that could potentially block each other's new technologies. To address this

---

1. U.S. Patent No. 7,069,308 (filed June 16, 2003).

Exhibit 6.1   **Blocking Patents and Negative Rights**

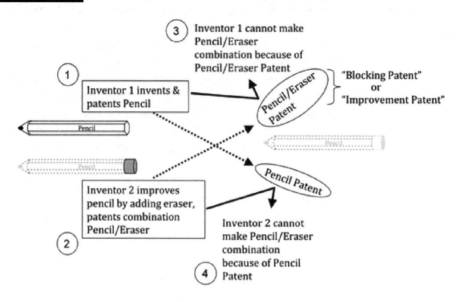

problem, industry players commonly engage in **cross-licensing**, whereby each party to the cross-licensing agreement is permitted to make, use, or sell the inventions protected by the other party's patents. Cross-licensing can be viewed as a less costly alternative to litigation and provides firms with room to innovate without fear of inadvertently infringing on the other party's patents. In 2014, for example, Twitter acquired 900 of IBM's patents and the parties entered into a cross-licensing agreement for an undisclosed amount that Twitter described as providing "freedom . . . to innovate."

Obtaining a Patent

Like trademarks, patents can be obtained by application to the USPTO. Unlike copyright and trademark rights, however, no patent rights arise until the USPTO grants the patent. In fact, publicly using, selling, or publicizing an invention without timely submitting a patent application can serve to bar later patenting by anyone, including the inventor.

Patent Prosecution

Inventors will normally hire a patent attorney to **prosecute** (apply for) the patent on behalf of the inventor. Note that the term "prosecute" is used in a different sense in patent law than it is in the context of criminal law, where "prosecution" refers to the bringing of an action by the government against an alleged criminal. Patent prosecution may last several years while a USPTO agent known as a **patent examiner** ensures that the invention described in the application meets the statutorily defined standards of patentability. Patent examination is much more

Exhibit 6.2	**U.S. Patent Grants, by U.S. and Foreign Ownership**

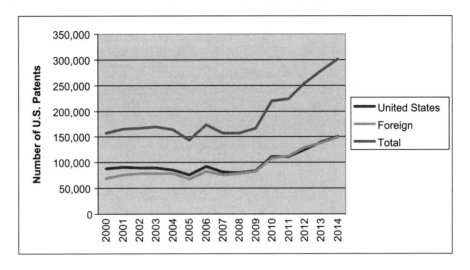

rigorous and therefore much more expensive and time consuming than copyright or trademark examination. Inventions are kept secret for a period of 18 months, after which time they are generally published and thereby made available to anyone. If the examiner determines the invention to be patentable, the patent will **issue** (be granted) and the inventor may at that point enforce the patent against others.

Despite the common image of the lone inventor toiling away in a garage or basement, more than 93 percent of United States patents issued between 2011 and 2014 were owned by corporations. Moreover, about 50 percent of U.S. patents issued during this period were owned by foreign entities, a figure that has been gradually increasing over the last several decades. In turn, individuals and businesses from the United States own many patents in other countries. See Exhibit 6.2.

Appeal from an Examiner's Adverse Decision

Sometimes a patent examiner will determine that an invention is not patentable. When this occurs, the inventor may choose to appeal the examiner's adverse decision to the Patent Trial and Appeal Board (PTAB), and if necessary seek further review in a specialized federal appeals court known as the Court of Appeals for the Federal Circuit (CAFC), often known simply as the **Federal Circuit**. The Federal Circuit hears both appeals originating from the applications rejected by the USPTO as well as appeals from district court patent decisions throughout the country.

Patent Searching

Individuals and businesses may search both issued patents and published applications at the USPTO website, http://www.uspto.gov, as well as via Google's patent search tool at http://www.google.com/patents. Note that, with some exceptions,

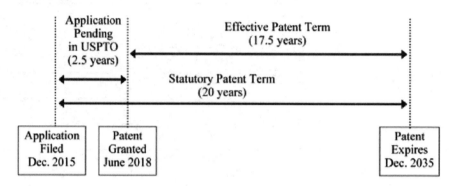

Exhibit 6.3 Patent Duration for Hypothetical Application Filed in 2015

patent applications pending for 18 months are published and therefore available to the public whether or not the patent eventually issues. Because publication creates a risk of piracy notwithstanding any patent rights that are eventually granted, businesses may sometimes wish to forgo patent protection in favor of trade secret protection, a topic that will be explored in the next chapter.

Patent Duration

Patents last for a nonrenewable term of 20 years—far shorter than copyrights, which may persist for 120 years or even longer. While the 20-year term begins to run from the date the patent application is filed with the USPTO, the patent owner may not assert the right to exclude until the patent actually issues. Because most patent applications take two or more years to undergo examination before they issue, the effective term may therefore be somewhat less than 20 years. Exhibit 6.3 illustrates how the patent term might play out for a patent application filed in December of 2015 that remained pending for two and a half years before issuing as a patent.

A Shorter Duration for Internet Patents?

Even the relatively short term of patents has sometimes received criticism as unnecessarily long. In 2000, Amazon.com's CEO Jeff Bezos made headlines when he published an open letter in which he recommended a much shorter three- to five-year term for Internet and software patents. Bezos' comments came as Amazon was embroiled in litigation with Barnes & Noble over Amazon's notorious "1-click" patent, which allowed Internet purchases to be made with a single click of the mouse. Critics claimed that the patented 1-click method was not an invention but instead an obvious variation of existing practices. Bezos, who was one of four named inventors on the patent in question, defended Amazon's right to assert its patent but believed that the existing patent term was too long and might even retard development of the Internet (see the opening chapter epigraph, which is excerpted from Bezos' letter). You will read an excerpt from the court opinion in *Amazon v. BarnesAndNoble* later in the chapter.

Although Congress has acknowledged the need for patent reform, as in the America Invents Act of 2011, it is highly unlikely that it will adopt a shorter patent term for Internet patents in light of the United States' international treaty obligations. In particular, more than 160 countries (including the United States) have agreed to a minimum patent term of 20 years for inventions in all fields of technology as required by the international Agreement on Trade-Related Aspects of Intellectual Property Rights (TRIPS) (see Chapter 14). Even in the absence of the TRIPS agreement, providing a different patent term for Internet patents would require a precise definition of what constitutes an "Internet patent" and could result in additional litigation regarding how a given invention should be classified.

Patent Duration, 1790 to the Present

The strong public reaction to the 1-click patent and Amazon's surprising response are indicative of the critical importance of patent duration to the continued evolution of the Internet. In fact, perhaps the most significant limitation on the exclusive rights of a patent owner, once a patent is granted, is the limited patent term.

Although the patent term has lengthened since the first patent act in 1790, the increases have been modest compared to the copyright extensions explored in the last chapter. Pursuant to the Constitution's Intellectual Property Clause, Congress enacted the first patent statute in 1790, which authorized patents for up to 14 years. In 1836, Congress provided for a single seven-year extension to the original 14-year term, but only if the inventor had "failed to obtain ... a reasonable remuneration for the time, ingenuity, and expense" devoted to the invention. The term was changed to a fixed 17-year nonrenewable term in 1861, a compromise between the 21-year period favored by some and the 14-year period favored by others. The 17-year patent term endured for over 130 years, until it was changed in 1995 to its present term of 20 years, measured from the date of filing. See Exhibit 6.4.

Patent Fees

Obtaining and maintaining a patent is expensive. The initial fees associated with filing an application with the USPTO total $1,600. If an examiner determines that an invention is patentable, a fee of $960 must be paid to the USPTO before the patent will issue. Since 1980, **maintenance fees** have been required in order to enjoy the full patent term. Fees must be paid to the USPTO at 3.5 years ($1600), 7.5 years ($3,600), and 11.5 years ($7,400) after the patent issues. Because patent fees change regularly, interested parties should consult the current fee schedule at http://www.uspto.gov.

Most fees can be reduced for applicants who meet certain size requirements. "Small entities," including individual inventors, nonprofit organizations, and businesses with fewer than 500 employees, pay 50% of the full fee rate. In addition,

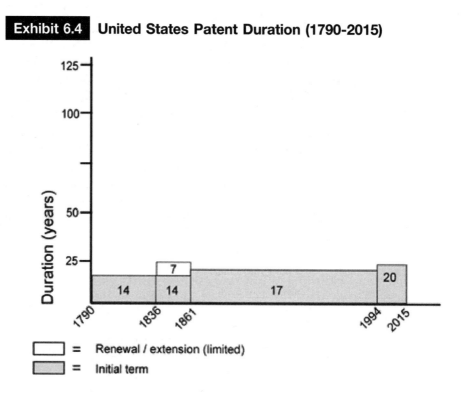

Exhibit 6.4   **United States Patent Duration (1790-2015)**

the 2011 Leahy-Smith America Invents Act created a new category of "micro entities," defined as applicants who have previously filed four or fewer patent applications and whose gross income does not exceed three times the median household income, which pay only 25% of the full fee rate.

The largest expense of prosecuting and maintaining a patent, however, consists of attorney fees. When attorney fees are added to the USPTO fees, the cost of obtaining a patent, not including maintenance payments, ranges from approximately $10,000 to $50,000. The exact cost will depend on a number of variables such as the type of technology involved, the number of variations to the invention sought to be patented, and the hourly rate and efficiency of the attorney prosecuting the patent application.

Maintenance Fees and Patent Duration

If maintenance fees are not timely paid, the patent may lapse and the invention will fall into the public domain. Research indicates that the second maintenance fee is paid for approximately two-thirds of patents, while the third maintenance fee is paid for only about half of patents. Thus, the average effective patent duration may be several years shorter than the nominal 20-year term. By comparison, copyrighted works created after January 1, 1978 do not need to be renewed and therefore enjoy their full statutory term of 70 years or more. Trademarks, although potentially perpetual if renewed every 10 years, have been calculated to have an average expected life of around 15 years due to nonrenewal—roughly the same as the average expected life of a patent.

Other Limitations to the Exclusive Rights

Once a patent expires, it becomes part of the **public domain** and may be used freely by anyone without restriction. During the term of the patent, the patent owner's rights are limited in a number of ways. As with copyright law, the **first sale doctrine** permits individuals to resell a product embodying a patented invention, so long as the initial sale of that product was authorized by the patent owner. Unlike copyright law, which has a broad fair use doctrine, patent law's analogous *experimental use* exception (35 U.S.C. § 271(e)(1)) is extremely narrow and does not meaningfully impact the Internet. Finally, Section 1498 of Title 28 provides an eminent-domain-like power to the federal government to practice any invention without the permission of the patent owner, though doing so will give the patent owner a right to seek "reasonable and entire compensation" from the federal government in court.

The Limited Territorial Reach of Patents

U.S. patents provide rights only within the United States and its territories. Thus, an owner of a U.S. patent seeking to prevent those in other countries from copying the invention could not do so unless patent protection had been obtained in each country. Although businesses might find it more convenient to obtain a single patent that could be enforced throughout the world, no such patent regime exists. However, responding to the practicalities of a global economy, an international agreement known as the Patent Cooperation Treaty was concluded in 1970 to streamline the process of obtaining patents in multiple countries. Nevertheless, businesses tend to be selective when determining in which countries to seek patent protection in light of the costs and complexity of obtaining and enforcing rights in multiple countries. The estimated costs of obtaining patents presented previously ($10,000-$50,000) apply only to the acquisition of U.S. patents. Acquiring patent rights in other countries requires significant additional investment.

Exporting Patented Inventions: *Microsoft* v. *AT&T*. Given that the law allows patent holders to exclude others from making an invention within the United States, what happens when a business makes components of an invention—but not the completed invention—in the United States and then exports those components for assembly abroad? In 1984, Congress answered this question by enacting 35 U.S.C. § 271(f), which prohibits exporting "all or a substantial portion" of a patented invention's components for assembly abroad. In other words, a competitor cannot get around the prohibition against "making" by leaving out the final step of assembly, which can be easily completed once outside the United States.

However, in a twist on this theme, the Supreme Court had to decide whether Section 271(f) prohibited the exportation of software to a recipient located abroad who would then copy the software for installation on computers made and sold abroad. In effect, the court had to determine whether exported software constituted a "component" under the statute. The case, *Microsoft v. AT&T*,[2] involved an assertion by AT&T of a patent covering a particular aspect of Microsoft's Windows software. Microsoft conceded that Windows, when installed on a computer, infringed the AT&T patent if the relevant code was executed in the United States but argued that Windows did not infringe when exported from the United States and installed in another country, notwithstanding Section 271(f). The Court agreed, thus finding no infringement and limiting the territorial reach of AT&T's patent. Central to the Court's decision was the fact that the foreign recipient made and installed *copies* of the software exported by Microsoft, not the exported software itself. Although critics charged that this holding exalted form over substance, the Court emphasized that Congress was free to alter the result if it wished but that in the absence of Congressional action the territorial boundaries of the patent law should be respected.

Patents versus Copyrights

Patents and copyrights are often studied and considered together, and for good reasons. Each is a type of government-sanctioned monopoly that lasts for a limited period of time. Each provides compensation for an individual's intellectual contribution with the ultimate aim of promoting the public good. Each is governed almost exclusively by federal law, the authority for which is provided by the Constitution's Intellectual Property Clause (simultaneously known as the "Copyright Clause" or the "Patent Clause," according to the context). Each has had an enormous impact on the development of the Internet.

Yet patents and copyrights are distinct rights and are quite different in a number of important respects. For example, patents last for a much shorter period of time than copyrights, are far more expensive to obtain, and can only be secured by application to the USPTO. Several of the more important differences are summarized in Exhibit 6.5.

The Anatomy of a Patent

Exhibit 6.6 illustrates the structure of a typical patent document, using as an example excerpted portions of the Amazon "1-click" patent that underlies the case you will read later in the chapter. The patent **specification** is the portion of the patent that describes the invention and the manner and process of making and using it. The patent concludes with one or more **claims** that particularly point out and distinctly claim the subject matter which the inventor regards as his invention. Although the specification is helpful in understanding the invention, it is the claims that define the scope of a patent owner's legal rights and therefore constitute a critically important part of the patent. The 1-click patent, for example, contains twenty-six claims, five of which are visible in Exhibit 6.6.

---

2. 550 U.S. 437 (2007).

Exhibit 6.5   **Comparing Copyrights and Patents**

	Copyrights	Patents
Subject Matter	Creative works	Inventions
Duration	• 120 years (works for hire) • life of author + 70 years	20 years
Duration in 1790	14 years (28 if renewed)	14 years
Registration	Not required	Required
Ease of Obtaining Right	Easy	Difficult
Cost	None ($35 if registered)	$10,000 - $50,000 / patent
Governing Statute	Copyright Act of 1976	Patent Act of 1952
Federal Agency	Copyright Office	USPTO
Public Right to Use	Broad, due to fair use	Extremely narrow

What Can Be Patented? Requirements for Patentability

The modern framework governing utility patents is set forth in the federal **Patent Act of 1952**, as amended, which provides that patents may only be granted for inventions that are:

1. Within the scope of patentable subject matter
2. Useful
3. Novel (new)
4. Nonobvious
5. Enabled

The reason patents are more difficult, time-consuming, and expensive to obtain than copyrights or trademarks is that patent attorneys must draft patent applications such that they comply with these statutory requirements, personnel at the USPTO must examine patent applications to ensure compliance, and, when the attorney and examiner disagree, both must work to determine whether the patent application can be revised so that it does comply. The five requirements are explored below.

The Broad Scope of Patents: Section 101 Subject Matter

In 35 U.S.C. § 101, Congress set forth four broad categories of subject matter for which utility patents can be granted:

Exhibit 6.6 **The Amazon "1-Click" Patent (excerpts)**

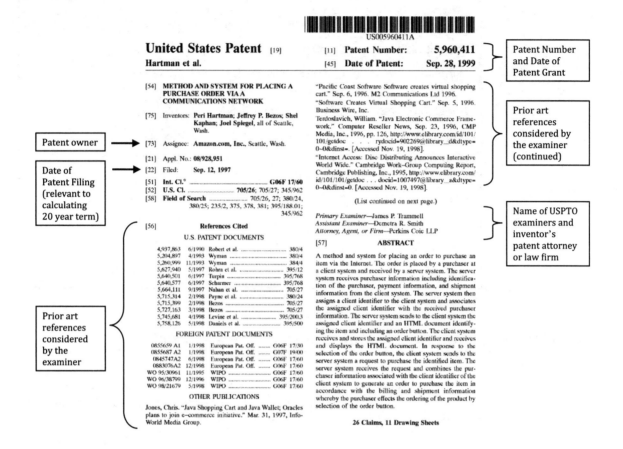

- Processes
- Machines
- Manufactures
- Compositions of matter

Under Section 101, patents have been issued on inventions as diverse as computer software, image compression technology, pharmaceutical ingredients, diapers, an isotope of the element Americium, a method of combing hair to conceal partial baldness, and a method of organizing and managing mutual funds using a computer.

From these examples it can be seen that the scope of patentable subject matter is extremely broad, encompassing virtually any invention that is novel, useful, and nonobvious. In fact, in the legislative history leading up to the Patent Act of 1952, Congress famously declared its intent that patents be granted on "anything under the sun that is made by man." This phrase gained renown when the Supreme Court quoted this portion of the legislative history in support of its decision in

Exhibit 6.6 Continued

5,960,411

1

METHOD AND SYSTEM FOR PLACING A PURCHASE ORDER VIA A COMMUNICATIONS NETWORK

TECHNICAL FIELD

The present invention relates to a computer method and system for placing an order and, more particularly, to a method and system for ordering items over the Internet.

BACKGROUND OF THE INVENTION

The Internet comprises a vast number of computers and computer networks that are interconnected through communication links. The interconnected computers exchange information using various services, such as electronic mail, Gopher, and the World Wide Web ("WWW"). The WWW service allows a server computer system (i.e., Web server or Web site) to send graphical Web pages of information to a remote client computer system. The remote client computer system can then display the Web pages. Each resource (e.g.,

2

vendors and purchasers want to ensure the security of such information. Security is a concern because information transmitted over the Internet may pass through various intermediate computer systems on its way to its final desti-5 nation. The information could be intercepted by an unscrupulous person at an intermediate system. To help ensure the security of the sensitive information, various encryption techniques are used when transmitting such information between a client computer system and a server computer 10 system. Even though such encrypted information can be intercepted, because the information is encrypted, it is generally useless to the interceptor. Nevertheless, there is always a possibility that such sensitive information may be successfully decrypted by the interceptor. Therefore, it 15 would be desirable to minimize the sensitive information transmitted when placing an order.

The selection of the various items from the electronic catalogs is generally based on the "shopping cart" model. When the purchaser selects an item from the electronic

Excerpt from page 14 of "1-click" patent

FIG. **7** is a flow diagram of a routine that implements an expedited order selection algorithm.

FIGS. **8A–8C** illustrate a hierarchical data entry mechanism in one embodiment.

DETAILED DESCRIPTION OF THE INVENTION

The present invention provides a method and system for single-action ordering of items in a client/server environment. The single-action ordering system of the present invention reduces the number of purchaser interactions needed to place an order and reduces the amount of sensitive 35 information that is transmitted between a client system and a server system. In one embodiment, the server system assigns a unique client identifier to each client system. The server system also stores purchaser-specific order information for various potential purchasers. The purchaser-specific 40 order information may have been collected from a previous order placed by the purchaser. The server system maps each client identifier to a purchaser that may use that client system to place an order. The server system may map the client

shopping cart section of that Web page for an item that may be ordered. The server system, however, only adds the 25 single-action ordering section when single-action ordering is enabled for that purchaser at that client system. (One skilled in the art would appreciate that a single Web page on the server system may contain all these sections but the single-action ordering section can be selectively included or 30 excluded before sending the Web page to the client system.) This example single-action ordering section allows the purchaser to specify with a single click of a mouse button to order the described item. Once the purchaser clicks the mouse button, the item is ordered, unless the purchaser then 35 takes some action to modify the order. The single-action ordering section contains a single-action ordering button **103a**, purchaser identification subsection **103b**, and single-action ordering information subsections **103c** and **103d**. The purchaser information subsection displays enough information so that the purchaser can verify that the server system correctly recognizes the purchaser. To reduce the chances of sensitive information being intercepted, the server system sends only enough information so that the purchaser is confident that the server system correctly identified the

Patent Specification

Excerpt from page 15 of "1-click" patent

Diamond v. Chakrabarty,[3] which held that living organisms that have been modified by humans are patentable.

Limits to Patentable Subject Matter

Although the scope of patentable subject matter is extremely broad, it is not unlimited. The Supreme Court in *Chakrabarty* noted that the following have been held not patentable:

- Laws of nature
- Physical phenomena
- Abstract ideas

3. 447 U.S. 303 (1980).

Exhibit 6.6   **Continued**

time. Thus, a user needs to scroll through the Web page to enter the information. When the data entry fields do not fit onto the display at the same time, it is difficult for the user to get an overall understanding of the type and organization of the data to be entered. The hierarchical data entry mechanism allows a user to understand the overall organization of the data to be entered even though the all data entry fields would not fit onto the display at the same time. FIG. **8A** illustrates an outline format of a sample form to be filled in. The sample form contains various sections identified by letters A, B, C, and D. When the user selects the start button, then section A expands to include the data entry fields for the customer name and address. FIG. **8B** illustrates the expansion of section A. Since only section A has been expanded, the user can view the data entry fields of section A and summary information of the other sections at the same time. The user then enters data in the various data entry fields that are displayed. Upon completion, the user selects either the next or previous buttons. The next button causes section A to be collapsed and section B to be expanded so that financial information may be entered. FIG. **8C** illustrates the expansion of section B. If the previous button is selected, then section A would collapse and be displayed as shown in FIG. **8A**. This collapsing and expanding is repeated for each section. At any time during the data entry, if an error is detected, then a Web page is generated with the error message in close proximity (e.g., on the line below) to the data entry field that contains the error. This Web page is then displayed by the client system to inform the user of the error. In addition, each of the data "entry" fields may not be editable until the user clicks on the data entry field or selects an edit button associated with the data entry field. In this way, the user is prevented from inadvertently changing the contents of an edit field. When the user clicks on a data entry field, a new Web page is presented to the user that allows for

the purchaser does not need to re-enter their customer identifier each time access is initiated. The scope of the present invention is defined by the claims that follow.

We claim:

1. A method of placing an order for an item comprising:
    under control of a client system,
       displaying information identifying the item; and
       in response to only a single action being performed, sending a request to order the item along with an identifier of a purchaser of the item to a server system;
    under control of a single-action ordering component of the server system,
       receiving the request;
       retrieving additional information previously stored for the purchaser identified by the identifier in the received request; and
    generating an order to purchase the requested item for the purchaser identified by the identifier in the received request using the retrieved additional information; and
    fulfilling the generated order to complete purchase of the item
       whereby the item is ordered without using a shopping cart ordering model.

2. The method of claim 1 wherein the displaying of information includes displaying information indicating the single action.

3. The method of claim 1 wherein the single action is clicking a button.

4. The method of claim 1 wherein the single action is speaking of a sound.

5. The method of claim 1 wherein a user of the client system does not need to explicitly identify themselves when placing an order.

> Patent Claims

Excerpt from page 18 of "1-click" patent

Thus, neither the law of gravity nor $E = mc^2$ would constitute patentable subject matter.

Another example of unpatentable subject matter is provided by the digital watermarking technology that you studied in Chapter 5. Recall that copyright owners have developed a means for embedding watermarks in digital audio or video files to help detect and prevent unauthorized copying. Unfortunately, embedding watermarks can cause distortions when the file is played, which can detract from the listener or viewer's experience. When an inventor named Petrus Nuijten developed a technique for reducing these distortions and tried to patent it, the Federal Circuit held that the *electromagnetic signal itself* in which the watermark was embedded did not constitute patentable subject matter because it was not a process, machine, manufacture, or composition of matter.[4] However, the Court did not upset the USPTO's determination that the *process used to create the signal* was patentable. Thus, Nuijten was able to obtain a patent on his invention, though one that was somewhat narrower than the one he initially sought.

---

4. *In re Nuijten*, 500 F.3d 1346 (Fed. Cir. 2007).

Utility

The **utility** (usefulness) requirement is a very low bar and rarely precludes patentability in the Internet context. To meet the minimal utility requirement, an invention must merely operate as described. Furthermore, there is no need for the invention to be any better than existing technologies or methods. Thus, patents have issued on:

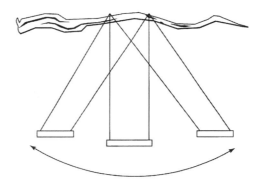

- A purportedly novel method of swinging on a swing that involves using a side-to-side motion rather than a front to back motion[5]

- A method of combing hair to conceal partial baldness[6]

---

5. U.S. Patent No. 6,368,227 (filed Nov. 17, 2000).
6. U.S. Patent No. 4,022,227 (filed Dec. 23, 1975).

FIG. 1

● A method of exercising cats by using a laser pointer to create a bright pattern of light that the cat will chase[7]

● A method of designating dating status by wearing a color-coded bracelet[8]

Despite the low bar of utility, patents may not issue on inventions that can only be used for illegal or fraudulent purposes. Thus, an attempt to patent a business method "useful" only for committing identity theft or for defrauding those seeking to purchase items on Craigslist or eBay would likely be rejected as failing the utility requirement.

Novelty

Even if an invention falls within the scope of patentable subject matter and meets the minimal utility requirement, a patent cannot be granted unless the invention is **novel** (new). This means at a minimum that the person seeking to patent the invention must be the person who actually invented it and must not have copied it from others. In addition, if the invention was on sale, in public use, described in a printed publication, or otherwise available to the public anywhere in the world prior to the filing date, the invention will be unpatentable due to lack of novelty.

Prior Art

Prior patents, publications, or uses that could negate novelty are known as **prior art**. If you go back and examine the 1-click patent illustrated in Exhibit 6.6, you will see that the prior art references considered by the examiner include previous U.S. patent documents, previous foreign patent documents, and a number of

---

7. U.S. Patent No. 5,443,036 (filed Nov. 2, 1993).
8. U.S. Patent No. 7,255,277 (filed Apr. 6, 2006).

Exhibit 6.7	Prior Art that Negates Novelty

Examples of Prior Art Under § 102

- Issued patents
- Published patent applications
- Other publications
- Public use or sales

news articles including two accessed online. Exhibit 6.7 provides examples of prior art that could render an invention unpatentable for lack of novelty if present before the date of filing.

First-to-Invent versus First-to-File

In the Leahy-Smith America Invents Act of 2011, Congress provided that patents would be granted to the first inventor to file a patent application in the USPTO (**first-to-file** system), regardless of the date of invention. Prior to this legislation, the United States stood virtually alone in following a **first-to-invent** system, which could result in costly adversarial proceedings where two individuals each claimed to have invented the same invention first. By switching to a first-to-file system, Congress created a clear date to help avoid competing claims of priority and brought the U.S. into greater harmony with prevailing practice around the world.

The first-to-invent system motivates inventors to file as early as possible, before others do so. In addition to the activities of others, a business's own activities could bar patentability. Once a company discloses an invention, it has a one-year **grace period** to file a patent application or it will lose the right to patent due to lack of novelty. For example, if Amazon.com had not filed an application for its 1-click patent within one year of using it in its website, the company would likely have been barred from receiving a patent. Similarly, researchers who publish papers describing their inventions must file a patent application within one year of the publication or they may lose the right to patent.

It is easy to understand why it is called a grace period by looking to the law of other countries, where the ability to patent may be lost the moment certain activities occur (such as publication or commercial use), with no grace period at all. Thus, businesses wishing to preserve their patent rights abroad should be careful to avoid selling, using, or disclosing the invention until the appropriate patent documents have been filed, regardless of where in the world those activities occur.

Nonobviousness

To be patentable, an invention must not only be novel, useful, and comprise appropriate subject matter, but must also be **nonobvious**. While the novelty requirement bars patentability where the invention is identical to a prior art reference, the nonobviousness requirement extends the bar to inventions that are only slightly different from the prior art. Whether an invention is obvious is judged from the perspective of a person ordinarily skilled in the relevant art. For example, whether a given software program is obvious would be determined from the perspective of an ordinarily skilled software engineer or computer programmer, rather than from the perspective of a layperson or a preeminent software engineer.

An invention is more likely to be held nonobvious and therefore patentable if:

- The differences between the prior art and the invention are many and large
- The level of ordinary skill in the art is low

Secondary Considerations

In addition to examining the prior art, level of skill in the art, and invention itself, the Supreme Court in *Graham v. John Deere*[9] instructed lower courts to examine secondary considerations when deciding whether a purported invention is obvious. **Secondary considerations**, also known as "objective indicia of nonobviousness," are thought to be easier for judges to evaluate than the sometimes highly technical aspects of new inventions and generally relate to how the invention was welcomed in the market or perceived by industry experts. An invention is more likely to be nonobvious and therefore patentable when one or more of the following secondary considerations are present:

- **Commercial Success.** The invention is a commercial success in the marketplace, displacing prior art products.
- **Long-Felt Need.** The invention solves a problem that had remained unsolved for a long period of time.
- **Failure of Others.** Others skilled in the art tried but failed to achieve the invention.
- **Copying.** The invention was copied by competitors who had other alternatives from which to choose.

As noted earlier, Amazon's patent for a 1-click ordering system was widely criticized as obvious. In the following opinion, the Federal Circuit had to determine whether defendant Barnes & Noble had presented sufficient evidence of patent invalidity to prevent a preliminary injunction. The court considered both whether the 1-click invention was novel and whether it was nonobvious, including an inquiry into evidence of secondary considerations.

---

9. 383 U.S. 1 (1966).

Amazon.com v. Barnesandnoble.com
239 F.3d 1343 (Fed. Cir. 2001)

Clevenger, Circuit Judge

[Facts] This is a patent infringement suit brought by Amazon.com, Inc. ("Amazon") against barnesandnoble.com, Inc. ["BN"]. . . .

The '411 patent [U.S. Patent No. 5,960,411] describes a method and system in which a consumer can complete a purchase order for an item via an electronic network using only a "single action," such as the click of a computer mouse button. . . . Amazon developed the patent to cope with what it considered to be frustrations presented by what is known as the "shopping cart model" purchase system for electronic commerce purchasing events. In previous incarnations of the shopping cart model, a purchaser . . . could select an item from an electronic catalog, typically by clicking on an "Add to Shopping Cart" icon, thereby placing the item in the "virtual" shopping cart. Other items from the catalog could be added to the shopping cart in the same manner. When the shopper completed the selecting process, the electronic commercial event would move to the check-out counter, so to speak. Then, information regarding the purchaser's identity, billing and shipping addresses, and credit payment method would be inserted into the transactional information base by the soon-to-be purchaser. Finally, the purchaser would "click" on a button displayed on the screen or somehow issue a command to execute the completed order, and the server computer system would verify and store the information concerning the transaction.

As is evident from the foregoing, an electronic commerce purchaser using the shopping cart model is required to perform several actions before achieving the ultimate goal of the placed order. The '411 patent sought to reduce the number of actions required from a consumer to effect a placed order. . . . How, one may ask, is the number of purchaser [actions] reduced? The answer is that the number of purchaser [actions] is reduced because the purchaser has previously visited the seller's web site and has previously entered into the database of the seller all of the required billing and shipping information that is needed to effect a sales transaction. Thereafter, when the purchaser visits the seller's web site and wishes to purchase a product from that site, the patent specifies that only a single action is necessary to place the order for the item. . . .

[Summary of Holding: No Preliminary Injunction] [W]e conclude that BN has mounted a serious challenge to the validity of Amazon's patent. We hasten to add, however, that this conclusion only undermines the prerequisite for entry of a preliminary injunction. Our decision today on the validity issue in no way resolves the ultimate question of invalidity. That is a matter for resolution at trial. It remains to be learned whether there are other [prior art] references that may be cited against the patent, and it surely remains to be learned whether any shortcomings in BN's initial preliminary validity challenge will be magnified or dissipated at trial. All we hold, in the meantime, is that BN cast enough doubt on the validity of the '411 patent to avoid a preliminary injunction, and that the validity issue should be resolved finally at trial.

[Analysis: First Prior Art Reference (Compuserve Trend System)]   One of the references cited by BN was the "CompuServe Trend System." The undisputed evidence indicates that in the mid-1990s, CompuServe offered a service called "Trend" whereby CompuServe subscribers could obtain stock charts for a surcharge of 50 cents per chart. . . . The district court failed to recognize the substantial question of invalidity raised by BN in citing the CompuServe Trend reference, in that this system appears to have used "single action ordering technology" within the scope of the claims in the '411 patent.

First, the district court dismissed the significance of this system partly on the basis that "[t]he CompuServe system was not a World Wide Web application." This distinction is irrelevant, since none of the claims mention either the Internet or the World Wide Web. . . . Moreover, the '411 patent specification explicitly notes that "[o]ne skilled in the art would appreciate that the single-action ordering techniques can be used in various environments other than the Internet."

More importantly, one of the screen shots in the record (reproduced below) indicates that with the CompuServe Trend system, once the "item" to be purchased (i.e., a stock chart) has been displayed (by typing in a valid stock symbol), only a single action (i.e., a single mouse click on the button labeled "Chart ($ .50)") is required to obtain immediate electronic delivery (i.e., "fulfillment") of the item. Once the button labeled "Chart ($.50)" was activated by a purchaser, an electronic version of the requested stock chart would be transmitted to the purchaser and displayed on the purchaser's computer screen, and an automatic process to charge the purchaser's account 50 cents for the transaction would be initiated. . . .

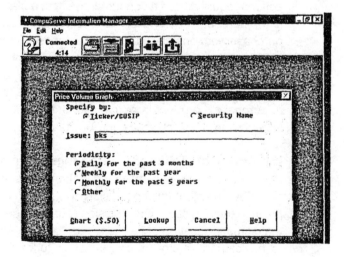

The final distinction drawn by Amazon's counsel between the claimed invention and the CompuServe Trend system was that—according to Amazon—the *only* reason that a purchaser would "call up" the screen would be to actually order an electronic stock chart, and that therefore an earlier action taken by a purchaser to invoke the screen should count as an extra purchaser action. According to this argument, the CompuServe Trend system would not meet the "single action" limitation because at least two actions would need to be taken to order an item: one action to invoke the ordering screen, and a second action to click on the ordering button. However, as the screen shot plainly indicates, a purchaser could use the display screen for purposes other than to order an electronic stock chart (e.g., to "Lookup" a stock symbol). . . .

In view of the above, we conclude that the district court erred in failing to recognize that the CompuServe Trend reference raises a substantial question of invalidity. Whether the CompuServe Trend reference either anticipates[10] and/or renders obvious the claimed invention in view of the knowledge of one of ordinary skill in the relevant art is a matter for decision at trial.

[Analysis: Second Prior Art Reference (Excerpt from a Book)] BN also presented as a prior art reference an excerpt from a book written by Magdalena Yesil entitled *Creating the Virtual Store* that was copyrighted in 1996. . . . BN focuses on the following passage from Appendix F of the book:

> **Instant Buy Option**
> Merchants also can provide shoppers with an Instant Buy button for some or all items, enabling them to skip check out review. This provides added appeal for customers who already know the single item they want to purchase during their shopping excursion.

The district court dismissed the significance of this passage, stating that "[r]ead in context, the few lines relied on by Defendants appear to describe only the elimination of the checkout review step, leaving at least two other required steps to complete a purchase." However, the district court failed to recognize that a reasonable jury could find that this passage provides a motivation to modify shopping cart ordering software to skip unnecessary steps. Thus, we find that this passage, viewed in light of the rest of the reference and the other prior art references cited by BN, raises a substantial question of validity. . . .

[Analysis: Third Prior Art Reference (Web Page Printout)] Another reference cited by BN, a print-out from a web page describing the "Oliver's Market" ordering system, generally describes a prior art multi-step shopping cart model. BN argued that this reference anticipates at least claim 9. The reference begins with an intriguing sentence:

> A single click on its picture is all it takes to order an item.

---

10. [If a prior art reference renders an invention unpatentable for lack of novelty, that reference is said to "anticipate" the invention.—Eds.]

Read in context, the quote emphasizes how easy it is to order things on-line. The district court failed to recognize that a reasonable jury could find that this sentence provides a motivation to modify a shopping cart model to implement "single-click" ordering as claimed in the '411 patent. In addition, the district court failed to recognize that other passages from this reference could be construed by a reasonable jury as anticipating and/or rendering obvious the allegedly novel "single action ordering technology" of the '411 patent. For example, the reference states that "[o]ur solution allows one-click ordering anywhere you see a product picture or a price." The reference also describes a system in which a user's identifying information (e.g., username and password) and purchasing information (e.g., name, phone number, payment method, delivery address) is captured and stored in a database "the very first time a user clicks on an item to order," and in which a corresponding cookie is stored on the client system. In this system, the stored information may be retrieved automatically during subsequent visits by reading the cookie. All of these passages further support BN's argument that a substantial question of validity is raised by this prior art reference, either alone or in combination with the other cited references.

[Analysis: Secondary Considerations] The district court also cited certain "secondary considerations" to support its conclusion of nonobviousness. Specifically, the district court cited (1) "copying of the invention" by BN and other e-commerce retailers following Amazon's introduction of its "1-Click" "feature, and (2) "the need to solve the problem of abandoned shopping carts." First, we note that evidence of copying Amazon's "1-Click®" feature is legally irrelevant unless the "1-Click®" feature is shown to be an embodiment of the claims. To the extent Amazon can demonstrate that its "1-Click®" feature embodies any asserted claims of the '411 patent under the correct claim interpretation, evidence of copying by BN and others is not sufficient to demonstrate nonobviousness of the claimed invention, in view of the substantial question of validity raised by the prior art references cited by BN and discussed herein.

With respect to the abandoned shopping carts, this problem is not even mentioned in the '411 patent. Moreover, Amazon did not submit any evidence to show either that its commercial success was related to the "1-Click®" ordering feature, or that single-action ordering caused a reduction in the number of abandoned shopping carts. Therefore, we fail to see how this "consideration" supports Amazon's nonobviousness argument.

CONCLUSION

BN has raised substantial questions as to the validity of the '411 patent. For that reason, we must conclude that the necessary prerequisites for entry of a preliminary injunction are presently lacking. We therefore vacate the preliminary injunction and remand the case for further proceedings.

Case Questions

1. Did the appeals court uphold the preliminary injunction issued by the district court? Did the appeals court find that the 1-Click patent was "obvious" and therefore invalid? Who would you say was winning the case at this stage?
2. Suppose the court found the patent nonobvious and therefore valid. How might BarnesAndNoble.com change its "Express Lane" feature so as to avoid further infringement of the patent?
3. *Ethical Consideration:* If you were a CEO or Chief Technical Officer (CTO) of a start up Internet company, would you seek to obtain patents for any new business method the law allowed, even if you thought it was obvious? Why or why not? Which stakeholders would you consider when making your decision?

After Amazon v. Barnes & Noble

After the case was **remanded** (sent back) to the district court the parties settled and no additional opinion was issued, leaving the issue of obviousness unresolved. Surprisingly, this was not the end of the story. In 2006 an individual from New Zealand, unrelated to either Amazon or Barnes & Noble, challenged the 1-click patent in an administrative action before the USPTO known as a reexamination proceeding. In 2007 the 1-click patent emerged from the reexamination proceeding somewhat narrower, but still valid. Although it might still be vulnerable to attack if its validity were again tested in court, an 11.5-year maintenance fee was paid in 2011 and the patent may remain in force until its 20-year term expires in 2017.

Enablement

The final element of patent eligibility requires that the patent document contain "a written description of the invention . . . in such full, clear, concise, and exact terms as to **enable** any person skilled in the art to which it pertains . . . to make and use [the invention]."

The primary purpose of the enablement requirement is to ensure that an inventor has disclosed enough information in the patent so that, when the patent expires, others can make and use it. A patent is therefore sometimes compared to a contract between an inventor and the public: In return for an enabling disclosure of the patent, an inventor receives a temporary right to exclude others.

The extent of the enabling disclosure must be commensurate with the breadth of what is claimed in the patent. For example, in *NetMoneyIN, Inc. v. Verisign, Inc.*,[11] the Federal Circuit held that a where a patent claim indicates that a general purpose computer will perform a claimed function, the claim will be invalid unless the specification explains *how* the computer will perform that function. That is, the patent must disclose the underlying algorithm.

The five major requirements for patentability just explored are summarized in Exhibit 6.8.

---

11. 574 F.3d 1371 (Fed. Cir. 2008).

| Exhibit 6.8 | Requirements for Patentability |

Requirement	United States Code (35 U.S.C.)
Appropriate subject matter	Section 101
Utility	Section 101
Novelty	Section 102
Nonobviousness	Section 103
Enablement	Section 112

Types of Patents

There are three types of statutorily defined patents in the United States:

- Utility patents (e.g., hardware/software patents, business method patents)
- Design patents
- Plant patents

By far the most common type of patent is the **utility patent**, which has the characteristics described throughout this chapter. In fact, utility patents are so common that they are usually referred to simply as "patents" rather than "utility patents." This text follows that convention, such that any reference to a "patent" should be understood to mean a utility patent unless otherwise specified. **Plant patents** protect new and distinct plant varieties that can be asexually reproduced. **Design patents** protect new, original, and ornamental designs on an article of manufacture. Exhibit 6.9 indicates the number of patents granted of each type in 2013.

Design Patents and the Internet

Whereas utility patents protect functional aspects of an invention, design patents protect the way a product looks. To prove infringement, a design patent owner must establish that an ordinary observer, familiar with prior art designs, would be deceived into believing that the accused product is the same as the patented design. Design patents last only 14 years from the date the patent is granted, in contrast to the 20-year duration of utility patents that begins on the date the application is filed. Whereas utility patents require maintenance fees, design patents (and plant patents) do not.

A number of design patents have issued for various ornamental aspects of software, hardware, and visual displays such as web page interfaces. For example,

Exhibit 6.9	Patent Grants by Patent Type (2013)

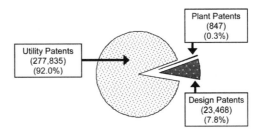

Exhibit 6.10	Design Patents, Examples

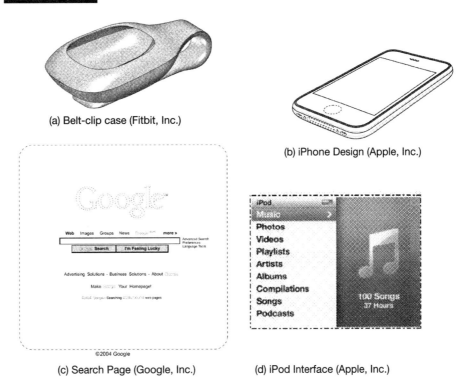

(a) Belt-clip case (Fitbit, Inc.)

(b) iPhone Design (Apple, Inc.)

(c) Search Page (Google, Inc.)

(d) iPod Interface (Apple, Inc.)

Fitbit, a company that makes fitness tracking devices, obtained a design patent for its belt clip case in 2014. Apple, Inc. has obtained a design patent for the iPod user interface and another for the design of the iPhone. Google has obtained a design patent for its minimalist search page interface. See Exhibit 6.10.

Overlapping Rights: Design Patents, Copyrights, and Trademarks

Because design patents protect visual appearances, it is often possible to obtain both design patent protection and copyright protection for the same ornamental design. For example, you can see in Exhibit 6.10(c) that Google is claiming a copyright in its search engine page, which is also pictured in an exhibit in its design patent.

If a design serves to indicate the source of the product, the design may be additionally protected by trademark law. For example, in Chapter 4 you learned that the three dimensional shape of the iPod has been registered as a trademark, while Exhibit 6.10(b) indicates that the shape of the iPod may also be protected by a design patent.

From Design Patents to Trademarks

Commentators have recommended that businesses desiring to trademark their product shapes first obtain a design patent on the product design, if possible. Then, during the 14-year term of the design patent, the business can advertise purposefully so as to establish the "secondary meaning" (public recognition) required for trademark protection of product designs. See Chapter 4. Because trademarks are renewable indefinitely, this strategy can potentially allow a business to secure a perpetual monopoly on its product design. Without the design patent, competitors would have a greater ability to create products with similar visual appearances, making it difficult or impossible to establish the distinctiveness required for trademark protection.

There are a number of factors to consider when deciding which type or types of intellectual property protection to pursue, and in which order. Businesses should therefore consult with their attorneys when facing such decisions.

Software Patents

Although software does not fit neatly into either the copyright or patent regimes, it may now be simultaneously protected by both. The Copyright Office announced that it would accept applications to register computer software in 1964. The patentability of software, however, was uncertain until the 1981 case of *Diamond v. Diehr*[12] in which the Supreme Court in a 5-4 decision ruled patentable a process of curing synthetic rubber that involved the use of a computer. Before Diehr's invention, the cure times had been estimated manually and the lack of precision sometimes led to undercuring or overcuring of the rubber. The claimed invention, however, allowed for the constant measuring of the temperature inside the mold and resulted in the ability to constantly recalculate, via use of the Arrhenius equation, the appropriate mold time.

---

12. 450 U.S. 175 (1981).

Although the process in *Diehr* required a computer to perform calculations, there was also a physical transformation of the rubber itself that formed part of the invention. An earlier Supreme Court case, *Gottschalk v. Benson*,[13] had suggested that a bare algorithm, unconnected to any particular physical transformation, was not patentable because such an algorithm would be merely an abstract idea. (An **algorithm**, according to the Supreme Court in *Benson*, is "a procedure for solving a given type of mathematical problem.") Although *Benson* and *Diehr* may have left some uncertainty as to which software-related inventions are patentable and which are not, software is currently treated as patentable subject matter by the USPTO and tens of thousands of patents that might be described as "software patents" have been issued.

Patent Protection or Copyright Protection?

The protection afforded to software by patent law differs in a number of respects from that afforded by copyright law. First, the patent term is much shorter than the copyright term, though given the rapid pace of software development it is doubtful whether the shorter patent term should be a significant factor in the decision to seek patent protection. Second, patent protection can be much more expensive to acquire than copyright protection, particularly for companies desiring protection in other countries. Third, patent protection requires disclosure of the invention to the public, and piracy may be difficult to prevent. On the other hand, patent protection of software is generally regarded as stronger than copyright protection because patents protect against independent invention, among other reasons.

Business Method Patents

A **business method patent**, though not statutorily defined, might be described as a patent covering methods for processing data or conducting business operations. Like software patents, business method patents are an informal subcategory of utility patents. For example, the following might be described as business method patents:

- Amazon's 1-click patent
- Friendster's (now Facebook's) patent on a method for connecting users within online social networks
- Google's PageRank patent on a method for ranking search results

As you might suspect, business method patents and software patents are not entirely distinct categories, and in fact many business method patents involve the use of computer software.

---

13. 409 U.S. 63 (1972).

Business Method Patents and Section 101 Subject Matter

In most fields of technology, the issue of patentable subject matter is rarely critical because the scope of patentable subject matter (Section 101) is so broad. On the Internet, however, the definition of patentable subject matter is at the heart of a heated debate over whether Internet business methods may be patented. Prior to 1996, the USPTO instructed its examiners that applications claiming methods of doing business—whether or not related to the Internet—could be rejected because they did not claim patentable subject matter. This policy was based on a judge-made "business method exception" to patentability often traced to the 1908 case of *Hotel Security Checking Co. v. Lorraine Co.*,[14] in which the court held unpatentable a "method of and means for cash-registering and account-checking designed to prevent frauds and peculation [theft] by waiters and cashiers in hotels and restaurants."

In 1996, the USPTO issued new guidelines indicating that business methods "should be treated like any other process claims." Under these guidelines, business methods could still be rejected as obvious or lacking novelty but could not be rejected simply because they were methods of doing business.

Business Method Patents: State Street v. Signature Corp

Soon after the new guidelines were issued, the Federal Circuit confirmed that business methods constituted patent-eligible subject matter in the landmark case of *State Street v. Signature Corp.*[15] In that case, State Street was accused of infringing Signature's patented Hub and Spoke® system of pooling the assets of mutual funds (spokes) into an investment portfolio (hub) that was organized as a partnership, a system that was advantageous because it combined the tax advantages of a partnership with the economies of scale associated with managing a large pool of funds. The Federal Circuit not only held the system to constitute patentable subject matter, but removed any doubt regarding the patentability of business methods:

> [T]he [district] court relied on the judicially-created, so-called "business method" exception to statutory subject matter. We take this opportunity to lay this ill-conceived exception to rest. Since its inception [in 1908], the "business method" exception has merely represented the application of some general, but no longer applicable legal principle. . . . Since the 1952 Patent Act, business methods have been . . . subject to the same legal requirements for patentability as applied to any other process or method.

The Rise of Business Method Patents

After *State Street's* rejection of the business method exception to patentability, the number of business method patents granted by the USPTO increased substantially.

---

14. 160 F. 467 (2d Cir. 1908).
15. 149 F.3d 1368 (Fed. Cir. 1998).

Exhibit 6.11 Business Method Patents Granted, 1990-2013

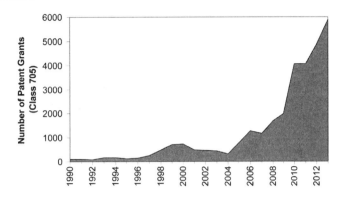

As noted above, there is no precise definition of "business method patent" and therefore the number of business method patents can only be approximated. The USPTO, however, organizes patents into more than 450 classes based on subject matter. For example, Class 24 includes inventions related to "buckles, buttons, and clasps," while Class 711 includes inventions related to computer memory. Often considered useful in estimating the number of business method patents is Class 705, entitled "Data processing: financial, business practice, management, or cost/price determination." Exhibit 6.11 illustrates the dramatic growth in the annual number of patents granted in Class 705 since 1990.

Against a backdrop of vigorous public debate and academic discussion, the Supreme Court issued a long-awaited decision in 2014 in which it weighed in on the continued viability of business method patents.

Alice Corp. Pty. Ltd. v. CLS Bank Int'l
134 S. Ct. 2347 (2014)

Justice Thomas, J.

[Facts] The claims at issue relate to a computerized scheme for mitigating "settlement risk"—*i.e.*, the risk that only one party to an agreed-upon financial exchange will satisfy its obligation. In particular, the claims are designed to facilitate the exchange of financial obligations between two parties by using a computer system as a third-party intermediary. The intermediary creates "shadow" credit and debit records (*i.e.*, account ledgers) that mirror the balances in the parties' real-world accounts at "exchange institutions" (*e.g.*, banks). The intermediary updates the shadow records in real time as transactions are entered, allowing only those transactions for which the parties' updated shadow records indicate sufficient resources to satisfy their mutual obligations. At the end of the day, the intermediary instructs the relevant financial institutions to carry out the "permitted" transactions in accordance with the updated shadow records, *ibid.*, thus mitigating the risk that only one party will perform the agreed-upon exchange. . . .

Respondents CLS Bank International and CLS Services Ltd. (together, CLS Bank) operate a global network that facilitates currency transactions. In 2007, CLS Bank filed suit against petitioner, seeking a declaratory judgment that the claims at issue are invalid, unenforceable, or not infringed. Petitioner counterclaimed, alleging infringement.

[Patentable Subject Matter] Section 101 of the Patent Act defines the subject matter eligible for patent protection. It provides:

> "Whoever invents or discovers any new and useful process, machine, manufacture, or composition of matter, or any new and useful improvement thereof, may obtain a patent therefor, subject to the conditions and requirements of this title." 35 U.S.C. § 101.

[Exceptions to Patentable Subject Matter] We have long held that this provision contains an important implicit exception: Laws of nature, natural phenomena, and abstract ideas are not patentable. . . . Laws of nature, natural phenomena, and abstract ideas are the basic tools of scientific and technological work. [M]onopolization of those tools through the grant of a patent might tend to impede innovation more than it would tend to promote it," thereby thwarting the primary object of the patent laws. We have repeatedly emphasized this concern that patent law not inhibit further discovery by improperly tying up the future use of these building blocks of human ingenuity.

At the same time, we tread carefully in construing this exclusionary principle lest it swallow all of patent law. At some level, all inventions embody, use, reflect, rest upon, or apply laws of nature, natural phenomena, or abstract ideas. Thus, an invention is not rendered ineligible for patent simply because it involves an abstract concept. Applications of such concepts to a new and useful end remain eligible for patent protection.

[The Court's Test] In *Mayo Collaborative Services v. Prometheus Laboratories, Inc.*, 132 S. Ct. 1289 (2012), we set forth a framework for distinguishing patents that claim laws of nature, natural phenomena, and abstract ideas from those that claim patent-eligible applications of those concepts. First, we determine whether the claims at issue are directed to one of those patent-ineligible concepts. If so, we then ask, what else is there in the claims before us? To answer that question, we consider the elements of each claim both individually and as an ordered combination to determine whether the additional elements transform the nature of the claim into a patent-eligible application. We have described step two of this analysis as a search for an "inventive concept," *i.e.*, an element or combination of elements that is sufficient to ensure that the patent in practice amounts to significantly more than a patent upon the ineligible concept itself.

[Step 1: Patent Ineligible Concept] We must first determine whether the claims at issue are directed to a patent-ineligible concept. We conclude that they are: These claims are drawn to the abstract idea of intermediated settlement. . . . We most recently addressed the category of abstract ideas in *Bilski v. Kappos*, 561 U.S. 593 (2010). The claims at issue in *Bilski* described a method for hedging against the financial risk of price fluctuations. . . . All members of the Court agreed that the patent at issue in *Bilski* claimed an abstract idea. . . . It follows from our prior cases, and *Bilski* in particular, that the claims at issue here are directed to an abstract idea. . . . On their face, the claims before us are drawn to the concept of intermediated settlement, *i.e.*, the use of a third party to mitigate settlement risk. Like the risk hedging in *Bilski*, the concept of intermediated settlement is a fundamental economic practice long prevalent in our system of commerce. The use of a third-party intermediary (or "clearing house") is also a building block of the modern economy.

[Step 2: Inventive Concept] [W]e must examine the elements of the claim to determine whether it contains an "inventive concept" sufficient to transform the claimed abstract idea into a patent-eligible application. A claim that recites an abstract idea must include "additional features" to ensure that the claim is more than a drafting effort designed to monopolize the abstract idea." *Mayo* [*v. Prometheus*] made clear that transformation into a patent-eligible application requires more than simply stating the abstract idea while adding the words "apply it." . . . The introduction of a computer into the claims does not alter the analysis. . . . [S]imply implementing a mathematical principle on a physical machine, namely a computer, is not a patentable application of that principle.

Stating an abstract idea while adding the words "apply it" is not enough for patent eligibility. Nor is limiting the use of an abstract idea to a particular technological environment. Stating an abstract idea while adding the words "apply it with a computer" simply combines those two steps, with the same deficient result.

[Conclusion] For the foregoing reasons, the judgment of the Court of Appeals for the Federal Circuit [holding the patent invalid] is affirmed.

[Justice Sotomayor (Joined by Ginsburg and Breyer), Concurring] I adhere to the view that any "claim that merely describes a method of doing business does not qualify as a 'process' under §101." *Bilski v. Kappos*, 561 U.S. 593 (2010) (Stevens, J., concurring in judgment); see also *In re Bilski*, 545 F.3d 943 (Fed. Cir. 2008) (Dyk, J., concurring) ("There is no suggestion in any of the early consideration [by Eighteenth Century English courts] of process patents that processes for organizing human activity were or ever had been patentable"). As in *Bilski*, however, I further believe that the method claims at issue are drawn to an abstract idea. I therefore join the opinion of the Court.

Case Questions

1. According to the court, which three categories of subject matter are excluded from patent eligibility?
2. After *Alice Corp.*, can business method patents still be obtained?
3. ***Ethical Consideration:*** It is easy to understand the desire to avoid doing business with parties that are unable to meet their financial obligations. This is particularly true as the volume of international transactions increases and the geographic and cultural distance between parties becomes greater. Do you think that very important inventions that have the potential to significantly impact welfare should be subject to patenting? Or should they be excluded from patent protection because they are so important? For example, should the law assure patents for, say, life-saving drugs because incentivizing their creation is so important? Or, should the law prohibit patents on such drugs because it would be unethical to deny their availability once they are created? How would you resolve this conflict?

Enforcing Patent Rights

Although federally granted patents provide the right to exclude others from making, using, or selling a patented invention, it is the responsibility of the patent owner—not the government—to enforce them. For this reason, critics sometimes derisively refer to patents as mere "rights to sue."

Google's Patents

Since it was incorporated in 1998, Google has amassed an intellectual property portfolio comprising at least 19,000 issued patents and patent applications. The most famous among these is the PageRank patent, invented by Google cofounder Larry Page. [The PageRank patent is actually assigned to Stanford University but has been exclusively licensed to Google.] The PageRank patent (U.S. Patent No. 6,285,999) was granted in 2001 and describes the underlying method employed by Google's search engine when returning Internet search results. Under the PageRank method, a web page is ranked according to the number of other pages that link to it. Thus, if a large number of web pages contain links to the home page of the USPTO, the USPTO home page will receive a high ranking and will appear toward the top of Google's organic search results based upon an Internet search using a term such as "patents." However, the rank of a page is determined not only by the number of pages linking to it but also by the rank of *those* pages, with more highly ranked pages more heavily weighted than lower ranked pages. The method is therefore recursive and must be calculated by an iterative process.

Not all of Google's patents pertain directly to online business methods. For example, Google has obtained a patent for a "Water-Based Data Center" in which computing facilities used to power the Internet could be housed on ships or floating platforms. The patent specification explains that the natural motion of the sea could be harnessed to generate electricity while sea water could be used to cool the computer equipment.

A few of the many other Internet-related patents and patent applications owned or controlled by Google address:

- A method of calculating suggested driving routes
- A system for facilitating online "micro-payments" while reducing the exposure of credit card information
- A method for translating Chinese pinyin (i.e., Chinese written phonetically using Roman characters) into Chinese characters
- A method of overlaying advertisements on images or videos
- A method for blocking unsolicited commercial email ("spam")

Finally, Google has obtained a patent covering a method of more effectively targeting advertisements to key members of social networks. The application notes that "certain members [of online social networks] are more popular than others and, consequently, wield enhanced influence over other members in the community." In order to determine who key influencers are and target advertisements accordingly, the patent describes a method of weighting the links between members and identifying the influencer to be targeted as the member with the highest rank—an idea seemingly inspired by Google's patented PageRank method.

The High Cost of Patent Litigation

By all accounts, patent litigation is expensive. A 2013 study by the American Intellectual Property Law Association found median patent litigation costs to be $5.5 million for each party, where more than $25 million is in dispute. In addition to these out-of-pocket costs, patent cases may often last for several years, and businesses should be aware that indirect costs such as the lost time and effort of key personnel and the burden of retaining relevant documents and email can be significant.

Cease-and-Desist Letters to Supreme Court Review

A patent owner who believes another party is making, using or selling a patented invention within the United States may first send a **cease-and-desist letter**, which will generally request that the other party either pay royalties or stop infringing the patent. If the other party declines to comply, the patent owner may file suit in federal district court. Parties dissatisfied with the district court's decision can appeal to the Federal Circuit which, as you learned earlier, also hears appeals from the USPTO regarding patent applications. The Supreme Court may in its discretion review Federal Circuit decisions by granting a party's request for a **writ of certiorari**.

Enforcement Against Unlawful Imports

Where infringing products are imported into the U.S. from abroad, the U.S. patent owner may seek relief via the **United States International Trade Commission** (**USITC**). The USITC is an administrative agency based in Washington,

Exhibit 6.12 **Patent Appeals in the United States**

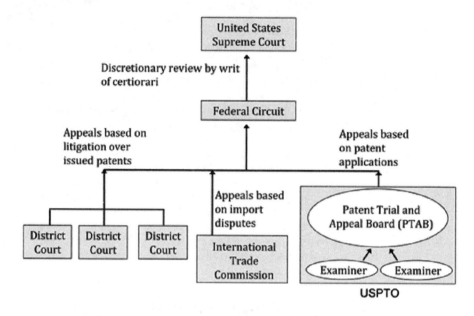

D.C., that has the authority to issue **exclusion orders** that bar the importation into the United States of articles that infringe a valid and enforceable U.S. patent (or U.S. copyright or registered trademark).[16] Investigations instituted by the USITC have increased substantially since the 1990s, with the majority of recent cases relating to computers, telecommunications equipment, consumer electronics, or other high technology products.

The major government institutions involved with patent appeals, including appeals from the USPTO and USITC, are illustrated in Exhibit 6.12.

Infringement

Determining whether an accused device or process infringes a patent involves a two-step analysis. First, the court must construe the claims. That is, the court must determine what the patent actually covers by looking at the claims and determining what they mean. These determinations take place at claim construction proceedings known as **Markman hearings** (named after the 1996 Supreme Court case of *Markman v. Westview Instruments*[17]), which occur in advance of the trial. Second, the court must compare the claims as construed to the accused device or process.

---

16. 19 U.S.C. § 1337.
17. 517 U.S. 370 (1996).

Literal Infringement and the Doctrine of Equivalents

Literal infringement will be found where the accused device or process includes every **limitation** (part or element) of a patent claim. Thus, an exact copy of the invention claimed in the patent would literally infringe the patent. It is difficult, however, for patent attorneys to draft patent claims so as to literally cover every conceivable equivalent element of an invention. Conversely it is easy for copyists to pirate an invention by making insubstantial changes to fall outside of the literal claim scope. For example, a copyist might substitute a software switch in place of a mechanical switch described in a claim.

Therefore, even where the defendant has not literally infringed the patent, infringement may nevertheless be found under the **doctrine of equivalents** if the accused device or process performs substantially the same function in substantially the same way to obtain the same result. The Supreme Court explained why the doctrine of equivalents is necessary:

> Courts have . . . recognized that to permit imitation of a patented invention which does not copy every literal detail would be to convert the protection of the patent grant into a hollow and useless thing. Such a limitation would leave room for—indeed encourage— the unscrupulous copyist to make unimportant and insubstantial changes and substitutions in the patent which, though adding nothing, would be enough to take the copied matter outside the claim, and hence outside the reach of law.[18]

Secondary Liability

As with copyright law, businesses may be secondarily liable for patent infringement committed by another. Selling a component of a patented invention, where the component is not capable of substantial noninfringing use, can give rise to a claim of *contributory infringement*. In addition, businesses that actively encourage infringement can be liable for *inducement*.[19]

Defenses

A defendant in a patent infringement suit may avoid liability by establishing that (1) the defendant's actions or products do not infringe the patent; (2) the patent is invalid or unenforceable; or (3) the claim was not timely filed with the court. Additionally a provision in the America Invents Act provides a defense from liability for those who commercially used the invention more than one year before the earlier of the patent application date or the public disclosure date (**prior-use defense**).

Not Infringed

The most obvious means of avoiding liability in a patent infringement suit is to establish that the accused device or process does not infringe the patent. Because

---

18. 339 U.S. 605 (1950).
19. 35 U.S.C. § 271(b)-(c).

infringement will be found only if the accused process contains every element of the claimed invention, a defendant whose process is lacking one or more elements of a claim will be found not to infringe. However, a defendant may not avoid infringement by adding an additional element. (Recall that improvement patents that contain all the elements of an earlier invention plus some additional improvement element will nevertheless infringe the earlier patent.) Thus, if a patent claim includes elements A, B, and C:

- An accused process containing elements A, B, and D will not infringe.
- An accused process containing elements A, B, C, and D will infringe.

Because the Internet facilitates coordination of activities, it may sometimes be easy for multiple parties to collectively perform all of the elements of a patented process, even though no single party performs all of the steps. If a business performs some steps of a patented process, and encourages its customers to complete the remaining steps, has infringement occurred? In 2014 the Supreme Court was called upon to answer this question in the context of a patent that enabled faster Internet usage.

Limelight Networks, Inc. v. Akamai Technologies, Inc.,
134 S. Ct. 2111 (2014)

Justice Alito, J.

[Facts] Akamai maintains many servers distributed in various locations. Proprietors of Web sites, known as "content providers," contract with Akamai to deliver their Web sites' content to individual Internet users. [Akamai's] '703 patent provides for the designation of certain components of a content provider's Web site (often large files, such as video or music files) to be stored on Akamai's servers and accessed from those servers by Internet users. The process of designating components to be stored on Akamai's servers is known as "tagging." By aggregating the data demands of multiple content providers with differing peak usage patterns and serving that content from multiple servers in multiple locations, as well as by delivering content from servers located in the same geographic area as the users who are attempting to access it, Akamai is able to increase the speed with which Internet users access the content of its customers' Web sites.

Petitioner Limelight Networks, Inc., also operates a CDN [content delivery network] and carries out several of the steps claimed in the '703 patent. But instead of tagging those components of its customers' Web sites that it intends to store on its servers (a step included in the '703 patent), Limelight requires its customers to do their own tagging. Respondents claim that Limelight "provides instructions and offers technical assistance" to its customers regarding how to tag, but the record is undisputed that Limelight does not tag the components to be stored on its servers. In 2006, [Akamai] sued Limelight in the United States District Court for the District of Massachusetts, claiming patent infringement.

[Infringement Analysis] A method patent [such as the one at issue in this case] claims a number of steps; under this Court's case law, the patent is not infringed unless all the steps are carried out. The Federal Circuit held in *Muniauction* [*v. Thomson Corp.*, 532 F.3d 1318 (Fed. Cir. 2008)] that a method's steps have not all been performed as claimed by the patent unless they are all attributable to the same defendant, either because the defendant actually performed those steps or because he directed or controlled others who performed them. [Here,] there has simply been no infringement of the method in which respondents have staked out an interest, because the performance of all the patent's steps is not attributable to any one person. And, as both the Federal Circuit and respondents admit, where there has been no direct infringement, there can be no inducement of infringement under § 271(b) [which imposes secondary liability on parties that induce others to infringe]. . . .

Section 271(f)(1) reinforces our reading of § 271(b). [Subsection 271(f)] imposes liability on a party who "supplies or causes to be supplied in or from the United States all or a substantial portion of the components of a patented invention . . . in such manner as to actively induce the combination of such components outside of the United States in a manner that would infringe the patent *if such combination occurred within the United States.*" . . . In *Deepsouth Packing Co. v. Laitram Corp.*, 406 U.S. 518 (1972), a manufacturer produced components of a patented machine and then exported those components overseas to be assembled by its foreign customers. (The assembly by the foreign customers did not violate U.S. patent laws.) In both *Deepsouth* and this case, the conduct that the defendant induced or contributed to would have been infringing if committed in altered circumstances: in *Deepsouth* if the machines had been assembled in the United States, and in this case if performance of all of the claimed steps had been attributable to the same person. In *Deepsouth*, we rejected the possibility of contributory infringement because the machines had not been assembled in the United States, and direct infringement had consequently never occurred. Similarly, in this case, performance of all the claimed steps cannot be attributed to a single person, so direct infringement never occurred. Limelight cannot be liable for inducing infringement that never came to pass.

CONCLUSION

The judgment below is reversed, and the case is remanded for further proceedings consistent with this opinion.

Case Questions

1. In the context of the technology involved in this case, what is "tagging," and how does it relate to the patented technology?
2. The Court notes that a process patent cannot be infringed unless all of the steps of the process are carried out. In *Akamai*, it was undisputed that all of the steps had been carried out. Why, then, did the Court find that the patent had not been infringed?
3. ***Ethical Consideration:*** Complex business activities are increasingly carried out by multiple parties that act independently but whose actions are coordinated or facilitated through the Internet, as *Akamai* demonstrates. Did the Supreme Court in *Akamai* create a giant loophole that immunizes otherwise infringing activity simply because it is carried out by two or more parties? If so, is it ethical for entrepreneurs to exploit this loophole, for example, by searching for valuable patents that can be implemented by performing some of the claimed steps and inviting others to perform the remaining steps?

Invalid as Anticipated

Defendants may also argue that irrespective of infringement, the patent should not have been granted by the USPTO in the first place because the invention is either **anticipated** (not novel) or obvious. A claim is said to be anticipated under Section 102 and therefore invalid if a single prior art reference contains each and every element of a claim. Patents issued by the USPTO are presumed to be valid and the defendant therefore has the burden of proving by clear and convincing evidence that the patent should not have been granted.[20]

An example of the anticipation defense is provided by Blackboard Inc., a leading provider of course management software that allows professors and students to exchange course-related documents and interact online. When Blackboard Inc. sued Desire2Learn, a company based in Canada, over alleged infringement of Blackboard's course management software patent, Desire2Learn defended on the ground of anticipation. The Federal Circuit agreed, issuing an opinion in which it held certain claims of the Blackboard patent invalid as lacking novelty in light of earlier course management software packages.[21] The parties eventually settled their remaining patent disputes and agreed to a cross license on undisclosed terms.

Invalid as Obvious

Even if the invention is not anticipated, it may still be obvious. Just as the doctrine of equivalents provides the patent owner some flexibility when the court determines infringement, the doctrine of *obviousness* provides alleged infringers some flexibility when the court determines validity. Patents on inventions

---

20. *Microsoft v. i4i Ltd. P'ship*, 131 S. Ct. 2238 (2011).
21. *Blackboard, Inc. v. Desire2Learn Inc.*, 574 F.3d 1371 (Fed. Cir. 2009).

that are novel but only slightly different from inventions described in the prior art will be invalid if the differences would have been obvious to a person ordinarily skilled in the relevant art.

Unenforceable Even if Valid

Even if a defendant has infringed a valid patent, the defendant may still prevail if the patent is found to be *unenforceable*. A patent may be found unenforceable if the patent owner (or the patent attorney) committed **inequitable conduct**, such as by intentionally failing to disclose relevant prior art to the USPTO examiner during prosecution. For example, when Netflix sued Blockbuster for infringement of Netflix's patents covering methods of renting movies through the mail, Blockbuster defended on the ground that Netflix had committed inequitable conduct by failing to disclose relevant prior art of which it was aware to the patent examiner. The court found that Blockbuster's accusations of inequitable conduct were strong enough to merit further review, which finding placed Blockbuster in a more favorable negotiating position.[22] The parties settled on undisclosed terms the following year, before the court could make a final ruling on whether inequitable conduct had in fact been committed.

Failure to Timely File Claim

Like other claimants who wish to assert rights, patent holders cannot wait indefinitely to file their claims. Under 35 U.S.C. § 286, a patent owner will generally be unable to collect damages for infringement occurring more than six years prior to the time the lawsuit is filed. A statute providing that suits cannot be brought or damages cannot be recovered after a specified period of time is known as a **statute of limitations**. Unlike many statutes of limitations, however, § 286 does not bar the claim altogether but instead limits damages to those sustained within the preceding six years. In addition to § 286, a court has discretion under the doctrine of **laches** to bar a claim entirely, even during the six-year period under § 286, if the claimant has "slept upon his rights" and failed to file within a reasonable period after becoming aware of the infringement.[23]

Remedies

Remedies available to patent owners who prevail in court include damages, attorney fees, and injunctions.

Damages and Attorney Fees

Plaintiffs that prevail in patent suits are entitled to **damages** (monetary compensation), which may be calculated by the court or jury as profits the plaintiff would

---

22. *Netflix, Inc. v. Blockbuster, Inc.*, No. C 06-02 361 WHA, 2006 WL 2458717 (N.D. Cal. Aug. 22, 2006).
23. *A.C. Aukerman Co. v. R.L. Chaides Constr. Co.*, 960 F.2d 1020 (Fed. Cir. 1992).

have earned if not for the infringement. Where lost profits cannot be established with certainty, the Patent Act provides that damages must be at least equal to a reasonable royalty for the use made of the invention by the infringer.

The court may award up to three times actual damages (**treble damages**) and attorney fees when appropriate, such as where the infringement was willful or the defendant engaged in misconduct during litigation.

z4 Technologies v. Microsoft Corp.   The case of *z4 Technologies v. Microsoft Corp.*[24] provides an example of the type of misconduct that can lead to an award of attorney fees. In that case, z4 Technologies held a patent on a method of reducing software piracy and unauthorized software use that required users to "activate" software products by using one or more passwords. A jury had earlier found that Microsoft's Office software included product activation features that infringed the patent and awarded $115 million in damages to z4. The district court judge held that Microsoft had committed litigation misconduct by withholding from z4 an important email unfavorable to Microsoft and by burying relevant exhibits amidst 3,449 marked exhibits "in the hope that they could conceal their trial evidence in a massive pile of decoys," among other bad acts. The court ordered Microsoft to pay almost $2 million to z4 for attorney fees and expenses.

Injunctions

Potentially the most potent remedy is the **injunction**, an order by the court that a defendant must refrain from infringing a patent. Injunctions are highly sought after by patent owners because they place the patent owner in a strong bargaining position. Unless the defendant is able to redesign the accused device or process so as to avoid further infringement, the defendant may be forced to choose between halting business and negotiating a license on terms acceptable to the patent holder.

eBay v. MercExchange.   In 2001, a small company called MercExchange sued eBay for the infringement of three business method patents related to operating an online marketplace, including one covering eBay's "Buy It Now" feature. At trial, a jury found that eBay had infringed two of the patents (including the one covering the Buy It Now feature) and the Federal Circuit held that an injunction should issue. Under the rule prevailing at the time, a patent holder would generally be entitled to an injunction absent exceptional circumstances. In 2006, however, the Supreme Court in the landmark case of *eBay v. MercExchange*[25] rejected this rule and thereby made it more difficult for patent holders to obtain injunctions. Under *eBay*, a patent holder is entitled to an injunction only if it can demonstrate:

---

24. No. 6:06-CV-142, 2006 WL 2401099 (E.D. Tex. Aug. 18, 2006).
25. 547 U.S. 388 (2006).

1. that it has suffered an irreparable injury;
2. that monetary damages are inadequate to compensate for that injury;
3. that, considering the balance of hardships between the plaintiff and defendant, an injunction is warranted; and
4. that the public interest favors a permanent injunction.

The Supreme Court in *eBay* thus brought the patent law rule into line with other areas of the law, where the four-factor test was already long established.

After *eBay v. MercExchange*. After *eBay* was remanded for further proceedings, the district court applied the four factor test and found that an injunction was not warranted. MercExchange and eBay entered into a settlement agreement in 2008 pursuant to which eBay purchased all three of MercExchange's patents as well as related intellectual property not asserted in the suit. The Buy It Now feature continues to be available on eBay.

Trolls, Landmines, and Other Metaphors

The USPTO granted 277,835 patents in 2013 compared to just 98,342 in 1993, bringing the total patents currently in force in the United States to about 2.1 million. The recent proliferation of patents has inspired a number of colorful metaphors and raised concerns among some observers that patents are inhibiting rather than promoting the progress of the useful arts. Before exploring these metaphors and criticisms, however, it will be helpful to understand why patents are thought to be beneficial in the first place.

Why Patents?

As with copyrights, the authority of Congress to enact patent legislation derives from the Constitution's Intellectual Property Clause:

> The Congress shall have Power . . . To promote the Progress of Science and useful Arts, by securing for limited Times to Authors and Inventors the exclusive Right to their respective Writings and Discoveries.[26]

To an even greater extent than copyrights, patents are usually justified as a tool to promote social welfare. Patent theory assumes that businesses will not invest resources in inventing and developing inventions if others can simply copy those inventions with impunity. Without patents, copyists could reap the benefits of the inventor's efforts without sharing invention and commercialization costs. An additional justification for patents is that they help to disseminate valuable information via the required patent disclosure.

---

26. U.S. CONST. art. I, § 8, cl. 8.

Patent Theory and Business Method Patents

Critics argue that the traditional social welfare rationale applies with less force to business method patents. These critics point out that the development of new business methods tends to require relatively small initial investment, and so does not require the patent incentive. Moreover, they argue, many business methods are easily observable by others when used (for example, the Amazon 1-click patent) and so no patent disclosure is needed to effectively disseminate knowledge of the invention.

Those favoring business method patents reply that, consistent with USPTO policy and court rulings, business methods should be treated like any other process. Moreover, some business methods may not be observable, such as financial trading strategies, back-office operations, or computer software algorithms. Finally, they argue that inventors of new and useful business methods deserve patent protection from freeriding just as other inventors do.

Patent Landmines

Recent scholarship suggests that only around 4 percent of defendants in patent suits are ultimately held liable for intentional copying, with even smaller figures for litigation relating to software and other computer-related patents. That is, it appears that most defendants in patent infringement suits independently invented or acquired the invention covered by the plaintiff's patent and did not freeride off of the plaintiff's efforts. These figures lend support to the commonly cited metaphor of businesses innovating in a competitive field while trying to avoid inadvertently stepping on a **patent landmine**. The risk of encountering a landmine exists not only because relevant published patents and applications may be difficult to identify or interpret, but because patent applications are kept secret for at least 18 months before being published.

The tendency of inventions to be independently developed around the same time, thus creating fertile ground for the proliferation of landmines, was noted by the Supreme Court in *Kewanee Oil Co. v. Bicron Corp.*[27]:

> The ripeness-of-time concept of invention, developed from the study of the many independent multiple discoveries in history, predicts that if a particular individual had not made a particular discovery others would have, and in probably a relatively short period of time. If something is to be discovered at all very likely it will be discovered by more than one person.

Patent Thickets

Because so many patents issue each year, a number of patents may cover similar subject matter or different aspects of the same subject matter. This dense network of related patents intertwined in a limited innovative space has led to the popular

27. 416 U.S. 470 (1974).

metaphor of the **patent thicket**, which consists of overlapping exclusive rights that businesses must cut through in order to conduct business.

Patent Hold-ups

Finally, some Internet-related products may be covered by hundreds or even thousands of different patents. Even if a product manufacturer were to negotiate licenses with most of the relevant patent owners, a single patent owner could **hold up** the manufacture of the entire product and would therefore be in a position to demand an exorbitant royalty. For example, one study found that the Linux operating system may be covered by as many as 283 separate patents owned by numerous different parties. A rule favoring an injunction would thus make businesses that are dependent on the Linux operating system vulnerable to hold-up. The hold-up problem was acknowledged by Justice Kennedy in a concurring opinion to *eBay v. MercExchange*, in which he and three other Justices expressed concern that a general rule favoring injunctions would give undue leverage to owners of patents covering only a small component of an accused product.

Patent Trolls

A **patent troll** is a pejorative term used to refer to an entity that asserts patents against others without itself practicing the inventions claimed in the patents. Justice Kennedy's concurrence in *eBay* alluded to the existence of trolls without using the term, noting the emergence of "[a]n industry . . . in which firms use patents not as a basis for producing and selling goods but, instead, primarily for obtaining licensing fees." Some patent trolls may not even invent the subject matter of the patents they wield, choosing instead to purchase others' patents and then assert them against third parties.

Critics argue that the royalties demanded by patent trolls are a "tax" on innovation and blame trolls for contributing to the landmine, thicket, and hold-up problems described above. Because trolls are nonpracticing entities, patent disputes are generally resolved through litigation rather than cross licensing, because a nonpracticing entity has no need to in-license a defendant's patents. More optimistic observers, on the other hand, view nonpracticing entities as intermediaries that create an important market where inventors can sell their patents, thus serving as a spur to innovation. They further argue that a rule requiring inventors to practice their inventions in order to assert patent rights would favor large, already-established businesses at the expense of individual inventors and start-up companies.

University Patenting: The Bayh-Dole Act of 1980

A number of Internet technologies have originated in university settings. Google's search engine patent, for example, was a culmination of the efforts of Larry Page while a graduate student at Stanford University. Another technology that allows interactive applications or "plugins" to be embedded in Internet browsers was patented by a researcher at the University of California, who founded a company called Eolas Technologies to exploit the invention. Because university research is often funded by the government, the question arises as to who (if anyone) should have the right to patent resulting inventions. The **Bayh-Dole Act of 1980** answered this question, providing that universities and other organizations may acquire patents on inventions developed with federal funds. The Act provides that the funding agency retains the right to practice the invention on a royalty-free basis, notwithstanding the patent owner's exclusive rights. Since the Bayh-Dole Act was enacted in 1980:

- More than 8,778 start ups have been established to develop academic research.
- The number of patents granted annually to universities has increased from in 267 in 1979 to 4,797 in 2012, an 18-fold increase.
- University technology transfer offices collectively report about $1.5 billion per year in licensing revenue.

Although these figures are optimistically cited by some as indicators of the success of Bayh-Dole in promoting university patenting, others fear that Bayh-Dole has wrongly shifted university science away from basic research and toward revenue-generating research while adversely affecting longstanding scientific norms of information sharing. Some economists add that patent litigation is not an efficient way to finance university research and that university licensing revenues are more than offset by the corresponding costs to businesses, particularly after attorney fees and other transaction costs are taken into account.

Because universities are nonpracticing entities but assert their patents against practicing entities, some have even compared them to patent trolls. From the perspective of businesses, this comparison may be apt. For example, in 2007 Northeastern University sued Google based on a patent covering Internet search technology obtained by a Northeastern University professor and assigned to the university. The parties settled in 2011 on undisclosed terms.

Responses to Patent Proliferation

Industry Responses

Businesses have responded in a number of ways to the proliferation of Internet-related patents. Those with large patent portfolios may engage in blanket *cross-licensing*, sometimes including "balancing payments" if necessary to account for the fact that one party's patent portfolio may be more valuable than the other party's portfolio. Another method of reducing the transaction costs associated with licensing individual patents is the **patent pool**, in which owners of related patents bundle their rights so as to provide "one stop shopping" for those who wish to make or sell a product or service covered by those patents. For example, patent pools have been formed that relate to the WiMAX wireless broadband standard, the MPEG audio and video compression standard, and certain DVD technology.

Consumer Advocate Responses: Patent Busting

Several nonprofit entities have sought to invalidate some patents by uncovering prior art that either anticipates those patents or renders them obvious. For example, the Public Patent Foundation, founded in 2003, has challenged a number of patents before the USPTO, including one related to the Joint Photographic Experts Group (JPEG) compression standard. The USPTO eventually rejected some, but not all, of the patent's claims for lack of novelty as a result of the Public Patent Foundation's efforts. The Electronic Frontier Foundation (EFF) initiated its Patent Busting Project in 2004. In a re-examination proceeding initiated by the EFF, the USPTO rejected patent claims to a method of quickly recording live performances on digital media that would enable performance venues to sell CDs to attendees as they exit the performance. In some cases, private individuals have challenged Internet-related patents, as in the New Zealander's challenge to the 1-click patent discussed earlier in the chapter.

Judicial and Legislative Responses

In the last several years, the Supreme Court has issued a number of decisions that moderate the ability to obtain and enforce patent rights. In 2006, the Court's *eBay* decision made it more difficult for patent holders to obtain injunctions, thereby reducing the ability of patent holders to negotiate favorable royalty agreements. In *KSR v. Teleflex*[28] the Court raised the obviousness standard, thereby making new patents more difficult to obtain and existing patents easier to invalidate. In 2014, the Supreme Court in *Nautilus v. Biosig*[29] set forth an elevated definiteness standard, thus reducing the patent owner's ability to include broad and imprecisely defined claims. A key Federal Circuit decision resulting from a dispute over hard drive technology made it more difficult for patent owners to establish that infringement was willful, thereby reducing the ability of patent owners to receive an enhanced damages award.[30] In addition, the 2011 America Invents Act included a number of provisions that limit patent rights. These include prohibitions against the issue of patents on human organisms or on methods of avoiding government tax liability, the creation of a broad defense for prior commercial use, and an expanded ability to challenge patents in an administrative procedure before the USPTO.

---

28. *KSR Int'l Co. v. Teleflex Inc.*, 550 U.S. 398 (2007).
29. *Nautilus v. Biosig*, 134 S. Ct. 2120 (2014).
30. *In re Seagate Technology, LLC*, 497 F.3d 1360 (Fed. Cir. 2007).

Conclusion

The patent landscape continues to evolve rapidly as online businesses acquire and assert patents with ever-increasing intensity. In the years ahead, significant judicial and legislative actions both domestically and at the global level will no doubt continue to shape the patent landscape, and businesses must stay on top of these developments in order to maximize their competitive position in the online marketplace.

Summary

Patents are temporary, government-sanctioned rights to exclude others from making, using, selling, offering to sell, or importing an invention that are granted in exchange for the inventor's public disclosure of how to make and use the invention. Thousands of Internet-related patents issue every year on hardware, software, and business methods employed by online companies. Although patent rights generally provide stronger protection than copyrights, patents last for only twenty years, measured from the date of filing and are more difficult to obtain. Prosecuting a patent may take several years and cost $50,000 or more. Only inventions of appropriate subject matter that are novel, useful, nonobvious, and enabled may be patented. Though only occasionally important in other contexts, the subject matter requirement is critical to Internet patents because software and business methods may not fit easily into the statutorily patentable subject matter categories, which include processes, machines, manufactures, and compositions of matter. Two of the three statutorily defined types of patents are relevant to the Internet: utility patents and design patents (the third type of patent is the plant patent). Software patents and business method patents are not precisely defined but are subcategories of utility patents. In some cases, a particular product design may be simultaneously protected by patent, copyright, and trademark law.

Key Terms

patent A government-granted, temporary *right to exclude*, awarded in return for an individual's public disclosure of a new and useful invention.

blocking patent An improvement patent of a second inventor that blocks a first inventor from making the improved version of the first inventor's own invention.

to license To authorize or allow.

royalties Money paid for the right to use a patented invention or other intellectual property.

cross-licensing An arrangement whereby two parties authorize each other to make, use, or sell the inventions protected by the other party's patents.

prosecute To apply for a patent.

patent examiner An employee of the USPTO that ensures that the invention described in a patent application meets the statutorily defined standards of patentability.

issue To grant (a patent).

Federal Circuit The federal court that hears appeals originating both from applications rejected by the USPTO as well as from district court patent decisions throughout the country.

maintenance fees Periodic fees paid to the USPTO to maintain a patent in force.

public domain The condition of a creation no longer under patent or copyright and that may thus be used freely by anyone without restriction.

first sale doctrine An exception to the exclusive rights of a patent or copyright owner, by which the owner of a particular copy of a copyrighted work or patented invention may resell or otherwise dispose of that copy or invention without the permission of the copyright or patent owner.

specification The portion of the patent that describes the invention and the manner and process of making and using it.

claims The portion of a patent that states explicitly and distinctly claims the particular subject matter the inventor regards as his or her invention.

Patent Act of 1952 The principal federal patent law.

utility A requirement of patentability that an invention be useful.

novel A requirement of patentability that an invention be new.

prior art Prior patents, publications, or uses that could negate novelty.

first-to-file A system by which patents are granted to the first inventor to file a patent application.

first-to-invent A system by which patents are granted to the first inventor to invent an invention.

grace period Once a company discloses an invention, it has a one-year grace period to file a patent application or it will lose the right to patent due to lack of novelty.

nonobvious A requirement that extends the novelty requirement to bar inventions only slightly different from the prior art.

secondary considerations Objective indicia of nonobviousness, such as the commercial success of an invention.

remand To send back a case (to a lower court).

enablement A requirement of patentability that a patent document enable any person skilled in the art to which it pertains to make and use the invention.

utility patent The most common type of patent; ordinarily referred to simply as a "patent."

plant patents A type of patent that protects new and distinct plant varieties that can be asexually reproduced.

design patents A type of patent that protects new, original, and ornamental designs on an article of manufacture.

algorithm A procedure for solving a given type of mathematical problem.

business method patent Though not statutorily defined, a type of patent that covers methods for processing data or conducting business operations.

cease-and-desist letter A letter that generally requests another party to either pay royalties or stop infringing a patent.

writ of certiorari The Supreme Court may in its discretion review Federal Circuit decisions by granting a party's request for a writ of certiorari.

United States International Trade Commission (USITC) An administrative agency based in Washington, D.C., that has the authority to issue exclusion orders that bar the importation into the United States of articles that infringe a valid and enforceable U.S. patent (or U.S. copyright or registered trademark).

exclusion order An order that bars the importation into the United States of articles that infringe a valid and enforceable U.S. patent (or U.S. copyright or registered trademark).

Markman hearings Claim construction proceedings associated with patent disputes.

literal infringement Where the accused device or process includes every limitation (part or element) of a patent claim.

limitation A part or element of a patent claim.

doctrine of equivalents A doctrine by which an accused device or process may be found to infringe if it performs substantially the same function in substantially the same way to obtain the same result.

prior-use defense A provision in the America Invents Act that provides a defense from liability for those who commercially use an invention more than one year before the earlier of the patent application date or the public disclosure date.

anticipated Not novel.

inequitable conduct Conduct before the USPTO that falls below the standard, such as intentionally failing to disclose relevant prior art to the examiner during prosecution.

statute of limitations A statutory provision providing that suits cannot be brought or damages cannot be recovered after a specified period of time.

damages Monetary compensation.

injunction An order by a court requiring a party to refrain from certain conduct.

patent landmine A metaphor used to describe the situation where a businessperson inadvertently infringes the patent of another.

patent thicket Overlapping patent rights that businesses must negotiate in order to conduct business.

hold-up A situation in which a single patent owner prevents third party use of a product even though other relevant rights owners have given authorization.

patent troll A pejorative term used to refer to an entity that asserts patents against others without itself practicing the inventions claimed in the patents.

Bayh-Dole Act of 1980 A federal law providing that universities and other organizations may acquire patents on inventions developed with federal funds.

patent pool An arrangement in which owners of related patents bundle their rights so as to provide "one stop shopping" for those who wish to make or sell a product or service covered by those patents.

Manager's Checklist

1. Before selling a new product or publishing research results, confer with an attorney to ensure the preservation of United States and foreign patent rights.

2. Establish a regular system of creating signed, written records of research activities in order to establish dates of invention and preserve patent rights.

3. Utilize (or ensure that your attorney utilizes) a calendar of maintenance fee due dates to ensure timely payment.

4. Consider the substantial costs of patenting and patent litigation when making business decisions.

5. Consider foreign patent laws, U.S. disclosure requirements, and the ability to prevent both domestic and foreign piracy when deciding whether to protect an invention with a patent.

Questions and Case Problems

1. Netflix rents movies to more than 13 million members via its online subscription service. Although some movies can be downloaded from the Internet, Netflix's signature service involves distributing movies through the mail. For a fixed monthly fee, members can receive as many movies as they like without the worry of late fees, limited only by the speed of the mail and rules regarding how many movies a member can have at one time. The service allows users to search online for movies they want, and then place those movies in a queue. When a customer returns one movie through the mail, Netflix automatically sends the next one in the queue. The rental method is covered by claim 1 of Patent No. 6,584,450 ("Method and Apparatus for Renting Items"), which

reads as follows: "A method for renting items to customers, the method comprising the computer-implemented steps of:

- Receiving one or more item selection criteria that indicates one or more items that a customer desires to rent;
- Providing to the customer up to a specified number of the one or more items indicated by the one or more item selection criteria; and
- In response to receiving any of the items provided to the customer, providing to the customer one or more other items indicated by the one or more item selection criteria, wherein a total current number of items provided to the customer does not exceed the specified number.

Imagine you are a defendant. Can you think of any prior art that might invalidate this patent? Remember that both lack of novelty and obviousness are potential theories of invalidity. The '450 patent was filed on April 28, 2000.[31]

2. Continuing from Question 1, suppose you were unable to think of prior art that might invalidate the Netflix '450 patent, or that the judge found that the prior art you presented did not render the invention either anticipated or obvious. *Present an argument that the patent should be invalid because it does not claim patentable subject matter.*

3. The chapter noted that Friendster, a former social networking site, obtained a number of social networking patents that it could potentially assert against other social networking sites such as Facebook. Suppose you are corporate counsel at Facebook and you expect that you may eventually be sued by Friendster. *In addition to contesting the validity or enforceability of the Friendster patents, what are some of your other options?*[32]

4. Mr. Antonious is the owner of U.S. Patent No. 5,482,279 ("the '279 patent"), which is directed to an improved perimeter weighting structure for metal golf club heads. Spalding sells the Intimidator golf club line. The Intimidator line includes drivers and fairway woods that use what Spalding refers to as "titanium insert technology." Antonious saw several Spalding Intimidator metal wood-type golf clubs in retail stores. He purchased one of the Intimidator drivers and cut open the club head. After inspecting the interior of the club head, Antonious concluded that Spalding's club infringed his '279 patent. *What are Antonious's legal options?*[33]

5. ***Ethical Consideration:*** If you found excerpted claim 26 from the '298 patent in *Hyperphrase Technologies v. Google* difficult to understand, you are not alone. Critics note that patents are often drafted deliberately to obfuscate the

---

31. *Netflix v. Blockbuster*, No. C 06-02361 WHA, 2006 WL 2458717 (N.D. Cal. Aug. 22, 2006).
32. See Caroline McCarthy, *Facebook's Newsfeed Patent Could Mean Lawsuits*, CNET News, http://www.cnn.com/2010/TECH/02/26/facebook.patent/index.html?hpt=T2.
33. *Antonious v. Spalding & Evenflo Co.*, 275 F.3d 1066 (Fed. Cir. 2002).

invention claimed and to provide as little information as possible, making relevant patents both difficult for businesses to find and challenging to decipher. *Why might businesses prefer to make their patents difficult to locate and understand? If you were a CEO of a business, would you instruct your patent department to try to draft patent applications as clearly as possible, or as opaquely as possible? Why?*

Additional Resources

Feldman, Robin. *Rethinking Patent Law* (Harvard Univ. Press 2012).

Google Patent Search. http://www.google.com/patents.

Merges, Robert P. *Justifying Intellectual Property* (Harvard Univ. Press 2011).

Orozco, David, and James Conley. *Shape of Things to Come*, WALL. ST. J., May 12, 2008, *available at* http://online.wsj.com/article/SB121018802603674487.html.

U.S. Patent and Trademark Office. http://www.uspto.gov.

World Intellectual Property Organization (WIPO). http://www.wipo.int.

 The Court is not persuaded that trade secret status should be deemed destroyed . . . merely by the posting of the trade secret to the Internet. To hold otherwise would do nothing less than encourage misappropriators of trade secrets to post the fruits of their wrongdoing on the Internet as quickly as possible and as widely as possible thereby destroying a trade secret forever.

—DVD Copy Control Ass'n v. McLaughlin (Cal. Super. Ct. 2000).

Trade Secrets

Learning Outcomes

After you have read this chapter, you should be able to:

- Describe the essential characteristics of a trade secret.
- Provide examples of trade secrets.
- Explain the significance of the Uniform Trade Secrets Act (UTSA) and the Economic Espionage Act (EEA).
- Describe the types of contracts businesses can use to protect secret information.

Overview

The Age of Big Data

We live in an age of "big data," where the potential to use large information datasets to transform the business and social environment is generating tremendous excitement: Google and Twitter data to track disease outbreaks; credit card data to improve marketing and detect fraud; and cell phone data to track urban congestion or to foil terrorist plots. Although the financial value of big data is difficult to quantify, many companies are now searching for ways to translate "big data" into competitive advantage. More generally, the value of information associated with new technology and business processes is growing ever larger.

An Information Explosion

To provide a sense of the amount of information being generated annually, the U.S. Copyright Office registered 509,112 creative works in a recent year, while the number of U.S. patents issued in 2013 exceeds the number issued during first 92 years of the nation's history. In the online environment, the U.S. Library of Congress reports that its web archive contains approximately 525 terabytes (1 terabyte = 1,000 gigabytes) of data as of 2014—a lot of data, but nothing compared to the more than 666 exabytes (1 exabyte = 1 million terabytes) of data estimated to have been transferred over the Internet in that year alone. Information, which constitutes the raw material on which many businesses depend for their vitality, is critical to the Information Economy.

Patents and Copyrights Cannot Protect All Data

Although information advantages may often be a key component of the competitive strategy of a business and a decisive factor in its success, a great deal of information cannot be protected by either copyright or patent law. For example, a secret recipe such as the formula for Coke may not exhibit a sufficient degree of creative expression to be copyrightable, while the public sale of Coke for more than 100 years prevents the Coca-Cola Company from patenting the recipe under the patent law novelty provisions (see Chapter 6). Even where information could be patented or registered as a copyright, a business may prefer trade secrecy for its potentially longer period of monopoly out of concern that disclosed information could be pirated or for other reasons.

This chapter explores the clandestine world of trade secrets, discussing what they are, how businesses can develop and protect them, and what a business can do to ensure against their loss.

What Is a Trade Secret?

By far the most famous example of a trade secret is the Coke formula mentioned above, which has remained secret since its creation by an Atlanta pharmacist in 1886. Similar examples include KFC's secret chicken recipe, McDonald's special sauce recipe for the Big Mac, the formula for the popular lubricant WD-40, and the formula for Listerine (which began as a trade secret in the 1880s but was disclosed in the *Journal of the American Medical Association* in 1931).

In addition to formulas and recipes, many other types of information can also qualify for trade secret status. Examples include:

- Computer software
- Customer lists that indicate purchasing histories and contact information
- Technical specifications for building or operating a device or service
- Marketing plans, including dates for new product launches

Virtually any information that provides economic value to a business can potentially be protected as a trade secret, and so the scope of subject matter covered by trade secret law tends to be broader and less precisely defined than it is for, say, patent law.

Trade Secrets: Governing Law

Unlike patents and copyrights, which are governed almost exclusively by federal law, trade secrets are primarily governed by state law and the precise definition may therefore vary somewhat from one state to another.

State Law: The Uniform Trade Secrets Act

The **Uniform Trade Secrets Act (UTSA)** has helped to harmonize trade secret law throughout the United States. The UTSA is one of more than 300 uniform laws that have been developed by a nonprofit organization known as the Uniform Law Commission (ULC). The ULC, although not itself a legislative body, drafts and proposes uniform laws that are then submitted to state legislatures. States may in their discretion decline to adopt the uniform laws, adopt them in their entirety as originally drafted, or adopt a partial or modified version as desired. The UTSA was originally submitted to the states for adoption in 1979. As of 2014, 48 states and the District of Columbia have adopted some version of the UTSA (only New York and Massachusetts have not done so).

Federal Law: Economic Espionage Act of 1996

Although trade secrets are still primarily governed by state law, there has been a trend toward increasing federal regulation. In the 1990s, as the Cold War ended and large-scale electronic commerce began to take root, Congress observed that classic military espionage was giving way to **economic espionage**—the deliberate theft of proprietary business information for the benefit of a foreign entity or government. The ease with which business information could be surreptitiously downloaded by insiders or even accessed at a distance through computer hacking was thought to have contributed to a quadrupling of economic espionage incidents over a four-year period, resulting in related losses to businesses of $63 billion annually. FBI investigations of alleged economic espionage by individuals or organizations from at least 23 different countries suggested that foreign governments were supporting the theft of information from American companies.

In order to provide federal law enforcement with the tools to combat both foreign and domestic trade secret theft, Congress enacted the **Economic Espionage Act of 1996** (EEA). As amended, the act criminalizes the theft of trade secrets and provides for penalties of up to $10 million (or three times the value of the stolen trade secret, whichever is greater) as well as imprisonment for up to fifteen years. In 2014, the first federal jury conviction under the EEA was obtained against Walter Lian-Heen Liew and Robert Maegerle in connection with a scheme to convey a secret process of producing titanium dioxide, owned by Delaware-based DuPont, to Chinese state-owned enterprises. Maegerle was sentenced to 2.5 years in prison and fined $367,679, while Liew received a 15-year prison term and was forced to forfeit $27.8 million in illegal profits.[1]

Trade Secrets Defined

The UTSA defines a **trade secret** as:

> *information, including a formula, pattern, compilation, program, device, method, technique, or process, that:*
>
>   (i) derives independent economic value . . . from not being generally known to, and not being readily ascertainable by proper means by, other persons who can obtain economic value from its disclosure or use, and
>
>   (ii) is the subject of efforts that are reasonable under the circumstances to maintain its secrecy.

The Economic Espionage Act provides a very similar definition, specifying that trade secrets include:

> [A]ll forms and types of financial, business, scientific, technical, economic, or engineering information, including patterns, plans, compilations, program devices, formulas, designs, prototypes, methods, techniques, processes, procedures, programs, or codes. . . .[2]

Like the UTSA, the Economic Espionage Act provides that information will only qualify as a trade secret if (1) the information is valuable because it is not generally known and would be difficult to lawfully acquire and (2) reasonable measures are taken to preserve secrecy. These two principal requirements for trade secret status will be explored in turn.

Valuable Because Not Generally Known

Information may be considered *generally known* if it is widely available on the Internet, published in a corporation's annual report, discernable via a public factory tour, or disclosed in marketing materials or professional journals. For example, when purported trade secrets regarding the Church of Scientology were posted to an Internet newsgroup where "competitors" of the Church were likely to look, the posted information became generally known.[3] However, the mere fact that information has been published on the Internet does not necessarily make it generally known, as this chapter's opening quote suggests. For example, where allegedly secret information regarding semiconductor chips was posted on a Chinese-language website but no evidence was proffered that any competitor was aware of the posted information, the court held that trade secret status had not been destroyed.[4]

---

1. http://www.justice.gov/sites/default/files/pages/attachments/2014/10/22/export-case-fact-sheet-201410.pdf.
2. 18 U.S.C. § 1839.
3. *Religious Tech. Ctr. v. Netcom On-line Commc'n Servs.*, 923 F. Supp. 1231 (N.D. Cal. 1995).
4. *Silicon Image, Inc. v. Analogix Semiconductor, Inc.*, 2008 WL 166950 (N.D. Cal. Jan. 17, 2008).

Even if information is not generally known to the *public*, it will still be ineligible for trade secret protection if it is clearly understood in the relevant industry. Under the UTSA definition provided above, the key is whether the information is generally known to "persons who can obtain economic value from its disclosure or use."

The determination of whether information is *generally known* can be compared to the patent law concept of novelty, but is not identical with it. For example, although patentability may be precluded based upon a relatively obscure but publicly available document, trade secret status might not be precluded so long as the information contained in the document is not generally known to competitors.

Not Readily Ascertainable. In addition to not being generally known, a trade secret must not be *readily ascertainable* by those who can obtain economic value from its disclosure or use. Information is **readily ascertainable** if it is available in trade journals, reference books, or published materials, or if it can be duplicated quickly and inexpensively or reverse engineered. Although there are no bright line rules, court decisions suggest that information is more likely to be readily ascertainable if it can be derived within a few minutes or hours and less likely if derivation would require months or years. Whether or not information is readily ascertainable might be compared to patent law's obviousness standard, in that the easier the information is to duplicate or acquire the less likely it is that the information will be eligible for protection.

Simultaneous Protection by Patent and Trade Secret Law? Information published in a domestic patent or patent application will ordinarily be considered generally known. This is important because it means that a business cannot simultaneously protect the same information as a patented invention and a trade secret. The business must choose one or the other.

Nevertheless, it is a common practice for businesses to obtain patents on inventions without disclosing certain information useful in making the invention commercially practicable, such as cost information, supplier information, or information about failures during the course of the invention's development. This additional information, not described within the patent itself, is instead kept as a trade secret and may be separately licensed as **know-how**. Know-how may also arise *after* the application for patent is filed. For example, when Larry Page applied for his Page Rank search engine patent in 1998, the Patent Act required him to describe the invention in sufficient detail so as to enable others to make and use it. However, because the Patent Act does not require inventors to update the patent disclosure if better techniques are later developed, any improvements by Page or others to the search engine algorithm, subsequent to the time of filing the patent application, could be kept as trade secrets. (Those improvements would not, however, be protected by the patent.)

Because businesses that **in-license** (receive) intellectual property generally desire the most commercially effective means of offering a product or service, intellectual property owners will often **out-license** (permit others to use) both patent and trade secret information.

Exhibit 7.1   Sample Document Marked as "Top Secret"

During the last five years, both Congress and the Supreme Court have been particularly active in considering some of the pressing issues in patent law in the context of a rapidly changing business environment. In this chapter you will explore the basic features of patents, study examples of how patents are being asserted in the online context, and examine the Supreme Court's recent pronouncement in the ongoing controversy over business method patents.

A *patent* is a government-granted, temporary right to exclude awarded in return for an individual's disclosure of a new and useful invention. In the United States, patents are granted by the United States Patent & Trademark Office (USPTO) and last for a non-renewable term of 20 years.

Patent owners enjoy the temporary right to exclude others from engaging in any of the following activities with respect to their inventions:

- making
- using
- selling (or offering to sell)
- importing into the United States

Although the patent term is much shorter than the copyright term, the exclusive rights of the patent owner are broader than those of the copyright owner. For example, while copyrights are limited by a generous fair use doctrine, patents are not subject to any comparably broad exception. Similarly, while independent creation of a copyrighted work is a defense to a copyright infringement action, independent invention is *not* a defense to a patent infringement action. The right to exclude others from making a patented invention applies even to those who later independently invent the same invention.

The fact that independent invention is not a valid defense to a patent infringement action means that online businesses must be aware of others' patent rights even if they do not copy other companies' business methods or technologies. For example, in 2002 Friendster launched its pioneering social networking website and became an early leader in a phenomenon that accelerated throughout the decade. Although it was eventually eclipsed in popularity by MySpace and later by Facebook, Friendster nevertheless succeeded in obtaining four patents between 2006 and 2009 including one entitled "System, Method and Apparatus for Connecting Users in an Online Computer System Based on Their Relationships Within Social Networks."[1] Even if MySpace and Facebook did not copy Friendster in designing and implementing their online businesses, they might nevertheless inadvertently infringe one or more of these patents by independently inventing the same patented subject matter. Although Friendster has declined in prominence in the United States, it continues to be a substantial social networking presence in Asia and could

Reasonable Measures to Maintain Secrecy

Not only must the information not be generally known, but businesses must take measures that are reasonable under the circumstances in order to maintain secrecy.

Although the circumstances may vary from case to case, reasonable measures might include:

- Restricting access to databases, such as by requiring the use of a password
- Restricting access to sensitive areas, such as by maintaining sensitive documents in locked cabinets or rooms
- Limiting sensitive information to employees that have a "need to know"
- Marking proprietary documents as "secret" or "confidential" (see Exhibit 7.1)
- Embedding watermarks in electronic documents to help identify the source of the disclosure
- Conducting "exit interviews" when employees leave the company to remind them about confidentiality obligations and the proper treatment of proprietary information

In addition to these operational and technological measures that businesses can take to maintain trade secret status, a number of contractual measures are available. These include requiring employees or others to sign nonsolicitation agreements, nondisclosure agreements, and covenants not to compete.

Nonsolicitation Agreements. A trade secret owner wishing to decrease the risk that its employees will be tempted to quit their jobs to work for one of the trade secret owner's business partners may ask those business partners to sign **nonsolicitation agreements.** These agreements deter partner businesses from attempting to lure away the trade secret owner's employees, who may possess valuable trade secrets. Similarly, a trade secret owner worried that its employees may try to start a competing enterprise may include a **nonsolicitation clause** as part of the employment contract in order to deter the employee from soliciting former colleagues to join the new enterprise.

Nondisclosure Agreements (NDAs). As the name implies, a **nondisclosure agreement** (**NDA**) is a contract that requires a party not to disclose certain specified information that a business considers important to its competitive advantage. Businesses may routinely enter into NDAs with employees, contractors, consultants, clients, business partners, and potential investors. The NDA should indicate what specific information is subject to nondisclosure and how long the nondisclosure obligation will persist.

Businesses should be aware that an NDA that imposes nondisclosure obligations for too short a duration can undermine a plaintiff's claim that "reasonable measures" have been taken. For example, one court concluded that plaintiff Silicon Image was unlikely to prevail in its trade secret misappropriation claim against competitor Analogix, noting that the plaintiff's NDAs imposed confidentiality obligations for only two to four years and that many of them had expired. The proprietary information in question related to the HDMI technology common to popular consumer electronics such as High Definition Televisions (HDTVs) and some cell phones. Although it was unclear to what extent the ruling was based on the NDA duration, the court cited earlier opinions where NDA durations of one to ten years had been held too short.

Covenants Not to Compete. A **covenant not to compete**, also called a non-compete agreement, is a provision in an employment contract in which an employee promises not to compete with the employer should the employment relationship end. Covenants not to compete will usually be enforced when they are reasonable, which requires courts to balance a number of factors. Courts must weigh the legitimate interests of the employer who has invested resources and effort in training an employee against the public interest in receiving the benefit of the employee's services as well as the employee's interest in earning a living.

In order to be enforced, covenants not to compete must generally be reasonable across three dimensions: (1) duration; (2) geography; and (3) scope (prohibited future activity cannot be broader than that currently performed by the employee). As a rule of thumb, noncompetition clauses that prohibit former employees from competing with the employer for a term of more than two years will tend to be unreasonable. However, the standard of reasonableness is highly dependent on the circumstances and tends to be shorter within the Internet context. For example, one early Internet trade secret case famously held that a one-year covenant was too long to be enforced because "in the Internet environment, a one-year hiatus from the workforce is several generations, if not an eternity."[5] Similarly, in *DoubleClick v. Henderson*,[6] the court granted an injunction enforcing a noncompete agreement for only six months rather than for the one-year period sought by plaintiff DoubleClick, an Internet advertising company.

Covenants Not to Compete in California

Although states generally disfavor covenants not to compete, California is one of a small number of states that uniformly refuse to enforce such covenants absent a specific statutory exemption. Because of the large number of Internet-related businesses located in California, its committed policy against covenants not to compete is notable.

Ethical Consideration: Employment-at-Will and Non-Compete Agreements.

As you will learn in Chapter 9, the default rule in the United States is "employment-at-will," meaning that, absent a contractual provision to the contrary, an employee can be discharged from employment at any time even if the employee has done nothing wrong. Tension arises between the at-will doctrine and the existence of non-compete agreements, which prevent employees from utilizing their most valuable skills for a limited period of time. Business managers should

---

5. *EarthWeb, Inc. v. Schlack*, 71 F. Supp. 2d 299 (S.D.N.Y. 1999).
6. No. 116914/97, 1997 WL 731413 (N.Y. Sup. Ct. Nov. 7, 1997).

Google

> In some cases, businesses seeking to hire employees who have signed noncompete agreements will make great efforts to have the dispute resolved by a California court. For example, when Google sought to hire Kai-Fu Lee as its Vice President of Engineering, the $10 million employment offer was cast into doubt by a one-year noncompete agreement that Lee had signed as part of his employment with Microsoft. Microsoft, seeking to prevent Lee's employment with Google, filed suit in Washington State. Google, seeking the benefit of California law in its efforts to overcome the covenant not to compete, then filed a separate suit in California. However, the California judge declined to rule in the case until the Washington court issued its decision, and the parties eventually settled the dispute on confidential terms with Lee heading up Google's China operations.

consider the ethics of exercising their at-will rights while simultaneously enforcing a non-compete agreement against the now-discharged employee.

Government Disclosure Under the Freedom of Information Act (FOIA). Under the **Freedom of Information Act** (**FOIA**, pronounced "foy-uh"), the public may obtain government documents from federal agencies upon request. Because businesses must frequently disclose information to the government as part of the ordinary regulatory process, secret business information may potentially be placed at risk. Anticipating this problem, FOIA provides a number of exceptions to its disclosure provisions for trade secrets and other sensitive information.

In some cases, businesses may find it advantageous to file requests for confidentiality with the relevant government agency in order to ensure nondisclosure and to help demonstrate that reasonable measures have been taken to maintain secrecy. For example, shortly before releasing the Surface 2 tablet computer in 2014, Microsoft reportedly submitted a request to the Federal Communications Commission to maintain in confidence certain details of the product, including associated schematics, photographs, user's manual, and antenna specification.

Justifying Trade Secret Law

Trade secret law and the contractual measures employed to protect trade secrets impose a number of costs on society. They can restrict employee mobility and limit employees, at least temporarily, from utilizing their most valuable skills. Conversely, they can create challenges for employers seeking to hire employees with relevant skills. Trade secret law can restrict the free flow of ideas, reduce competition, and slow technological and business development. Moreover, trade secret litigation and the desire to avoid litigation impose significant transaction costs in the form of uncertainly, attorney fees, and paperwork. Given these disadvantages, it might be wondered why trade secret law exists at all!

Two principal rationales have been offered in justification of the legal protection of trade secrets. First, trade secret law can promote innovation, particularly with respect to subject matter that may not satisfy the requirements for patentability. Second, trade secret law reinforces standards of commercial ethics. These two rationales are explored below.

Innovation and Efficiency

Like trademark, patent and copyright law, trade secret law is thought to promote innovation by ensuring that those who have invested in developing information can benefit from their efforts without the fear of free riding. In addition, trade secret law can help to promote business efficiency. For example, without trade secret law employers might hesitate to hire strangers of unknown loyalty and instead engage in **nepotism** (hiring of relatives) or **cronyism** (hiring of friends) even if other more qualified workers are available. By providing a right of action for misappropriation, trade secret law encourages employers to select their employees from a broad range of applicants, fully train them, and share information with them as required for efficient business operations. More generally, by providing a legal structure within which information may be shared yet maintained in confidence, trade secrets encourage the formation of stable business relationships.

Business Ethics

Trade secret law can also be justified on the basis of a number of ethical or moral dimensions. Trade secret law provides a legal basis for reinforcing loyalty and confidentiality obligations that many believe are inherently part of the relationship between employer and employee. The definition of misappropriation includes within its reach the acquisition of a trade secret by bribery or misrepresentation, both of which have obvious ethical dimensions. In addition, trade secret law prohibits economic espionage, which can be characterized as a form of theft that may sometimes involve deceit. In short, trade secret laws can be justified on principles of good faith and fair dealing in addition to principles of market efficiency.

"Obtaining" and Maintaining a Trade Secret

Unlike trademarks, copyrights, and patents, there is no process by which a trade secret can be registered, and in fact no generally accepted procedure by which particular information becomes a trade secret. Instead, trade secrets come into existence when valuable information that is not generally known to competitors is developed or acquired and reasonable efforts are made to maintain the information as a trade secret.

In the Internet context, the passage of time could potentially terminate trade secret status if the information is no longer valuable. For example, in a long-running dispute between CarsDirect.com, an online automobile comparison and buying portal, and a competing software firm, a court refused to grant injunctive relief in part because of the rapid pace of technological advancement in the software industry. The court found that it was "highly unlikely" that the trade secrets at issue were still valuable fourteen years after the misappropriation.[7]

Trade Secret as Alternative to Patent and Copyright

Trade secret protection is sometimes considered an alterative to patent or copyright protection, though the various types of intellectual properly may provide overlapping rights in some cases. For example, different aspects of a single computer program may be simultaneously protected by patent law, copyright law, and trade secret law.

When determining which type or types of intellectual property to pursue, a number of important differences should be borne in mind. For example, copyrighted works reflect creative expression and therefore tend to derive value from being publicly observable, while information may be protected as a trade secret only if it is *not* generally known to the public. Other differences relate to the duration of protection and costs associated with maintaining information in confidence.

Costs of Trade Secrets

Trade secrets are often described as a less expensive alternative to patents, in part because they do not require registration or maintenance fees. Yet trade secrets do impose costs on businesses. For example, designing and maintaining secure computer systems that have appropriate password, encryption, and firewall controls is not costless. In addition, there are transaction costs associated with limiting access to information and requiring business partners, suppliers, and clients to enter into nondisclosure and other agreements. Finally, some employees may find the security measures inconvenient or distasteful, particularly where contractual provisions frustrate their ability to accept future employment.

Duration of Trade Secrets

In light of the fact that trade secrets are not registered with the government, they also do not need to be "renewed" nor do they expire after a statutorily prescribed period of time. So long as the trade secret remains secret and continues to confer economic value, the owner's rights in the trade secret under state and federal law will persist. Trade secrets are therefore potentially perpetual, in contrast to the limited terms of copyrights and patents.

In the online environment, the rapid pace of development may mean that information will lose much of its value before the 20-year patent term expires. The potentially perpetual duration of trade secrets may therefore be of only nominal added value. Businesses may nevertheless prefer trade secret protection

---

7. *Versata Software, Inc. v. Internet Brands, Inc.*, No. 2:08-cv-313-WCB (E.D. Tex. July 30, 2012).

over patent protection, however, because the patent law disclosure requirement increases the chance of unauthorized copying. Although patents confer the right to prevent others from making, using, or selling an invention, infringement of patented processes or business methods may be difficult to detect. Moreover, copying may occur in other countries where patent rights have not been secured at all. Maintaining information as a trade secret avoids the need to obtain patent protection in multiple countries or to engage in expensive and time-consuming litigation to enforce those patents.

Unsuccessful Patenting Places Secret Information at Risk

Although trade secrets are potentially perpetual, the public disclosure of a secret could bring a premature and abrupt end to trade secret status. For example, if a business were to file a patent application, the application, including its detailed description of the invention, would typically be made public after eighteen months under applicable law. However, if the USPTO examiner ultimately determined that the invention described in the application was unpatentable, the business would have destroyed its trade secret without securing the benefit of a patent. A similar result would occur if a patent was issued by the USPTO but later invalidated by a court.

Third Party Patents May Limit Trade Secret Duration

In addition, if a business decides to protect information as a trade secret and a third party independently develops and patents an invention based on the same information, the business could find itself unable to continue using its own trade secret information. The 2011 Leahy-Smith America Invents Act lessened but did not eliminate this risk by providing a defense to patent infringement for those who commercially used an invention more than one year prior to the patent's filing date. Businesses wishing to assert this defense must be able to prove commercial use prior to the relevant date, suggesting the need for careful recordkeeping.

A business's own partners may even attempt to patent the business's trade secrets. This was the case in *Corbis Corp. v. Stone*,[8] which pitted a small start up company that had developed a digital image, video, and music tracking system against Corbis Corp., a photograph licensing corporation owned by Microsoft's Bill Gates. Originally business partners, the two companies found themselves embroiled in litigation with each party accusing the other of trade secret misappropriation. Ultimately, the dispute was resolved by a jury, which found that Corbis had misappropriated trade secrets by secretly filing a patent application based on Stone's proprietary technology. The court ordered Corbis to pay more than $49 million, including $750,000 in attorney fees and costs based on its determination that the misappropriation was "willful and malicious."

---

8. *Corbis Corp. v. Stone*, 167 Wash. App. 1019 (Wash. Ct. App. 2012); *see also* No. 07-2-03244 (Wash. Super. Ct. Feb. 9, 2010).

Exhibit 7.2	**Comparing Trade Secrets with Patents**	

	Trade Secret	**Patent**
Governing Law	UTSA, EEA	Patent Act of 1952
State/Federal	Mostly state law	Federal law
Subject Matter	Information that is valuable and not generally known	Inventions that are novel, useful, and nonobvious
Duration	Perpetual (potentially)	20 years
Protection Against Independent Invention	No	Yes
Third Party Patent	Third party patent could end trade secret rights	"Blocking patents" limit innovative freedom
Registration	No	Yes
Disclosure	Undermines secrecy	Required
Costs	No registration costs (but transaction costs)	High registration (and maintenance) costs
Prevention of Copying	Secrecy impedes piracy	Right to sue infringer

Independent Invention and Trade Secrets

In contrast to patents, trade secrets provide no protection against others who independently develop the same information, regardless of whether those third parties attempt to patent the information. Exhibit 7.2 summarizes some of the differences between patent and trade secret protection.

Trade Secrets and Software

It was noted above that software could be simultaneously protected by both copyright and trade secret law. Given that copyright registration involves making a copy available for public inspection in the Copyright Office, it might be wondered how software code can remain secret while simultaneously fulfilling copyright registration requirements. The answer in part is that under Copyright Office regulations only the first and last twenty-five pages of source code need be deposited, and the portions of the source code that contain trade secrets may be **redacted** (blocked out). Because large software programs may be composed of millions of lines of code, the Copyright Office deposit requirements can result in only a tiny fraction of the code being made available to the public. For example, in *Two Palms Software, Inc. v. Worldwide Freight Management LLC*, a court found that the deposit of only 50 pages of more than 80,000 lines of source code did not preclude trade secret status.[9]

In addition, although creative works deposited with the Copyright Office are available for public *inspection*, a member of the public wishing to view deposited material must sign an agreement not to *copy* the material pursuant to formal Copyright Office policies. Thus, when a software company deposited unredacted copies of its software instruction manuals with the Copyright Office, a court found that trade secret protection was not lost owing to the restrictions on public copying and the lack of evidence that anyone had actually viewed the deposited material.[10]

A Dynamic Business Environment Places Trade Secrets at Risk

Trade secrets can be lost if information leaks cause once-secret information to become generally known by competitors. One of the greatest threats to the maintenance of secret information is disclosure by employees, who can be viewed as living repositories of a business's economically valuable information, whether financial, strategic, or technological. The skills, experiences, and business knowledge acquired by an employee over the course of employment are as mobile as the employee who possesses them. And employees are indeed mobile, with some reports indicating that the average person will change jobs ten or more times over the course of the person's career. Employment in the Internet sector is particularly fluid.

Employee Mobility

Although employee mobility and associated knowledge spillovers have been cited as key contributors to the success of technology centers such as Silicon Valley, every change in personnel brings with it the risk that proprietary information will fall into the hands of a competitor. In fact, the most common scenarios that give rise to trade secret litigation include:

- An employee leaving an employer to begin work for a competitor
- An employee leaving an employer to start a new competing company
- An employee disclosing proprietary information on the Internet (either directly or via a third party)
- A relationship between business partners that ends poorly

Many trade secret disputes therefore arise as a result of a broken employment or business relationship, which one scholar has analogized to a "bitter divorce." For example, in 2004 a social networking site called ConnectU sued a then-fledgling Facebook based upon allegations that Facebook's founder Mark Zuckerberg stole ConnectU's source code and business plan. Zuckerberg and

---

9. No. 4:10-CV-1045(CEJ), 2012 WL 2418913 (E.D. Mo. June 26, 2012).
10. *Compuware Corp. v. Serena Software Int'l Inc.*, 77 F. Supp. 2d 816 (E.D. Mich. 1999).

ConnectU's founders had originally worked together to design a social networking site while they were classmates at Harvard before the relationship soured.

In the following case, the court had to determine whether Accenture, a global consulting firm, could be liable for trade secret misappropriation based on a confidential relationship with one of its former clients.

Wellogix, Inc. v. Accenture L.L.P.

716 F.3d 867 (5th Cir. 2013)

Higginson, Circuit Judge

[Facts] The oil and gas industry spends billions of dollars each year to construct oil wells. Yet, traditionally, oil companies planned such projects over "coffee and doughnuts," using paper records to track and pay costs. And, to the extent that they employed computer software, they relied on basic tools such as Excel. Due, in part, to this paper process, oil companies struggled to estimate certain well construction costs—known as "complex services." Even modest improvements in how companies estimated such costs could save hundreds of millions of dollars. Wellogix, Inc.—motto: "making the complex simple"—sought to modernize this process. Wellogix developed software that allowed oil companies to "plan, procure, and pay for complex services"—all online. . . .

To promote its software, Wellogix entered into six marketing agreements with the consulting firm Accenture, L.L.P. Wellogix also participated in pilot projects with oil companies. Wellogix shared source code and access to its technology with both Accenture and the oil companies [including BP], subject to confidentiality agreements. . . .

Without notifying Wellogix, Accenture and [a software company called] SAP began developing the complex services component of the global software for BP. As they developed the component, Accenture and SAP apparently accessed Wellogix technology—including flow diagrams, design specifications, and source code critical to Wellogix's software—that had been uploaded to [a confidential website set up as part of the prior collaboration between BP and Wellogix]. Wellogix sued BP, Accenture and SAP in district court in 2008, alleging that they had stolen and misappropriated Wellogix trade secrets. . . .

[Misappropriation of Trade Secrets] Trade secret misappropriation under Texas law is established by showing: (a) a trade secret existed; (b) the trade secret was acquired through a breach of a confidential relationship or discovered by improper means; and (c) use of the trade secret without authorization from the plaintiff. . . .

[Existence of Trade Secret] A trade secret is any formula, pattern, device, or compilation of information used in one's business, and which gives an opportunity to obtain an advantage over competitors who do not know or use it. To determine whether a trade secret exists, we consider six factors, weighed "in the context of the surrounding circumstances":

> (1) the extent to which the information is known outside of his business; (2) the extent to which it is known by employees and others involved in his business; (3) the extent of the measures taken by him to guard the secrecy of the information; (4) the value of the information to him and to his competitors; (5) the amount of effort or money expended by him in developing the information; (6) the ease or difficulty with which the information could be properly acquired or duplicated by others.

In re Bass, 113 S.W.3d 735, 739–40 (Tex. 2003).

Here, Wellogix presented sufficient evidence and testimony to support the jury's finding that Wellogix's technology contained trade secrets. Wellogix showed that, because it was the only company offering complex services software from 2000 to 2005, its software—and, in particular, the underlying proprietary source code—gave it an opportunity to obtain an advantage over competitors. Wellogix also showed that the six *Bass* factors weigh in its favor. For example, Wellogix introduced evidence that it guarded the secrecy of its technology by placing its software behind a firewall, and sharing it subject to confidentiality agreements. . . .

[Improper Means] Improper means of acquiring another's trade secrets include theft, fraud, unauthorized interception of communications, inducement of or knowing participation in a breach of confidence, and other means either wrongful in themselves or wrongful under the circumstances of the case. Here, Wellogix presented sufficient evidence and testimony to support the jury's finding that Accenture improperly acquired Wellogix's trade secrets. Wellogix showed: that it entered into six confidential agreements with Accenture; that, through the marketing agreements, Accenture had access to Wellogix trade secrets; that Accenture also had access to Wellogix trade secrets uploaded to the confidential [Web] portal; and that an Accenture email referenced "harvesting IP" from Wellogix.

[Use] As a general matter, any exploitation of the trade secret that is likely to result in injury to the trade secret owner or enrichment to the defendant is a "use." Thus, marketing goods that embody the trade secret, employing the trade secret in manufacturing or production, relying on the trade secret to assist or accelerate research or development, or soliciting customers through the use of information that is a trade secret, all constitute "use." . . . Here, Wellogix presented sufficient evidence and testimony to support the jury's finding that Accenture used its trade secrets. Wellogix showed: that Accenture joined with SAP to develop a complex services component for BP's P2P pilot; that, around the time that Accenture and SAP partnered, they were able to access Wellogix's dynamic templates source code that had been uploaded to the confidential eTrans portal; that an Accenture document referenced the "creation of . . . complex service templates," and then right below stated: "Use Wellogix content"; that the same document provided that the templates "better deliver similar or better functionality than Wellogix or we may have a problem" . . .

CONCLUSION

[The Fifth Circuit upheld a jury award of $18.2 million in punitive damages plus $26.2 million in compensatory damages.]

Case Questions

1. What are the three elements needed to establish trade secret misappropriation under Texas law?
2. According to the court, are confidentiality agreements relevant to the issue of trade secret misappropriation? If so, how are they relevant?
3. *Ethical Consideration:* If you were in Accenture's position and wanted to pursue a business relationship with BP, how might you do so in a way that minimizes the risk of liability for misappropriating Wellogix's trade secrets?

Inadvertent Disclosure

Secret information may also be placed at risk inadvertently by well-intentioned but perhaps overzealous employees who, for example, tout product benefits online or at trade shows in an attempt to generate business. In some cases business partners, consultants, or law firms may inadvertently disclose confidential information. For example, although ConnectU and Facebook attempted to keep their 2008 settlement agreement confidential, ConnectU's law firm inadvertently boasted in its newsletter that it had achieved a $65 million settlement for ConnectU. Although the settlement figure might not itself qualify as a trade secret, the incident serves to demonstrate how easily confidential information can be disclosed.

Third Party Espionage

Secret information may also become vulnerable as a result of intentional espionage by competing businesses or even foreign governments, a concern that resulted in the passage of the Economic Espionage Act described above.

The Internet

Computers, smart phones and the Internet have served to magnify the risk of trade secret loss. Networked computers enable departing employees to easily email confidential information to themselves or others, or download large volumes of data to a tiny flash drive. Unrelated third parties may be able to hack into networks to view or download information from across the street or around the globe. Even loyal employees can place trade secrets at risk by mistyping an

Google

WHAT GOOGLE DOESN'T WANT YOU TO KNOW

Just because Google is known for its highly effective information search tool doesn't mean that the company is eager to share its own information with anyone who happens to be curious. Like most companies with competitive strategies based on technology, Google develops and protects various types of technical and strategic information as trade secrets.

Perhaps Google's most closely guarded secret relates to its patented PageRank method of ranking Internet search results by relevance. Although the patent publicly discloses certain information as required by law, the details of the search algorithm remain largely unknown. It should hardly be surprising that the patent (U.S. Patent No. 6,285,999), which is only eleven pages long, does not disclose the more than 200 signals, 500 million variables, and 2 billion terms that Google claims constitute part of its PageRank system. Moreover, even if such details were disclosed in the patent, Google is reported to make frequent changes to its algorithm—as many as one every day.

Google is also secretive when it comes to the hardware and technology infrastructure that allow it to process the hundreds of millions of queries that it receives on a daily basis. It is not publicly known, for example, how many computer servers Google maintains throughout the world in its various data centers, though estimates suggest the figure may exceed 1 million. When Google built its Internet data center near Portland, Oregon, the center's design and details were intentionally kept shrouded in secrecy, with local officials unable to publicly comment due to the nondisclosure agreements they had signed with Google.

In some cases, however, Google has decided that the benefits of disclosure outweighed the advantages of secrecy. For example, in 2009 Google cracked open the door to its storehouse of proprietary information, surprising industry observers by disclosing that each of its servers had been designed to include its own 12 volt battery. The design constituted a break from the traditional practice of using a centralized backup power source and, according to Google, allowed it to operate its data centers with greater efficiency and lower energy consumption.

email address or by traveling with a company laptop or smart phone that is then vulnerable to theft by a third party. In addition, the ability to post information on the Internet dramatically increases the speed with which secret information can be disseminated as well as the number of people who may potentially access it.

An example of the risks posed by departing employees is provided by iRobot, the maker of both the well-known Roomba floor vacuuming robot as well as a military reconnaissance and bomb-disposal robot known as the PackBot. When engineer Jameel Ahed resigned from iRobot to start competing enterprise known as Robotic FX, he allegedly sent confidential documents from his iRobot email account to a Robotic FX email account and worked to build a less expensive version of the PackBot. Ahed's former employer iRobot filed suit against Robotic FX and Ahed alleging misappropriation of trade secrets and breach of a nondisclosure agreement. Although the dispute settled before trial, iRobot largely prevailed: Certain assets of Robotix FX were transferred to iRobot and Ahed was prohibited from competing in the robotics industry for five years.

Trade Secret Litigation

It is preferable to appropriately guard against trade secret loss by proactively engaging in the measures described above, such as limiting access to confidential information and utilizing nondisclosure agreements. In some cases, however, it may be necessary to protect trade secrets through litigation.

Asserting Trade Secret Rights in Court

Plaintiffs in trade secret cases must generally establish that (1) the information in question qualifies as a trade secret, (2) reasonable measures were taken to protect the information, and (3) despite these measures the information was misappropriated.

Information Qualifies as a Trade Secret

Plaintiffs must provide evidence that the information in question qualifies as a trade secret under the particular version of the UTSA that has been enacted in the relevant jurisdiction. As noted earlier, the plaintiff must therefore prove that the information alleged to be a trade secret is valuable because it is not generally known to those who could gain economic value from its disclosure or use and that reasonable measures were taken to maintain secrecy.

Businesses should be aware that not all confidential information will necessarily be considered valuable. For example, in *MicroStrategy, Inc. v. Business Objects, S.A.*,[11] the court found that a confidential email regarding the financial condition of the plaintiff did not constitute a trade secret because it was unclear that the email had any economic value. Similarly, information which is merely embarrassing may not qualify as a trade secret absent a finding of independent economic value.

Moreover, the value of information must be proven convincingly to the court. In *Yield Dynamics v. TEA Systems Corp.*,[12] a California appeals court declined to classify as trade secrets eight segments of software code used to facilitate the fabrication of integrated circuits, quoting with approval the trial court's finding that "[n]o evidence was admitted relating to [the code's] value to a competitor."

Reasonable Measures to Maintain Secrecy

Although a trade secret plaintiff must establish that reasonable measures were taken to maintain secrecy, the law does not require the plaintiff to have taken all available measures. For example, in the landmark case of *E.I. DuPont de Nemours & Co. v. Christopher*,[13] the Fifth Circuit held that aerial photography by a competitor of a partially built chemical plant could constitute trade secret

---

11. 331 F. Supp. 2d 396 (E.D. Va. 2004).
12. 154 Cal. App. 4th 547 (Cal. Ct. App. 2007).
13. 431 F.2d 1012 (5th Cir. 1970).

misappropriation. Although it would have been possible for DuPont to build a cover over its facility, such a measure could not be reasonably required of DuPont given the enormous expense involved.

In contrast, where a software developer failed to include confidentiality provisions in a contract with its customer and could not point to any affirmative steps it took to maintain the secrecy of its software interface, the Sixth Circuit held that the plaintiff had not taken reasonable measures to maintain secrecy and that the information was therefore not a trade secret.[14]

Inadvertent Disclosure of Information During Litigation. Businesses must take care when seeking to enforce their trade secrets not to inadvertently disclose their trade secrets through court filings, which are generally open to public inspection. If disclosure occurs and court documents are not sealed, the ironic result might be that the trade secrets sought to be enforced could become "generally known" and trade secret status would then be destroyed. Recognizing this unfair result, the UTSA instructs courts to preserve the secrecy of an alleged trade secret by reasonable means, which may include:

- Holding **in-camera** hearings (i.e., proceedings without public spectators)
- **Sealing** (making unavailable to the public) the records of the action
- Ordering any person involved in the litigation not to disclose an alleged trade secret without prior court approval

In *Religious Technology Center v. Lerma*,[15] the plaintiff, a religious organization, sought to enjoin the defendant from posting on the Internet some of its religious documents, which the plaintiff alleged contained trade secrets. Before the court ordered the documents sealed, the *Washington Post* learned of the case and sent a news aide stationed near the court to obtain the court records, which contained the documents in question. In light of the public availability of the court records, the court held that the documents could not be trade secrets and that the *Post* could not be liable for misappropriation. The availability of the documents on the Internet reinforced the court's conclusion that the documents were not trade secrets.

Information Was Misappropriated

Under the UTSA, a plaintiff may be entitled to remedies based on the misappropriation of trade secrets. **Misappropriation** is defined as the "acquisition of a trade secret by someone who knows or has reason to know that the trade secret was acquired by improper means" or "disclosure or use of a trade secret of another without express or implied consent."

Misappropriation can therefore arise based upon three different types of activities. First, a person can misappropriate a trade secret by wrongfully *acquiring* it.

---

14. *R.C. Olmstead, Inc. v. CU Interface, LLC*, 606 F.3d 262 (6th Cir. 2010).
15. 897 F. Supp. 260 (E.D. Va. 1995).

Second, a person can misappropriate a trade secret by wrongfully *using* it. Finally, misappropriation can occur when a person wrongfully *discloses* it to others. The acquisition, use, or disclosure of a trade secret will be wrongful if the information was acquired by improper means or if the use or disclosure was made possible based upon acquisition by improper means.

Acquisition by Improper Means. Misappropriation by improper means may include:

- Theft
- Bribery or misrepresentation
- Breach or inducement of a breach of a duty to maintain secrecy
- Espionage through electronic or other means

In addition, the violation of particular federal laws would likely constitute improper means. For example, the **Computer Fraud and Abuse Act** (**CFAA**) prohibits individuals from accessing a computer without authorization. Similarly, the federal **Electronic Communications Privacy Act** (**ECPA**) prohibits the interception of an electronic communication (such as an email message) while in transit. Engaging in activities prohibited by the CFAA or the ECPA in order to obtain trade secrets would likely be classified as "improper means." (See Chapter 13 for further discussion of the CFAA and ECPA.)

Acquisition by Proper Means. Although the acquisition of secret information by improper means is prohibited, there are several ways to acquire information that do not constitute improper means and therefore will generally not give rise to trade secret liability. As mentioned above, trade secret laws do not prevent third parties from independently inventing the subject matter of the trade secret. Similarly, third parties may generally reverse engineer a product that is subject to trade secret protection absent a contractual prohibition. **Reverse engineering** occurs when one starts with a known product and works backward to determine the process which aided in its development or manufacture. Finally, if information is acquired by examining publicly available documents or engaging in an ordinary Internet search, such acquisition will ordinarily not constitute misappropriation.

Even where a defendant breaches a security measure to obtain allegedly secret information, however, the defendant's action may not constitute misappropriation of trade secrets if the information is not in fact secret. For example, in *Storage Technology Corp. v. Custom Hardware Engineering & Consulting*,[16] the Federal Circuit declined to impose liability for trade secret misappropriation where the defendant circumvented plaintiff's passwords because the information protected by those passwords had been publicly available for several years.

---

16. 421 F.3d 1307 (Fed. Cir. 2005).

Suits Based Upon Inevitable Disclosure

Section 2 of the UTSA authorizes courts to enjoin actual *or threatened* misappropriation. Under the **inevitable disclosure** doctrine, a court may enjoin a departing employee from accepting employment at a competing enterprise if there is a high probability that the employee would inevitably use or disclose the former employer's trade secrets to the benefit of the new employer. Inevitable disclosure is more likely to be found where the similarities between the businesses are such that the employee could not reasonably be expected to perform the duties of the new position without relying on trade secrets of the previous employer. One court famously compared the plaintiff in an inevitable disclosure case to "a coach, one of whose players has left, playbook in hand, to join the opposing team before the big game."[17]

However, it should be noted that while employees may be enjoined from prospective employment based on the inevitable disclosure of a former employer's trade secrets, such injunctions are relatively uncommon. Moreover, employees are free to use the general knowledge and skills gained in their former positions. The line between general knowledge and skills on the one hand and trade secrets on the other may be difficult to draw, and may ultimately need to be determined by a court.

By authorizing injunctions as to prospective employment, the inevitable disclosure doctrine can reinforce a covenant not to compete or, in the absence of such a covenant, may be used by a trade secret plaintiff to achieve a similar result. In *Janus et Cie v. Kahnke*, below, a New York court had to decide whether to apply the inevitable disclosure doctrine to prevent a sales manager with knowledge of a customized account management system from accepting employment with his employer's direct competitor. Recall that New York has not yet adopted the UTSA, and so the court had to apply the judicially created common law of trade secrets that guides New York courts.

Janus et CIE v. Kahnke
No. 12 Civ. 7201 (WHP), 2013 WL 5405543 (S.D.N.Y. Aug. 29, 2013)

Pauley, District Judge

[Facts] In February 2008, Kahnke was employed as a sales associate by Janus, a provider of high-end residential and commercial furnishings. . . . Kahnke and Janus executed a non-disclosure agreement that prohibited Kahnke from sharing Janus' confidential information, defined as "all information that has actual or potential economic value to [Janus]." Kahnke did not execute any non-compete agreement with Janus. . . . As part of his responsibilities, Kahnke developed and customized Janus' account management system and other resource documents

---

17. *PepsiCo v. Redmond*, 54 F.3d 1262, 1270 (7th Cir. 1995).

which detail key points about customers and competitors, financial, marketing and new production information, . . . inventory management, logistics, historical customer information and customized management systems.

On August 20, 2012, Kahnke notified Janus that he had accepted a very similar position with Dedon, Inc., a direct competitor of Janus. . . . According to the Complaint, Dedon hired Kahnke hoping to exploit the information he learned at Janus in order to develop its own customized account management system. Janus now brings this action for inevitable disclosure of trade secrets, seeking a permanent injunction barring him from disclosing any of Janus' trade secrets or confidential information and from working for Dedon in any area where Janus and Dedon are direct competitors. Janus does not allege that Kahnke breached the nondisclosure agreement. Nor does Janus assert any facts indicating that Kahnke actually misappropriated or disclosed any of Janus' trade secrets. Rather, Janus seeks an injunction based on the theory that Kahnke's position with Dedon is so similar that he cannot possibly perform the functions of his position without using and/or disclosing confidential information and trade secrets belonging to Janus.

[Inevitable Disclosure Under New York Law] Fourteen years ago, in *Earth-Web, Inc. v. Schlack*, 71 F. Supp. 2d 299 (S.D.N.Y. 1999), this Court explored the parameters of the inevitable disclosure doctrine under New York law. There, EarthWeb sought to use inevitable disclosure of trade secrets as a basis to enjoin Schlack preliminarily from working for a competitor even though the parties' non-compete agreement did not prohibit it. Critically, like Janus here, EarthWeb had no evidence that Schlack had copied or otherwise absconded with documents allegedly containing trade secrets. In such cases, the court is essentially asked to bind the employee to an implied-in-fact restrictive covenant based on a finding of inevitable disclosure. This runs counter to New York's strong public policy against such agreements and circumvents the strict judicial scrutiny they have traditionally required. This Court refused to re-write the parties' employment agreement under the rubric of inevitable disclosure, holding that the doctrine treads an exceedingly narrow path through judicially disfavored territory. Absent evidence of actual misappropriation by an employee, the doctrine should be applied in only the rarest of cases. . . .

The parties' non-disclosure agreement mandates that any breach be governed by California law, which does not recognize inevitable disclosure of trade secrets as a valid cause of action. . . . Janus contends that its Complaint survives a Rule 12(b)(6) motion [i.e., a motion to dismiss at an early stage of the proceedings] merely because it alleges certain factors that courts consider in weighing the appropriateness of granting injunctive relief based on the inevitable disclosure doctrine; namely that "(1) the employers in question are direct competitors providing the same or very similar products or services; (2) the employee's new position is nearly identical to his old one, such that he could not reasonably be expected to fulfill his new job responsibilities without utilizing the trade secrets of his former employer; and (3) the trade secrets at issue are highly valuable to both employers." *EarthWeb*, 71 F. Supp. 2d at 310. But this argument . . . does not persuade this Court that it has threaded the "exceedingly narrow path through judicially disfavored territory."

CONCLUSION

Absent any wrongdoing that would constitute a breach under the confidentiality agreement, mere knowledge of the intricacies of a business is simply not enough. . . . Andrew Kahnke's motion to dismiss Janus et Cie's Complaint is granted.

Case Questions

1. What steps did Janus take, with respect to Mr. Khanke, to prevent the loss of its valuable business information? Did the court find these steps sufficient?
2. List the three factors that courts consider in weighing the appropriateness of granting injunctive relief based on the inevitable disclosure doctrine.
3. *Ethical Consideration:* Why did the court deny relief for Janus? What policy considerations support, or call into question, the court's decision?

Breach of Contract

In addition to pursuing a cause of action for trade secret misappropriation under a given state's version of the UTSA, a trade secret owner may also be able to assert a separate cause of action for breach of contract. If the defendant signed a valid nonsolicitation agreement, nondisclosure agreement (NDA), or covenant not to compete, the trade secret owner could bring suit to enforce the terms of the contract subject to the caveat that agreements that restrict employee mobility are disfavored to varying degrees in different states.

Pretrial Discovery. Prior to trial, litigants engage in the mandatory exchange of documents and other forms of information relevant to the litigation in a process known as **discovery**. For trade secret owners who find their confidential information posted online, one of the critical issues during discovery is whether Internet blogs or other sites can be compelled to disclose the identity of the individuals who provided the allegedly secret information posted on those blogs.

In *O'Grady v. Superior Court,*[18] a California court of appeal answered this question in the negative. According to the court, the dispute developed after Apple sought to obtain the identity of individuals—presumably Apple employees—who had provided confidential information that appeared on a website operated by O'Grady. The information was related to an interface for Apple's GarageBand music creation product and included not only product information but also certain confidential financial information such as expected quarterly earnings. The trial court authorized Apple to serve a **subpoena** (order to appear or to

---

18. 139 Cal. App. 4th 1423 (Cal. Ct. App. 2006).

produce documents) on O'Grady and his email service provider so that it could obtain the identities of the proper defendants. The appellate court, however, concluded that the subpoenas should be **quashed** (declared void). Its decision was based in part on the First Amendment protection of the press, which helps to shield reporters and publishers such as O'Grady from liability for refusing to disclose their information sources. The *O'Grady* court held that online journalists seeking to protect the identity of their sources were to be treated no differently than traditional journalists.

Protective Orders. Discovery in noncriminal federal court proceedings is governed by the **Federal Rules of Civil Procedure** (**FRCP**), which allow parties to resist discovery requests where disclosure would place trade secrets at risk or be otherwise unduly burdensome or expensive. Under FRCP 26(c), courts have wide discretion to grant protective orders limiting discovery of certain information or barring it altogether.

For example, when Viacom sued YouTube for $1 billion for its alleged role in facilitating online copyright infringement, Viacom moved to compel the disclosure of YouTube's search algorithm. Viacom hoped to show that YouTube had intentionally designed its algorithm to help users find infringing content on the YouTube site. In granting YouTube's request for a protective order barring discovery, the court noted that "YouTube . . . should not be made to place this vital asset [i.e., the search algorithm] in hazard merely to allay speculation."[19] As noted in Chapter 5, YouTube ultimately prevailed in the underlying copyright litigation based on the Digital Millennium Copyright Act's (DMCA) safe harbor provisions.

Discovery from Nonparties. The Federal Rules of Civil Procedure allow for the discovery of information not only from parties to a lawsuit, but also from nonparties who have information relevant to the underlying dispute. For example, when the American Civil Liberties Union (ACLU) challenged the constitutionality of the Child Online Protection Act (COPA), the government served a subpoena on Google, a nonparty, requesting it to produce a statistically significant sample of Google's search index URLs. The government sought the data so that it could test the effectiveness of blocking and filtering software, which was relevant to its assertion that the COPA was constitutional. Although the court noted that the discovery request created a risk to Google's secret search algorithm information, it nevertheless granted the government's motion to compel limited disclosure by Google on the condition that any documents produced be subject to a protective order indicating their status as "Confidential."

Defending a Trade Secret Suit

A defendant in a trade secret suit may be able to prevail upon showing that the information in question is not in fact secret, that reasonable measures were not

---

19. *Viacom Int'l Inc. v. YouTube, Inc.*, 253 F.R.D. 256 (S.D.N.Y. 2008).

taken to maintain secrecy, or that the defendant did not misappropriate the information. In addition, a statute of limitations provision under the UTSA allows a defendant to avoid liability if the plaintiff failed to bring its claim within three years (modified by some states to five years) of the discovery of the misappropriation.

Information Is Not Secret

Posting information to the Internet can destroy a trade secret by making it generally known, even if the information is eventually taken down. Nevertheless, two caveats are worth noting.

First, the person who initially posts the information on the Internet may be liable for misappropriation even if the posting destroys the trade secret. To relieve the misappropriator from liability because the misappropriator posted the information on the Internet, thereby making it generally known, would reward wrongful conduct and undermine the goals of trade secret law. Similarly, subsequent posters may be liable for misappropriation if they acquired the information with knowledge that the person from whom they obtained the information acquired the information by improper means.

Second, as this chapter's opening quote suggests, courts have sometimes hesitated to conclude that the posting of information on the Internet destroys a trade secret even as to third parties because such a conclusion would only serve to encourage the posting of trade secrets on the Internet. If the Internet disclosure is sufficiently limited in both time and scope, it is more likely that the trade secret can be preserved. Therefore, if Internet disclosure occurs businesses should move as quickly as possible to have the information removed.

A list of customers is a classic example of information that may be protected as a trade secret, in part because such a list, if known by competitors, could allow those competitors to efficiently target marketing and communication efforts. What if a business maintains a social networking site where its list of "friends" is publicly viewable on the Internet? Does public visibility prevent this "customer list" from achieving trade secret status? In answering this question in the negative, a federal district court explained that the trade secret is not merely the list of "friends" but also their email address, interests, and preferences, as well as the ability to promote directly to them via their social networking accounts.[20] The court noted that this ancillary information was not readily ascertainable from outside sources.

Defendant Did Not Misappropriate Information

Even if the information is secret, a defendant may defend on the basis that it did not misappropriate the information. For example, a defendant may be able to establish that it obtained the information by reverse engineering or by independently developing the information. For example, in *Sarkissian Mason, Inc. v.*

---

20. *Christou R.M.C. Holdings, L.L.C. v. Beatport, LLC*, 849 F. Supp. 2d 1055 (D. Colo. 2012).

Exhibit 7.3 **Example of Quick Response (QR) Code**

Enterprise Holdings, Inc.,[21] a digital marketing agency presented Enterprise, a car rental company, with the idea of placing QR codes on rental car key fobs. The QR codes would lead consumers to a website designed to encourage purchases of the type of car the renter was driving. While the parties were still negotiating, Enterprise developed its own QR-code based service that differed in at least two important respects. The court found no misappropriation because the "broad concept" of using QR codes to connect consumers to manufacturers via their smartphones was already in the public domain, and the plaintiff's detailed marketing program was not used by Enterprise.

A First Amendment Right to Post on the Internet?

The First Amendment to the U.S. Constitution provides that "Congress shall make no law . . . abridging the freedom of speech, or of the press. . . ." Defendants in trade secret cases seeking to justify the disclosure of information on the Internet have sometimes asserted that their actions are protected by the First Amendment. Most courts, however, have concluded that the First Amendment does not create a right to publicly disclose others' trade secrets on the Internet, at least where the trade secrets do not address matters of public concern.

There have been exceptions, however. For example, in *Ford Motor Company v. Lane,*[22] the court declined to enjoin the Internet disclosure of corporate trade secrets in favor of First Amendment rights, explaining that some of the documents posted by the defendant revealed aspects of Ford's approach to fuel economy standards and therefore did address matters of public concern. Similarly, the court in *Rain CII Carbon LLC v. Kurczy*[23] declined to preliminarily enjoin an "email alert" that disclosed Rain's confidential financial information. The *Rain* court noted that the defendant was a member of the media, heightening First

---

21. 955 F. Supp. 2d 247 (S.D.N.Y. 2013).
22. 67 F. Supp. 2d 745 (E.D. Mich. 1999).
23. No. 12-2014, 2012 WL 3577534 (E.D. La. Aug. 20, 2012).

Amendment concerns, and that the plaintiff's financial information was a matter of public concern in part because the plaintiff was a major world supplier of petroleum coke, a raw material used to make aluminum.

In the following landmark case, the California Supreme Court had to decide whether the First Amendment protected a defendant's posting to the Internet of DeCSS, a computer program that could be used to make copies of copyrighted movies without authorization.

DVD Copy Control Ass'n v. Bunner
75 P.3d 1 (Cal. 2003)

Justice Brown, J.

[Background] Digital versatile discs (DVD's) are five-inch wide disks capable of storing more than 4.7 [Gigabytes] of data. In the application relevant here, they are used to hold full-length motion pictures in digital form. . . . Recognizing [that the digital nature of DVDs creates a] risk of widespread piracy, the motion picture industry insisted that a viable protection system be made available to prevent users from making copies of motion pictures. . . .

[T]wo companies, Toshiba and Matsushita Electric Industrial Co., Ltd., developed the Content Scrambling System (CSS). CSS is an encryption scheme that employs an algorithm configured by a set of "keys" to encrypt a DVD's contents. . . . The motion picture, computer, and consumer electronics industries decided to use the CSS technology to encrypt copyrighted content on DVD's and agreed that this content should not be subject to unauthorized (i) copying or (ii) transmission, including making the content available over the Internet. . . . These industries later established the DVD Copy Control Association, Inc. (DVD CCA) as the entity charged with granting and administering the licenses to the CSS technology.

Despite . . . efforts to safeguard the CSS technology, Jon Johansen, a Norwegian resident, acquired the proprietary information embodied in the technology . . . by reverse engineering software created by a licensee. . . . [The licensee's software] is licensed to users under a license agreement, which specifically prohibits reverse engineering. Using the proprietary information culled from this software, Johansen wrote a program called DeCSS that decrypts movies stored on DVD's and enables users to copy and distribute these movies. . . . Johansen posted the source code of DeCSS on an Internet Web site in October 1999.

Soon thereafter, DeCSS appeared on other Web sites, including a Web site maintained by Andrew Bunner. Bunner posted DeCSS on his Web site allegedly because "it would enable Linux users to use and enjoy DVDs available for purchase or rental in video stores" and "make Linux more attractive and viable to consumers." Bunner also claimed he wanted "to ensure [that] programmers would have access to the information needed to add new features, fix existing defects and, in general, improve the DeCSS program." . . .

DVD CCA then filed this action against Bunner and numerous other named and unnamed individuals who had published or linked to web sites publishing DeCSS (collectively defendants), alleging trade secret misappropriation. . . .

[Legal Issue] [T]he narrow question before us is whether the preliminary injunction violates Bunner's right to free speech under the United States and California Constitutions even though DVD CCA is likely to prevail on its trade secret claim against Bunner. . . . [24]

[Is Computer Code "Speech" Under the First Amendment?] As computer code . . . is a means of expressing ideas, the First Amendment must be considered before its dissemination may be prohibited or regulated. . . .

[Level of First Amendment Scrutiny] In determining the appropriate level of scrutiny [that the court should apply], the critical question is whether the injunction is content neutral or content based. Content-based injunctions are subject to [heightened scrutiny and thus more likely to be held unconstitutional]. . . . By contrast, content-neutral injunctions are subject to [a] lesser level of scrutiny [and thus more likely to be held constitutional]. . . . [25]

[W]e conclude that the preliminary injunction [barring Bunner from posting DeCSS on the Internet] is content neutral. . . . [T]he trial court issued the injunction to protect DVD CCA's statutorily created property interest in information—and not to suppress the content of Bunner's communications. Because the injunction is justified without reference to the content of Bunner's communications, it is content neutral.

Indeed, the governmental purpose behind protecting trade secrets like the CSS technology through injunctive relief is wholly unrelated to their content. "Trade secret law promotes the sharing of knowledge, and the efficient operation of industry; it permits the individual inventor to reap the rewards of his labor by contracting with a company large enough to develop and exploit it." The law also maintains important standards of commercial ethics. Assuming, as we do, that the trial court properly applied California's trade secret law, the preliminary injunction necessarily serves the broader governmental purpose behind the law. Because the injunction does not purport to restrict DVD CCA's trade secrets based on their expressive content, the injunction's restrictions on Bunner's speech properly are characterized as incidental to the primary purpose of California's trade secret

---

24. [Norwegian authorities brought a criminal action against Johansen in Norway at the urging of the Motion Picture Association of America (MPAA). Johansen was eventually acquitted, a ruling described by the MPAA as reflecting "an apparent defect in Norwegian law."—Eds.]

25. [Government limitations on speech, based on the content of the speech, are a type of censorship. Such limitations are therefore much more difficult to justify under the First Amendment and courts will "strictly scrutinize" them. In contrast, limitations on speech imposed without reference to the content of the speech—such as limiting noise after a certain hour or, as in this case, preserving trade secrets—are more likely to survive First Amendment scrutiny.—Eds.]

law—which is to promote and reward innovation and technological development and maintain commercial ethics. . . .

[Bunner as Misappropriator] Bunner contends the preliminary injunction [should not have issued] because it enjoins disclosures by those with no connection to DVD CCA or those people who acquired its trade secrets by improper means. . . . [However, the trial] court found that . . . Bunner knew or should have known that Johansen acquired these trade secrets by improper means when [Bunner] posted DeCSS on [his] Web site. . . . [A] person who knowingly exploits the illegal acquisition of property owned by another should be in no better position than the illegal acquirer himself . . .

[Matter of Public or Private Concern] In this case, the content of the trade secrets neither involves a matter of public concern nor implicates the core purpose of the First Amendment. . . . DVD CCA's trade secrets in the CSS technology are not publicly available and convey *only* technical information about the method used by specific private entities to protect their intellectual property. Bunner posted these secrets in the form of DeCSS on the Internet so Linux users could enjoy and use DVD's and so others could improve the functional capabilities of DeCSS. He did not post them to comment on any public issue or to participate in any public debate. Indeed, only computer encryption enthusiasts are likely to have an interest in the *expressive* content—rather than the uses—of DVD CCA's trade secrets. Thus, these trade secrets, as disclosed by Bunner, address matters of purely private concern and not matters of public importance.

CONCLUSION

We . . . hold that the preliminary injunction [issued against Bunner] does not violate the free speech clauses of the United States and California Constitutions. . . .

Case Questions

1. Did Bunner obtain the DeCSS code by reverse engineering? Who is Jon Johansen? Why was the reverse engineering in question alleged to be wrongful in this case, given that reverse engineering is normally a proper means of acquiring trade secrets?
2. Did the court find that the trial court's injunction was a content-neutral restriction on Bunner's free speech rights? Or was it a content-based restriction? How did this determination affect the level of scrutiny applied by the court?
3. *Ethical Consideration:* Do you think Bunner is more analogous to a common criminal who has given out the combination to a warehouse of goods so that others may steal them? Or, is he to be commended for performing a valuable public service that contributes to technological development and consumer enjoyment?

After DVD Copy Control Ass'n v. Bunner

The California Supreme Court's decision in *Bunner* meant that preliminary injunctions against the Internet disclosure of trade secrets do not necessarily violate the First Amendment. Although the ruling was a significant victory for the movie industry and trade secret owners in general, the victory was short lived with respect to the claim against Bunner. On remand, the California appeals court found that DeCSS had been disseminated so quickly to anyone interested in it that by the time Bunner posted the information on his webpage it likely no longer qualified as a trade secret. The court therefore declined to impose a preliminary injunction. Johansen, who faced criminal charges in Norway, was acquitted in 2003 after a Norwegian court concluded that his actions in reverse engineering the code did not violate Norwegian law.

Although the posting of DeCSS could not be prevented in *Bunner* on the basis of trade secret law, it does not necessarily follow that anyone may post DeCSS to the Internet without risking liability. Recall from Chapter 5 that the Digital Millennium Copyright Act (DMCA) prohibits trafficking in devices that are primarily designed for the purpose of circumventing copyright protection measures and that the Second Circuit enjoined the posting of or linking to DeCSS in *Universal City Studios v. Corley*.[26] No claims under the DMCA were asserted in *Bunner*.

Remedies

A number of remedies are available to successful trade secret plaintiffs, including damages, attorney fees, and injunctions. In addition, contractual remedies may be available as mentioned above.

Damages and Attorney Fees Under the UTSA

Under the UTSA, successful plaintiffs may recover either the actual loss they experience as a result of the trade secret misappropriation or the gain to the defendant owing to the misappropriation. Damages may alternately consist of a reasonable royalty for the misappropriator's unauthorized disclosure or use of the trade secret. Unlike patent and trademark law, under which plaintiffs may in certain cases be entitled to treble damages (three times actual damages), trade secret plaintiffs may recover up to *twice* their actual damages where willful and malicious misappropriation is demonstrated. A finding of willful misappropriation also makes available the remedy of attorney fees, which may be awarded to the plaintiff in the court's discretion.

---

26. 273 F.3d 429 (2d Cir. 2001).

Injunctions Under the UTSA

The most potent remedy available to trade secret plaintiffs is the injunction, authorized by Section 2 of the UTSA. Such an injunction might involve, for example, an order to remove content from the Internet, a prohibition on further use or dissemination of information, or a constraint on the ability of a defendant to accept employment at a competitor's business under the inevitable disclosure doctrine.

Because trade secret litigation may last for months or years, a **permanent injunction** granted by the court after trial may come too late to prevent information posted on the Internet from becoming generally known. Courts may therefore issue **preliminary injunctions** at earlier stages of the litigation, but only after notifying the other party and offering that party a chance to respond. In some cases of extreme urgency, courts may issue a **temporary restraining order** (**TRO**) that enjoins certain activities or disclosures without providing the other party a chance to be heard. For example, a lower court in *Rain* initially issued a TRO against the defendant news publisher in the litigation over the unauthorized email alert mentioned above.

An Expedited Remedy for Internet Postings?   Even TROs may require several days to obtain, however, during which time information could spread rapidly on the Internet. One scholar has proposed that Congress address this problem by enacting **notice and takedown** legislation analogous to that which is available to copyright holders under the Digital Millennium Copyright Act (DMCA) (see Chapter 5). Such legislation could require third parties to expeditiously remove (take down) alleged trade secrets from the Internet even without a court order upon notification by the trade secret owner, provided that certain conditions are met. Any Internet takedown requests would, of course, be subject to judicial review. No such legislation has been enacted to date.

Conclusion

Proprietary information is an increasingly important asset for online businesses, with one government estimate placing the aggregate value of intellectual property owned by United States companies at $5 trillion. Laws such as the Economic Espionage Act and those based on the UTSA can help to reinforce company efforts to maintain secrecy, but the most important weapon against trade secret misappropriation is prevention. Utilizing encryption and passwords, marking documents as "secret," and entering into appropriate confidentiality and employment agreements can avoid significant future litigation costs and can potentially avoid the need for litigation altogether. More than with any other type of intellectual property, appropriate trade secret policies should reflect the adage that an ounce of prevention is worth a pound of cure.

Summary

Online businesses operate within a dynamic business environment where employees are especially mobile and where the volume of new and valuable information generated proceeds at a tremendous and ever-increasing pace. Electronic communications and the Internet have only increased the risk of trade secret loss by magnifying the speed and ease with which secret information can be communicated. The Uniform Trade Secrets Act has helped to harmonize trade secret law throughout most of the United States, though differences remain. In addition, the Economic Espionage Act of 1996 allows the government to bring criminal actions based on the interstate or international theft of trade secrets. Although virtually any type of information can qualify as a trade secret, the information must (1) derive independent economic value (2) from not being generally known by competitors and (3) be the subject of reasonable efforts to maintain its secrecy. Nondisclosure agreements and covenants not to compete may be used both to inform employees of their obligations toward the employer's proprietary information and to enhance the ability of those employers to enforce against use or disclosure of trade secrets if necessary. Trade secrets may serve to complement or substitute for patent protection and in some cases may be more appropriate for certain types of information than either copyright or patent protection. Businesses should consider differences in subject matter eligibility, duration, effectiveness in preventing copying, and cost when deciding how best to protect their proprietary information.

Key Terms

Uniform Trade Secrets Act (UTSA) One of more than 300 uniform laws that have been developed by a nonprofit organization known as the Uniform Law Commission.

economic espionage The deliberate theft of proprietary business information for the benefit of a foreign entity or government.

Economic Espionage Act of 1996 (EEA) An act that criminalizes the theft of trade secrets and provides for penalties of up to $10 million.

trade secret Information that derives independent economic value from not being generally known by competitors and that is the subject of efforts that are reasonable under the circumstances to maintain its secrecy.

readily ascertainable Information is readily ascertainable if it is available in trade journals, reference books, or published materials, or if it can be duplicated quickly and inexpensively or reverse engineered.

know-how Information that is not described within a patent and that may instead be kept as a trade secret and separately licensed.

in-license To receive authorization to utilize intellectual property.

out-license To permit others to use intellectual property.

nonsolicitation agreements Agreements that prohibit partner businesses from attempting to lure away a trade secret owner's employees.

nonsolicitation clause A provision in an agreement (such as an employment agreement) that prohibits a departing employee from attempting to lure away the employee's former colleagues.

nondisclosure agreement (NDA) A contract that requires a party not to disclose certain specified information that a business considers important to its competitive advantage.

covenant not to compete A provision in an employment contract in which an employee promises not to compete with the employer should the employment relationship end.

Freedom of Information Act (FOIA) A federal law under which the public may obtain government documents from federal agencies upon request.

nepotism The hiring of relatives.

cronyism The hiring of friends.

redact To block out or omit a portion of text so that it is not visible.

in camera Out of view of the public.

seal To make unavailable to the public.

misappropriation The acquisition of a trade secret by someone who knows or has reason to know that the trade secret was acquired by improper means or disclosure or use of a trade secret of another without express or implied consent.

Computer Fraud and Abuse Act (CFAA) A federal law that prohibits individuals from accessing a computer without authorization.

Electronic Communications Privacy Act (ECPA) A federal law that prohibits the interception of an electronic communication (such as an email message) while in transit.

reverse engineering When one starts with a known product and works backward to determine the process which aided in its development or manufacture.

inevitable disclosure A doctrine under which a court may enjoin a departing employee from accepting employment at a competing enterprise if there is a high probability that the employee would inevitably use or disclose the former employer's trade secrets to the benefit of the new employer.

discovery A process, prior to trial, in which litigants engage in the mandatory exchange of documents and other forms of information relevant to the litigation.

subpoena An order to appear or to produce documents.

quash To declare void.

Federal Rules of Civil Procedure (FRCP) Rules which govern the process by which federal civil litigation is conducted.

injunction, permanent An order of a court prohibiting a party from engaging in some action, after a final judgment.

injunction, preliminary An order of a court prohibiting a party from engaging in some action, prior to a final judgment.

temporary restraining order (TRO) A court order that enjoins certain activities or disclosures without providing the other party a chance to be heard.

notice and takedown Proposed legislation that would require third parties to expeditiously remove (take down) alleged trade secrets from the Internet even without a court order upon notification by the trade secret owner.

Manager's Checklist

1. Require employees, contractors, consultants, and business partners to sign nondisclosure agreements (NDAs).

2. Include reasonable noncompete clauses in employment contracts; but be aware that some states such as California may not enforce these clauses.

3. Redact trade secrets from source code when registering with the Copyright Office.

4. Utilize passwords, firewalls, encryption, and other forms of digital and physical security measures to control access to proprietary information.

5. Conduct exit interviews with departing employees to remind them of their contractual confidentiality and noncompetition obligations.

Questions and Case Problems

1. Suppose you independently develop a new, useful, and nonobvious method of conducting an online auction. The novel aspects of the method relate to the minimum amount of bid increments, the time at which bidders must submit bids, and the mathematical algorithm for calculating the price that the winning bidder must pay (which price is *not* the same as the highest bid price). *Would you seek patent protection, trade secret protection, or both? What problems might you face in attempting to secure patent or trade secret rights, and what advantages and disadvantages might you consider in making your decision?*

2. The CEO of a small but promising start-up company is in need of an experienced engineer to head up a key aspect of the business, and has selected Sam as a leading candidate. If hired, Sam would not only be exposed to the proprietary technology that already provides a significant advantage in the market, but would be tasked with developing additional proprietary information and software. Sam is currently an employee of XYZ Corp., a competitor of

the start-up. *What potential problems might the CEO want to consider? What steps could the CEO take to address these problems?*

3. A medical foundation used IDX's medical billing software. IDX's competitor is Epic. Two Epic employees left and went to work directly for the medical foundation, and soon thereafter, the foundation switched its software supplier—to Epic. IDX alleges that these two employees used their new positions to transfer valuable information to Epic, about how IDX software works, and so on, thus enabling Epic to enhance its own software package. IDX filed suit alleging the two employees misappropriated IDX's trade secrets. *What should be the result?*[27]

4. Suppose a well-financed start-up company seeks to compete in the provision of Internet search services. The company has developed a proprietary system of organizing and cooling its servers that it believes is faster, cheaper, and more scalable than existing methods. These servers, designed to be housed in waterproof units that float just below the surface of the water, are located several miles off the coast of Washington State. A competitor, seeking to uncover the trade secrets embodied in the floating server units, sends a boat and team of divers to examine one of the floating units and successfully obtains valuable information. The start-up could have foiled the competitor's efforts by stationing a patrol boat at all times near the floating server units, but failed to do so. *Assuming the law of the state of Washington applies and that Washington has adopted the UTSA without modification, present an argument that the competitor should be liable for trade secret misappropriation.*

5. *Ethical Consideration:* California's policy strongly disfavoring claims based upon covenants not to compete is complemented by its policy strongly disfavoring injunctions based upon inevitable disclosure. *What do covenants not to compete and the inevitable disclosure doctrine have in common? Is a contract required in order to assert each type of claim (in states which recognize such claims)? Construct an argument that both types of claims should be recognized in California, including within your argument the effect of the claims on the welfare of (1) the employee, (2) the trade secret owner, (3) the competitor, and (4) the public.*

Additional Resources

Digital Media Law Project: Trade Secrets, Berkman Center for Internet & Society, http://www.dmlp.org/legal-guide/trade-secrets.
Federal Bureau of Investigation. *Economic Espionage: Protecting America's Trade Secrets*, http://www.fbi.gov/about-us/investigate/counterintelligence/economic-espionage-1.

27. *IDX Systems Corp. v. Epic Systems Corp.*, 285 F.3d 581 (7th Cir. 2002).

National Conference of Commissioners on Uniform State Laws. http://www.uniformlaws.org.

Paine, Lynn Sharp. *Trade Secrets and the Justification of Intellectual Property: A Comment on Hettinger*, 20(3) PHIL. & PUB. AFF. 247 (1991).

Pierce, Shannon S., and Matthew Digesti. *To Protect Trade Secrets, Companies Must Get Smart About Smart Phones*, 22-MAY NEV. LAW. 8 (2014).

Risch, Michael. *Why Do We Have Trade Secrets?*, 11 MARQUETTE INTELL. PROP. L. REV. 1 (2007).

Rowe, Elizabeth A. *Proposing a Mechanism for Removing Trade Secrets from the Internet*, 12 No. 3 J. INTERNET L. 3 (2008).

World Intellectual Property Organization (WIPO). *What Is a Trade Secret?*, http://www.wipo.int/sme/en/ip_business/trade_secrets/trade_secrets.htm.

three

Part III

Transactional Law: Creating
Wealth and Managing Risk

 Thoroughly read all of your contracts. I really mean thoroughly.
—Bret Michaels, musician

Contracts and Licensing

Learning Outcomes

After you read this chapter, you should be able to:

- Understand the process of engaging with business partners to accomplish goals through drafting and executing agreements.
- Learn that much of contracts has to do with performance obligations, trust, timing, quality and communication issues.
- Learn that software and site licenses are legally binding and enforceable contracts.
- Understand how licensing and intellectual property rights are closely related in businesses.
- Understand how agreements have potential for anti-competitive effects on markets that can trigger regulatory scrutiny.

Overview

Contracts and licenses are integral to our work and personal lives. Agreements are the means by which we transfer goods and services, and in this way, create relationships, opportunities, wealth, as well as diffuse technology and speed innovation. All ventures start with ideas, and agreements are the means by which the ideas are actualized, other needed technology is added, the employees are hired, risk is managed, the products are commercialized, and more. For example, say Zirka and Darby created a video sharing startup. As to the idea, they will need a founders' agreement, a contribution agreement, another to assign any technology to the startup, and more. Sometimes other technology is needed, and in this case, the founders will need a website, servers, or maybe they will opt for cloud hosting instead and contract with, for example, Amazon Web Services. And maybe they need a technology covered by someone else's patent for this; they will need to negotiate licensing rights. Employees are needed and there are a number of other agreements there, too, to manage them. Managing risk is a constant, and one issue, for example, is what users will post and share on the site. To the extent they wish to maintain a certain vibe and decorum, the founders will want to carefully write their Terms of Use license, another type of agreement. Finally, some of the videos posted may go viral and these nascent stars may be able to produce added revenue for the site and additional agreements will be needed. And the site is supported by third-party ads, also the product of agreements.

Contracts, also known as agreements, are created to accomplish a desired end, which is to obtain some good or service a business is not able or willing to make itself. For example, NBC Universal paid the International Olympic Committee $7.75 billion for the exclusive broadcast rights to the six Olympic Games between 2022 and 2032. ESPN paid $15.2 billion for the exclusive right to broadcast Monday Night Football games; Comcast negotiated broadcast rights with Disney to show the film *Frozen* to its cable subscribers, and so forth. Most agreements are negotiated (*i.e.*, such as those just mentioned, and other examples include technology transfer, or joint venture agreements). Still other "agreements" are not (*i.e.*, consumer arbitration, or software license, site license end user license agreements), and so construing these as agreements is clearly more controversial. Both types of agreements are the means to create wealth, manage risk, all while creating a blueprint for successful transfer of goods and services.

Contracts are in a sense a road map for the parties to follow as they both perform their duties under the agreement. Contracts are the system for creating a mutual set of performance conditions and obligations, whereby each party attempts to maximize their control and reward, while minimizing their risk and responsibilities. Contracts are a type of transactional law, ranging from simple purchase and sales agreements, to complex transactions. For this, the parties plan, negotiate, make proposals, draft, review, modify, and then finally execute these agreements.

Engaging in transactions means taking on risk to reach a goal. This chapter opens with introductory contract concepts, and then addresses contracts of particular relevance to entrepreneurial Internet and technology companies. Contracts in these sectors are concentrated on intangibles including services, site licenses, intellectual property licenses, and software goods. There are a number of significant differences from contracts involving, for example, employment, physical goods or real property. Finally, mention of anticompetitive issues that are triggered by restrictive agreements is made, since this is increasingly becoming a compliance challenge for businesses.

General Contract Law Principles

Contracts form the legal foundation of all commercial transactions. Parties voluntarily form contracts to effectuate commercial goals. Each party has something to give, as well as gain, from the agreement. One party may give up money for a good; another may offer time and services in return for payment, and so forth. Contracts create a legal relationship. They are voluntarily entered into agreements, whereby each party has legal capacity and is bound by obligations, in order to pursue lawful objectives. Everything about contracts is the result of intentional purposeful engagement and bargaining; it is a process that occurs over a period of time, with each party conducting due diligence on the other, generating an initial working draft, then suggesting—or demanding—revisions, resulting in more bargaining, drafts, and then the execution copy is finalized. The terms are a reflection of the parties' needs, hopes, and fears. The terms are detailed and provide for substantive terms of performance, as well as for a process should the contract obligations not be met. Finally, based on the principle of parties' freedom to contract, courts favor upholding contracts, and therefore are reluctant to overturn any terms in the agreements.

Formation of Contracts

Contracts are, at their most basic, a bet. They involve calculated risk-taking for a reward, driven by optimism, but also backstopped with clauses hedging against the possibility of failure and limitations to liability or loss. Composing an agreement clearly takes creativity and diligence: creativity to imagine what could be accomplished, and diligence to think about what could go wrong and plan for such an eventuality.

The basic elements for every contract include 1) an offer, 2) acceptance, 3) consideration, 4) with legal capacity, for a legal purpose. Each element is necessary for a valid contract. Defects in the process can render a contract unenforceable and either void or voidable. Examples of contracts that are unenforceable span quite a range. It could be that the offer was not sufficiently definite, that the acceptance was not done in a way as to properly notify the offeror, and so forth. It could be that the consideration was nonexistent, thus the contract is unenforceable (unless an alternative form of consideration is found). It could be that the terms of the contract are so unconscionable (though not illegal) that the court will refuse to enforce the contract on grounds that it would violate public policy. It could be that the contract is void because of incapacity based on age, intoxication, or mental condition. It could be that the contract did not sufficiently legally bind one party to the contract and so the agreement is illusory.

It could be that there was a mistake, misrepresentation, duress, or fraud in the making of a contract. For example, in cases where there is unreasonable behavior, the defense of unconscionability can be raised at any time, and is a complete bar to enforcement of the contract. There are three scenarios under which a contract is unfair or oppressive to a party in a way suggesting the formation process was flawed. Unconscionability claims will be successful based upon proof of an absence of meaningful choices such as: (a) undue influence; (b) duress, and (c) unequal bargaining power. Undue influence exists where one party exercises unreasonable pressure in order to get the other party to sign the contract. Duress exists where one party uses threats to get the other to agree to contract terms.

Unequal bargaining power exists where one party has an unusual advantage over the other and uses this to disadvantage the other party.

In short, there are many hazards to consider when drafting a contract. Overall though, courts favor enforcement rather than destruction of contracts as a matter of public policy, with some courts even going so far as to imply terms before striking down the contract.

Negotiating and agreeing to terms is the process by which a final agreement is finally developed, and signed. The offer, acceptance and consideration are key to the formation. To further clarify, offer and acceptance represent a mutual assent to be bound to agreed-upon terms that are sufficiently definite. The acceptance should generally be the "mirror image" of the offer. Any term in the offer that is not specifically agreed to could otherwise be construed as a counteroffer, or even a rejection. Consideration represents something of value given up in exchange for the promise. This could be a payment, an act, or even forbearance to act. The exact value or adequacy of the consideration is not a matter of concern. In the process of the exchange, a bargain is created. As an example of contract negotiations, consider Amazon and its negotiations with Hachette Publishing Group, which is first among the world's top publishers. Amazon developed as an online bookseller before moving into other goods. It successfully built an e-books business following the successful introduction of the Kindle reader, and now Amazon controls about 50% of the e- and physical books market. The parties engaged in a famously public spat with two points in contention during the negotiations. First was the price control of books, especially e-books. Amazon wanted the ability to set it own prices for Hachette Books. Hachette, however, wanted to use the legacy model of setting a uniform price for its books across retailers. Second was the current form of marketing, co-op marketing, also known as pay-for-display advertising. While publishers generally pay for some marketing in stores, Amazon asked Hachette for a far more significant payment for placement on its website. As of this time, negotiations are stalled over these points.

Regarding when the obligations mature, this is typically a matter of which type of contract the parties created. There are two main categories of contracts: bilateral and unilateral. Bilateral contracts are a promise for another promise and this forms a contract and binds both parties immediately. Examples of bilateral contracts are above, in which for example, Comcast pays Disney for public performance and distribution rights for *Frozen*. Unilateral contracts are a type of contract in which an offer can be accepted only by performance, and thus the contract is not formed until the contract has been completed by successfully performing all obligations. An example of unilateral contract is Amazon Publishing's contest, in which the company offered five publishing contracts, one of whom will be selected as the grand prize-winner of a $50,000 publishing contract. The offers are the *possibility* of being selected for a prize; acceptance is given by performance—writing a work that is selected for a prize. In the meantime, and while hopefuls are toiling away writing, it could be that Amazon Publishing will decide to cancel this promotion; it will not be liable for damages because Amazon is not legally bound by its unilateral offer until performance by a writer.

re Amazon: **Hachette Statements on Contract Negotiations**

ADAPTING TO DISRUPTIVE INNOVATIONS

Currently, Amazon and Hachette Book Group are negotiating terms for Amazon to carry Hachette's 5,000 titles. Negotiations collapsed at one point over terms, and the disruptive innovation of e-books. How to split profits between distributors and producers, and whether there is even room for producers in the future, are central points of contention.

Excerpts of the parties' statements

Amazon:

"We are currently buying less (print) inventory and "safety stock" on titles from the publisher, Hachette, than we ordinarily do, and are no longer taking pre-orders on titles whose publication dates are in the future. These changes are related to the contract and terms between Hachette and Amazon.

Hachette:

"We will spare no effort to resume normal business relations with Amazon. Once we have reached such an agreement, we will be happy to discuss with Amazon its ideas about compensating authors for the damage its demand for improved terms may have done them, and to pass along any payments it considers appropriate."

During formation, negotiations, and throughout the life of the contract, parties are bound by the implied covenant of good faith and fair dealing. These additional requirements, implied in every contract, require honesty in fact and the observance of reasonable commercial standards of fair dealing in all transactions.

Contracts are governed by state law, and therefore legal decisions and rules can be quite variable, and this lack of national uniformity creates enforcement and compliance challenges for businesses. The Uniform Commercial Code is relevant to some extent, for even if states have not adopted the UCC, it nevertheless informs courts on standards concerning: formation, unconscionability, sales, leases, allocation of risk, output and requirement contracts, warranties, performance conditions, repudiation, breach and remedies.

Performance of Contracts: Conditions and Obligations

Once the parties finish negotiations and execute the agreement, the parties begin performance of their contractual obligations. In most instances, there are benchmarks in the contract, points of reference for the parties to measure progress and assess whether the other contract partner is performing as expected. As an example, in a construction contract, the contractor is obligated to work diligently to reach a certain stage in building a house, such as completing the framing portion, and then performance obligations turn to the site owner to pay the contractor a percentage of the contract price. Contracts can provide a system of rewards and punishments, but they are not instruments for micro-managing contracts partners. Governed by the reasonable person standard, there is a great deal of autonomy and leeway afforded to performance of contractual obligations.

In contracts with conditions, such as conditions precedent or subsequent, the contracts cite specific events that will trigger obligations. As a contract is being performed, though, there are often other outside events occurring that can have the effect of causing parties to question the purpose or rationale of the contract going forward, or worse, stop performing. Changed conditions in the larger environment clearly impact attitudes and incentives. It is quite possible to renegotiate contracts, but barring this, the contract remains in force. Material obligations that are not met in an adequate or timely manner will cause that party to be in breach, though it is possible to excuse performance under certain limited conditions.

Completion of Contracts: Discharge, Repudiation, Breach, Remedies

Contracts are discharged, or completed, upon satisfactory performance, or when performance is excused. Adequate or reasonable performance is all that is required. Any other, higher standard must be clearly stipulated. Furthermore, in the process of construing contracts, courts adhere to a number of doctrines. The four corners doctrine is a rule of construction in which courts are hesitant to add context or further meaning into the parties' actual worded agreement. Further oral agreements that can be completed within one year (and do not involve the transfer of real estate are valid, though their existence and proof of terms is an evidentiary challenge and therefore enforcement of oral agreements is problematic. For all other agreements, the statute of frauds requires that certain classes of contract must be in writing in order to be enforceable. Once the contract is discharged, parties have no further rights, duties, or obligations toward one another. Should either party fail in any way to satisfactorily complete performance benchmarks, or fail to adequately correct failures in a reasonable amount of time, there is a breach of the contract. A breach occurs when there is a material failure to act or perform obligations as outlined by the contract.

The remedies provisions of the contract are triggered at this point. The injured party is entitled to a range of damage remedies including compensatory, consequential, and special damages, and in the meantime, the injured party is responsible to mitigate damages. Equitable relief is potentially available in extraordinary cases only, since in most instances a monetary award will fully compensate for breaches of contract.

Contracts for Entrepreneurial Startups

Companies engage in a web of contractual arrangements. Each agreement seeks to accomplish an end such as to commercially develop goods and services, or to control a risk such as disclosure of trade secrets. Some contracts are for services required by law, such as an independent audit; others are for goods and services such as office computers. Each contract is individually drafted and intentionally and voluntarily entered into. The agreements span the range subject matter covered throughout the text. For example: contribution agreements for startups, and buy-sell agreements for changes in control; voting rights agreements for shareholders, term sheets for venture capital investors; technology transfer agreements for the use of intellectual property, and employment agreements for confidentiality, non-compete, and more. Finally another class of contracts is not negotiated at all—the downstream contracts with customers for software, covered by software license agreements that courts construe as contracts.

Negotiated Contracts between Businesses

Beyond the basics of transactional law concepts and the elements common to contracts generally, there are a number of specialized agreements to highlight in this chapter as the one most regularly used by tech and Internet companies to leverage their assets. This section of contracts covers agreements negotiated between businesses for the purpose of developing commercially viable goods and services.

Overall, there is a range of terms common to negotiated commercial contracts, though each agreement is individualized in that it represents the goals of those parties (and these provisions are covered more completely throughout the chapter discussion and cases):

- **Statement as to ownership of the rights and title in the goods and services.**
- **Number of licensed devices:** The software vendor agrees to provide access to, for example, 1,000 devices at the licensee's office, and if licensee hires 20 extra people, the licensee will have to re-negotiate this term.
- **Proprietary rights:** The software vendor clarifies that the software is entirely owned by the vendor, and usually inclusive of any upgrades or modifications that the licensee makes.
- **Usage rules**: The software vendor clarifies what are permissible uses of the software, such as for creating 3D software for architectural renderings of buildings, and that same software may not be used for example, for design of automobiles, even though the software may be capable of being used for that purpose.
- **Pricing for licenses:** The software vendor may charge one price for a desktop device and a different price for access to that same software running on a mobile device.
- **Prohibitions** (such as reverse engineering, re-distribution, copying): Any violations of these prohibitions could have the potential to trigger claims of breach of terms of the contract for violating the terms of the license.
- **Copyright and trademark and patent policies** (including no-challenge clauses): The software vendor will specify allowed and prohibited uses of the software, and oftentimes feature a clause in which the licensee "agrees" to not challenge the validity of the IP in any way.

- **Termination**: The software vendor specifies events that will trigger a termination of the parties' agreement.
- **Clauses that survive termination:** The software vendor specifies events that are excepted from the terminating events, so that the contractual relationship of the parties continues.
- **Scope of license rights:** Similar to the usage rules, the software vendor clarifies permitted uses.
- **Export restrictions:** Much software is restricted from export, and further there is an export control office that scrutinizes transactions to countries in a watch list, and so the software vendor will add this and any other of its own restrictions to this clause.
- **Duration of license rights:** The software vendor will state when the license expires, and this becomes a time-sensitive date for the licensee as access to the software programs, and all associated data terminate on that date.
- **Resale price maintenance:** Software vendors attempt to restrict the licensees' right or ability to re-sell uses of the software.
- **Confidentiality provisions:** These could include matters relating to negotiations, pricing, functionality, access, and so forth, and this protects the software vendor's business information.
- **Testing period**: Software vendors often allow potential licensees to test the software as part of the diligence and evaluation process in purchasing software as a service, and clauses reflect the parties' agreement during this short-term evaluation period.
- **Rights over adaptations, improvements** (also known as grant-back clauses): Software vendors will attempt to capture any of the modifications that licensees make to the licensed software.
- **Acceptance date:** The date on which the license payments start and the parties' performance obligations commence.
- **Audit:** Software vendors usually retain the right to audit licensees' uses of software, on and off-site, and analyze the data for their business purposes.
- **Non-disclosure**: See *confidentiality provisions,* above.
- **Disclaimers:** Software vendors attempt to disclaim responsibility for bugs in the software or other issues that may not be readily apparent at the time of the agreement.
- **Indemnification:** Software vendors attempt to escape any obligations should the licensee get sued based on the use of the software. For example, Oracle would state in such a clause for software it developed for doctor's office that Oracle is not responsible for any doctor-patient issues, such as if a doctor miswrites a prescription in the software for four times the correct amount of a drug therapy.
- **Advertisers and other third-party use of data:** Software vendors provide that they and their affiliates may be collecting information, that, while not the exact data the licensee is producing, is the usage information.
- **Limitations on liability**: Software vendors attempt to limit any of the events it specifies, such as a power outage at the licensees' business and any associated loss or corruption of data due to the outage.

- **DMCA notice and takedown provisions**: Software vendors will require that any sites will feature a provision for resolution of contested uses of others' works.
- **Rules of conduct:** Software vendors may specify conduct requirements and thereby avoid liability for any non-permitted uses.
- **Exclusive or non-exclusive license:** Software vendors may make a deal with just one licensee (exclusive), or with many licensees (non-exclusive).
- **Dispute escalation and resolution process**: This provision specifies the protocols for licensees to use when there is a functionality or other issue with the software.
- **Transferable or assignable license** (see also *resale price maintenance*): Software vendors may attempt to restrict the licensees' rights to sell or rent the software (also known as passive sales), or otherwise change the agreed upon scope of permitted uses.
- **Warranties and warranty disclaimers**: To the extent states require certain minimums (of merchantability, and so forth), software vendors may attempt to add further warranties or disclaimers thereto.
- **Jurisdiction**: Software vendors will specify the locus should any dispute need to be litigated.
- **Choice of law**: Software vendors will specify what state's law governs the dispute—notably, some states' laws are more consumer-friendly than others.
- **Venue**: Software vendors may stipulate whether the dispute is to be arbitrated, mediated, or litigated, and in which state.
- **Arbitration**: Software vendors may stipulate that all disputes are to be arbitrated, and that the result is final, and non-appealable.
- **Disruptions to operations:** Software vendors may provide for equipment or software work-arounds to the extent to which there occurs a material failure of the software to perform for a substantial period of time.
- **Remedies:** Software vendors may attempt to limit remedies to actual financial losses suffered by the licensee and thereby eliminate consequential and other damages.

Non Compete and Non solicitation

Joint Venture Agreements

Joint ventures are a commercial collaboration in which two or more businesses share or integrate some of their resources for a limited purpose while staying independent. These agreements between two or more businesses are formed for a particular purpose and for a defined period of time. For example, Ford and Toyota, sometime competitors, have teamed up to form a joint venture with the specific purpose of building big hybrid vehicles. Microsoft and GE formed a joint venture to deliver data intelligence to health care professionals. Johnson & Johnson formed JVs with six new biotech startups in order to leverage their talent and resources in this relatively new and rapidly expanding sector. Typically, each business is ongoing, and they may want to enter a new market quickly but, as individual businesses way not have sufficient overall expertise in all areas, and wish to scale up quickly.

8-K 1 d678625d8k.htm 8-K

UNITED STATES
SECURITIES AND EXCHANGE COMMISSION
Washington, D.C. 20549

FORM 8-K

CURRENT REPORT
Pursuant to Section 13 or 15(d)
of the Securities Exchange Act of 1934

February 19, 2014
Date of Report
Date of earliest event reported

BLUCORA, INC.
(Exact name of Registrant as specified in its charter)

DELAWARE	000-25131	91-1718107
(State or other jurisdiction of incorporation)	(Commission File Number)	(I.R.S. Employer Identification No.)

10900 N.E. 8th Street, Suite 800
Bellevue, Washington 98004
(Address of Principal Executive Offices)

425-201-6100
Registrant's Telephone Number, Including Area Code

Check the appropriate box below if the Form 8-K filing is intended to simultaneously satisfy the filing obligation of the registrant under any of the following provisions:

☐ Written communication pursuant to Rule 425 under the Securities Act (17 CFR 230.425)

☐ Soliciting material pursuant to Rule 14a-12 under the Exchange Act (17 CFR 240.14a-12)

☐ Pre-commencement communications pursuant to Rule 14d-2(b) under the Exchange Act (17 CFR 240.14d-2(b))

☐ Pre-commencement communication pursuant to Rule 13e-4(c) under the Exchange Act (17 CFR 240.13e-4(c))

Item 1.01 ENTRY INTO A MATERIAL DEFINITIVE AGREEMENT

On February 19, 2014, InfoSpace, LLC ("*InfoSpace*"), a subsidiary of Blucora, Inc. ("*Blucora*"), entered into the Google Services Agreement (the "*GSA*") with Google, Inc. ("*Google*"). The term of the GSA begins on April 1, 2014 and runs to March 31, 2017, and accordingly it will replace the current Amended and Restated Google Services Agreement (as amended, the "*Prior Agreement*") between InfoSpace and Google, when the Prior Agreement expires in accordance with its terms on March 31, 2014. In addition, the term of the GSA may be extended until March 31, 2018 upon the mutual agreement of the parties.

Under the terms the GSA, InfoSpace can display search results and advertisements from Google on InfoSpace's owned and operated search websites and provide Google search results and advertisements to the websites in InfoSpace's distribution network. Google pays InfoSpace a percentage of the revenue collected by Google as a result of Internet users clicking on advertisements provided by Google and displayed by InfoSpace and its distribution partners.

In general, the material terms of the Prior Agreement and the GSA are similar. However, beginning on April 1, 2014, InfoSpace will no longer display ads provided by Google's AdSense for Search for search traffic that originates from mobile and tablet devices. For this mobile and tablet traffic, InfoSpace instead intends to display mobile advertisements from other sources, including Yahoo!'s ad network. While the impact of this change is limited to a relatively small subset of our current search business and may be partially offset by the alternative advertising sources, we expect this change will result in slowing of InfoSpace's search business revenue growth rate and, if we are unsuccessful or limited in our ability to transition our search services to provide value to mobile and tablet end-users, this change may result in a longer term negative impact on InfoSpace's search business.

InfoSpace will continue to display ads provided by Google's AdSense for Search for search traffic that originates from desktops and laptops. This traffic constituted approximately 85% of the revenue generated by InfoSpace's search business in the fourth quarter of fiscal 2013, and the revenue share percentages that determine the payments that InfoSpace receives from Google for this traffic remain unchanged from the Prior Agreement.

The other changes in the GSA consist of revisions to Google's form of service agreement, minor changes to the legal terms of the Agreement, and updates to reflect changes in the relationship since the Prior Agreement was signed in 2005. These other changes are not expected to materially affect InfoSpace's operations or financial results.

The foregoing description is a summary, does not purport to be a complete description of the GSA, and is qualified in its entirety by reference to the GSA, a copy of which will be attached as an exhibit to Blucora's Quarterly Report on Form 10-Q for the first fiscal quarter of 2014.

This Current Report on Form 8-K contains forward-looking statements within the meaning of Section 27A of the Securities Act of 1933 and Section 21E of the Securities Exchange Act of 1934. The impact of the changes to the operations of InfoSpace's search business caused by new and changed provisions in the GSA are currently unknown. The forward-looking statements above are based on assumptions regarding matters that include, but are not limited to: the operational impact of these new and changed provisions, the continuation of current business trends, the ability of InfoSpace and its partners to comply with Google policies and requirements, and the likely future types and sources of traffic for InfoSpace's search business. However, if those assumptions are incorrect, the new and changed provisions in the GSA may have a material negative impact on the operations and financial results of Blucora. Investors are cautioned not to place undue reliance on these forward-looking statements, which speak only as of the date of this Current Report. Blucora undertakes no obligation to update any forward-looking statements to reflect new information, events, or circumstances after the date of this release or to reflect the occurrence of unanticipated events.

Item 2.02 RESULTS OF OPERATIONS AND FINANCIAL CONDITION

On February 20, 2014, Blucora announced its financial results for the quarter and year ended December 31, 2013. Copies of the press release and a supplemental investor presentation are furnished to, but not filed with, the Commission as Exhibits 99.1 and 99.2 hereto.

Item 9.01 FINANCIAL STATEMENTS AND EXHIBITS

99.1 Press release dated February 20, 2014

99.2 Investor presentation dated February 20, 2014

-2-

SIGNATURES

Pursuant to the requirements of the Securities Exchange Act of 1934, the Registrant has duly caused this report to be signed on its behalf by the undersigned hereunto duly authorized.

Date: February 20, 2014

BLUCORA, INC.

By: /s/ Eric M. Emans
Eric M. Emans
Chief Financial Officer

-3-

EXHIBIT INDEX

Exhibit No	Description
99.1	Press release dated February 20, 2014
99.2	Investor presentation dated February 20, 2014

-4-

Businesses find mutually beneficial reasons to pursue a common purpose. Increasingly, entrepreneurs with a specialty are forming joint ventures with ongoing businesses, and in that way, the entrepreneur can leverage that company's infrastructure, capital, market, and operations. The project scope is limited to specific activities, such as marketing, R&D, and so forth. In these strategic alliances for a limited purpose, each business retains ownership of their assets, and is taxed according to their status. Finally, in a similar form to the JV, US government agencies increasingly are negotiating agreements with private companies, and such contracts are known as CRADAs—Cooperative Research and Development Agreements. Created by the Federal Technology Transfer Act, 15 U.S.C. §§ 2701-3722 (2012), CRADAs are intended to accelerate the commercialization of government-sponsored basic research and technology development, by promoting private sector participation. Participating businesses file patents and retain rights to inventions developed under a CRADA.

Joint venture (and CRADA) agreements have a number of provisions that deserve mention. A checklist for any JV will include the following terms:

- **Scope, or purpose clause:** what do the JV expressly intend to do (and refrain from doing)? This will cover corporate opportunity issues (a statement of existing non-JV business activities of each JV partner, and any potential future conflicts); non-compete and confidentiality provisions; either JV partner's proprietary technology or IP to be assigned or licensed by the JV.

- **Form of JV:** whether it is an S corporation, LLC, jointly owned corporation, and so forth.
- **Regulatory:** identification of risk factors in terms of compliance, foreign jurisdictional differences, antitrust, export control, and so forth. The US construes export controls broadly. For example, if a US nanotechnology company that makes products for mobile phones wanted to participate in China's continuing expansion and need for this product (about half the world's mobile phone market), it would probably create a JV with a Chinese company, which would have to take into account export control requirements.
- **Internal considerations:** tax considerations, accounting, auditing, banking and reporting requirements.
- **Letter of intent/Term Sheet:** this evidences the parties' intent as to whether this is binding at this point or not. If it is not immediately binding, this clause will describe the conditions upon which it becomes binding, for example, when the full board signs off, approving the contract. The clause covers all key points of the agreement (and therefore any subsequent business points are not incorporated into this JV agreement). Arbitration, if agreed upon, for dispute resolution, will be provided for in this clause. If either business is a public company, appropriate disclosure is required. A covenant to negotiate in good faith is optional, and while this is implied into every agreement, some parties opt to add this explicit language.
- **Governance:** this clause specifies governance structure, and whether the JV is to be managed by a simple representation of the two businesses, or whether they need a new management team for the JV. Also covered, are the authority to hire, fire, create a business plan and budget, finance the JV, distribution of profits, authority to make significant decisions, meeting and voting requirements, what actions require consent, and protocols for resolving conflicts of interest or opportunities.
- **Intellectual property or technology:** the parties could agree that the JV is to license the tech from one or both of the parties, or that the JV is to purchase it. The tech usually comprises both the actual tech, along with any necessary support and documentation, including know-how. This aspect of a JV agreement overlaps licensing and is more fully covered in licensing materials that follow in this chapter.
- **Corporate opportunity:** this doctrine provides that each of the JV partners are required to offer to the JV entity any business opportunity that is within the scope of the JVs business. The JV then has the opportunity to pursue this opportunity first, and if the JV declines, then either of the individual businesses may exploit that opportunity.
- **Non-compete, non-solicitation:** this clause covers whether the JV is subject to any restrictions on hiring personnel from either of the individual businesses, and the length of any restriction. Further, either party may negotiate for restrictions on the JV hiring from either of their competitors.

- Breach, non-performance. The JV partners may wish to make clear ahead of time what actions/failures to act constitute a breach, including what is considered material to the agreement (and therefore on its own, a breach), and possibly, what non-material breaches, when considered in the aggregate, constitute a material breach.
- Share transfer or pledges, exit and termination rights: the parties will specify restrictions on transfer of shares, and what events trigger an exit or termination of the JV. This is especially relevant to minority shareholders and particular attention is needed in this area so as to effectuate the intent of the parties.

In this next case, the court ruled on a JV and considered both parties' claims against each other after their JV unraveled. The judge's opinion is 91 pages in length, with 339 footnotes! (The abstracted form of the case is presented here.)

In re: Mobilactive Media, LLC,
Civ. Action No. 5725-VCP
Del. Ct. Chancery (Jan. 25, 2013)

Facts: This case is between two 50% members of a joint venture (JV) to take advantage of mobile marketing opportunities in North America. One member, Terry Bienstock, a former general counsel of Comcast Cable, would provide industry contacts, and the other member, Silverback Media, a United Kingdom company that owns proprietary mobile marketing technologies, would provide technical resources.

After Bienstock left Comcast to start his own consulting business, he negotiated with Silverback terms of the JV. They signed a limited liability company agreement for Mobilactive that described the Purpose of Business as: "The purpose of the Company is to license, develop and own and market technology, content and applications for the purpose of enabling and enhancing interactive video programming and advertising content. . . ."

This same section also contained a carve-out that excluded certain activities from the JV's business. The carve-out provided: "It is expressly acknowledged that the Business shall not include Silverback's and its subsidiaries' North American non-video based mobile and online marketing businesses and the Members . . . shall be free to engage in any business activities except those whose primary purpose involve enabling and enhancing of interactive video programming and advertising content across multiple digital platforms."

At the outset, the JV had bright prospects, including promising meetings with senior executives in the telecom and ad industries. Bienstock introduced Amsellem and Doane to, among others, the Comcast CEO as well as the head of marketing and, beyond that, executives at Saatchi & Saatchi, BBDO, and ESPN. It developed marketing materials and a website. The JV, however, met with limited success. Silverback's COO proposed, internally, that, "things would be easier down the road if we owned Mobilactive 100%." They tried to buy out Plaintiff Bienstock's interest, but he declined. This same day, Doane instructed Amsellem and others to "spend as little time as possible on Mobilactive . . . it is a 50% business for us, not a 100% business. Provide the platform for Mobilactive and fulfill on deals Bienstock can close." Doane warned Amsellem in an email to "be careful because there are things in the agreement with Bienstock that could be prejudicial to Silverback. Please monitor him closely."

Amsellem informed Bienstock that he (Amsellem) would not come to the U.S. to serve as Mobilactive's COO despite their previous understanding and a provision in the agreement that Amsellem would serve as Mobilactive's COO. A few month's later, Silverback's COO asked Doane, "When do you think we should terminate Bienstock and get out of that deal?" Doane responded, "It's a tough call. I don't think we should fund anymore, but Bienstock said they were expecting checque in from Comcast which would cover the burn for another 6 weeks or so. . . . My sense is we should wait until we close the $10M before pulling the plug."

In the meantime, Silverback (on its own, not part of the JV) bought other companies that had similarities to Mobilactive. For example, one company was involved in text messaging platforms, gateways and a payment system; another was a traditional advertising and marketing boutique; a third was a database analytics business; and a fourth was an SMS network with technology to deliver ads to the network. Silverback never presented these opportunities to Mobilactive. Bienstock sent a demand letter reiterating Silverback's obligation to present opportunities within Mobilactive's business to Mobilactive.

Mobliactive did obtain some contracts for services, but for small amounts. Tyler Nelson replaced Doane as Silverback's CEO, and he wrote to Doane asking, "How do we unwind [the joint venture]?" In 2010, Nelson emailed Bienstock suggesting that they dissolve the JV. The parties met, and Nelson suggested that rather than being an owner, Bienstock personally consult to projects instead. Bienstock rejected this proposal as materially less than what the JV's potential represented. Nelson replied that, nevertheless, "the joint venture will still need to be wound down." Thereafter, Bienstock sent a demand letter to Nelson and Silverback alleging that Silverback had breached the JV Agreement. Silverback was reorganized and merged into another entity, Adenyo. In the same time period, PriceWaterhouseCoopers valued Silverback at $79 million, and Bienstock notified the liquidators of Silverback of his claim against Silverback. Bienstock filed this lawsuit against Silverback and its successor, seeking damages based on allegations of breach of the Agreement (by engaging in the Business of Mobilactive in North America), and breach of fiduciary duties (by engaging in business activities specifically reserved for the JV).

Judicial Opinion. Vice Chancellor Parsons:

Analysis Bienstock bears the burden of proving his claims by a preponderance of the evidence. Under this standard, Bienstock is not required to prove his claims by clear and convincing evidence or to exacting certainty.

Prior Material Breach A party is excused from performance under a contract if the other party is in material breach thereof. The converse of this principle is that a slight breach by one party, while giving rise to an action for damages, will not necessarily terminate the obligations of the injured party to perform under the contract. The question whether the breach is of sufficient importance to justify non-performance by the non-breaching party is one of degree and is determined by weighing the consequences in the light of the actual custom of men in the performance of contracts similar to the one that is involved in the specific case. Here, Silverback contends that Bienstock's claims should be barred because he failed to make his initial capital contribution in full, and thereby materially breached the Agreement.

The Restatement (Second) of Contracts identifies a number of relevant factors for determining whether a failure to render or to offer performance is material. Those factors include: (a) the extent to which the injured party will be deprived of the benefit which he reasonably expected; (b) the extent to which the injured party can be adequately compensated for the part of that benefit of which he will be deprived; (c) the extent to which the party failing to perform or to offer to perform will suffer forfeiture; (d) the likelihood that the party failing to perform or to offer to perform will cure his failure . . . ; and (e) the extent to which the behavior of the party failing to perform or to offer to perform comports with standards of good faith and fair dealing. Here . . . [b]oth members were to contribute Initial Capital of $75,000. Bienstock asserts that he was willing to fund his share of the Initial Capital. Because I find that Bienstock offered to make capital contributions to Mobilactive, his actions [demonstrate that he offered performance of his obligations and therefore] cannot be considered a material breach. More importantly, Silverback asked Bienstock to, and Bienstock did, render other performance under the Agreement. Silverback accepted the benefits of Bienstock's performance of the Mobilactive Agreement, but now asserts that his failure to perform a part of the Agreement, which Silverback itself failed to perform, should preclude Bienstock from recovering. By continuing to accept the benefits of the contract . . . Silverback essentially admitted to its validity, and is estopped from arguing voidability. There is no dispute that both Bienstock and Silverback contributed $46,500.00 of their Initial Capital obligation. The relatively insignificant failure by Bienstock to contribute the full amount of his Initial Capital, therefore, should not preclude Bienstock's ability to recover under the Agreement.

Breach of Contract To prove a breach of contract claim, a plaintiff must show: the existence of a contract, the breach of an obligation imposed by that contract, and resulting damages to the plaintiff . . . [and] prove the elements of its claim by a preponderance of the evidence. Bienstock asserts that Silverback breached the Agreement by (1) refusing to honor Mobilactive as the exclusive vehicle for engaging in the Business in North America; (2) diverting acquisition opportunities away from Mobilactive; and (3) establishing a competing business to capitalize on those opportunities.

Bienstock . . . contends that the scope of the Business includes 'interactive video programming' and 'interactive advertising.' Silverback interprets the 'purpose' of Mobilactive [more narrowly thus leaving other opportunities for its own subsidiaries]. I hold that Bienstock's [broader] interpretation of 'interactive video programming] is correct. The advertising and marketing material drafted by Silverback provide further insight into the scope of the joint venture. The Mobilactive website also reinforces this conclusion.

Meaning of the Carve-Out. [The court finds as to its scope, that] Silverback and its existing subsidiaries would be free, notwithstanding [the JV], to continue conducting their non-video based mobile and online marketing businesses. Any future opportunities for new or expanded Business that included a business activity having a primary purpose to do such things [within the purpose clause] would have to be presented to Mobilactive as a corporate opportunity.

The [evidence] show[s] that Silverback infringed on the Business [of the JV] by providing interactive advertising content in North America through mobile platforms independently of Mobilactive, and therefore breached the Agreement.

Usurpation of Corporate Opportunity I next examine whether Silverback breached the . . . fiduciary duties it owed to Mobilactive and Bienstock by acquiring companies within the same line of business as Mobilactive. Defendants seek dismissal of Bienstock's breach of fiduciary duty claims as being merely duplicative of his breach of contract claims. Defendants ignore, however, the Agreement's express imposition of fiduciary duties on the members of Mobilactive.

Moreover, the remedies for breach of contract and breach of fiduciary duty in this case are different. [U]nder Delaware law, 'the relationship of the joint adventurers is fiduciary in character and imposes upon all of the participants the utmost good faith, fairness and honesty in dealing with each other with respect to the enterprise.' As the core of the fiduciary duty is the notion of loyalty—the equitable requirement that, with respect to the property subject to the duty, a fiduciary always must act in a good faith effort to advance the interests of his beneficiary. It forbids one joint adventurer from acquiring solely for himself any profit or secret advantage in connection with the common enterprise. [After broadly interpreting whether a corporation has an overlap in a line of business, the court held that three of the companies Silverback acquired were] opportunities . . . within Mobilactive's line of business . . . [and] that the [JV was] financially able to exploit the opportunity. Silverback [therefore] usurped several corporate opportunities [from the JV] and exploited those . . . on its own behalf rather than sharing the benefits with Bienstock and Mobilactive.

CONCLUSION

I find in favor of Bienstock. [On his claim for breach of contract, Bienstock is entitled to compensatory damages only. On his claim for breach of fiduciary duty, Bienstock is entitled to disgorgement of the profits Defendant obtained through its inequitable conduct, and so the court analyzed each of the four successfully challenged acquisitions, to evaluate their profits.] Finally, I deny Silverback's counterclaim for dissolution of Mobilactive.

Case Questions

1. On what basis did the court find that the Silverback's carve-out was inapplicable as to business activities that it participated in without its JV partner Bienstock?
2. The court made an initial finding that Bienstock's failure to make his initial JV contribution in full, was not a material breach. Silverback will surely want to challenge this on appeal; prepare an argument to present to the appeals court.
3. The court rejected Silverback's request to dissolve the JV, and therefore it is ongoing until it expires—either due to a time specified in the JV agreement, or by agreement of the JV partners. How is the JV to be operational under such conditions?

Technology Transfer/Material Transfer Agreements

Tech transfer describes the process by which a business transfers to another business assets, including facilities, technology, know-how or expertise, in order commercialize or improve a product or process. Investing in new technology may be expensive and with too much risk, since the innovation process has many uncertainties. The tech transfer practice area accelerated after 1980 when Congress passed the Bayh-Dole Act, 35 U.S.C. §§ 200-212 (2012). Also mentioned in the Patents and Inventions chapters, this law gives universities, small businesses and nonprofits the ability to elect title to inventions resulting from federally financed research. The federal government actively supports commercialization of inventions, and this public sector approach to permissive technology transfer is credited with creatively leveraging public research funding for the public benefit.

Businesses engage in tech transfer to scale quickly on a process or a product, and it may be that it is more feasible to negotiate rights for technology than attempt to make it, and risk that the in-house version infringes another business's IP rights. This creates another risk however, in that there is now technological dependence on other businesses' technology, and continued access to it. For the licensor, it is an opportunity to turn an infringer and competitor into a customer-licensee and ally. It is an opportunity to experiment and enter new markets, which otherwise may be inaccessible, and the licensee will agree to ensuring all conditions necessary for entering this new market are met, including: localization requirements on labeling, manufacturing, and marketing.

In-bound, Out-bound, and Cross-licensing

In this era of accelerated R&D and innovation, oftentimes it does not make economic sense to negotiate a purchase or sale of the technology. The rapid rate of change means that many products or services become obsolete quickly, and as a result licensing this technology is a better approach. It is also exceedingly difficult for an individual company to develop all of its own technology. To scale these shortcomings, companies transfer technology from, and to, each other. There are three ways tech transfer is effectuated.

In-licensing

This describes the process of contracting to receive another business's technology. In-licensing technology means that businesses gain quick access to technology that is proven, market-ready, non-infringing, and compliant with standards and specifications. For example, a computer-maker would want to have a high-speed connections port as a feature for its customers. Because interoperability is desirable, the manufacturer likely wants to license one of the standards, such as the Firewire or USB port technology, and therefore, would seek an in-licensing tech transfer agreement. In-licensing also creates a business relationship between the two businesses that generates immediate benefits, and it also may yield substantial benefits subsequently as it sets the foundation for other collaborations.

Out-licensing

This describes the process of granting rights in your technology to another business. This is commonly used in the tech and Internet sectors, such as when original equipment manufacturers license out their hard drives, keyboard, and more, and leave the branding to their retail partners. For example, Microsoft licenses out a variety of technologies, monitors, etc. But the Android patents that they license to mobile phone manufacturers earned over $400 million for Microsoft in 2012. In another example, IBM's Intellectual Property Licensing page features an impressive array of technology for out-licensing, and further, it represents that its scientists, researchers, engineers, developers and technologists support the agreements through consulting with their know-how and expertise. Further, out-licensing is a low-risk way to enter a new market. It also represents a defensive strategy, in that, to the extent a business out-licenses its tech to a business, it increases the chance that this other business cannot become a competitor in making its own version of this technology. Out-licensing promotes diffusion of the technology while it discourages development of competing technology. Finally, in some cases, when businesses experience a reorganization or work-out when they emerge, they may find they have tech that does not fit into their new focus, and so this tech is appropriate for an out-bound tech transfer agreement.

Cross-licensing

This describes agreements for which each business grants rights to the other for specified technologies. With such agreements, each business is able to freely use the covered technology and therefore innovate and create products and services without risk of infringing. Further, cross-licensing limits the possibility that the technology will be used as a leverage point, since the negotiating power of both businesses is more even, and there are reciprocal rights and interest in each others' technologies. For example, Cisco, a market leader in networking technologies, and

Samsung, a device maker, announced that they entered into a broad patent cross-licensing agreement, in which each gains access to each other's patent portfolios for a wide range of products and technologies. The agreement covers existing patents, as well as those filed for the next 10 years. Cross-licensing is also a key business strategy in that it enhances the possibility for collaboration and innovation. It is controversial, however, in that cross-licensing potentially produces anticompetitive consequences.

Terms in tech transfer agreements

The transfer is typically for specific rights for a limited time, although it could be an outright sale or assignment of all rights. Depending on the nature of the technology, the agreement may be simple, or quite involved. Tech transfer agreements have a number of provisions that deserve mention. Tech transfer agreements will include the following provisions in addition to the other clauses:

1. The agreement will describe whether the parties contemplate a sale or assignment of the technology. Any assignments of IP are recorded and this terminates all rights of the transferor in that technology. [Documents affecting title to patents and trademarks are filed at the Assignment Recordation Branch in the Public Records Division; copyright assignments are filed with the U.S. Copyright Office.]
2. The agreement could be in the form of a license to use the technology, that is, permission to use the technology limited to the terms and uses the transferor agrees to.
3. The agreement will specify if know-how is included. Know-how can be comprised of tangible form such as reports, blueprints, microfilm, documents, photographs, diagrams, manuals and so forth. Intangible know-how includes training, manufacturing oversight, professionals of the transferor explaining information to professionals of the transferee. Further, the agreement will feature provisions detailing limitations to disclosure of this information.

Contract Manufacturing Agreements

Also known as supply chain agreements, these are increasingly popular as the means of production are easier to split and outsource offshore. What holds the entire process of design, procurement, manufacturing, quality control, shipping, and retailing together is the contract manufacturing agreement. Each company is producing custom goods or services for the client company. These agreements make financial sense when offshore labor costs and transportation costs are comparatively lower. Automation has increasingly made labor cost differences less of a factor though, and further, transportation costs are higher due to rising global activity. Each contract manufacturing relationship is formalized by an agreement. The business attempts to capitalize on increased productivity, including lower cost inputs, while avoiding a number of complex international business risks and associated legal issues involved in foreign manufacturing, employment, and raw materials procurement. A site called iSuppli shows all the inputs in the supply chain that combine to create these types of goods and services. Isaac Wang, an iSuppli analyst, noted, "It takes 3,000 procedures to assemble an H.P. computer. If a contract manufacturer can find a way to save 10 percent of the procedures, then it gets a real good deal."[1] Additionally a number of sites that display schematics of products, posting what are known as "tear-down reports," which detail the parts, accessories, and suppliers of products investigators have taken apart.

Although these agreements are in widespread use and seem to transcend traditional domestic manufacturing limitations as to price, capacity, and quality, there are risks. Supply chain agreements seek to match ideas for goods and services, with production and distribution expertise, and the contract must be clear as to expectations, including, for example, quality and timeliness. Compliance by supply chain partners on employment conditions and wages is a recurring concern (covered more in the Employment chapter) and is a major factor in the due diligence process when selecting supply chain partners. No matter how agile the management is in this area however, there are a number of risks, including:

- Expectations of cost savings (which may not occur);
- Loss of knowledge, know-how, trade secrets, and other sensitive business information to partners (with risk that it will be revealed to competitors);
- Inability to translate work to partners using a mature and systematized process (because they can perform the contract only if there is a standardized repeatable model);
- Data compliance liability (especially in countries with strict privacy laws);
- Government regulatory risk (host country's laws may become more burdensome, especially in wages, hours, health, safety, and environmental issues);
- Contract partner's failure to deliver (in material ways including quality, timeliness, record keeping, etc.);
- Scope or mission creep (the project goes beyond that described in the agreement, and the resulting lack of clarity leads to problems);
- Lack of cultural alignment (leaving a divide that needs to be bridged, as to religion, gender, appropriate garb, holidays, hours, and so forth).

The leader in the use of these innovative agreements is Apple, Inc., whose demand-shaping strategies have produced outstanding results. Supply chain transparency is a trending issue, as are fair trade and sustainability as corporate social responsibility matters. As an example of the extent to which they have to address supply chain agreements, consider their *Supplier Responsibility 2014 Progress Report*, which starts, "At Apple, we believe in making complex things simple. We strive to design products that are intuitive and enrich people's lives. Behind that simplicity lies ones of the biggest supply chains on the planet. Products like iPhone, iPad, and Mac all depend on the contributions of more than a million people across the globe, employed by both Apple and hundreds of their manufacturing partners." In this report, Apple addresses its contract suppliers'

---

1. David Barboza, "Supply Chain for iPhone Highlights Costs in China," *New York Times,* July 5, 2010.

conditions relating to training, age, pay, union representation, sourcing of minerals, health and safety, environment, and accountability.

One area of supply chain contracting of particular focus for Internet and tech companies is conflict minerals, since these are (at this time) necessary components for device makers. In response to reported human rights abuses surrounding the extraction and sale of 'the three Ts'—tin, tantalum, and tungsten—as well as gold, Congress passed legislation in 2010 requiring public companies to disclose their use of covered conflict minerals extracted or processed in the Democratic Republic of Congo and nine adjacent countries. Section 1502 of the Dodd-Frank Wall Street Reform and Consumer Protection Act (relevant parts codified in the Exchange Act at 15 U.S.C. §78m(p) (2012). The purpose of the law is to promote transparency of businesses' use of these minerals, and discouraging them from continuing to trade in ways that support regional conflicts.

Congress directed the SEC to implement rules to effectuate the disclosure requirements, rules that impact approximately 6,000 companies. The SEC created a multi-step process for companies to engage in if they contract for these minerals in their supply chains.

1. Companies must determine if they are covered (i.e., they are a public company, or these minerals are necessary for the production or functionality of their products.
2. Companies must conduct a 'reasonable country of origin inquiry' to establish preliminarily whether the necessary minerals originated in the covered countries.
3. If companies have 'reason to believe' minerals 'may have originated' in covered countries, they must 'exercise due diligence on the source and chain of custody of its conflict minerals.'
4. If, after performing due diligence, this is the case, companies must file a report with the SEC (a) describing its due diligence; (b) have a private sector audit of its efforts; and (c) report that those products have 'not been found to be DRC conflict free.'

This next case is a recent ruling on an industry challenge to the SECs conflict mineral disclosure regulations.

National Association of Manufacturers v. Securities and Exchange Commission,

214 U.S. App. LEXIS 6840 (D.C. Cir. April 14, 2014)

Facts: For the last fifteen years the Democratic Republic of Congo has endured war and humanitarian catastrophe. Millions have perished, mostly civilians who died of starvation and disease. Communities have been displaced, rape is a weapon, and human right violations are widespread. Armed groups fighting the war finance their operation by exploiting the regional trade in several kinds of minerals. Those minerals—gold, tantalum, tin, and tungsten—are extracted from technologically primitive mining sites in remote eastern Congo. They are sold at regional trading houses, smelted nearby or abroad, and ultimately used to manufacture many different products (including: turbines, camera lenses, medical devices, mobile phones and computers, plastics, automobile parts, lighting, power tools, and golf clubs). Armed groups profit by extorting, and in some cases directly managing, minimally regulated mining operations.

In 2010, Congress devised a response to the Congo war. Section 1502 of the Dodd-Frank Wall Street Reform and Consumer Protection Act (relevant parts codified in the Securities Exchange Act, 15 U.S.C. §78m(p) and note (2012)) requires the SEC to issue regulations requiring firms using "conflict minerals" to investigate and disclose the origin of these minerals, to the extent they are necessary to the functionality or production of a product.

Congress directed the SEC to develop implementation rules for this law. For this, the SEC proposed rules and solicited comments on a range of issues. The SEC received a mass of replies, and twice extended the Comment Period. Finally, by a 3-2 vote the SEC promulgated final rules. The first disclosure reports were due from companies May 31, 2014, applicable only to large companies–securities issuers who file reports with the SEC under sections 13(a) or 15(d) of the Exchange Act.

Overall, this challenge focuses on the statute and final rule requiring issuers to state their products have "not been found to be DRC conflict free" if it is found to be so after due diligence and an audit. The final rule adopts a three-step process. At step one, a company must determine if the rule covers it. The final rule does not include a *de minimis* exception and so applies even to issuers who use very small amounts of conflict minerals. The rule also extends to issuers who only contract for the manufacture of products with conflict minerals, as well as issuers who directly manufacture those products. Step two requires issuers to conduct a "reasonable country of origin inquiry." If, as a result of the inquiry, an issuer knows—or has reason to believe—that its necessary conflict minerals may have originated in covered countries, then it must proceed to step three and exercise due diligence. Step three requires issuers to exercise due diligence on the source and chain of custody of its conflict minerals. If issuers still have reason to believe its conflict minerals may have originated in covered countries, it must file a conflict minerals disclosure report. The report must describe both its due diligence efforts, including a private sector audit, and those products that have "not been found to be DRC conflict free." The report must also provide detailed information about the origin of the minerals used in those products. The report must describe measures taken to establish "the course and chain of custody" of the minerals, including a "private sector audit." The report to the SEC must also list "the products manufactured or contracted to be manufactured that are not DRC conflict free." A product is "DRC conflict free" if its necessary conflict minerals did not 'directly or indirectly' finance or benefit armed groups in the adjoining countries.

During a two-year phase-in period (four years for small issuers), issuers may describe certain products as "DRC undeterminable." The SEC estimated initial costs of the final rule to be $3-4 billion, and between $207-609 million annually thereafter. The SEC was "unable to readily quantify" the "compelling social benefits" the rule was designed to achieve: reducing violence and promoting peace and stability in Congo. The SEC instead relied on Congress's judgment that supply-chain transparency would promote peace and stability by reducing the flow of money to armed groups. That judgment grounded many of the SECs discretionary choices in favor greater transparency.

The National Association of Manufacturers (NAM) challenged the statute and final rule, on grounds that they violate both the Administrative Procedure Act and the First Amendment. The district court rejected NAMs claims and granted summary judgment for the SEC.

Judicial Opinion. Judge Randolph: Under the Administrative Procedure Act, a court must hold unlawful and set aside agency action . . . found to be arbitrary, capricious, an abuse of discretion, or otherwise not in accordance with law or in excess of statutory jurisdiction.

[Two of NAMs challenges are abstracted here: that there is no de minimus exception to the reporting requirement; and there is an inadequate cost-benefit analysis.] The Act does not include an exception for *de minimis* uses of conflict minerals . . . [and NAM] claims that the rule should have . . . and that the SEC erred. Although the SEC acknowledges that it had the authority to create such an exception, it stated [that] "would be contrary to the statute and Congressional purpose." The SEC did not act arbitrarily and capriciously by choosing not to include a *de minimis* exception, [because it reasoned that] conflict minerals are often used in products in very limited quantities. Though costly [the SECs] decision bears a "rational connection" to the facts. The SECs explanation was "rational," and that is enough.

NAM . . . alleges that the SEC violated [its mandate] because it did not adequately analyze the costs and benefits of the final rule. We do not see any problems with the SEC cost-side analysis [when it] concluded that the rule would impose competitive costs, but have relatively minor or offsetting effects on efficiency and capital formation. NAM argues on the benefit side that the SEC failed to determine whether the final rule would actually achieve its intended purpose. But we find it difficult to see what the SEC could have done better. Congress intended the rule to achieve compelling social benefits, but it was unable to readily quantify those benefits because it lacked data about the rule's effects. That determination was reasonable. An agency is not required 'to measure the immeasurable.' And need not conduct a 'rigorous, quantitative economic analysis' unless the statute explicitly directs it to do so. Here, the rule's benefits would occur half-a-world away in the midst of an opaque conflict about which little reliable information exists. Even if one could estimate how many lives are saved or rapes prevented as a direct result of the final rule, doing so would be pointless because the costs of the rule—measured in dollars—would create an apples-to-bricks comparison. Despite the lack of data, the SEC *had* to promulgate a disclosure rule. Promulgating some rule is exactly what Dodd-Frank required the SEC to do.

This brings us to NAMs First Amendment claim. NAM challenges . . . the requirement that an issuer describe its products as 'not DRC conflict free' in the [disclosure] report. That requirement, according to NAM, unconstitutionally compels speech. The SEC argues that rational basis review is appropriate because the conflict free label discloses purely factual non-ideological information. We disagree. [R]ational basis review applies to certain disclosures . . . limited to cases in which disclosures requirements are reasonable related to the State's interest in preventing deception of consumers.

[I]t is far from clear that the description . . . "conflict free"—is factual and non-ideological. The label . . . is a metaphor that conveys moral responsibility for the Congo war. It requires an issuer to tell consumers that its products are ethically tainted, even if they only indirectly finance armed groups. By compelling an issuer to confess blood on its hands, the statute interferes with that exercise of the freedom of speech under the First Amendment.

Under *Central Hudson* [a case explaining use of the intermediate standard of review in applicable First Amendment cases], the government must show (1) a substantial government interest that is; (2) directly and materially advanced by the restriction; and (3) that the restriction is narrowly tailored. The narrow tailoring requirement invalidates regulations for which narrower restrictions on expression would serve the government's interest as well. Although the government need not choose the least restrictive means of achieving its goals, there must be a reasonable fit between means and ends. The SEC has provided no such evidence here. [NAM suggested alternatives including] issuers could use their own language to describe their products, or the government could compile its own list of products that it believes are affiliated with the Congo war, based on information the issuers submit. The SEC . . . simply assert[s] that those proposals are less effective. The SEC has failed to explain why (much less provide evidence that) NAMs intuitive alternatives to regulating speech would be any less effective. Without any evidence that alternatives would be less effective, we . . . cannot say that the restriction here is narrowly tailored. We therefore hold that [the statute] and the SECs final rule . . . violate the First Amendment the statute and rule require regulated entities to report to the SEC and to state on their website that any of their products 'have not been found to be DRC conflict free.' [Affirmed in part and reversed in part and the case is remanded to the district court.]

So ordered.

Case Questions

1. Describe the court's analysis for review of the Agency's rulemaking process.
2. Describe the court's legal analysis for reviewing the SEC's mandatory disclosure rule that in some circumstances companies must add this label if any of their products "have not been found to be DRC conflict free."
3. Devise a label that the SEC can mandate for contract manufacturing partners that will satisfy First Amendment jurisprudence.

EDGAR Online

APPLE INC

FORM SD
(Specialized Disclosure Report)

Filed 05/29/14

Address	ONE INFINITE LOOP
	CUPERTINO, CA 95014
Telephone	(408) 996-1010
CIK	0000320193
Symbol	AAPL
SIC Code	3571 - Electronic Computers
Industry	Computer Hardware
Sector	Technology
Fiscal Year	09/27

UNITED STATES
SECURITIES AND EXCHANGE COMMISSION
Washington, D.C. 20549

FORM SD

S PECIALIZED D ISCLOSURE R EPORT

Apple Inc.
(Exact name of registrant as specified in its charter)

California	**000-10030**	**94-2404110**
(State or other jurisdiction of incorporation or organization)	(Commission File Number)	(IRS Employer Identification No.)

1 Infinite Loop
Cupertino, California   **95014**
(Address of principal executive offices)   (Zip Code)

D. Bruce Sewell
Senior Vice President,
General Counsel and Secretary
(408) 996-1010
(Name and telephone number, including area code, of the
person to contact in connection with this report.)

Check the appropriate box to indicate the rule pursuant to which this form is being filed, and provide the period to which the information in this form applies:

☒   Rule 13p-1 under the Securities Exchange Act (17 CFR 240.13p-1) for the reporting period from January 1 to December 31, 2013.

Section 1 – Conflict Minerals Disclosure

Items 1.01 and 1.02 Conflict Minerals Disclosure and Report, Exhibit

Conflict Minerals Disclosure

A copy of Apple Inc.'s ("Apple's") Conflict Minerals Report for the reporting period January 1, 2013 to December 31, 2013 is provided as Exhibit 1.02 hereto and is publicly available at investor.apple.com/sec.cfm. Apple's determination and related disclosures relating to materials that may come from recycled and scrap sources are included in Apple's Conflict Minerals Report and incorporated by reference herein.

Section 2 – Exhibits

Item 2.01 Exhibits

Exhibit 1.02 – Conflict Minerals Report for the reporting period January 1, 2013 to December 31, 2013

* * * * *

SIGNATURE

Pursuant to the requirements of the Securities Exchange Act of 1934, the registrant has duly caused this report to be signed on its behalf by the duly authorized undersigned.

APPLE INC.

By: /s/ D. Bruce Sewell   Date: May 29, 2014
   D. Bruce Sewell
   Senior Vice President, General Counsel and Secretary

EXHIBIT 1.02

Apple Inc.

Conflict Minerals Report

Introduction

This Report has been prepared pursuant to Rule 13p-1 under the Securities Exchange Act of 1934, as amended, for the reporting period from January 1 to December 31, 2013.

This Report relates to the process undertaken for Apple products that were manufactured, or contracted to be manufactured, during calendar 2013 and that contain gold, columbite-tantalite (coltan), cassiterite, wolframite, tantalum, tin, and tungsten (collectively, the "Subject Minerals").

These products are Apple's iPhone, iPad, Mac, iPod, Apple TV, displays, and accessories. Third-party products that Apple retails but that it does not manufacture or contract to manufacture are outside of the scope of this Report.

Apple's Conflict Minerals Program

The ethical sourcing of minerals is an important part of Apple's mission to ensure safe and fair working conditions in its supply chain. Apple is determined to use "conflict free" minerals in its products.

Apple began investigating the uses of tantalum, tin, tungsten, and gold in its products in 2009. In 2010, Apple became one of the first companies to begin mapping its supply chain to the smelter or refiner level, in order to identify the smelters and refiners its suppliers use and to understand potential entry points into its supply chain for tantalum, tin, tungsten, and gold.

Rather than simply funneling its demand through a limited number of verified smelters or those that are not sourcing in the Democratic Republic of the Congo ("DRC") or adjoining countries, Apple is focused on expanding the verified smelter and refiner base. Apple believes the best way to impact human rights abuses on the ground in the DRC is to have a critical mass of smelters verified as conflict-free, so that demand from other questionable sources is reduced. Apple is pushing smelters and refiners to comply with the Conflict-Free Sourcing Initiative's Conflict-Free Smelter Program (the "CFSP") or equivalent independent third-party audit programs, and Apple is holding accountable the smelters and refiners in its supply chain by publishing their names, countries, and CFSP participation status. In February 2014, Apple announced that all tantalum smelters in its supply chain had been designated "conflict free" by the CFSP or an equivalent independent third-party audit program. Apple is also continuing to increase the number of verified smelters and refiners for tin, tungsten and gold, and the majority of the smelters and refiners in Apple's supply chain are either designated "conflict free" by the CFSP or an equivalent independent third-party audit program or are undergoing conflict minerals audits. Apple will keep up the pressure until all unaudited smelters and refiners are either certified or removed from Apple's supply chain.

To drive economic development and create opportunities to source "conflict free" minerals from the DRC and adjoining countries, Apple has provided financial support for in-region programs, including the Conflict-Free Tin Initiative, KEMET's Partnership for Social and Economic Sustainability, Solutions for Hope, and the Public-Private Alliance for Responsible Minerals Trade. Apple is also working with other non-governmental organizations, trade groups, government agencies, and others to promote change.

Apple requires all of its suppliers to adhere to its conflict minerals policy and supplier code of conduct. This policy and code of conduct are on Apple's website, along with Apple's annual supplier responsibility progress reports. Apple expects its suppliers to implement policies and due diligence measures in accordance with its conflict minerals standards, and the suppliers are required to make their polices available to Apple. If a supplier fails to comply with Apple's conflict minerals policy, Apple will take measures up to and including termination of its relationship with the supplier.

Understanding Sources of Minerals

In order to understand the sources of the Subject Minerals used in its complex and multi-tiered supply chain, Apple has implemented an extensive survey program. Apple's conflict minerals policy requires that all of its suppliers map their supply chains through all levels down to the smelters and refiners and report the results to Apple. Accordingly, between 2010 and 2013, Apple surveyed more than 400 suppliers.

Apple worked to verify the smelters and refiners that its suppliers reported by, among other things, making in-person site visits, engaging third-party investigators, and collaborating with industry partners. Apple has identified to date 205 different smelters and refiners of Subject Minerals for 2013. Apple continues to work with suppliers throughout its supply chain to re-validate, improve, and refine their reported information, taking into account supply chain fluctuations and other changes in status or scope and relationships over time.

Due Diligence

Design of Due Diligence

Apple designed its due diligence measures to conform to the Organisation for Economic Co-operation and Development Due Diligence Guidance for Responsible Supply Chains of Minerals from Conflict-Affected and High-Risk Areas: Second Edition, including the related supplements on tantalum, tin, tungsten and gold. Apple believes that auditing smelters and refiners through the CFSP or equivalent independent third-party audit programs provides a reasonable basis for determining if the smelters and refiners process minerals originating from "conflict free" sources.

Due Diligence Measures Performed

Based on its assessment of survey responses received from suppliers, Apple implemented due diligence measures with approximately 400 survey respondents that reported use of Subject Minerals. These due diligence measures included engaging directly with smelters and refiners to drive them to comply with the CFSP or equivalent third-party audit program. Apple personnel also conducted on-site visits of smelters and refiners, and established action plans with particular smelters and refiners, to prepare for and undergo conflict mineral audits.

Apple also directed its suppliers to ensure that their smelters and refiners undergo audits to verify compliance with the CFSP or equivalent audit program. Where particular smelters or refiners were unwilling to engage with Apple or seek compliance with the CFSP or equivalent independent third-party audit programs, Apple required its suppliers to terminate their relationships with those smelters and refiners.

Risk Mitigation and Future Due Diligence Measures

Apple will keep improving its due diligence measures by taking the following steps, among others:

- Continuing to drive suppliers to ensure that their smelters and refiners obtain a "conflict free" designation from an independent third-party auditor of Subject Minerals;

- Continuing to pressure smelters and refiners directly to become verified as having "conflict free" sources of Subject Minerals, or have them removed from Apple's supply chain; and

- Continuing to drive its suppliers to obtain current, accurate, and complete information about their smelters and refiners of Subject Minerals.

Determination

Based on the information provided by Apple's suppliers and its own due diligence efforts with known smelters and refiners through December 31, 2013, Apple believes that the facilities used to process the Subject Minerals in Apple products include the smelters and refiners listed in Annex I below.

Based on its due diligence efforts, Apple does not have sufficient information to conclusively determine the country of origin of the Subject Minerals in its products or whether the Subject Minerals are from recycled or scrap sources. However, based on the information provided by Apple's suppliers, smelters, and refiners, as well as from other sources, Apple believes that the countries of origin of the Subject Minerals contained in its products include the countries listed in Annex II below, as well as recycled and scrap sources.

Of the 205 smelters and refiners of Subject Minerals identified for calendar 2013, 21 smelters and refiners were identified as sources of Subject Minerals from the DRC or adjoining countries. Of these 21, 17 were found CFSP-compliant. The 4 remaining smelters and refiners have not yet undertaken a third-party audit. Apple commissioned a third-party review of publicly available information and found no reasonable basis for concluding that any of these smelters and refiners sourced Subject Minerals that directly or indirectly finance or benefit armed groups. Apple will continue to drive these 4 smelters and refiners to become CFSP-compliant or, if necessary, will require its suppliers to remove them from its supply chain.

Apple has provided information as of the date of this Report. Subsequent events, such as the inability or unwillingness of any suppliers, smelters or refiners to comply with Apple's conflict minerals policies, may affect Apple's future determinations under Rule 13p-1.

3

ANNEX I

Subject Mineral	Smelter or Refiner Name	Country Location of Smelter or Refiner
Gold	AIDA Chemical Industries Co., Ltd.	Japan
Gold	Allgemeine Gold- und Silberscheideanstalt A.G.	Germany
Gold	Almalyk Mining and Metallurgical Complex	Uzbekistan
Gold	AngloGold Ashanti Corrego do Sitio Minercao	Brazil
Gold	Argor-Heraeus SA	Switzerland
Gold	Asahi Pretec Corporation	Japan
Gold	Asaka Riken Co., Ltd.	Japan
Gold	Atasay Kuyumculuk Sanayi Ve Ticaret A.S.	Turkey
Gold	Aurubis AG	Germany
Gold	Bangko Sentral ng Pilipinas (Central Bank of the Philippines)	Philippines
Gold	Boliden AB	Sweden
Gold	Caridad	Mexico
Gold	Cendres & Metaux SA	Switzerland
Gold	Chimet SpA	Italy
Gold	Chugai Mining Co., Ltd.	Japan
Gold	Codelco	Chile
Gold	DOWA	Japan
Gold	ECO-System Recycling Co., LTD.	Japan
Gold	FSE Novosibirsk Refinery	Russia
Gold	Guangdong Jinding Gold Ltd.	China
Gold	Hangzhou the Fuchun River Smelting Co., Ltd.	China
Gold	Heimerle and Meule GmbH	Germany
Gold	Heraeus Ltd. Hong Kong	China
Gold	Heraeus Precious Metals GmbH & Co. KG	Germany
Gold	Hunan Chenzhou Mining Industry Co., Ltd.	China
Gold	Inner Mongolia Qiankun Gold and Silver Refinery Share Co., Ltd.	China
Gold	Ishifuku Metal Industry Co., Ltd.	Japan
Gold	Istanbul Gold Refinery	Turkey
Gold	Japan Mint	Japan
Gold	Jiangxi Copper Co., Ltd.	China
Gold	Johnson Matthey Inc.	United States

4

Gold	Johnson Matthey Ltd.	Canada
Gold	JSC Ekaterinburg Non-Ferrous Metal Processing Plant	Russia
Gold	JSC UralElectromed	Russia
Gold	JX Nippon Mining & Metals Co., Ltd	Japan
Gold	Kazzinc Ltd.	Kazakhstan
Gold	Kennecott Utah Copper LLC	United States
Gold	Kojima Chemicals Co., Ltd.	Japan
Gold	Kyrgzaltyn JSC	Kyrgyzstan
Gold	L'azurde Company For Jewelry	Saudi Arabia
Gold	Lingbao Jinyuan Tonghui Refinery	China
Gold	LS-Nikko Copper Inc.	Republic of Korea
Gold	Materion	United States
Gold	Matsuda Sangyo Co., Ltd.	Japan
Gold	Met-Mex Peñoles, S.A.	Mexico
Gold	Metalor Technologies (Hong Kong) Ltd	China
Gold	Metalor Technologies Ltd. (Suzhou)	China
Gold	Metalor Technologies SA	Switzerland
Gold	Metalor Technologies Singapore Pte Ltd	Singapore
Gold	Metalor USA Refining Corporation	United States
Gold	Mitsubishi Materials Corp.	Japan
Gold	Mitsui Mining and Smelting Co., Ltd.	Japan
Gold	Moscow Special Alloys Processing Plant	Russia
Gold	Nadir Metal Rafineri San. Ve Tic. A.S.	Turkey
Gold	Navoi Mining & Metallurgy Combinat	Uzbekistan
Gold	Nihon Material Co., Ltd.	Japan
Gold	Ohio Precious Metals	United States
Gold	Ohura Precious Metal Industry Co., Ltd.	Japan
Gold	OJSC "The Gulidov Krasnoyarsk Non-Ferrous Metals Plant" - (OJSC Krastvetmet)	Russia
Gold	OJSC Kolyma Refinery	Russia
Gold	Pamp SA	Switzerland
Gold	Prioksky Plant of Non-Ferrous Metals	Russia
Gold	PT Aneka Tambang (Persero) Tbk	Indonesia
Gold	PX Precinox SA	Switzerland
Gold	Rand Refinery (Pty) Ltd.	South Africa
Gold	Royal Canadian Mint	Canada

5

Gold	Sabin Metal Corp.	United States
Gold	Samwon Metals Corp.	Republic of Korea
Gold	Schone Edelmetaal	Netherlands
Gold	SEMPSA Joyeria Plateria, S.A.	Spain
Gold	Shandong Zhaojin Gold & Silver Refinery Co., Ltd.	China
Gold	SOE Shyolkovsky Factory of Secondary Precious Metals	Russia
Gold	Solar Applied Materials Technology Corp.	Taiwan
Gold	Sumitomo Metal Mining Co., Ltd.	Japan
Gold	Tanaka Kikinzoku Kogyo K.K.	Japan
Gold	The Great Wall Gold & Silver Refinery of China	China
Gold	The Refinery of Shandong Gold Mining Co. Ltd.	China
Gold	Tokuriki Honten Co., Ltd.	Japan
Gold	Tongling Nonferrous Metals Group Holdings Co., Ltd	China
Gold	Torecom	Republic of Korea
Gold	Umicore Brasil Ltda	Brazil
Gold	Umicore SA Business Unit Precious Metals Refining	Belgium
Gold	United Precious Metal Refining, Inc.	United States
Gold	Valcambi SA	Switzerland
Gold	Western Australian Mint trading as The Perth Mint	Australia
Gold	Xstrata Canada Corp.	Canada
Gold	Yantai Guoda Safina High-Advanced Refining Co. Ltd.	China
Gold	Yokohama Metal Co. Ltd	Japan
Gold	Zhongyuan Gold Smelter of Zhongjin Gold Corporation	China
Gold	Zijin Mining Group Co. Ltd	China
Tantalum	Conghua Tantalum and Niobium Smeltery	China
Tantalum	Duoluoshan	China
Tantalum	Exotech, Inc.	United States
Tantalum	F&X	China
Tantalum	Gannon & Scott	United States
Tantalum	Global Advanced Metals	United States
Tantalum	H.C. Starck Gmbh	Germany
Tantalum	Hi-Temp Specialty Metals, Inc.	United States
Tantalum	JiuJiang JinXin Nonferrous Metals Co. Ltd.	China
Tantalum	JiuJiang Tanbre Co. Ltd.	China
Tantalum	Kemet Blue Powder	United States

6

Tantalum	Metallurgical Products India Pvt Ltd.	India
Tantalum	Mitsui Mining & Smelting	Japan
Tantalum	Ningxia Orient Tantalum Industry Co., Ltd.	China
Tantalum	Plansee	Austria
Tantalum	RFH Tantalum Smeltry Co., Ltd	China
Tantalum	Shanghai Jiangxi Metals Co., Ltd	China
Tantalum	Solikamsk Metal Works	Russia
Tantalum	Taki Chemical Co., Ltd.	Japan
Tantalum	Tantalite Resources	South Africa
Tantalum	Telex	United States
Tantalum	Ulba	Kazakhstan
Tantalum	Zhuzhou Cement Carbide	China
Tin	Alpha	United States
Tin	CFC Cooperativa dos Fundidores de Cassiterita da Amazônia Ltda.	Brazil
Tin	China Rare Metal Material Co., Ltd.	China
Tin	China Tin Group	China
Tin	CNMC (Guangxi) PGMA Co. Ltd.	China
Tin	Cooper Santa	Brazil
Tin	CV Duta Putra Bangka	Indonesia
Tin	CV Gita Pesona	Indonesia
Tin	CV JusTindo	Indonesia
Tin	CV Makmur Jaya	Indonesia
Tin	CV Nurjanah	Indonesia
Tin	CV Serumpun Sebalai	Indonesia
Tin	CV United Smelting	Indonesia
Tin	EM Vinto	Bolivia
Tin	Estanho de Rondonia SA	Brazil
Tin	Fenix Metals	Poland
Tin	Gejiu Non-Ferrous Metal Processing Co. Ltd.	China
Tin	Gejiu Zi-Li	China
Tin	Gold Bell Group	China
Tin	Huichang Jinshunda Tin Co., Ltd	China
Tin	Kai Unita Trade Limited Liability Company	China
Tin	Linwu Xianggui Smelter Co	China
Tin	Magnu's Minerais Metais e Ligas LTDA	Brazil

7

Tin	Malaysia Smelting Corporation	Malaysia
Tin	Melt Metais e Ligas Ltda.	Brazil
Tin	Metallo Chimique	Belgium
Tin	Mineração Taboca S.A.	Brazil
Tin	Minmetals Ganzhou Tin Co., Ltd.	China
Tin	Minsur	Peru
Tin	Mitsubishi Materials Corp.	Japan
Tin	Novosibirsk Integrated Tin Works	Russia
Tin	O.M. Manufacturing (Thailand) Co., Ltd.	Thailand
Tin	OMSA	Bolivia
Tin	PT Alam Lestari Kencana	Indonesia
Tin	PT Artha Cipta Langgeng	Indonesia
Tin	PT Babel Inti Perkasa	Indonesia
Tin	PT Babel Surya Alam Lestari	Indonesia
Tin	PT Bangka Kudai Tin	Indonesia
Tin	PT Bangka Putra Karya	Indonesia
Tin	PT Bangka Timah Utama Sejahtera	Indonesia
Tin	PT Bangka Tin Industry	Indonesia
Tin	PT Belitung Industri Sejahetra	Indonesia
Tin	PT Billi Tin Makmur Lestari	Indonesia
Tin	PT Bukit Timah	Indonesia
Tin	PT DS Jaya Abadi	Indonesia
Tin	PT Eunindo Usaha Mandiri	Indonesia
Tin	PT Fang Di Multindo	Indonesia
Tin	PT HP Metals of Indonesia	Indonesia
Tin	PT Koba Tin	Indonesia
Tin	PT Mitra Stania Prima	Austria
Tin	PT Panca Mega	Indonesia
Tin	PT Prima Timah Utama	Indonesia
Tin	PT Refined Bangka Tin	Indonesia
Tin	PT Sariwiguna Binasentosa	Indonesia
Tin	PT Stanindo Inti Perkasa	Indonesia
Tin	PT Sumber Jaya Indah	Indonesia
Tin	PT Tambang Timah	Indonesia

8

Tin	PT Timah	Indonesia
Tin	PT Timah Nusantara	Indonesia
Tin	PT Tinindo Inter Nusa	Indonesia
Tin	PT Yinchendo Mining Industry	Indonesia
Tin	Rui Da Hung Business Co., Ltd.	Taiwan
Tin	Soft Metais, Ltda.	Brazil
Tin	THAISARCO	Thailand
Tin	VQB Mineral and Trading Group Joint Stock Co.	Vietnam
Tin	White Solder Metalurgia	Brazil
Tin	Yunnan Chengfeng Non-Ferrous Metals Co., Ltd.	China
Tin	Yunnan Tin Company, Ltd.	China
Tungsten	A.L.M.T. Corp.	Japan
Tungsten	ATI Tungsten Materials	United States
Tungsten	Chaozhou Xianglu Tungsten Industry Co. Ltd.	China
Tungsten	Chongyi Zhangyuan Tungsten Co. Ltd	China
Tungsten	Dayu Weiliang Tungsten Co., Ltd.	China
Tungsten	FuJian JinXin Tungsten Co., Ltd.	China
Tungsten	Ganzhou Grand Sea W & Mo Group Co. Ltd	China
Tungsten	Ganzhou Huaxing Tungsten Products Co., Ltd.	China
Tungsten	Global Tungsten & Powders Corp.	United States
Tungsten	H.C. Starck GmbH	Germany
Tungsten	Hunan Chenzhou Mining Group Co	China
Tungsten	Hunan Chun-Chang Nonferrous Smelting & Concentrating Co., Ltd.	China
Tungsten	Japan New Metals Co., Ltd.	Japan
Tungsten	Jiangxi Gan Bei Tungsten Co., Ltd.	China
Tungsten	Jiangxi Rare Earth & Rare Metals Tungsten Group Corp.	China
Tungsten	Jiangxi Xinsheng Tungsten Industry Co., Ltd.	China
Tungsten	Kennametal Inc.	United States
Tungsten	Tejing (Vietnam) Tungsten Co. Ltd	Germany
Tungsten	Wolfram Bergbau und Hütten AG	Austria
Tungsten	Wolfram Co., CJSC	Russia
Tungsten	Xiamen Tungsten (H.C.) Co. Ltd	China
Tungsten	Xiamen Tungsten Co. Ltd	China
Tungsten	Xinhai Rendan Shaoguan Tungsten Co., Ltd.	China
Tungsten	Zhuzhou Cemented Carbide Group Co. Ltd	China

9

ANNEX II

Angola	Laos
Argentina	Luxembourg
Australia	Madagascar
Austria	Malaysia
Belgium	Mongolia
Bolivia	Mozambique
Brazil	Myanmar
Burundi	Netherlands
Central African Republic	Nigeria
Chile	Peru
China	Portugal
Colombia	Republic of Congo
Côte D'Ivoire	Republic of Korea
Czech Republic	Russia
Democratic Republic of the Congo	Rwanda
Djibouti	Sierra Leone
Egypt	Singapore
Estonia	South Africa
Ethiopia	South Sudan
France	Suriname
Germany	Switzerland
Guyana	Tanzania
India	Thailand
Indonesia	Uganda
Ireland	United Kingdom
Israel	United States
Japan	Zambia
Kenya	Zimbabwe

10

Additionally, lithium is another mineral that is necessary for the Internet and tech industries; and it, too, is the subject of supply chain contracts. Lithium ion batteries are increasingly the technology of choice for the tech as well as the automotive industry's hybrid vehicles, since both require mobile electrical energy storage. The U.S. lithium production and reserves are quite low; it is estimated that South America holds about 80 percent of the lithium to be developed, and the depletion rates are a concern. Therefore, sustainability is in question.

Professional Services Contracts and Software Licenses

These are negotiated contracts that typically include software as well as implementation. Software contracts are highly specialized agreements granting licensees limited rights of use, and protecting the licensors' investment in creation of the code, and subsequent dissemination. The unique aspect of software contracts is that the agreements are not for an outright sale of software. Rather, they are a license to use the software in specific ways that are agreed upon. Software publishers originally claimed that the software was licensed and not sold, so as to avoid the first sale/exhaustion of rights doctrine recognized in both patent and copyright law. A license is the permission to use the software, which, in the absence of the permission, would amount to infringement of that property. The software publishers' position that the software is licensed, and not sold, and therefore it may not be re-sold, is controversial. In *Vernor v. Autodesk*, the Ninth Circuit reversed the district court court's finding of ownership. The appeals court held that software licensees were not "owners," and therefore not entitled to invoke the first sale doctrine as a defense to copyright infringement claims made by the software publisher.[2] (Software is also unusual in that it is possibly covered by patent, copyright or trade secret, and therefore licensing is quite involved.)

Professional software and license agreements have a number of provisions that deserve mention. This is a checklist with mention of major terms:

- **License grant:** This will clarify what parties are entitled to use the software. It could include, or carve out, subsidiaries, divisions, and subsequently acquired, or sold, companies, for example.
- **Term:** a perpetual or fixed-term license: Perpetual terms extend for so long as the licensee pays for the license, and fixed terms are specified in the agreement, and pricing is re-negotiated for each subsequent term.
- **Revocation of the license:** It is almost always the case that licenses are revocable upon breach. Irrevocable licenses are the exception, since licensees, even if in breach, may continue using the software.
- **Exclusivity:** Software publishers will typically license the software non-exclusively and therefore be able to license it to multiple parties. Rarely, software will be licensed exclusively and so payments are in such cases, made earlier in the parties' relationship.

---

2. 621 F.3d 1102 (9th Cir. 2010), *cert. denied*, 132 S. Ct. 1102 (2011).

- **Territorial restrictions:** If no restrictions are agreed to, licensees have rights everywhere. However, licenses are typically granted for certain territories. For example, NBC Broadcasting negotiated for the exclusive right to broadcast the Olympics in the U.S. The BBC has broadcasting rights for the UK, and Sportfive has broadcast rights for Europe.
- **User licenses:** This may be based on the number of devices, employees, offices, and so forth. This becomes highly relevant when licensee businesses are rapidly expanding.
- **Field of use:** Licenses may be for certain purposes, and should a licensee expand into other endeavors, this present license does not extend to those uses.
- **Installation, training, support, fixes, patches, updates, licensee modifications:** This covers installation specifications of hardware, compatibility, servers, etc., for successful execution.
- **Payments:** This covers deposits, escrows, updated versions, bankruptcy or merger.
- **Exports:** This covers any licenses that may be required, and any country restrictions.
- **Warranties:** This covers those that are implied (merchantability, fitness for a particular purpose); disclaimers (allowed only if conspicuous)
- **Integration clause:** This specifies that the contract is the entire sum of the parties' agreement and its provisions supersede all other agreements and representations.
- **Performance specifications:** This covers what the licensee expects to accomplish with the software.
- **Remedies:** Licensors limit liability for direct damages by adding a provision that remedies are limited to repair or replacement so as to avoid licensees from finding a more expensive replacement. Consequential damages cover lost data and profits and such losses can be quite costly.
- **Invalidity:** Each states' laws are different on which aspects of a contract render it invalid (such as for duress, unconscionability, etc.). Licensors should be aware of local law and provide that should any clause be invalidated, the rest of the license agreement survives.
- **Jurisdiction, choice of law, and conflicts of law:** Since contract law is state-based, these clauses are particularly concerning and each party wants its own jurisdiction and its own laws applied. Both will agree that conflicts of laws provisions do not apply.
- **ADR:** Both parties should contemplate arbitration or mediation and agree to a forum for any disputes.

Of course, the parties in a contract have common interests, such as in the success of their agreement, even as some aspects of their relationship are at cross-purposes. In order to manage the risks of any disputes, each side has its own exigencies to consider when negotiating. For example, licensees will prefer the agreement to be irrevocable, preventing the licensor from terminating or suspending access to the technology during a dispute. In another example, licensees will want restrictions on audits that licensors can request. As to licensors, they will seek a significant up-front payment so as to diminish the licensees' withholding of payments as leverage. Licensors will also want to control disputes concerning invoices, and request that any disputes are 'in good faith,' and further, that after a certain period from date of invoice, the right to dispute the invoice is forfeited. For both parties, reducing ambiguity and promoting effective communications are highly desirable. The next cases, when considered together, provide a highly illuminating look at professional contracts for software and services. They show the complications involved with providing software to ongoing businesses that need to integrate new software with the present systems. Further, international differences in software rights matter, and present software companies with acute challenges as they move into international markets and other opportunities.

Montclair State Univ. v. Oracle, Inc.,
2012 U.S. Dist. LEXIS 119509 (D. N.J. Aug. 23, 2012)

Facts: Plaintiff Montclair State University (MSU) decided to replace its enterprise resource planning (ERP) software system with a new system. In seeking a primarily 'off-the-shelf' version of a system that it could use, MSU identified over 3,200 business requirements for the new system. Then it issued a Request for Proposals (RFP) to Oracle, and two other ERP software companies. In the RFP, MSU directed the bidder to specify which of its business requirements could be satisfied by their "base product." In Oracle's RFP response, it allegedly represented that its base system would address the overwhelming majority of MSUs business requirements; that only 156 of the 3,200 could not be satisfied by its base system. Thereafter Oracle gave a live demonstration of its system to MSU.

MSU asserts that Oracle made additional representations during the negotiation and bidding process. After hearing that MSU was concerned with having enough personnel resources for the software migration, Oracle represented it could accelerate implementation and would conclude successfully. MSU further asserts that Oracle misrepresented its intention to implement the agreement at the agreed-upon price. Software fees totaled $4.3 million and the fixed fee for implementation was $15.75 million for a phase-in over 25 months. The project's scope was massive. The parties entered into several contracts that altogether comprise their agreement, and include the: (1) the Services Ordering Document; (2) Oracle License and Services Agreement (LSA); (3) first amendment to the LSA; (4) second amendment to the LSA; and (5) fixed price exhibit. Following execution of the agreement Oracle began its work on developing and implementing MSUs transition to the new ERP system, scheduled to take place over a 25 month period.

Once its work project began, MSU alleges it was dissatisfied with Oracle's work on several fronts—that the software did not possess the 'critical functionality' that Oracle represented it would possess, and contrary to its representations, needed substantially more customizations. As a result, Oracle did not meet the project's first "go-live date." Oracle asked for additional fees for work that it contended was beyond the scope of the parties' agreement. Oracle's additional charges amounted to $7 million, though Oracle indicated that it was willing to accept approximately $4 million. MSU asserts that based on these post-agreement developments, Oracle never intended to abide by the fixed price term.

MSU alleges Oracle's staff engaged in dishonest and bad-faith business practices by failing to take responsibility for software problems, blaming MSU for Oracle's own errors, and finally repudiating the agreements by walking off the project. MSU filed its initial complaint in New Jersey state court covering four different theories: claims of fraudulent inducement, gross negligent misrepresentations, two breaches of contract, and a breach of implied covenant of good faith and fair dealing. MSU asserted that it would incur $10-20 million beyond the original amount to complete the job with assistance of a third party systems integration specialist. Oracle removed the case to this federal district court and seeks to dismiss all claims.

Judicial Opinion, Judge Wolfson: When reviewing a motion to dismiss, courts accept all factual allegations as true, construe the complaint in the light most favorable to the plaintiff, and determine whether, under any reasonable reading of the complaint, the plaintiff may be entitled to relief. [There is no] probability requirement at the pleading stage, but instead simply [this initial inquiry] calls for enough facts to raise a reasonable expectation that discovery will reveal evidence of the necessary element[s of a claim.].

A. FRAUDULENT INDUCEMENT CLAIM

Oracle first argues that [this] claim is barred by New Jersey's economic loss doctrine. Under New Jersey law, a plaintiff may not recover in tort for damages caused by a breach of contract: the economic loss rule defines the boundary between the overlapping theories of tort law and a contract law barring the recover of purely economic loss in tort. [P]laintiffs may be permitted to proceed with tort claims sounding fraud in the inducement so long as the underlying allegations involved misrepresentations unrelated to the performance of the contract, but rather preceded the actual commencement of the agreement. In the past twenty-two years, the New Jersey Supreme Court has still not expressed its view on what precise sort of fraud claims may proceed alongside breach of contract claims . . . [n]or have any appellate court decisions. In my view, District Courts would greatly benefit from the guidance of the New Jersey Supreme Court in this regard . . . to clarify this area of law. The Third Circuit has made clear that where the scope of the state law is unsettled, federal courts are to adopt the approach that limits recovery rather than expands it. The alleged misrepresentations here are not extraneous to the parties' agreement; to the contrary [they] relate to Oracle's performance of the terms. Here, there are two sophisticated parties who were represented by counsel at each stage of their relationship—from early negotiations through the termination of the agreement. Indeed, MSU does not dispute the validity of the agreement or argue that its terms are unconscionable. Permitting MSU to pursue its fraudulent inducement claim . . . would permit MSU to recover remedies beyond those embraced by the contract. I conclude that . . . MSU [is barred from pursuing a] fraudulent inducement claim.

B. NEGLIGENT MISREPRESENTATION CLAIM

[I]n determining whether a negligent misrepresentation claims is properly asserted, New Jersey courts focus on the course of dealings between the parties and the express contractual undertaking and will upload [such a] claim alongside a contract claim where an independent duty exists. As MSU has not pointed to any such independent duty, its negligent misrepresentation claims must be dismissed.

C. BREACH OF CONTRACT CLAIMS

Count III is captioned: Breach of Contract (Grossly Negligent Performance of Contractual Obligations), and Count IV is captioned: Breach of Contract (Willful Anticipatory Repudiation of Contract). The LSA [provides] "The limitations stated in this section shall not apply to . . . damages resulting from acts of *gross negligence or intentional wrongdoing*." [Because there are claims for which relief may be granted, if they are proven] Counts III and IV will not be dismissed.

Post-script The decision above was a ruling on MSUs complaint. Oracle filed a $5.3 million countersuit alleging that MSU failed to pay it for work completed. In this lawsuit, Oracle alleges that MSU did not adequately understand the technology and the steps necessary to complete the project. Further, that instead of working out problems, MSUs project leaders, "motivated by their own agenda and fearful of being blamed for delays, escalated manageable differences into major disputes . . . which, unfortunately . . . is costing taxpayers of N.J. millions of dollars."

Post-post-script In March 2013, the parties settled all claims out of court.

Case Questions

1. As it turns out, there was not a formal project tracking system. While there was an "issues and risks" log, it was not kept up to date. The only reporting system that was active was Oracle's weekly status report that it sent to MSU. Describe a better way to manage this business issue so as to avoid it becoming a legal dispute.

2. If Judge Wolfson allowed damages in tort to be considered along with damages for any contract breaches, how would this alter the dynamic of the parties' negotiations?

3. It is apparent that many experts and professionals were involved in the negotiation and execution of this agreement. Overall, what are your top three recommendations for businesses that are considering external software purchases?

This next case concerns a challenge to Oracle's licensing terms, highlighting how the European Court is not bound by U.S. precedent. This provides valuable insights into the risks of doing business internationally.

UsedSoft GmbH v. Oracle Int'l Corp.,

Judgment C-128/11
European Ct. of Justice, Grand Chamber (3 July 2012)

Facts: Oracle develops and markets mostly database software, most of which is downloaded from its site, and is known as "client-server-software." Oracle is the proprietor of the exclusive rights to this software under copyright laws. User rights are granted through a software license agreement (SLA). SLAs describe the parties' relationship, responsibilities, product features and extent of rights, as well as a number of provisions and limitations on users' rights. The user right for the programs here include the right to store a copy of the program permanently on company servers, and allow a certain number of users to access it by downloading it. On the basis of a separate maintenance agreement, updated versions and patches can be downloaded from Oracle's site. Programs can also be supplied on disks.

Oracle offers group licenses for a minimum of 25 users each. An undertaking requiring licenses for 27 users thus has to acquire two licenses. At issue here is Oracle's 'Grant of Rights' clause, providing: "With the payment for services you receive, exclusively for your internal business purposes, for an unlimited period a non-exclusive non-transferable user rights . . . ." Additionally, there is a separate maintenance agreement for users to download updates and patches from Oracle's site.

UsedSoft deals in secondhand software. It acquires from Oracle customers their user licenses, or parts of them, and then it sells these current "used" Oracle licenses to later purchasers.

The EU Directive (relevant provisions):

Article 4(1): the computer program rights holder has the exclusive right to do or authorize: (a) the reproduction of the program; (b) the translation or other alteration of the program; and (c) any form of distribution to the public of the program.
Article 4(2): the first sale in the Community of a copy of a program by the rightholder or with his consent shall exhaust the distribution right within the Community of that copy.

Article 5(1): [none of the above] require authorization by the rightholder where they are necessary for the use of the computer program by the lawful acquirer.

Oracle filed a complaint against UsedSoft in Munich Regional Court, and the court ruled for Oracle thereby restraining UsedSoft from engaging in this business. UsedSoft appealed to the German Federal Court (BDH). The BDH referred a number of questions on the interpretation of Directive 2009/24/EC (codifying an earlier Directive 91/250/EEC), concerning the legal protection of computer programs. The BDH stayed proceedings and asked the EU Court of Justice for responses to a number of questions.

Judicial Opinion: [The BGH referred] the following questions to the Court for a preliminary ruling:

1. Is the person who can rely on exhaustion of the right to distribute a copy of a computer program a 'lawful acquirer' within the meaning of Article 5(1) of Directive 2009/24?
2. If the reply to the first question is in the affirmative: is the right to distribute a copy of a computer program exhausted in accordance with . . . Article 4(2) of Directive 2009/24 when the acquirer has made the copy with the rightholder's consent by downloading the program?
3. If the reply to the second question is also in the affirmative: can a person who has acquired a 'used' software license for generating a program copy as 'lawful acquirer' . . . also rely on exhaustion of the right to distribute the copy of the computer program made by the first acquirer with the right holder's consent by downloading the program . . . if the first acquirer has erased his program copy or no longer uses it?

CONSIDERATION OF THE QUESTIONS REFERRED

QUESTION 2

By its second question, which should be addressed first, the referring court essentially seeks to know whether and under what conditions the downloading from the Internet . . . can give rise to exhaustion of the right of distribution of that copy. It should be recalled that under Article 4(2) . . . the first sale in the European Union of a copy of a computer program by the rightholder or with his consent exhausts the distribution right within the European Union of that copy.

To determine whether . . . the copyright holder's distribution right is exhausted, it must be ascertained, first, whether the contractual relationship between the rightholder and its customer . . . may be regarded as a 'first sale of a copy of a program' within the meaning of Article 4(2). A uniform interpretation of the term 'sale' is necessary in order to avoid . . . varying [results within the EU].

According to a commonly accepted definition, a 'sale' is an agreement by which a person, in return for payment, transfers to another person his rights of ownership in an item of tangible or intangible property belonging to him. Oracle submits that it does not sell copies of its computer programs. It says that it makes available . . . a copy of the program. The copy . . . may not, however, be used by the customers unless they have concluded a user licence agreement. Oracle submits that neither the making available of a copy . . . nor the . . . user agreement involves a transfer of the right of ownership of that copy. [These actions though, downloading a copy and agreeing to terms] are thus intended to make the copy usable . . . permanently, in return for payment.

[T]he operations . . . examined as a whole, involve the transfer of the right of ownership of the copy of the computer program. Consequently, in a situation such as that at issue . . . the transfer . . . of a copy . . . accompanied . . . by a . . . licence agreement, constitutes a 'first sale of a copy of a program.' [The Court therefore adopts] a broad interpretation as encompassing all forms of product marketing characterised by the grant of a right to use a copy of a computer program for an unlimited period, in return for payment of a fee. [Otherwise] suppliers would merely have to call the contract a 'licence' rather than a 'sale' in order to circumvent the rule of exhaustion and divest it of all scope. [Also] it does not appear from Article 4(2) . . . that the exhaustion of the right of distribution of copies . . . is limited to copies of programmes on a material medium. [T]hat provision . . . makes no distinction according to the tangible or intangible form of the copy.

[T]he objective of the principle of . . . exhaustion . . . is, in order to avoid partitioning of markets, to limit restrictions of the distribution of those works to [only] what is necessary to safeguard the specific subject-matter of the intellectual property.

[I]t must also be examined whether, as Oracle claims, the maintenance agreement concluded by the first acquirer prevents in any event the exhaustion of the right . . . since the copy . . . no longer corresponds to the copy he downloaded but to a new copy of the program. Article 4(2) . . . only concerns copies which have been the subject of a first sale in the [EU]. It does not relate to contracts for services, such as maintenance agreements, which are separable from such a sale. None the less, the . . . maintenance agreement . . . has the effect that the copy originally purchased is patched and updated. [T]he functionalities . . . form an integral party of the copy . . . and can be used by the acquirer of the copy for an unlimited period, even in the event that the acquirer subsequently decides not to renew the maintenance agreement.

It should be pointed out, however, that if the licence acquired by the first acquirer relates to a greater number of users than he needs . . . the acquirer is not authorized by the effect of . . . exhaustion . . . to divide the licence and resell only the user right.

An original acquirer who resells a . . . copy . . . must, in order to avoid infringing the exclusive right of reproduction of a computer program which belongs to its author . . . make his own copy unusable at the time of its resale. On the basis of all the foregoing, the answer to Question 2 is that Article 4(2) . . . must be interpreted as meaning that the right of distribution of a copy of a computer program is exhausted if the copyright holder who has authorised, even free of charge, the downloading of that copy . . . in return for payment of a fee intended to enable him to obtain a remuneration corresponding to the economic value of the copy of the work of which he is the proprietor, a right to use that copy for an unlimited period.

QUESTIONS 1 AND 3

By its first and third questions the referring court seeks essentially to know whether and under what condition an acquirer of used licences . . . such as those sold by UsedSoft, may, as a result of the exhaustion of the distribution right . . . be regarded as a 'lawful acquirer' within the meaning of Article 5(1) . . . who . . . enjoys the right of reproduction of the program . . . in order . . . to use the program in accordance with its intended purpose.

Admittedly . . . the original acquirer . . . must, in order to avoid infringing . . . make the copy downloaded onto his computer unusable at the time of its resale. As Oracle rightly observes, ascertaining whether such a copy has been made unusable may prove difficult. To solve that problem, it is permissible for the distributor–to make use of technical protective measures such as product keys.

The argument put forward by Oracle, Ireland and the French and Italian Governments that the 'lawful acquirer' in Article 5(1) . . . relates only to an acquirer who is authorised, under a licence agreement . . . cannot be accepted. That argument would have the effect of allowing the copyright holder to prevent the effective use of any used copy. It follows from the foregoing that the answers to Questions 1 and 3 is that Article 4(2) and 5(1) . . . must be interpreted as meaning that, in the event of the resale of a user licence . . . the second acquirer of the licence, as well as any subsequent acquirer of it, will be able to rely on the exhaustion of the distribution right . . . and hence be regarded as lawful acquirers of a copy.

Case Questions

1. Under the EU's construction of software and ownership, when can software developers make money from their software?
2. Describe the distribution rights licensees have in the EU for software they lawfully purchased.
3. This opinion is in contravention of the U.S. law which limits applicability of the exhaustion doctrine to lawfully purchased physical goods (therefore developers are able to maintain distribution limits on digital goods). How should software developers manage this dichotomy?

Non-negotiated Contracts/Licenses for Sites, Services and Software

Even though these contracts are anything but negotiated, courts construe and classify these as agreements under contract law. As we increasingly do not own physical goods or products (think: books, music), but rather license uses of that product in digital format, consumer rights to digital versions are remarkably diminished. For example, instead of owning a book, and having rights to fairly use or sell it, we license a copy of an encrypted e-book, and "agree" to what the distributor dictates regarding price, format, device limits, no device interoperability, no lending, no selling. These licenses are the means by which businesses execute their business models, maximize their control, and minimize their responsibility.

Software license agreements

SLAs are ubiquitous in our lives. They greet users at the beginning activation stage of every new app, program, device. SLAs are presented on a take-it, or leave-it basis. Significantly at this time, SLAs are valid and enforceable, though there is developing caselaw that suggests otherwise. This section explores selected SLA provisions and their legal significance. The following are excerpted from actual SLAs and, collectively, give readers the sense of the lack of mutuality in these contracts:

1. Acceptance of terms: This provides that in order to use the software and related services, you must first agree to the license agreements. The licensor retains all rights, title, and interest in the software and any updates. If You do not agree to these terms, You are not permitted to use the software or services.
2. Waiver of rights: The company grants to You a limited, non-exclusive, personal, revocable, non-sublicensable and non-transferable license. . . .
3. Digital rights software: You acknowledge that the software may be "locked" and agree to give up rights users have under copyright to fairly copy, use, sell re-distribute, transform and reverse engineer, or sub-license . . . (this is known as "enclosure"). What is remarkable about this provision, is that rights that users have under copyright law, rights set out in the US Constitution, may be abolished by agreement of the parties. Yet in a non-negotiated SLA, this is clearly not the case that users voluntarily, knowingly agreed to forgo constitutionally derived rights.

Further Examples of Non-negotiated Clauses in SLAs

For example, a prospective app developer applies to the Apple Developer program and by doing so, agrees not to release the useful software on any other platform, and further, Apple can make its own version of your app. Some sites have broad confidentiality provisions and do not allow users to speak to the press, write benchmark reports, blog about their experience, and so forth. The Cheerios maker, General Mills, stated in its terms that users waive their right to sue the company by downloading coupons, joining their Facebook community, entering any company contests, and more. iPad users download Smurfs' Village and then their children make in-app purchases of smurfberries and, according to the Terms of Use, agree to all charges, which in some cases have run into the thousands of

EDWARD J. MARKEY
7TH DISTRICT, MASSACHUSETTS

2108 RAYBURN HOUSE OFFICE BUILDING
WASHINGTON, DC 20515–2107
(202) 225–2836

DISTRICT OFFICES:

5 HIGH STREET, SUITE 101
MEDFORD, MA 02155
(781) 396–2900

188 CONCORD STREET, SUITE 102
FRAMINGHAM, MA 01702
(508) 875–2900

http://markey.house.gov

Congress of the United States
House of Representatives
Washington, DC 20515–2107

February 8, 2011

The Honorable Jon Leibowitz
Chairman
Federal Trade Commission
600 Pennsylvania Avenue, NW
Washington, DC 20580

Dear Chairman Leibowitz:

According to a report in today's <u>Washington Post</u> ("In-app purchases in iPad, iPhone, iPod kids' games touch off parental firestorm", February 8, 2011), companies such as Apple and Google are offering applications that are free to download but subsequently enable the companies to charge users for products and services after the application has been launched. The article referenced above contains quotations from unsuspecting parents whose children downloaded the free games and then purchased, in one case, more than $1,000 worth of virtual game accessories without comprehending the consequences.

I am concerned about how these applications are being promoted and delivered to consumers, particularly with respect to children, who are unlikely to understand the ramifications of in-app purchases. Accordingly, I am interested in any actions the Commission has taken to investigate this issue. I also encourage the Commission to pursue measures to provide consumers with additional information about the marketing and delivery of these applications. I request that the Commission assess current industry activities in this area to determine whether they constitute unfair or deceptive acts or practices.

Thank you for your attention to this important matter. If you have questions, please have a member of your staff contact Mark Bayer on my staff at 202-225-2836.

Sincerely,

Edward Markey

PRINTED ON RECYCLED PAPER

dollars. Further, the in-app purchase feature is defaulted to "on." Credit card company mails its terms of use with the statement and it provides: "Reasons we can share your personal information . . . for our marketing purposes–to offer our products and services to you." The credit card company can share our information with its affiliates and customers are not allowed to limit the sharing. Since

SLAs are considered contracts, and courts aspire to uphold all valid contracts, these clauses have received little scrutiny. The pushback has begun, however. Then-Congressman (and now-Senator) Markey began an inquiry of the in-app purchasing imbroglio. California residents recently filed suit against General Mills, and a judge refused to grant General Mills' motion to dismiss the charges.

This next case is an important Supreme Court decision on the enforceability of an SLA mandating arbitration of customer disputes, and further, not allowing for the consolidation of claims among other customers. Known as class action waivers, such clauses are used in order to block plaintiffs from consolidating their small claims into one large class action, thereby making it highly unlikely that any single customer will file suit over their own, relatively small individual loss.

AT&T Mobility, LLC v. Concepcion,
131 S. Ct.1740 (2011)

Facts: Vincent and Liza Concepcion entered into an agreement for the purchase and servicing of a mobile phone. Their original contract was with Cingular Wireless. AT&T acquired Cingular in 2005 and renamed the company AT&T Mobility. The contract provided for arbitration of all disputes between the parties, but required that claims be brought by parties in an "individual capacity" and not as class members of any purported class of plaintiffs. Further, that "the arbitrator may not consolidate more than one person's claims, and may not otherwise preside over any form of a representative or class proceeding." The agreement authorized AT&T to make unilateral amendments, which it did to the arbitration provision on several occasions.

The revised agreement provides, inter alia, that customers may initiate proceedings by completing a one-page Notice of Dispute form available on AT&T's site. AT&T may then offer to settle the claim. If it does not, or if the dispute is not resolved within 30 days, the customer may invoke arbitration by filing a Demand for Arbitration. For that AT&T must pay all costs for nonfrivolous claims, the arbitration must take place in the customer's billing county, and if the amount in question is $10,000 or less, the customer may choose to pursue the case in person or by telephone. Further, if the arbitration award exceeds AT&T's last written settlement offer, AT&T must pay a minimum recovery award and double attorney's fees.

The Concepcions made the purchase. It was advertised as including a free phone. However they were charged $30.22 in sales tax based on the phone's retail value. The Concepcions filed a complaint against AT&T for false advertising and fraud by charging sales tax on phone it advertised as free.

AT&T moved to compel arbitration under the terms of its contract. The Concepcions opposed the motion, contending that the arbitration clause was unconscionable and unlawfully exculpatory under California law because it disallowed class actions among many such claimants. (California statutes and public policy encourages the use of the class action device.) The District Court denied AT&T's motion, finding that while the arbitration agreement had many favorable features, the clause was overall unconscionable and illegal because AT&T had not shown that the arbitration clause was an adequate substitute for the deterrent effects of class action lawsuits. The Ninth Circuit affirmed, also finding the provision unconscionable under California law. It held that state law was not pre-empted by the Federal Arbitration Act (FAA) because it was simply a refinement of federal law. The FAA encourages and facilitates arbitration of legal disputes and applies to both state and federal courts. We granted *certiorari*.

Judicial Opinion. Justice Scalia (joined by Chief Justice Roberts and Justices Kennedy, Thomas and Alito): The FAA was enacted . . . in response to widespread judicial hostility to arbitration agreements. We have described this provision as reflecting both a liberal federal policy favoring arbitration . . . and the fundamental principle that arbitration is a matter of contract. In line with these principles, courts must place arbitration agreements on an equal footing with other contracts . . . and enforce them according to their terms. Arbitration agreements [may] be declared unenforceable "upon such grounds as exist at law or in equity for the revocation of any contract." This savings clause permits agreements to arbitrate to be invalidated by generally applicable contract defenses, such as fraud, duress, or unconscionability, but not by defenses that apply only to arbitration or that derive their meaning from the fact that an agreement to arbitrate is at issue. The question in this case is whether § 2 preempts California's rule classifying most collective-arbitration waivers in consumer contracts as unconscionable.

Under California law, courts may refuse to enforce any contract found 'to have been unconscionable at the time it was made' or may 'limit the application of any unconscionable clause.' A finding of unconscionability requires a procedural and a substantive element, the former focusing on oppression or surprise due to unequal bargaining power, the latter on overly harsh or one-sided results.

In [the] *Discover Bank* [case], the California Supreme Court applied this framework to class-action waivers in arbitration agreements and held:

"[W]hen the waiver is found in a consumer contract of adhesion in a setting in which disputes between the contracting parties predictably involve small amounts of damages, and when it is alleged that the party with the superior bargaining power has carried out a scheme to deliberately cheat large numbers of consumers out of individually small sums of money, then . . . the waiver becomes in practice the exemption of the party from responsibility for its own fraud, or willful injury to the person or property of another. Under these circumstances, such waivers are unconscionable under California law and should not be enforced."

The Concepcions argue that the *Discover Bank* rule . . . is a ground that exists at law or in equity for the revocation of any contract under the FAA. When state law prohibits outright the arbitration of a particular type of claim, the analysis is straightforward. The conflicting [state] rule is displaced by the FAA. But the inquiry [such as is the case here] becomes more complex when . . . unconscionability is alleged to have been applied in a fashion that disfavors arbitration. [I]t is worth noting that California's courts have been more likely to hold contracts to arbitrate unconscionable than other contracts. Although § 2's saving clause preserves generally applicable contract defenses, nothing in it suggests an intent to preserve state-law rules that stand as an obstacle to the accomplishment of the FAA's objectives. In other words, the {FAA} cannot be held to destroy itself. The overarching purpose of the FAA . . . is to ensure the enforcement of arbitration agreements according to their terms so as to facilitate streamlined proceedings. Requiring the availability of classwide arbitration interferes with fundamental attributes of arbitration and thus creates a scheme inconsistent with the FAA. The point of affording parties discretion in designing arbitration processes is to allow for efficient streamlined procedures tailored to the type of dispute. California's *Discover Bank* rule . . . interferes with arbitration.

First, the switch from bilateral to class arbitration sacrifices the principal advantage of arbitration—its informality—and makes the process slower, more costly, and more likely to generate procedural morass than final judgment. Second, class arbitration requires procedural formality. Third, class arbitration greatly increases risks to defendants. Arbitration is poorly suited to the higher stakes of class litigation. The judgment of the Ninth Circuit is reversed, and the case is remanded for further proceedings consistent with this opinion.

Dissenting Opinion. Justice Breyer (joined by Justices Ginsburg, Sotomayor and Kagan): The California *Discover Bank* rule does not create a blanket policy . . . against class action waivers. [It] is consistent with the federal Act's language. [It] is also consistent with the basic purpose behind the [FAA]. [E]ven though contract defenses, *e.g.*, duress and unconscionability, slow down the dispute resolution process, federal arbitration law normally leaves such matters to the States. The *Discover Bank* rule amounts to a variation on this theme. California is free to define unconscionability as it sees fit, and its common law is of no federal concern so long as the State does not adopt a special rule that disfavors arbitration. By using the words "save upon such grounds as exist at law or in equity for the revocation of any contract," Congress retained for the States an important role incident to agreements to arbitrate. Through those words Congress reiterated a basic federal idea that has long informed the nature of this Nation's laws. Here, recognition of that federalist ideal, embodied in specific language in this particular statute, should lead us to uphold California's law. We do not honor federalist principles in their breach. With respect, I dissent.

Case Questions

1. The majority held that federal law preempts conflicting state law rules. Can you suggest any strategies for states to address this result?
2. The majority wrote, "The point of affording parties discretion in designing arbitration processes is to allow for efficient streamlined procedures tailored to the type of dispute. California's *Discover Bank* rule . . . interferes with arbitration." How can it be that the Court finds there is a negotiated contract?

3. The dissent advocates for the position that the state rule is not exactly conflicting, that the state rule supports arbitration unless there is, for example, duress or unconscionability, and that both the federal and state laws should be read together in our federalist system. Whose view do you credit more, the majority's, or the dissent's? Why?

This next case was decided after *Concepcion*. Note the similarities to *Concepcion*, though a different legal theory is used.

Grosvenor v. Qwest Corp., and Qwest Broadband Services, Inc.,

854 F. Supp.2d 1021 (D. Colo. 2012), appeal dismissed, 733 F.3d 990 (10th Cir. 2013)

Facts: Qwest provides consumer communications services. Grosvenor was attracted to their marketing campaign to purchase Internet service through a "Price for Life Guarantee," under which the monthly cost remains the same for so long as he remained a customer. He alleges that Qwest breached its contractual promise to provide service at a fixed price when it later raised the monthly rate.

In the Complaint he alleges claims for breach of contract, promissory estoppel, unjust enrichment, and a claim under the Colorado Consumer Protection Act. Shortly after Grosvenor filed this lawsuit, Qwest moved to compel arbitration of the claims. Judge Miller denied Qwest's motion, finding that (i) the court had jurisdiction over challenges to the validity of the agreement to arbitrate; and (ii) there were genuine disputes of fact as to the circumstances under which Grosvenor agreed to Qwest's Subscriber Agreement (if at all), thus requiring further discovery. Judge Miller directed that the parties "schedule a trial to determine whether a valid arbitration agreement exists."

The parties proceeded to conduct discovery with regard to disputes relating solely to contract formation, and now both parties seek summary judgment on the question of whether there is a binding and enforceable agreement to arbitrate the claims. Qwest argues that the facts indicate Grosvenor accepted all of the terms of the Subscriber Agreement, and thus bound to arbitrate his claims. Mr. Grosvenor's motion argues that any agreement to arbitrate is rendered illusory by the fact that Qwest claims an unfettered right to modify the arbitration provision.

Judicial Opinion. Judge Krieger: The Court begins with Qwest's motion, insofar as the question of whether a contract was formed must precede the question of whether the terms of that contract might be illusory. This motion presents the most fundamental of contract law questions—when is a contractual agreement formed. Colorado law provides that a contract is formed when one party makes an offer and the other party accepts it, and the agreement is supported by consideration. Both parties must mutually assent to all essential elements of the agreement. The terms of the offer must be sufficiently definite such that promises and performances required of each party are reasonably certain. If the parties agree as to some issues, but fail to reach a meeting of the minds as to other material issues, the contract is not sufficiently formed.

The matter involves contract formation questions attendant to a party manifesting its agreement to have a contract's terms by "clicking on a button during the installation of a software program." The Court has not located Colorado authority for the proposition that objective indicia of assent can be overcome whether the terms of the agreement were inconspicuous or concealed from the offeree.

The Court turns to the parties' evidence. The Court assesses what a reasonable user would understand from the installation. The users would be aware that there are terms of service including arbitration and limits on liability. The users would also understand that those terms are viewed at the link for the web address qwest.com/legal. If users clicked on this link, they would find that the main body of the page consisted of various legal notices unrelated to the software installation, and not find a place to click "I accept." There are additional agreements—and for each, there was a separate link directing users to a different page from the installation page. The "I Accept" link indicating assent to each of the terms was back on the install page. Users therefore had to "accept" the terms without actually reviewing the relevant terms page. The question then, is whether these facts constitute 'reasonably conspicuous notice' of the agreement's terms.

Mr. Grosvenor could not review Qwest's terms of service simply by clicking on the legal link. The Court cannot say that, as a matter of law, requiring a user to navigate through two links in order to review the terms of an offer prevents any contractual formation [but] each additional step required of the user tips against a finding that the terms were sufficiently conspicuous. [H]ere, Qwest's program did not allow him to review the applicable documents, and there was no way of assessing the terms until *after* he completed installation of the software, and completion of the installation would not occur until Mr. Grosvenor manifested his acceptance of the terms. Thus, despite the representations made as to the effect of pressing the "I Accept" button, the Court has some doubt that doing so created an enforceable contract. [A]nd perhaps more importantly, the fact that a user must navigate to a web page in order to ascertain terms of an offer is particularly difficult where the software being installed is the means by which the Internet can be accessed.

Second, it is undisputed that . . . Qwest followed up [the] activation of his Internet service by sending a "Welcome Letter" . . . . reading, "Please review the important information about service and terms for use . . . on the back of this letter."

[It read:] Qwest High-Speed Internet Service and related products are offered under the Subscriber Agreement terms, which are located at www.qwest.com/legal. Please review the terms, which include arbitration and limits on Qwest liability. If you do not agree, call Qwest to cancel your service within 30 days.

The Welcome Letter alleviates some of the issues noted above. The Welcome Letter, having arrived after Internet service software was installed, also addresses the users' potential difficulty in accessing the terms of Qwest's offer in the absence of Internet service. Finally, their Letter provides time in which to consider the terms of the Subscriber Agreement. Mr. Grosvenor did not cancel his Qwest Internet service.

Taking the circumstances as a whole, the Court finds that . . . [his] conduct constitutes an objective manifestation of assent to the contractual terms. Although the presentation of the terms is hardly a model of clarity, the Court nevertheless finds that they were sufficiently conspicuous as to permit a reasonable user the opportunity to review them. To the extent the presentation of the terms via the installation softer can be said to be . . . unclear, the Welcome Letter would be sufficient to cure . . . users' confusion.

Accordingly, the Court finds that Mr. Grosvenor entered into a contractual agreement with Qwest . . . in which he agreed to arbitrate disputes. Consistent with the terms of the letter, Mr. Grosvenor's continued use of the service manifested his continuing acceptance of those terms. Thus, [his] breach of contract claims are subject to that agreement to arbitrate, unless that obligation to arbitrate is somehow rendered unenforceable.

Grosvenor . . . argues that any agreement to arbitrate that he may have entered into is illusory and thus unenforceable because Qwest reserved the unilateral right to change terms of the agreement. The Subscriber Agreement provides that 'Qwest may . . . modify the Service and/or any of the terms and conditions of this Agreement.' This, Mr. Grosvenor argues renders the agreement illusory. Qwest offers several arguments in response. First, it contends that challenges . . . are questions that are reserved to the arbitrator, not the courts. Second Qwest argues . . . [it] was to not required to post notice of any changes to its agreement. A notice requirement becomes significant when it is coupled with the right to accept or reject the changes. Here, nothing in the Subscriber Agreement indicates that Qwest's changes . . . are subject to delayed effect for consideration by the user. The agreement simply states that changes become "effective upon posting. . . ."

Mr. Grosvenor argues quite persuasively that the terms of the Agreement treat his act of accessing the Internet to see if changes have been made to the agreement, as "assent." By conflating the review of the changes with assent to them, there is no right to reject changed terms. Qwest also argues that there is no evidence of record establishing that it has changed the arbitration terms. This is true, but irrelevant. [The *Dumais* Court] recognized that it was the unilateral power of one party to change the arbitration terms that rendered the arbitration provision illusory. The Court finds that *Dumais* controls the outcome of Mr. Grosvenor's motion. Because Qwest retained an unfettered ability to modify the existence, terms and scope of the arbitration clause, it is illusory and unenforceable.

CONCLUSION

For the foregoing reason, Qwest's Motion for Summary Judgment is GRANTED insofar as it finds that Mr. Grosvenor entered into a contractual agreement.

However, Mr. Grosvenor's Motion for Summary Judgment is also GRANTED, insofar as the Court finds that the arbitration clause in that agreement is illusory and thus unenforceable.

Post-script The Court of Appeals for the Tenth Circuit reviewed this decision. It dismissed Qwest's appeal concluding that "in order to properly invoke appellate jurisdiction under the FAA, the movant (Qwest) must either explicitly move to stay litigation and/or compel arbitration . . . or it must be unmistakably clear from the four corners of the motion that the movant seeks relief provided for in the FAA. Because we conclude Qwest has not satisfied this standard, we dismiss this appeal."

Case Questions

1. On what basis is the ADR clause invalidated in this case, and how does this case differ from *Concepcion*?
2. How should Qwest re-write its agreement after this decision?
3. What does this mean for businesses outside of the Tenth Circuit, and how do businesses respond to this case throughout the United States?

Free and Open Source Software Agreements (FOSS)

Beyond the proprietary/closed model of software rights characterized by businesses' ownership and control, there are two additional models of software rights, characterized by more permissive agreements as to ownership and control. Software coding began as a freely shared hobbyists' endeavor. Early computer programs, software and source code were built out by collaboration and sharing. Software was therefore reciprocally available, and not the subject of contract. The industry changed by the 1960s when companies began selling proprietary software directly, usually bundled with their hardware. Further, Congress gave software publishers legal protections when it extended copyright subject matter to computer programs (Pub. L. No. 96-517, 94 Stat. 3015, 3028 (1980)), giving software creators more rights. Later on, technical protections for software were developed (such as DRM encryption technologies) that helped software creators control uses. Proprietary software companies have flourished with these legal and technological protections, with Oracle being a well-known example of this model, in which licensors control most rights and uses.

In response to these developments, members of the nascent software community, notably Richard Stallman, founded the Free Software Foundation in the 1980s, and began development of the GNU operating system, a free and open software system. The concept is that software should be available to all users, who should be free to use, study, share, and modify it ("free" as in "free speech," and not as in "free beer."). Importantly, even this free software is wrapped in a license agreement and requires users to agree to terms. Specifically, any free software users who modify it must release their iteration free and under the same free-to-use license.

There are a number of variants on the two models: proprietary/closed, and free/open software. Open source software is a hybrid and is neither fully closed nor "anti-commercial." Prime examples are Mozilla Firefox, Apache, and Android. The "kernels" of these were built out, and are maintained by a network of volunteer programmers. This freely available software also have licenses, though they are permissive, granting users rights to use, study, change, and re-release and distribute it, charge money for, and exert control over this modified software. It becomes evident that organizations may have many types of software in their stack, along with a range of vendors and licenses to manage. Clearly negotiating, and managing software licenses is a key business challenge.

Complementary Theory of Liability in Contracts Cases: Tortious Interference with Contract Rights

Tortious Interference with Contract Rights.

This is a tort-based theory providing a cause of action against a defendant for intentionally damaging the plaintiff's contractual relationship with another. This occurs when the defendant disrupts the performance, induces the breach, or prevents the other person from performing obligations required by the contract, and so the plaintiff files suit against that defendant for tortious interference with contract rights. Elements of the cause of action are, in most jurisdictions: (1) existence of a contractual relationship; (2) knowledge of that relationship; (3) intent to induce a breach of contract; (4) breach of contract; and (5) damages. As an accompaniment to breach of contract claims, successfully pleading tortious interference with contract rights allows plaintiffs to seek a number of additional remedies, including punitive damages and equitable relief.

This next case concerns claims of tortious interference with contract rights, the contract being the SLA between the *World of Warcraft* creators and their users.

MDY Indus., LLC v. Blizzard Entm't, Inc. and Vivendi Games, Inc.,

2011 U.S. App. LEXIS 3428 (9th Cir. Feb. 17, 2011), motion denied, 2011 U.S. Dist. LEXIS 68735 (D. Ariz. June 27, 2011)

Facts: Blizzard Entertainment is the creator of World of Warcraft (WoW), a multi-player role-playing game phenomenon with 10 million players, in which players interact in a virtual world while advancing through the game's 70 levels. Players' central objective is to advance characters in quests and engaging in battles with monsters. As players advance, characters collect rewards including in-game currency, weapons and armor. There are chat features to interact with other players.

WoW software has two components: (1) the game client software players install on their devices; and (2) the game server software that players access by subscription so to connect with WoWs servers. There is no single-player or offline play. MDY Industries and its sole member Michael Donnelly developed and sold the software program, Glider, that automatically plays the early levels of WoW for players.

Each WoW player must read and accept Blizzard's Terms of Use (ToU) on multiple occasions. Players who do not accept the terms may return the game client for a refund. Donnelly is a WoW player and software programmer. He developed Glider, a software bot that automates the play of WoWs early levels, for his personal use. A user of this software need not be at the computer while Glider is running through these early levels. MDY describes Glider on its site this way:

> "Glider . . . moves the mouse around and pushes keys on the keyboard. You tell it about your character, where you want to kill things, and wen you want to kill. Then it kills for you, automatically. You can do something else, like eat dinner or go to a movie, and when you return, you'll have a lot more experience and loot."

Glider does not alter or copy WoWs game client software, does not allow a player to avoid paying monthly subscription dues to Blizzard, and has no commercial use independent of WoW. Glider was not initially designed to avoid detection by Blizzard. Blizzard's terms, at least initially, did not prohibit bots.

Then MDY changed its design so that the bots would avoid detection, and subsequently MDY began selling Glider for $15-20 per license, and it had at least 120,000 users. Blizzard changed its terms to prohibit bots, then launched "Warden," a technology to detect bots and prevent MDY software from connecting to its servers. Then to comply, MDY modified its site to indicate that using Glider violated Blizzard's ToU. Blizzard claims that it received half a million complaints about WoW bots, and that it spends almost $1 million annually on responding to these complaints, and it introduced evidence that it may have lost subscription fees from Glider users who reached WoWs highest levels in fewer weeks than other players.

Blizzard sent MDY a cease-and-desist letter. Then MDY initiated a software update to make its bots evade notice of Blizzard's Warden program. MDY immediately commenced this lawsuit seeking a declaration that Glider does not infringe Blizzard's copyright or other rights. Blizzard filed counterclaims against MDY for copyright and DMCA violations, and tortious interference with contract [the part of the lawsuits and claims that is abstracted here].

The parties dispute Glider's impact on the WoW experience. Blizzard contends that Glider disrupts WoWs environment for non-Glider players by enabling Glider users to advance quickly and unfairly through the game, and to amass assets. MDY contends that Glider has a minimal effect on non-Glider players, enhances the WoW experience for Glider users, and facilitates disabled players' access to WoW by auto-playing the game for them.

The district court granted Blizzard a partial summary judgment, finding that MDYs Glider sales tortiously interfered with Blizzard's contracts [the subscribers' agreement with Blizzard and formalized in the ToU]. The court ruled that Donnelly was personally liable, and entered judgment against him for $6.9 million. Both parties filed appeals.

Judicial Opinion. Judge Callahan: To recover for tortious interference with contract . . . Blizzard must prove: (1) the existence of a valid contractual relationship; (2) MDY's knowledge of the relationship; (3) MDY's intentional interference in inducing or causing the breach; (4) the impropriety of MDY's interference; and (5) resulting damages. Blizzard satisfies four of these five elements based on undisputed facts.

First, a valid contractual relationship exists between Blizzard and its customers based on the operative ToU. Second, MDY was aware of this relationship; it does not contend that it was unaware of the . . . ToU, or unaware that using Glider breached their terms. In fact, after Blizzard first attempted to ban Glider users, MDY modified its website to notify customers that using Glider violated the ToU. Third, MDY intentionally interfered with Blizzard's contracts. After Blizzard used Warden to ban a majority of Glider users . . . MDY programmed Glider to be undetectable by Warden . . . [and] Blizzard has proffered evidence that it was damaged by MDY's conduct. [A]s to the fourth element of its tortious interference claims: whether MDY's actions were improper . . . Arizona employs the seven-factor test of Restatement (Second) of Torts § 767.

The seven factors are (1) the nature of MDY's conduct, (2) MDY's motive, (3) Blizzard's interests with which MDY interfered, (4) the interests MDY sought to advance, (5) the social interests in protecting MDY's freedom of action and Blizzard's contractual interests, (6) the proximity or remoteness of MDY's conduct to the interference, and (7) the relations between MDY and Blizzard. A court should give greatest weight to the first two factors. We conclude that summary judgment was inappropriate here, because on the current record, taking the facts in the light most favorable to MDY, the first five factors do not clearly weigh in either side's favor, thus creating a genuine issue of material fact.

1. NATURE OF MDY'S CONDUCT AND MDY'S MOTIVE

The parties have presented conflicting evidence with respect to these two most important factors. Blizzard's evidence tends to demonstrate that MDY helped Glider users gain an advantage over other WoW players. Thus, MDY knowingly assisted Glider users to breach their contracts, and then helped to conceal those breaches from Blizzard. Blizzard was negatively affected by MDY's Glider sales, because Glider use (1) distorts WoW's virtual economy by flooding it with excess resources; (2) interferes with WoW players' ability to interact with other human players; and (3) strains Blizzard's servers because bots spend more continuous time in-game than do human players.

2. THE BLIZZARD' INTEREST, WITH WHICH MDY INTERFERES; THE INTEREST THAT MDY SEEKS TO ADVANCE; THE SOCIAL INTEREST IN PROTECTING MDY'S AND BLIZZARD'S RESPECTIVE INTERESTS

Blizzard argues that it seeks to provide its millions of WoW players with a particular role-playing game experience that excludes bots . . . that MDY's interest depends on inducing Blizzard's customers to breach their contracts. In contrast, MDY argues that Glider is an innovative . . . software program that has positively affected its users' lives by advancing them to WoWs more interesting levels. We . . . note that, if the fact-finder decides that Blizzard did not ban bots at the time that MDY created Glider, the fact-finder might conclude that MDY had a legitimate interest.

3. PROXIMITY OF MDY'S CONDUCT TO THE INTERFERENCE; RELATIONSHIP BETWEEN MDY AND BLIZZARD

MDY's Glider sales are the but-for cause of Glider users' breach of the operative ToU. Moreover, Blizzard and MDY are not competitors in the online role-playing game market; rather; MDY's profits appear to depend on the continuous popularity of WoW. Blizzard, however, chose not to authorize MDY to sell Glider to its users. Even accepting that these factors favor Blizzard, we do think that they independently warrant a grant of summary judgment to Blizzard.

We cannot hold that five of the seven 'impropriety' factors compel a finding in Blizzard's favor at this stage, including the two (nature of MDY's conduct and MDY's motive) that the Arizona courts deem most important. Because we conclude that there are triable issues of material fact, we vacate [the district court's grant of summary judgment to Blizzard] and remand for trial.

Case Questions

1. Besides this legal strategy, articulate other strategies Blizzard can use to address the challenge from MDY.
2. Is there some way that Blizzard can work with MDY, rather than suing MDY?
3. Identify additional legal theories Blizzard can assert against MDY.

Contracts in Employment

While these agreements are covered in Chapter 9, on employment, they are included in a brief mention here since each is a contract.

- **Visitor confidentiality clause:** Signed by everyone who enters the workplace, including vendors, professional service providers, interviewees, and so forth. This is essentially a non-disclosure agreement along with behavioral standards during the site visit, along with a waiver of liability.

● **Employment agreement:** Negotiated by the Board with incoming executives, these agreements cover a range of issues, including performance targets and incentives, stock options and a vesting schedule, termination with and without cause, and so forth.

● **Invention assignment:** Signed by all incoming employees, contractors, free-lancers, and temps, the workers agree that all work, inventions, know-how, etc., belongs to the employer and this agreement effects an assignment of all rights to the employer. To the extent the worker presently owns any inventions or technologies that are clearly not contemplated as being claimed by the employer, there is a provision for excluding these from the invention assignments, and is known as a 'carve-out' of this invention.

● **Stock option agreement:** A perquisite of many Internet and tech companies that at the outset may be short on cash, and therefore the companies compensate workers with grants of stock in the business. The future value of these stock options is unclear, and so financial and accounting technique for valuing and expensing these is quite complicated.

● **Non-disclosure/confidentiality agreement:** Written into all contracts, the parties acknowledge they both have sensitive confidential information that yields a competitive advantage, disclosed only because of necessity, and this contract restricts use and dissemination or disclosure. The disclosure period may last even beyond the parties' working relationship.

● **Non-compete agreement:** Increasingly used in a wide range of jobs, the parties acknowledge the job relationship and departing employees agree to not compete with the employer. Restrictions concern three areas: duration of time the restriction lasts, geographic range of the restriction, and scope of job overlap that would be considered to be competing.

● **Non-solicitation agreement:** Parties agree that departing employees may not directly or indirectly solicit other employees, or company vendors, customers, suppliers, etc., to join them in their new venture, for a defined period of time.

● **Forfeiture agreement:** Usually found in executive compensation agreements, the parties agree that a departing employee forfeits any unvested compensation if they elect to leave for a competitor.

● **Separation agreement:** An agreement covering all aspects of the post-employment term, including severance payments, unreimbursed vacation or compensation, continuation of health coverage, rights to vested options, release of all other claims, non-disparagement clause, ownership of any company social media, return of all proprietary technologies. And this agreement will also clarify other restrictive covenants that have already been executed that continue in force, such as non-solicitation agreements, and so forth.

● **Independent contractor agreement:** Start-ups often hire independent contractors at the beginning for specialty work and since there is no defined and ongoing business yet, it is crucial for the business to clarify the scope of work, and especially to ensure all works created for the business are assigned to the business as the legal owner of the works.

- **Work-for-hire agreement:** This provides that the worker is hired for the specific purpose of creating the desired work; that the work created is within the scope of the job, and that all rights to it immediately vest in the hiring employer. The employer is thereby considered the legal author of this work.

- **No-poaching agreement:** These are considered illegal agreements in restraint of trade, but since they are contracts, and quite commonly used, mentioned here. Companies enter into these agreements to refrain from hiring each other's employees. This limits competition between firms for workers and therefore affects a restraint on employees' ability to be recruited and hired, which depresses wages and mobility (and potentially innovation).

Policy Issues and Antitrust Concerns in Agreements

As businesses increasingly turn to tech transfer, contract manufacturing, collaboration agreements to accomplish ever more specialized inventions, and goods and services, such agreements could create antitrust concerns. There are two main factors for this. First, there is a trend in which collaboration agreements frequently involve competitors, or at least potential competitors, which, when combined, may have an outsize market share reaching the threshold for government oversight of the agreement. Second, the provisions in the agreements can be incompatible with competition. Clauses covering exclusivity, field-of-use or non-compete restrictions, territorial or customer restrictions, are vulnerable to antitrust challenge. The business risk is substantial in that should such a clause be invalidated, it could undermine a key goal of the agreement.

There are an increased number of enforcement actions in IP and software licensing as the Department of Justice has made this a priority. Concerning cross-licensing and the creation of patent pools, and the reasonableness of terms upon with the agreements are offered (especially if the technology is a standards-essential), the Department is especially vigilant. In a recent report, the Department aptly stated the challenge this way, "In many industries, the patent right[s] necessary to commercialize a product are frequently controlled by multiple rights holders. This fragmentation of rights can increase the costs of bringing products to market due to the transaction costs of negotiating multiple licenses . . . .Portfolio cross licenses and patent pools can help solve the problems created . . . by reducing transaction costs for licensees while preserving the financial incentives for inventors to commercialize their [work . . . .yet] they also may generate anticompetitive effects if the arrangement result in price fixing, coordinated output restrictions among competitors, or foreclosure of innovation."[3]

---

3. U.S. Dep't of Justice & Fed. Trade Comm'n, Antitrust Enforcement and Intellectual Property Rights: Promoting Innovation and Competition, Chap. 3, *Antitrust Analysis of Portfolio Cross-Licensing Agreement and Patent Pools* (2007).

As the parties attempt to maximize control through their agreements, this tends to result in anticompetitive effects. One key aspect common to tech companies is in the area of IP and licensing. Intellectual property gives the holder monopoly-like power for a limited time, and in some cases for a potentially unlimited time. This occurs most especially with copyrights and patents. For example, businesses may try to leverage a patent in a number of ways, such as tying the licensing of a patent to other of its goods and services, or containing a covenant not to compete, or placing restrictions on field of use, customers or territory, price, quantity or output, exclusivity arrangements, or charging excessive royalties to certain parties, or by grant-back clauses requiring the licensee to grant back any technology improved or developed out of the original license. IP and licensing is an area of antitrust concern currently, and is regulated by the Department of Justice (DOJ) and the Federal Trade Commission (FTC). The government is conscious of regulating in a way that maximizes business opportunities, while fostering competition and innovation.

To an extent, software goods tend towards monopoly share, and contracts typically restrict competition, and so when there is a contract for software, it is very likely there are antitrust concerns. Software goods and services achieve the most value when they capture the biggest share of the market (think Facebook—it only achieves maximum utility if all of your friends use it, too). Software utility increases with market share (in contrast to, say, certain goods that achieve more value due to scarcity, like certain vintage cars, limited edition art, and so forth). This "network effect" phenomenon can be seen for example with office software. Say you want to send your digital presentation to a colleague. The presentation software you use is useful only if your colleague has that same software or there is interoperability to different software programs. Software goods and services reach maximum value in many cases only when they grow to monopoly-size market share. This alone does not make for an actionable claim. Businesses with monopoly power must engage in monopolistic acts before there might be any actionable claim. In one example, Advanced Micro Devices (AMD) filed suit against rival chip maker Intel, which held 80 percent of the market for chips, alleging Intel required original equipment manufacturers (OEMs) to forgo using AMD products in order to receive rebates on pricing. The parties later settled all claims based on these acts, with Intel reportedly making a large payment to AMD. In another example, in the *United States v. Microsoft* litigation, the government accused Microsoft, which at that time held a 90 percent share of the OS market, of achieving that position through creating barriers to entry for others. The complaint alleged such practices as onerous licensing restrictions and terms with partners. Specifically, Microsoft's licensing terms prohibited OEMs like Dell from altering the icons, folders, start menu, or boot sequencing, and through these tactics and others, effectively denied competitors access to the OEMs to start their own licensing relationships. In this respect, courts more closely scrutinize contractual agreements, and there is an effective statutory framework for guidance on resolution of such charges.

The antitrust laws were originally passed to regulate large businesses—monopolies engaging in monopolistic practices—but the modern view of antitrust regulation encompasses a broader mandate, and now government regulation of markets includes promoting competition and efficiency.

The Sherman Antitrust Act prohibits contracts, combinations, and conspiracies in restraint of trade. Restraints include price fixing, tying, and monopolization. "Every person who shall monopolize, or attempt to monopolize, or combine or conspire with any other person or persons, to monopolize any part of the trade or commerce among the several States, or with foreign nations, shall be deemed guilty of a felony."

Courts follow a two-part test for considering Sherman Antitrust Act claims:

- First, courts analyze whether there is monopoly power, whether the business has market power in the relevant market (generally defined as the ability to control price and exclude competitors in that market); and
- Second, courts analyze whether there is monopolistic conduct (defined as anticompetitive conduct, or willful acquisition or maintenance of that monopoly power—in contrast to business growth through superior products, business acumen, or historic accident).

While the language of the statute appears to impose absolute, or *per se* liability on every monopolistic act, the regulatory environment has shifted on this line of thought to encompass a more nuanced approach for tech licensing agreements, and is governed by a less stringent "rule of reason" test. Thus, anticompetitive consequences are balanced against asserted business justifications for the practices and any pro-competitive impacts that may exist. Defendants may counter antitrust allegations with claims of business justification. Thus, if Plaintiff establishes a violation, Defendants may present a defense of business justification for their actions, that such business practices are justified because of, for example, quality control, that such a configuration or integration is necessary for quality, or for other reasons, including to maintain performance, speed, or accuracy. In a recent high-profile civil antitrust case over the cost of e-books, the court found the publishers liable for conspiring to create an agreement for price-fixing e-books. Further, the judge found that Apple's participation in the horizontal-price fixing conspiracy, was like that of a retailer, and amounted to vertical price-fixing which is a *per se* violation of Sherman Act § 1.[4]

Further, Sections 12 through 27 of the Clayton Act outlaw other agreements that tend to lessen competition, including: (1) exclusive dealing clauses and tie-ins; (2) price discrimination; (3) mergers and acquisitions; and (4) interlocking directorates in which two or more Directors on a Board also are on the Boards of competitors. Antitrust issues in the Internet and tech sectors are more fully covered in the chapter on Government Regulation.

Internationally, the EU has been quite active in its antitrust oversight of technology transfer agreements, since one of the EU's main principles is ensuring

---

4. United States v. Apple, Inc., Civil Action No. 1:12-CV-2826 (S.D.N.Y. April 11, 2012).

freedom of movement, and goods and services among member states. Its antitrust enforcement focuses on removal of barriers in agreements, such as those that distort competition. The EU has allowed "block exemptions" from antitrust laws for certain agreements (tech transfer, R&D, distribution agreements) that it considers acceptable, to the extent they stay within the safe harbors.

In May 2014, the revised Technology Transfer Block Exemption Regulation (TTBER) was enacted. The new TTBER exempts agreements from antitrust enforcement when the parties have limited market power. The critical market share threshold is 20 percent for agreements between competitors, and 30 percent for agreements when parties are not competitors. If the market share exceeds these thresholds, the parties lose their exemption and will have to consider Article 101's prohibitions on anticompetitive agreements. Further, in 2014 the European Commission adopted new revised guidelines on the application of Article 101 of the Treaty on the Functioning of the European Union to Technology Transfer Agreements, 2014/C, 89/01(Guidelines). The Guidelines foster competition and are more strict than is the US on the allowance of no-challenge, grant-back, and passive (unsolicited) sales clauses.

Summary

Contracts are used for a variety of strategic purposes. Offensively, they are a way to earn revenue, secure access to a new technology, enter a new field, scale up quickly. Defensively, they prevent competitors from accessing a new technology, limit employee movement, disclosure, and more. These are voluntarily entered into, privately negotiated agreements, and therefore courts make every effort to uphold and enforce contracts, limiting any unenforceability to just the offending clauses. Drafting contracts takes foresight and care, in an effort to leverage all opportunities and to limit the potential for, and magnitude of, any harms. These issues are especially relevant in this era of technology convergence and the Internet of things, which demands that products, goods and services be seamlessly integrated. Technology licensing decisions are some of the most important companies make. Currently software licensing is a matter of concern for government regulators and it is important to draft agreements to comport with formation and unconscionability standards, as well as antitrust guidelines.

Key Terms

contract Contracts create a legal relationship; voluntarily entered into agreements, whereby each party has legal capacity and is bound by obligations in order to pursue lawful objectives.

technology transfer/material transfer agreement The process by which a business transfers to another business assets, including facilities, technology, know-how or expertise, in order commercialize or improve a product or process.

contract manufacturing/supply chain agreement A series of contracts with different partners throughout the entire creation and deployment process covering design, procurement, manufacturing, quality control, shipping, and retailing.

joint venture agreement A commercial collaboration in which two or more businesses share or integrate some of their resources for a limited purpose while staying independent.

in-licensing The process of contracting to receive another business's technology.

out-licensing The process of granting rights in your technology to another business.

cross-licensing Each business grants rights to the other for specified technologies to freely use the covered technology and therefore innovate and create products and services without risk of infringing.

software licensing agreement (SLA) Also known as end user license agreements, courts construe these non-negotiated documents as agreements and therefore are governed by contract law)

free and open source software agreement (FOSS) A contract for software rights characterized by more permissive agreements as to ownership and control.

proprietary software Software that is completely owned and therefore all rights are controlled by the publisher.

tortious interference with contract rights Tort-based theory providing a cause of action against a defendant for intentionally damaging the plaintiff's contractual relationship with another, for which enhanced damages are available if successfully proven.

Manager's Checklist

1. Regarding negotiated agreements, businesses should carefully draft clauses, being able to articulate which clauses are necessary, and which ones can be bargained away.

2. During execution of the negotiated agreements, it is important to ensure each benchmark is acceptably completed, and to communicate the extent the other party needs to cure any breach.

3. Businesses that own technology should consider whether to, and with what other businesses they want to target for out-, or cross-licensing purposes.

4. Businesses that do not own the technology should consider whether to make it, or to in-license it.

5. Regarding non-negotiated agreements, presently these can be written with impunity, though some states' courts have begun reviewing these agreements with a more critical point of view.

6. Manager should review all agreements for compliance with antitrust laws.

Questions and Case Problems

1. Neon Enterprise Software is a small company that writes and sells software utilities for use by businesses that are users of IBM mainframe computers and operating systems. Neon's software virtualizes the work and enables the IBM mainframe to offload work to specialty computers and this saves time and resources. But IBM's negotiated software agreement with Neon specifically prohibited such offloading. IBM customers pay IBM metered usage fees for mainframes, so such a utility as Neon's would diminish IBM revenues. What do you expect for a result in this lawsuit?

2. BusyBox, a collection of software applications highly valued for its use in embedded software, was created by a group of developers, and is released under a GNU free software license. Another company borrowed some of the BusyBox code for its software and released it without any reciprocal offer to share the source code as required by the BusyBox license. What causes of action can BusyBox allege?

3. The headline in a recent news story reads, "Another Year, Another ERP Lawsuit," in reaction to a lawsuit filed by ScanSource against Avanade, the Joint Venture between Accenture and Microsoft. ScanSource alleges Defendants purposefully underestimated costs, misrepresented their skills and abilities, used "bait and switch" tactics, and a revolving door of implementation consultants, leading to an incomplete and defectively designed system with extensive flaws and needing extensive remedial work. ScanSource filed a breach of contract suit, and Avanade filed counterclaims. What can a court do to change the outcomes of this type of litigation?

4. The patent dispute between Apple and HTC began in 2010 and quickly Apple filed a number of lawsuits throughout the world, seeking damages and injunctions against HTC. At one point Apple won a ban on the importation and sale of HTC Android devices. After much more litigation, they subsequently agreed to a ten-year exclusive cross-licensing deal that applies to all past and future patents for the companies. Describe how this deal is potentially anti-competitive with other mobile device manufacturers such as Samsung.

5. Facebook users found out that the company was sharing their personal information with third parties without their permission and in violation of the license agreement, and so they filed suit. What will result?

6. *Ethical Consideration:* As a business entity, say you developed an invention that many other businesses wish to incorporate into their hardware as well (something, for example, that is comparable to a USB-port invention). Should you license the invention on the same terms to every business that wants it? Should you favor some businesses (those that you would like to work with), over others (those that are your arch-competitors)? What do you charge on a licensing agreement to a promising start up that cannot pay anything at the moment?

Additional Resources

Department of Justice and US Patent & Trademark Office. *Policy Statement on Remedies for Standards-Essential Patents Subject to Voluntary F/RAND Commitments*, Jan. 8, 2013.

General Accountability Office. *IT Supply Chain*, March 2012.

Gilbert, Richard, and Carl Shapiro, *Antitrust Issues in the Licensing of Intellectual Property: The Nine No-No's Meet the Nineties*, Brookings Papers: Microeconomics 283 (1997).

Rustad, Michael, and Thomas F. Lambert, Jr., *Software Licensing: Principles and Practical Strategies* (2010).

White House. *National Strategy for Global Supply Chain Security* (Jan. 2012).

 Google is interviewing candidates . . . who are willing to relocate, are in top physical condition and are capable of surviving with limited access to such modern conveniences as soy low-fat lattes and a steady supply of oxygen. Google will be conducting experiments in entropized information filtering, high-density, high-delivery hosting (HiDeHiDeHo) and de-oxygenated cubicle dwelling.

—**Excerpt from Google's Job Opportunities page:**
http://www.google.com/jobs/lunar_job.httnl

The Employment Relationship

Learning Outcomes

After you have read this chapter, you should be able to:

● Understand the issues specific to employment in the Internet and tech sectors.
● Learn about different worker status of employees that exist and that are prevalent in the Internet and tech sectors.
● Understand how the employment relationship is governed by a variety of laws as well as private agreements between the parties.

Overview

The employment relationship in the Internet and technology sector is highly dynamic, dominated by creative and talented individuals, where rapid deployment of the technology is mission-critical. Strategic assets are as much the technology as the workers themselves, and changes in company ownership are the norm. The tech sector is dominated by knowledge workers who are highly educated and mobile, often with multiple cultural links. Managing these employees and this dynamic employment relationship is a core challenge for tech businesses.

Consider Dr. Kai-Fu Lee who in 2000 was VP for Research and Development at Microsoft. At Microsoft, Dr. Lee signed a noncompete agreement and a nondisclosure agreement in which he promised Microsoft, among other things, that he would not accept employment or engage in activities that competed with products or services he worked on at Microsoft; the agreements were governed by the laws of the state of Washington. In 2005, Dr. Lee accepted a position at Google, a California company, as VP of Engineering at an R&D plant in China. Microsoft sued Google and Lee in Washington for breaching the noncompete and nondisclosure agreements, and Google and Lee filed their own suit against Microsoft in California.

The situation Dr. Lee, Google, and Microsoft find is typical in the tech industry: a very mobile workforce, off-shoring certain parts of operations, and using contracts to maintain control over confidential information when an employee moves to another company. As we will see, this control can survive even after the employment relationship is over.

Another aspect of the tech sector that the Internet and Web have changed dramatically is the workplace itself. Complicated information and data projects can be disaggregated, then collaboratively designed and completed across various and unconnected locations, and finally reaggregated for the client. Work and workplaces are more mobile and unstructured (work gets done at the beach, at WiFi-enabled coffee shops, etc.); work and nonwork tasks are accomplished seamlessly throughout the day. The ability to move work out of the office network has created unparalleled threats to company assets as work is emailed to personal accounts, workers write blogs about their work environments and their coworkers, and more. The workplace has undergone radical changes with notable losses of control, hierarchy, and secrecy and as a result the relationship between workers and employers has had to adapt. This chapter surveys the employment relationship in the tech sector along with discussion of agreements between employers and employees common to Internet and technology companies.

The Work Environment

Preemployment

Employer Search for Qualified Candidates

Employee search, screening, interviewing, and hiring are special challenges in the high-tech sector, forcing employers and start ups to confront topics ranging from immigration and visa issues, to questions, to complications with candidates locked into noncompete and other agreements with previous employers. Even after candidates have survived a vetting process, unexpected financial constraints could arise requiring reclassification of the position as work for a subcontractor, temp, or even an unpaid intern. Some may want to accept a job offer, but perhaps an unwritten understanding exists between the former and prospective employers to not hire each other's workers.

Exhibit 9.1	Questions Candidates Were Reportedly Asked When Interviewing at Google

> **Q:** How many golf balls can fit in a school bus?
>
> **Q:** How many times a day does a clock's hands overlap?
>
> **Q:** You are at a party with a friend and 10 people are present including you and the friend. Your friend makes you a wager that for every person you find that has the same birthday as you, you get $1; for every person he finds that does not have the same birthday as you, he gets $2. Would you accept the wager?
>
> **Q:** You are shrunk to the height of a nickel and your mass is proportionally reduced so as to maintain your original density. You are then thrown into an empty glass blender. The blades will start moving in 60 seconds. What do you do?
>
> **Q:** Explain a database in three sentences to your eight-year-old nephew.
>
> **Q:** How many gas stations would you say there are in the United States?

Selection: Legal process of choosing employee's

There are many considerations for all parties during this process, in which each company is now competing with the rest of the world's companies for the top talent. Related to this intense competition are the high-profile company perquisites that act to brand and distinguish companies as they compete for talent. Company perquisites may include onsite medical care, salons, laundry, massage, game rooms, cafeteria, transportation, pool, gym, referral bonuses, child care, doggie day care, reimbursement for education, stock ownership plan, retirement plan, sabbaticals, surfboards, volleyball courts, bike trails, tickets, and reimbursement for egg freezing for female employees.[1]

Promising candidates may be brought in for a site visit where potential employers may ask candidates to read and sign a **visitor's confidentiality and nondisclosure agreement**. In such contracts, all visitors promise, in consideration for being admitted to the workplace, to not disclose any information about the company, its employees, or their impressions thereof for a defined period of time. During this visit, candidates may interview with a number of constituencies at the workplace. Interview questions must comply with all laws regarding queries on age, citizenship, national origin, religion, disability, and so forth. If everything checks out, including references, companies will transmit an offer letter of employment. Offers are typically conditioned on the candidate's employment eligibility and acceptance of a number of terms, including many of the agreements in this chapter.

---

1. Sabrina Parsons, "Female Tech CEO: Egg-Freezing 'Benefit' Sends the Wrong Message to Women," *BusinessInsider .com*, Oct. 20, 2014. http://www.businessinsider.com/apple-facebook-egg-freezing-benefit-is-bad-for-women-2014-10.

Exhibit 9.2 **Excerpt from the IBM-Papermaster NCA**

NONCOMPETITION AGREEMENT ". . . You acknowledge and agree that: (i) the business in which IBM . . . [is] engaged is intensely competitive . . . that you have access to, and knowledge of, confidential information of the Company, including, but not limited to, certain or all of the Company's methods, information, systems, plans for acquisition or disposition of products, expansion plans, financial status and plans, customer lists, client data, personnel information and trade secrets of the Company, which are of vital importance to the success of the Company's business; (ii) the disclosure of any of the foregoing could place the Company at a serious competitive disadvantage and could do serious damage . . . ; (iii) you have been given access to, and developed relationships with, customers of the Company at the time and expense of the Company; and (iv) by your training, experience and expertise, your service to the Company are, and will continue to be, extraordinary, special and unique."

Contract Obligations

Noncompete Agreements (NCAs)

Problems can potentially surface at any time during the hiring process, particularly when employers face two impediments. First, employers may be limited in hiring candidates because a candidate may be contractually bound to their former employer through a **noncompete agreement (NCA)**. Employers rely on NCAs to prevent former employees from using all they have learned to the advantage of a competitor.

NCAs should cover three points:

- *Time:* Employees agree to refrain from working for competitors for a specified period of time;
- *Place:* Employees agree to refrain from working for competitors within a certain geographic area; and
- *Scope:* Employees agree to refrain from working for competitors whose business consists of similar work, or those whose business could expand into that field of work.

Employees have access to customer lists, strategic business plans, salary information, production and design materials, costs, and so forth; employees who leave and start up a competing business start with a significant advantage based on that knowledge. Employees naturally disfavor NCAs because they prevent employment at certain companies, which not coincidentally are those with which employees have the most compatible skill set, and may be unduly burdensome for employees to earn a living.

Courts understand that employers have invested time and resources in their employees and these are protectable interests, but that employees have the right to earn a living and to job mobility in a free-market economy. Not every state recognizes NCAs. For those that do, employers are favored at the expense of talented individual employees, tending to lead to static markets, less job mobility, less innovation, and lower salary structures. For those jurisdictions that do not recognize NCAs, talented individual employees are favored at the expense of employers, tending to lead to dynamic unpredictable markets, higher job mobility, more innovation, and higher salary structures. This also creates higher personnel and administrative costs for businesses. Historically, NCAs were presumptively invalid, but they have gained legitimacy as large businesses gained bargaining power over employees. Nevertheless, the status of NCAs is unsettled, as states' laws differ. For example, NCAs are void in California, but valid in a number of other states, including New York.[2] Although NCAs are still valid in Massachusetts, the Governor has proposed a bill similar to the law in California banning noncompetes for workers in the tech, life sciences, and other industries.[3] Scholars have tracked the results of NCAs and innovation and concluded that there is a competitiveness gap between states that enforce NCAs and those that do not: those that do not have higher productivity and higher economic rewards from creativity, such as more start ups, risk-taking, and the spillover of know-how.[4]

In those jurisdictions that recognize NCAs, a **rule of reason test** is used when considering the validity of the terms.

Courts consider:

- Whether the restraint is designed to protect some legitimate interest of the employer (or is it merely to restrain ordinary competition); and
- Whether each of the restraints is reasonable as to time, place and scope.

Some jurisdictions have adopted the *blue pencil* rule,[5] which means that even if there is a finding that the NCA is an unreasonable restraint under the rule of reason test, the court can strike or modify terms that violate an otherwise valid NCA. Because this rule works to completely frustrate employers' goals, employers are advised to manage this risk by including a "step-down provision" in their NCAs, permitting courts to rewrite provisions as a substitute for any terms found to be unreasonable.

Employers may be limited in hiring candidates to the extent these candidate employees are still bound to a legally recognized noncompete agreement. Employers should not make any assumptions in this area. It may seem possible to pay off

---

2. See David P. Twomey and Marianne Moody Jennings, Business Law, p. 420 (3d ed. 2011).

3. Callum Borchers and Michael Farrell, "Patrick Looks to Eliminate Tech Noncompete Agreements," The Boston Globe, 4/10/14 http://www.bostonglobe.com/business/2014/04/09/gov-patrick-pushes-ban-noncompete-agreements-employment-contracts/kgOq3rkbtQkhYooVIicfOO/story.html.

4. See Ronald J. Gibson, "The Legal Infrastructure of High Technology Industrial Districts: Silicon Valley, Route 128, and Covenants Not to Compete," 74 N.Y.U. L. Rev. 575 (1999). Further, legislators in Massachusetts are drafting a bill to eliminate restrictive employer covenants. For updates, see the Boston Bar Association's page, http://www.bostonbar.org.

5. See Restatement (Second) of Contracts, § 184 (1981). Courts generally will not re-write contracts; rather they will strike unreasonable terms.

the former employer for costs associated with an employee's departure, but in certain instances the competitive disadvantage is too great for the soon-to-be former employer and they may seek an **injunction**. An injunction is a court order that prohibits a person from engaging in certain conduct, or that compels them to perform a certain act. Here, an injunction would prohibit the employee from assuming certain job duties for a defined period of time at the prospective employer's company. Injunctions are a powerful counterpoint to employee mobility.

In the following case, an employee left IBM to join HP, despite his NCA with IBM. HP tried to "fence off" the new hire so he would not work on matters covered by the noncompete. Was this good enough?

IBM v. Visentin
2011 U.S. Dist. LEXIS 15342 S.D.N.Y. (2011)

Facts IBM is a leading technology company with 400,000 employees in over 170 countries. The company is organized into several business segments, including Global Technology Services (GTS). GTS has four business segments, one of which is Integrated Technology Services (ITS), which provides clients with nearly 180 different infrastructure technology services.

Hewlett-Packard (HP) is a global technology provider and an IBM competitor, and has 300,000 employees in more than 170 countries. HP is organized into several business segments including Enterprise Services (ES).

Mr. Visentin worked for IBM for twenty-six years; he is a business manager, not a technical expert, and during his career with IBM held several management positions in different geographic areas and business divisions. In 2007, Mr. Visentin became General Manager of the ITS business. The ITS business generates about 5000-9000 deals per quarter and total revenue of $2.5 billion annually.

IBM requires over 1700 employees to sign noncompetition agreements, and Mr. Visentin signed two: one in 2008 and the other in 2009. The 2009 agreement states that during Mr. Visentin's employment with IBM "and for twelve (12) months following termination of [his] employment . . . [Mr. Visentin] will not directly or indirectly within the 'Restricted Area' (i) Engage in or Associate with (a) any 'Business Enterprise' or (b) any competitor of the Company." This includes working as an employee, consultant, or contractor for any business that competes with any business unit or division of IBM.

On January 18, 2011, Mr. Visentin accepted a position at HP and he immediately notified IBM. In his resignation letter, Mr. Visentin offered to stay for a reasonable transition period but IBM declined. HP hired Mr. Visentin because he is a "process-oriented thinker" and has skills in managing large teams. His new role at HP was Senior Vice President, General Manager, Americas for Enterprise Services. In this position, Mr. Visentin was responsible for managing three business units within the ES group.

Although Mr. Visentin did not provide any IBM confidential information or trade secrets to HP, he did provide an IBM client list that included nothing but the names of clients, most of which are well-known to HP and the industry. Mr. Visentin provided this list for the sole purpose of allowing HP to assess his noncompetition agreement with IBM and determine how to "fence" him off from those clients. After discussing the nature of the position at HP, both Mr. Visentin and HP's decision-maker, Mr. Iannotti, determined that it was feasible to structure the HP job so that it was different from Mr. Visentin's previous position at IBM in terms of subject area, geographic scope, and level of responsibility. HP offered Mr. Visentin a high-level management job and agreed to narrow the job during an appropriate time period to minimize any potential overlap with his previous position at IBM.

IBM filed suit against Mr. Visentin for breach of the noncompetition agreement, misappropriation of trade secrets, and sought an injunction to prevent him from working at HP for twelve months.

Judicial Opinion   Judge Preska

Preliminary Injunction   A preliminary injunction is "an extraordinary and drastic remedy which should not be routinely granted." To obtain a preliminary injunction, a party must prove: "(1) that [it] would be irreparably harmed if an injunction were not granted, and (2) either (a) a likelihood of success on the merits or (b) sufficiently serious questions going to the merits to make them a fair ground for litigation, and a balance of hardships tipping decidedly in its favor."

IBM bears the burden of demonstrating that these circumstances warrant such a "drastic remedy." This Court presided over an exhaustive four-day hearing and concludes that IBM failed to carry its burden of demonstrating that these facts warrant granting a preliminary injunction.

I. IRREPARABLE HARM

A demonstration of irreparable harm is the most important factor for the issuance of an injunction. The harm must be imminent, not speculative or a mere possibility.

TRADE SECRETS

In New York, noncompetes are enforceable to protect an employer's legitimate interests, such as trade secrets and confidential information, provided the agreement poses no undue hardship on the employee. IBM claims that if Mr. Visentin works at HP, he will inevitably reveal the trade secrets of IBM.

At IBM, Mr. Visentin's primary job was as a "general manager" and the real thrust of his position was to manage his teams to make them as efficient as possible. Mr. Iannotti confirmed that these qualities were the driving factors behind HP hiring him; he hired Mr. Visentin because "[h]e had good general IT services knowledge, broad experience." Mr. Visentin's job at HP will be to "manage people" and he is not expected to be involved in the pricing, design, or staffing of new business.

IBM claims that through his job, Mr. Visentin was in possession of information that deserved protection. However, IBM's fact witnesses failed to provide specific examples of confidential or trade secret information that could actually be used to IBM's detriment should Mr. Visentin work at HP. There are two areas of information—potential IBM acquisition and client pipeline information—that may warrant protection as trade secrets. Regarding potential acquisitions, Mr. Visentin acknowledges that he is subject to a separate nondisclosure that applies to this information, but in any event at IBM Mr. Visentin was not responsible for making acquisitions and he will not have that responsibility at HP. Regarding client pipeline information, while Mr. Visentin might have seen the name of a client and the total dollar value of a prospective deal, Mr. Iannotti testified that simply knowing the client and the projected amount of the deal would not tell Mr. Visentin about the scope of the services to be provided, the length of the contract, or the cost to IBM. At most, IBM has established the possibility of some confidential information that Mr. Visentin testified he will not disclose and which at HP he does not have to disclose to do his job.

That Mr. Visentin had access to some confidential information is not sufficient to show irreparable harm. The Court must still determine whether Mr. Visentin actually misappropriated those trade secrets or if his new position will inevitably require disclosure of these trade secrets. Two factors used to determine inevitable disclosure are: how similar is the new position to the old position, and whether the trade secrets at issue are valuable to HP.

It is undisputed that Mr. Visentin did not leave IBM with any documents, and he and HP agreed to limit the scope of his responsibilities for the first twelve months at HP. Moreover, Mr. Visentin's new position at HP is not the same as his old position at IBM. In fact, in his new position the scope of his new responsibility is significantly larger and includes areas of supervision that he had no prior exposure to in his position at IBM. Thus inevitable disclosure is not likely.

II. LIKELIHOOD OF SUCCESS ON THE MERITS

IBM must show that the restrictions in the agreement are no greater than is required for the protection of the legitimate interest of the employer, they do not impose an undue hardship on the employee, and are not injurious to the public.

IBM has not demonstrated that the restrictions in Mr. Visentin's noncompetition agreement are no greater than required to protect IBM's legitimate interests. First, the agreement prohibits competition in areas where IBM has no legitimate interest. And second, it has been established that there are areas of Mr. Visentin's new position that are unrelated to what he did for IBM.

IBM also cannot show that it seeks to protect a legitimate interest such as protection from competition by a former employee whose services are unique or extraordinary. Neither party asserts that Mr. Visentin's skills as a manager are "unique or extraordinary," and IBM did not produce any persuasive evidence to contradict that assertion. Moreover, IBM has not demonstrated that it seeks to protect trade secrets or confidential information from misappropriation by Mr. Visentin. In sum, the evidence produced by IBM fails to demonstrate affirmatively any legitimate interest IBM needs to protect. Even though the Court need go no further, the agreement imposes an undue hardship on Mr. Visentin because if he cannot work for HP for the next twelve months, although he will draw a paycheck he will not be guaranteed the same position at HP and not working will hamper significantly his ability to prove his value to HP.

Based on the facts in the record, the Court concludes that IBM has failed to satisfy its burden of showing that it is likely to succeed on the merits. Request for injunction denied.

Case Questions

1. What is IBM's "inevitable disclosure" argument? Is there a way to ever fully protect against this?
2. Once IBM knew Mr. Visentin had resigned, what could it have done differently to avoid the time and expense of seeking a preliminary injunction but still protect its interests?
3. *Ethical Consideration*: What facts in the case demonstrate Mr. Visentin's good faith, that is, his intentions to not disclose IBM's trade secrets? Do you think this is important? Why or why not?

Employers may also be limited in hiring candidates to the extent the employers have agreed among themselves to not hire each other's employees. In the ultra-competitive high-tech market where there is a constant struggle for skilled workers, it is widely reported that companies have unwritten agreements to not actively hire employees of companies that partner or have joint ventures with each other.[6] (Hiring employees from *direct competitors* is not an aspect of this legal issue.) Often called *no poaching agreements* or *hands-off lists,* the Department of Justice is actively pursuing confidential investigations of the software, Internet, technology, and biotech industries for evidence of anticompetitive acts in violation of the antitrust laws because such agreements, if proven, amount to collusion in hiring decisions that have the effect of restricting job mobility and suppressing wages. Agreements to hold down labor costs are as anticompetitive as agreements to fix prices.

For example, in April 2014, Apple, Google, Intel, and Adobe Systems agreed to a $324 million settlement of a class action lawsuit covering more than 64,000 tech workers.[7] The suit alleged that the high tech companies entered "no-poaching" agreements with each other, which hampered the workers' job mobility and suppressed their salaries.

---

6. See Thomas Catan and Brent Kendall, "U.S. Steps Up Probe of Hiring in Tech," Wall Street Journal, April 9, 2010; Miguel Helft, "Unwritten Code Rules Silicon Valley Hiring," New York Times, June 4, 2009.
7. David Streitfeld, "Tech Giants Settle Antitrust Hiring Suit," The New York Times, 4/25/14 http://www.nytimes.com/2014/04/25/technology/settlement-silicon-valley-antitrust-case.html?_r=0.

According to court documents, Apple co-founder Steve Jobs sent an email to Google co-founder Sergey Brin stating "if you hire a single one of these people that means war."[8] As further evidence of collusion among the companies, the workers cited an email from Google Chairman Eric Schmidt to Steve Jobs in 2007 explaining that Google terminated a recruiter who contacted an Apple employee in violation of the companies' "do not call policy," and Jobs responded to the message with a smiling emoticon.

The civil class action came after a 2010 settlement between the tech companies and the U.S. Department of Justice whereby Apple, Google, Intel, and Adobe agreed not to enter into no-hire agreements. The government did not pursue fines in that settlement; however, the workers' civil action focused on monetary damages. The $324 million settlement is about one-tenth of the $3 billion the workers would have sought had the case gone to trial. As this text went to press, the $324 million settlement was still awaiting court approval because presiding Justice Lucy Koh had concerns whether the amount was fair to the 64,000 workers.[9]

The cases in this area are guided by *Todd v. Exxon Corp.*,[10] where the court ruled that employees adequately pleaded antitrust violations against Exxon and thirteen other companies in the integrated oil and petrochemical industries for colluding in their hiring decisions for oil geologists and petroleum engineers. The oil companies controlled 80-90 percent of the industry's revenues and employed 80-90 percent of the industry's workers, and they exchanged a broad range of employment and salary data, including past and current salaries along with future salary budget information. This data was aggregated and distributed to third-party recruiters confidentially without being distributed to the employees themselves, even though the companies allegedly participated in numerous meetings to share this data. The court ruled that the companies had monopoly power and engaged in monopolistic acts that were anticompetitive and lacked any pro-competitive benefits or impacts.

Employer Verification of Employment Eligibility of Non-US Workers

The high-tech work sector in the U.S. is characterized by a multinational and extremely mobile workforce; it is common for employees to have been born in one country, schooled in another, and seek work in yet a third country. Sorting out employment eligibility is an involved process for human resource departments and daunting for start ups. It is the employer's responsibility nevertheless to verify that the employee is eligible to work in the U.S. and must certify this through completing Form I-9 with the employee. To understand this in more

---

8. Jeremy Quittner, "How Steve Jobs Undercut Silicon Valley's Greatest Asset: Engineers," Inc. 4/22/14 http://www.inc.com/jeremy-quittner/silicon-valley-wage-collusion-class-action.html.
9. Zach Miners, "Judge Not Sold on $324M Settlement in Silicon Valley Tech Worker Case," PCWorld, 6/19/14 http://www.pcworld.com/article/2365940/judge-not-sold-on-324m-settlement-in-silicon-valley-tech-worker-case.html.
10. 275 F.3d 191 (2d Cir. 2001).

detail, a government publication on employment eligibility is reproduced in Appendix 9.A.

Employment and immigration issues are regulated by two departments: the Department of Justice and the Department of Homeland Security, along with three agencies: Immigration and Customs Enforcement, Citizenship and Immigration Services, and Customs and Border Protection.

U.S. start ups Pfizer, Sun, Intel, Yahoo!, DuPont, eBay, Procter and Gamble, and Google were all begun by foreign-born founders. So were Nvidia, Akamai, PayPal, Hotmail, Red Hat, Computer Associates, and Flickr. Nearly half of all Silicon Valley companies have at least one founder that is foreign-born. The proportion of immigrant- started businesses has dropped 8.5 percent since 2005 to 44 percent.[11] "Their departure means gains for technology hubs in other countries, such as Brazil, China, and India."[12]

The U.S. immigration system features a series of visa preference categories based on certain criteria. Permanent worker visa preference categories are known as the EB series (**EB-1-EB-5**). The EB-3 is popularly called the *Green Card;* these visas are reserved for certain workers, including those with "extraordinary ability," and ten years' experience, or those who are investors with at least $1 million of capital to invest in the United States.

H1-B visas are temporary work permits allocated to high-skill workers in specialty occupations. This is the main preference category used by the tech industry, and the visa status is dependent on the worker's employment status with the sponsoring employer, meaning the worker must stay employed at that employer. This program was begun in recognition of the growing importance of technology to our economy, and in 1990 Congress approved a temporary (non-immigrant track) work visa program for skilled workers sponsored by companies, making available 65,000 H1-B visas annually designated for nonimmigrant aliens who are highly skilled workers. Due to demand, the government holds a lottery for these visas. There are over 500,000 workers waiting for permanent legal residence through this preferred category.

Not surprisingly, the political discussion of immigration reform and the role of the H1-B visa in the larger effort for comprehensive reform are fraught with conflict and controversy. The U.S. Senate's version of immigration reform includes a bill that would increase the number of H1-B visas from 65,000 to 110,000 and ultimately to 185,000. Although this bill is part of a larger reform effort, it is the part of most interest to tech companies as these companies have applied for hundreds of thousands of such visas on behalf of potential workers.

Critics claim that tech companies use H1-B visas as a way to bring in cheap labor at the expense of U.S. jobs. In response, Facebook CEO Mark Zuckerberg created a group, FWD.us, which claims that each H1-B visa holder helps create

11. Jeremy Quittner, "How Silicon Valley is Transforming the Immigration Debate," Inc. 7/9/13, http://www.inc.com/jeremy-quittner/silicon-valley-immigration-reform.html.
12. Quittner, http://www.inc.com/jeremy-quittner/silicon-valley-immigration-reform.html.

two to three U.S. jobs.[13] The debate continues as Republicans and Democrats introduce new bills for their version of reform.[14]

Employment Status and Relationship

Employer Classification of Employee Status

When the employer hires workers, it is the employer's responsibility to negotiate the terms and conditions of employment. The different work configurations made possible by the Internet and Web are myriad, and thus it is crucial to clearly establish the status of workers. No longer does work have to be performed in one office. Knowledge work can theoretically be performed anywhere by anyone. Under these conditions, workers might be employed by the company, or self-employed, or even employed by another company—perhaps the main company's supply chain partner halfway around the world. The classification of workers is relevant to the legal obligations of employers; therefore, a short description of each employment classification is necessary.

Self-Employed Professional Subcontractors, Work for Hire Professionals, and **independent contractors** are nonemployee workers who perform defined tasks for a client company, but remain independent from the client and maintain a separate professional identity with the right and ability to work simultaneously for other client companies. This class of workers include outside attorneys, accountants, auditors, programmers, and so forth. Client companies have immediate access to qualified workers and reduced overhead expenses, but there is not the same ability to control these workers as there is with employees. Also, the pay rates may be variable and there is a risk of loss of sensitive business information or trade secrets.

There are fewer compliance and reporting responsibilities for client companies that hire independent contractors. Companies do not have to withhold or pay any taxes on payments to independent contractors. Prudent companies will enter into an **Independent Contractor Agreement**[15] with these workers to spell out the nature of the job, payment and other terms, and a declaration that both parties understand the relationship to be that of independent contractor. Should there be any confusion over worker status, companies file a Form SS-8 to determine worker status, responding to such questions as behavioral and financial control over the worker and the benefits, if any, extended to the worker. Generally, the more control a client company exerts over the person, the more likely it is that the IRS will classify the person as an employee.

Also, factors relevant in one situation may not be relevant in another. The key is to look at the entire relationship, consider the degree or extent of the right to direct and control According to the IRS:

13. http://www.nbcnews.com/business/careers/senator-tech-ceos-support-comprehensive-immigration-reform-n70166.
14. For more information, see http://www.foreignlaborcert.doleta.gov/h-1b.cfm.
15. See Exhibit A for sample Independent Contractor Agreement.

● **Behavioral:** Does the company control or have the right to control what the worker does and how the worker does his or her job?
● **Financial:** Are the business aspects of the worker's job controlled by the payer? (These include things like how worker is paid, whether expenses are reimbursed, who provides tools/supplies, etc.)
● **Type of Relationship:** Are there written contracts or employee-type benefits (i.e., independent contractor agreement, pension plan, insurance, vacation pay, etc.)? Will the relationship continue and is the work performed a key aspect of the business?

Businesses must weigh all of these factors when determining whether a worker is an employee or an independent contractor. There is no "magic" or set number of factors that "makes" the worker an employee or an independent contractor, and no one factor stands alone in making this determination. Finally, to document each of the factors used in coming up with the determination.[16]

Companies are required to submit IRS Form 1099 for every contractor paid more than $600 in a calendar year. Mistakes in misclassifying workers will have financial consequences for client companies, such as liability for back taxes, penalties, and interest, even when the contractor paid taxes in full.

Liability for independent contractors' torts is also a differentiating factor. Unlike for employees, a company's liability for the accidents and intentional torts of an independent contractor is limited to legal claims for **negligent hiring** or **negligent supervision** of that contractor. Thus, if an independent contractor got into a car accident while travelling from one work location to another, the hiring company would not be liable for any injuries unless the injured person could show that the company knew its independent contractor had a bad driving record and hired them anyway, didn't do a background check which would have revealed multiple traffic violations and hired them, or knew of her terrible driving and did nothing to supervise her more appropriately. Lastly, and importantly, many federal employment laws do not apply to independent contractors, such as Title VII of the Civil Rights Act, which prohibits discrimination in all aspects of employment based on race, color, gender, national origin, and religion. However, because state laws can differ from federal law, many state discrimination laws do cover independent contractors.

Clearly this work arrangement is very attractive for companies in start up mode.[17] During the 2010 legislative cycle, Congress passed health care legislation and included provisions related to 1099 workers that dramatically expanded reporting requirements for client companies.[18] According to the IRS, the law "will require businesses to report a wider range of payments to contractors,

---

16. See Stephen Fishman, *Working with Independent Contractors*, pp. 14–15 (6th ed., 2008) (citing as the key determinant for employee status the employer's right to control, or tell the employee what to do).
17. For information in the mis-classification crackdown see https://info.sequent.biz/blog/the-crackdown-on-independent-contractors-what-you-need-to-know.
18. The new reporting requirements are in § 6041 of the Internal Revenue Code, amended by § 9006 of the Patient Protection and Affordable Care Act of 2010, Pub. L. No. 111-148, 124 Stat. 119.

vendors and others,"[19] noting that this will be an enormous burden and compliance cost for small businesses.

Self-employed professionals are also pursuing legislative changes in states. For example, in Massachusetts where there is a high proportion of tech professionals engaged in creative work, Senate Bill 2345, *An Act Relative to Economic Development Reorganization* (2010), Amendment No. 4 supports independent contractors by making it easier for businesses to classify workers as such. The bill would modify the current treatment of professionals as interpreted by enforcement actions under Mass. Gen. Laws Ann. Ch. 149, Section 148B (2008).

In California, Assembly Bill 1897 would require an employer to share all of the legal responsibility and liability for wages, taxes and workers compensation if the contracting company does not. Opponents of this bill claim that not having these responsibilities is the main reason businesses subcontract out work.[20]

Work for Hire Professionals

A related work arrangement involves work made for hire. **Work for hire** is an issue that is quite common to tech start ups in which companies need software, coding, documentation, and so forth, and for these defined needs, a professional completes the task. A work made for hire is a work prepared by an employee within the scope of their employment, but the employer/client is considered the author or creator for copyright purposes.[21] All ownership rights, including copyright, credit, and right to control that work, vest in the employer/client.[22]

For work possibly beyond the employee's scope of employment (such as work done after hours, at home, etc.), the question becomes more difficult, and employers may have, at best, **shop rights** in the work. Shop rights permit employers to claim merely a nonexclusive license with limited rights to use the work, all without ultimate ownership rights. In such instances therefore, the employer would not be able to prevent the creator from selling or licensing the creation to others, even competitors.[23]

In cases where an independent contractor performs the work (such as when the ConnectU team asked a number of acquaintances, including Sanjay Mavinkurve, Victor Gao, and eventually, Mark Zuckerberg, for programming help on their early website concept), it may or may not be a work for hire. This category of work for hire addresses **specially commissioned works**. In this category of work for hire the parties enter into a written agreement explaining that the work commissioned is a work for hire. Even with this agreement, the question of ownership of the work is more complicated. In the analysis of whether it is a

---

19. IR-2010-79, July 1, 2010.
20. Allen Young, "Bill Would Make Employers Legally Responsible for Subcontractor Employees", Sacramento Business Journal, 4/1/14, http://www.bizjournals.com/sacramento/news/2014/04/01/subcontractor-workers-legal-responsibility-bill.html.
21. See 17 U.S.C. § 201 (2012).
22. See 17 U.S.C. § 101 (2012), and Copyright Office Circular 9, Works Made for Hire under the 1976 Copyright Act (featured in Appendix 10).
23. The Copyright Office provides guidance as to works for hire in Circular 9: http://copyright.gov/circs/circ09.pdf.

work for hire, and therefore owned by the hiring client company (rather than by the individual creator), three conditions must be met according to the copyright statute:

- The work must be specially ordered or commissioned (not yet in existence);
- The work must fall within one of the categories recognized by the Copyright Office, (Refer to Circular 9, in Appendix 10); and
- There must be an express agreement before the work begins specifying that this is a work for hire.

For protection, companies should require blanket copyright assignments to all works from employees, and most especially from all professional sub-contractors. A *Work for Hire Agreement* is not enough; it is critical to execute an assignment as well, wherein the creator of the work agrees to assign all rights and duties in the work to the company in order to avoid the perils of negotiating for creative work to be completed only to find out later that the creator owns rights rather than the company. This next case highlights some of these difficulties.

State v. Kirby
141 N.M. 838, 161 P.3d 883 (2007), 2009 N.M. App. LEXIS 213 (2009)

Facts Defendant Richard Kirby owned a small business, Global Exchange Holding, LLC, and for this venture, he hired Loren Collett, a sole proprietor operating under the name Starvation Graphics Company, to design and develop a website. They entered into a contract for website design services with Kirby agreeing to pay Collett $1,890.00 for the work.

Collett did the work requested but was never paid. When Kirby changed the site password and locked Collett out from the site, Kirby was charged with one count of fraud, a fourth degree felony, using means of fraudulent conduct, practices, or representations. On appeal, Kirby challenged the sufficiency of the evidence that Collett was the actual owner of the site, an element required under the fraud statute. In effect, Kirby took the position that he, not Collett, owned the site, and therefore, he could not defraud himself. We granted certiorari to address the issue of who is the owner of a website under these circumstances: the designer or the person who hires the designer.

Judicial Opinion, Judge Bosson

We first turn our attention to the legal document between Collett and Kirby, the "Website Design Contract." According to that contract, Collett was engaged "for the specific project of developing and/or improving a World Wide Website to be installed on the client's web space on a web-hosting service's computer." Thus, the end product of Collett's work was the website, and the client, Kirby, owned the web space. Kirby was to "select a web hosting service" which would allow Collett access to the website. Collett was to develop the website from content supplied by Kirby.

While the contract did not explicitly state who owned the website, it did specify ownership of the copyright to the web pages. "Copyright to the finished assembled work of web pages" was owned by Collett, and upon final payment Kirby would be "assigned rights to use as a website the design, graphics, and text contained in the finished assembled website." Collett reserved the right to remove web pages from the Internet until final payment was made. Thus, the contract makes clear that Collett was, and would remain, the owner of the copyright to the web pages making up the website. Upon payment, Kirby would receive a kind of license to use the website.

There are two exceptions to the general rule that the author of the work is the sole copyright owner. First, the creator of the work may not be the copyright owner in a "work made for hire" arrangement. This includes works prepared by an employee within the scope of his or her employment. The second work for hire exception applies to the independent contractor scenario, as exists here. To apply in the independent contractor context, the parties must expressly agree in a signed written instrument that the work will be work for hire and the work must be commissioned for one of the uses specified in the Copyright Act. Because these elements are lacking in this case, the work made for hire exceptions do not apply and therefore Collett remains the owner.

Kirby argues that because he owned certain elements that are part of a website and make it functional, he was the owner regardless of who owned copyright to the web pages. Specifically, Kirby purchased a domain name for the site, and contracted with a web hosting service, and owned the password that enabled him to control access to the site. While these elements are all necessary components of a website, none of these rises to the importance of the web pages that provide content. It is the information that creates substance and value. Ownership of the site follows from ownership of the copyright, unless otherwise agreed. Based on the evidence, a rational jury could have concluded that under the Website Design Contract, Collett owned the site, and . . . Kirby committed fraud by taking property that belonged to another.

We affirm the Court of Appeals.

Case Questions

1. How could businesses manage the employment relationship so as to avoid this risk?
2. Assuming Collett no longer wants to work with Kirby (he did sue him, after all) how should Collett structure their agreement so they permanently part ways?
3. *Ethical Consideration*: Can you contract ethics? Without knowing more about what transpired between Collett and Kirby leading up to the lawsuit, are there contract clauses that could have been added to "motivate" the parties to do the right thing in the case of a disagreement?

Temporary Workers

Temp workers are contingent workers who typically have specialty credentials and are not employed by the company, but rather by a staffing agency. This is an ideal way to quickly secure much-needed talent when scaling up. Likewise, this is an ideal strategy for staffing work that is cyclical in nature. Agencies screen, employ, and handle payroll and taxes for temp workers, who take direction from and report to the client company. Temps are not eligible for client company benefits, though possibly eligible for some perks. Client companies are able to take on more risk with such staffing flexibility and shed staff as market conditions merit, which may be ideal for uncertain business environments.

The status of temp workers as employees of the business will be scrutinized by the IRS if there is evidence that the same temps work for many months at the same client employer's company. In *Vizcaino v. Microsoft,*[24] the IRS successfully challenged the company's characterization of the workers as temps, and asked that these "permatemps" be reclassified as employees of Microsoft. The Ninth Circuit agreed, resulting in a $97 million settlement including payments to workers, penalties, and back employment taxes. Microsoft and others subsequently reevaluated their business practices and created new guidelines and hiring practices for temp workers.

Unpaid Interns

Another classification of worker common to start ups, and well-known to students, is the unpaid intern. Dubbed "full-time nonemployees" by Laurie Pike of Entreprenuer.com, this practice, too, has come under the scrutiny of regulators. While nonprofits and government employers may agree with workers for a long-term full-time unpaid internship placement, private employers do not enjoy this same benefit. While such employment arrangements can be mutually advantageous to companies with lean budgets and workers with little experience, there is the potential for exploiting workers and relying on this labor to sustain a business model over the long term. Sacrificing pay for experience has become an extremely common, almost well-settled route to professional salaried jobs, so much so that the Department of Labor addressed this practice in April 2010.

The federal Department of Labor's Wage and Hour Division issued Fact Sheet 71, *Internship Programs Under The Fair Labor Standards Act* (which is featured in Appendix 11) listing six criteria for determining "whether interns must be paid the minimum wage and overtime . . . for the services that they provide to 'for-profit' private sector employers" in that to qualify as an internship (rather than as unpaid work for which wages are owed) employers must demonstrate that the internship:

- includes training;
- benefits the intern;

---

24. 290 F.3d 1043 (9th Cir.), cert. denied sub nom., Vizcaino v. Waite, 2002 U.S. LEXIS 8338 (Nov. 11, 2002).

- does not displace regular employees and is closely supervised by existing staff;
- the employer does not derive immediate advantage from intern's contributions and employer operations may actually be impeded;
- the intern is not entitled to a job after the internship ends; and
- both parties understand the intern is not entitled to wages.

In the following case, unpaid interns claimed they did the work of employees and the court applied the Department of Labor's six criteria. Do you agree with the result?

Glatt v. Fox Searchlight Pictures, Inc.,
293 F.R.D. 516 (S.D.N.Y. 2013)

Facts Eric Glatt and Alexander Footman were unpaid interns who worked on production of the film *Black Swan* in New York. After production ended, Glatt took a second unpaid internship relating to post-production of the film. Fox Entertainment Group (FEG) is the parent corporation of approximately 800 subsidiaries including Fox Searchlight Pictures (FSP). FSP produces and distributes feature films, but does not produce the films itself, it enters into production agreements with corporations created for the sole purpose of producing particular films.

FSP entered into a production agreement with Lake of Tears, Inc. (LOT) a company created by director Darren Aronofsky and producer Scott Franklin for the sole purpose of producing Black Swan. The production agreement was typical for the industry, it gave FSP the power to hire and fire production personnel, set budgets, and monitor the progress of films.

LOT hired Glatt and Footman, and both were based in LOT offices and both worked exclusively on *Black Swan*. Among Glatt's duties were obtaining documents from personnel files, picking up paychecks for co-workers, tracking and reconciling purchase orders and invoices, writing cover letters, making copies, and running errands. Footman's internship duties were similar, including assembling office furniture, arranging travel plans, taking out the trash, taking lunch orders, answering phones, and making deliveries.

Both Glatt and Footman claim that FSP and FEG violated federal law by classifying them as unpaid interns instead of paid employees. Both sides filed motions for summary judgment on the issue of whether FSP was the "employer" of Glatt and Footman.

Opinion The Fair Labor Standards Act (FLSA) defines "employ" as "to suffer or permit to work." The law also allows for joint employers and "all joint employers are responsible, both individually and jointly, with all applicable provisions of the [FLSA]." This is a broad definition that might cover some parties who would not qualify as an employer under stricter agency law. Whether an employer-employee relationship exists should be based on economic reality rather than technical concepts.

In this case there are two questions that must be answered: first, is FSG a joint employer with LOT; and if so, was FSG an employer of all production interns?

For FLSA joint employer analysis control is key, and courts in New York use two tests to determine control: the formal control test and the functional control test. Neither test is a set of rigid rules and may have overlapping factors, but when used together the analysis provides the broad evaluation of "employer" required by the FLSA.

FORMAL CONTROL

There are four factors of a formal control evaluation: whether the alleged employer 1) had the power to hire and fire the employees, 2) supervised and controlled work schedules or conditions of employment, 3) determined the rate and method of pay, and 4) maintained employment records. Although LOT hired Glatt and Footman, we find that FSG is a joint employer with LOT.

Here, the *Black Swan* production agreement required FSP's approval to hire key production staff including department heads where Glatt and Footman interned, and FSG's power to fire production staff was unbridled as FSG reserved the right "in its sole reasonable discretion" to require LOT to fire any person working on *Black Swan*. Although FSG argued that it could only fire employees if certain conditions were met, it did have the right to require LOT to fire any worker based on FSG's sole reasonable discretion. In any event, control may be restricted or only exercised occasionally; however, that does not diminish the significance of its existence.

The second factor is supervision and control of work schedules or working conditions. Status as a joint employer does not require constant monitoring, it is enough that an employer is apprised of operations by receiving periodic reports from employees.

Here, FSG closely supervised work on *Black Swan*: it sent 'crew lists' with contact information for all staff, including interns; required production to send daily "call sheets" listing scenes to be filmed the next day, "wrap reports" listing scenes actually filmed, the hours worked by production employees and scenes scheduled to be filmed the next day; morning and evening calls to the Executive Vice President of production informing her of the time production began and wrapped each day; and weekly cost and expense reports.

FSG set the overall budget for *Black Swan* and set the allocations for each line item, and Glatt and Footman argue that because of this, FSG set the wages for all production workers. We agree. Even though LOT hired the men, LOT needed FSG's permission to have an unpaid intern who was not receiving college credit. Moreover, FSG withheld employee pay until they signed FSG-approved employment agreements and was involved in the method of pay.

Lastly, FSG required employment records such as confidentiality agreements and employment agreements. The fact that neither Glatt nor Footman actually entered into one of these agreements with FSG does not defeat this element; FSG exercised control over the supervisory employees of both men through such employment agreements.

FUNCTIONAL CONTROL TEST

This test has six factors: 1) whether FSG's premises and equipment were used in Glatt and Footman's work; 2) whether LOT could move from one employer to another; 3) extent to which Glatt and Footman performed discrete jobs that were integral to FSG's production; 4) whether responsibility could pass from one subcontractor to another; 5) the degree to which FSG supervised the men's work; and 6) whether the interns worked exclusively or predominantly for FSG.

The analysis using this test is less clear; however, four factors clearly weigh in favor of joint employer status. It is true that Glatt and Footman's internships were based at the LOT offices not FSG offices; however, production of *Black Swan* could not move from one studio to another because the production agreement between LOT and FSG prohibited LOT from taking *Black Swan* elsewhere. The economic reality in the film industry is a film is produced by a single-purpose entity whose operations cease after the film is made. But, Glatt and Footman did not work as part of an integrated, discrete production unit comparable to a production line as required by element three. For the fourth element, responsibility could pass from one subcontractor to another because the crew of *Black Swan* was tied to FSG, not to LOT. FSG in its "sole reasonable discretion" had the power to replace key production personnel without a material change to those underneath them. So, if FSG fired one person, another would be hired to take their place without much disruption or change. This is especially true because LOT would dissolve once production wrapped and the movie was delivered to FSG.

Looking at the fifth element and the degree to which FSG supervised Glatt and Footman's work, supervision weighs in favor of joint employment only if it demonstrates effective control of the terms and conditions of their employment. Here, FSG closely monitored work on *Black Swan* production and exercised effective control. Lastly, Glatt and Footman worked exclusively on *Black Swan*, which weighs in favor of finding joint employment. FSG claims that there is no evidence the men were ever controlled by FSG, but this argument ignores the relevance of the totality of the circumstances.

The second question we must now answer is whether FSG was the employer of Glatt and Footman. Glatt and Footman claim that they were employees of FSG and not merely trainees and thus entitled to wages for their work, and the Court agrees. We look to the six factors established by the Department of Labor Wage and Hour Division to guide us. Using those standards it is clear that neither man received formal training or education during their internship, and neither acquired new skills aside from those specific to *Black Swan's* back office such as how to use the coffee pot and photocopier. It is not enough that the men "learned what the function of a production office was through experience" because that they learned simply by being there, just as their paid co-workers did. Undoubtedly, both men received some benefit from their internship such as a resume listing and contacts, but again those benefits were incidental to working in that office like any other employee and not the result of their internship specifically. FSG, however, did receive the benefits of Glatt and Footman's unpaid work which otherwise would have required paid employees. Glatt's supervisor stated that "if Mr. Glatt had not performed this work, another member of my staff would have been required to work longer hours to perform it, or we would have needed a paid production assistant or another intern to do it." Footman performed similar chores, had he not a paid employee would have been needed. Menial as it was, their work was essential and FSG received an immediate advantage.

Lastly, there is no evidence that either man was entitled to a job at the end of their internships and both understood that they would not be paid. But these factors add little because the FLSA does not allow employees to waive their right to be paid.

Considering the totality of the circumstances, Glatt and Footman were improperly classified as unpaid interns and are "employees" covered by the FLSA.

Case Questions

1. What are the benefits for both the intern and the employer of an unpaid internship?
2. What do you think the long-term impact of this case might be on the status of unpaid internships? What about if Glatt and Footman had lost?
3. *Ethical Considerations*: Is it fair for a business not to pay a person if that person willingly sought out and accepted an unpaid internship? Is the bargaining power even?
4. *Ethical Considerations*: It seems the court evaluated three different perspectives in making its decision: the short-term view, the industry standard, and the long-term view. What facts support each, and which view did the court determine was the most important?

The question of what will trigger a wage and hour claim is difficult to predict, and businesses are often left wondering what work they may ask interns to do on occasion, such as coffee and lunch runs, but it is clear that there must be a formalized structure to the unpaid internship experience.

Foreign Workers of Off-Shore Businesses, Partnering with your Supply Chain

The capital markets have become highly efficient, making possible a global economy, and with more countries' markets opened, the Internet has brought even more efficiencies to global business. Companies, under intense pressure to become more productive and to lower costs are leveraging these capabilities through outsourcing. And as the work itself is in digital format and mostly intangible and service oriented, such as software programming, drafting legal documents, reading medical and diagnostic results, the work is easily disaggregated. Companies can accomplish this by entering into supply chain agreements and joint ventures with foreign partners.

Outsourcing

Outsourcing involves the process of transferring work to a third-party subcontractor. It is a signature feature of capitalism with its emphasis on division of labor and productivity to optimize shareholder wealth. Outsourcing intensified with the introduction of modern telecommunications networks, the digitization of content, and broadband Internet connections, all of which create an optimal platform to engage in business transactions with different contract partners.

Offshoring

Offshoring is a subset of outsourcing and describes the process of locating some function or division of a business in a different country. As an example, consider IBM. Its employment peaked in 1985 when it employed over 400,000 workers. By 1992 it suffered losses in the billions, and by 1994, its workforce shrunk to about 200,000. IBM focused on what it thought was a core strength: business consulting. Its employee numbers grew during this period, with at least half working as IT professionals. In 2009, IBM announced that it would lay off thousands of its U.S. employees and offer them jobs in new offshored locations in India, Nigeria, Russia, Argentina, Brazil, China, Czech Republic, Hungary, Mexico, Poland, Romania, Slovakia, Slovenia, South Africa, Turkey, or the United Arab Emirates. IBM workers who chose to relocate had their salaries reassessed too and worked on a different wage scale based on local wages and cost of living.

Working with foreign contract partners is a further variation in which entire operations are outsourced to separate companies; workers (typically off-shore in another country) are not officially employed by U.S. companies, and there is no direct responsibility to comply with U.S. regulation. Moreover, the regulatory environment in the contract partner's country may be permissive or lacking in enforcement. Important ethical questions are raised with this relationship, including: where does responsibility by the company start and end for these workers? For the environmental impacts of the work performed? For example, most technology is manufactured in China by Hon Hai Precision Industries (under the Foxconn brand), contract manufacturer for Apple, HP, and many other companies. Hon Hai was the subject of tragic reports that during just the first half of 2010, ten workers leaped off company roofs—all apparently suicides. The tech manufacturing industry is plagued with similar reports, including a Microsoft supplier said to force teens to work in unbearable conditions.[25]

---

25. For two different perspectives on global supply issues, see http://www.ted.com/talks/auret_van_heerden_making_global_labor_fair?language=en and https://www.ted.com/talks/leslie_t_chang_the_voices_of_china_s_workers?language=en.

Employer/Employee

Employees in the U.S. generally are **at-will**. An at-will employee can be fired at any time, for any reason, unless that reason is illegal or violates public policy. For example, an at-will employee cannot be fired for exercising their legal right to take Family and Medical Leave Act leave, or for complaining about illegal activity.

In an important distinction with the EU nations, the U.S. follows more closely a free-market system for labor that is regulated minimally, for wages, hours, health, and safety. Comparatively few constraints are placed on employers. In the EU, countries embrace a social charter and more centralized government planning, with employment and wages guaranteed to workers, who are considered social and economic partners with their companies. In the U.S., it is easy to hire and fire based on need and market conditions, not so in the EU.

Employees are governed by principal-agency law whereby each party has rights and owes duties to the other party. **Fiduciary duties** are implied in the employment relationship. For example, employers as *principals* hire employees, the *agents*, to operate under their control and on their behalf. Employers are obligated to disclose all relevant information to employees so that they can perform their tasks and are also obligated to pay a reasonable wage for all services. Employees are obligated to act on behalf of the employer and put their needs second to those of their employer. Under the theory of **Respondeat Superior**, employers are liable for the negligence of employees operating within the scope of their employment. This means that if an employee of IBM driving from one IBM location to another for work purposes gets into a car accident, IBM will be liable to a third party for any damage they suffered as a result of the IBM employee's negligence.

Employees owe their employer a **duty of loyalty** to act solely on behalf of the employer, free from conflicts of interest such as self-dealing. For example, an employee violates her duty of loyalty when she secretly bids on a contract her employer is seeking to fill. Employees also owe a **duty of care** to act reasonably on the employer's behalf, in accordance with industry standards, free from negligence or recklessness. However, with employees less tethered to the physical office, it is increasingly difficult for employers to have a clear sense of their employees' conduct and its consequences.

Despite these duties, knowledge learned on-the-job or creations made for the employer present specific issues that can best be protected by going further than relying on an employees' duties of loyalty and due care. For example, **Invention Assignment Agreements (IAAs)** are meant to capture and assign to the company all inventions of the employee. The employee agrees to surrender all ownership rights in the invention and assign them to the company (the assignee) who then owns the invention regardless of whether the employee still works there. Thus if an employee departs or is fired, their ideas conceived during the term of employment belong to the company and not to the employee or their subsequent employer.

IAAs commonly cover all work pursued during the term of employment that relates to the company's current or anticipated areas of business research or development, while using the company's property (including physical and intellectual property), equipment, supplies—in essence any company resource. IAAs are governed by state law, and therefore parties should expect that there will be wide differences among jurisdictions on these agreements. Notably, California Labor Code Section 2870 provides that IAAs do not apply "to an invention that the employee developed entirely on his or her own time without using the employer's equipment, supplies, facilities, or trade secret information. . . ."

The following case illustrates a high-stakes competitive environment with departing employees, ideas, copyrights, trademarks, and an invention assignment agreement that may, or may not, be applicable.

Mattel, Inc. v. MGA Entertainment, Inc.
2009 U.S. App. LEXIS 29187 (9th Cir. July 22, 2010)

Facts Mattel employee Carter Bryant worked in the "Barbie Collectibles" department where he designed fashion and hairstyles for the dolls. In August 2000, while still employed by Mattel, Bryant pitched his idea for the Bratz line of dolls to MGA, one of Mattel's competitors. Bryant received a callback from MGA's CEO, and for that meeting Bryant brought preliminary sketches as well as a crude dummy constructed out of a doll head from a Mattel bin, a Barbie body, and Ken boots. Bryant signed a consulting agreement with MGA dated Sept. 18, 2000. He resigned from Mattel and gave Mattel two weeks' notice on October 4th, and continued working there until October 19th. During this period he was also working with MGA to develop Bratz, even creating a preliminary sculpt (a mannequin-like plastic doll body without skin coloring, face paint, hair or clothing).

MGA kept Bryant's involvement with the Bratz project secret, but Mattel eventually found out. This led to a number of lawsuits. Proceedings were split into two phases: Phase 1 dealt with the claims relating to the ownership of Bratz; Phase 2 is pending and will deal with the remaining claims. This is an appeal from the equitable orders entered at the conclusion of Phase 1. During Phase 1, Mattel argued that Bryant violated his employment agreement by going to MGA with his Bratz idea instead of disclosing and assigning it to Mattel. Mattel claimed it was the rightful owner of the sketches and sculpt, and therefore the subsequent Bratz dolls infringed on those rights. Mattel won virtually every point. The jury awarded Mattel $10 million along with a constructive trust over all trademarks and copyrights, and prohibited MGA from marketing any Bratz-branded products.

Judicial Opinion. Chief Judge Kozinski

I. WHO OWNS BRATZ?

Barbie was the unrivaled queen of the fashion-doll market throughout the latter half of the 20th Century. But 2001 saw the introduction of Bratz, "The Girls With a

Passion for Fashion!" This spunk struck a chord, and Bratz became an overnight success. Mattel, didn't relish the competition, and it was particularly unhappy when it learned that the man behind Bratz was its own former employee, Carter Bryant.

A constructive trust would be appropriate only if Bryant assigned his ideas for Bratz to Mattel in the first place. Whether he did turns on the interpretation of Bryant's 1999 employment agreement, which provides: "I agree to communicate to the Company . . . all inventions conceived or reduced to practice by me . . . at any time during my employment by the Company. I hereby assign to the Company . . . all my right, title and interest in such inventions, and all my right, title and interest in any patents, copyrights, patent applications or copyright applications based thereon."

The contract specifies that the term "invention" includes, but is not limited to all discoveries, improvements, processes, developments, designs, know-how, data computer programs and formulae. The district court held that the agreement assigned Bryant's *ideas* to Mattel, even though ideas are not specifically listed in the contract.

Mattel points out that the list of examples of what constitutes an invention is illustrative rather than exclusive. Ideas, however, are markedly different from most of the listed examples. Designs, processes, computer programs, etc. are concrete, unlike ideas, which are ephemeral and often reflect bursts of inspiration that exist only in the mind. On the other hand, the agreement also lists less tangible inventions such know-how and discoveries. We conclude that the agreement could be interpreted to cover ideas, but the text doesn't compel that reading. Plus during litigation, the parties introduced other contracts, one for example Mattel drafted for employees in which they expressly assigned their ideas as well as their inventions which tends to show that the term inventions alone doesn't include ideas. The district court thus erred in holding that the agreement clearly covered ideas.

Mattel also claimed ownership of Bryant's preliminary Bratz drawings and sculpt under Bryant's employment agreement, and that the MGA dolls infringed its copyrights in those works. The drawings and sculpt clearly were inventions as that term is defined in Bryant's employment agreement with Mattel. However, MGA argued that the employment agreement didn't assign the items because Bryant created them outside the scope of his employment at Mattel, on his own time. The district court held that the agreement assigned inventions even if they were not made during working hours, so long as they were created during the time period Bryant was employed by Mattel. The jury was not asked to find whether Bryant made the drawings and sculpt during Mattel work hours, and it's unclear whether the record contained any evidence on this point.

The phrase "at any time during my employment" is ambiguous. It could easily refer to the entire calendar period he worked for Mattel, including nights and weekends. But it can also be read more narrowly to encompass only those inventions created during work hours, possibly including lunch and coffee breaks. Extrinsic evidence doesn't resolve the ambiguity. For example, an employee testified that it was "common knowledge that a lot of people were moonlighting and doing other work," which wasn't a problem so long as it was done on their own time. However, another employee testified, "Everything I did for Mattel belonged to Mattel. Actually, everything I did while I was working for Mattel belonged to Mattel." The issue should have been submitted to the jury, which could then have been instructed to determine (1) whether Bryant's agreement assigned works created outside the scope of his employment at Mattel, and (2) whether Bryant's creation of the Bratz sketches and sculpt was outside the scope of his employment.

II. CONSTRUCTIVE TRUST

Bryant's employment agreement may not have assigned his ideas for the Bratz name to Mattel at all, and the district court erred by holding that it did so unambiguously. Even if Bryant did assign his ideas, the district court abused its discretion in transferring the entire Bratz trademark portfolio to Mattel. We therefore vacate the constructive trust and injunction. The district court may impose a narrower constructive trust on remand only if there's a proper determination that Mattel owns Bryant's ideas.

The district court also erred in holding, at summary judgment, that the employment agreement assigned works created outside the scope of Bryant's employment. We therefore vacate the copyright injunction. On remand, Mattel will have to convince a jury that the agreement assigned Bryant's preliminary sketches and sculpt, either because the agreement assigns works made outside the scope of employment or because these works weren't made outside of Bryant's employment.

America thrives on competition; Barbie, the all-American girl, will too.

Case Questions

1. As a result of this case, identify the most important changes Mattel should make to its employee agreements.
2. As a result of this case, identify how the state law could be amended in order to add clarity to the definition of what is work time.
3. *Ethical Considerations:* What did Carter do while he was working for Mattel that revealed his intentions in terms of future employment with MGA? Do these actions indicate loyalty to Mattel?
4. *Ethical Considerations:* In what way(s) does this case highlight the difference between what is legal and what is ethical?

Nondisclosure Agreements (NDAs) are related to IAAs in that employers use these agreements to retain control over the disclosure of any proprietary or sensitive business information that employees use, learn about, or even helped develop during the employment term. NDAs cover two main points. First, they create a confidential relationship between the parties and outline the scope of materials and information covered, which can be broader than trade secrets

---

Twitter and IPAs

Assignment agreements between engineers, designers, and their company are standard procedure in the tech industry. The agreements give the company irrevocable ownership of any creation, including patents filed related to the employee's creation. Typically the engineer or designer sells, assigns, and transfers all of their title and interest in the invention to the company and the company can use the invention or patent in any way they see fit, including producing the invention, selling the rights, or doing nothing at all with it. Using a patent could include any number of things, such as using patents offensively to restrict the innovation and activities of competitors, or simply to extract licensing fees.

Twitter has developed a new type of agreement: the Innovator's Patent Agreement (IPA). In an IPA, the creators would retain partial control of the patent thereby fostering innovation; the inventor assigns the patent to the company but the company makes important promises in return. For example, under an IPA the company cannot start a patent war or try to shut out a competitor. Also, patents can only be used as intended by the original inventors even if the IPA is sold to someone else. If the company or a future owner of the IPA were to breach a clause in the IPA, the inventors can hold them accountable by granting a license to others. For example, if the company sells the patent to someone who decides to sue others offensively, in violation of the IPA, the inventor could license the invention to the person being sued, thereby protecting that person from liability.[26]

---

and specifies that the information is confidential. Second, the length of the agreement starts at the term of employment and may remain in effect beyond the term of employment.

The scope of NDAs is subject to agreement. Employers favor broadly worded agreements, while employees favor agreements that are specific and limited in their terms and term length. Again, there is tension between employers' need for secrecy of strategic business information in order to maintain a competitive advantage, and employees who may wish to change jobs. Generally, an employee upon termination may carry away and use the general skills, technical know-how, or knowledge acquired during the course of employment. This promotes the public interest in employment and freedom to practice one's profession, as well as in mitigating monopoly tendencies of employers.

Some jurisdictions construe NDAs quite broadly and will grant injunctions against departing employees when there is a risk of "inevitable disclosure" of trade secret or other sensitive business information. The most widely acknowledged precedent for this doctrine is *PepsiCo., Inc. v. Redmond,*[27] in which the court granted an injunction enjoining a departing employee's disclosure of trade secrets or even work in beverage pricing, sales, marketing, and distribution. This ruling was based on inference, without proof of the employee's actual or threatened use of this information. This doctrine has been repudiated in California, but is still followed in a number of other jurisdictions.

---

26. Brian Lee, "Twitter's Surprising Solution to the Patent Problem: Let *Employees* Control Them," Wired.com 2/21/13 http://www.wired.com/2013/02/twitters-ingenious-solution-to-the-patent-problem-let-inventors-control-the-patents/.
27. 54 F.3d 1262 (7th Cir. 1995).

In contrast, recall *IBM v. Visentin,* where the court stated that just because Mr. Visentin had access to confidential information it did not mean that disclosure was inevitable. IBM needed to show, and the court had to find, that there was an actual misappropriation of a trade secret or that because of the similarities between his old job at IBM and his new job at HP he would inevitably disclose the information. Because IBM could show neither, Visentin was free to work at HP despite the NCA and the NDA.

States favor the enforceability of NDAs, provided the scope of covered information is written into the agreement and it is reasonable, based upon the employees' job status and work duties. There are limits, such as when the information alleged to be covered is otherwise publicly available, when the employee had access to the information prior to the term of employment, or as the court noted in *Visentin*, the old job and the new job are not similar and the information in possession of the departing employee is not valuable to the old employer.

Forfeiture Agreements

Forfeiture agreements are a complementary, and perhaps more useful strategy than NCAs for managing key employee attrition. Under these clauses, nonsalary compensation (such as bonuses, stock, stock options, and so forth) paid out during a specified period that will be forfeited upon an employee's departure to any company in the same industry. Courts generally will not uphold agreements that require forfeiture of salary as this is considered too harsh a penalty. Forfeiture clauses are widely recognized as valid and therefore hold more promise for enforceability than NCAs.

For example, Anne Houghton worked for Viad Corporation as a Senior Vice President of Design and Creative, primarily in Exhibit Services. In this role, Houghton was privy to internal strategic planning and knew Viad's costs for providing services. Because of her senior position, Houghton was eligible to participate in a voluntary Incentive Plan. Under the Plan, participants couldn't work or provide services for competitors for two years after leaving Viad. If they did, they would forfeit all bonuses paid under the plan during the last twelve months of employment. In 2007, Houghton received a $102,000 bonus under the Plan and in 2008 she resigned from Viad to take a similar job for a direct competitor. Viad demanded repayment of the $102,000 payout and when Houghton refused Viad sued. The court held that Houghton had to pay Viad back because although her new job was not identical to her job at Viad it was "concerned with" the services he provided at Viad. Forfeiture in this case did not stifle job mobility because Houghton could still work for her new employer.

Nonsolicitation Agreements (NSAs)

In this agreement, employees agree that during the term of employment and for a designated time thereafter, they will not solicit coworkers, customers, prospective customers, or company vendors when they leave the company for another employer. As an employment relationship ends, departing employees have the right to let these groups know about the departure, but they may not solicit business for any new venture they may be undertaking. To the extent that the customer or coworker is also a personal friend of the departing employee, courts are less inclined to find an actionable claim due to the intertwined nature of the parties' relationship. Issues inevitably arise in litigation concerning the meaning of "solicitation" in instances when a customer or a coworker follows the departing employee to a new venture.

What if your old customers contact you first? Is that solicitation? In Massachusetts, the First Circuit Appellate Court answered this by ruling in favor of Corporate Technologies' (CT) nonsolicitation agreement. In this case, a former sales employee went to work for a competitor of CT, and the new employer sent an email blast to the new hire's former CT customers announcing the sales employee's new position. In response to the email, several CT customers contacted the new company and the employee began working with them. In upholding the validity of the nonsolicitation agreement, the court said that it was irrelevant that the first contact came from the customer and not the former employee: "[B]ecause initial contact can easily be manipulated—say, by a targeted announcement that piques customers' curiosity—a per se rule would deprive the employer of its bargained-for protection."[28]

Employee Separation Agreements

Separation agreements are necessary to manage the postemployment term. Employee separation agreements are usually signed during the exit interview when employees return company property and receive relevant departure information on unemployment insurance, pension plans, retirement plans, health, or other benefits programs. These agreements cover severance pay if any, along with a host of other clauses, including: a pledge of future cooperation, nondisparagement of the company, confidentiality of company information, noncompetition with the company, and most critically, a release from any present or future claims against the company.

Summary

Employment in the Internet and technology industries is dynamic: there is intrigue as employees leave for start ups. It is not surprising therefore that there is high company turnover, which fuels demand for employee mobility. Courts and legislatures are called upon to calibrate the relative rights of employers and employees. Employment agreements for the most part attempt to control the employment relationship, and most clauses inure to the employers' favor, so to the extent agreements are upheld, employees' mobility and ability to leverage one's skills are limited. Innovation likely suffers. However, to the extent such

---

28. *Corporate Technologies, Inc. v. Harnett*, 731 F.3d 6, 9 1st Cir. (2013).

agreements are invalidated, companies incur tremendous losses and wages can get out of control. Here, innovation likely flourishes. Employers balance rights and duties while also protecting their information in the event that the employees depart. Employment agreements are meant to provide guidelines, benchmarks, and rules for this process.

Key Terms

visitor's confidentiality and nondisclosure agreement An agreement by which site visitors promise, in exchange for being admitted to the workplace, to not disclose any information about the company, its employees, or their impressions thereof for a defined period of time.

noncompete agreement A contract between employee and employer to prevent employees, upon switching jobs, from using what they have learned to the advantage of a competitor.

rule of reason test A test used to determine the validity of the terms of a noncompete agreement. Factors include whether the restraint is designed to protect a legitimate interest of the employer, and whether the restraint is reasonable as to time, place, and scope.

Injunction A court order that prohibits a person from engaging in certain conduct, or that compels them to perform a certain act.

E-B (1-5) visa Permanent worker visa preference, commonly called the *Green Card*, reserved for workers with "extraordinary ability" and ten years' experience, or those who are investors with at least $1 million of capital to invest in the United States.

H1-B visa Temporary work permits for high-skilled workers in specialty occupations.

independent contractor agreement An agreement between employer and worker declaring that both parties understand the relationship to be that of independent contractor.

negligent hiring Legal claim made by an injured party against an employer alleging the employer knew or should have known about the independent contractor's background which, if known, indicates a dangerous or untrustworthy character.

negligent supervision Failure to reasonably supervise.

work for hire A work prepared by an employee within the scope of their employment, but the employer/client is considered the author or creator for copyright purposes.

shop rights A right permitting employers to claim merely a nonexclusive license with limited rights to use the work, all without ultimate ownership rights.

specially commissioned work Work undertaken by an independent contractor under a written agreement between the parties stating that the work commissioned is a work for hire.

temporary workers Contingent workers who typically have specialty credentials and are not employed by the company, but rather by a staffing agency.

unpaid internships An arrangement under which individuals work for a company or organization for free to gain experience.

outsourcing The practice of transferring work to a third-party subcontractor.

offshoring The process of locating some function or division of a business in a different country.

at-will employee An employee who can be fired at any time, for any reason, unless that reason is illegal or violates public policy.

fiduciary duty The obligation of an agent requiring that the needs of the principal be put ahead of those of the agent. Employers are obligated to disclose all relevant information to employees so that they can perform their tasks and are also obligated to pay a reasonable wage for all services. Employees are obligated to act on behalf of the employer and put their needs second to those of their employer.

Respondeat Superior A legal theory whereby employers are liable for the negligence of employees operating within the scope of their employment.

duty of loyalty A duty to act solely on behalf of the employer, free from conflicts of interest such as self-dealing.

duty of care A duty to act reasonably on the employer's behalf, in accordance with industry standards, free from negligence or recklessness.

invention assignment agreement (IAA) An agreement to capture and assign to the company all inventions of the employee. The employee agrees to surrender all ownership rights in the invention and assign them to the company (the assignee) who then owns the invention regardless of whether the employee still works there.

nondisclosure agreement (NDA) An agreement used by employers to retain control over the disclosure of any proprietary or sensitive business information that employees use, learn about, or even helped develop during the employment term.

forfeiture agreement Nonsalary compensation (such as bonuses, stock, stock options, and so forth) paid out during a specified period that will be forfeited upon an employee's departure to any company in the same industry.

nonsolicitation agreement An agreement whereby employees agree that during the term of employment and for a designated time thereafter, they will not solicit coworkers, customers, prospective customers, or company vendors when they leave the company for another employer.

employee separation agreement An agreement covering severance pay if any, along with a host of other clauses, including: a pledge of future cooperation, nondisparagement of the company, confidentiality of company information, noncompetition with the company, and most critically, a release from any present or future claims against the company.

Manager's Checklist

1. Human Resources should carefully review present agreements to which potential hires are bound and understand any constraints on hiring that individual.

2. Managers should make an effort to understand each state's laws with respect to employment agreements and plan accordingly.

3. To the extent managers can control the terms of employment agreements, they will be better able to manage their employee turnover.

4. Managers should be prepared to follow up on departing employees as a way to ensure no company information is being disclosed to the new employer.

5. Managers should work closely with the information technology group to identify what each employee needs access to and limit access accordingly.

Questions and Case Problems

1. CEO and officer compensation has been reported, studied, and criticized. In this era of multimillion-dollar compensation packages, agreed to by compliant (or is it complacent?) boards at the expense of shareholder return and share value, it can be difficult to see the value to shareholders by offering outsized compensation packages. For example, in 2009, Oracle CEO Lawrence Ellison's taxable earnings were: $1 million in salary; $3.5 million as a bonus; $1.5 million in perks; and $78 million in exercised stock options. Oracle's stock price rose from $14.72 in December, 2008 to close 2009 at $21.51. Using these figures, can you make a guess whether Ellison's pay is a good value for shareholders?

2. According to the 2013 AFL-CIO Executive Pay Watch database, U.S. CEOs of 350 companies made almost 331 times that of the average U.S. worker. In Switzerland, executives earned about 148 times that of the average Swiss worker, Germany 147 times, France 104 times, and the UK 84 times that of the average UK worker. There has been movement in both the U.S. and the EU to pass laws requiring companies to disclose the pay ratio between executives and average worker salary, but thus far there is no requirement. Why would the public want this information? Why would businesses not want to disclose this information? Can you justify the disparity?

3. Dana Owens signed an NCA when she began work at King Capital. She later resigned from King Capital with the intention to go work for Goldman Sachs. Goldman told Owens they would hire her only if she secured a release from the King NCA. After she was unable to (and out of the Goldman job), she sued King. *What result can be expected?*

4. Two Merrill Lynch financial advisors, who had signed employment agreements, resigned in order to go to work for Ameriprise Financial. They had given their new employer contact information for their old clients, and Ameriprise sent them announcements that these brokers now worked for Ameriprise. Merrill Lynch immediately filed a lawsuit and requested an injunction based on allegations that they took proprietary business information including client lists, and solicited Merrill Lynch clients. The court considered the four-factor test for issuing an injunction (irreparable harm to plaintiffs; balance of harms; the public interest; likelihood that plaintiff will succeed on the merits of the case).[29] *What result can be expected?*

5. Immunomedics was alerted that there was some negative buzz about the company in a chat room. The poster used a pseudonym, and therefore the company was unable to identify the poster for lawsuit purposes. The only information the company could ascertain was the poster's ISP. So the company decided to subpoena the ISP for identity information of the poster in order to file suit against the poster.[30] *How should courts handle these cases, where the company's complaints may, or may not rise to the level of an actionable legal claim?*

6. Defendant Jeff Smith worked for KKC Filtration, and then left that job to go work for another company. He had communicated information about KKC prior to leaving KKC. KKC filed suit, alleging that Smith signed an NDA and that he breached this agreement. (Just after the suit was filed, Smith drove 20 miles and threw his computer in a construction site dumpster in an effort to prevent KKC from discovering potentially damaging evidence.) Smith also defended these charges, asserting that while there might have been an NDA with his original compensation agreement, his agreement was revised over the years, and a new NDA was never attached to these revised copies. Smith argues therefore that he is not subject to any NDA. KKC countered that the original NDA was in force at all times, even after Smith left the company. *What result can be expected?*

---

29. Merrill Lynch, Pierce, Fenner & Smith, Inc. v. Baxter, 2009 U.S. Dist. LEXIS 31326 (D. Utah 2009).
30. Immunomedics, Inc. v. Doe, 342 N.J. Super. 160 (2001).

Additional Resources

Alliance for Open Competition. http://opencompe tition.wordpress.com/.

Information Technology Association of America. http://www.itaa.org/.

Tech Recruiting Clashes with Immigration Rules. http://www.nytimes.com/2009/04/12/business/12immig.html.

U.S. Citizenship and Immigration Services. Employer Information. http://www.uscis.gov/portal/site/uscis.

Wadhwa, Vivek, AnnaLee Saxenian, Richard B. Freeman, and Gary Gereffi. *America's Loss Is the World's Gain: America's New Immigrant Entrepreneurs, Part 4,* March 2, 2009. http://papers.ssrn.com/sol3/papers.cfm?abstract_id=1348616.

Social Media: Risk and Liability

Learning Outcomes

After you have read this chapter, you should be able to:

- Understand the prevalence of social media use by businesses.
- Discuss potential risks to intellectual property via social media.
- Identify risks with online reviews: are they speech or defamation? Do you have to reveal the personal information of those who post reviews?
- Understand social media space as the new "workspace" and the risks to employers and their confidential information.

Overview

In April 2014, an employee of U.S. Airlines responded to a customer complaint on Twitter by inadvertently attaching a pornographic image to the tweet. The airline quickly removed the tweet and issued an apology, but the image reached hundreds of thousands of U.S. Airline followers.[1] Brixx Pizza is a small restaurant in North Carolina. Ashley Johnson, a server at Brixx complained on her Facebook page about a couple that sat at one of her tables for three hours and only left a $5.00 tip, mentioning the restaurant by name and calling the customers cheap. Brixx fired Ms. Johnson for disparaging customers. While certainly embarrassing,

---

1. Laurel Friedel, "Social Media Poses Grave Danger to Companies' Confidential Information," Insidecounsel.com, May 8, 2014.

399

the true danger these examples highlight is the combination of the growing role social media plays in communication between businesses and customers and the ease of sharing information. No business is immune; large or small they all have vital assets that can be jeopardized in this new era of communication.

Almost three-quarters of all adults use social media sites.[2] Facebook recently passed 1.23 billion active monthly users,[3] Twitter has 284 million active monthly users,[4] Instagram boasts 150 million users,[5] LinkedIn 300 million users,[6] and YouTube reaches more U.S. adults than cable.[7] This in only the tip of the iceberg. The number of social media sites with active users ranges from 200 to 700, depending on what source you use and what you consider "social media." Despite its ubiquity, a full 25 percent of Facebook users do not bother with their privacy settings.[8] Businesses of all sizes have embraced social media as an effective way to communicate with customers. Among Fortune 500 companies, a whopping 97 percent have a presence on LinkedIn, 83 percent have corporate Twitter accounts, 80 percent are on Facebook, 67 percent have YouTube accounts, 51 percent are on Foursquare, and 36 percent are on Pinterest.[9] Small and medium-sized businesses overwhelmingly (81 percent) use social media, mostly for marketing purposes.

Twitter and Small Businesses

Most companies agree that engaging with customers on social media helps boost brands and may result in higher sales. This boost, however, is not necessarily apparent when using Twitter to reach customers. Twitter blogged that small and medium-sized businesses often ask the company for "proof that their efforts on Twitter can lead to real business results." As a result, Twitter joined with Market Probe International to conduct a study of 500 adults who follow small and medium-sized businesses on Twitter.[10] Here are the results:

- 60 percent have purchased something because of Twitter.
- 72 percent are more likely to buy something from a business they follow.
- 86 percent are more likely to visit a business if a friend recommends it.
- 85 percent feel more connected with a business after following it.[11]

2. PewResearch, Social Networking Fact Sheet.
3. Emil Protalinski, "Facebook passes 1.23 billion monthly active users," Thenextweb.com, January 29, 2014.
4. https://about.twitter.com/company.
5. Cooper Smith, "Here's Why Instagram's Demographics are so Attractive to Brands," BusinessInsider.com, August 17, 2014.
6. Cheryl Conner, "New Research: 2014 LinkedIn User Trends," Forbes.com, May 4, 2014.
7. Belle Beth Cooper, "10 Surprising Social Media Statistics that Will make You Rethink Your Social Media Strategy," Fast Company, November 13, 2013.
8. Id.
9. Nora Ganim Barnes and Ava Lescault, *The 2014 Fortune 500 and Social Media*, Charlton College of Business Center for Marketing Research, University of Massachusetts, Dartmouth.
10. Robin Madell, "10 Ways Twitter Can Help (or Hurt) Your Business," *U.S. News & World Report Money*, Sept. 3, 2014.
11. https://business.twitter.com/basics/grow-and-engage-your-follower-base.

The popularity and perceived anonymity of social media as a method of communication can pose specific risks for businesses. For example, in 2007 it became public that John Mackey, CEO of Whole Foods, used a fictional identity on a Yahoo message board for almost eight years to tout his company's performance and disparage competitors. Mackey's social media posts came to light during an FTC investigation into Whole Foods' merger with Wild Oats. While this may have been embarrassing for Mr. Mackey and Whole Foods, more is at stake for businesses: the Securities and Exchange Commission opened an informal inquiry into whether Mackey violated securities laws with his posts. Ultimately, the agency took no action against the CEO.[12]

Intellectual Property

For centuries land was the most valuable source of property, but as our economy has migrated to more service and idea-based commerce, **intellectual property** has become one of the most valuable assets for businesses. Patents, logos, business methods, customer/client lists, and databases are typically well-guarded intellectual property assets. We saw in Chapter 9 that many businesses require employees and contractors to enter into contracts to keep certain information confidential during the term of employment and sometimes even after the employment relationship has ended. But ensuring that confidential information or other intellectual property remains private can be tricky, even with contracts in place. What if a disgruntled employee purposely leaks private information as revenge against their employer? Microsoft alleges that that is what happened in 2013 when an internal investigation revealed that a former employee in Lebanon released confidential information to a blogger in France. Allegedly Alex Kibkalo was upset about a poor performance review he received in 2012 while working at Microsoft, and threatened to resign if the review was not amended. Instead, he shared trade secrets and other confidential information about Windows 8 RT and ARM devices as well as the Microsoft Activation Server Software Development Kit. Microsoft believed Kibkalo encouraged the blogger to share the kit online so others could crack protections on Microsoft products. Kibkalo is currently facing criminal charges in the U.S.[13]

In an effort to address innovations in emerging media and communications, Congress passed the **Electronic Communications Privacy Act (ECPA)** in 1986. The ECPA was created to extend the coverage of the federal Wiretap Act. The **Wiretap Act** covered communications that could be heard by the human ear and in-person communications, but did not account for the development of emails, blogs, and social media as a means of communication. The ECPA prohibits the intentional interception of emails and generally allows an employer to monitor emails sent and received on its servers. The **Stored Communications Act (SCA)**, which is part of the broader ECPA, prohibits "intentionally access[ing] without authorization a facility through which an electronic communication service is

12. Steven Taub, "Whole Foods 'Blogging' Probe Dropped by SEC," *CFO.com*, April 28, 2008.
13. Shannon Stapleton, "Ex-Microsoft Employee Charged with Leaking Trade Secrets to Blogger," Reuters, March 20, 2014.

provided . . . and thereby obtain[ing] . . . access to a wire or electronic communication while it is in electronic storage in such system."

To complicate matters, confidential information may be leaked in such a way that you do not know the source of the leak. Whether the SCA authorizes the release of information in order to learn the identity of anonymous leakers is currently an open question. In the following case, Apple tries to persuade the court to force the publishers of the websites where confidential information was published to reveal the posters. The court must balance the SCA and the Constitution with the rights of news gathering.

O'Grady v. The Superior Court of Santa Clara County
139 Cal. App. 4th 1423 (2006)

Facts Jason O'Grady owns and operates "O'Grady's PowerPage," an online news magazine devoted to news and information about Apple computers and compatible software and hardware. PowerPage has been published daily since 1995, and today publishes about 15 to 20 items per week with an average of 300,000 unique visits per month. PowerPage has nine editors and reporters. "Apple Insider," another online news magazine devoted to Apple computers, has been in operation since 1998 and publishes about 15 articles per week and in July 2004 received 438,000 unique visits. Apple Computer is a manufacturer of computer hardware and software.

Over several days in November 2004, PowerPage and Apple Insider published several articles about a new Apple product called the Asteroid (or Q97). Power-Page, under O'Grady's byline, stated that it had "gotten it's [sic] hands on this juicy little nugget about a new FireWire breakout box for GarageBand that Apple plans to announce at Mac World Expo SF 2005 in January." According to the article this new product would allow users of GarageBand to record analog audio sources like guitars and microphones. The article also included a drawing of the FireWire box and details of its physical features. Another article appeared a few days later on PowerPage, also under O'Grady's byline, and described more product details including target price, "target intro date . . . [and] target intro quantity," and a concept drawing. A third article by O'Grady ran on PowerPage the same day and described Asteroid's integration into GarageBand: "today we have some juice on new GarageBand functionality for extremely easy setup, recording and playback through Asteroid."

Apple Insider also ran similar articles during the same time period. One article authored by "Kasper Jade" said the device would "allow users to directly record audio using any Mac and Apple's GarageBand music studio application" and that "according to reputable sources, the company is on track to begin manufacturing the device overseas next month." This article also included a rendering of the device based "on Apple's prototype design" and noted that the device "code-named 'Q97' or 'Asteroid'" had been "under development" for "the better part of a year." Details about the history of the product including the name of Apple's subsidiary that participated in the design and the company with whom Apple had already contracted for manufacture were spelled out in the article. References were also made to "internal company estimates" about quarterly earnings from FireWire.

According to Apple, most of the information published on both sites appears to have originated from an electronic file presentation created by Apple and conspicuously marked "Apple Need-to-Know Confidential." There are striking similarities between the presentation and the articles, especially the images and drawing. Other parts of the file are paraphrased and in some cases copied verbatim, especially in the PowerPage articles. However, the PowerPage articles also include information not from the Apple files, including alternate drawings of FireWire.

Apple lawyers contacted O'Grady and referred to the PowerPage articles as "references to an unreleased Apple product, namely the Asteroid." Apple demanded that O'Grady remove all references to the product from PowerPage, as the information includes trade secrets published without Apple's authorization and demanded to know the sources of the information.

Apple then sued "Doe 1, an unknown individual and Does 2-25 unidentified persons or entities." As part of the suit, Apple served subpoenas on PowerPage and Apple Insider to produce information on the true identities of the defendants as Apple could not learn of them any other way, and on Nfox.com, the company that hosted the email account for PowerPage. Apple claimed that as part of its internal investigation it interviewed 29 employees who were known to have had access to the Asteroid presentation file. All 29 employees denied sharing the contents of the file with anyone outside of the group. Apple claims that although it did not question its employees under oath, it nevertheless did everything possible to determine the source of the leak because all of its employees were obligated to tell the truth or risk losing their job.

Both O'Grady and "Kasper Jade" objected to the subpoena claiming that their sources and unpublished information were protected under the reporter's shield in the California Constitution and the First Amendment to the U.S. Constitution, and O'Grady claimed the subpoena for Nfox.com violated the Stored Communications Act. The trial court denied O'Grady and "Kasper Jade's" motion for a protective order and stated that their constitutional claims were overstated because reporters and their sources do not have a license to violate criminal laws, and that the subpoena to Nfox.com could go forward because much of the information posted on PowerPage was marked by Apple as confidential, therefore they are relevant to Apple's claim. O'Grady and "Kasper Jade" filed this motion to set aside the trial court's ruling.

Judicial Opinion. Nfox.com

We first must look at the subpoena served on Nfox.com and determine whether the disclosures sought by that subpoena violate the Stored Communications Act (SCA). The purpose of the SCA is to lessen the disparities between protections given more traditional methods of communication and those accorded newer modes of communication. Mail and telephone services have long enjoyed protection in a variety of forms, and with the SCA Congress sought to not only shield private electronic communications from government intrusion, but also to encourage "innovative forms" of communication by granting them protection against unwanted disclosure to anyone. Otherwise, potential users might be deterred from using newer forms of communication out of fear of intrusion.

According to the SCA, a person providing an electronic communication service to the public "shall not knowingly divulge to any person or entity the contents of a communication while in electronic storage by that service." There are exceptions, for example, disclosures are authorized if they are incidental to the provision of the service or incidental to the protection of property of the service provider.

Apple claims that Nfox.com can disclose the emails on its servers pursuant to the subpoena because doing so is incidental to protecting its (Nfox.com's) rights and property. But, the most that can be said about Apple's property argument is that Nfox.com would incur *costs* in defending against an invalid subpoena, and if costs were enough to trigger this exception, the mere threat of litigation would necessitate disclosure and a subpoena would be unnecessary. Apple next claims that the "safe harbor" provision in the SCA allows Nfox.com to release the information. The **"safe harbor" provision** states that if a service provider relies in good faith on a court order the service provider has a complete defense to any action brought against it under the SCA. This argument fails because the "safe harbor" provision does not make compliance lawful; it just provides a defense if a service provider relies in good faith on an unlawful subpoena. This argument would make sense if Nfox.com had voluntarily complied with the subpoena and then been charged with a violation of the SCA, but that is not what happened here. The "safe harbor" does not compel disclosure.

Given the purpose of the SCA, it makes sense that Congress requires those that are seeking disclosure of the content of an email to ask the author of the email and not the service provider. Similarly, it doesn't make sense that someone seeking disclosure of the contents of an old-fashioned letter ask the letter carrier for the contents rather than the author of the letter. Imposing this requirement does not create any new burden on litigants; the denial of discovery here makes Apple no worse off than if an employee had printed the presentation file onto paper, placed it in an envelope and handed it to O'Grady and "Kasper Jade."

Turning to the subpoenas issued to O'Grady and "Kasper Jade" we must determine whether both are protected under California's **reporter's shield law**. The California Constitution states that a "publisher, editor, reporter . . . shall not be adjudged in contempt . . . for refusing to disclose the sources of any information procured while so connected or employed for publication in a newspaper, magazine or other periodical publication."

Apple claims that O'Grady and "Kasper Jade" are not entitled to this protection because they were not engaged in legitimate journalistic activities when they acquired the confidential information, only trade secret misappropriation. They merely took the confidential information, turned around and put it on PowerPage and Apple Insider with no added value. Without getting into the discussion of what constitutes "legitimate journalism," the shield law is designed to protect the gathering and dissemination of news, and that is what O'Grady and "Kasper Jade" did here. Even if neither added any editorial content, that is not a basis for denying protection. A reporter who uncovers newsworthy documents cannot be denied protection because the publication for which she works chose to publish copies of the actual documents rather than editorial summaries. Given the ease and speed with which information is shared today, editorial content may be on the decline. Digital communication and storage, especially when coupled with hyper-linking text, makes it possible to present readers with an unlimited amount of information in connection with a story or report. The only constraint is time—the publisher's and the reader's. The purpose of both PowerPage and Apple Insider was to disseminate information, and toward that end they gathered information by a variety of means including confidential sources. Thus they do not appear to differ in any material respect from a traditional reporter.

But, are PowerPage and Apple Insider "newspaper[s], magazine[s], or other periodical publication[s]" as enumerated in the shield law? O'Grady and "Kasper Jade" describe their sites as "magazines" and Apple does not offer any argument to the contrary. It is questionable whether the sites are "periodical publications" within the shield law, but the sites are much like printed publications: they consist of text on pages which the reader opens and reads at her own pace, then closes. The main distinction between this and traditional periodicals is the medium by which readers access the material. Moreover, the material on both PowerPage and Apple Insider is updated as it becomes available, not at regular intervals like traditional periodicals. But, both sites are recurring and ongoing much like a news publication as compared to a book. Given the intent of the shield law, we find these ambiguities must fall in favor of protection and O'Grady and "Kasper Jade" are protected from punishment for refusing to disclose the sources of the information.

O'Grady and "Kasper Jade" also claim that the U.S. Constitution protects them from divulging their sources. The essence of this protection is that a news gatherer cannot be compelled to disclose their sources without a showing of need sufficient to overcome the chilling effect disclosure would have on the free flow of ideas and information. We hold that there is no sufficient need here. First, O'Grady and "Kasper Jade" are not parties to the underlying action. This is pertinent because Apple has control over whom it sues, and if it had not included O'Grady and "Kasper Jade" as defendants in the underlying suit it cannot now demand discovery from them as if they had been defendants. Next, Apple did not exhaust all other means to identify the sources of the leaks. Although it did conduct an internal investigation, Apple did not question its employees under oath, which it could have done by asking permission to depose them. Apple claims it did every-thing it could because the employees would risk losing their job if they did not tell the truth; however, questioning under oath exposes a person to criminal liability, a far more persuasive incentive.

Accordingly, we direct the trial court to set aside its denial of O'Grady and "Kasper Jade's" protective order.

Case Questions

1. Why didn't Apple depose its employees in order to learn the source of the leak?
2. The court considered PowerPage a news gatherer and akin, but not identical, to a newspaper, even though in this instance they didn't include much editorial content to the posts in question. Do you think a broader look at the site was warranted? What if they typically do not contribute editorial content to their posts, should that matter?
3. *Ethical Considerations*: If editorial content in generally is on the decline, as the court notes, what might this decision mean for businesses in the era of thousands of social media sites and blogs? What might this mean for the sites that publish reviews? Is there an incentive for them to be honest?

Compare the result in *O'Grady* to a later case, *Juror Number One*, involving Facebook. In *Juror Number One*, a juror was accused of misconduct during a criminal trial because he posted to his Facebook page comments about evidence as it was being presented during the trial. One of the defendants in the trial, who was convicted, filed a subpoena to Facebook to produce all of Juror Number One's posts. Facebook claimed such disclosure would violate the SCA, and directed the defendant to request the information from Juror Number One, as he owns and has access to his own Facebook account. Juror Number One objected and the court stated that the SCA only applies to providers of electronic communication services, such as Facebook, not to Juror Number One the owner of the Facebook account. According to the court, Juror Number One, like any party in litigation, has an obligation to disclose information pursuant to the rules of civil procedure and a court can compel parties to litigation to make such disclosures. If the court can compel Juror Number One to disclose his Facebook posts, it can compel Juror Number One to consent to Facebook disclosing his posts as well.[14]

Ensuring confidential information remains confidential in the era of social networking can be difficult. In a 2010 case, *Sasqua Group v. Courtney*, Sasqua Group accused Courtney, a former employee, of stealing confidential customer lists when she left to start her own competing business. Courtney claimed, and the court agreed, that the customer lists were not confidential because Sasqua obtained the information in the lists from LinkedIn and other social media sites, thus the information was publicly available. The ubiquity of social media as a means of communication can defeat the classification of confidential information as actually confidential, and therefore any business value gained from that information may be non-existent or lost.

Defamation

Three decades ago, almost 95 percent of the average corporation's value was tangible assets. Today as much as 75 percent of that value consists of intangible

14. *Juror Number One v. Superior Court of Sacramento*, 206 Cal. App. 4th 854 (2012).

assets like its good name, brand, and reputation. In a recent survey released by the World Economic Forum three-fifths of chief executives believed that brand and reputation represented more than 40 percent of their company's market capitalization.[15] Reputation management has become a priority for many businesses as review sites like Yelp and Angie's List play an increasingly important role for businesses and consumers. Some companies are spending between $100,000 to $300,000 to build and maintain their social media presence.[16] Every interaction with a customer is a chance to build or maintain trust, and that trust is valuable. One company with an online reputation problem did a Google search of itself and found that seven of the top ten Google results were negative. An online reputation management expert reviewed the company's rankings and prior-year revenues and estimated it was losing nearly $2 million a year because of the negative search results. The company confirmed that the estimates were accurate but low.

Search engine results can change at any time based on news, social media, or changes in any number of things. But because social media happens in real time a real-world crisis will become a reputation crisis on social media immediately. When this happens, two competing interests go head-to-head: a business's right to protect its reputation and the right to free speech. In the following case, what can a hotel owner do when a TripAdvisor survey lists his hotel as the "Dirtiest Hotel in America"?

Seaton v. TripAdvisor
728 F.3d 592 (6th Cir. 2013)

Facts Kenneth Seaton is the sole proprietor of the Grand Resort Hotel and Convention Center in Pigeon Forge, Tennessee. Seaton has operated the Grand Resort since 1982 and has established it as a valuable business in the state and for tourists travelling to the Great Smoky Mountains. TripAdvisor, a worldwide company in the business of conducting surveys on hotels and restaurants throughout the world, published a survey on January 25, 2011 which concluded that the Grand Resort was the "dirtiest hotel in America." The survey, entitled "The 2011 Dirtiest Hotels as reported by travelers on TripAdvisor" also included a photo of a ripped bedspread, a quote that "there was dirt at least ½ inch thick in the bathtub which was filled with lots of dark hair" and a thumbs-down image next to the statement "87% of reviewers do not recommend this hotel."

Seaton sued TripAdvisor for defamation and TripAdvisor filed a motion to dismiss the complaint stating that Grand Resort's placement on the list was protected speech under the First Amendment to the U.S. Constitution. The trial court granted TripAdvisor's motion to dismiss and Seaton appealed.

15. Alexander Brigham and Stefan Linssen, "Your Brand Reputational Value is Irreplaceable. Protect It!," Forbes, February 1, 2010.
16. Chris Bennett, "Social Media's Role Will Soon Shift from Driving Awareness to Creating Revenue," Entrepreneur.com, November 19, 2014.

Opinion To establish a case of **defamation**, Seaton must show that 1) a party published a statement, 2) with knowledge that the statement is false and defaming to the other; or 3) with reckless disregard for the truth of the statement or with negligence in failing to ascertain the truth of the statement. The **First Amendment** protects statements that cannot reasonably be interpreted as stating actual facts, those statements using "loose, figurative, or hyperbolic language" would defeat the impression that a statement is an assertion of fact. In other words, mere hyperbole or exaggeration are not defamatory statements.

Here, Seaton cannot make a plausible claim for defamation because TripAdvisor's "2011 Dirtiest Hotels" list cannot reasonably be interpreted as stating an assertion of fact that the Grand Resort is, in fact, the dirtiest hotel in America. First, TripAdvisor's use of the word "dirtiest" is a loose, hyperbolic terms because it is the superlative of an adjective. No reader of TripAdvisor's list would understand the Grand Resort to be, objectively, the dirtiest hotel in all of the Americas. Thus, it is clear to us, as it would be to any reader, that TripAdvisor is not stating that Grand Resort is the dirtiest hotel in America as an actual assertion of fact.

Next, the general tenor of the list supports this conclusion. On the webpage where the list appears, TripAdvisor clearly states that the list is "reported by travelers on TripAdvisor." The implication is clear: the rankings are based on the subjective reviews of TripAdvisor users, not on objectively verifiable facts. Based on this, readers would know that TripAdvisor did not conduct a scientific study to determine which ten hotels were objectively the dirtiest in America, but instead would understand the list to be the opinions of travelers who use TripAdvisor.

Seaton claims that the placement of the Grand Resort on the list connotes a statement of fact when you look at the list in the broader context of what TripAdvisor does. TripAdvisor, according to Seaton, considers itself to give the "World's Most Trusted Travel Advice" and to "share the whole truth about hotels." While this may be true, neither statement has any bearing on whether placement on the list can be construed as stating an actual fact. TripAdvisor's claim of trustworthiness refers to its relaying of users' personal opinions, not the credibility of the "2011 Dirtiest Hotels" list.

For the above reasons, we affirm the district court's grant of TripAdvisor's motion to dismiss Seaton's complaint.

Case Questions

1. Do you think the placement of the Grand Resort on TripAdvisor's "2011 Dirtiest Hotels" list hurt Seaton's business? Why isn't this defamation?
2. What can a business do to counter the effects of being placed on a list like TripAdvisor's "2011 Dirtiest Hotels" list?
3. *Ethical Considerations*: Should companies like TripAdvisor consider the long-term consequences to businesses when it creates lists like its "2011 Dirtiest Hotels" list? Who are some other stakeholders in this decision?

The court in *Seaton* made it clear that context matters when evaluating whether online reviews rise to the level of defamation. In a world where a single negative comment can have a lasting impact on a business, it makes sense that businesses will pursue claims against posters and social media sites in court. In the following case, like the *O'Grady* case, a business seeks the identity of posters, but with a much different result.

Yelp v. Hadeed Carpet Cleaning
62 Va. App. 678 (2014)

Facts Yelp is a social networking site that allows its users to post and read reviews of local businesses. In the first quarter of 2013, Yelp had an average of 102 million monthly, unique visits and contributors to Yelp have written over 39 million local reviews. Yelp users must register by providing a valid email address, but users are not required to provide their actual name or address, can choose their own user name, and pick a zip code as their location. During registration, users agree to the Terms of Service (TOS) which require users to have actually been customers of the business in question before posting a review, and to base their review on their own personal experience.

Hadeed Carpet Cleaning is a business located in Virginia. As of October 19, 2012 Yelp's website displayed seventy-five reviews of Hadeed, many of them critical of the business. In seven of the reviews, the authors implicitly held themselves out to be Hadeed customers. Hadeed tried to match the seven negative reviews with its customer database but could find no record that the negative reviewers were actually Hadeed customers.

Hadeed filed suit against the Doe authors for defamation because the reviews falsely stated that Hadeed had provided substandard service to each author. Pursuant to its complaint, Hadeed issued a *subpoena duces tecum* to Yelp requesting documents revealing information about the authors of each of the challenged reviews. The court issued an order enforcing the *subpoena duces tecum* but Yelp refused to comply stating that the subpoena violated the First Amendment to the U.S. Constitution. Yelp claimed that the First Amendment requires a showing of merit by Hadeed on both the law and the facts of his complaint before a *subpoena duces tecum* to reveal an anonymous speaker could be enforced. Yelp was held in contempt of court for failing to comply with a court order, and Yelp filed this appeal.

Opinion The First Amendment to the U.S. Constitution states that "Congress shall make no law . . . abridging the freedom of speech." This protection includes protection for anonymous speech; therefore, Internet users do not lose their free speech rights at the log-in screen. The right to free speech is guarded in all mediums of expression: from anonymous pamphleteering to anonymous postings on the Internet. This veil of anonymity cannot be pierced simply because another person disagrees with them.

However, the freedom to speak, including the freedom to speak anonymously, is not absolute. Because the speech here is **commercial speech**, that is, speech related solely to the economic rights of the speaker and its audience, the First Amendment rights of the speaker are limited. If we assume the Yelp reviews of Hadeed are lawful, then the speakers can remain anonymous. But, if the reviews are unlawful because they are defamatory, then the speakers do not have the right to remain anonymous because defamation is not entitled to constitutional protection.

A person's or business's reputation is a precious commodity and defamation law evolved as a means of allowing an individual to vindicate his, or his business's good name. In order to prove defamation in Virginia, the plaintiff needs to show that the statement is false and defamatory and that it was published with intent. This claim must be balanced with First Amendment protections, thus statements that cannot be proven true or false because they are opinions are protected.

In this case, we have the added complexity of anonymous speakers. Virginia has a specific law, an **unmasking statute** that addresses this very issue: the identity of persons communicating over the Internet. According to the unmasking statute, a procedure must be followed when a person files a subpoena seeking to learn the identity of an anonymous Internet speaker. Generally, Hadeed must show that he gave notice to the anonymous speakers via the internet service provider, that the posts made by the anonymous speakers are or may be tortious or illegal, or that he has a good faith belief that he is the victim of actionable conduct, that he tried to learn the identity of the speakers on his own, and that the identity of the anonymous speakers is necessary in order for him to move forward with his claim. For this last element, courts must balance Hadeed's need to know the information against the rights of the anonymous communicator.

Hadeed provided notice to Yelp, and Yelp conceded that point. For the second prong, whether the posts were tortious or that Hadeed had a good faith belief that they were actionable, if the Doe defendants were not customers of Hadeed then their Yelp reviews are defamatory. A Yelp review is entitled to First Amendment protection because it is a person's opinion about a business. But this protection relies on the underlying fact that the reviewer was actually a customer of the business and posted their review based on their actual experience with that business. Hadeed proved to the court that he made a thorough review of its customer database to determine whether all of the Yelp reviews were written by actual customers, and it could not match the seven Doe defendants' reviews with actual customers in its database. This, we hold, is sufficient to show that the reviews may be defamatory if not written by actual customers.

Turning to the third prong, Hadeed took reasonable steps to identify the anonymous posters and those efforts proved fruitless. After it reviewed its database, Hadeed contacted Yelp to obtain the identity of the Doe defendants but Yelp refused to comply. Hadeed had no choice but to use a subpoena *duces tecum* to learn the identity of the Doe defendants. Lastly, we find that the identity of the Doe defendants are necessary for Hadeed to advance his claim; without their identity Hadeed cannot move forward, he has no other option.

Based on our examination of the whole record, we affirm the circuit court's decision.

Dissent Hadeed's supporting material did not justify issuance of the subpoena *duces tecum.* The law requires that the communications "are or may be tortious" and to be tortious the statements must be false. Six of the seven Doe defendants' claimed in their reviews that Hadeed overcharged them but nowhere does Hadeed claim that those statements are false. Rather, Hadeed claims that these Doe defendants *may* not have been customers, and *if* they were not customers then the statements may be tortious.

Moreover, the unmasking statute requires "reasonable efforts" for identification to have been fruitless and the identities are needed to advance the claim. Here, Hadeed stated to the court "I don't know whether that person is a customer or not, and we suspect not." Obviously, Hadeed cannot say that the Doe defendants are *not* customers until he learns their identities. This, I suggest, is a self-serving argument—one that proceeds from a premise the argument is supposed to prove.

Anonymous speech is protected by the Constitution. A business subject to critical commentary, commentary here not even claimed to be false, should not be permitted to force disclosure of the identity of the anonymous speakers simply by alleging that those speakers may not be customers because they cannot find them in their database.

Case Questions

1. Why are the holdings different in *Seaton* and *Hadeed*?
2. What might be a long-term consequence of this decision on sites like Yelp?
3. *Ethical Considerations*: Watch the following clip: http://abcnews.go.com/GMA/video/fake-yelp-reviews-19-companies-fined-york-attorney-20354563. Does Yelp have an obligation to investigate these claims? If they do not, what impact could this have on the online review industry, including sites like TripAdvisor and Angie's List? What, if any, advice would you give the young woman in the video?

Social Media and the New Definition of "Workspace"

In the opening scenarios we met Ashley Johnson, a server at a pizza place called Brixx. Ms. Johnson was fired after Brixx discovered her Facebook posts disparaging customers of the business. But shouldn't our personal social media communication remain private? After all, what Ms. Johnson said on her personal Facebook account to her Facebook friends was more like a conversation she had at home than a conversation in the workplace.

That isn't how courts view many personal conversations on social media. One of the first cases to address this issue was *Blakey v. Continental Airlines* in 2000. Bonnie Blakey, a pilot for Continental Airlines, included in her complaint for sexual harassment against her employer comments posted on the Crew Member Forum (the Forum). The Forum is an online virtual community for crew members to exchange ideas and information. The Forum was accessible to all Continental pilots through the Internet service provider CompuServe, and Continental management was not allowed to post or reply to messages posted on the Forum.

In deciding whether the Forum was sufficiently integrated into Continental's workplace, the court determined that there was no difference between the Forum and an actual bulletin board used exclusively by the pilots and crew of the airline. The fact that the electronic bulletin board was not physically located at work was not decisive. Because the Forum is considered a workplace setting, liability rests on whether Blakey gave notice to Continental of the harassment by her co-workers.

If an online forum may be considered a workplace where sexual harassment can happen, then it follows that an online forum may be an appropriate place to give notice to an employer of sexual harassment. Well, not yet. In 2013, the Tenth Circuit Court of Appeals held that a Facebook post was not a report of sexual harassment because it was not in accordance with the employer's flexible reporting system for sexual harassment complaints, and the post, by itself, did not provide notice to the employer especially because the alleged victim denied writing the post.[17]

If personal social media can be considered a workplace, does that give employers free rein to monitor our personal social media posts? In the following case, the court used the SCA to evaluate this question.

Pietrylo v. Hillstone Restaurant Group
U.S. Dist. LEXIS 108834 2008 and U.S. Dist. LEXIS 88702 2009

Facts Brian Pietrylo and Doreen Morino worked as servers at Houston's, a restaurant owned by Hillstone Restaurant Group (Hillstone). Pietrylo created a group on MySpace called "Spec-Tator" and described the site as a place to "vent about any BS we deal with out (sic) work without any outside eyes spying in on us. This group is entirely private, and can only be joined by invitation . . . Let the s**t talking begin." The icon for the group, Houston's trademarked logo, would appear only on the MySpace profiles of those who accepted their invitation to join. The invitation included past and present Houston's employees, including Marino, and once a member joined the group they could access the Spec-Tator at any time to read, comment on, and add posts.

---

17. *Debord v. Mercy Health System of Kansas, Inc.*, 737 F.3d 642 (10th Cir. 2013).

Karen St. Jean, a greeter at Houston's, was invited to join the Spec-Tator. While having dinner at TiJean Rodriguez's house, a Houston's manager, St. Jean accessed the Spec-Tator through her MySpace account using Rodriguez's home computer and showed him the site. At some point thereafter, another manager, Anton, asked St. Jean to provide him her password so that he could access the Spec-Tator site. Although St. Jean said that she was never explicitly threatened with any consequences, she stated that she gave her password to members of management only because she thought she "would have gotten in some sort of trouble" and that she understood that once the managers had access to the site, all of the managers would know about it. Anton used St. Jean's password to access the Spec-Tator site through St. Jean's MySpace page and printed copies of the contents. Other members of senior management and human resources reviewed the contents of the site.

The posts on the Spec-Tator included sexual remarks about management and customers of Houston's, jokes about some of the specifications that Houston's had established for customer service and quality, references to violence and illegal drug use, and a copy of a new wine test that was to be given to employees. Pietrylo claimed the remarks were just jokes, but Marano, the regional supervisor of operations, found the comments to be "offensive" and was concerned that they would affect the operations of Houston's by contradicting Houston's core values of professionalism, positive mental attitude, aim-to-please approach, and team-work. Marano fired Pietrylo and Marino.

Pietrylo and Marino sued Hillstone Restaurant Group for, among other things, a violation of the Stored Communications Act. The case went to trial and a jury found in favor of Pietrylo and Marino and awarded them $2,500 and $900 respectively, plus punitive damages four times the amount of compensatory damages. Hillstone's filed a motion for a new trial claiming Pietrylo did not present enough evidence to the jury showing Hillstone managers were not authorized users of the Spec-Tator.

Decision New trials because the verdict is against the weight of the evidence are proper only when the record shows that the jury's verdict resulted in a miscarriage of justice or where the verdict, on the record, cries out to be overturned or shocks our conscience. In order to determine this, we must look at the evidence Pietrylo presented to the jury.

Pietrylo was required to offer sufficient evidence to allow the jury to conclude that Houston's managers knowingly, intentionally, or purposefully accessed the Spec-tator without authorization. According to the SCA, if access to the Spec-Tator was authorized "by a user of that service with respect to a communication of or intended for that user," there is no violation. Houston's claims that there was no evidence that an invited member of the group did not authorize Houston's managers to use her password to access the Spec-Tator, and that Pietrylo and Marino did not present evidence that Houston's managers had the required state of mind for their actions to constitute a violation of the SCA.

Specifically, Houston's claims that St. Jean was undisputedly an authorized user of the Spec-Tator, and not only showed the website to Rodriguez on her own, but also willingly provided her MySpace.com log-in information to Anton and Marano without indicating any reservations. Thus, says Houston's, St. Jean authorized Anton, Marano, and other Houston's employees to access the Spec-Tator and that, therefore, precludes a finding by the jury that Houston's violated the SCA.

Pietrylo claims that there was ample evidence on which the jury based its verdict that Houston's violated the SCA. St. Jean's testimony was critical to the jury's finding because St. Jean established that she had not authorized access to the Spec-Tator. St. Jean testified that she felt she had to give her password to Anton because she worked at Houston's and for Anton. She also testified that she would not have given Anton her password if he had not been a manager and that she would not have given her information to other co-workers. St. Jean stated that she felt something would happen to her if she did not give Anton her password and "felt that [she] would probably have gotten in trouble." The jury could reasonably infer from her testimony that St. Jean's purported "authorization" was coerced or provided under pressure, and as a result was not, in fact, authorized.

The jury could also reasonably infer that Houston's managers acted with the requisite state of mind proscribed by the SCA. Pietrylo and Marino presented evidence that Houston's managers accessed the Spec-Tator on several different occasions, even though it was clear on the site that the Spec-Tator was intended to be private and only accessible to invited members. A reasonable jury could conclude that these repeated visits were on purpose and not by accident, and that Houston's managers knew that they were not authorized to access the content of the password-protected Spec-Tator. Houston's managers continued to access the Spec-Tator after realizing that St. Jean had reservations about having provided them her password information. Marano testified that he knew that "St. Jean was very uneasy with the fact that she had given me and the rest of the managers her password" and that she worried about the consequences of having provided such information. Based on this, a jury could reasonably conclude that the managers knew they were not authorized to access the Spec-Tator but that they continued to do so through St. Jean's MySpace page using her password, further supporting their conclusion that management's access was not authorized in accordance with the SCA.

This Court does not find that the jury's verdict resulted in a miscarriage of justice, nor a verdict that shocks the conscience. Accordingly, we deny Houston's motion for a new trial.

Case Questions

1. The court in *Pietrylo* agreed that a business has a right to enforce its policies and code of professional behavior. If you were Rodriguez and were shown the site as Ms. St. Jean showed him, what would you have done with that information? Is there a way for a manager to use this information in a constructive way that does not run afoul of the law?

2. *Ethical Considerations*: Which is a bigger concern for employees: a website where they can complain about work or a workplace where managers monitor your social media use? Why?
3. *Ethical Considerations*: Can you identify some long-term impacts of both scenarios in Question 2 on workplace culture and decision-making?

Passwords

In the *Peitrylo* case we saw the consequences of a co-worker revealing her password to management in order for them to gain access to her social media site. Some employers are more proactive and ask for social media passwords during job interviews. During an interview with the Maryland Department of Corrections, Mr. Collins was asked for his Facebook login and password. Mr. Collins sat with the interviewer as they logged onto his account, and not only read his posts, but also those of his family and friends.[18] Shocked, he nevertheless turned over his password: "I needed my job to feed my family. I had to."[19] The North Carolina Department of Public Safety goes so far as to ask for an applicant's Facebook and MySpace password on his or her application.[20] While courts grapple with applying legal theories to this new reality, state legislatures have been quick to respond: as of 2014, seven states have passed laws, and legislation is pending in 28 more prohibiting employers from requesting passwords to personal internet accounts to get or keep a job.

[Handwritten margin note: Pretext: Lying to cover up the real reason you are being fired. (very hard to prove)]

Social Media Consumer Reports

Given the ease with which online information is accessed, prudent employers will engage in at least a superficial online search of job applicants. Given the changing legal landscape of accessing others' social media, new businesses have emerged providing a partial solution: social media consumer reports. A social media consumer report is similar to a traditional background check, but moved online. Businesses use algorithms and proprietary technology to search people online and link aliases and online names. Like the data storage industry, businesses contract with a social media-reporting firms who produce reports on applicants' or current employees' online histories. Firms mine publicly available data to investigate a person's entire online footprint, from Facebook and LinkedIn, to blogs, wikis, Flickr, and YouTube, which can reveal a library of information.

However, there are legal risks for both the social media reporting business and the company that hires them. For example, **Title VII of the Civil Rights Act** prohibits the use of race, gender, religion, national origin, or color in any employment decision. However, a quick social media search may reveal wedding photos,

---

18. *Id.*; American Civil Liberties Union, *Want a Job? Password, Please!*, ACLU.ORG (Feb. 18, 2011), http://www.aclu.org/blog/technology-and-liberty/want-job-password-please.
19. Valdes & McFarland, *supra* note 1.
20. Mike Wehner, *Could Employers Begin Asking for Facebook Passwords on Applications?*, TECCA.COM (Nov. 29, 2011), http://www.tecca.com/news/2011/11/30/facebook-password-jobs.

attendance at cultural events, or a "friend" of the Italian-American Club. **The Americans with Disabilities Act (ADA)** prohibits employers from discriminating against someone with a disability if they can do the essential functions of the job with, or without, a reasonable accommodation. Yet a quick Google search may reveal someone as a cancer survivor, or active in mental health support groups. Businesses like Social Intelligence and Reppify offer their customers one possible solution: they can provide vital information to corporate clients, and both companies claim to scrub information of any facts that could indicate a protected category under laws like Title VII and the ADA.

As with many cyber businesses, Social Intelligence and Reppify have bumped up against traditional laws. For instance, the **Fair Credit Reporting Act (FCRA)** which was passed in 1970 and protects consumers and their personal financial information by requiring that consumer reporting agencies follow strict accuracy and disclosure procedures.[21] Key to this protection is the creation of a "**consumer report**." Under the law, a consumer report includes, among other things, any communication, whether written or oral, that includes information on a consumer's credit worthiness, credit standing, character, general reputation, personal characteristics, or lifestyle which is used or intended to be used in employment decisions.[22] According to the Federal Trade Commission (FTC), Social Intelligence creates consumer reports because it "assembles information that is furnished to third parties that use such information as a factor in establishing a consumer's eligibility for employment."[23] As a result, Social Intelligence and companies like it must comply with the safeguards and procedures outlined in the FCRA as a credit reporting agency, such as ensuring its clients notify applicants when negative information turns up in their social media consumer report, and providing a dispute procedure for consumers to challenge information in the report they deem inaccurate.

The FTC closed their investigation of Social Intelligence, finding that the procedures in place at the company are in compliance with the FCRA.[24] Reppify also complies with the FCRA and only shares social media reports with clients if the client has proof that the applicant has consented to a social media consumer report and completes FCRA certification. Spokeo is a data broker that collects personal information about consumers from both online and offline sources, combines this data to create a personal profile, and then markets their reports to human resources professionals and recruiters. The FTC filed a complaint against Spokeo alleging a violation of the FCRA when Spokeo did not disclose the source of its data, allow individuals a chance to dispute inaccurate information, or let individuals know who sought their information. Spokeo settled the complaint for $800,000.[25] Aggressive FTC enforcement highlights the need for businesses in this new age of consumer reporting to pay careful attention to the

---

21. 15 U.S.C. 1681.

22. 15 U.S.C. § 1681a, see http://www.law.cornell.edu/uscode/text/15/1681a for the complete definition.

23. Letter from FTC to Renee Jackson, counsel for Social Intelligence, May 9, 2011. http://www.ftc.gov/sites/default/files/documents/closing_letters/social-intelligence-corporation/110509socialintelligenceletter.pdf.

24. Kashmir Hill, "Feds OK Start-up That Monitors Employees' Internet and Social Media Footprints," *Forbes*, June 15, 2011.

25. Kim Zetter, FTC Fines Spokeo $800K for Peddling False Employee Background Check Info, WIRED.com (June 12, 2012).

requirements of the FCRA in both their collection procedures and customer contracts.

Concerted Activity

Courts and government agencies are making headway, albeit slowly, into the new world of social media by applying traditional laws to this nontraditional form of communication. Consistent with this trend, the National Labor Relations Board (NLRB) has stepped up its enforcement of the National Labor Relations Act (NLRA) as it applies to employee communications online. From confidential information to pay secrecy policies, the NLRB has begun to examine closely the behavior of businesses when it comes to their employees' personal social media activities.

Under section 7 of the NLRA, private sector employees, whether or not in a union, have the right to get together to discuss the terms and conditions of work with each other or third parties. Employers violate the NLRA when they establish workplace rules that tend to chill the communication protected in Section 7.

Like most employers, Hooters and Lily Transportation had workplace policies to protect the companies' confidential information. The Hooters policy stated that the unauthorized dispersal of sensitive company operation materials or information to any unauthorized person might result in discipline up to and including termination. Lily Transportation had a similar rule that stated disclosure of confidential information, including company customer lists, could result in termination. In both cases, NLRB administrative judges found the rules violated Section 7 because they were overbroad. Employees reasonably would believe the policies prohibited them from discussing wages or other terms and conditions of employment with nonemployees, and nothing about the rules limited their scope by exempting these **protected activities**.[26]

Pay secrecy policies are quite common in U.S. workplaces. In fact, over one-third of employers have rules prohibiting discussion of pay, salaries, or other forms of compensation.[27] In a car manufacturer's social media policy, the NLRB found unlawful portions that prohibited employees from revealing any non-public information on a public site, where non-public information included: information related to the financial performance of the company, personal information about another employee such as performance, compensation or status in the company. The NLRB stated that this provision is a violation of the NLRA because it specifically encompasses topics related to Section 7 activities and employees would reasonably construe the policy as precluding them from discussing the terms and conditions of work among themselves or with non-employees.

Answering the question of what constitutes protected activity in the era of social media is a work in progress. In the following case, an employee posted two pictures with comments to Facebook. One is protected and the other is not.

---

26. Philip Gordon and Lauren Woon, *Littler: Six Recent NLRB Cases Provide Further Insight on Structuring Employer's Social Media Policies*, July 23, 2014.
27. Leonard Bierman and Rafael Gely, *Love, Sex and Politics - Sure - Salary - No Way: Workplace Social Norms and the Law*, 25 Berkeley J. Emp. & Lab. L. 167 (2004).

Knauz Motors, Inc. D/B/A Knauz BMW
358 NLRB No. 164 (Sept. 28, 2012)

Facts Robert Becker began working at Knauz's Land Rover dealership in 1998, which is located in the same automall, and then transferred to its nearby BMW dealership where he worked until he was fired in 2004. Becker's pay, like all Knauz salespeople, was based on a combination of commission from sales, volume of sales, and customer satisfaction feedback.

The Ultimate Driving Event (Event) was held in June to introduce the redesigned BMW 5 Series, the best-selling model BMW at Knauz, considered its "bread and butter" product. To make this event more special, BMW representatives, rather than Knauz salespeople, would be at the event to take potential customers on test drives. Shortly before the Event, Knauz salespeople met with Cerullo, the general sales manager, to discuss the event and what was expected of them. Cerullo informed the salespeople that they were going to serve food at the Event for customers: a hot dog cart, cookies, and chips. Many salespeople rolled their eyes and expressed their concern that they were not doing more for the Event, stating that at a Mercedes event that dealership served hors d'oeuvres with servers. Moreover, sales people felt that because BMW is a luxury brand, the food selection did not convey that brand image. Cerullo responded that the Event was not a food event.

On the day of the Event, there was a hot dog cart, bags of Doritos, cookies, bowls of apples, and water. Becker took pictures of sales people holding hot dogs and bottles of water and told them that he was going to post them on his Facebook page. A few days after the event, at the nearby Land Rover dealership, a person showing a customer a car let the customer's 13-year-old son sit in the driver's seat while the salesperson was in the passenger seat while the door was open. The boy must have stepped on the gas pedal and the car drove down a small embankment, over the foot of the customer, and into an adjacent pond. The sales person was thrown into the water but otherwise unharmed. Becker was told of the Land Rover incident and could see it from the BMW facility; he got his camera and took pictures of the Land Rover in the pond.

On June 14, Becker posted pictures of the Event as well as the Land Rover accident on his Facebook page. Of the Event, Becker wrote "I was happy to see that Knauz wen 'All Out' for the most important launch of a new BMW in years . . . a car that will generate tens of millions of dollars in revenues . . . the . . . chips, and the $2.00 cookie plate from Sam's Club . . . were such a nice touch . . ." Another post had a picture of a salesperson with Becker's comment: "No, that's not champagne or wine, its 8 oz. water. Pop or soda would have been out of the question." Of the Land Rover accident, Becker posted two pictures: one with the front end of the car in the pond and the second with the sales person with a blanket around her sitting next to a woman with a young boy holding his head, with the comment "This is your car: This is your car on drugs." Both posts generated several comments, some to which Becker responded.

Two days later, Becker's supervisors met with him and asked him "What were you thinking?" to which Becker responded that it was his Facebook page and it was none of their business. Management informed Becker that they received calls from other dealers who had seen Becker's Facebook postings and said he had embarrassed management and his co-workers at Knauz. Management then told Becker that they were going to have to think about what they were going to do. Later that night, Becker called William Knauz to apologize, and Knauz responded that Becker should have apologized during the meeting with management. A week later, Becker was fired.

Becker filed a complaint with the NLRB stating that his firing violated the NLRA.

Decision The two crucial issues in this case are whether Becker was fired because of both postings, the hot dog cart incident at the Event and the Land Rover accident, or only for the postings of the Land Rover accident, and were these postings protected concerted activity under Section 7 of the NLRA.

Concerted activities do not require that two or more people act in unison to protest, or protect, their working conditions. Concerted activity can include individual activity where a person seeks to initiate or induce a group to actions as well as an individual bringing group complaints to the attention of management. Because Becker and other salespeople spoke up at the meeting for the Event commenting on the food being offered, and the subject was further discussed by the salespeople after the meeting, even though Becker was the only person to complain on his Facebook page does not mean that his actions were not concerted activity. I find that it was protected concerted activity: there may have been customers who were turned off by the food offerings at the Event and either did not purchase a car because of it, or gave the sales person a lower rating on the customer satisfaction feedback survey. Knauz claims that this was not protected activity because neither Becker now any other salesperson made management aware that their true complaint was about sales commissions rather than the food. This, however, is not a requirement of protected concerted activities. And although Becker's tone in his Facebook posts was mocking and sarcastic, they did not rise to the level of disparagement, which would disqualify such comments from protection under the NLRA.

On the other hand, I find that Becker's posts of the Land Rover incident was neither protected nor concerted activities. The pictures and posts were made as a lark, without any discussion prior with employees and had no connection to any employees' term and conditions of work. It is so obviously unprotected that it is unnecessary to discuss whether the mocking tone of the posts impacts this conclusion.

Whether Becker's firing was based on the Event posts or the Land Rover posts requires further analysis. Management told Becker that his posts embarrassed his co-workers at BMW, and that "the photos at Land Rover are one thing, but the photos at BMW, that's a whole different ball game." However, management testified that in meetings to discuss the consequences of the posts, they thought the posts of the Event were more comical, but in the Land Rover posts

Becker had satirized a serious accident and were unforgiveable. Although management discussed both posts leading up to their decision to terminate Becker, I find that the termination was based on the Land Rover accident and therefore not a violation of Section 7.

Case Questions

1. What did Knauz management mean when it told Becker "the photos at Land Rover are one thing, but the photos at BMW, that's a whole different ball game"?
2. Do you agree with Knauz management that Becker's posts embarrassed management and co-workers? If so, how should management have responded?
3. *Ethical Considerations*: It seems Becker felt he had no choice but to post the photos of the Event on his Facebook page. What might have driven him to this? If you were Knauz management, how could you impact the culture at Knauz to influence decision-making and avoid this problem in the future?

We learned in *Knauz* that individuals engage in concerted activity by trying to induce group activity or by raising group complaints about the terms and conditions of employment. Given the subtle differences among social media platforms, that could mean that comments on one platform, like Becker's comments about the Event on Facebook, might be protected but comments on another platform might not deserve the same protection. For example, a former homicide reporter at the Arizona Daily Star tweeted the following:

Aug. 27: "You stay homicidal Tuscon. See Star Net for the bloody deets."

Aug. 30: "What?!?! No overnight homicide? WTF? You're slacking Tuscon."

Sept. 10: "Suggestion for new Tuscon-area theme song: Doening (sic) pool's 'let the bodies hit the floor.'"

In another tweet, the reporter called local TV station staff stupid. The reporter was suspended and then fired because the paper had "no confidence" that he could meet their expectation of professional courtesy and mutual respect. The NLRB declined to hear the reporter's complaint because the tweets were not protected by the NLRA as concerted activity.[28]

Summary

Social media is the new normal in terms of communication. What was once discussed around water coolers or over the phone is now discussed on line in a medium that reaches thousands of people rather than two or three. Facebook is

---

28. http://blogs.phoenixnewtimes.com/valleyfever/2011/05/arizona_daily_star_allowed_to.php.

trying to make it easier for us to use its social media platform to communicate at work, too. In November 2014, Facebook announced its "Facebook at Work" platform to facilitate internal collaboration among workers. Given the volume of social media users, it is a platform with unprecedented potential in terms of customer relations, brand imaging, and sales. However, social media also poses serious risks for businesses—especially cyber businesses. It could threaten confidential information, reputation, employee moral, and liability exposure for defamation, speech, or employment law violations. Courts are learning how to navigate the intersection of social media and traditional laws and a body of case law is developing that can provide a road map for managers and businesses in this growing industry. The cases in this chapter underscore the dangers when business owners or managers react to customer or employee conduct on-line rather than pausing and thoroughly investigating the conduct in the post.

Key Terms

Intellectual Property Idea-based property such as patents, logos, business methods, customer/client lists, and databases.

Electronic Communications Privacy Act An act prohibiting the intentional interception of emails and generally allows an employer to monitor emails sent and received on its servers.

Stored Communications Act An act prohibiting "intentionally access[ing] without authorization a facility through which an electronic communication service is provided . . . and thereby obtain[ing] . . . access to a wire or electronic communication while it is in electronic storage in such system."

Safe harbor provision Part of the SCA that states if a service provider relies in good faith on a court order the service provider has a complete defense to any action brought against it under the SCA.

Reporter's Shield Law A law stating that a "publisher, editor, reporter . . . shall not be adjudged in contempt . . . for refusing to disclose the sources of any information procured while so connected or employed for publication in a newspaper, magazine or other periodical publication."

defamation Legal claim for injury to reputation. To establish a claim the plaintiff must show that 1) a party published a statement, 2) with knowledge that the statement is false and defaming to the other; or 3) with reckless disregard for the truth of the statement or with negligence in failing to ascertain the truth of the statement.

First Amendment The First Amendment to the U.S. Constitution, which protects speech.

commercial speech Speech related solely to the economic rights of the speaker and its audience.

Unmasking statute A law addressing the identity of persons communicating over the Internet. Specifically, a procedure must be followed when a person files a subpoena seeking to learn the identity of an anonymous Internet speaker.

Title VII of the Civil Rights Act An act prohibiting the use of race, gender, religion, national origin, or color in any employment decision.

The Americans with Disabilities Act (ADA) An act prohibiting employers from discriminating against someone with a disability if they can do the essential functions of the job with, or without, a reasonable accommodation.

Fair Credit Reporting Act (FCRA) An act, passed in 1970, to protect consumers and their personal financial information by requiring that consumer reporting agencies follow strict accuracy and disclosure procedures.

consumer report Any communication, whether written or oral, that includes information on a consumer's credit worthiness, credit standing, character, general reputation, personal characteristics, or lifestyle which is used or intended to be used in employment decisions.

pay secrecy Rules prohibiting discussion of pay, salaries, or other forms of compensation.

protected activity Discussion of wages or other terms and conditions of employment with nonemployees.

concerted activity Action in unison to protest, or protect, their working conditions. Concerted activity can include individual activity where a person seeks to initiate or induce a group to actions as well as an individual bringing group complaints to the attention of management.

Manager's Checklist

1. Managers should make sure confidentiality agreements are in place for key employees with access to confidential information, proprietary information, or trade secrets.

2. Compliance with the SCA requires ISPs, electronic communication providers, or publishers to have authorization before they are allowed to reveal the identity of a poster.

3. If your business posts reviews, recommendations, or rankings of your users, make sure it is clear that these posts are their opinions.

4. Because social media space is considered part of the "workplace," conduct that takes place online may be considered taking place at work; therefore, managers should be aware of and respond to what is going on in the actual workplace if they do not have access to virtual workspaces.

5. Businesses that provide social media consumer reports or sell consumer data must follow the strict collection and discloser procedures set out in the FCRA.

Questions and Case Problems

1. The lure of anonymity attracts millions of users to social media, some of them executives of well-known businesses, magazine critics, political operatives, and others.

   a. At the criminal fraud trial of Hollinger International's chief executive Conrad Black, prosecutors introduced evidence that Black once proposed joining a Yahoo! Finance chat room to blame short sellers for his company's stock performance. When his chief investment officer refused to post the message, Black wrote in an email "don't be so strait-laced . . . Get our story out." Prosecutors alleged Black posted the message himself using the name "nspector."

   b. Patrick Byrne, the founder and chief executive of Overstock.com has for years been accused of anonymously resorting to the Internet to do battle with critics.[29]

2. Why do you think, using these examples, executives are drawn to social media to communicate about their company despite the enormous risks? Some employees share confidential information in an attempt to harm their employer. Most sharing, however, is inadvertent or the result of an employee not understanding what he or she is doing. What are the hidden dangers in the following posts?

   a. On Facebook, Dec. 23: "Ding dong the deal is dead! Turns out I won't have to work all week . . . Christmas is saved!"

   b. On Twitter: First sale is in the books! Thanks XYZ Company!"

3. Anna Rose worked for the ambulance service American Ambulatory Response (AAR). Ms. Rose had to prepare a response to a customer's complaint about her work, and she requested representation from her union to accompany her to a meeting with management about her handling of the complaint. When her request was denied, Ms. Rose took to her Facebook page and posted negative comments about her supervisor, calling him, among other vulgarities, a "scumbag."[30] Some of Ms. Rose's co-workers supported her through their comments to her post: "I'm sorry hon! Chin up!"

   A week later, AAR fired Ms. Rose for violating the company's Internet policy, which prohibits employees from posting anything about the company without permission. AAR also claimed that Ms. Rose was fired because of "multiple serious complaints about her behavior." Ms. Rose sued claiming her firing violated Section 7 of the NLRA.[31] Do you think Ms. Rose's posts were protected, concerted activity? Why or why not?

---

29. Brad Stone and Matt Richtel, "The Hand That Controls the Sock Puppet Could Get Slapped," *The New York Times*, July 16, 2007.

30. Sara Yin, "Connecticut Woman Fired Over Face book Rant," PCMAG.COM (Nov. 11, 2010), http://www.pcmag.com/article2/0,2817,2372465,00.asp.

31. Press Release, National Labor Relations Board, Office of the General Counsel, Complaint Alleges Connecticut company illegally fired employee over Facebook comments (Nov. 2, 2010), *at* http://www.nlrb.gov/shared_files/Press%20Releases/2010/R-2794.pdf.

Additional Resources

Federal Trade Commission. FTC Guide to Using Consumer Reports in Employment. http://www.ftc.gov/tips-advice/business-center/using-consumer-reports-what-employers-need-know.

National Conference of State Legislatures. States with Laws Prohibiting Disclosure of Passwords as a Condition of Employment. http://www.ncsl.org/research/telecommunications-and-information-technology/employer-access-to-social-media-passwords.aspx.

National Labor Relations Board. NLRB Guidelines on Acceptable Social Media Policies. http://www.emspring.com/sites/default/files/Sample-Legis-Brief-NLRB-Guidelines-for-Acceptable-Social-Media-Policies.pdf.

four

Part IV

Regulatory, Compliance, and Liability Issues

Dispute Resolution: Jurisdiction, Litigation, and ADR

Learning Outcomes

After you have read this chapter, you should be able to:

- Explain jurisdiction.
- Discuss some jurisdictional issues with firms doing business in cyberspace instead of one jurisdiction.
- Identify problems that 21st-century businesses encounter when they resort to the traditional litigation method of resolving disputes and proposed alternatives.
- Describe issues relevant to high tech businesses that manage data for companies involved in information.

Overview

Many companies with online operations engage in a wide range of transactions with individuals and entities from all over the world. Unfortunately, these transactions do not always go quite as smoothly as one might like and expect when they initially agree to the transaction. When this occurs, and a dispute evolves, parties may want to resolve the matter in court. But first, before we can file a lawsuit, we must determine where the dispute can or must be resolved and the law that will apply to the resolution.

Consider Apple. Apple, Inc. is headquartered in Cupertino, California. In addition to a number of products and services, Apple offers its widely popular iTunes service to online consumers. Consider, hypothetically, that technical glitches arose with the service and some users in several different countries (France, several states in the Northwest United States, Brazil, and Korea) suddenly could no longer access and use the music that they had downloaded through Apple's iTunes service. Consider that at the same time, music distributors from Canada suddenly had all their music removed from the service just as a major new release was ready to hit the market. In this case, Apple would clearly have a problem on its hands and would also be facing a number of disgruntled customers and business partners. Assuming Apple is unable to resolve the matters amicably with its various stakeholders, what next?

Jurisdiction

First, Apple must determine where any of the numerous claims can be heard— that is, where is there jurisdiction. **Jurisdiction** is the authority of a court or arbitration panel to hear a case and resolve a dispute. It is important to note that jurisdiction *does not resolve the issue of liability;* it just resolves where the case will be tried. The Fourteenth Amendment to the U.S. Constitution ensures due process and equal protection under the laws to any person within its jurisdiction:

> All persons born or naturalized in the United States, and subject to the jurisdiction thereof, are citizens of the United States and of the state wherein they reside. No state shall make or enforce any law which shall abridge the privileges or immunities of citizens of the United States; nor shall any state deprive any person of life, liberty, or property, without due process of law; nor deny to any person within its jurisdiction the equal protection of the laws.

The right to due process is the entitlement to certain procedures (**procedural due process**) before one is deprived of life, liberty, or property. From the Due Process Clause springs the jurisdictional principle that each state has jurisdiction over persons within its territory. Whether a state has **personal jurisdiction** over a particular individual is determined by application of tests developed by the U.S. Supreme Court. Generally, a state has jurisdiction over a person who is present within the state, lives in the state, or has consented to the exercise of the state's jurisdiction over him or her.[1]

Jurisdiction over the person and over the subject matter (**subject matter jurisdiction**) are two key elements of any civil lawsuit in the United States. Subject matter jurisdiction refers to a court's power to hear specific types of claims. For example, the U.S. Tax Court can only hear claims relating to taxes, thus it does not have subject matter jurisdiction over a murder case, for example. When a person initiates a suit by filing a complaint, the complaint must include

---

1. See Denis T. Rice & Julia Gladstone, *An Assessment of the Effects Test in Determining Personal Jurisdiction in Cyberspace*, 58 Bus. Law. 601 (Feb. 2003).

basic statements that describe the **plaintiff** (the person suing) and the **defendant** (the person being sued), and state on what basis the court has personal and subject-matter jurisdiction. For instance, a breach of contract complaint filed in a California trial court might state that the plaintiff is a company residing and doing business in California; the defendant is incorporated in Delaware and does business in California; and the parties entered into a contract on a particular date in a particular location in California. The allegation that the defendant does business in California is a basic statement of personal jurisdiction over the defendant, and the fact that the complaint asserts a breach of contract in California is an assertion of the California trial court's jurisdiction over the subject matter (i.e., civil contract law). This California court would not have personal jurisdiction over a nonresident who had no connection to California and would not have subject-matter jurisdiction over a contract matter arising in Massachusetts.

In general, where the effect of an event takes place is where the case should be tried.[2] For example, if a plane crashes in New York, the resulting legal case should be tried in New York regardless of the plane's departure location. However, there are a number of reasons why parties involved in litigation and/or their counsel might wish to have a matter adjudicated elsewhere. Many clients and their counsel prefer to pursue their legal claim in their local courts. When the local court has jurisdiction over the matter, local law will apply, attorneys will not need to travel, it will not be necessary to hire attorneys from another state, and the judge may be familiar and even sympathetic to business. A lawyer who is familiar with the local judge and his or her decisions is in a legal comfort zone.

Long-arm statutes are an important part of the determination of jurisdiction. A long-arm statute is a law that allows a state to exercise jurisdiction over an out-of-state party; like a long arm reaching out to grab a party from another state and pulling them into your state to stand trial. In order for the court to have personal jurisdiction over a nonresident defendant, the plaintiff must prove: (1) the state long-arm statute applies; and (2) satisfaction of the Due Process Clause. All fifty states have their own version of a long-arm statute. Some are very liberal, such as California's statute, which allows jurisdiction in any case in which the Due Process Clause is not violated. Other states enumerate specific activities that must have occurred in the state in order for its court to have jurisdiction. In Massachusetts, for example, a defendant must have transacted business in Massachusetts, and the plaintiff's claim must have arisen from that transaction.

Traditional Concepts of Jurisdiction

As demonstrated in the opening scenario with Apple, the concept of personal jurisdiction is essential to any analysis of jurisdiction in cyberspace. The Due Process Clause of the Fourteenth Amendment to the U.S. Constitution allows a court to require a nonresident defendant to stand trial only in the state in which the court properly exercises personal jurisdiction over the defendant.

---

2. *An Assessment of the Effects Test, supra,* note 2 at 601.

A court may exercise **general jurisdiction** over a nonresident defendant only if the defendant is physically present in the *forum state*, that is the state where the court is located, or maintains continuous and systematic contacts with that forum state.[3] **Specific jurisdiction** may be exercised over a nonresident defendant via the long-arm statute of a forum state if the defendant has *minimum contacts* with the forum state such that being haled into court in that state is fair and reasonably foreseeable.[4]

The **minimum contacts test** is used to determine what contacts count toward jurisdiction. This test contains three elements necessary to find personal jurisdiction[5] First, the defendant must have *purposefully availed* themselves of the benefits of the forum state. "Purposeful availment" exists when the defendant has purposefully directed their actions towards the forum state and shows a substantial connection with the forum state.[6] Second, the claim must arise from the defendant's activities with the forum state[7] For example, the president of a software company incorporated in Virginia has his office in Boston. If he sold software to a customer in Massachusetts that customer could sue the software company in Massachusetts for a claim arising from the software—like it didn't work as described or the software destroyed the customer's data. But if the defendant's contacts with the forum state are not related to the incident, then sufficient minimum contacts do not exist and the action against the defendant cannot be heard in that forum. Third, the court's exercise of jurisdiction over the defendant must be reasonable.[8] Factors used in determining reasonableness include the burden placed on the defendant such as whether the defendant must travel a great distance to reach the forum state, the forum state's interest in the outcome, the plaintiffs interests in obtaining relief, the judicial system's interest in a most efficient resolution, and furthering social policies shared by the states.[9] When the minimum contacts analysis is satisfied, due process is also satisfied and the court may then exercise personal jurisdiction over the out-of-state defendant.[10]

Term	Definition
Personal Jurisdiction	A court's authority over a person who is present within the state, lives in the state, or has consented to the exercise of the state's jurisdiction over him or her.
Subject Matter Jurisdiction	A court's authority to hear specific types of claims. For example, the U.S. Tax Court can only hear claims relating to taxes.
Specific Jurisdiction	A court's authority over a non-resident defendant through a long-arm statute if the defendant has minimum contacts with the forum state.

3. *Helicopteros Nacionales de Colombia, S.A. v. Hall*, 466 U.S. 408, 414–16 (1984).
4. *World-Wide Volkswagen, Corp. v. Woodson* 444 U.S. 286, 291.
5. See *Reynolds v. Int'l Amateur Athletic Fed'n*, 23 F.3d 1110, 1116 (6th Cir. 1994).
6. See *Burger King Corp. v. Rudzewicz*, 471 U.S. 462, 475 (1985).
7. *Reynolds*, 23 F.3d at 1116.
8. See *World-Wide Volkswagen*, 444 U.S. at 293.
9. *Reynolds*, 23 F.3d at 1117.
10. See *World-Wide Volkswagen*, 444 U.S. at 291–92 (discussing that the minimum contacts requirement protects defendants from litigating in a distant and inconvenient forum).

Personal Jurisdiction and the Internet

The Internet raises questions regarding the "presence" of a business in a particular location or jurisdiction because, arguably, an online business is present wherever the Internet reaches. But despite near-universal accessibility, it is often hard to prove that someone accessed a site in a specific state unless a transaction was made. In the Apple hypothetical, where did the effect of the event take place—at Apple's headquarters or in all of the countries in which iTunes became unavailable?

Notwithstanding these difficulties, a body of case law has developed addressing personal jurisdiction in the digital age. Courts have exercised personal jurisdiction over defendants who were not physically in the territory of the court based on the traditional concepts of jurisdiction. For example, one of the earliest and most important cases on this issue is *Calder v. Jones*. In this case, the plaintiff was an entertainer from California who sued the *National Enquirer* for publishing a libelous article about her. The Enquirer was a Florida corporation with its principal place of business in Florida, and the article was written and edited in Florida. The Plaintiff filed suit in California, the forum state. The U.S. Supreme Court decided that the circulation of the paper in California was enough to establish personal jurisdiction in that state because the story concerned the activities of a California resident, impugned the character of a person whose career was centered in California, and was drawn from California sources. In addition, the paper knew that the piece would be widely circulated in California and all of the damage from the tort (libel) was in California.

Although *Calder* did not involve the Internet, the *Calder* test has become a key test for courts determining personal jurisdiction in the age of Internet transactions. Even if a tort occurs across the Internet rather than by publication in a newspaper or magazine, the court will look to where the party was injured when deciding whether to exercise personal jurisdiction.

For example, in *Tamburo v. Dworkin,* the court examined whether a tort committed against a company over the Internet, by sending blast emails and urging customers to boycott another company's products, can be a basis for personal jurisdiction in a foreign state. Using the *Calder* test, the court said because the defendant's "defame[d] and tortuously generate[d] a consumer boycott against [plaintiff] knowing that he lived and operated his software business in Illinois and would be injured there" it is fair for the federal court of Illinois to exercise jurisdiction over the defendant in Illinois.[11]

Another way that personal jurisdiction might exist is by operation of a website. In the last decade, courts have considered various uses of websites and to what extent a website operator's actions or the content of the website can form the basis for jurisdiction over the defendant. While there has been debate over the general topic of Internet jurisdiction ever since the Internet came into existence, concern over facing civil or criminal liability in foreign jurisdictions because of the content

---

11. *Tamburo v. Dworkin*, 601 F.3d 693 (2010).

of one's website is a relatively new issue, fostered in large part by the experiences of Yahoo! in France.[12]

Yahoo!, Inc. v. La Ligue Contre Le Racisme Et l'ANTISEMITISME
433 F.3d 1199 9th Cir. (2006)

Facts France enacted a law making it illegal and punishable with both civil and criminal penalties to display or sell Nazi artifacts. Nazi material was being made available through Yahoo's online auction service hosted out of the United States (although Yahoo! France complied with the French law). In April 2000, La Ligue Contre Le Racisme et l'Antisemitisme ("LICRA") and l'Union des Etudiants Juifs de France ("UEJF")[13] filed suit in a French court, claiming that Yahoo! violated the French Penal Code, which prohibits exhibition or sale of racist materials. The French court found it had jurisdiction, held Yahoo! liable, and ordered Yahoo! to use all means necessary to prevent French users from accessing its auction site. It further ordered Yahoo! "to remove from 'all browser directories accessible in the territory of the French Republic,'" the "negationists" heading, as well as all links "bringing together, equating, or presenting directly or indirectly as equivalent' sites about the Holocaust and sites by Holocaust deniers."[14]

Yahoo! then brought suit in a federal district court in California seeking a declaration that the French court's order was unenforceable. The California court found that it had jurisdiction over the two French organizations[15] and decided that there was an actual controversy causing a real and immediate threat to Yahoo!. However, the court also held that that enforcement of the French order in the United States would violate the First Amendment of the U.S. Constitution. This decision was overturned by the Court of Appeals for the Ninth Circuit, which concluded that the district court erred in finding that it had personal jurisdiction over the French organizations.[16] Jurisdiction in a U.S. court could only be obtained, and Yahoo!'s First Amendment claim heard, if the French parties sought enforcement of the French judgment in the United States—and that had not yet happened.

Judicial Opinions In the first Ninth Circuit Court of Appeals decision, the three-judge panel used the familiar test to determine jurisdiction: whether sufficient minimum contacts existed such that trying the case in that forum would not offend fair play and justice. This would be the case if LICRA and UEJF had purposefully directed their activities with the forum, the claims arose out of, or related to,

---

12. See Richard Raysman and Peter Brown, *Yahoo! decision fuels e-commerce sovereignty debate*, New York Law Journal, December 12, 2000, at 3.
13. The International League against Racism and Anti-Semitism, and the Union of French Jewish Students.
14. Cited in 433 F.3d at 1202–03.
15. *Yahoo!, Inc. v. La Ligue Contre le Racisme et L'Antisémitisme*, 169 F. Supp. 2d 1181 (N.D. Cal. 2001).
16. 379 F.3d 1120 (9th Cir. 2004).

LICRA and UEJF's forum-related activities, and the exercise of jurisdiction would be reasonable.

Here, because LICRA and UEJF took action to enforce their rights under French law and because Yahoo! makes no allegation that could lead a court to conclude that there was anything wrongful in the organization's conduct, the District Court did not properly exercise personal jurisdiction over LICRA and UEJF.

Yahoo! sought and was granted a rehearing *en banc,* that is, by the entire 11-member Ninth Circuit Court of Appeals. Eight judges—a majority—decided that California *did* have jurisdiction over the French organizations based on its actions in California, but that the case should be dismissed for other reasons. There were several opinions issued in the appeal.

The Majority (Judge W.A. Fletcher, joined by Chief Judge Schroeder and Judges Hawkins, Fisher, Gould, Paez, Clifton, and Bea) A majority
of eight judges concluded that the U.S. district court properly exercised personal jurisdiction over the defendants because the French court order required Yahoo! to take actions in California (where Yahoo! was headquartered) and the order was under threat of substantial penalty. "The case before us is the classic polar case for specific jurisdiction described in *International Shoe*, in which there are very few contacts but in which those few contacts are directly related to the suit."[17]

The court reviewed the French organizations' actions under the applicable *International Shoe* test, holding that a court in California could exercise personal jurisdiction over LICRA based on its sending a cease-and-desist letter to Yahoo! in California, serving process on Yahoo!, and obtaining and serving a French court order. Together, these contacts were enough to confer jurisdiction. Under the *Calder v. Jones* test the first two requirements are: that LICRA and UEJF 1) committed an intentional act and 2) expressly aimed at the forum state. Both requirements are satisfied here: LICRA intentionally filed suit in the French court and the suit was expressly aimed at California. The suit sought, and the French court granted, orders directing Yahoo! to perform significant acts in California. Although the effect of the order would be felt in France, that does not change the fact that significant acts were to be performed in California. The servers that support Yahoo.com are located in California, and compliance with the French court's orders necessarily would require Yahoo! to make some changes to those servers. Lastly, to the extent that any financial penalty might be imposed, the impact of that penalty would be felt by Yahoo! at its corporate headquarters in California.[18] Therefore, the federal court had jurisdiction over the French organizations.

Despite the majority's conclusion that jurisdiction existed, the action was dismissed by a majority of six—only three of whom found jurisdiction. Three judges (Chief Judge Schroeder and Judges W.A. Fletcher and Gould) concluded

---

17. 433 F.3d at 1210.
18. Id. at 1209 (citations omitted).

"that the suit is unripe," that is, not ready for litigation. When their votes were combined with "those of three dissenting judges who conclude that there is no personal jurisdiction over LICRA and UEJF, there are six votes to dismiss Yahoo!'s suit."[19]

The Concurrence (Judges Ferguson, O'Scannlain, and Tashima) Dismissal was appropriate because personal jurisdiction was *not* present. LICRA did not expressly aim its French litigation activities at California as required to find jurisdiction under *Calder*. An intentional act aimed exclusively at a location other than the forum state, which results in harm to a plaintiff in the forum state, does not satisfy the "express aiming" requirement under Calder.[20]

LICRA and UEJF's suit sought French court orders directing Yahoo! to perform significant acts in France, such as preventing surfers calling from France from viewing anti-Semetic services on their computer screen, identifying the geographical origin of a visiting site from the caller's IP address, which should enable it to prevent surfers calling from France from accessing services and sites which when displayed on a screen installed in France is liable to be deemed an offence in France and/or to constitute a manifestly unlawful act; and taking all measures to dissuade and make impossible any access by a surfer calling from France to disputed sites and services of which the title and/or content constitutes a threat to internal public order. Thus, there is no evidence that LICRA and UEJF had any intention to expressly aim their suit at California.[21]

Judge O'Scannlain's Separate Concurrence (Joined by Judges Ferguson and Tashima) Dismissal was appropriate, however under *Calder* the rule of jurisdiction applies to intentional tortious actions directed at the forum state. Here, neither LICRA nor UEJF has ever carried on business or any other activity through which they have availed themselves of the benefits and protections of California's laws, nor should either party have reasonably anticipated that it would be haled into court in California to answer for the legitimate exercise of its rights in France.[22]

Moreover, despite the Majority opinion, the personal jurisdiction requirement is not merely a rule of civil procedure; it is a constitutional constraint on the powers of a State, as exercised by its courts, in favor of the due process rights of the individual. Case law does not support the majority's unprecedented holding that by litigating a bona fide claim in a foreign court and receiving a favorable judgment, a foreign party automatically assents to being haled into court in the other litigant's home forum.[23]

---

19. Id. at 1224.
20. Id. (citation omitted).
21. Id. at 1225.
22. Id. at 1230.
23. Id. at 1229.

Twitter

Twitter has developed technology so it can now censor messages on a country-by-country basis in order to help the micro-blogging company expand into countries with laws that run counter to the company's free expression protections. Prior to this new technology, if Twitter erased a tweet, it was deleted throughout the world. Now, a tweet that runs counter to a specific country's law can be deleted in that country but still be available elsewhere.

This targeted censorship was necessary, according to Twitter, because if Twitter breaks the law in a country where it has employees, those employees could be arrested. "One of our core values as a company is to defend and respect each user's voice . . . we try to keep content up wherever and whenever we can."[24]

Twitter is feeling the impact of not censoring unlawful material in France. There, a French court ruled that Twitter must hand over the details of people who tweeted racist and anti-Semitic remarks in violation of French law. The company is also being sued for $50 Million (€ 38.5m) by the Union of French Jewish students who are demanding that Twitter reveal the names of the users so the police can prosecute them for hate speech.[25]

Case Questions

1. Does a U.S. court have jurisdiction over a foreign organization that obtains a judgment against a U.S. defendant in a foreign court?
2. *Ethical Consideration:* Yahoo's French subsidiary, and eventually Yahoo! itself, took all Nazi paraphernalia from the site, complying with French law. What does this say about the values of the French people? The values of Yahoo!? Was Yahoo! motivated by the obligation to comply with a court order or by the adherence to the values of the French people? Or by the value of doing business in the French market?
3. The litigation took approximately six years and involved multiple appeals and some related criminal proceedings. What does this tell us about the actual costs of complex cyber-litigation?

Although the *Yahoo!* case generated a significant amount of media attention[26] and should serve as a wake-up call to many, website operators may find themselves running afoul of foreign laws for activities much more mundane than offering Nazi materials. There are many examples of how domestic U.S. websites can find that they have violated the law of one country by virtue of the kinds of materials they have placed on their website. In the early days of the Internet, for example, CompuServe decided to deny its subscribers worldwide access to certain

---

24. Associated Press, The Guardian, January 26, 2012.
25. Ian Steadman, "Twitter sued £32 for refusing to reveal anti-semites," The Guardian, March 22, 2013.
26. See, e.g., Randall E. Stoss, "Pardon My French. If It's a World Wide Web, Why Is France Censoring Yahoo!?" U.S. News & World Report, Feb. 12, 2001, p. 41.

sex-related discussion groups because of the potential for liability under German antipornography laws.[27] In 1996, a number of German Internet service providers attempted to block American and Canadian websites that contained neo-Nazi material.[28] As national and local governmental authorities continue to enact laws and regulations concerning the Internet, conflicts such as these are likely to continue and even intensify.

Whether a state has personal jurisdiction in cases involving the Internet is often unclear. The test laid out in *Calder v. Jones* still currently serves as the starting point for many courts when determining personal jurisdiction when an intentional tort is alleged.

The other significant test courts employ to find personal jurisdiction is the **sliding scale test** that comes from *Zippo Manufacturing Co. v. Zippo Dot Com, Inc.*[29] This test is used in lieu of *Calder* in negligence cases where defendants do business over the Internet. It is used to determine if a defendant has the requisite "minimum contacts" in the forum state sufficient to establish personal jurisdiction. Under *Zippo,* personal jurisdiction is based on a sliding scale, that balances the defendant's Internet presence with "the nature and quality of commercial activity" the defendant engages in over the Internet.

There are two competing approaches to dispute resolution in Internet-based cases: let "law" control, or let the parties control. When law—that is, the state—controls, the boundaries of authority are stretched because the state is unable to completely control conduct that has a global impact even though it is initiated locally.[30] Internet activists argue that "the underlying fight is a profound struggle against the very right of sovereign states to establish rules for online activity."[31]

For example, Italian authorities took issue with a video that showed an autistic child being subjected to cruel bullying. The video, made by four students enrolled at a secondary school in Turin, Italy, was posted to Google Video in September of 2006, where it remained until November 2007, when it was taken down after Google received a complaint from Italian police. Italian authorities contended that Google was negligent for failing to take the content down sooner. An Italian court eventually found three Google executives guilty of privacy violations and they were given six-month suspended sentences.

Similarly, the *Pirate Bay* case demonstrates that the state's arm can reach far to find personal jurisdiction.

27. See John Markoff, "Online Service Block's Access to Topics Called Pornographic", NY Times, Dec. 29, 1995, at A1. Subsequently, CompuServe reinstated all but five of the discussion groups and provided screening software to users. See Peter H. Lewis, "An Online Service Halts Restriction on Sex Materials," NY Times, Feb. 14, 1996, at A4.
28. See Nathaniel C. Nash, "Germans Again Bar Internet Access, This Time to Neo-Nazism", NY Times, Jan. 29, 1996, at D6.
29. 952 F. Supp. 1119 (W.D. Pa. 1997).
30. See generally Joel R. Reidenberg, *Technology & Internet Jurisdiction*, 153 U. Pa. L. Rev. 1951 (2005).
31. Id. at 1954.

In Re Pirate Bay

Case No. 13301-06 (Stockholm District Court, Apr. 17, 2009)

Facts The *Pirate Bay* trial was a joint criminal and civil prosecution in the Swedish legal system against Fredrik Neij, Gottfrid Svartholm Warg, Peter Sunde Kolmi-soppi and Carl Lundstrom. The four men were charged with illegally promoting the copyright infringement of others with their torrent-tracking website, The Pirate Bay. The website carries links to copies of music, television programs, and films, and is the world's most well-known file-sharing site. The prosecution argued that facilitating file-sharing constitutes the crime of accessory to theft, just as a person holding the jacket of someone while he commits battery can and should be held responsible for the battery.

The four men were convicted by the Stockholm District Court on April 17, 2009, and sentenced to one year in jail each. Additionally, the defendants were ordered to pay a total of 30 million Swedish krona (equal to approximately $3.5 million) in fines and damages. Both sides appealed.

Opinion (Judge Tomas Horstrom)[32] The Copyright Act distinguishes between copyright and rights associated with copyright. Copyright belongs to the person who has created a literary or artistic work, such as a film or a computer program. A right associated with copyright belongs to a producer of a sound recording or a recording of moving pictures, e.g. a record company that records an artist's music on a certain medium, and a film producer who records a film. The indictments for breach of the Copyright Act are based on an allegation of infringement of both associated rights and actual copyright, which belong to US film and computer game companies.

Under the Copyright Act, a work or a right is made available to the general public when it is broadcasted to the general public. The District Prosecutor alleged that files containing copyright-protected performances have been made available to the general public through Internet transfers. This can happen when a work or a right, either by way of a wired or wireless connection, is made available to the general public from a place other than where the public can enjoy the work. In addition, broadcasting to the general public includes a transfer which takes place in such a way that individuals can gain access to the work or right from a place and at a time of their own choosing.

The investigation into the case revealed that some of The Pirate Bay's users, whose making available is the subject of the action, were located outside Sweden when they made the works available to the general public. Under Chapter 2 § 1 of the Criminal Code, Swedish law applies when an offence has been committed in Sweden. The law applies if it is uncertain where the offence was committed but there is reason to assume that it was committed in Sweden. Under § 4, an offence

---

32. Quotations are from a translation into English commissioned by the International Federation of the Phonographic Industry (IFPI), which is one of the music trade groups that brought the case against the four defendants. The translation was not endorsed by the Stockholm District Court.

is regarded as having been committed where the criminal act was committed, as well as where the infringement took place. One issue in the case is where the principal offence should be regarded as having taken place.

According to the District Court, there is reason to regard an offence which involves the making available of something on the Internet as having been committed in a country where the Internet user can obtain the information which has been made available, provided that the making available has legal implications in the country.[33] This applies when the information—as in this case—is published in a language spoken in that country. This suggests that all principal offences, even those committed by persons located outside Sweden, should be regarded as having been committed in Sweden. This conclusion is further reinforced by the fact that the servers hosting The Pirate Bay's website and the tracker were located in Sweden. Thus, all the principal offences alleged by the District Prosecutor must be regarded as having been committed in Sweden and being offences in Sweden.

Case Questions

1. On what basis did the Stockholm District Court assert jurisdiction over the four *Pirate Bay* defendants?
2. What does the *Pirate Bay* decision tell us about jurisdiction? About the strengths and weaknesses of litigation?
3. *Ethical Consideration:* Can a company that does business on the Internet escape the reach of a country's domestic laws by simply locating elsewhere? What are the consequences of relocation on the business, the community, users, and other stakeholders?
4. *Update:* http://www.csmonitor.com/Innovation/Horizons/2015/0202/Cops-can-t-kill-The-Pirate-Bay-but-maybe-Spotify-can-video.

Based on the case law, it is clear that jurisdiction involving transactions or crimes on the Internet is not at all clear. The *International Shoe* two-step process gives some guidance for businesses in the United States. First, does the forum state asserting authority have a long-arm statute, and second, was there sufficient minimum contact between the defendants and the forum state. Although many courts currently follow the sliding scale test laid out in *Zippo* to determine whether there was sufficient minimum contacts, many district courts are split on whether *Zippo* is applicable in determining whether an Internet presence establishes the minimum required contacts with the foreign state under due process.

Litigation

In the opening scenario, some Apple customers and business partners were not happy about their service: technical problems with iTunes left customers without the music they purchased and distributors without any music at all. If Apple

---

33. Cf Schonning, phavsretsloven with commentary, 3rd edition, p. 686.

cannot resolve these issues on their own, the customers and distributors might resort to litigation to enforce their rights against Apple. **Litigation** is the process of taking legal action. In civil litigation, this means filing a lawsuit in court to enforce particular rights. Criminal law, while perhaps more familiar thanks to television shows, serves a different purpose than litigation. In a **criminal prosecution**, the government seeks to impose a punishment on a defendant for violating the law. The punishment can include fines, imprisonment, other losses of freedom, and even death. The purpose of prosecution and punishment varies from deterrence, to retribution, to rehabilitation, to incapacitation to protect the public.

In litigation, private parties ask the court to help them resolve a dispute. Although you have seen these terms in other places in this chapter, a **plaintiff** is the person, or corporation, that sues the **defendant**. The Plaintiff asks the court to resolve the dispute in their favor and award them **damages**. Damages could be money for their injury, which could be property damage or personal injury, money for losses as a result of breaking a promise, or the plaintiff could ask the court to perform a specific act like returning or destroying property.

The plaintiff starts the litigation process by filing a **complaint** in a court with proper jurisdiction. The complaint is a short and plain statement of the factual and legal basis of the plaintiff's claim.[34] Next, the defendant **answers** the plaintiff's complaint by admitting or denying the allegations in the complaint, or the defendant can file a **motion to dismiss** the plaintiff's complaint. A motion to dismiss, if granted, would end the case without a trial. At this early stage, motions to dismiss are usually based on improper jurisdiction, improper service of the complaint, expiration of the statute of limitations, or that the complaint does not state a legal claim.

Assuming the defendant survives a motion to dismiss, if one is filed, the action then moves into the **discovery** phase. Discovery involves the identification, preservation, collection, review, and production of relevant information in a party's possession, custody, or control. Discovery could also include relevant information in the possession, custody, or control of a non-party such as a witness. Changes to federal litigation rules expanded the scope of discovery to account for the increasing amount of business conducted electronically. For example, a "document" includes electronically stored information (ESI) such as Microsoft Word, Excel

Term	Definition
Civil Litigation	Filing a suit in court to enforce private rights between private parties (i.e. not the government). For example, ABC Co. files a breach of contract case in civil court when Acme failed to pay for the goods purchased from ABC.
Criminal Prosecution	The government seeks to impose punishment on a defendant for breaking a criminal law (usually a law with punishment of imprisonment or some deprivation of rights).

---

34. As an example, see: http://docs.justia.com/cases/federal/district-courts/massachusetts/madce/1:2007cv10593/ 108516/1 for the complaint filed in the *ConnectU v. Facebook* case.

and PowerPoint files, Adobe PDF files, database records, and CAD/CAM files. Evaluating a party's effort to preserve and collect documents during discovery is judged by a "reasonableness" standard. According to the court in *Pension Committee v. Bank of America Securities, LLC*, "the duty to preserve means what it says and that failure to preserve records—paper or electronic—and to search the in right places for those records will inevitably result in spoliation of evidence."[35]

But what happens when data storage is outsourced? Suppose Joe's Deli has fifteen years of electronic personnel and payroll records they can no longer store themselves. Joe's would hire a data storage provider to store this data. Suppose further that Joe's Deli is sued for overtime pay violations and the plaintiff is requesting payroll records for the past several years. Joe's will now look to their data storage provider for help complying with the discovery request. The data storage provider must be able to locate the relevant data and have taken steps to preserve Joe's data. The obligation to preserve ESI is triggered once a company, such as Joe's Deli, reasonably anticipates litigation. Thus the data storage provider must have policies in place that require customers to notify them of reasonably anticipated litigation. It will also be helpful at this point to review data destruction and retention policies to ensure compliance with the obligation to preserve ESI.

A data storage provider may receive a subpoena to produce a customer's ESI. A **subpoena duces tecum**[36] is a request for the production of documents, materials, or other tangible things and is usually served during the discovery phase of litigation by a party to the lawsuit and can be served on other parties to the litigation or on non-parties. In the case of a non-party, such as a data storage provider, a subpoena duces tecum will generally demand the production of documents. In 2013 the federal litigation rules were amended to require, among other things, that if the subpoena requires the production of ESI then other parties to the action must be given notice and a copy of the subpoena before the subpoena is served on the non-party. If Joe's Deli is sued and the plaintiff requests ESI help by a non-party, the plaintiff must give Joe's a copy of the subpoena before it is served on the data storage provider.

Several issues arise specific to non-parties and the handling of ESI. For example, although receiving a subpoena duces tecum triggers a non-party's duty to preserve ESI, that duty to preserve might begin long before a subpoena is ever served if the non-party has a contractual relationship with the party, such as a customer contract, or if they know their customer is involved in litigation and have a reasonable basis to know that ESI in their possession is relevant to that litigation.

Production of ESI can be expensive and time-consuming for a non-party. Courts have recognized that non-parties such as data storage businesses should not be required to subsidize litigation in which they have no stake in the outcome.[37] This does not mean that there are no costs associated with preserving, retrieving,

---

35. *Pension Committee v. Banc of America Securities, LLC*, No. 05 Civ. 9016 (SAS), 2010 WL 184312, at 1 (S.D.N.Y. Jan. 15, 2010).

36. For an example, please see https://www.nycourts.gov/courts/6jd/forms/SRForms/subpducestecum_instructwithsamp .pdf.

37. The Sedona Conference Commentary on Non-Party Production and Rule 45 Subpoenas, April 2008.

reviewing, and producing ESI, and courts will not automatically assume that complying with discovery creates an undue financial burden just because ESI exists. A non-party must make "a particular and specific demonstration of fact as distinguished from stereotyped and conclusory statements"[38] that they will incur an undue financial burden. Because of the expense of producing ESI, non-parties have begun to pursue cost-shifting for compliance with discovery requests. Although the body of cost-shifting case law seems to favor the non-party, that does not mean that the party requesting the ESI bears all of the expense. Some factors courts consider in deciding whether shifting the costs of production of ESI to the requesting party makes sense include whether the non-party is really an innocent bystander in the action, the scope of the request, the cost both financially and in time and resources of complying, and the reasonableness of the costs sought by the non-party.

Managing the Litigation Risk

It was estimated in 2008 that the total cost of litigation among Fortune 500 companies was around $210 billion, or about one-third of those companies' after-tax profits. And this cost could be even higher. Although it is easy to calculate litigation defense costs, these costs are only a portion of a corporation's litigation expenses, which also includes payouts to plaintiffs. The average case takes three years to resolve and almost always ends in settlement despite the fact that the company prepares to defend most disputes as if they will go to trial. Preparing for trial—even if the case never gets there—means exhaustive discovery and filing or defending multiple motions which adds costs. And it is hard to ignore the noneconomic costs of a litigious corporate culture: a combative reputation, which makes plaintiffs less willing to settle early and alienates customers, employees, shareholders, and the larger community.

Forum Selection and Choice of Law Clauses

One strategy to reduce litigation is to discourage claims in the first place through the use of forum selection and choice of law clauses. The Terms of Use of a business's website can specify that the website is only intended for use by residents of certain countries. Some website operators might require website users to enter their zip code or country of residence on the home page. If the user enters a location in which the website operator does not intend to submit to jurisdiction, the individual will not be able to proceed onto the website. Another method is to require a user to click on an online box indicating that he or she is not from any of certain prohibited jurisdictions.

These strategies have limits; they can be easily defeated by most users. If, for example, an American user wanted to access a website in France and was aware that it was off-limits to American users, the user could just type that he or she resided in another country. Also, the legal effect of such methods is clear,

---

38. *Black & Veatch Corp. v. Aspen Insurance* (UK), 2014 U.S. Dist. LEXIS 25896 D. Kan. (2014).

especially in jurisdictions outside the United States. Alternatively, website operators might find that they do not have to prohibit individuals from certain countries from accessing the website altogether but instead can control access to certain parts of the website. For example, online trading services might contain news and other information that can be viewed freely by individuals from all jurisdictions, but enable only individuals who are residents in certain jurisdictions such as the United States to open online trading accounts.

Another technique to manage litigation risk is to include a forum selection clause in the Terms of Service agreement. In a **forum selection clause**, the parties agree that if any dispute arises between them, the dispute will be resolved in a particular agreed-upon forum, such as the state where the business is located. Any forum selection clause must (1) be reasonable, (2) be conspicuous, and (3) not work a hardship on the defendant. Courts generally will enforce them. Increasingly, forum selection clauses go beyond selecting a particular court system that will have jurisdiction over potential disputes and state that the parties agree to resolve disputes by alternative dispute resolution.

Typically, the companion to a forum selection clause is a **choice of law provision**, which states that the law of a particular jurisdiction will apply. Often, the choice of law will be based upon where the company's headquarters are located, where the business operates, and/or where it stores its stock.

For example, the User Agreement of eBay provides[39]:

> **Law** and **Forum for Disputes**—This Agreement shall be governed in all respects by the laws of the State of California as they apply to agreements entered into and to be performed entirely within California between California residents, without regard to conflict of law provisions. You agree that any claim or dispute you may have against eBay must be resolved exclusively by a state of federal court located in Santa Clara County, California, except as otherwise agreed by the parties or as described in the Arbitration Option paragraph below. You agree to submit to the personal jurisdiction the courts located within Santa Clara County, California for the purpose of litigating all such claims or disputes.

One criticism of forum selection clauses is whether they are fair to end users who, in the case of eBay, do not reside in Santa Clara, California, will need to bear the costs of traveling there in order to pursue their case. In addition, by using the website, the customer will often be deemed to have consented to the Terms of Use (including the forum selection clause). There is not always an opportunity to decline or assent to the Terms of Use, including the forum selection clause, when using the website.

Although choice of law provisions can be very helpful, courts do not always uphold them, especially when they are in consumer agreements. Jurisdiction issues arise over whether a company had sufficient contacts with the forum state. For example, in *Feeney v. Dell Inc.,*[40] the contracts at issue were between

39. For other examples, such as Google, Yahoo!, MySpace, and others, see http://www.kentlaw.edu/perritt/courses/civpro/forum-selection-provisions.htm
40. 454 Mass. 192, 908 N.E.2d 753 (July 02, 2009).

consumers in Massachusetts, and Dell, a Texas computer manufacturer and seller. The contracts contained Texas choice of law clauses, as well as clauses binding the consumers (but not Dell) to individual arbitration and prohibiting class action either by litigation or arbitration. The class-action waivers, while enforceable under Texas law, were not enforceable under Massachusetts law. In determining that the clauses would be unenforceable in Massachusetts, the court contended that the enforcement of the class-action waivers would be contrary to a fundamental policy embodied in Massachusetts consumer protection law. As a result, businesses must be particularly careful when constructing choice of law clauses for use in agreements with consumers.

The Role of Alternative Dispute Resolution

Going to court is becoming less desirable given jurisdiction issues and skyrocketing costs. Increasingly, there is a global shift towards **alternative dispute resolution (ADR)**. ADR is the name for a variety of processes that are alternatives to a court trial. The most common ADR processes are mediation, arbitration, and neutral evaluation. Alternatives to litigation are attractive because they are almost always cheaper, faster, and less stressful than a typical court case. Some speculate that someday litigation will be the alternative to so-called ADR methods of resolving disputes.

Mediation is a method of resolving a dispute without going to court. This method involves a neutral third party, the mediator, who listens to each party's issue separately. After meeting with the parties, sometimes several times, the mediator presents them with a resolution, which the parties may or may not accept. If the parties do not accept the resolution proposed by the mediator, they may pursue their claim in court.

In **arbitration** a neutral "arbitrator" conducts a hearing taking arguments and evidence from both parties and then, much like a judge, renders a decision in favor of one party or the other. The arbitrator has legal or other dispute resolution training and often is educated and experienced in the particular subject area of the dispute—such as labor, securities, or finance. With **binding arbitration**, parties agree beforehand to accept the arbitrator's decision as final and forgo pursuing the matter in court. In this case, the decision of the arbitrator generally cannot be appealed in court.

Arbitration is such a favored method of resolving disputes, according to a recent study of the top 200 online stores, (such as Amazon, eBay, OKCupid, The Wall Street Journal, BuzzFeed, Dropbox, and others,) over one-third included a mandatory arbitration clause or something similar in their Terms of Service rules. Facebook and Google stand out from this group because they do not limit whether users can sue.[41] Sites like Travelocity use "**clickwrap**" agreements where visitors to the site click on a box indicating that they agree to the terms of service when they create an account or make a purchase. Other sites, like Zappos, make

---

41. Jeremy Merrill, "One-Third of Top Websites Restrict Consumers' Right to Sue," *The New York Times*, October 23, 2014.

acceptance of the terms of service a condition of simply browsing the site, called a **"browsewrap"** agreement.

Arbitration agreements or clauses have received considerable judicial scrutiny in the last decade regarding whether parties have truly agreed to arbitrate from positions of relative equal power, or if the agreement has been foisted on the weaker party, often unknowingly. In the following case the court had to decide whether users of Zappos.com actually agreed to the site's arbitration clause.

In re Zappos.com, Inc., Customer Data Security Breach Litigation
893 F. Supp. 2d 1058, 2012

Facts: In mid-January 2012, a computer hacker attacked Zappos.com and attempted to download files containing customer information such as names and addresses from a Zappos server. On January 16, 2012, Zappos notified customers via email that their personal information had been compromised by hackers. Several customers sued for damages resulting from the security breach.

Zappos filed a motion to compel arbitration citing the arbitration agreement in its Terms of Use that the customers agreed to and accepted when they used its website. The customers claim they never agreed to the arbitration clause because they didn't see it.

Opinion The Federal Arbitration Act states that contractual arbitration agreements "shall be valid, irrevocable, and enforceable, save upon such grounds as exist in law or in equity for the revocation of any contract." The Act demonstrates Congress' liberal favoring of arbitration agreements; however, arbitration clauses are still a matter of contract and no party may be required to submit to arbitration if they have not agreed to do so. A court's discretion to compel arbitration is limited to a two-step process of determining 1) whether a valid agreement to arbitrate exists, and if it does 2) whether the agreement encompasses the dispute at issue. In assessing whether the first step has been satisfied, a court should apply ordinary state-law principles that govern contracts. Under Nevada law an enforceable contract must include an offer and acceptance, meeting of the minds, and consideration.

Zappos arbitration agreement found in its Terms of Use on the Zappos.com website, states in pertinent part:

> Any dispute relating in any way to your visit to the Site or to the products you purchased through the Site shall be submitted to confidential arbitration in Las Vegas, Nevada . . . The arbitrator's award shall be final and binding and may be entered as a judgment in any court of competent jurisdiction.

The first paragraph of the Terms of Use states that Zappos "reserve[s] the right to change this Site and these terms and conditions at any time. ACCESSING, BROWSING OR OTHERWISE USING THE SITE INDICATES YOUR AGREEMENT TO ALL THE TERMS AND CONDITIONS IN THE AGREEMENT."

It is undisputed that this type of agreement is a "browsewrap" agreement whereby a website owner seeks to bind users to terms and conditions by posting the terms, typically accessible through a hyperlink located somewhere on the website. In contrast, a "clickwrap" agreement requires users to indicate assent to terms by clicking an "I accept" button. Browsewrap agreements are dubious because no affirmative action is required by the user to agree to the terms of the contract other than their use of the website. The validity of the agreement, however, rests on whether the user had notice of the website's terms and conditions.

Here, the Terms of Use hyperlink is on every Zappos webpage between the middle and the bottom of each page, it is inconspicuous as it is in the same size, font, and color as most of the other non-significant links. The website does not direct a user to the Terms of Use when creating an account, logging in to an existing account, or making a purchase. Without direct evidence that the customers clicked on the Terms of Use, we cannot conclude that they manifested their assent to the Terms of Use. No reasonable user would have reason to click on the Terms of Use, and as a result, we find that there was no acceptance by the customers, no meeting of the minds, and no manifestation of intent as required under Nevada law.

The customers also argue that because Zappos reserved the right to change the Terms of Use at any time the arbitration clause is illusory because Zappos can avoid the promise to arbitrate simply by changing the Terms of Use, but users of Zappos.com are bound by the agreement. Most courts have held, and we agree, that if a party retains the unilateral, unrestricted right to terminate the arbitration agreement it is illusory and unenforceable. Thus the arbitration provision found in the Terms of Use is unenforceable.

Today, the link for the Terms of Use on the Zappos.com website is highlighted in blue directly beneath the site's login section. When browsewrap agreements look more like clickwrap agreements, that is they require the user to click an "I accept" button, courts are more willing to uphold them. However, when there is no affirmative acceptance of the terms, courts are more reluctant to uphold browsewrap agreements. For example in *Nguyen v. Barnes & Noble*, the court refused to bind a consumer to a browsewrap agreement found on the Barnes & Noble website because "[t]he defining feature of browsewrap agreements is that the user can continue to use the website or other services without visiting the page hosting the browsewrap agreement or even knowing that such a web page exists."[42] And the onus is on the website owner to put users on notice of the terms to which they seek to bind the user. Courts will look at the design and content of the website: is the link to the terms of use hidden at the bottom of the page or in obscure corners of the website? If so, that might not be sufficient notice.

---

42. *Kevin Khoa Nguyen v. Barnes & Noble Inc.*, 2014 U.S. App. LEXIS 15868 (9th Cir. 2014),

Case Questions

1. Why are "clickwrap" and "browsewrap" agreements treated differently under the law? What contract element(s) is/are present in one but arguably not in the other?
2. What is an illusory promise? Why was the arbitration clause in this case illusory?
3. What interests are businesses trying to protect by binding visitors to the Terms of Service simply by visiting the site?
4. *Ethical consideration:* As more of everyday life moves online, critics state that including clauses prohibiting suing, such as arbitration clauses, in Terms of Service that people rarely read, if they see them at all, is damaging to society. How so? What could be some long-term consequences to consumers and the balance of power between businesses and individuals if customers do not have access to the courts?

Neutral evaluation is an alternative step on the way toward dispute resolution, although the process is not designed to actually resolve the dispute. The parties present short arguments and evidence to a neutral "evaluator" with subject-matter expertise. The evaluator reviews the cases and provides the parties with an evaluation of each side's strengths and weaknesses and the likely outcome if the parties went to court. The goal is to reach settlement rather than initiate litigation.

Even among attorneys, ADR is widely viewed as having advantages over litigation:

- It is less expensive than litigation. Arbitration filing fees, which start at $25, hearings fees, and optional attorney's fees, are much less than the same costs in a litigation system.[43]
- The parties reach resolution faster than they do in the court system.
- There is flexibility in scheduling times to meet.
- Solutions can be more creative than a jury verdict or court decision.
- Rules of negotiation and document submission are less confusing and more flexible.
- The parties have more of a say in the outcome, as well as in the process.
- Hostility is less likely to accelerate and can even be eliminated by the process of working together toward a solution. Ongoing and future business dealings between the parties are more likely to remain positive and operational.

Like many aspects of business, ADR has moved online. Online dispute resolution (ODR) has its roots in basic dispute resolution principles and practice,

---

43. See, e.g., Paul Moss & Peter Phillips, "How to Stop Costly Litigation from Ruining Your Results," FAC [facultative reinsurance] Magazine, 25 (February 2007) (observing that mediation is quick, it works, it saves money—an open litigation file is a costly one—and it preserves relationships).

Term	Definition
Mediation	A neutral third party (mediator) listens to each party's issues separately and presents them with a potential resolution, which the parties may or may not accept. If the parties do not accept the mediator's proposal, they may pursue their claim in court.
Arbitration	A neutral third party (arbitrator) conducts a hearing taking arguments and evidence from both parties and makes a decision.
Binding Arbitration	Parties agree ahead of time to accept the arbitrator's decision as final and forgo pursuing the matter in court.
Neutral Evaluation	Parties present short arguments and evidence to a neutral evaluator who reviews the case and provides the parties with an evaluation of each side's strengths and weaknesses and the likely outcome if the parties went to court. The goal is to reach settlement.

including reaching resolution by mediation, arbitration, or neutral evaluation. Unlike traditional ADR, however, ODR uses Internet technology that may enable communication between the parties and resolution professionals; real-time online communication; resolution rooms, in which the parties organize their arguments and evidence in response to specific questions; evidence assessment and evaluation by resolution professionals; online blind-bidding negotiation tools; or online community courts. The parties are better able to understand each other's positions through informal discovery and can decide to settle their dispute before the neutral party becomes involved.

An example of the successful use of ODR is PayPal's Dispute Resolution, launched in 2006. PayPal is an online payment service that allows members to send money to a website electronically by using their account balances, bank accounts, credit cards, or personal financing. It has over 75 million active accounts in 190 markets and 19 currencies around the world. PayPal Dispute Resolution was designed to help PayPal sellers and buyers resolve transaction problems automatically and directly—that is, without requiring involvement by a customer service representative and without resorting to litigation. Buyers and sellers work with each other directly to solve problems at the Dispute Resolution's on-site, member-to-member communication forum. The site has a fully integrated tracking, delivery, and communication center.

Colin Rule,[44] Director of Online Dispute Resolution at eBay.com, which acquired PayPal in 2002, has described the Dispute Resolution program as "empower[ing] buyers to proactively take control of a problem in a productive way; [and] empower[ing] sellers by giving them a framework in which to solve the buyers' problems." By using direct negotiation, investigation, and arbitration, "PayPal Dispute Resolution gets problems resolved more quickly and to

---

44. Colin Rule is the Director of Online Dispute Resolution for eBay and PayPal, having worked in the dispute resolution field as a mediator, trainer, and consultant.

everyone's satisfaction . . . As we say in the dispute resolution field, it's a win-win!"[45] Rule reports that between 2006 and 2008, "buyer claims against sellers decreased by 50 percent, and seller losses on PayPal due to chargebacks decreased 20 percent."[46] Over 80 percent of eBay's disputes are resolved automatically between the parties by using ODR.

How PayPal Dispute Resolution works:

1. First, if you paid or collected payment through PayPal, PayPal's Dispute Resolution service will hold the money in escrow until the matter has been resolved.

2. In the Resolution Center, the seller can post and the buyer can read a customer service message about shipping delays or other issues. Often, this is enough to stop the PayPal Dispute Resolution process before it begins.

3. To open a dispute, simply click on your item number in your PayPal account and open the dispute and clearly describe the problem.

4. If the other party has initiated a dispute, you're notified of the new dispute by email and on your account overview page. You clearly and promptly respond to the complaint. (If you don't respond, the issue may be escalated to a PayPal claim.)

5. You and the other party communicate directly on the PayPal site. During this process, buyers and sellers trade messages, negotiate partial refunds, and share shipment and tracking information. Did you misread or misdescribe the item? Whose mistake was it? If it was your mistake and you are the seller, you can offer a partial refund. If you are the buyer, clearly state what it is you want from the seller. Do you want a refund? To return the item? All messages from the seller and buyer are on record, where PayPal can view them.

6. Come through with the resolution you've agreed to in the Dispute Resolution process. If you promised a refund, refund the money. If you're going to return the item, do so immediately and let the seller know that you have shipped it back to him or her.

7. If no resolution is reached, the buyer (or seller) may escalate the dispute to a PayPal claim. If this happens, PayPal will review the case and render a decision, free of charge. If a buyer escalates a dispute, PayPal's dedicated claims specialists will gather information from both parties, examine the case, work with both parties to fairly and efficiently resolve the claim, and render a decision.

If the dispute is not escalated to a claim within twenty days, it will be closed automatically.[47]

The American Arbitration Association provides many examples of contract clauses in which the parties provide for various alternatives for dispute resolution. For example, instance, a sample construction contract "step mediation-arbitration

---

45. Posted in "The Chatter: eBay's Blog About the Company and the Community" (June 1, 2006), http:// ebay-chatter.typepad.com/the_chatter/2006/06/paypal_dispute_.html.
46. Interview with Rule by Practical eCommerce Staff, "Quick Query: PayPal Exec on Payment Disputes" (April 7, 2008), Practical eCommerce: Insights for Online Merchants, http://www.practicalecommerce.com/articles/709-Quick-Query-PayPal-Exec-On-Payment-Disputes.
47. Summary of process posted on www.paypal.com.

clause" that provides for mediation first and then, if the dispute is not resolved within the specified time frame, the issues that remain will be resolved by arbitration:

> Any controversy or claim arising out of or relating to this contract, or breach thereof, shall be settled by mediation under the Construction Industry Mediation Procedures of the American Arbitration Association. If a party fails to respond to a written request for mediation within 30 days after service or fails to participate in any scheduled mediation conference, that party shall be deemed to have waived its right to mediate the issues in dispute. If the mediation does not result in settlement of the dispute within 30 days after the initial mediation conference or if a party has waived its right to mediate any issues in dispute, then any unresolved controversy or claim arising out of or relating to this contract or breach thereof shall be settled by arbitration administered by the American Arbitration Association in accordance with its Construction Industry Arbitration Rules and judgment on the award rendered by the arbitrator(s) may be entered in any court having jurisdiction thereof.[48]

As noted, ADR has the benefit of preventing conflict. And even if a conflict is not resolved until an ADR process is complete, the process usually deescalates acrimony and fosters positive continuing relations between the parties.

Some critics have concerns about the legitimacy of ADR as somehow second-rate to traditional litigation, even though ADR settlements are as enforceable as court judgments. Some argue ADR encourages compromise, which is a good thing, except in a case of a serious miscarriage of justice, which should not be resolved by compromise. Finally, many ADR procedures are private, which leads to charges of a lack of transparency and public scrutiny.

In anticipation of the 2010 meeting of the United Nations Commission on International Trade Law ("UNCITRAL"), the Institute of International Commercial Law at Pace Law School, and numerous organizations and institutions including the Cairo Regional Centre for International Commercial Arbitration, Egypt; the China Society of Private International Law; the Global Business Dialogue on e-Society; the Internet Bar Organization; and the Latin American E-commerce Institute, presented a "Paper Supporting the Possible Future Work on Online Dispute Resolution by UNCITRAL." The organizations took the position that an increase in information and communications technology presented a significant opportunity for a uniform and focused use of ODR to provide access to justice for buyers and sellers concluding cross-border commercial transactions by the way of Internet and mobile platforms.

Recognizing that efforts to increase the use of ODR have brought with them various issues—such as utilization of different standards, application primarily in domestic disputes to the exclusion of international disputes, absence of effective mechanisms for enforcement, and lack of awareness of and accessibility to buyers—the authors of the UNCITRAL paper posited that "it is crucial that a global harmonizing instrument or set of principles be created in the near future to support online dispute resolution systems that can handle cross-border disputes

---

48. *The AAA Guide to Drafting Alternative Dispute Resolution Clauses for Construction Contracts* 7 (2007).

across the commercial spectrum, including the potential millions of small-value B2B, B2C and C2C disputes that occur annually."[49] They concluded that "UNCITRAL is uniquely positioned to establish instruments or guidelines particularly suited for redress in the online commercial environment, reflecting the needs of the developed and developing world," and provided detailed guidelines for developing such unified rules or guidelines for ODR.[50] Clearly, with such concentrated efforts to grow and improve ODR systems, resolution of disputes in online forums will become the choice of buyers and sellers in both small and complex domestic and cross-border electronic transactions.

Summary

While the Internet offers unprecedented opportunities for businesses, it also raises new risks. Cyberspace does not recognize legal boundaries, and companies must be aware of this reality when engaging in transactions in this medium. Once a company makes a website, products, services, contents or other goods available through cyberspace, it may be pulled into a foreign court and subject to the laws of foreign jurisdictions or become involved in a lawsuit as a non-party custodian of ESI. Companies can prepare for this through risk management strategies, including the utilization of various technological measures and the use of choice of law and forum selection clauses. In the future, alternative forms of dispute resolution, including arbitration and various forms of online dispute resolution are likely to play an increasingly important role in the resolution of online disputes.

Key Terms

due process The entitlement to certain procedures before one is denied life, liberty, or property.

jurisdiction The authority of a court or arbitration panel to hear a case and resolve a dispute.

personal jurisdiction Authority of a court over a particular individual; a state court has personal jurisdiction over people who are present within the state, live in the state, or have consented to the exercise of the state's jurisdiction over them.

subject matter jurisdiction A court's power to hear certain types of legal claims.

long-arm statute A law that allows a state to exercise jurisdiction over an out of state party.

---

49. Note submitted by the Institute of International Commercial Law (Pace Law School), and other Organizations and Institutions, *Paper supporting the possible future work on online dispute resolution by UNCITRAL*, United Nations Commission on International Trade Law, Forty-third session, New York, 21 June–9 July 2010.
50. Id.

forum state The state where the court is located.

minimum contacts test Used to determine what contacts with a forum state can be used to determine jurisdiction.

Complaint Court filing that starts the litigation process; a short and plain statement of the factual and legal basis of the plaintiff's claim.

Answer The defendant's response to the plaintiff's compliant. In the answer the defendant either admits or denies the allegations made in the complaint.

Discovery Phase in litigation that involves the identification, preservation, collection, review, and production of relevant information in a party's, or nonparty's, possession, custody, or control.

Electronically Stored Information (ESI) Documents stored electronically, such as Microsoft Word, Excel, and PowerPoint files, Adobe PDF files, database records, and CAD/CAM files.

subpoena duces tecum A request for the production of documents, materials, or other tangible things served by a party during discovery on other parties or nonparties.

forum-selection clause A clause included in a contract or terms of service in which the parties agree that if a dispute arises between the parties, that dispute will be resolved in a particular agreed-upon forum.

choice-of-law provision A clause in a contract or terms of service that states that the law of a particular jurisdiction will apply.

alternative dispute resolution (ADR) A variety of processes that are alternatives to resolving disputes in court.

mediation A form of ADR in which a neutral third-party, the mediator, listens to each party separately then presents the parties with a resolution that they are free to accept or reject. If the parties reject the resolution, they may still pursue their claim in court.

arbitration A neutral "arbitrator" conducts a hearing taking arguments and evidence from both parties and then, much like a judge, renders a decision in favor of one party or the other.

binding arbitration Parties agree beforehand to accept the arbitrator's decision as final and forgo pursuing the matter in court

clickwrap agreement An agreement whereby visitors to a website click on a box indicating that they agree to the terms of service when they create an account or make a purchase.

browsewrap agreement An agreement whereby acceptance of the terms of service is a condition of simply browsing the site.

online dispute resolution (ODR) A dispute resolution approach with roots in basic dispute resolution principles and practice, including reaching resolution by mediation, arbitration, or neutral evaluation, but uses Internet technology that may enable communication between the parties and resolution professionals; real-time online communication; resolution rooms, in which the parties organize their arguments and evidence in response to specific questions; evidence assessment and evaluation by resolution professionals; online blind-bidding negotiation tools; or online community courts.

Manager's Checklist

1. Website operators should consider including a forum selection and a choice of law clause in the website's Terms of Use as a condition of doing business with the website. Be aware, however, that not all courts will be obliged to follow the clause.

2. Companies should be aware that soliciting business worldwide through a website may subject the company to jurisdiction almost anywhere, and ensure that they have adequate insurance to cover the additional costs of defending lawsuits in remote jurisdictions.

3. Consider including disclaimers in the Terms of Use to stipulate that users from certain jurisdictions are not able to use the website.

4. Companies engaging in transactions in cyberspace may wish to consider alternative forms of dispute resolution, including arbitration and/or online dispute resolution.

Questions and Case Problems

1. To prevent piracy of DVDs, a coalition of motion picture and DVD companies developed the Content Scrambling System CSS. CSS is encryption technology that assures DVDs cannot be copied and can be viewed exclusively on those players that, by license, have the algorithms and keys necessary to decrypt the data on the DVDs.

   In December 1998, the motion-picture and DVD industries created the DVD Copy Control Association, Inc. DVD CCA—the plaintiff in this case, a California-based nonprofit trade organization, to control and administer licensing of CSS. Approximately one year later, in December 1999, DVD CCA was the sole entity offering licenses for CSS in the DVD video format. While in college, the defendant, a resident of Texas, founded and led the "LiVid project," whose purpose was to support DVD and video technology on the freely available Linux computer operating system—and had as a goal defeating CSS and allowing easy copying of DVDs. As part of this effort, the LiVid project operated an Internet website that, as early as October 1999, posted the source code of a computer program called DeCSS. DeCSS allows its users to decrypt data on CSS-protected DVDs and enables the placement of this data on computer hard drives or other storage media, for later use. In this way, users can make copies of DVDs as well as view them on unlicensed players.

DVD CA sued the defendant (and others who publicized DeCSS) in Santa Clara County Superior Court for misappropriations of the CSS trade secrets, which are allegedly found in or used by DeCSS. The defendant filed a motion to quash service of the summons and complaint, arguing that the California court did not have personal jurisdiction over him, as a Texas resident.

The trial court denied the motion, which would have allowed the lawsuit to proceed. Defendant obtained review in the intermediate court of appeal, but that court also rejected his arguments. The dispute then moved to the California Supreme Court. *Decide and state your reasons why there is or is not personal jurisdiction in California.*[51]

2. A couple living in Idaho purchased a Porsche on eBay from a seller living in Indiana. The conditions of the sale included that the buyers pick up the vehicle in Indiana. The buyers hired an automobile transportation company to pick up the car in Indiana and deliver it to them in Idaho. Thereafter, the buyers sought to rescind the transaction based upon the car's condition. Ultimately, the purchasers were successful in having the $5,000 charge removed from their credit card. The sellers filed suit in Indiana, seeking $5,900 in damages. The buyers responded with a motion to dismiss on the grounds of lack of personal jurisdiction. *Should the Indiana courts have jurisdiction over the purchasers? Why or why not? If the Indiana courts should have jurisdiction over the defendants, under what theory would they have jurisdiction?*[52]

3. In February, 2004, two companies, Consulting Engineering Corporation (CEC), based in Virginia with two offices in India, and Geometric Software Solutions (Geometric), a corporation based in India, entered into a nondisclosure agreement that provided, among other things, that each company would not hire certain employees from the other. The agreement provided for Virginia law to govern the contract. This was contemporaneous with the two companies working with a third company, Structure Works, a Colorado corporation, in negotiating a software project. A few months later, Geometric hired one of the employees that it had agreed not to hire. Structure Works then decided not to pursue the project.

CEC filed suit in the Virginia state court against both Geometric and Structure Works, and the court dismissed the claim for lack of personal jurisdiction over the defendants. CEC appealed. The contacts that it alleged Structure Works had with the forum state were several phone calls and emails. Almost all of the correspondence was in reference to the nondisclosure agreement. The basis for personal jurisdiction over Geometric, according to CEC, was that it falls under the "effects test." The effects test has three prongs: 1) that the defendant committed an intentional tort, 2) the brunt of the harm was felt by the plaintiff in the forum state, making the forum state the focal point of the harm, and 3) the defendant aimed the tort at the forum state. *Should the*

51. *Pavlovich v. Superior Court*, 29 Cal. 4th 262, 58 P.3d 2, 127 Cal. Rptr. 2d 329 (2002).
52. *Attaway v. Omega*, 903 N.E.2d 73 (Ind. Ct. App. 2009).

court of appeals affirm or reverse the district court's dismissal of the case for lack of personal jurisdiction? Why or why not?[53]

4. An important part of operating Internet websites is owning the affiliated domain name (www.example.com). Anyone in the world can own any domain name that is available and the facts of this case arise from this concept.

Weather Underground Corporation (WUC), a Michigan corporation, is a commercial weather service. It owns and operates several domain names so that people can access their company through their websites. Navigation Catalyst Systems, Incorporated (NCS), a Delaware corporation, owns many domain names that are similar to the plaintiff's company name (some would result from people misspelling the correct domain name for WUC). NCS profits from consumers going to one of these websites and clicking on links that are on them.

WUC filed suit against NCS and several of its companies in Michigan. Because NCS and the others were not incorporated in Michigan, personal jurisdiction was questioned. Appellate courts have held that in order to establish specific personal jurisdiction (showing that this company has established contacts with the forum state), one must show three things: 1) the defendant purposefully availed himself of the privilege of acting in the forum state, 2) the cause of action arises from the defendant's activities there, and 3) the defendant's acts were so substantial as to make the exercise of personal jurisdiction there reasonable.

The district court is considering whether the exercise of personal jurisdiction is proper. *What should it decide and why?*[54]

5. Best Van Lines, Inc., (BVL), a New York based moving company, claims to have been defamed by Tim Walker ("Walker"), a resident of Iowa, who runs a website that is exclusively meant to provide information and opinions about household movers. Walker allegedly posted statements on his website claiming that BVL had just received its license and it should not be used for moving purposes. These postings were made from Iowa and, of course, were viewable by people around the world including in New York, where the company is based.

BVL filed suit against Walker in New York. The action was dismissed because of lack of personal jurisdiction. *Decide whether jurisdiction is proper based on purposeful availment in the forum state and whether the court of appeals should affirm or reverse the district court's ruling.*[55]

---

53. *Consulting Eng'rs Corp. v. Geometric Ltd.*, 561 F.3d 273 (4th Cir. 2009).
54. *Weather Underground Inc. v. Navigation Catalyst Sys. Inc.*, No. 09-10756, 2009 WL 3818191 (E.D. Mich. Nov. 13, 2009).
55. *Best Van Lines, Inc. v. Walker*, 430 F.3d 239 (2d Cir. 2007).

Additional Resources

American Arbitration Association (AAA). Available at: www.adr.org.

CyberSettle. Available at: www.cybersettle.com Center for Electronic Dispute Resolution, available at: www.cedire.org.

Katsh, Ethan, and Leah Wing. *Ten Years of Online Dispute Resolution (ODR): Looking at the Past and Constructing The Future, 38 U. Tol. L. Rev. 41 (2006).*

Mediate.com. Resources on online dispute resolution, available at: www.mediate.com/ODR.

Mediation Arbitration Resolution Services (MARS), available at: www.resolvemydispute.com.

National Arbitration and Mediation. Available at: www.namadr.org.

The National Center for Technology and Dispute Resolution. Available at: www.odr.info.

 Regulation needs to catch up with innovation.
—Henry Paulson, Former U.S. Secretary of the Treasury

Government Regulation

12

Learning Objectives

After you have read this chapter, you should be able to:

- Explain the concept of net neutrality and identify the competing perspectives of government regulators versus broadband providers.
- List and discuss the important elements of wireless spectrum management.
- Differentiate between various regulatory schemes for government regulation of Internet content.
- Categorize the methods used in government regulation of e-commerce and discuss the dilemmas faced by users of digital currency and current Internet tax policy.
- Identify and explain how the government regulates markets and its impact on e-commerce.

Overview

The dilemmas created by the lag between the need for regulation and the actions necessary to regulate businesses are particularly acute in cyberspace. While the Internet presents enormous opportunities for business managers and entrepreneurs, the nature of transacting business through the use the Internet is still largely unregulated. This can create uncertainty. A firm grasp of current regulatory trends in cyberspace is necessary to reduce risk and should be part of any business strategy that involves integration of the Internet into its business model. This

457

chapter examines the issue of net neutrality, government regulation of content, laws that impact e-commerce and digital currency, and preserving competition through regulation of markets.

Net Neutrality

Net neutrality is a principle that all movement and content on the Internet should receive equal treatment. Proponents of net neutrality—typically users, content providers, and online businesses—argue that a *neutral* Internet encourages innovation and that telecommunications providers' restriction of bandwidth for certain Internet services stifles advances by entrepreneurs. They oppose broadband providers blocking Internet content and applications of competitors on the basis that users paying for the same level of service should receive the same level of service. The net-neutrality argument is another aspect of the larger question about the scope of competition regulation in cyberlaw in the modern age.

Opponents of the concept of complete net neutrality argue that some regulation is necessary. Some ISPs, other members of the telecommunications industries (especially cable companies such as Comcast and Verizon), and large hardware companies have argued that some data discrimination, such as packet filtering of viruses, is positive and even necessary to a functional Internet. They insist that more regulation by the Federal Communications Commission (FCC) would actually discourage innovation by preventing ISPs from charging higher fees for tiered services.

Initial FCC Regulation

The Federal Communications Commission (FCC) is the primary regulator to issue rules on net neutrality because their jurisdiction includes oversight of broadband providers. In 2005, the FCC adopted its first *Policy Statement* with regard to the neutrality of the Internet. The FCC's purpose was to ensure that broadband networks are widely deployed, open, affordable, and accessible to all consumers. Specifically, the FCC adopted four principles:

- To encourage broadband deployment and preserve and promote the open and interconnected nature of the public Internet, consumers are entitled to access the lawful Internet content of their choice.
- To encourage broadband deployment and preserve and promote the open and interconnected nature of the public Internet, consumers are entitled to run applications and use services of their choice, subject to the needs of law enforcement.
- To encourage broadband deployment and preserve and promote the open and interconnected nature of the public Internet, consumers are entitled to connect their choice of legal devices that do not harm the network.
- To encourage broadband deployment and preserve and promote the open and interconnected nature of the public Internet, consumers are entitled to

competition among network providers, application and service providers, and content providers.[1]

The Comcast Case

In 2007, some of the subscribers to Comcast's high-speed Internet service found out that Comcast was interfering with their use of applications for peer-to-peer networking. These peer-to-peer programs, which allow users to directly share large files with one another, consume large amounts of bandwidth.

Two nonprofit advocacy organizations filed a complaint with the FCC against Comcast seeking a declaratory ruling that Comcast's actions violated the FCC's 2005 Policy Statement entitling consumers to access "the lawful Internet content of their choice," and "to run applications and use services of their choice." Comcast's response was that it had to interfere with peer-to-peer programs in order to manage its limited capacity.

The FCC ruled that Comcast had significantly impeded consumers' ability to access the content and use the applications of their choice, and that Comcast's method of bandwidth management contravened federal policy because there were other options it could use to manage network traffic without discriminating against peer-to-peer communications. On appeal, Comcast challenged the FCC's authority to impose net neutrality obligations on broadband providers such as Comcast. Comcast contested that the FCC was trying to officially set net neutrality regulations and that it did not have the jurisdiction to do so.

In *Comcast Corp. v. FCC,*[2] decided in 2010, the U.S. Court of Appeals for the D.C. Circuit held that the Federal Communications Commission (FCC) did not have the legal authority to regulate the way Internet service providers (ISPs) manage user traffic. Therefore, the FCC did not have the authority to enforce net neutrality in accordance with their 2005 policy.

FCC's Open Internet Order

Prior to the ruling in the Comcast case in 2010, the FCC revamped their approach but still rejected reclassifying broadband Internet services as telecommunications services. Instead, it sought comments on a proposed rule that eventually became the Open Internet Order.[3] The Order required broadband providers to 1) publicly disclose accurate information regarding their network management systems, 2) adhere to anti-blocking requirements and refrain from blocking consumers from accessing a particular edge provider such as Netflix, and 3) adhere to an anti-discrimination rule in which all network traffic is treated as neutral.

In the following case, an appellate court considers Verizon's challenge to the Open Internet Order.

---

1. Federal Communications Commission, Policy Statement, FCC 05-151 (Sept. 23, 2005).
2. 600 F.3d 642 (D.C. Cir. 2010).
3. 25 F.C.C.R., at 17907.

Verizon v. FCC

740 F. 3d 623 (D.C. Cir. 2014)

Facts Prior to the D.C. circuit court's 2010 ruling in the Comcast v. FCC net neutrality case, the Federal Communications Commission (Commission) sought comment on a set of proposed rules that led to the issuance of the Open Internet Order. The Open Internet Order established two sets of prophylactic rules designed to incorporate longstanding openness principles that are generally in line with current practices. One set of rules applies to fixed broadband providers — i.e., those furnishing residential broadband service and, more generally, Internet access to end users primarily at fixed end points using stationary equipment. The other set of requirements applies to "mobile" broadband providers — i.e., those serv[ing] end users primarily using mobile stations," such as smart phones.

The Order first imposes a transparency requirement on both fixed and mobile broadband providers. Second, the Order imposes anti-blocking requirements on both types of broadband providers. It prohibits fixed broadband providers from "block[ing] lawful content, applications, services, or non-harmful devices, subject to reasonable network management." Similarly, the Order forbids mobile providers from "block[ing] consumers from accessing lawful websites" and from "block[ing] applications that compete with the provider's voice or video telephony services, subject to reasonable network management." The Order defines "reasonable network management" as practices designed to "ensur[e] network security and integrity," "address[] traffic that is unwanted by end users," "and reduc[e] or mitigat[e] the effects of congestion on the network." The anti-blocking rules not only prohibit broadband providers from preventing their end-user subscribers from accessing a particular edge provider altogether, but also prohibit them "from impairing or degrading particular content, applications, services, or non-harmful devices so as to render them effectively unusable." Third, the Order imposes an anti-discrimination requirement on fixed broadband providers only. The Commission explained that "[u]se-agnostic discrimination" — that is, discrimination based not on the nature of the particular traffic involved, but rather, for example, on network management needs during periods of congestion — would generally comport with this requirement.

Although the Commission never expressly said that the rule forbids broadband providers from granting preferred status or services to edge providers who pay for such benefits, it warned that "as a general matter, it is unlikely that pay for priority would satisfy the 'no unreasonable discrimination' standard." Declining to impose the same anti-discrimination requirement on mobile providers, the Commission explained that differential treatment of such providers was warranted because the mobile broadband market was more competitive and more rapidly evolving than the fixed broadband market, network speeds and penetration were lower, and operational constraints were higher.

As authority for the adoption of these rules, the Commission relied on the Telecommunications Act, which directs it to encourage the deployment of broadband telecommunications capability. According to the Commission, the rules furthered this statutory mandate by preserving unhindered the "virtuous circle of innovation" that had long driven the growth of the Internet.

Verizon challenged the Open Internet Order on several grounds: 1) the Commission lacked affirmative statutory authority to promulgate the rules, 2) that its decision to impose the rules was arbitrary and capricious, and 3) that the rules contravene statutory provisions prohibiting the Commission from treating broadband providers as common carriers.

Judicial Opinion "Before beginning our analysis, we think it important to emphasize that although the question of net neutrality implicates serious policy questions, which have engaged lawmakers, regulators, businesses, and other members of the public for years, our inquiry here is relatively limited. Accordingly, our task as a reviewing court is not to assess the wisdom of the Open Internet Order regulations, but rather to determine whether the Commission has demonstrated that the regulations fall within the scope of its statutory grant of authority . . .

I . . .

The [first] question, then, is this: Does the Commission's current understanding of section 706(a) as a grant of regulatory authority represent a reasonable interpretation of an ambiguous statute? We believe it does.

Recall that the provision directs the Commission to "encourage the deployment . . . of advanced telecommunications capability . . . by utilizing . . . price cap regulation, regulatory forbearance, measures that promote competition in the local telecommunications market, or other regulating methods that remove barriers to infrastructure investment." 47 U.S.C. § 1302(a). As Verizon argues, this language could certainly be read as simply setting forth a statement of congressional policy, directing the Commission to employ "regulating methods" already at the Commission's disposal in order to achieve the stated goal of promoting "advanced telecommunications" technology. But the language can just as easily be read to vest the Commission with actual authority to utilize such "regulating methods" to meet this stated goal. As the Commission put it in the Open Internet Order, one might reasonably think that Congress, in directing the Commission to undertake certain acts, "necessarily invested the Commission with the statutory authority to carry out those acts." . . .

Of course, we might well hesitate to conclude that Congress intended to grant the Commission substantive authority in section 706(a) if that authority would have no limiting principle. But we are satisfied that the scope of authority granted to the Commission by section 706(a) is not so boundless as to compel the conclusion that Congress could never have intended the provision to set forth anything other than a general statement of policy . . . .

Section 706(a) thus gives the Commission authority to promulgate only those regulations that it establishes will fulfill this specific statutory goal—a burden that, as we trust our searching analysis below will demonstrate, is far from "meaningless." . . .

II.

Even though section 706 grants the Commission authority to promote broadband deployment by regulating how broadband providers treat edge providers, the Commission may not, as it recognizes, utilize that power in a manner that contravenes any specific prohibition contained in the Communications Act. . . . According to Verizon, the Commission has done just that because the anti-discrimination and anti-blocking rules "subject[] broadband Internet access service . . . to common carriage regulation, a result expressly prohibited by the Act." . . .

An unwarranted government interference in a functioning market is likely to persist indefinitely, whereas a failure to intervene, even when regulation would be helpful, is likely to be only temporarily harmful because new innovations are constantly undermining entrenched industrial powers . . .

This regulation essentially provides an economic preference to a politically powerful constituency, a constituency that, as is true of typical rent seekers, wishes protection against market forces. The Commission does not have authority to grant such a favor . . .

[T]he Commission begins with the rather half-hearted argument that the Act referred to in sections 153(51) and 332 is the Communications Act of 1934, and that when the Commission utilizes the authority granted to it in section 706—enacted as part of the 1996 Telecommunications Act—it is not acting "under" the 1934 Act, and thus is "not subject to the statutory limitations on common-carrier treatment." But section 153(51) was also part of the 1996 Telecommunications Act. And regardless, "Congress expressly directed that the 1996 Act . . . be inserted into the Communications Act of 1934." The Commission cannot now so easily escape the statutory prohibitions on common carrier treatment.

Thus, we must determine whether the requirements imposed by the Open Internet Order subject broadband providers to common carrier treatment. If they do, then given the manner in which the Commission has chosen to classify broadband providers, the regulations cannot stand. We apply Chevron's deferential standard of review to the interpretation and application of the statutory term "common carrier." After first discussing the history and use of that term, we turn to the issue of whether the Commission's interpretation of "common carrier"—and its conclusion that the Open Internet Order's rules do not constitute common carrier obligations—was reasonable. . . .

We have little hesitation in concluding that the anti-discrimination obligation imposed on fixed broadband providers has "relegated [those providers], . . . , to common carrier status." In requiring broadband providers to serve all edge providers without "unreasonable discrimination," this rule by its very terms compels those providers to hold themselves out "to serve the public indiscriminately.

Having relied almost entirely on the flawed argument that broadband providers are not carriers with respect to edge providers, the Commission offers little response on this point. . . .

The Commission has provided no basis for concluding that in permitting "reasonable" network management, and in prohibiting merely "unreasonable" discrimination, the Order's standard of "reasonableness" might be more permissive than the quintessential common carrier standard. To the extent any ambiguity exists regarding how the Commission will apply these rules in practice, we think it is best characterized as ambiguity as to how the common carrier reasonableness standard applies in this context, not whether the standard applied is actually the same as the common carrier standard.

Decision For the forgoing reasons, although we reject Verizon's challenge to the Open Internet Order's disclosure rules, we vacate both the anti-discrimination and the anti-blocking rules. We remand the case to the Commission for further proceedings consistent with this opinion.

Case Questions

1. The Open Internet Order imposed an anti-discrimination requirement on fixed broadband providers. What does that mean? Discriminate against whom?
2. Why does the court conclude that the FCC had the authority to regulate, but did not have the authority to impose net neutrality rules?
3. The court called one of the FCC's arguments "half-hearted." What do think the court was indicating by using that phrase?

Political and Public Response

Shortly after the court's decision in the Verizon case, Netflix struck a deal with Comcast in which it paid Comcast for a direct connection into its broadband network so subscribers experience less delay in viewing Netflix's streaming video. The case also set off a decidedly pro-neutrality political and public reaction. The FCC issued a statement that promised to lay out a framework that would promote net neutrality and still fit within the court's ruling. The FCC's work was endorsed by the White House and members of Congress. President Obama became an outspoken opponent of allowing cable and telephone companies from providing special access to some content providers and in 2014 he urged the FCC to treat consumer broadband service as a public utility and regulate them in the public's interest.

The Internet Association, a trade group of 36 web companies such as Google, Inc., Netflix, and Amazon.com, made their views known through an FCC filing that urged the government to restrict the ability of Internet providers including mobile carriers to strike deals for faster delivery of some web traffic. Indeed, the FCC reported that over 3.7 million people had submitted comments that largely favored regulations that impose net neutrality on broadband providers.

The public net neutrality backlash even crept into pop culture after the FCC's antiquated Electronic Comment Filing System crashed when fans of comedian John Oliver responded to his pro-neutrality video. Oliver's video, aired on his HBO show, encouraged viewers to weigh in on the net neutrality debate via the

FCC's website. According to the Washington Post, more than 45,000 new comments on net neutrality were likely sparked by Oliver's barbs.

FCC's Regulation of the Internet as a Public Utility

Soon after the Verizon case was decided, political and industry leaders called on the FCC to take aggressive action by promulgating regulations that would regulate the Internet as a public utility. Initially, the FCC favored a "hybrid approach" that would place certain controls on the commercial relationship between Internet service providers and content companies. However, in 2015, the FCC announced that high-speed Internet service was to be regulated as a public utility pursuant to their authority under Title II of the Communications Act[4] that governs common utility carriers (such as landline phone systems). Although the FCC did not prohibit the use of paid-peering agreements between broadband providers and large content providers (e.g., Netflix) and network intermediaries (e.g., Level 3 Communications), the agency would have authority to police such agreements and prevent any deals that were not in the public interest. Opponents of FCC regulation have promised to challenge the FCC's approach in court and argue that regulation of broadband providers would saddle providers with outdated regulations and create regulatory uncertainty that will stifle innovation.

FTC Regulation: Throttling

Another recent development of net-neutrality related principles is regulation of what the Federal Trade Commission (FTC) calls **throttling**. Throttling is the practice of broadband providers slowing down a consumer's Internet speed once they exceeded a certain amount of data—even when the consumer has paid for an unlimited data plan. In 2014, the FTC sued AT&T alleging that the mega-wireless carrier engaged in deceptive trade practices by selling unlimited data plans and then throttling users speed as much as 90 percent slower than usual. The government alleged that more than 3.5 million customers with legacy unlimited data plans had their Internet speeds slowed more than 25 million times by AT&T's throttling practices. AT&T denied the allegations claiming that they had been completely transparent with customers, that only 3 percent of their customers were affected, and that the practice was necessary to manage network resources.

Government Regulation and Twitter

After months of failed negotiation over how transparent Twitter can be about how much information it provides in response to the government's national security requests for data, the world's largest micro-blogging platform sued the U.S. government in 2014. Twitter alleged that the Justice Department's restrictions on what the company can say publicly about the government's national security requests for user data violate the firm's

---

4. 47 U.S.C. § 151.

First Amendment rights. The lawsuit goes a step beyond steps taken by five other technology companies that already reached a settlement with the government on the permissible scope of disclosure at a time of heightened concern about the scale of government surveillance.

Wireless Spectrum Management

Management of the **wireless spectrum** is another area in which the FCC plays a key role. One hears similar arguments as those made in the net neutrality debate when studying the question of the extent to which the federal government should manage the wireless spectrum. On the one hand are those who urge centralized governmental ownership and regulation of the wireless spectrum. On the other are those who advocate for a hands-off approach.

Electromagnetic waves move through space at different frequencies and together make up the electromagnetic spectrum. The radio frequency (RF) spectrum is the part of the electromagnetic spectrum for radio frequencies. The range of frequencies from 3kHz to 300 kHz can be used for wireless communication.

In most countries, the RF spectrum is the property of the state. The main purpose of managing the RF spectrum is to maximize the amount of available RF, optimizing its use and, conversely, to minimize radio spectrum "pollution" (i.e., interference). Other spectrum management goals include designing allocations for short- and long-range frequencies, coordinating wireless communications with others, and advancing the invention and introduction of new wireless technologies.

Among United Nations member-states, the International Telecommunications Union (ITU) manages the use of the RF spectrum. The ITU is divided into three sectors, including the Radio Communication Sector, which decides the operational procedures and technical characteristics for wireless services and performs other spectrum management functions; the Telecommunication Standardization Sector, which develops technical and operating standards; and the Telecommunication Development Sector, which works to expand the telecommunications infrastructure in developing nations.

In the United States, the FCC regulates domestic nonfederal spectrum use. The National Telecommunications and Information Administration (NTIA) manages the spectrum for the federal government. Like other regulators, the FCC and NTIA use the so-called "command-and-control" approach to spectrum management in which the regulator is a centralized authority. Because the command-and-control approach initiated with early wireless communications when interference was more of an issue such that each band needed to be dedicated to a single provider, some argue that such an exclusive approach is outmoded and no longer necessary.

Those who support the command-and-control model argue that some beneficial communication services would not be profitable enough to attract private providers, that such services are enforced by way of license agreements, and that the there is an advantage to standardization, especially in networked industries. Critics of this approach contend that RF spectrum management should be cooperative. It should balance stakeholder interests through user education and regulatory enforcement. Regulations should address politics, economics, physics, and practical reality. The argument is that RF spectrum management in the United States especially is outdated and unnecessarily complex in some areas but too permissive in others.

Spectrum scarcity has emerged as a major issue for those trying to initiate new wireless services, yet studies have shown that there is unused spectrum available. This artificial limitation to accessing parts of the RF spectrum arguably could be remedied by changes to the current approach to spectrum management.

Two suggested approaches are the **spectrum commons** and the **spectrum property rights** models. Under the spectrum commons approach, the spectrum is like a physical commons to which the people have certain access rights, although no one owns the commons as property. Under the spectrum property rights approach, portions of the spectrum may be privately owned. Allocation of parts of the spectrum is dictated by market forces. Most famously, economist Ronald Coase advocated for ownership of parts of the spectrum as the most efficient use of the spectrum. Advocates argue that such an approach would promote innovation efficiency. Critics argue that individual spectrum owners could hold up parts of the spectrum for high compensation in return for its use.

Regulation of Content

User-generated content (UGC) refers to various kinds of content created by end-users (as opposed to a website operator, for example) and made publicly available. Some common examples include customer reviews, social networking content, videos and photos uploaded by users, blog posts, and wikis.

For many websites, UGC constitutes only a portion of content. For example, on many e-commerce websites, the majority of content is prepared by website operators, but the site also displays user reviews of the products being sold submitted by visitors to the website. On other sites, UGC is the primary content of the site. The names of UGC websites have become part of our common language. Examples include Yelp (consumer comment site focused primarily on restaurants), Flickr or Pinterest (photo sharing sites), Facebook (social networking), YouTube (video sharing site), TripAdvisor (consumer comment site focused on travel information, including reviews of hotels and other travel-related goods and services), Wikipedia (information resource created with UGC), and Twitter (a social/community communication).

Often UGC is partially or totally monitored by website administrators. Monitoring can be undertaken for a number of purposes, including avoiding offensive content or language, copyright infringement issues, and to determine if the content posted is relevant to the site's general theme.

While UGC is an important part of the online world, it is not without its legal risks and concerns. Content created by others, including website users, can, for instance, give rise to intellectual properly concerns, violate individual privacy rights, result in criminal liability, and raise other concerns. Website operators can attempt to mitigate the potential risks of UGC by implementing systems for reviewing UGC before it is posted, but for most companies this is not practical. Moreover, even the most thorough review policies and procedures are incapable of detecting all unacceptable UGC. Fortunately, as will be discussed herein, certain laws provide some protection against liability for some forms of UGC. Moreover, websites can also protect themselves with the use of appropriate agreements and disclaimers. Many websites aim to protect themselves through the use of comprehensive provisions in their website agreements. Consider, for instance, the following provision from TripAdvisor.com:

> TripAdvisor takes no responsibility and assumes no liability for any Content posted, stored or uploaded by you or any third party, or for any loss or damage thereto, nor is TripAdvisor liable for any mistakes, defamation, slander, libel, omissions, falsehoods, obscenity, pornography or profanity you may encounter. As a provider of interactive services, TripAdvisor is not liable for any statements, representations or Content provided by its users in any public forum, personal home page or other Interactive Area. Although TripAdvisor has no obligation to screen, edit or monitor any of the Content posted to or distributed through any Interactive Area, TripAdvisor reserves the right, and has absolute discretion, to remove, screen or edit without notice any Content posted or stored on the Site at any time and for any reason, and you are solely responsible for creating backup copies of and replacing any Content you post or store on the Site at your sole cost and expense.[5]

As noted above, UGC can give rise to privacy concerns. By posting UGC, users may inadvertently disclose more information about themselves and/or others than they had intended to. This can make users vulnerable to a range of harms, including identity theft. UGC can also give rise to privacy issues when individuals post private photographs and other content of third parties.

Operators of websites on which users are permitted to post UGC may also face liability risks arising from the nature of the content. One of most significant risks is copyright infringement. Given the in-depth examination of these issues in Chapter 5 we will not focus on them in too much detail here. However, issues particular to UGC are worthy of some discussion. Consider, for instance, if you host a site where users are invited to share their opinions on movies, music, and the like. What if, when commenting upon a certain video, a website user posts the video without permission of the rights holder?

The key law for analyzing the website operator's liability in such a situation is the Digital Millennium Copyright Act (DMCA).[6] Section 512 of the DMCA establishes a safe harbor under which an Internet service provider (ISP) can escape liability for copyright infringement, as long as the ISP meets certain conditions. Of course, the ISP seeking immunity must not have been involved in

---

5. http://www.tripadvisor.com/pages/terms.html.
6. 17 U.S.C. § 512.

the infringement. Additionally, ISPs are required to adopt a special take-down policy, which allows individuals to respond to alleged copyright violations. If the individual moves expeditiously to remove the infringing material, he or she usually avoids liability. When the company removes the infringement, it is then required to notify the user that their material has been taken down. If the user then submits a counter-notification claiming a good faith belief that the material is not infringing, the company must put the material back online unless the original company claiming the infringement brings a suit against the user.

Of course, copyright infringement is not the only potential liability about which websites hosting UGC must be concerned. In the context of third-party copyright violations, it is important to consider the liability issues between the content provider and the ISP. There are two distinct models of liability: the "publishing information doctrine" and "storing information doctrine." According to the former view, ISP controls, or at least has the ability to control, the content published by virtue of the fact that the user is using its services. In other words, the ISP has the editorial control to take down and monitor content posted online. In order to establish secondary liability, it is pivotal to evaluate the level of control practiced by the ISP. The more control the ISP has before the content is posted, the more likely it will be subjected to greater liability, but it also greatly decreases the risk objectionable material will be posted on the Internet. The latter view applies to situations in which the ISP acts as a mere host, lacking any editorial role to the content posted online. Even though the ISP might have awareness of the content run by using their services, it cannot monitor or modify posted information.

First Amendment Concerns

Any content regulation by the government will always carry the risk of violating First Amendment rights of the content provider. Although the First Amendment is not absolute, user generated content has been one of the issues which has tested its limits. For example, should a user be entitled to First Amendment protection for advocating lawlessness or violence? Can role-playing online and depiction of violent acts be protected by the First Amendment? Although the U.S. Supreme Court has held that "abstract advocacy" of lawlessness is protected under the First Amendment,[7] some courts have held that anything used to aid or abet a violent act is not protected speech. For example, a federal court ruled that the publisher of *Hitman: A Technical Manual for Independent Contractors* was not entitled to a First Amendment defense for civil liability as a conspirator in a triple contract murder performed in accordance with the manual.[8] Most courts have held that role-playing typically falls into the "abstract advocacy" category unless the role-playing crosses the line between fantasy and reality. In 2014, a federal court overturned the conviction of a New York City police officer, dubbed by the media as the "cannibal cop," for plotting to kidnap, cook, and eat women after prosecutors discovered online postings by Officer Gilberto Valle on a website

7. *Brandenburg v. Ohio*, 395 U.S. 444 (1969).
8. *Rice v. Paladin Enterprises*, 128 F. 3d 233 (4th Cir. 1997).

devoted to fantasizing online about cannibalism. Prosecutors contended that Valle went beyond the online fantasy by using a law enforcement database to gather personal information on potential targets. They contended that Valle had specific plans to abduct women for purposes of committing cannibalism. However, the federal court reversed the conviction on the grounds that Valle's conduct had amounted to mere fantasy and despite the "highly disturbing nature of Valle's deviant and depraved sexual interests, his chats and emails about those interests are not sufficient" to convict him for kidnapping.[9]

Website Liability and the Communications Decency Act

The **Communications Decency Act (CDA)** of 1996[10] plays a very important role in insulating website operators from liability for UGC. To understand the role and importance of the CDA, one can look at traditional common-law principles. Under those principles, a person who publishes a defamatory statement by another would bear the same liability for the statement as if he or she had initially created it. Accordingly, a book publisher or a newspaper publisher could be held liable for anything that appeared within its pages. This common law rule is based on the notion that a publisher has the knowledge, opportunity, and ability to exercise editorial control over the content of its publications.

Conversely, under common law, the liability of *distributors* of content is much more limited. Generally, distributors, such as newsstands, bookstores, and libraries, are not held liable for the content of the material they distribute. The theory behind this principle is clear: it would be difficult, if not impossible, for distributors to read every publication before they sell or distribute it.

In the early days of the Internet, a number of lawsuits were brought that tested how websites should be classified—as distributors or publishers. The early cases in this area, such as *Cubby v. CompuServe, Inc.*[11] and *Stratton Oakmont v. Prodigy,*[12] resulted in an interesting scenario. Efforts by online information providers to restrict or edit user-submitted content faced a much higher risk of liability if the provider failed to eliminate all defamatory material than if it simply did not try to control or edit the content of third parties at all.

This eventually led to the passage of the Communications Decency Act. Of most relevance is Section 230, which provides: "No provider or user of an interactive computer service shall be treated as the publisher or speaker of any information provided by another information content provider" and further that "[n]o cause of action may be brought and no liability may be imposed under any State or local law that is inconsistent with this section."

Section 230 of the CD A applies to "interactive computer service [s]," a term that is defined broadly to include any "information service, system, or access software provider that provides or enables computer access by multiple users to

---

9. *U.S. v. Valle,* No. 12 cr 847 (S.D.N.Y. 2014)
10. 47 U.S.C. § 230.
11. 776 F. Supp. 135 (S.D.N.Y. 1991).
12. 23 Media L. Rep. 1794 (N.Y. Sup. Ct. 1995).

a computer server." Courts have interpreted this term to include a wide variety of Internet services, including websites, blogs, forums, and listservs.

Section 230 has most frequently been applied to bar defamation-based claims. In the next case, a federal appeals court considers the scope of immunity provided by the CDA.

Johnson v. Arden
614 F.3d 785 (8th Cir. 2010)

Facts Johnson owns and operates an exotic cat breeding business known as the Cozy Kitten Cattery in Missouri. He obtained a registered federal trademark and service mark for "Cozy Kitten Cattery" in 2004 and operated the cat breeding business under that trademark, including advertising their trademark on the Internet and hosting a website called CozyKittens.com.

After an unknown user posted several defamatory statements about the Cozy Kitten Cattery on an interactive consumer website called ComplaintsBoard.com, Johnson filed suit against Arden and others who maintained the website and also against InMotion, the ISP who hosted ComplaintsBoard.com. Johnson alleged that the parties conspired to post false statements about Cozy Kittens including statements that the Johnson kills cats, cheats cat breeders, and that Johnson and his wife were con artists. The suit alleged that the false statements caused damages in the form of lost revenue and lost goodwill. The trial court dismissed the claims against InMotion after finding that they were immune from liability under the Communications Decency Act. Johnson appealed.

Judicial Opinion . . .

A. Communications Decency Act "[Johnson] first argues that the district court erroneously dismissed their claims after concluding InMotion is immune under the CDA. Johnson contends that 47 U.S.C. § 230(c)(1) and (e)(3) merely provide that a provider of Internet services shall not be treated as the publisher or speaker of information on the Internet provided by another party but does not immunize a provider from suit.

InMotion responds that the district court correctly found that InMotion was immune from suit under the CDA. Additionally, In Motion asserts that it maintained no control and had no influence over the content that the Johnsons alleged was posted on www.ComplaintsBoard.com by unrelated third parties. Because of this, InMotion maintains, it could not have "acted in concert" or "intentionally inflicted emotional distress" in a manner that caused any damage to the Johnsons.

This case presents an issue of first impression for this court, as we have not previously interpreted § 230(c). . . . The CDA states that "[n]o provider or user of an interactive computer service shall be treated as the publisher or speaker of any information provided by another information content provider," 47 U.S.C.

§ 230(c)(1), and expressly preempts any state law to the contrary. . . .   The CDA defines an "information content provider" as "any person or entity that is responsible, in whole or in part, for the creation or development of information provided through the Internet or any other interactive computer service." Id. at § 230(f)(3).

Read together, these provisions bar plaintiffs from holding ISPs legally responsible for information that third parties created and developed. See Fair Housing Council of San Fernando Valley v. Roommates.com, LLC (holding that CDA immunity did not apply to the website that was designed to force subscribers to divulge protected characteristics, but that CDA immunity did apply to the "Additional Comments" section of the website where the information was created by third parties and not required by the website ISP). "Congress thus established a general rule that providers of interactive computer services are liable only for speech that is properly attributable to them." Nemet Chevrolet, Ltd. v. Consumer-affairs.com, Inc.

"The majority of federal circuits have interpreted the CDA to establish broad 'federal immunity to any cause of action that would make service providers liable for information originating with a third-party user of the service.'" Almeida v. Amazon.com, Inc., (quoting Zeran v. Am. Online, Inc.,. The district court, following majority circuit precedent, held that § 230(c)(1) blocks civil liability when web hosts and other ISPs refrain from filtering or censoring the information that third parties created on their sites. Green v. Am. Online, 318 F.3d 465, 471 (3d Cir.2003) (holding that under the CDA the defendant ISP is not liable for failing to monitor, screen, or delete allegedly defamatory content from its site).

It is undisputed that InMotion did not originate the material that the Johnsons deem damaging. InMotion is not a "publisher or speaker" as § 230(c)(1) uses those terms, therefore, the district court held that InMotion cannot be liable under any state-law theory to the persons harmed by the allegedly defamatory material. Five circuit courts agree. See Universal Commc'n Sys., Inc. v. Lycos, Inc., 478 F.3d 413, 419 (1st Cir.2007) (affirming dismissal of a claim brought by a public-traded company against an Internet message board operator for allegedly false and defamatory postings by pseudonymous posters); Batzel v. Smith, 333 F.3d 1018 1032-33 (9th Cir.2003) (holding that even if operator of internet services could have reasonably concluded that the information was sent for internet publication, he was immunized from liability for the defamatory speech as a "provider or user of interactive computer services" under the CDA and . . . finding that defendant ISP was immune to the defamation claim under the CDA when it made its own editorial decisions with respect to third-party information published on its website); Zeran, 129 F.3d at 332-34 (holding that the CDA barred claims against defendant ISP that allegedly delayed in removing defamatory messages posted by unidentified third party, refused to post retractions of those messages, and failed to screen for similar postings thereafter).

. . .

Johnson cites the [Craigslist case] for support. Craigslist held that "§ 230(c) as a whole cannot be understood as a general prohibition of civil liability for website operators and other online content hosts. . . ." However, while the Seventh Circuit construes § 230(c)(1) to permit liability for ISPs, it limited that liability to ISPs that intentionally designed their systems to facilitate illegal acts, such as stealing music. Specifically, Craigslist held that an ISP could not be held liable for allowing third parties to place ads in violation of the Fair Housing Act on its website if the ISP did not induce the third party to place discriminatory ads.

The record contains no evidence that InMotion designed its website to be a portal for defamatory material or do anything to induce defamatory postings. We conclude that the CDA provides ISPs like InMotion with federal immunity against state tort defamation actions that would make service providers liable for information originating with third-party users of the service such as the other defendants in this case.

Therefore we decline the Johnsons' invitation to construe § 230(c)(1) as permitting liability against InMotion for material originating with a third party. . . .

Because InMotion was merely an ISP host and not an information content provider . . . the district court properly dismissed the claims.

III. Conclusion   Accordingly, we affirm the judgment of the district court [in favor of defendants InMotion].

Case Questions

1. Why did the court rule that InMotion was not a "publisher or speaker" under the CDA?
2. How did the Johnsons use the "Craigslist" case to bolster their arguments?
3. Should website providers have such broad immunity? Is it good for public policy? Why or why not?

Exhibit 12.1   Summary of CDA Best Practices

- A website that passively hosts third-party content will be protected under § 230 of the CDA.
- A website that exercises traditional editorial functions over user-submitted content, such as deciding whether to publish, remove, or edit material, will not lose immunity unless the edits materially alter the meaning of the content.
- A website operator that prescreens objectionable content or corrects, edits, or removes content, will not lose its immunity.
- A website operator that encourages or pays third parties to create or submit content will not lose its immunity.
- A website that uses drop-down forms or multiple-choice questionnaires should be cautious of allowing users to submit information through these forms that might be deemed illegal.
- Subject to limited exceptions, § 230 of the CDA provides broad protection from liability from a number of different claims.

In *Barnes v. Yahoo! Inc.*, the Ninth Circuit Court of Appeals considers whether a computer service provider can be held liable for negligently failing to remove unauthorized material about the plaintiff posted by a third party.

Barnes v. Yahoo!, Inc.
570 F.3d 1096 (9th Cir. 2009)

Facts In 2004, Barnes, an Oregon resident, broke up with her boyfriend. He responded by posting indecent profiles of her on a website run by Yahoo!. According to Yahoo!'s Member Directory, "[a] public profile is a page with information about you that other Yahoo! members can view. You[r] profile allows you to publicly post information about yourself that you want to share with the world. Many people post their age, pictures, location, and hobbies on their profiles." After the profiles were posted, men who Barnes's ex-boyfriend had contacted using her identity began to harass her.

In accordance with Yahoo! policy, Barnes mailed Yahoo! a copy of her photo ID and a signed statement denying her involvement with the profiles. She then requested their removal. One month later, Yahoo! had not responded and Barnes again requested that Yahoo! remove the profiles. The following month, when the profiles were still not removed, Barnes sent Yahoo! two more requests to have the profiles removed. Only then, the day before a local news program was preparing to broadcast a report on the incident, did a Yahoo! representative call Barnes and ask her to fax directly the previous statements she had mailed. Barnes was told that the representative would "personally walk the statements over to the division responsible for stopping unauthorized profiles and they would take care of it."

Barnes took no further action regarding the profiles and the trouble they had caused. Following another two months without action by Yahoo!, Barnes filed suit against Yahoo! in Oregon state court. After Barnes initiated her suit, the profiles were permanently removed from Yahoo!'s website. The court was asked to find that Yahoo! was negligent in removing the profiles. Yahoo! claimed that the Communications Decency Act, barring courts from treating certain Internet service providers as publishers or speakers, protected Yahoo! from liability. The lower court granted Yahoo!'s motion to dismiss, and the plaintiff appealed to the Court of Appeals for the Ninth Circuit.

Judicial Opinion The court first addressed whether § 230(c)(1) of the Communications Decency Act rendered it immune from liability for the content that Barnes's former boyfriend had posted. The section states: "One who undertakes, gratuitously or for consideration, to render services to another which he should recognize as necessary for the protection of the other's person or things, is subject to liability to the other for physical harm resulting from his failure to exercise reasonable care to perform his undertaking." . . . Initially, the court recognized two specific purposes for the enactment of the statute.

> We have recognized in this declaration of statutory purpose two parallel goals. The statute is designed at once "to promote the free exchange of information and ideas over the Internet and to encourage voluntary monitoring for offensive or obscene material."[13]

The court then considered whether Yahoo! fell within the protected immunity for publishers or speakers of third-party content.

> [C]ourts must ask whether the duty that the plaintiff alleges the defendant violated derives from the defendant's status or conduct as a "publisher or speaker." If it does, section 230(c)(1) precludes liability. . . . Subsection (c)(1), by itself, shields from liability all publication decisions, whether to edit, to remove, or to post, with respect to content generated entirely by third parties.
>
> [T]he duty that Barnes claims Yahoo[!] violated derives from Yahoo[!]'s conduct as a publisher–the steps it allegedly took, but later supposedly abandoned, to depublish the offensive profiles. It is because such conduct is publishing conduct that we have insisted that section 230 protects from liability "any activity that can be boiled down to deciding whether to exclude material that third parties seek to post online."
>
> [S]ection 230(c)(1) precludes courts from treating [I]nternet service providers as publishers not just for the purposes of defamation law, with its particular distinction between primary and secondary publishers, but in general. The statute does not mention defamation, and we decline to read the principles of defamation law into it.[14]

After dismissing Barnes's claim under CDA § 230 (c)(1), the court considered whether she could make a claim under an alternative legal theory.

> . . . Barnes's complaint could also be read to base liability on section 90 of the Restatement (Second) of Contracts, which describes a theory of recovery often known as promissory estoppel. . . . The "principal criteria" that determine[s] "when action renders a promise enforceable" under this doctrine are: "(1) a promise[;] (2) which the promisor, as a reasonable person, could foresee would induce conduct of the kind which occurred[;] (3) actual reliance on the promise[;] (4) resulting in a substantial change in position." . . . Contract liability here would come not from Yahoo[!]'s publishing conduct, but from Yahoo[!]'s manifest intention to be legally obligated to do something, which happens to be removal of material from publication.
>
> [W]e conclude that, insofar as Barnes alleges a breach of contract claim under the theory of promissory estoppel, subsection 230(c)(1) of the Act does not preclude her cause of action.[15]

13. 570 F.3d 1096, 1099-1100 (9th Cir. 2009).
14. *Id.* at 1102, 1103, 1104, 1105.
15. *Id.* at 1106, 1109.

Case Questions

1. How can you explain the difference between the court's denial of Barnes's claim to hold Yahoo! liable as the publisher of a third-party act and its willingness to accept Barnes's quasi-contractual claim under a promissory estoppel theory?

2. *Ethical Consideration:* What do you think was the underlying reason for the court finding that the CDA permitted Yahoo! to avoid liability in this case? Should the CDA help to insulate website operators from liability?

Regulation of E-Commerce

Conducting commercial transactions online has changed rapidly both in terms of how often consumers use the web to purchase products and the structure of the transactions. While e-contracts and licensing issues are covered in Chapter 8 on contracts and licensing, this chapter focuses on government regulation of digital currency and Internet taxation issues.

Bitcoins

Bitcoins are the most well-known, and controversial, form of digital currency. They exist only online and are not controlled by a central authority such as the Federal Reserve, but rather depend on a decentralized peer-to-peer payment network powered by its users. All transactions using Bitcoins take place in an online marketplace where users are typically unable to be identified. Owners of Bitcoins store them in an online wallet through use of "wallet firms" that are set up through a secure third-party website. The wallet firms do not invest or lend deposited money like banks, and there is no regulation of these firms that protect the Bitcoin owners from virtual theft. There are approximately 11 million Bitcoins in existence and owners acquire Bitcoins in one of four ways. First, a seller of goods or services may receive Bitcoins as payment from the buyer. Second, consumers may purchase Bitcoins through a Bitcoin exchange such as Coin Café or expresscoin. Third, users may arrange a private sale from another owner through a website such as LocalBitcoins.com. Fourth, consumers may actually discover new coins through a process called competitive mining. Mining requires users to contribute to the system by solving a complex mathematical problem and successful miners are rewarded with twenty-five new Bitcoins. According to Bitcoin protocols, no more Bitcoins will be released once 21 million are in existence.

While Bitcoins do carry some significant advantages when it comes to payment freedom and lower fees than credit cards, the biggest downside to owning Bitcoins is reluctance by the overwhelming majority of business owners to accept them. The anonymity of Bitcoin owners has attracted those interested in illegal transactions such as illicit drug sales on the infamous, but now defunct, Silk Road marketplace. The Silk Road is covered in more detail in Chapter 14, on security and computer crime. Lack of regulation also carries significant risk for Bitcoin owners. In 2014, Mt. Gox, the world's largest Bitcoin exchange, filed for bankruptcy claiming that $480 million in Bitcoins belonging to their customers had been stolen. Mt. Gox's customers filed a lawsuit accusing the firm of being complicit in a massive fraud scheme.

The increasing coverage of Bitcoins by the media led to increased governmental and law enforcement scrutiny of the use of Bitcoins. The Mt. Gox bankruptcy caused the U.S. Department of Justice to launch an investigation that resulted in criminal charges against the operators of several Bitcoin exchanges who were allegedly involved criminal enterprises. Agencies ranging from the New York bank regulator to the Commodity Futures Trading Commission are actively considering some regulatory plan for virtual currencies. A string of state banking regulators issued warnings to potential investors that virtual currencies were highly volatile and unregulated.

The IRS issued a 2014 revenue ruling that classified Bitcoins as property rather than as currency for tax purposes. The ruling means that Bitcoins are treated more like stocks in that investors would be required to pay capital gains taxes on any profit upon a sale of a Bitcoin. The tax is paid based on any increase in the value of the Bitcoin from the time the investor obtained the Bitcoin until the time it was sold.

Taxation

The debate over the taxation of e-commerce transactions has grown increasingly important to strategies of firms that sell products over the Internet because more consumers and business owners are using web-based sales and the volume of online purchases continues to expand rapidly. The taxation debates centers primarily on two areas: direct taxation of Internet services and tax applied to online purchases.

Internet Tax Freedom Act

In response to efforts by states and local municipalities to tax Internet access via user fees charged to Internet Service Providers, Congress passed the **Internet Tax Freedom Act**[16] which banned any direct taxation of Internet access by state and local government. It also bars discriminatory Internet-only taxes such as bandwidth taxes or taxes on e-mail and prohibits multiple taxes on e-commerce. Seven states that already had their use taxes in place in 1996 were exempted from the law.[17] In theory, the law is temporary, but it has been extended four times. In 2014, the House of Representatives passed the Permanent Internet Tax Freedom Act in an effort to make the ban permanent. The bill was controversial because it ended the state exemptions from the original law and would result

---

16. 47 U.S.C. § 151.
17. Hawaii, New Mexico, North Dakota, Ohio, South Dakota, Texas, and Wisconsin.

in the exempt states losing approximately $500 million a year in combined taxes. The bill ultimately failed to garner Senate support and did not become law.

Sales Tax

The stakes in collecting state and local sales taxes are high. Because states are typically prohibited from requiring any out of state vendors to collect **sales tax** from consumers, state and local sales tax losses from ecommerce are estimated by economists to be about $12.65 billion.[18] The ability of states to impose a sales tax on e-commerce is limited by federal law that requires taxing authorities to prove that an out of state vendor has some physical presence within state boundaries before requiring them to collect sales tax on the transaction. *Stays in state border*

The ability of states to impose sales tax on ecommerce transactions is limited by the Due Process Clause and the Commerce Clause of the U.S. Constitution. From a constitutional perspective, there are a number of requirements that must be met for a tax to be valid. The tax must be fairly related to the services provided by the state. The tax cannot discriminate. The tax must be fairly apportioned, and the business at issue must have a substantial nexus with the taxing state.

1. The tax must be fairly related to services

2. The tax must not discriminate

3. The tax must be fairly portioned.

Problems with e-commerce taxation arise due to the fact that sales taxes are generally imposed based upon the physical presence of a business, while online services and products are generally sold from remote locations. The out-of-state e-business must have a **nexus** or physical connection with the taxing state in which the customer is located before it is obliged to collect and remit sales tax to the state taxation authorities. The physical presence requirement usually takes the form of a retail store, warehouse, employees, or sale representatives doing business in the taxing state. The taxing state must prove this nexus before an out-of-state company is required to collect tax from the buyer and remit it to the state. States may not require online companies to collect and remit sales taxes from their customers when those companies do not have a physical presence in the state.

In *Quill v. North Dakota,*[19] the U.S. Supreme Court held that the Commerce Clause of the U.S. Constitution requires an out-of state merchant to have a physical presence in a state before it can be obligated to collect its taxes.

Quill Corp. v. North Dakota
504 U.S. 298 (1992)

Facts The state of North Dakota filed an action in state court to require Quill Corporation (Quill), an out-of-state mail order house, to collect and pay a use tax on goods purchased for use in the state. The trial court determined that a seller whose only connection with the customers in the state was by common carrier or

---

18. For a detailed review of state and local tax revenues lost, see Prof. Donald Bruce's paper "State and Local Government Sales Tax revenue Losses from Electronic Commerce", www.cber.bus.utk.edu/ecomm.htm.
19. 504 U.S. 298 (1992).

the mail lacked the requisite minimum contacts with the state. The state supreme court reversed, holding that the Commerce and Due Process Clauses did not any longer require a physical presence in the state in order for the state to exercise its power over a company. Despite the fact that Quill, a Delaware corporation, had no employees living or working in North Dakota, the court held that advancements in technology and the mail order business as a whole rendered obsolete the law that required a physical presence in the state.

Judicial Opinion The Supreme Court of the United States described North Dakota's tax in the following way:

> North Dakota imposes a use tax upon property purchased for storage, use, or consumption within the State. North Dakota requires every "retailer maintaining a place of business in" the State to collect the tax from the consumer and remit it to the State.[20]

The statute included a person who engages in regular or in systematic solicitation of a consumer market in North Dakota in the meaning of a retailer. The Supreme Court analyzed the Due Process Clause and the Commerce Clause separately in evaluating the state supreme court's decision.

"The Due Process Clause 'requires some definite link, some minimum connection between a state and the person, property or transaction it seeks to tax.'"[21] This standard has been construed in the past to mean that any company that purposefully avails itself of the benefits of an economic market is considered to have minimum contact with the state. As long as the tax is related to that benefit, the tax would be proper under the Due Process Clause.

The Commerce Clause, observed the Court,

> . . . expressly authorizes Congress to "regulate Commerce with foreign Nations, and among the several States." It says nothing about the protection of interstate commerce in the absence of any action by Congress. Nevertheless, . . . the Commerce Clause is more than an affirmative grant of power; it has a negative sweep as well. The Clause . . . "by its own force" prohibits certain state actions that interfere with interstate commerce.[22]

One of the instances in which the Commerce Clause would prohibit state actions would be when the state taxes someone who does not have a substantial nexus with the taxing state. The state supreme court reasoned that when one has minimum contacts with the state, the substantial nexus test for Commerce Clause purposes would also be fulfilled. But the U.S. Supreme Court ruled that it is possible to have minimum contacts for purposes of the Due Process Clause, and still not have a substantial nexus for purposes of the Commerce Clause. The history of the Commerce Clause dictates that in order to have a substantial nexus with a state, one must have a physical presence there.

---

20. *Id.* at 302 (citing statute).
21. *Id.* at 306 (citation omitted).
22. *Id.* at 309 (citations omitted).

Case Questions

1. Based on the standards articulated in the case summary, should the state be allowed to impose a use tax on Quill even though it does not have a physical presence in the state?

2. Is this the right decision? Should a state be able to impose income taxes on a company whether or not it has a physical presence, as the state supreme court held? Or, was the U.S. Supreme Court correct?

3. ***Ethical Consideration:*** Is this decision fair? Does the decision have the effect of withholding taxes from states that really rightfully deserve them? Quill was doing business in North Dakota. Shouldn't Quill be ethically obligated to pay taxes to a state that generated so much revenue?

Although the *Quill* decision explicitly allowed Congress to enact legislation for the states to impose sales and use taxes on products sold by an out-of-state merchant, to date it has failed to do so. This has not, however, stopped states from attempting to collect sales tax for e-commerce transactions from retailers based outside of the state. Businesses often resist and many cases have resulted. Exhibit 12.2 summarizes the positions commonly taken by the parties in these cases.

Exhibit 12.2 Summary of Positions in Tax Cases

Party	Position
Plaintiff (always a state)	Plaintiff asserts the Defendant business has a sufficient presence in the state to justify imposition of the tax collection burden; because the business takes advantage of the benefits of doing business in this state, it must pay its way.
Defendant (always a business)	Defendant asserts that the state taxation law violates the Constitution because the federal government regulates interstate commerce and the state tax is unduly burdensome to interstate commerce. In the alternative, the business's contacts with the state are not sufficient to justify imposition of the tax collection burden.

An out-of-state web retailer might have a physical presence for tax jurisdiction purposes without having a retail store in the taxing state. In order to avoid being subject to collecting and paying a sales tax to the taxing state, an online company should be aware that other in-state activities may establish a tax nexus with the ebusiness:

- Renting an office or warehouse in the taxing state
- Holding trade shows at which employees or agents take orders from customers in the taxing state

- Using a web merchant's server
- Working with a server in the taxing state
- Licensing software to licensees in the taxing state
- Hiring agents in the taxing state
- Maintaining a business relationship with a brick-and-mortar company in the taxing state

States have been successful in arguing that presence and nexus may also be shown when a business generates revenue through its intellectual property rights. In the next case, a state appellate court considers the assessment of a state tax on a famous toy retailer who received licensing royalties from retailers located in their state.

Geoffrey, Inc. v. Commissioner
453 Mass. 17, 899 IM.E.2d 87 (2009)

Facts   Appellant Geoffrey, Inc. (Geoffrey) was given, and now owns, several trademarks, trade names, and service names that are associated with Toys "R" Us, Inc. Geoffrey's business consisted of licensing out these trademarks (through contracts) to various Toys "R" Us retail locations, including the one that is the subject of this case, Toys "R" Us Mass. Inc, which operated twenty-six Toys "R" Us locations in Massachusetts. Geoffrey had the rights to conduct inspections and oversee activities primarily to ensure that the trade names did not become generic. Geoffrey also received royalties from the retail locations throughout Massachusetts.

In 2002, during a state audit of Geoffrey, the tax commissioner discovered that Geoffrey was not filing corporate excise returns in Massachusetts and provided it with a notice of deficiency for not paying taxes on the royalties earned from the retail locations there. The basis for this tax was Massachusetts General Laws Ch. 63 § 39, which states:

> [E]very foreign corporation, exercising its charter, or qualified to do business or actually doing business in the commonwealth, or owning or using any part or all of its capital, plant or any other property in the commonwealth, shall pay, on account of each taxable year, the [specified] excise.[23]

Geoffrey filed an application for abatement, claiming that it was not required to pay taxes in Massachusetts on the royalties since it did not have a physical presence in the state. The commissioner and the board denied the application. Geoffrey filed appeal to the appellate tax board, which affirmed the denial. The tax board's reasoning in denying the application was that Geoffrey had a substantial

---

23. 899 N.E.2d 87, 91 (Mass. 2009).

nexus with the state and it purposefully entered into that state to reap economic benefits, factors that would allow an income tax to be imposed on it.

Judicial Opinion The Supreme Court of Massachusetts stated that the standard that it must apply in assessing the board's decision is that:

> A decision by the board will not be modified or reversed if the decision "is based on both substantial evidence and a correct application of the law." We presume that a tax is constitutionally valid unless the party challenging it establishes its invalidity "beyond a rational doubt." While we give deference to the board's expertise in interpreting the tax laws of the Commonwealth, we apply our independent judgment as to both the law and the facts on constitutional issues.[24]

The Supreme Court of Massachusetts held that a physical presence is not necessary in order for a state to impose an income tax on interstate commerce. Rather, only a substantial nexus is required. The court specifically held that an income tax may be imposed when the following is fulfilled: (1) the tax is applied to an activity with a substantial nexus in that state, (2) it is fairly apportioned, (3) it does not discriminate against interstate commerce, and (4) it is fairly related to the services provided by the state. To establish a substantial nexus, the business activities must be more than a mere slight presence, and if economic activities are performed in-state by the business's personnel or on the business's behalf, a substantial nexus can be established. In this case, Geoffrey's trademarks appeared in many places in the Massachusetts locations including on signs, packaging, and store displays.

> Here, Geoffrey engaged in business activities with a substantial nexus to Massachusetts during the tax years at issue. Geoffrey entered into contractual relationships, in the form of licensing agreements, with TRUMI and Baby Superstore and permitted those entities to use the trademarks exclusively in Massachusetts; Geoffrey encouraged Massachusetts consumers to shop at Toys "R" Us, Kids "R" Us, and Babies "R" Us through an implicit promise, manifested by the trademarks, that the products at those stores would be of good quality and value; Geoffrey relied on employees at TRUMI to maintain a positive retail environment, including store cleanliness and proper merchandise display; and Geoffrey reviewed licensed products and materials that would be sold in the Commonwealth to ensure high standards and to maintain its positive reputation with Massachusetts consumers, thereby generating continued business and substantial profits. Geoffrey's annual royalty income from retail stores in the Commonwealth for the tax year ending February 1,1997, was $5,928,567, and it increased to $7,423,420, by the tax year ending February 3, 2001. Based on the findings of the board, we conclude that Geoffrey's activities established a substantial nexus with Massachusetts, and, therefore, the assessment of the corporate excises, pursuant to G.L. c. 63, § 39., for the tax years at issue comported with the commerce clause.[25]

---

24. *Id.* at 91 (citations omitted).
25. *Id.* at 93.

Case Questions

1. Based on the standards articulated in *Geoffrey, Inc.,* should the state be allowed to impose a tax on the income that Geoffrey receives from royalties from the Massachusetts chain stores?

2. It seems as though all Geoffrey would have to do in order to prevent taxation in Massachusetts would be to license out the name for a set price and then not have anything else to do with the locations there. Why would Geoffrey hesitate to do that?

3. *Ethical Consideration:* Did the *Geoffrey* court reach the right decision? Should a company have to pay income taxes in a state where it receives royalties even though it has no presence there? Surely the company pays federal and state taxes on the income it receives. Should it have to first pay royalty taxes in Massachusetts?

"Amazon" Laws: Current Trends in Internet Taxation

State legislatures and brick-and-mortar business owners have lobbied for federal laws that would enable state governments to collect sales taxes from remote retailers with no physical presence in their state. The traditional retailers have complained that online retailers have a distinct advantage due to what amounts to tax free shopping on the Internet. Some members of Congress tried to address those concerns through the Marketplace Fairness Act, a bill supported by state legislatures and brick-and-mortar retailers. The law was proposed in 2011 and 2013, but did not gain sufficient support and the proposed law was never enacted.

State legislatures became frustrated over the federal government's refusal to step into the sales tax controversy and have acted on their own. In the past few years, New York, Minnesota, Illinois, and Maine have led the way by imposing various taxes related to Internet sales that involved downloading digital audio works like songs, audio books, speeches, ring tones and other recordings. In 2008, the New York state legislature redefined "presence" for purposes of establishing a tax nexus by including any website based in the state that earns a referral fee for sending customers to an online retailer. The law was meant to sweep hundreds of thousands of Amazon affiliates (everyone from large publishers to microbloggers) into the definition of the necessary physical presence for purposes of forcing Amazon to collect state sales tax. Although some Amazon laws have survived judicial scrutiny thus far, other attempts by states to tax Internet sales have been struck down. For example, in 2011, the Illinois legislature passed the Main Street Fairness Act, their own version of the Amazon-tax law, which expanded the scope of its sales tax collection law to include any business affiliated with large Internet retailers such as Amazon. In the following case, the Illinois Supreme Court considers a challenge to the validity of the Main Street Fairness Act.

Performance Marketing Association v. Hamer

998 N.E.2d 54 (Ill 2013)

Facts Sales tax in the State of Illinois is comprised of two complementary taxes, the Retailers' Occupation Tax Act, which is the principal means for taxing the retail sale of tangible personal property in Illinois, and use tax. Use tax is imposed "upon the privilege of using in this State tangible personal property purchased at retail from a retailer." The purpose of the use tax is "primarily to prevent avoidance of the [retailers' occupation] tax by people making out-of-State purchases, and to protect Illinois merchants against such diversion of business to retailers outside Illinois. The Retailers' Occupation Tax and the use tax are imposed at the same rate.

The ultimate responsibility for paying the use tax falls upon the consumer. However, because it is impractical to collect the tax from individual purchasers, the burden of its collection is imposed upon the out-of-state retailer. In Illinois, any retailer "maintaining a place of business in this State" is required by statute to collect use tax from its customers and remit it to the Illinois Department of Revenue.

In 2011, the Illinois General Assembly enacted the Main Street Fairness Act (Act). In relevant part, the Act amended the definition of a retailer or serviceman "maintaining a place of business in this state" in Illinois' Use Tax and Service Use Tax Acts.

Thus, pursuant to the Act, out-of-state internet retailers and servicemen are required to collect state use tax if they have a contract with a person in Illinois who displays a link on his or her website that connects an Internet user to that remote retailer or serviceman's website. There is no requirement under the Act that sales be made to Illinois residents to subject the out-of-state retailer or serviceman to Illinois use tax obligations, and there is no requirement that the computer server hosting the Illinois affiliate's website be located in Illinois. Both new definitions are limited, however, to referral contracts that generate over $10,000 per year.

The type of contractual relationship taxed by the new definitions in the Act is known as "performance marketing." Performance marketing refers to marketing or advertising programs in which a person or organization that publishes or displays an advertisement (often referred to as an "affiliate" or "publisher") is paid by the retailer when a specific action, such as a sale, is completed. In performance marketing, the retailer tracks the success or "performance" of the marketing campaign and sets the affiliate's compensation accordingly. Such contractual arrangements are not limited to the Internet. They are also used in print and broadcast media, where promotional codes are used to generate and track sales.

After the Act was enacted, plaintiff, a trade group that represents businesses engaged in performance marketing, filed a complaint against defendant in the circuit court of Cook County. In count I of its complaint, plaintiff alleged that the new definitions in the Act were unconstitutional under the commerce clause of the United States Constitution (U.S. Const., art. I, § 8), because they authorized the collection of use tax with respect to an activity that lacked a substantial nexus with the state of Illinois. In count III of its complaint, plaintiff alleged that the provisions of the Act were expressly preempted by the Internet Tax Freedom Act (ITFA), which prohibits "discriminatory taxes on electronic commerce." Plaintiff and defendant filed cross-motions for summary judgment.

Judicial Opinion Plaintiff argues that the relevant provisions of the Act are expressly preempted under section 1101(a)(2) of the ITFA (47 U.S.C. §151 note). That section prohibits a state from imposing "discriminatory taxes on electronic commerce." Section 1105(2)(A)(iii) of the ITFA defines a discriminatory tax, in part, as:

> "(A) any tax imposed by a State or political subdivision thereof on electronic commerce that—
>
> * * *
>
> (iii) imposes an obligation to collect or pay tax on a different person or entity than in the case of transactions involving similar property, goods, services, or information accomplished through other means." 47 U.S.C. §151 note.

The term "tax" in turn is defined in sections 1105(8)(A)(i) and (ii) of the ITFA to include both revenue-raising measures and "the imposition on a seller of an obligation to collect and to remit to a governmental entity any sales or use tax imposed on a buyer by a governmental entity." "Electronic commerce" is defined in section 1105(3) as "any transaction conducted over the Internet *** comprising the sale *** of property, goods, [or] services."

Plaintiff argues that, under the plain language of the ITFA, the relevant provisions of the Act constitute a prohibited, discriminatory tax on electronic commerce. According to plaintiff, the amended definitions of retailer and serviceman "maintaining a place of business in this State" result in the "imposition on a seller of an obligation to collect and remit" use tax, and thus constitute a "tax" within the meaning of the ITFA. Further, the Act's tax-collection obligation is targeted at out-of-state Internet retailers who enter into agreements with Internet affiliates for online performance marketing arrangements and, thus, applies to electronic commerce as defined in the ITFA . . . .

According to defendant, this provision covers "offline" performance marketing contracts that are similar to those entered into with Internet affiliates. Thus, in defendant's view, the Act is not discriminatory within the meaning of the ITFA. We disagree.

Under paragraph 3 of the definition section of the Use Tax Act, retailers who enter into contracts with Illinois publishers and broadcasters for advertising "disseminated primarily to consumers located in this State," i.e., locally, are obligated to collect use tax. But Internet advertising is different. As the parties' joint stipulation of facts states: "The home page and other publicly-available pages of any Internet website can be accessed from a computer, or other digital device, located anywhere in the world that is connected to the Internet via wire or radio signal. Thus, information appearing on a webpage is available and disseminated worldwide." Illinois law does not presently require out-of-state retailers who enter into performance marketing contracts for "offline" print or broadcast advertising that is disseminated nationally, or internationally, to collect Illinois use tax. However, under the Act, out-of-state retailers who enter into such contracts with Illinois Internet affiliates for the publication of online marketing—which is inherently national or international in scope and disseminated to a national or international audience—are required to collect Illinois use tax. In this way, by singling out retailers with Internet performance marketing arrangements for use tax collection, the Act imposes discriminatory taxes within the meaning of the ITFA. . . .

In short, under the Act, performance marketing over the Internet provides the basis for imposing a use tax collection obligation on an out-of-state retailer when a threshold of $10,000 in sales through the clickable link is reached. However, national, or international, performance marketing by an out-of-state retailer which appears in print or on over-the-air broadcasting in Illinois and which reaches the same dollar threshold will not trigger an Illinois use tax collection obligation. The relevant provisions of the Act therefore impose a discriminatory tax on electronic commerce within the meaning of the ITFA. Accordingly, we affirm the circuit court's judgment that the definition provisions contained in the Act, quoted above and codified at 35 ILCS 105/2(1.1) (West 2010), and 35 ILCS 110/2(1.1) (West 2010), are expressly preempted by the ITFA and are therefore void and unenforceable. Because we hold that the provisions of the Act are void based on preemption, we do not reach plaintiff's alternative argument that the new definitions provisions of the Act violate the commerce clause of the United States Constitution. . . .

CONCLUSION

For the foregoing reasons, the judgment of the circuit court granting summary judgment in favor of [Performance Marketing Association] and denying [State Commissioner of Revenue's] motion for summary judgment is affirmed.

Affirmed.

Case Questions

1. Why did the court decide that the ITFA conflicted with Illinois statute?
2. What was the State of Illinois main argument to support the law?
3. How did the Illinois statute expand the definition of out-of-state Internet retailers?

Regulation by Local Authorities

While much of the regulation of Internet firms and users comes from federal and state authorities, local governments also play a role in day-to-day operations of business owners and managers. For example, ridesharing services such as UberX, Lyft, and Sidecar have all been the subject of enforcement efforts in San Francisco,

Los Angeles, and Philadelphia. The services are running afoul of local ordinances that regulate common carriers such as taxis. In Los Angeles, the local District Attorney threatened to take action against drivers using such services because the cars and drivers were not licensed according to the public utilities code. In Philadelphia, the city's parking authority began to impound cars and issue fines to users of UberX after the company launched its service there contrary to warnings issued by city officials.

Another attempt to regulate by local authorities that garnered substantial media attention was when a California motorist who drove while wearing Google Glass was cited by police under a section prohibiting the operation of a television or video screen while driving. Although the traffic court judge made clear that the law was broad enough to apply to Google Glass, the citation was dismissed since there was no evidence that the device was activated while the driver was operating the car.

Regulation of Markets

Governments are concerned with concentrations of economic power that distort optimum market conditions—a sort of free, unregulated marketplace. This marketplace has many sellers and many buyers who freely enter into transactions with full knowledge of the terms and the bargained-for goods or services. **Antitrust** laws regulate and encourage competition.

Overview of U.S. Antitrust Law

United States antitrust law is the body of laws that prohibits anticompetitive behavior and related unfair business practices. At the core of antitrust law is prohibition of any monopoly that restrains competition using its size to unfairly compete. Antitrust laws seek to allow competition in the marketplace, targeting activities that lessen or discourage competition. Regulators generally look at whether a company is erecting a barrier of entry into a market for other companies. Outside of the United States, antitrust law is known simply as competition law.

The two main U.S. antitrust laws are the **Sherman Act** and the **Clayton Act**. The Sherman Antitrust Act, 15 U.S.C. Sections 1-7, limits cartels and monopolies, and empowers the federal government to investigate and prosecute companies and organizations that violate the Act. Its purpose is to halt the combination of entities that might harm competition.

Section 1 of the Sherman Act states, "Every contract, combination in the form of trust or otherwise, or conspiracy, in restraint of trade or commerce among the several States, or with foreign nations, is declared to be illegal." Thus, in prosecutions for violating the Act, the government is required to prove 1) that an agreement has been reached 2) that unreasonably restrains competition and 3) that affects interstate commerce.

Section 2 states, "Every person who shall monopolize, or attempt to monopolize, or combine or conspire with any other person or persons, to monopolize any part of the trade or commerce among the several States, or with foreign nations, shall be deemed guilty of a felony. . . ." Thus, proof of a violation of Section 2 of the Sherman Act requires a showing of (1) monopoly power in a particular market and (2) willful acquisition or maintenance of that power.

The Clayton Antitrust Act of 1914, 15 U.S.C. Sections 12-27 and 29 U.S.C. Sections 52-53, supplements the Sherman Act and focuses on prevention of anticompetitive practices. There are four sections of the Clayton Act.

- One section prohibits **price discrimination** between different purchasers of the same product, when the discrimination substantially lessens competition or creates or furthers a monopoly.
- Another part prohibits sales conditioned on 1) a purchaser agreeing not to deal with the seller's competitors or 2) the purchaser also buying a different product at the same time (tying), if one of these acts substantially lessens competition.
- Another section prohibits any merger or acquisition that substantially lessens competition.
- There is a section that prohibits an individual from being a director or corporate officer of competing corporations (**interlocking directorates**). In 2009, interlocking directorates made headlines when Google's CEO resigned from Apple's board of directors following the FTC's investigation into a possible Section 8 violation. Shortly thereafter, another individual resigned from the boards of both Apple and Google, and then a third person, a director at Google, resigned from the board of Amazon amid the FTC's investigation into the Google-Amazon relationship. Although such overlapping roles are not uncommon, the FTC warned that "co-opetition"—marketing and developing products or services in one market while competing in another—poses the risk of improper agreements and information-sharing that could hurt consumers, running afoul of U.S. antitrust laws.

Enforcement

In the United States, the Federal Trade Commission (FTC) through its Bureau of Competition and Bureau of Economics, and the Department of Justice (DOJ) via its Antitrust Division, enforce the federal antitrust laws. Additionally, state attorney generals enforce state antitrust statutes, and private persons "injured" in their "business or property" by an antitrust law violation may file civil suits against alleged violators. In an antitrust case like the cases discussed below, the plaintiff is usually the government. The defendant is a business or an organization.

Tying

Another aspect of antitrust law with frequent application to the online realm is **tying**. When a seller requires the buyer to purchase a second product or service in conjunction with the purchase of the buyer's choice, and the tying substantially affects competition, the antitrust laws are triggered.

Apple has allegedly run afoul of antitying laws on several occasions. In 2009, Apple told software developers making applications for Apple's iPhone, iPod Touch, and iPad, that they had to use Apple programming tools. In *In Re Apple & AT&TM Antitrust Litigation,* the court considers Apple's position (just after it introduced the iPhone), in seeking to contractually bind consumers to use only Apple applications on their iPhones and only a particular carrier—AT&T Mobility—for their phone service.[26]

In Re Apple & AT&TM Antitrust Litigation
596 F. Supp. 2d 1288 (N.D. Cal. 2008)

Facts This litigation arose from Apple, manufacturer of cellular telephone equipment, joining with AT&T Mobility (AT&TM), supplier of voice and data services, to provide to consumers a cell phone with service. Pursuant to an arrangement between the companies, the purchaser of an Apple iPhone became bound contractually to use AT&TM as its cell phone service provider.

> Plaintiffs allege that consumers were offered iPhones only if they signed a two-year service agreement with AT&T Mobility. Plaintiffs allege, however, that unknown to consumers, the companies had agreed to technologically restrict voice and data service in the aftermarket for continued voice and data services, i.e., after the initial two-year service period expired?[27]

In the proceedings on Apple's motion to dismiss, Apple contended that the plaintiffs did not state a claim under § 2 of the Sherman Act. Apple argued that the plaintiffs alleged neither legally cognizable markets under the Sherman Act, nor legally sufficient monopolization of those markets.

Judicial Opinion Denying Defendants' Motion to Dismiss, the court determined that Plaintiffs stated a cause of action upon which relief could be granted.

> Section 2 of the Sherman Act prohibits monopolization, attempted monopolization and conspiracy to monopolize "any part of the trade or commerce among the several States." 15 U.S.C. § 2. To state a valid claim under the Sherman Act, a plaintiff "must allege that the defendant has market power within a 'relevant market.'" *Newcal Industries, Inc. v. IKON Office Solution*, 513 F.3d 1038, 1044 (9th Cir. 2008) (citing *Eastman Kodak Co. v. Image Technical Services, Inc.*, 504 U.S. 451, 481, 112 S. Ct. 2072, 119 L. Ed. 2d 265 (1992))[28]

---

26. See Mark DeFeo, *Unlocking the iPhone: How Antitrust law Can Save Consumers From the Inadequacies of Copyright law,* 49 B.C. L. Rev. 1037 (2009).
27. 596 F. Supp. 2d at 1294.
28. *Id.* at 1301.

Thus, the two factors that must be proven are (1) a legally cognizable market and (2) monopolization of that market.

In *In re Apple,* the district court looked at the plaintiffs' market allegations relating to two markets: 1) an aftermarket in voice and data services for the iPhone, and 2) an aftermarket in iPhone applications. Apple contended there was no relevant aftermarket for the iPhone voice and data services. But the plaintiffs alleged that although they agreed to the two-year plan, they "did not agree to use AT&TM for five years," yet "Apple and AT&TM enforced this exclusivity by programming and installing software locks on each iPhone to prevent purchasers from later switching to another wireless carrier," which bound consumers for five years and prevented them switching carriers, even if they paid a $175 termination fee to AT&TM.[29] The court found that these allegations recited facts that, when presumed to be true, supported the existence of an aftermarket for iPhone voice and data services under the *Newcal* standard.

> Principally, Plaintiffs have alleged an aftermarket for iPhone voice and data services that "would not exist without" the primary market for iPhones, and is thus "wholly derivative from and dependent on the primary market." *Newcal*, 513 F.3d at 1049. Plaintiffs' Complaint is also adequate to the extent the alleged aftermarket is predicated on an initial contractual relationship between Defendants and iPhone purchasers.[30]

Further, the plaintiffs alleged a present injury, even if they had not yet tried to switch their voice and data service.

> Plaintiffs are alleging that at the point of purchase and initiation of service, Defendants involuntarily impose on consumers a contract exclusivity restriction which restricts their freedom from that point forward for at least the next five years and conceivably for the life of the iPhone . . . The fact that some consumers might not have sought to switch service and thus do not realize the restriction which the Apple/AT&TM Agreement has imposed on them does not alter the effect of Plaintiffs' allegation that their freedom in the aftermarket has already been taken from them.[31]

Likewise, the plaintiffs sufficiently alleged an after-market for iPhone applications. Not only did Apple create iPhone-specific applications, it also built technological restrictions into the phone and policed those restrictions. This was sufficient to state a claim under §2 of the Sherman Act.[32]

Having found that these two markets existed, the court then concluded that Apple possessed power in the relevant markets—a key factor to a finding of monopolization.

> Plaintiffs have alleged that Defendants "achieve[d] market power through contractual provisions that they obtain[ed] in the initial market" for iPhones and attendant two-year

---

29. *Id.* at 1303.
30. *Id.*
31. *Id.* at 1304.
32. *Id.*

service contracts. Through the initial iPhone purchase and contracting, Defendants are alleged to have gained the "special access" to consumers by which they are then able to lock purchasers into use of AT&TM . . . [and] into use of only applications in which Apple maintained a financial interest. Apple is then alleged to have enforced its special position through technological controls. . . .[33]

Accordingly, the court denied Apple's motion to dismiss the plaintiffs' antitrust claims relating to both the iPhone voice and data services and iPhone applications aftermarkets.

Case Questions

1. On what basis did the district court reject Apple's argument that the plaintiffs' claims should be dismissed because they had not actually suffered any injury?
2. *Ethical Consideration:* Suppose your company's engineers figured out how to manufacture applications that worked on the iPhone or another Apple product. Should you manufacture and sell them, so you can share in some of Apple's success? Would such a move find support in antitrust law? On the other hand, is it possible without running afoul of antitrust laws for a competitor to make a similar product?
3. Suppose a customer purchases several Apple devices, downloads Apple-compatible applications, and puts her personal data on the devices. Apple then makes it impossible for this consumer to use her own data on another device of her choice. Should regulators step in? Why or why not? Are consumers really harmed if various services are bundled together, but everything is free?

Maintaining a competitive marketplace is one of the U.S. government's primary areas of regulatory interest. While the Sherman Act and the Clayton Act were created long before the information age, their relevance to the computer industry, especially software goods and online services, is apparent. As the *In re Apple* case illustrates, companies that provide information goods and services must operate within the parameters of existing antitrust regulations. Federal enforcers will prosecute statutory violations, and they will scrutinize—and possibly prevent—proposed actions that threaten to lessen competition.

Antitrust and Employee Poaching in the Tech Sector

In 2010, the U.S. Department of Justice (DOJ) launched an antitrust investigation against tech giants Google, Apple, Adobe, Intel, Intuit, Pixar, and Lucasfilm, over their involvement in a secret anti-poaching conspiracy which resulted in an artificial restraint to keep their employees' wages lower by agreeing not to recruit each other's employees, sharing wage scale information, and punishing violators.

---

33. *Id.* at 1305, 1306.

The DOJ filed an antitrust suit which alleged that the so-called "no cold call" agreement was a per se violation of the Sherman Act. The defendant companies settled the DOJ lawsuit and agreed to a broad prohibition against entering, maintaining, or enforcing any agreement that interferes with competition for employee talent. The investigation led to a class action suit against the firms by more than 64,000 Silicon Valley tech workers. An attempt to settle the case for $324.5 million was rejected by the court in 2014 as insufficient to protect the plaintiffs' interests.

International Perspectives: Google's EU Antitrust Woes

A four-year battle between the European Union's antitrust chief and Google is likely to continue well into the future. EU officials launched the investigation in 2010 alleging that Google had abused its dominant position in online searches. Google reached a tentative deal with antitrust regulators by agreeing to display rivals' links more prominently in its search results, but EU competition chief Margrethe Vestager issued a statement that indicated her intent to continue the investigation. According to Vestager, the EU probe raised "very important questions" about access to vital markets.

Summary

Like all businesses, entrepreneurs and managers of firms that use the Internet as part of their business model face government regulation. Regulating businesses in cyberspace is a particular challenge because the nature of e-commerce can be too fluid to regulate. Regulators struggle with issues such as net neutrality and regulation of traditional common carriers by the FCC. Federal and state governments also regulate Internet content and e-commerce transactions including digital currency such as Bitcoins as well as whether and how to tax Internet use and sales. Finally, governments also regulate firms competitiveness through use of antitrust laws.

Key Terms

net neutrality Principle that all movement and content on the Internet should be treated similarly by service providers.

throttling Practice by broadband providers of slowing down a consumer's Internet speed once they exceeded a certain amount of data.

wireless spectrum management Managing radio frequency spectrum to maximize use and minimize interference.

user-generated content (UGC) Various types of content created by end-users rather than by the website operator.

Communications Decency Act (CDA) Federal law that provides certain immunity to providers of Internet services and website hosts.

bitcoins Most well-known form of digital currency that is based on a decentralized peer-to-peer network.

Internet Tax Freedom Act Federal law that bans direct taxation of Internet access by state and local government.

sales tax Tax levied by state and local governments on the sale of certain products or services.

nexus Legal requirement that states justify sales tax based on a connection between the vendor and the taxing state.

antitrust Federal laws that regulate and encourage competition.

Sherman Act Federal law which is the centerpiece of antitrust regulation.

Clayton Act Federal law focused on prevention of anticompetitive practices.

price discrimination Anticompetitive practice of price determination which leads to a monopoly.

interlocking directorates Prohibited by the Clayton Act, this is the practice of having the same individuals act as officers/directors in competing corporations.

tying Requiring the buyer to purchase a second product in conjunction with the first product chosen by the buyer.

Manager's Checklist

1. Managers of e-businesses must be aware of the impact of law, market-forces, funding, and technology on the regulation of their businesses. The regulation of e-commerce and other online conduct continues to evolve and, as a result, companies engaging in online transactions must remain vigilant about changes that will impact their businesses.

2. Net neutrality is the idea that all information going across the Internet should be treated equally, but in reality, some information, such as streaming videos, creates more Internet congestion. The debate over net neutrality is being played out in Congress and the marketplace. Although it remains to be seen how Internet information will be regulated by the government, multi-tier users are likely going to be required to pay extra fees. From the standpoint of an Internet business manager using data-rich content, it is smart to be aware that the cost of Internet usage might be higher.

3. Although the general trend is to limit the liability of website operators for defamatory statements posted by their end users, website operators should nonetheless have an aggressive antidefamation policy and act to remove offending information whenever it is found.

4. Operators of e-commerce businesses must stay abreast of changes and be prepared to adjust their operations when necessary. Noncompliance with tax law can result in substantial penalties for the e-business. Managers should work closely with tax advisors to ensure that they are collecting tax in a manner that complies with applicable legal requirements.

Questions and Case Problems

1. Plaintiff LiveUniverse, Inc. (LiveUniverse), and Defendant MySpace, Inc. (MySpace) are social networking companies that operate websites on the Internet allowing users to create profiles, view friends' profiles, and perform other social activities. MySpace created a system that does not allow users to view videos posted through LiveUniverse's website, Vidilife.com, and it also deleted any references by MySpace users to the Vidilife website. LiveUniverse alleges that these actions violate the Sherman Act by monopolizing, or attempting to monopolize, the market for social networking. LiveUniverse filed a complaint in the District Court for the Central District of California.

   According to the district court, in order to establish a claim for monopolization, one must prove three elements: "(i) possession of monopoly power in the relevant market, (ii) the willful acquisition or maintenance of that power as distinguished from growth or development as a consequence of a superior product, business acumen, or historic accident, and (iii) causal antitrust injury." Possession of monopoly power in a relevant market means that the company has the power to exclude competition in an identified market of goods or services in a certain geographic region by owning dominant shares of the market and putting up barriers to entry. The second monopolization prong requires that the alleged violator of the Act engaged in exclusionary conduct. This means that its actions harmed the competitive process *and* thereby harmed consumers. Mere harm to one of its competitors is not enough to show monopolization. Finally, one must show causal antitrust injury, which means injury to the competitive process that flows from the defendant's anticompetitive actions. If one cannot establish that the defendant's actions were anticompetitive by satisfying the second prong, the third prong is obviously impossible to prove.

   Based on the foregoing, discuss whether or not LiveUniverse should be able to claim monopolization by MySpace on the market for social networking. What should the district court conclude, and why?[34]

2. Defendant Consumeraffairs.com, Inc. (Consumeraffairs) operates a website that allows consumers to comment on their experiences with various businesses, goods, and services. The subject of this suit is a car dealership, Nemet Chevrolet (Nemet), the plaintiff, which claimed it was defamed by Consumeraffairs by several negative postings about Nemet on Consumeraffairs's website.

---

34. *LiveUniverse, Inc. v. MySpace, Inc.,* No. CV 06-6994 AHM, 2007 WL 6865852 (CD. Cal. June 5, 2007).

Nemet filed suit in the United States District Court for the Eastern District of Virginia. Consumeraffairs moved to dismiss the case on the ground that it was barred by Section 230 of the CDA, which precludes plaintiffs from holding interactive computer service providers liable for publication of information created by a third party. The motion to dismiss was granted and the case was appealed to the United States Court of Appeals for the Fourth Circuit.

On appeal, Nemet contended that Consumeraffairs was an *information content* provider, which would preclude it from receiving immunity under the CDA. The basis of this allegation is the fact that some of the postings had no apparent author, such that allegedly Consumeraffairs must have been the author, thereby making it an information content provider.

In order to overcome a motion to dismiss, a plaintiff must make more than mere conclusory statements and bare assertions.

Is Nemet's claim that Consumeraffairs should not have immunity, valid? Is the fact that Nemet cannot ascertain the author of the posts enough to support its allegation that Consumeraffairs is the author—thus categorizing Consumeraffairs as an information content provider that does not have immunity?[35]

3. The Jenkins Act, a federal law, requires any out-of-state sellers of cigarettes to submit customer information to the states in which it sells its cigarettes. The purpose of the Act is to ensure that purchasers of cigarettes pay the appropriate taxes when purchasing. The Racketeer Influenced and Corrupt Organizations Act (RICO), another federal law, provides for criminal penalties for racketeering activities, which includes mail and wire fraud.

In this case, Plaintiff, the City of New York, brought an action based on these two federal statutes against Hemi Group (Hemi), a New Mexico based company, for not filing the Jenkins Act report when selling cigarettes over the Internet to customers in New York City. New York alleged that the failure to file the report constituted mail and wire fraud under RICO. The District Court for the Southern District of New York dismissed the action. The Court of Appeals for the Second Circuit vacated the judgment and remanded the case. It was appealed to the Supreme Court of the United States.

In order to establish a claim based on RICO, New York would have to show that the taxes that it should have received from the customers purchasing the cigarettes was "by reason of Hemi not complying with the Jenkins Act reporting requirements and thereby violating RICO. To satisfy the requirement of "by reason of," New York would have to show that it was not only a "but for" cause, but also a proximate cause of its lost taxes. *Decide and state your reasons why or why not the Supreme Court should affirm the judgment of the district court dismissing New York's claim of Hemi's violation of RICO.*[36]

4. In a stated effort to enforce laws concerning child pornography, the United States Department of Justice asked a number of leading Internet companies,

---

35. *Nemet Chevrolet Ltd. v. Consumeraffairs.com, Inc.,* 591 F.3d 250 (4th Cir. 2009).
36. *Hemi Group, LLC v. New York,* _____ U.S. _____, 130 S. Ct. 983 (2010).

including Yahoo!, Google, America Online and Microsoft to turn over records concerning Internet users' online searches. Although Yahoo!, America Online and Microsoft complied with the request, Google resisted, choosing to fight the government's subpoena in court. This case shows how companies in private industry are often called upon to provide information to assist the government in its law enforcement and antiterrorism activities. *Consider and discuss whether the government should make such requests of companies operating in the private sector and whether companies should comply with those requests, even when compliance requires the company to breach privacy promises made to its customers.*

5. Users of the popular Internet website Craigslist are able to post advertisements for housing that permit statements regarding the preference, limitation, or discrimination of others based on race, religion, sex, or family status. The Fair Housing Act (FHA), however, prohibits making, printing, or publishing a notice, statement, or advertisement for sale or rental of dwellings indicating preference, limitation, or discrimination based on protected classes. As such, Chicago Lawyers Committee for Civil Rights Under Law, Inc. brought suit against Craigslist alleging a violation of the FHA. In defense, Craigslist claimed that it was immune from liability based on Section 230(c)(1) of the CDA, which protects interactive computer services from liability for unlawful third-party content. *Should Craigslist be subject to liability for FHA violations? Why or why not? Cite to appropriate legal principles when explaining your answer.*[37]

Additional Resources

American Civil Liberties Union. ACLU on Net Neutrality. www.aclu.org/net-neutrality.

Bitcoins. http://Bitcoin.org/en/faq.

Educause. Educause Resources on Net Neutrality. http://www. educause.edu/Resources/Browse/Net%20Neutrality/ 31666.

Electronic Frontier Foundation. Electronic Frontier Foundation: Legal Guide for Bloggers. http://www.eff.org/issues/bloggers/legal.

Federal Communications Commission. Federal Communications Commission Resources on Broadband Network Management. http://www.fcc. gov/broadband_network_management.

Federal Trade Commission. Federal Trade Commission Business Guide to Consumer Protection Issues. http://www.ftc.gov/bcp/business.shtm.

---

37. *Chicago Lawyers Committee for Civil Rights Under Law, Inc. v. Craigslist,* 519 F.3d 666 (7th Cir. 2008).

 Today, data is more deeply woven into the fabric of our lives than ever before. We . . . use data to solve problems, improve well-being, and generate economic prosperity. The collection, storage and analysis of data is on an upward . . . trajectory. But the volume of information that people create themselves [emails, texts, photos, etc.]—pales in comparison to the amount of digital information created about them each day."

—Big Data: Seizing Opportunities, Preserving Values, Executive Office of the President, May 2014, at 1-2.

Data Privacy and Management

Learning Outcomes

After you have read this chapter you should be able to:

- Understand the relationship between the First and Fourth Amendments, and the concept of privacy.
- Understand the sources of privacy at both the federal and state levels: constitutional, statutory, agency, tort theories, case law, and emerging theories.
- Understand that the U.S. sectoral, reactive approach to data privacy combined with industry self-regulation differs from the E.U. approach, which is comprehensive, and learn how to manage cross-border transactions.
- Understand that the big data era has vastly broadened the impact and scope of managing data.
- Identify who should have responsibility for data in enterprise, and how to tier access, govern uses, and inventory data throughout the business, and develop legal compliance and governance protocols.

Overview

The Internet has made a remarkable impact on communications and the ways that we communicate. As they have multiplied, the data trails they leave has, too. Sensors and the Internet of things is trending, and our devices now will be communicating too. Every chat/text/video/like/tweet/Instagram moment is a data moment, and every click/swipe/send and end is a data point that has value.

We pay for "free" apps and software with our data, our privacy. This data, mined through surveillance and tracking, then aggregated, analyzed, mapped and modeled, can play a useful economic role. For users, they benefit from enhanced relevancy, personalization, and knowledge. Businesses use this data to deliver these more meaningful results. This presumably translates into higher user satisfaction and retention rates. There are a number of internal data privacy challenges for businesses within this matrix of data use concerning, for example, cross-border transactions between supply chain partners, vendors, customers and employees, many of whom bring their own devices—all of which requires extensive data privacy and management controls. Data is the signature asset of the information age, and more especially in the era of big data and the Internet of things. Entire business models and crucial elements of businesses' value chains are built out around this asset.

This chapter provides an overview of data privacy through presentation of a number of recent important cases and legislation. This practice area is expanding in large part because users' norms point towards wanting more control of their data and privacy, structural changes in the workforce, the internationalization of transactions, legislative initiatives to protect data, and most especially, we are now in the era of big data. Because this practice area is rapidly changing, we consider the challenges of managing this dynamic legal environment, and include best practices, along with compliance strategies.

Data Privacy and Management

This broadly describes the concepts covering the collection of individual users' data, and then the subsequent re-use of this data by others, including commercial uses of tracking and sharing by businesses. The collected data of others is widely considered a valuable asset, though there is no consensus over ownership or control of this data, and there are multiple stakeholders who can claim an interest in, and rights to, the data. The privacy concern, and consequent legal and compliance risks exist for individuals as well as businesses. For individuals, this risk emerges to the extent the data contains **personally identifiable information (PII)** or other sensitive information, such as where you are, who you are speaking to, what you searched, what prescription you just paid for, who you are in a relationship with, what you plan to do this evening, and so forth. For businesses, the risk emerges as they collect, purchase or lease data, and how they process, manage and secure it, with such regulatory issues that arise when processing highly regulated data such as children's, or student or patient information, securities transactions, and more.

The challenge is essentially not so much about privacy as it is about control and management: to control the data so as to share data (without revealing the PII), while also protecting it from unauthorized or unlawful uses. To manage the data within complex and multinational enterprises to maximize the possibilities that data presents, while also being in compliance with data protection laws and transfer obligations. For example, as you do a Google search for spring break destinations, who can access parts or all of your data trail of information? Your college IT staff; the network connection provider; Google; sites you click on (they even know what site you were on before you clicked on their site). Then, if any web bugs or cookies are used, this information is shared with ad networks and these marketers track you across multiple sites. In reference to just one business partner in this chain, Google, this one company will analyze your search methodology and location, which link you first clicked on, how long you stayed on each link, and so forth, as a means to provide better, more meaningful relevant search results. Each of those sites you clicked on will likewise measure interest and more as a means to provide insights into what goods and services you buy and to make you a more loyal, free-spending customer. Can you choose or otherwise control this process? Do you have data privacy concerns? Clearly all of this data sharing helps businesses, while only some of this data sharing is directly or immediately beneficial to individuals. By way of example, Google just lost a case in the European Union, featured in this chapter, in which the Court ruled that it improperly shared data by failing to protect information about individuals from unauthorized uses. Now Google faces a re-set on managing data privacy and compliance after this case, especially in the EU where it currently enjoys an enormous market share.

Just a few years ago, consideration of data privacy and management as an important substantive practice area to cover was trending towards "not terribly relevant." There was little will or meaning within the legal environment, and further, individual users, so busy sharing on Facebook, had not shown any direct preference for data privacy. In fact, in 2010, Facebook's CEO announced that privacy was no longer a social norm. Since then, however, there has been a complete change in direction on data privacy—from governments, courts, legislators and users. Now this topic is trending in a major way. For example, the state of California has issued a number of new laws on data privacy. Even Facebook re-engineered its privacy tools as a result of user feedback, legal setbacks, and the emergence of privacy-friendly services like Whisper, and more, as competitive threats. Now for example, Facebook's over one billion users' posts will be defaulted to "friends," where previously the default was set to "public."

Data Privacy: Defining the Concept

We present four constructs concerning a right to privacy, as there is no accepted standard definition. First, the United States' definition, then the United Nations' promulgation, followed by the European Union's. Finally, the State of California's right to privacy is included because it has become a bellwether state concerning the legal environment of privacy whose views are often adopted by other jurisdictions. Understanding these different legal standards becomes highly important for businesses from a compliance and liability perspective. For example, even if a U.S. company complies with U.S. federal data protection laws, and bases its servers, and data processing, storage, etc., in the U.S., EU compliance is still necessary. For example, if an EU citizen's data is processed (say if an EU citizen buys an American Airlines ticket), the transaction must adhere to EU laws.

Knowledge of the international data protection legal environment is clearly important.

The Concept of Privacy as a Right (U.S.)

The concept of a privacy right in the United States, in historic terms, is relatively new and notably absent from the U.S. Constitution. The concept of a privacy right is borrowed from the **Fourth Amendment,** which stands as a right against unreasonable government searches and seizures (discussed below). Otherwise, any additional privacy rights have been inferred into the Bill of Rights' overall guarantee of personal freedoms and limits on government powers. The closest accepted construct of a generalized right of privacy is was developed in an essay in 1890.

The Right to Be Let Alone (U.S.)

The "Right to Be Let Alone" is the expression of the expectation of a broader right as to all interactions, not just concerning government searches. This concept as a stand-alone right, applicable even beyond government actions, extending to social and business interactions, was developed by Samuel Warren and Louis Brandeis for their influential article, *The Right of Privacy*, 4 Harvard Law Review 193, 193 (1890) in which they articulated this primarily as a "right to be let alone." Their approach was in response to intrusive technological developments of that time, such as photography and journalism. Later, Associate Justice of the Supreme Court Brandeis authored a memorable dissent in a Fourth Amendment case challenging the Government's warrantless telephone wiretapping, in which he referred to the right to be let alone as "the most comprehensive of rights and the right most valued by civilized [people.]" *Olmstead v. United States*, 277 U.S. 438, 478 (1928) (Brandeis, J., dissenting in a 5-4 decision that was subsequently overruled by *Katz v. United States*, 389 U.S. 347 (1967) when the Court extended Fourth Amendment protections).

The Right to Personal Autonomy and Liberty (U.N.)

The U.N. Human Rights Council defines privacy as "the presumption that individual should have an area of autonomous development, interaction and liberty, a 'private sphere' with or without interaction with others, free from State intervention and from excessive unsolicited intervention by other uninvited individuals. The right of privacy is also the ability of individuals to determine who holds information about them and how is that information used."

(HRC/23/40, 17 April 2013. The result of resolution 16/4, the U.N. report "analyses the implications of States' surveillance of communications on the exercise of the human rights to privacy and to freedom of opinion and expression. While considering the impact of significant technological advances in communications, the report underlines the urgent need to further study new modalities of surveillance and to revise national laws regulating these practices in line with human rights standards.")

The Right to Govern Businesses' Uses of Individuals' Data in the Name of Protecting Users' Privacy (E.U.)

The E.U. promulgated Directive 95/46/EC on the protection of individuals with regard to the processing of personal data and on the free movement of data. This Directive is intended to protect individuals with regard to the processing and movement of their personal data by others. Declaring that privacy is a fundamental human right and freedom, this charter binds EU members and businesses interacting with EU residents to comply with stringent data protections (though each country has made minor changes on implementing the law). Recently European lawmakers approved a new, more protective law of privacy that includes a right of erasure of data, the so-called right to be forgotten. See below.

As a State Constitutional Right

California's own state constitution, Article 1, is a declaration of rights, and it provides, "All people . . . have inalienable rights. Among these are pursuing and obtaining . . . privacy." Because of the prominent inclusion of a privacy right, the State's Attorney General targeted this as a top enforcement priority. The state's Department of Justice now features a Privacy Enforcement and Protection Unit, tasked with "protecting the inalienable right to privacy" concerning any PII data uses.

The Supreme Court's Privacy Jurisprudence

The Supreme Court's rulings on privacy are based on two sources: either a Fourth Amendment theory (our focus in this section), or on a more indeterminate source: that the Constitution implicitly grants a fundamental right of privacy against a wide range of other governmental intrusions into private lives on the theory that such a right emanates from a reading of the sum-total of constitutional protections. This right has been the basis for a variety of civil liberties cases challenging government regulations covering marriage, education, birth control and sodomy. We consider in this section two separate constitutional provisions that impact data privacy law: the Fourth Amendment as well as the First Amendment.

The Fourth Amendment

The Fourth Amendment, recall, is centrally concerned with protecting citizens from unreasonable government intrusions. Any intrusions require a judicially-issued warrant, supported by probable cause of criminal activity and particularly describes the place to be searched and the persons or things to be seized. Under current Fourth Amendment doctrine, the Court has created a two-part construct for analysis of government intrusions that occur without a warrant. First, the Court asks whether the defendant has a subjective expectation of privacy (in his house, in her workplace desk, in his mobile phone, in their discarded trash, etc.). Second, the Court asks whether this expectation of privacy is one that society would concur is objectively reasonable. If the answers to both questions are in the affirmative, courts will rule that a search has occurred, and since it was done without a warrant, the search is presumptively unreasonable, and unconstitutional in violation of the Fourth Amendment. Evidence gathered from warrantless or non-compliant searches (*i.e.*, the search exceeds the parameters of the area okayed to be searched), likely will be successfully challenged by defendants in a pre-trial motion to suppress the evidence.

There may be support for a different analysis of whether a search has occurred for purposes of the Fourth Amendment. In *United States v. Jones,* 132 S. Ct. 945 (2012), concurring Justices indicated support for an alternative theory by which courts should evaluate the entire sequence of government activity, and then consider whether in the aggregate, there is an unlawful search. This view could invite trial courts to experiment with the *Jones* concurrence as a possible new approach to Fourth Amendment search doctrine.

Exceptions to the Fourth Amendment

The Supreme Court stresses the importance of warrants, cautioning that searches without warrants should be the exception. Searches conducted outside the oversight of judges, without prior approval, are *per se* unreasonable is the general rule. There are exceptions to the warrant requirement, however including: consent to the search, search incidental to a lawful arrest, evidence in plain view/open fields, caretaker function, third-party doctrine, impounded vehicles and motor vehicles, border or airport searches, administrative searches, and exigent circumstances. In such cases as these, compliance with the warrant requirement is unnecessary, and therefore, the search does not violate the target's Fourth Amendment guarantees. Fourth Amendment cases are extremely fact-specific. Each presents unique challenges in balancing investigational work, public safety and the target's constitutional rights.

The Third Party Doctrine in the Digital Age

One of these exceptions merits further discussion because it has had tremendous play in this era of warrantless electronic data-gathering: the **third-party doctrine**. A controversial rule, this doctrine essentially relies on the notion of consent—that since an individual turned over information to a third party, the individual relinquishes any future claim to privacy in the information. Information lawfully held by third parties is obtainable with merely a subpoena. A subpoena differs from a warrant in that the standards for granting one are lenient in comparison to the probable cause standard. Subpoenas are issued if there is any reasonable possibility that the data will produce information relevant to an investigation.

Since our information increasingly is in digital form and stored by others, the third party doctrine would suggest that Fourth Amendment protections do not extend to this information. This is another example of the ways in which technology is on a collision course with privacy. As an example of the Court's rulings on the third party doctrine, in *Smith v. Maryland,* 442 U.S. 735 (1979) the Court found the target had no legitimate expectation of privacy in his phone records, reasoning that he voluntarily conveyed the numbers dialed to the telephone company, the third party, so it could connect his call. *United States v. Miller,* 425 U.S. 435 (1976) confirmed this view, when the Court ruled the target had no expectation of privacy in his bank records (deposits slips, etc.), voluntarily provided to the bank. What about our email and Dropbox accounts on the cloud, our mobile phones and other data, location, credit card transactions, and more? The third party doctrine is clearly of central concern to the privacy debates. In fact, one recent Supreme Court case, *United States v. Jones,* 132 S. Ct. 945 (2012), challenged the warrantless use of a GPS tracker that communicated the target's location data to a third party. Justice Sonia Sotomayor wrote in a concurring opinion, "It may be necessary to reconsider the premise that an individual has no reasonable expectation of privacy in information voluntarily disclosed to third parties."

This next case is a recent Fourth Amendment challenge to a warrantless government search. Note how the telecom companies are implicated as the government, when undertaking investigations, looks first and foremost to the data trail that is the byproduct of our daily lives.

Klayman v. Obama

957 F. Supp. 2d 1 (D.D.C. 2013), injunction granted in part and denied in part, and stay granted, 2013 U.S. Dist. LEXIS 177169 (D.D.C. Dec. 16, 2013), cert. denied, 134 S. Ct. 1795 (April 7, 2014)

Facts: Plaintiffs brought this lawsuit challenging the constitutionality of certain intelligence-gathering practices by the United States government relating to the wholesale collection of the phone record metadata of all U.S. citizens. This case arose from public revelations that the federal government, through the National Security Agency (NSA), and with participation of certain telecommunications and Internet companies, has conducted surveillance and intelligence-gathering programs that collect data about the telephone and Internet activity of American citizens within the United States.

In 2013, the British paper, *The Guardian* reported the first of several "leaks" of classified material from Edward Snowden, a former NSA contract employee which have revealed multiple U.S. government intelligence collection and surveillance programs. For example, he disclosed that the Foreign Intelligence Surveillance Court, in an Order dated April 25, 2013, compelled Verizon to produce to the NSA on "an ongoing daily basis . . . all call detail records or telephony metadata." The government confirmed the authenticity of the April 25th FISC Order.

Soon thereafter, plaintiffs filed their complaint alleging that the Government, with participation of private companies, is conducting "a secret and illegal government scheme to intercept and analyze vast quantities of domestic communications," and this violates their individual rights under the Fourth Amendment of the Constitution.

Congress passed the Foreign Intelligence Surveillance Act (FISA) in large measure as a response to [past] revelations that warrantless electronic surveillance in the name of national security has been seriously abused. In the view of the Senate . . . the act went "a long way in striking a fair and just balance between protection of national security and protection of personal liberties." FISA created a procedure for the Government to obtain ex parte judicial orders authorizing domestic electronic surveillance upon a showing that . . . the target . . . was a foreign power or an agent of a foreign power. FISA was subsequently expanded, enabling physical searches, pen registers and trap-and-trace devices. Congress further expanded government searches of foreign intelligence after 9/11 with a business records provision authorizing the FBI to seek business records.

Information that the FBI acquires through such a production order may be used and disclosed without the consent of the U.S. target. Meanwhile, recipients of the production orders [the telecom companies] are obligated *not* to disclose the existence of the orders. Further, only the recipient, and not the targets, has a right of judicial review of the order.

Plaintiffs seek a preliminary injunction barring the Government from collecting plaintiffs' metadata during the pendency of the lawsuit, and requiring defendants to destroy all data collected thus far, and prohibiting defendants from using the metadata.

Judicial Opinion. Judge Leon: To say the least, plaintiffs and the Government have portrayed to scope of the Government's surveillance activities very differently. For purposes of resolving these preliminary injunction motions . . . it will suffice to accept the Government's description of the phone metadata collection and querying Program. The records collected under this Program consist of metadata, such as information about what phone numbers were used to make and receive calls, when the calls took place, and how long the calls lasted. The metadata records . . . do not include any information about the contents of those calls, or the names, addresses or financial information of any party to the calls. Through targeted computerized searches of those metadata records, the NSA tries to discern connections between terrorist organizations and previously unknown terrorist operatives located in the United States. The Government has conducted the Bulk Telephony Metadata Program for more than seven years [based on reasonable articulable suspicion (RAS) that the call record is linked to foreign terrorist organizations approved for targeting].

According to Government officials, this aggregation of records . . . creates "an historical repository that permits retrospective analysis." When an NSA intelligence analyst runs a query using a "seed" [number] . . . in plain English, this means that if a search starts with telephone number (123) 456-7890 as the 'seed,' the first hop will include all the phone numbers that (123) 456-7890 has called or received calls from in the last five years (say, 100 numbers). The second hop will include all the phone numbers that each of *those* 100 numbers has called or receive calls from in the last five years (say, 100 numbers for each one of the 100 first hop numbers, or 10,000 total), and the third hop will include all the phone numbers that each of *those* 10,000 numbers has called or received calls from in the last five years (say, 100 numbers for each one of the 10,000 second hop numbers, or 1,000,000 total).

In January 2009, the Government reported to the [surveillance court] that the NSA had improperly . . . search[ed] the bulk telephony metadata. Judge Reggie Walton of the FISC concluded that he had no confidence that the Government was doing its utmost to comply with [FISC] orders, and that the NSA had engaged in "systematic noncompliance" . . . since the inception of the . . . Program, and had also repeatedly made misrepresentations and inaccurate statements about the program to the FISC judges. [T]he Government apparently has had further compliance problems relating to its collection programs in subsequent years.

Constitutional Claims While Congress has great latitude to create statutory schemes like FISA, it may not hang a cloak of secrecy over the Constitution.

When ruling on a motion for preliminary injunction, a court must consider whether (1) the plaintiff has a substantial likelihood of success on the merits; (2) the plaintiff would suffer irreparable injury were an injunction not granted; (3) an injunction would substantially injure other interested parties; and (4) the grant of an injunction would further the public interest. I will address each of these factors.

1. PLAINTIFFS HAVE SHOWN A SUBSTANTIAL LIKELIHOOD OF SUCCESS ON THE MERITS

In addressing plaintiffs' likelihood of success on the merits of their constitutional claims, I will focus on their Fourth Amendment arguments, which I find to be the most likely to succeed. The NSAs . . . Program involves two potential searches: (1) the bulk collection of metadata and (2) the analysis of that data through the NSAs querying process. The Fourth Amendment protects 'the right of the people to be secure in their person, houses, papers, and effects, against unreasonable searches and seizures.' That right 'shall not be violated, and no Warrants shall issue, but upon probable cause, supported by Oath or affirmation, and particularly describing the places to be searched, and the persons or things to be seized.' A Fourth Amendment 'search' occurs either when the Government obtains information by physically intruding on a constitutionally protected area, or when the government violates a subjective expectation of privacy that society recognizes as reasonable.

The threshold issue that I must address, then, is whether plaintiffs have a reasonable expectation of privacy that is violated when the Government indiscriminately collect their telephony metadata along with the metadata of hundreds of millions of other citizens without any particularized suspicion of wrongdoing, retains all of that metadata for five years, and then queries, analyzes, and investigates that data without prior judicial approval of the investigative targets. If they do—and a Fourth Amendment search has thus occurred—then the next step of the analysis will be to determine whether such a search is reasonable.

[T]he FISC has said [*Smith v. Maryland*] squarely controls when it comes to the production of telephone service provider metadata. The Supreme Court held that

Smith had no reasonable expectation of privacy in the numbers dialed from his phone because he voluntarily transmitted them to his phone company, and because it is generally known that phone companies keep such information in their business records. I disagree [with the Government]. The question before me is not the same question that the Supreme Court confronted in *Smith*. The Court in *Smith* was not confronted with the NSA Bulk . . . Metadata Program. Nor could the Court in 1979 have ever imagined how the citizens of 2013 would interact with their phones. I am convinced that the . . . Program now before me is so different from a simple pen register [a trace that was operational only for a few days, no evidence records would be retained], that *Smith* is of little value in assessing [whether this] Program constitutes a Fourth Amendment search. I believe that the bulk . . . collection and analysis almost certainly does violate a reasonable expectation of privacy. It's one thing to say that people expect phone companies to occasionally provide information to law enforcement; it is quite another to suggest that our citizens expect all phone companies to operate what is effectively a joint intelligence-gathering operation with the Government. [T]he almost-Orwellian technology that enables the Government to store and analyze the phone metadata of every telephone user in the United States is unlike anything that could have been conceived in 1979.

[T]he ubiquity of phones has dramatically altered the *quantity* of information that is available and, *more importantly*, what that information can tell the Government about people's lives. The rapid and monumental shift towards a cell phone-centric culture means that the metadata from each person's phone reflects a wealth of detail about her familial, political, professional, religious, and sexual associations' that could not have been gleaned from a data collection in 1979.

Whereas some may assume that these cultural changes will force people to reconcile themselves to an inevitable diminution of privacy that new technology entails, I think it is more likely that these trends have resulted in a greater expectation of privacy and a recognition that society views that expectation as reasonable. For the many reasons set forth above, it is significantly likely that . . . I will answer that question [whether people have a reasonable expectation of privacy] that is violated when the Government, without any basis whatsoever to suspect them of any wrongdoing, collects and stores for five years their telephony metadata for purposes of subjecting it to high-tech querying and analysis without any case-by-case judicial approval], in plaintiffs' favor.

[T]here is no indication that [any information was] immediately useful or that the [Government] prevented an impending attack. [The Program's Assistant Director conceded limited success.] Such candor is as refreshing as it is rare.

There is a significant likelihood Plaintiffs will succeed in showing that the searches are unreasonable. Having found that a search occurred in this case, I next must examine the totality of the circumstances to determine whether the search is reasonable within the meaning of the Fourth Amendment. As a general matter, warrantless searches are *per se* unreasonable [and] the Supreme Court has recognized only a few specifically established and well-delineated exceptions to that general rule.

The basic purpose of the Fourth Amendment . . . is to safeguard the privacy and security of individuals against *arbitrary invasions by governmental officials*. I cannot imagine a more indiscriminate and arbitrary invasion than this [Program]. I have little doubt that the author of our Constitution, James Madison, who cautioned us to beware 'the abridgement of freedom of the people by gradual and silent encroachments by those in power,' would be aghast.

2. PLAINTIFFS WILL SUFFER IRREPARABLE HARM ABSENT INJUNCTIVE RELIEF

It has long been established that the loss of constitutional freedoms, for even minimal periods of time, unquestionably constitutes irreparable injury.

3. THE PUBLIC INTEREST AND POTENTIAL INJURY TO OTHER INTERESTED PARTIES ALSO WEIGH IN FAVOR OF INJUNCTIVE RELIEF

It is always in the public interest to prevent the violation of a party's constitutional rights. That interest looms large in this case, given the significant privacy interests at stake and the unprecedented scope of the NSAs collections and querying effort, which likely violate the Fourth Amendment. Thus, the public interest weighs heavily in favor of granting an injunction. The Government responds that the public's interest in combating terrorism is of paramount importance—a proposition that I accept without question. But the Government offers no real explanation as to how granting relief to these plaintiffs would be detrimental to that interest. I am not convinced at this point in the litigation that the NSAs database has ever truly served the purpose of rapidly identifying terrorists in time-sensitive investigations, and so I am *certainly* not convinced that the removal of two individuals from the database will "degrade" the program in any meaningful sense.

CONCLUSION

This case is yet the latest chapter in the Judiciary's continuing challenge to balance the national security interests of the United States with the individual liberties of our citizens.

ORDERED that the Motion for Preliminary Injunction . . . is GRANTED as to plaintiffs; it is further ORDERED that the Government:

(1) is barred from collecting . . . any telephony metadata associated with [plaintiffs'] personal Verizon [accounts]; and

(2) must destroy all such metadata already collected . . . .and it is further

ORDERED that this Order is STAYED pending appeal.

Case Questions

1. Articulate what is the role of telecoms, such as Verizon, in this case.
2. Do you agree with Judge Leon that the *Smith v. Maryland* case is so old and irrelevant as to not be binding precedent in this case? Why or why not?
3. Why do you suppose the Government did not fill out an application for a warrant along with the affidavit in support of this application?

Fourth Amendment challenges to electronic evidence gathering is a rapidly evolving practice area. Starting in approximately 2010, a number of Magistrates on the front lines of responding to government warrant requests have increasingly pushed back on what they perceive as wide-ranging, almost open-ended warrant applications. The so-called Magistrates Revolt is so-named for their perception that many of the government's electronic evidence gathering requests are overly broad and in contravention with citizens' constitutional rights. The Magistrates have demanded more focused searches, insisting the government delete collected data deemed irrelevant rather than keep it on file, and even notifying a target that his Gmail account was the focus of a warrant (when the government did not want to notify the target). Setting a high threshold for collecting digital evidence will continue to be the subject of challenges, and a current case to watch is *In the Matter of the Search of Information Associated with [Redacted]@mac.com That is Stored at Premises Controlled by Apple, Inc.,* opinion by Magistrate John M. Facciola, (D.D.C. March 7, 2014) (No. 14-228) (rejecting the Government's "facially overbroad search and seizure warrant"), a decision the Department of Justice has appealed.

The First Amendment

Though this may appear to be an anomaly in a data privacy discussion, the First Amendment impacts the legal environment, because to an extent, businesses have First Amendment rights, and are asserting this right in the context of using individuals' data for their commercial purposes. The First Amendment provides, "Congress shall make no law . . . abridging the freedom of speech, or of the press. . . . "

Corporations are recognized as individuals under the law in most contexts. For example, corporations can contract, sue others and be sued, and own land. And therefore, corporations may hold and exercise certain rights under the Constitution. With regard to the First Amendment, historically corporations have had fewer speech rights than persons, and therefore, regulations of corporate speech have largely been upheld. This difference in the extent of free speech rights as between individuals and corporations has been the accepted status quo. This, too, has evolved, and since the *Citizens United v. Federal Election Commission,* 558 U.S. _____ (2010) decision, a majority of Justices agree that corporations have speech rights co-extensive with individuals' speech rights at least in the realm of elections to fund advertising initiatives. This decision had the effect of elevating protections for corporate speech, and thereby allowing for more scrutiny of laws that impact corporate speech.

The Court has developed three constructs for reviewing laws that impact speech as a means for deciding whether the law is too burdensome and unlawfully restricts speech impermissibly in violation of the First Amendment. For example, political speech receives the most protection under the First Amendment, and therefore any regulations on individuals' political speech receive the most scrutiny. Commercial speech, such as ads by companies promoting their products receives less protection under the First Amendment, and therefore any regulations receive less scrutiny by courts—just a cursory review. [Further, criminal speech, such as obscenity or language inciting violence or hate crimes, receives little-to-no protection under the First Amendment, and may be highly regulated, or in extreme circumstances, banned.]

Strict Scrutiny Review: Content-based Speech Regulation

Courts ask whether the law has an important, indeed, compelling government interest (something crucial, in contrast to merely something preferred), and if so, courts then ask whether the means used to accomplish this goal are narrowly tailored, so as to effectuate that interest/goal. The law has to be the least restrictive means for achieving that goal and an imperfect, overly broad regulation will violate the First Amendment.

Intermediate Level Review: Content-neutral Speech Regulation

Courts ask whether the speech concerns a lawful activity and is not misleading, and if so courts then ask whether the asserted state interest is substantial, and if it is, whether the law furthers this important government interest in a way that is substantially related to the goal.

Rational Basis Review: Economic Speech Regulation

Courts ask merely whether the regulation is a rational way to achieve its goal.

This next case considers the First Amendment in relation to a state's regulation of a datamining company that buys physician prescribing data from pharmacies. Readers will gain a better understanding of how the Court reviews state regulations that impact speech.

Sorrell v. IMS Health Inc.,

_____ U.S. _____, 131 S. Ct. 2653 (2011), and
2012 U.S. Dist. LEXIS 99105 (D. Vt. July 17, 2012)

Facts: Pharmaceutical manufacturers promote drugs to doctors through a process known as "detailing." Pharmacies receive "prescriber-identifying information" when processing prescriptions and then sell this information to data miners, who produce reports on prescriber behavior and lease them to pharmaceutical manufacturers. The reports are subject to nondisclosure agreements. Detailers employed by the manufacturers then use the reports to refine their marketing tactics and increase sales to doctors.

Vermont found . . . that the goals of marketing programs often conflict with the goals of the state, and that the marketplace for ideas on medicine safety and effectiveness is frequently one-sided in that brand-name companies invest in expensive . . . campaigns to doctors. Detailing, in the legislature's view, caused doctors to make decisions based on incomplete and biased information. The legislature further found that detailing increases the cost of health care and health insurance.

In 2007, Vermont enacted the Prescription Confidentiality Law, Vt. Stat. Ann. Tit. 18, § 4631 (Supp. 2010), (also known as Act 80). The central provision, subsection (d) provides:

> "[no business] shall sell, license, or exchange for value regulated records containing prescriber-identifiable information, nor permit the use of regulated records containing prescriber-identifiable information for marketing or promoting a prescription drug, unless the prescriber consents. . . . Vermont law restricts the sale, disclosure, and use of pharmacy records that reveal the prescribing practices of individual doctors. Subject to certain exceptions, the information may not be sold, disclosed by pharmacies for marketing purposes, or used for marketing by pharmaceutical manufacturers."

The present case involves two consolidated lawsuits. One suit was brought by Vermont data miners, the other by an association of pharmaceutical manufacturers that produce brand-name drugs. They sought declaratory and injunctive relief contending that the law violates their rights under the Free Speech Clause of the First Amendment. The district court denied relief, but the Court of Appeals for the Second Circuit held that the state law unconstitutionally burdens the speech of pharmaceutical marketers and data miners without adequate justification. The decision of the Second Circuit in this case is in conflict with the First Circuit. The State of Vermont appealed to the Supreme Court.

Judicial Opinion (6-3 opinion). Justice Kennedy: Vermont law restricts the sale, disclosure, and use of pharmacy records that reveal the prescribing practices of individual doctors - subject to certain exceptions.

Speech in aid of pharmaceutical marketing . . . is a form of expression protected by the Free Speech Clause of the First Amendment. As a consequence,

Vermont's statute must be subjected to heightened judicial scrutiny. The law cannot satisfy that standard.

Detailers . . . visit . . . a doctor's office to persuade the doctor to prescribe a particular pharmaceutical. Detailer bring drug sample as well as medical studies that explain the "details" and potential advantages of various prescription drugs. Interested physicians listen, ask questions, and receive follow-up data. Salespersons can be more effective when they know the background and purchasing preference of their clientele, and pharmaceutical salespersons are no exception. Knowledge of a physician's prescription practices . . . enables a detailer better to ascertain which doctors are likely to be interested in a particular drug and how best to present a particular sales message. Detailing is an expensive undertaking, so . . . companies most often use it to promote high-profit brand-name drugs protected by patent (detailers do not highlight unpatented low-cost generic drugs that may provide the same benefits).

On its face, Vermont's law enacts content- and speaker-based restrictions on [speech]. The provision first forbids sale subject to exceptions based in large party on the content of a purchaser's speech. Finally, the provision's second sentence . . . disfavors marketing, that is, speech with a particular content. More than that, the statute disfavors specific speakers. Detailers are likewise barred from using the information for marketing, even though the information may be used by a wide range of other speakers.

Act 80 is designed to impose a specific, content-based burden on protected expression. It follows that heightened judicial scrutiny is warranted. The First Amendment requires heightened scrutiny whenever the government creates a regulation of speech because of disagreement with the message it conveys. A government bent on frustrating an impending demonstration might pass a law demanding two years' notice before the issuance of parade permits. Even if the hypothetical measure on its face appeared neutral as to content and speaker, its purpose to suppress speech and its unjustified burdens on expression would render it unconstitutional. Commercial speech is no exception.

The State argues that heightened judicial scrutiny is unwarranted because its law is a mere commercial regulation. It is true that restrictions on protected expression are distinct from restrictions on economic activity. But §4631(d) imposes more than an incidental burden on protected expression. [The] law imposes a burden based on the content of speech and identity of the speaker.

Vermont further argues that §4631(d) regulates not speech but simply access to information. This argument finds some support [in previous cases, but the Court eventually rejected this argument.] [Vermont] also contends the heightened judicial scrutiny is unwarranted in this case because sales, transfer, and use of [this] information is conduct, not speech. Consistent with that submission, the United States Court of Appeals for the First Circuit has characterized [this] information as a mere commodity with no greater entitlement to First Amendment protection than "beef jerky." This Court has held that the creation and dissemination of information are speech within the meaning of the First Amendment.

[For this Court's] inquiry, it is the State's burden to justify its content-based law as consistent with the First Amendment. To sustain the targeted, content-based burden §4631(d) imposes on protected expression, the State must show at least that the statute directly advances a substantial governmental interest and that the measure is drawn to achieve that interest. [This is to] ensure not only that the State's interests are proportional to the resulting burdens placed on speech, but also that the law does not seek to suppress a disfavored message.

The State's asserted justifications for §4631(d) come under two general headings. First, the State contends that its law is necessary to protect medical privacy, including physician confidentiality, etc. Second, the State argues that §4631(d) is integral to the achievement of policy objectives—namely, improved public health and reduced healthcare costs. Neither justification withstands scrutiny. It may be assumed that, for many reasons, physicians have an interest in keeping their prescription decisions confidential But §4631(d) is not drawn to secure that interest [in confidentiality]. [T]he statute allows the information to be studied and used by all but a narrow class of disfavored speakers. [As to the State's second argument] that detailing make people anxious about whether doctors have their patients' best interests at heart . . . it cannot explain why detailers' use of . . . information is more likely to prompt these objections than many other uses permitted by §4631(d). While Vermont's stated policy goals may be proper, §4631(d) does not advance them in a permissible way. Vermont may be displeased that detailers who use [this] information are effective in promoting brand-name drugs. The State can express that view through its own speech.

The State nowhere contends that detailing is false or misleading within the meaning of this Court's First Amendment precedents. The State's interest in burdening the speech of detailers instead turns on nothing more than a difference of opinion. The State has burdened a form of protected expression that it found too persuasive. At the same time, the State has left unburdened those speakers whose messages are in accord with its own views. This the State cannot do. The judgment of the Court of Appeals is affirmed.

Dissent. Justice Breyer: The Vermont statute before us adversely affects expression in one, and only one, way. It deprives pharmaceutical and data-mining companies of data, collected pursuant to the government's regulatory mandate, that could help pharmaceutical companies create better sales messages. In my view, this effect on expression is inextricably related to a lawful governmental effort to regulate a commercial enterprise. [T]he Court should uphold the statute as constitutional.

[T]his Court has distinguished for First Amendment purposes among different contexts in which speech takes place. Thus, the First Amendment imposes tight constraints upon government efforts to restrict, *e.g.*, "core" political speech, while imposing looser constraints when the government seeks to restrict, *e.g.*, commercial speech, the speech of its own employees, or the regulation-related speech of a firm subject to a traditional regulatory program. [T]he Court should review Vermont's law under the standard appropriate for the review of economic regulation not under a heightened standard appropriate for the review of First Amendment issues. And with respect, I dissent.

Post-script: IMS Health as the prevailing party filed motions in federal district court for an award of attorney's fess, expenses and costs. The Court determined a reasonable attorney's fee in this case to be $2,137,050 (calculated by multiplying a reasonable hourly rate by the reasonably expended hours). Expenses in the amount of $106,989.63 were awarded. The Clerk of Court was charged with determining the appropriate award of costs.

Case Questions

1. How does Vermont have to amend its law following this decision?
2. Say the dissent's view was the majority opinion, and therefore, the law. How would that impact IMS Health's business model?
3. Describe how the Court's ruling impacts the state, and how it impacts individuals who reside in Vermont?

Federal Data Privacy Laws

Beyond the Constitutional sources of a right of privacy, there are a number of federal statutes governing data privacy. Because there is no overall right to privacy, Congress has crafted a number of sector-specific laws that regulate data in discrete ways. For example, there is a law governing children's privacy, another for medical records, and so forth. Each regulation is targeted at a particular use of data by a certain commercial entity. The U.S. system is grounded on the notion of industry self-regulation, and so there is a "light-touch" regulatory approach, and only when there is a complaint or grievous outcome will this trigger a change in the legal environment, such as a new law, a lawsuit, or an enforcement proceeding by a government agency.

Due to questions over the widespread and vast collection and use of consumers' personal information by data brokers, the U.S. Government Accountability Office produced a report for Congress. The GAO found that "no overarching federal privacy law governs the collection and sale of personal information. The current statutory framework for consumer privacy does not fully address new technology—such as the tracking of online behavior or mobile devices—and the vastly increased marketplace for personal information, including the proliferation of information sharing among third parties . . . no federal statute provides consumers with the right to learn what information is held about them and who holds it . . . consumers also do not have the legal right to control the collection or sharing with third parties of sensitive person information (such as their shopping habits and health interests) for marketing purposes. Some privacy advocates have cited the need for legislation that would [protect] consumers. At the same time, industry representatives have asserted that restrictions on the collection and use of personal data would impose compliance costs, inhibit innovation and efficiency, and reduce consumer benefits, such as more relevant advertising and beneficial products and services. The challenge will be providing privacy protections without unduly inhibiting the benefits to consumers, commerce, and innovation that data sharing can accord." (*Information Resellers, Consumer Privacy Framework Needs to Reflect Changes in Technology and the Marketplace*, GAO Rep't 13-663, Sept. 2013, at 3).

With this in mind, we present a summary of the primary federal laws addressing data privacy.

[handwritten margin note: Signed consent form to pull credit. They can contested / challenge / (you can still hold your decision,]

[handwritten note above list: should be included in the pre_____ pack]

- **Fair Credit Reporting Act**, 15 U.S.C. §§ 1681-1681x (2012): FCRA applies to consumer reporting businesses and protects the security and confidentiality of consumer data collected or used in decisions concerning eligibility for credit, employment, or insurance. The act limits resellers' use and distribution of personal data and imposes security requirements on the businesses to safeguard the data.

- **Gramm-Leach-Bliley Act**, codified in scattered sections of titles 12 and 15 of the U.S. Code (2012): GLBA protects nonpublic personal information individuals provide to financial businesses. These sharing and disclosure restrictions apply even to nonaffiliated third parties that receive this information. Financial regulators are tasked with establishing safeguards and security requirements to protect the data.

[handwritten margin note: medical provider must keep medical information private.]

- **Health Insurance Portability and Accountability Act**, codified in scattered sections of titles 18, 26, 29, and 42 of the U.S. Code (2012): HIPAA protects certain health information. The law aims to strike a balance that permits uses of the information in the provision of healthcare while protecting patient privacy. HIPAA governs the use and disclosure of this health information. Patients must give written consent for their information to be used for marketing purposes. The law requires healthcare providers to safeguard protected information from unauthorized uses or disclosures.

- **Children's Online Privacy Protection Act**, 15 U.S.C. §§ 6501-6506 (2012): COPPA governs the mobile app and online collection of personal information of children under 13. The law specifically provides protections regarding the collection of name, email address and geolocation information so as to safeguard the child's identity and location. Sites are required to obtain verifiable parental consent before collecting such information. This law does not apply to collection of this same information from adults.

- **Electronic Communications Privacy Act**, (including the **Wiretap Act**, and the **Stored Communications Act**), 18 U.S.C. §§ 2510-2522; 2701-2712 (2012): The acts are designed to prevent unauthorized government access to the contents of private electronic communications. The ECPA prohibits the interception and disclosure of the contents of communications, unless an exception applies. For example, Verizon cannot sell the contents of customers' text messages to a data broker without the customers' consent. It is a criminal offense to either intentionally access without authorization; or intentionally exceed the authorization, to any electronic communications, and then hack or prevent authorized access. Notably, the ECPA limits protections for non-content information, such as name, mailing or IP address information, reasoning that this information is less deserving of protection than is content information. Further, information in storage or information that is older than six months receives less privacy protection than information less than six months old.

As this chapter was being written, the next case was still being litigated. It represents the first case on consent. The decision by Judge Lucy Koh is prominent in the widening debate over online privacy and how Internet companies use personal data. Similar cases are surging, and to date decisions are pending in lawsuits against Apple, Facebook, LinkedIn and Yahoo! This next case concerns the ECPA's Wiretap provisions.

In re: Google, Inc. Gmail Litigation,
2013 U.S. Dist. LEXIS 172784 (N.D. Cal. Sept. 26, 2013)

Facts: Plaintiffs allege that Defendant Google, Inc., violated state and federal privacy laws in its operation of Gmail. Google's processing of email to and from its users has evolved over time. Plaintiffs allege, however, that in all iterations of Google's email routing processes since 2008, Google has intercepted, read, and acquired the content of emails that were sent or received by Gmail and non-Gmail users while the emails were in transit for the purposes of sending an advertisement relevant to that email communication to the recipient, sender, or both, in violation of the Wiretap Act.

According to the Complaint, this interception and reading of the email was separate from Google's other legitimate businesses processes, including spam and virus filtering. Moreover, Plaintiffs allege that relevance and targeted advertising was not the sole purpose of the interception. Rather, Plaintiffs allege that a number of Google devices intercepted the emails, read and collected content as well as affiliated data. Plaintiffs further allege that Google used these data to create user profiles and models to serve their profit interests in ways that were unrelated to providing email services to their users. Accordingly, Plaintiffs allege that Google has intercepted emails of both Gmail and non-Gmail users for the dual purposes of providing advertisements and creating user profiles to advance its profit interests.

The Complaint seeks damages on behalf of Gmail users and non-Gmail users for Google's interception of email. Plaintiffs seek the certification of several classes, preliminary and permanent injunctive relief, declaratory relief, statutory damages, punitive damages, and attorneys' fees. Google filed a Motion to Dismiss the Complaint. For the reasons stated below, the Court DENIES in part and GRANTS in part Google's Motion to Dismiss with leave to amend.

Judicial Opinion. Judge Koh: The operation of Gmail implicates several legal agreements. The Terms of Service reference Google's Privacy Policies, which have been amended three times. These . . . state Google could collect information that users provided to Google, cookies, log information, user communications to Google, information that users provide to affiliated sites, and the links that a user follows. Importantly, Plaintiffs who are not Gmail or Google Apps users are *not* subject to any of Google's express agreements. But because non-Gmail users exchange emails with Google users, their communications are nevertheless subject to these same actions by Google.

A defendant may move to dismiss an action for failure to allege enough facts to state a claim to relief that is plausible on its face. For purposes of ruling on [this] motion, the Court accepts factual allegations in the complaint as true and construes the pleading in the light most favorable to the non-moving party.

1. The Wiretap Act . . . generally prohibits the interception of "wire, oral, or electronic communications." More specifically, the Wiretap Act provides a private right of action against any person who 'intentionally intercepts, endeavors to intercept, or procures any other person to intercept or endeavor to intercept, any wire, oral, or electronic communication.

Plaintiffs contend that Google violated the Wiretap Act in its operation of the Gmail system by intentionally intercepting the content of emails that were in transit to create profiles of Gmail users and to provide targeted advertising. Google contends that Plaintiffs have not stated a claim with respect to the Wiretap Act for two reasons. First, Google contends that there was no interception because there was no "device." [The Wiretap Act excludes devices if they are] ". . . being used by a provider of wire or electronic communication service in the ordinary course of its business." Google [asserts] that reading . . . users' email occurred in the ordinary course of its business. Plaintiffs counter that [this] exception is narrow and applies only when an electronic communication service provider's actions are necessary [operationally] for the routing, termination, or management of the message.

In fact, Google's alleged interception of email content is primarily used to create user profiles and to provide targeted advertising—neither of which is related to the transmission of emails. The Court further finds that Plaintiffs' allegations that Google violated [its] own agreements and internal policies with regard to privacy also preclude application of the ordinary course of business exception. The legislative history of the [ordinary course of business exception] . . . suggests that Congress intended to protect . . . providers from liability [for limited functions such as to] route, terminate, and manage messages. Accordingly, the Court concludes that the legislative history supports a narrow reading of the . . . exception. Google's broader reading of the exception would conflict with Congressional intent. The case law . . . also suggests that courts have narrowly construed the [ordinary court of business exception]. Plaintiffs have plausibly alleged that Google's reading of their email was not within this narrow ordinary course of its business. [T]he alleged interception of emails at issue here is both physically and purposively unrelated to Google's provision of email services.

Google's alleged interceptions are neither instrumental to the provision of email services, nor are they an incidental effect of providing these services.

Furthermore, the D.C. Circuit has held . . . that a defendant's actions may fall outside the "ordinary course of business" exception when the defendant violates its own internal policies. Google has violated its own policies and therefore is acting outside the ordinary course of business. Google's Privacy Policies explicitly limit the information that Google may collect to any enumerated list of items, and that this list does not include content of emails. [T]he language of the Privacy Policy . . . states that Google 'may collect the following types of information' and then lists (1) information provided by the user (such as personal information submitted on the sign-up page), (2) information derived from cookies, (3) log-in information, (4) user communications to Google, (5) personal information provided by affiliated Google services and sites, (6) information from third party applications, (7) location data, and (8) unique application numbers from Google's toolbar. Accordingly, the Court DENIES Google's Motion to Dismiss.

2. Consent. Google [further defends the charges] contend[ing] that all Plaintiffs have consented to any interception. [I]t is not unlawful . . . where one of the parties . . . has given prior consent to such interception. Specifically, Google contends that by agreeing to its Terms of Service and Privacy Policies, all Gmail users have consented to Google reading their emails. Google further suggests that even though non-Gmail users have not agreed [to the policies] all non-Gmail users impliedly consent to Google's interception when non-Gmail users send an email to or receive an email from a Gmail user. If either party to a communication consents to its interception, then there is no violation of the Wiretap Act. Consent . . . can be explicit or implied, but any consent must be actual. Courts have cautioned that implied consent applies only in a narrow set of cases. The critical question . . . is whether the parties whose communications were intercepted had adequate notice of the interception. That the person communicating knows that the interceptor has the capacity to monitor the communication is insufficient to establish implied consent. Moreover, consent is not an all-or-nothing proposition. Rather, a party may consent to the interception of only part of a communication or to the interception of only a subset of its communications.

Google marshals both explicit and implied theories of consent. Google contends that by agreeing to [its policies], Plaintiffs who are Gmail users expressly consented to the interception of their emails . . . and that because of the way that email operates, even non-Gmail users knew that their emails would be intercepted, and accordingly that non-Gmail users impliedly consented to the interception. The Court rejects Google's contentions with respect to both explicit and implied consent. Rather, the Court finds that it cannot conclude that any party—Gmail users or non-Gmail users—has consented to Google's reading of email for the purposes of creating user profiles or providing targeted advertising.

The . . . policies did not explicitly notify Plaintiffs that Google would intercept users' emails for the purposes of creating user profiles or providing targeted advertising. Section 8 . . . stated that 'Google reserves the right . . . to pre-screen, review, flag, filter, modify, refuse or remove any or all Content.' Later, section 17 . . . stated that "advertisements may be targeted to the content of information stored on the Services, queries made through the Services or other information."

The Court finds that Gmail users' acceptance of these statements does not establish explicit consent. [The clauses do] not suggest to the user that Google would intercept emails for the purposes of creating user profiles or providing targeted advertising.

Section 17 . . . is defective in demonstrating consent . . . it demonstrates only that Google has the *capacity* to intercept communications, not that it will. As such, these . . . policies do not demonstrate explicit consent, and in fact suggest the opposite. Furthermore, the policies do not put users on notice that their emails are intercepted to create user profiles. The Court therefore finds that a reasonable Gmail user who reads the . . . Policies would not have necessarily understood that her emails were being intercepted to create user profiles or to provide targeted advertisements. Accordingly, the Court finds that it cannot conclude at this phase that the new policies demonstrate that Gmail user Plaintiffs consented to the interceptions.

Finally, Google contends that non-Gmail users . . . nevertheless impliedly consented to Google's interception of their emails. . . . Google's theory is that all email users understand and accept the fact that email is automatically processed. Google has cited no case that stands for the proposition that users who send emails impliedly consent to interceptions and user of their communications by third parties other than the intended recipient. Accepting Google's theory of implied consent . . . would eviscerate the rule against interception. The Court does not find that non-Gmail users . . . have impliedly consented to Google's interception of their emails to Gmail users. The court DENIES Google's Motion to Dismiss on the basis of consent.

[Furthermore, the Court denied Google's Motion to dismiss a claim under California state law. The Court rejected Google's contention that the state law applied only to a person who *has been injured* by a violation, reasoning that any invasion of privacy involves an affront to human dignity which the Legislature could conclude is worth at least $3,000 per violation.] IT IS SO ORDERED.

Case Questions

1. How do you recommend Google re-write its Privacy Policy after this case?
2. What should Google expect users to argue on the California state claims concerning their injury and a dollar amount on their plea for damages?
3. Can you recommend to Google any tweaks, or alternatives to their present business model of providing services (such as gmail) free to users, and earning revenue from selling relevant ads to businesses?

Federal Trade Commission Act, 15 U.S.C. § 45 (2012)

Congress delegated some of its regulatory authority in this area to the Federal Trade Commission. The FTC's mandate is as a consumer protection agency and it has become the de facto regulator of consumer data privacy in the U.S. as the act has been interpreted to apply to deceptions or violations of written privacy policies. The agency has authority to prohibit unfair or deceptive acts or practices. It has the power to bring enforcement actions, fine companies, make legislative recommendations to Congress, promote best practice recommendations to industry, hold industry workshops and seminars, and research and draft reports.

The Federal Trade Commission's 2014 Consent Order Regarding Snapchat

UNITED STATES OF AMERICA FEDERAL TRADE COMMISSION, IN THE MATTER OF SNAPCHAT, INC. AGREEMENT CONTAINING CONSENT ORDER

The Federal Trade Commission ("Commission") has conducted an investigation of certain acts and practices of Snapchat, Inc. ("Snapchat" or "proposed respondent"). Proposed respondent, having been represented by counsel, is willing to enter into an agreement containing a consent order resolving the allegations contained in the attached draft complaint. Therefore,

IT IS HEREBY AGREED by and between Snapchat, Inc., by its duly authorized officers, and counsel for the Federal Trade Commission that:

1. Proposed respondent Snapchat, Inc., the successor corporation to Toyopa Group LLC, is a Delaware corporation with its principal office or place of business at 63 Market Street, Venice, California 90291.

2. Proposed respondent neither admits nor denies any of the allegations in the draft complaint, except as specifically stated in this order. Only for purposes of this action, proposed respondent admits the facts necessary to establish jurisdiction.

3. Proposed respondent waives:

    A. any further procedural steps;
    B. the requirement that the Commission's decision contain a statement of findings of fact and conclusions of law; and
    C. all rights to seek judicial review or otherwise to challenge or contest the validity of the order entered pursuant to this agreement.

4. This agreement shall not become part of the public record of the proceeding unless and until it is accepted by the Commission. If this agreement is accepted by the Commission, it, together with the draft complaint, will be placed on the public record for a period of thirty (30) days and information about it publicly released. The Commission thereafter may either withdraw its acceptance of this agreement and so notify proposed respondent, in which event it will take such action as it may consider appropriate, or issue and serve its complaint (in such form as the circumstances may require) and decision in disposition of the proceeding.

5. This agreement is for settlement purposes only and does not constitute an admission by proposed respondent that the law has been violated as alleged in the draft complaint, or that the facts as alleged in the draft complaint, other than the jurisdictional facts, are true.

6. This agreement contemplates that, if it is accepted by the Commission, and if such acceptance is not subsequently withdrawn by the Commission pursuant to the provisions of Section 2.34 of the Commission's Rules, the Commission may, without further notice to proposed respondent, (1) issue its complaint corresponding in form and substance with the attached draft complaint and its decision containing the following order in disposition of the proceeding, and (2) make information about it public. When so entered, the order shall have the same force and effect and may be altered, modified, or set aside in the same manner and within the same time provided by statute for other orders. The order shall become final upon service. Delivery of the complaint and the decision and order to proposed respondent's address as stated in this agreement by any means specified in Section 4.4(a) of the Commission's Rules shall constitute service. Proposed respondent waives any right it may have to any other manner of service. The complaint may be used in construing the terms of the order. No agreement, understanding, representation, or interpretation not contained in the order or the agreement may be used to vary or contradict the terms of the order.

7. Proposed respondent has read the draft complaint and consent order. Proposed respondent understands that it may be liable for civil penalties in the amount provided by law and other appropriate relief for each violation of the order after it becomes final.

The FTC's increasingly active oversight of data privacy is evident. For example, it recently entered into a consent agreement with Snapchat after finding the company was inaccurate in describing its app. The FTC found Snapchat deceived users in these ways: inaccurate promises about the disappearing nature of the message, the amount of personal data it collects, and the security measures taken to protect users. The FTC found many other misrepresentations as well.

Drivers Privacy Protection Act, 18 U.S.C. §§ 2721-2725 (2012)

The act generally prohibits the use and disclosure of select personal information in states' motor vehicle records. The act details permitted uses, such as by government agencies carrying out their functions.

Family Educational Rights and Privacy Act, 20 U.S.C. § 1232g (2012)

This act governs access to and disclosure of students' educational records. Schools may not release student data or PII other than directory information to third parties without written consent (though students 18 or older may provide consent, and further, withhold data from their parents).

UNITED STATES OF AMERICA
FEDERAL TRADE COMMISSION
WASHINGTON, D.C. 20580

Jessica L. Rich
Office of the Director
Bureau of Consumer Protection

May 22, 2014

The Honorable Shelley C. Chapman
United States Bankruptcy Judge
Bankruptcy Court for the Southern District of New York
One Bowling Green
New York, NY 10004-1408

   Re: *ConnectEdu, Inc.*, No. 14-11238 (Bankr. S.D.N.Y.)

Dear Judge Chapman:

   The Federal Trade Commission ("FTC"), is the United States' leading consumer protection authority. Among other laws, the FTC enforces Section 5 of the Federal Trade Commission Act, which prohibits unfair or deceptive acts or practices.

   I am the Director of the FTC's Bureau of Consumer Protection (BCP) and am writing to express BCP's concerns about the ConnectEDU matter referenced above. It is our understanding, based on publicly available information, that ConnectEDU and its subsidiaries, including Academic Management Systems, Inc., have filed for Chapter 11 bankruptcy protection and have proposed selling substantially all of their assets, potentially including personal information about individuals. *In re ConnectEdu, Inc.*, No. 14-11238 (Bankr. S.D.N.Y.). Further, it is our understanding that this information (hereafter "ConnectEDU PI") was collected over 12 years from users of the www.ConnectEDU.com and affiliated websites and services operated under the ConnectEDU brand name. We are writing to express our concern that a sale that includes ConnectEDU PI may violate Section 363(b)(1)(A) of the Bankruptcy Code, as well as the prohibition on deceptive practices under the Federal Trade Commission Act, 15 U.S.C. § 45(a).

ConnectEDU and Its Privacy Practices

   During the time it was in operation, the ConnectEDU website collected a substantial amount of personal information from its user base, including high school and college students. This personal information includes name, date of birth, address, e-mail address, telephone number, grade level, and additional information required to provide services to users. ConnectEDU also collected personal information in the form of student records made available by contracting with high schools and community colleges.

The ConnectEDU Privacy Policy also describes what will happen to user information in the event of a company sale. ConnectEDU has expressly represented "*In the event of sale or intended sale of the Company, ConnectEDU will give users reasonable notice and an opportunity to remove personally identifiable data from the service*. In any event, any purchaser of ConnectEDU's assets will abide by the terms of this Privacy Policy in the form effective as of any transfer." (Emphasis added).

Many users would likely consider the protection of their personal information to be very important. In addition, information about teens is particularly sensitive and may warrant even greater privacy protections than those accorded to adults. These users as well as their parents would likely be concerned if their information transferred without restriction to a purchaser for unknown uses.

Respectfully Submitted,

Jessica L. Rich

Video Privacy Protection Act, 18 U.S.C. § 2710 (2012)

This act prohibits a videotape service provider from knowingly disclosing PII concerning rental and sales records, including the videos' title or subject matter, to third parties. There are several exceptions to the privacy protections.

This next case construes the privacy protections of this law in relation to the Internet service.

In re Hulu Privacy Litigation,
No. 3:11-cv-03764-LB (N.D. Cal. April 28, 2014)

Facts: Hulu provides access to shows, movies and other pre-recorded content from networks and studios on its site. Hulu pays license fees to rights holders for video content that Hulu then offers to its users. Hulu offers a free service as well as a paid service that features more content, as well as viewing options. A Hulu user does not need to register for an account, either. To register for a Hulu account, users enter their name, birthdate, gender, and email address. Users are not required to provide their legal name during registration. To register for the paid service, users must provide the same information, plus payment and billing address information. Hulu assigned each new registered user a User ID, a unique numerical identifier of at least seven digits.

The videos are displayed on "watch pages." Hulu wrote and deployed code for these pages, which downloads to registered users' browsers so their browser can display the content. The code also allowed information to be transmitted to comScore and Facebook. The URL of Hulu's watch pages included the name of the video on that page, and then Hulu began providing each registered user with a public profile page, which users could not opt-out of.

Hulu makes money mostly from ad revenue, and to a lesser extent from monthly premiums paid by Hulu Plus members. Advertisers pay Hulu to show their ads at periodic breaks during playback time. Advertisers pay based on how many times an ad is viewed. Hulu thus gathers information/metrics about its audience size. Advertisers require verified metrics, which means that Hulu needs to hire trusted metrics companies, and comScore is that company in this case.

comScore collects metrics on digital media consumption, and as of 2013, it had captured 1.5 trillion digital interactions each month and has over 2,000 clients. According to Hulu, comScore gives it reports containing metrics regarding the size of the audience for programming, and Hulu uses the reports to obtain programming and sell advertising. The reports never identify users by name; instead the data is presented in an aggregated and generalize basis, without reference to UserIDs. Hulu uses the comScore metrics to show other content owners that the Hulu audience is a desirable outlet for their programming, and to convince advertisers of the value of reaching Hulu's audience.

comScore uses "beacon" technology to track audience metrics. A beacon is triggered by defined events during the playing of a video, such as when a video starts, when the ad starts, when the video ends and re-starts. Every time users watch videos, therefore, Hulu transmits information to comScore.

How Hulu Interacts with Facebook Facebook collects information and processes content share by its users. It provides that information to marketers when it sells them its products (ads, analytics, insights and so forth). Facebook shares its members' information with marketers. Marketers can specify the types of users they want to reach based on information that users choose to share. Ad revenue is how Facebook makes money.

Certain information was transmitted from Hulu to Facebook via the Facebook "Like" button, as Hulu included a Like button on each Hulu watch page. The URL for each watch page included the title of the video being watched. The IP address of the registered user's computer also was sent to Facebook. Facebook also received the following cookies: (1) a "datr" cookie (identifies the browser); (2) a "lu" cookie (this can contain the Facebook user ID of the previous Facebook user to log in on that same browser, and has a lifetime of two years; and (3) a "c_user" cookie, if the user logged into Facebook using default setting with in the previous four weeks. Facebook would know the title of the video being viewed. The c_user cookie would give the name of the currently-logged in Facebook user. The lu cookie might too.

Plaintiffs are registered Hulu users, and allege that Hulu wrongfully disclosed their video viewing selections and PII to third parties comScore and Facebook in violation of the Video Privacy Protection Act (VPPA).

Judicial Opinion. Judge Beeler: The Video Privacy Protection Act and Disclosures of User IDs

The VPPA . . . protects certain personal information of an individual who rents [or otherwise obtains] video materials. The protected information is information that identifies a person as having requested or obtained specific video materials. The issue is whether the information transmitted to comScore and Facebook is "information which identifies a person as having requested or obtained specific video materials." If it is, then the transmission violates the VPPA.

A. THE VPPA PROHIBITS DISCLOSURES THAT TIE SPECIFIC PEOPLE TO THE VIDEOS THEY WATCH

The VPPA prohibits a videotape service provider from (1) knowingly disclosing to any person (2) personally identifiable information (PII) concerning any consumer. Hulu [is] a video tape service provider within the meaning of the act. The VPPA allows certain disclosures including the following: (1) disclosures to the consumer; (2) disclosures to any person with the informed, written consent of the consumer; (3) disclosures to law enforcement; or (4) disclosures that are incident to the ordinary course of business. The VPPA does not require proof of actual injury that is separate from a statutory violation . . . and requires only injury in the form of a wrongful disclosure.

The issue is whether Hulu's disclosures here are PII under the VPPA. The statute's plain language prohibits disclosure of information that "identifies a person" as having (in the Hulu context) viewed specific video content. It does not say "identify by name" and thus plainly encompasses other means of identifying a person. That being said . . . the language supports the conclusion that the disclosure must be pegged to an identifiable person (as opposed to an anonymous person). The statute's plain language is ambiguous about whether it covers unique anonymous user IDs such as the Hulu ID. The court thus turns to the legislative history. Congress's impetus for passing the VPPA was a newspaper's obtaining a list of video tapes that Supreme Court nominee and D.C. Circuit Judge Robert Bork rented from his local video store and then publishing an article about his viewing preferences. The Senate Report shows the legislature's concern with disclosures linked to particular, identified individuals. It states that VPPAs purpose was to preserve personal privacy with respect to the rental, purchase or delivery of videotapes or similar audio-visual materials.

As Senator Leahy explained in S. Rep. 100-599 (1988), "In an era of . . . computers, it would be relatively easy at some point to give a profile of a person and tell what they buy in a store, what kind of food they like, what sort of television programs they watch . . . I think that is wrong, I think that really is Big Brother, and I think it is something that we have to guard against. [T]he trail of information generated by every transaction that is now recorded and stored in sophisticated record-keeping systems is a new, more subtle and pervasive form of surveillance. These "information pools" create privacy interests that directly affect the ability of people to express their opinions, to join in association with others and to enjoy the freedom and independence that the Constitution was established to safeguard."

The plain language of the statute suggests, and the Senate Report confirms, that the statute protects PII that identifies a specific person and ties that person to particular videos that the person watched. The issue then is whether the disclosures here are merely an anonymized ID or whether they are closer to linking identified persons to the videos they watched. Hulu argues that it is not liable for these three disclosures because it never combined or linked the user IDs to identifying data such as a person's name or address. It characterizes plaintiff's comScore case as "the theoretical possibility that comScore could have used the anonymous ID . . . to find the user's name . . . and there is no evidence that Facebook ever linked the anonymized identifier to a person's name, or to the title of a video that person watched."

No case has addressed directly the issues raised by Plaintiffs. [Hulu cited three cases in support of its] argu[ment] that the disclosure has to be the person's actual name. That position paints too bright a line. One could not skirt liability under the VPPA, for example, by disclosing a unique identifies and a correlated look-up table. The statute does not require a name. The legislative history [confirms this]. One can be identified in many ways: by a picture, by pointing. . . . [What is required is] the identification of a specific person tied to a specific transaction, and support the conclusion that a unique anonymized ID alone is not PII but context could render it not anonymous and the equivalent of the identification of a specific person. The next sections apply this analysis to the three disclosures, which differ in the information disclosed.

1. Disclosure to comScore of Watch Page and Hulu User IDs. The disclosure to comScore is of a watch page URL containing the video name and the user's unique seven-digit Hulu User ID. This meant that comScore could access the profile page and see the user's first and last names. There is no evidence that comScore did this. The issue is only that it could. That information likely is relevant to an advertiser's desire to target ads to them. It does not suggest any linking of a specific, identified person and his video habits. The court grants summary judgment to Hulu on this theory.

2. The comScore UID Cookie. Sent by Hulu, this allowed comScore to link the identified user and the user's video choices with information that comScore gathered from other sites that the same user visited. Looking at the evidence very practically, comScore doubtless collects as much evidence as it can about what webpages Hulu users visit. There may be substantial tracking that reveals a lot of information about a person. [But] there is a VPPA violation only if that tracking necessarily reveals an identified person and his video watching. [T]he court grants summary judgment to Hulu on this theory.

3. Disclosure to Facebook of Watch Page and Transmission of Facebook Cookies to Facebook. Hulu sent code and information to load the Facebook Like button. At summary judgment state, it is not clear to the court whether the datr cookie alone establishes a VPPA violation because it apparently reveals only the browser, and it is not clear that it is the linking of the specific, identified person to his watched videos that is necessary for a VPPA violation. But the lu and the c_user cookies—sent with the datr cookie at the same time the watch page loaded—together reveal information about what the Hulu user watched and who the Hulu user is on Facebook. It also is a Hulu-initiated transmission of information. This is not merely the transmission of a unique, anonymous ID; it is information that identifies the Hulu user's actual identity on Facebook. Hulu argues that it needs to send an actual name to be liable and that it sent only cookies. The statute does not require an actual name and requires only something akin to it. Code is a language and languages contain names, and the string is the Facebook user name. The court cannot conclude on this record . . . that there was [user] consent. The court . . . denies the motion [for summary judgment regarding] the disclosures to Facebook.

IT IS SO ORDERED.

Case Questions

1. This judge could have read the provisions of the statute more broadly, and therefore ruled in Hulu's favor. Many have, in fact, in past years. It is only recently courts are hewing closer to the statutory language. What do you recommend to Hulu in managing this litigation risk?
2. This case exposes an aspect of the widespread data sharing that is the foundation of a free user experience. What is the top recommendation you have for Congress after this case?
3. comScore's metrics are used by Hulu to show to prospective advertisers the value proposition of placing ads on their site. What data do you suppose is in comScore's records?

Computer Fraud and Abuse Act

The **Computer Fraud and Abuse Act**, 18 U.S.C. § 1030 (2012), is covered more completely in Chapter 14 as it criminalizes specified computer-related acts, but listed here as it is peripherally related to data privacy since it restricts third parties from collecting PII from sites when the collection violates the sites' TOS. The CFAA provides, in pertinent part, "whoever intentionally accesses a computer without authorization or exceeds authorized access, and thereby obtains information . . . shall be punished." Under the civil enforcement provisions of the CFAA, "any person who suffers damage or loss by reason of a violation of this section may maintain a civil action against the violator to obtain compensatory damages and injunctive relief."

Telecommunications Act

The **Telecommunications Act**,codified in scattered sections of titles 15 and 47 of the U.S. Code (2012), requires telecom companies to protect the PII that they receive or obtain in their provision of telecom services. Known as CPNI (customer proprietary network information), telecoms have a duty to protect the confidentiality of this customer data, as well the CPNI of their customers' contacts, and may not use this CPNI for any marketing purposes. However, telecoms may, under 47 U.S.C. § 222 (2012) "use, disclose, or permit access to aggregate customer information [*i.e.*, CPNI that has been de-identified]."

In drawing some conclusions about the current federal data privacy legal environment, privacy protections are quite limited, and businesses have few regulatory or compliance obligations. There is no transparency or choice in data privacy policies. There are no common standards yet, such as rights of consent, or to access, review, control or correct PII, or to challenge the denial of these rights. There is no collection limitation standard. There are no data security standards. There is no liability for data security breaches. The default has been to grant autonomy to businesses to create their own data governance standards, and there is no common right to "opt-out" of each business's data collection protocol. There are no limitations to tracking technologies such as cookies (small text files placed by sites on users' computers once they visit the site). Furthermore, flash cookies are now commonly used, which circumvent users' settings, and thereby combat users' ability to delete cookies. Some web browsers have enhanced privacy settings to block cookies, as well as do-not-track features. But sites do not necessarily honor do-not-track settings. No federal law covers history sniffing, which records browsing history of page visitors. No federal law applies specifically to data privacy of mobile app's (software programs downloaded onto mobile devices), and so information generated is used by a number of businesses—even mobile payment systems. And with the exception of COPPA, no federal law explicitly addresses location data, location-based technology and data privacy.

State Data Privacy Laws

A few states broadly protect data privacy. California is at the forefront of states regulating data privacy and therefore some select provisions are presented here. California's "Shine the Light Law" is among the earliest attempts by a state to regulate data privacy. (Cal. Civ. Code § 1798.83 (2012).) Residents are entitled to disclosure of business's data sharing practices, and businesses must notify requesting customers of any sensitive user information shared with third parties (information concerning customers' height, weight, race, religion, telephone number, number of children, medical conditions, social security number, bank account numbers, and credit card balances). One other California data privacy law of note is the California Information Privacy Act (CIPA) (Cal. Penal Code §§ 630-638 (2012).) Enacted to protect residents' state constitutional right of privacy, CIPA prohibits eavesdropping, monitoring or recording of private communications that result in an invasions of privacy. California's legislature passed three bills

Executive Summary to Making Your Privacy Practices Public, Kamala D. Harris, Attorney General California Department of Justice

Meaningful privacy policy statements safeguard consumers by helping them make informed decisions about which companies they will entrust with their personal information. They are also an opportunity for companies to build their brands and to develop goodwill and trust through transparency. Many privacy policies, however, are overly long and difficult to read without offering meaningful choices to consumers. Indeed, research shows that consumers do not understand, and many do not even read, the privacy policies on the websites they visit.

The Attorney General's Office, in furtherance of its mission to protect the inalienable right to privacy conferred by the California Constitution, offers these recommendations to support companies in their work to provide privacy policy statements that are meaningful to consumers. To be specific, the guidance set forth here is intended to encourage companies to craft privacy policy statements that address significant data collection and use practices, use plain language, and are presented in a readable format.

The California Online Privacy Protection Act of 2003 (CalOPPA), the first law in the nation with a broad requirement for privacy policies, is a privacy landmark. The Act applies to operators of commercial web sites and online services that collect personally identifiable information about Californians. It requires them to say what they do and do what they say—to conspicuously post a privacy policy and to comply with it. The Act was amended in 2013 to address the issue of online tracking—the collection of personal information about consumers as they move across websites and online services. Do Not Track (DNT) technology exists, enabling consumers to communicate their desire not to be tracked through their browsers. However, many consumers do not know how sites and services are responding to their browsers' Do Not Track signals. The 2013 amendments to CalOPPA require web site operators and online services to inform consumers of just this, and the recommendations set forth here address these new provisions.

This document is another of the Attorney General's recommendations on privacy and security practices, including the recently released *Cybersecurity in the Golden State*.

in 2013 covering children's right to erase social media posts, making it a misdemeanor to publish identifiable nude photos online without permission, and requiring businesses to let users know if they abide by do not track signals on browsers. A "right to know" bill was not passed—it would have required businesses that retain PII to share a copy of that with users at their request as well as disclose with third parties received that information.

Other states have enacted regulations variously: promoting data security standards (Massachusetts); requiring warrants for email searches (Texas); requiring warrants for smartphone searches (Montana); privacy of student data (Oklahoma); inheritance of digital data (Connecticut, Idaho, Indiana, Nevada, Oklahoma, Rhode Island, and Virginia); limiting the use of license plate data (Vermont); limits on drone surveillance (Florida, Idaho, Illinois, Montana, North Carolina, Oregon, Tennessee, Texas, Virginia). A high number of states have passed laws in two prominent areas. First, restricting employers from demanding access to employees' social media accounts, and second, requiring businesses to notify customers of data breaches. The patchwork of rules creates another layer of compliance to adhere too, and therefore becomes quite a burden and logistical challenge for businesses.

Right of Publicity

Approximately half the states recognize this right, and it is construed as the right of individuals to control their name, image and likeness, and therefore a corresponding right to limit the public use of their name, likeness, and/or identity for commercial purposes. Claims typically involve the use of a plaintiff's identity, appropriated by the defendant for defendant's commercial advantage, without plaintiff's consent, and a resulting injury. Identity is construed broadly so as to be any image that evokes identity, including name, look-alikes, sound-alikes, and even a robot dressed up as a celebrity.

This next case construes the **right of publicity** in the context of an electronic image of a college football player. Note how the First Amendment impacts this right. Further, this was a split decision, and there is a split of opinion among the courts as well on analysis of these issues.

In re: Student-Athlete Name & Likeness Licensing Litigation v. Electronic Arts, Inc.

724 F.3d 1268 (9th Cir. 2013), petition for cert. filed, 82 U.S.L.W. 3137 (U.S. Sept. 23, 2013 (No.13-377), motion by NCAA for leave to intervene to file a petition for writ of certiorari denied, 134 S. Ct. 980 (Jan. 13, 2014)

Facts: Samuel Keller was the starting quarterback for Arizona State University before he transferred to the University of Nebraska. Electronic Arts (EA) is the producer of the *NCAA Football* series of video games, which allow users to control avatars representing college football players as the avatars participate in virtual games. In *NCAA Football*, EA seeks to replicate each school's entire team as accurately as possible. Every real college football player on each team included in the game has a corresponding avatar in the game with the collage player's actual jersey number, identical height, weight, build, skin tone, hair color, and home states. EA attempts to match any unique, highly identifiable playing behaviors by sending detailed questionnaires to team equipment managers. Additionally, EA creates realistic virtual versions of actual stadiums; populates them with the virtual athletes, coaches, cheerleaders, and fans realistically rendered by EA's graphic artists and incorporates realistic sounds such as the crunch of the players' pads and the roar of the crowd.

EA omits the players' names from the virtual jerseys and changes the hometown from the actual players' hometowns. However, users may upload rosters from third party sources and add them to the avatars' jerseys. In such cases, EA then allows images from the games containing the real names to be posted.

In EA's 2005 edition, the virtual starting quarterback for Arizona State wears number 9, as did Keller, and has the same height, weight, skin tone, hair color, hair style, handedness, home state, play style, visor preference, facial features, and school year as Keller.

Objecting to this use of his likeness, Keller filed a class-action complaint asserting that EA violated his right of publicity under California Civil Code § 3344, and California common law. EA moved to strike the lawsuit and raised four affirmative defenses derived from the First Amendment: the "transformative use" test, the Rogers test, the "public interest" test, and the "public affairs" exemption in order to defeat the right-of-publicity claims of Keller. The district court rejected EA's defenses to Keller's claims and ruled in favor of Keller.

Judicial Opinion. Judge Bybee: Video games are entitled to the full protections of the First Amendment, because like the protected books, plays, and movies that preceded them, video games communicate ideas—and even social messages—through many familiar literary devices (such as characters, dialogue, plot, and music) and through features distinctive to the medium (such as the players' interaction with the virtual world). Such rights are not absolute, and states may recognize the right of publicity to a degree consistent with the First Amendment. In this case, we must balance the right of publicity of a former college football player against the asserted First Amendment right of a video game developer to use his likeness in its expressive works. The appeal turns on the applicability of the four affirmative defenses. We take each one in turn.

The element of a right-of-publicity claim under California common law are: "(1) the defendant's use of the plaintiff's identity; (2) the appropriation of plaintiff's name or likeness to defendant's advantage, commercially or otherwise; (3) lack of consent; and (4) resulting injury." The same claim under § 3344 requires a plaintiff to prove all the elements of the common law cause of action, plus a knowing use by the defendant as well as direct connection between the alleged use and the commercial purpose.

The Transformative Use Defense

The California Supreme Court formulated the transformative use defense in the *Comedy III Productions* case. The defense is "'a balancing test between the First Amendment and the right of publicity based on whether the work in question adds significant creative elements so as to be transformed into something more than a mere celebrity likeness or imitation." When a work contains significant transformative elements, it is not only especially worthy of First Amendment protection, but it is also less likely to interfere with the economic interest protected by the right of publicity. [C]ourts [have] rejected the wholesale importation of the copyright "fair use" defense into right-of-publicity claims, but recognized that some aspects of that defense are particularly pertinent.

Comedy III gives us at least five factors to consider in determining whether a work is sufficiently transformative to obtain First Amendment protection. First, if the celebrity likeness if one of the "raw materials" from which an original work is synthesized, it is more likely to be transformative than if the depiction is the very sum and substance of the work in question. Second, the work is protected if it is primarily the defendant's own expression—something other than the likeness of the celebrity. This factor requires an examination of whether a likely purchaser's primary motivation is to buy a reproduction of the celebrity, or to buy the expressive work of that artist. Third . . . whether the literal and imitative, or the creative elements predominate in the work. Fourth, whether the marketability and economic value of the challenged work derive primarily from the fame of the celebrity depicted. Lastly, the court indicated that when the artist's skill and talent is manifestly subordinated to the overall goal of creating a conventional portrait of a celebrity so as to commercially exploit his or her fame, the work is not transformative.

EA is only entitled to the defense as a matter of law if no trier of fact could reasonably conclude that the game is not transformative. California courts have applied the transformative use test in relevant situation in four cases. First, in *Comedy III* itself, the California Supreme Court applied the test to t-shirts and lithographs bearing a likeness of *The Three Stooges* and concluded that it could discern no significant transformative or creative contribution . . . reason[ing] that the artist's undeniable skill is manifestly subordinated to the overall goal of creating literal, conventional depictions of *The Three Stooges* so as to exploit their fame [and so the artist's depictions were not protected by the First Amendment]. Finally, in *No Doubt v. Activision's Band Hero* video game . . . . users simulate performing in a rock band . . . the court held that *No Doubt's* right of publicity prevailed . . . because the [avatars] were literal recreations of the band members doing the same activity by which the band achieved and maintains its fame. The fact that avatars appear in the context of a videogame that contains many other creative elements does not transform the avatars into anything other than exact depictions of *No Doubt's* members doing exactly what they do as celebrities.

With [these and other] cases in mind as guidance, we conclude that EAs use of Keller's likeness does not contain significant transformative elements such that EA is entitled to the defense as a matter of law. The facts of *No Doubt* are vey similar to those here. EA is alleged to have replicated Keller's physical characteristics in NCAA Football, just as the member of *No Doubt* are realistically portrayed in Band Hero. [They are performing] the same activity for which they are known in real life. The context in which the activity occurs is also similarly realistic—real venues in Band Hero and realistic depictions of actual football stadiums in *NCAA Football*.

EA suggests that the fact that *NCAA Football* users can alter the characteristics of the avatars . . . is significant. We believe *No Doubt* offers a persuasive precedent. The Third Circuit came to the same conclusion in *Hart v. Electronic Arts, Inc.* Though the Third Circuit was tasked with interpreting New Jersey law, the court looked to the transformative use test developed in California. Given that *NCAA Football* realistically portrays college football players in the context of college football games, the district court was correct in concluding that EA cannot prevail as a matter of law based on the transformative use defense.

EA urges us to adopt, for right-of-publicity claims, [a different and] broader First Amendment defense than we have previously adopted in the context of false endorsement claims under the Lanham Act: the *Rogers* test. Th[at] case involved a suit brought by the famous performer Ginger Rogers against the producers ... who [created a new work that] imitated Rogers. The *Rogers* court determined that ... artistic ... works were less likely to be misleading than the names of ordinary commercial products, and thus that Lanham Act protections applied with less rigor when considering ... artistic ... works than when considering ordinary products.

Although we acknowledge that there is some overlap between the transformative use test and the *Rogers* test, we disagree that the *Rogers* test should be imported wholesale for right-of-publicity claims. [That test] was designed to protect consumers from the risk of consumer confusion. The right of publicity, on the other hand, does not primarily seek to prevent consumer confusion. Rather, it primarily protects a form of intellectual property [in one's person] that society deems to have some social utility. The right of publicity protects the *celebrity*, not the *consumer*. Keller's publicity claim is not founded on an allegation that consumers are being illegally misled into believing that he is endorsing EA or its products. Instead, Keller's claim is that EA has appropriated, without permission and without providing compensation, his talent and years of hard work on the football field. The reasoning of the *Rogers* ... court—that artistic ... works should be protected unless they explicitly mislead consumers—is simply not responsive to Keller's asserted interests here. The right of publicity yields to free use of a public figure's likeness only to the extent reasonably required to report information to the public or publish factual data, and [this applies] only to broadcasts or accounts of public affairs.

Under California's transformative use defense, EA's use of the likenesses of college athletes like Samuel Keller in its video games is not, as a matter of law, protected by the First Amendment. We reject EA's suggestion to import the *Rogers* test into the right-of-publicity arena, and conclude that state-law defenses for the reporting of information do not protect EA's use. AFFIRMED.

Judge Thomas, dissenting: Because the creative and transformative elements of EAs NCAA Football video game series predominate over the commercial use of the athletes' likenesses, the First Amendment protects EA from liability. Therefore, I respectfully dissent.

The majority confines its [transformative use] inquiry to how a single athlete's likeness is represented in the video game, rather than examining the transformative and creative elements in the video game as a whole. The logical consequence of the majority view is that all realistic depictions of actual persons, no matter how incidental, are protected by a state law right of publicity regardless of the creative context. The salient question is whether the entire work is transformative, and whether the transformative elements predominate, rather than whether an individual persona or image has been altered. When EA's *NCAA Football* video game series is examined carefully, and put in proper context, I conclude that the creative and transformative elements of the games predominate over the commercial use of the likenesses of the athletes within the games.

Case Questions

1. Which view is more protective of individuals' rights to control their likeness? Do you think this holding extends to individuals who are not famous?
2. What do you recommend for businesses that create likenesses of people?
3. There is a split of opinion on this issue among the circuit courts and therefore, the only way to harmonize these holdings is for the Supreme Court to take a case and make a ruling in this area. If you were on the Supreme Court, which view would you vote for, and why?

Additional Data Privacy Theories: Tort Laws Protecting Individuals' Privacy

Restatement (Second) of Torts § 652 (1977)

Beyond federal and state laws, tort law recognizes privacy-related protections. In the Restatement (Second) of Torts § 652 (1977), individuals may seek damages and injunctive relief for violations based on unreasonable or unwarranted invasions of privacy.

- **Intrusion upon seclusion**, § 652B: The Restatement defines intrusion upon seclusion as intentionally intruding, physically or otherwise, upon the solitude of another or his privacy affairs or concerns, in ways that average persons objectively would find highly offensive and unreasonable.

- **Misappropriation of a person's name or likeness causing injury to reputation**, § 652C: This typically involves a living person's name or likeness that is appropriated by another for commercial, non-newsworthy purposes, without the person's permission.

- **Public disclosure of private facts causing injury to reputation**, § 652D: This tort covers the public disclosure of highly personal facts or information about a person that results in injury to reputation. Plaintiffs must show that the facts were private and then publicly disclosed to a significant segment of the community. Courts require proof that the facts publicized would be highly offensive to a reasonable person and that they have no legitimate concern to the public. *much like the defamation*

- **Publicly placing another in false light**, § 652E: This tort covers claims that involve falsely connecting a person to an immoral, illegal or embarrassing situation resulting in injury to one's reputation. Plaintiff must show that defendant gave publicity to a matter concerning plaintiff in a false light, that is highly offensive to a reasonable person, and defendant did this with knowledge, and acted in reckless disregard as to the falsity of the publicized matter, and the false light in which plaintiff would be placed.

International Data Privacy Law

Significant differences in perceptions of and legal protections for data privacy are emerging as key conflict points between countries—and as between countries and U.S. companies. As an example of the former, in a November 2013 press release by the EU, Ms. Viviane Reding, President of the European Commission and the EU justice commissioner, demanded that the U.S. take greater care in protecting EU citizens' data. As an example of the latter, the EU is rigorously enforcing its data privacy laws on U.S. companies accessed by EU citizens even though in many instances, these companies are not physically operating in the EU. EU data protection laws are much more stringent and therefore, U.S. companies find themselves in a precarious legal position: in compliance with U.S. law, but not with EU law, and subject to fines, oversight and other penalties.

Currently, the EU's Data Protection Directive 95/46/EC governs, but fundamental changes to this are underway, with proposed amendments more stringent than these. Selected articles of the present Directive are presented below. Overall, these rules provide citizens with control over what data is collected, where it is kept, which companies and governments have access to it, and restrictions on what data can be sent to countries that do not have identical data protections.

- *Article 1*: protects the fundamental rights and freedoms of persons, and in particular, recognizes their right to privacy with respect to the processing of personal data.
- *Article 2*: personal data is any information relating to an identified or identifiable person; processor of data is any operation or set of operations which is performed on personal data, whether or not by automatic means
- *Article 6*: personal data must be processed fairly, accurately and lawfully, for specified explicit and legitimate purposes and not further processed in a way incompatible with those purposes.
- *Article 7*: data subjects must give consent to the processing.
- *Article 12*: data subjects have the right to obtain from the controller, as appropriate: the rectification, erasure, or blocking of data, the processing of which is noncompliant.
- *Article 14*: data subjects have the right to object at any time to the processing of data relating to him/her personally, except if otherwise provided. If the objection is justified, the processing must cease.
- *Article 25*: prohibits the export of personal data to nonmember countries that do not have laws that 'adequately' protect personal data.

This last article has significant implications for U.S. companies that EU citizens patronize. In response to the Directive, the U.S. Department of Commerce in consultation with the EU drafted Safe Harbor principles for data flows between the US and EU. U.S. Companies will be certified Safe Harbor compliant to the extent they meets the seven principles.

- Notice: data subjects must be informed that data is being collected and how it will be used;

- Choice: data subjects may opt-out of collection and forward transfer of data to third parties;
- Onward Transfer: allowed only if these third parties are Safe Harbor certified too;
- Security: data controllers must make reasonable efforts to prevent loss of subjects' data;
- Data Integrity: data must be relevant and reliable as to the purpose for which it was collected;
- Access: as to data about them, subjects must be able to access it, correct it, or delete it if inaccurate;
- Enforcement: an effective protocol for enforcing these principles.

Excerpt from European Commission Press Release, November 27, 2013

EUROPEAN COMMISSION CALLS ON THE U.S. TO RESTORE TRUST IN EU—U.S. DATA FLOWS

Today the European Commission has set out the actions that need to be taken to restore trust in data flows between the EU and the U.S. following deep concerns about revelations of large-scale U.S. intelligence collection programmes have had a negative impact on the transatlantic relationship. The Commission's response today takes the form of (1) **a strategy paper (a Communication) on transatlantic data flows** setting out the challenges and risks following the revelations of U.S. intelligence collection programmes, as well as the steps that need to be taken to address these concerns; (2) **an analysis of the functioning of 'Safe Harbour'** which regulates data transfers for commercial purposes between the EU and U.S.; and (3) **a report on the findings of the EU-US Working Group** (see MEMO/13/1059) on Data Protection which was set up in July 2013. In addition, the European Commission is also presenting its review of the existing agreements on **Passenger Name Records (PNR)** (see MEMO/13/1054) and the **Terrorist Finance Tracking Programme (TFTP)** regulating data exchanges in these sectors for law enforcement purposes (see MEMO/13/1060).

"Massive spying on our citizens, companies and leaders is unacceptable. Citizens on both sides of the Atlantic need to be reassured that their data is protected and companies need to know existing agreements are respected and enforced. Today, the European Commission is setting out actions that would help to restore trust and strengthen data protection in transatlantic relations, *"said Vice-President Viviane Reding, the EU's Justice Commissioner."* There is now a window of opportunity to rebuild trust which we expect our American partners to use, notably by working with determination towards a swift conclusion of the negotiations on an EU-U.S. data protection 'umbrella' agreement. Such an agreement has to give European citizens concrete and enforceable rights, notably the right to judicial redress in the U.S. whenever their personal data are being processed in the U.S."

"European citizens' trust has been shaken by the Snowden case, and serious concerns still remain following the allegations of widespread access by U.S. intelligence agencies to personal data. Today, we put forward a clear agenda for how the U.S. can work with the EU to rebuild trust, and reassure EU citizens that their data will be protected. Everyone from Internet users to authorities on both sides of the Atlantic stand to gain from cooperation, based on strong legal safeguards and trust that these safeguards will be respected." *said Cecilia Malmström, European Commissioner for Home Affairs.*

Presently, each of the twenty-eight EU member countries has a right to tweak the Directive in minor ways to make the laws more in accord with their individual country's views. Under proposed changes slated for 2015, companies will have fewer localization requirements and compliance obligations within the EU because they will only be required to comply with just one country's data protection protocols. Increasingly, businesses' focus is on Ireland as the country of choice for compliance certification. Ireland's Law on Data Protection is more moderate than France or Germanys' data protection laws. Furthermore, as it turns out, many U.S. tech companies already base their regional headquarters in Ireland due to its favorable tax laws (a 12.5% corporate tax rate, whereas the U.S. federal corporate tax rate is 35%). To the extent that companies do not comply with the country-specific version of the Data Protection Directive or the Safe Harbor principles, the EU reserves the right to levy multimillion dollar fines on companies that misuse EU citizens' data.

This next case concerns a recent EU decision on Google Spain's handling of an EU citizen's personal data. Though the company complied with U.S. law, the EU decision was quite a surprise to Google and it has caused the company to make a number of changes to its search business within the EU.

Google Spain, SL v. Agencia Espanola de Proteccion de Datos,
Court of Justice, Grand Chamber, European Union,
Case No. C-131/12 (13 May 2014) [translated]

Facts: Mario Costeja Gonzalez discovered that a Google search of his name produced results that linked to legal notices from fifteen years earlier from the online version of *La Vanguardia Ediciones, SL* that detailed his social security debts, the forced sale of his property, and, further, that his home was being repossessed to pay off these debts. The notice was placed by the Ministry of Labor and Social Affairs, and was intended to give maximum publicity to the auction in order to secure as many bidders as possible. Gonzalez subsequently paid his debts and resolved the claims, yet the original articles resurfaced whenever Gonzalez's name was searched on Google. His concern was the article's prominent position among Google search results, and this affects his reputation.

In February 2010, Gonzalez requested first that *La Vanguardia* be required either to remove those pages or to use certain tools made available by search engines in order to protect the data. Gonzalez also contacted Google Spain to request removal of the links. Google Spain forwarded the request to Google, Inc. in California, and thereafter he filed a complaint with the Spanish Data Protection Agency, on the theory that he had long resolved his debts and the information was no longer relevant, yet this information kept coming up in Google search results, which he said violated his privacy and data protection rights.

The Agency rejected Gonzalez's complaint against the newspaper, ruling that it was within its rights to publish the information at the time of the auction.

However, the Agency ruled that Google had no right to further disseminate the new about Gonzalez, and ruled that that Google must remove the link from its search results. Google appealed this ruling before the Audiencia Nacional (National High Court).

That Court referred the following questions to the EU Court of Justice:

1. Territorial scope: whether it is possible to apply EU legislation on data protection, privacy and erasure, to a U.S. company with a worldwide presence, and a local language site, www.google.es, and therefore, whether Google, Inc., which orients its activity towards the residents of an EU-member State on this site, is bound by the EU laws of data privacy and protection.
2. Material scope: whether the activity of Google, a search engine and provider of content in the form of links, makes it a 'data processor,' and therefore subject to the EU's strict laws for data processors.
3. Scope of data subjects' rights: whether the rights granted by the EU extend to data subjects being able to require Google to remove from the list of its results links to pages published lawfully by third parties (the newspaper) that contain true information, on the theory that the information may be prejudicial to him, or that he wishes it to be 'forgotten' after a certain time (rights of privacy and erasure).

Judicial Opinion: Regarding Question 1, the territorial scope and whether it is possible to apply EU national legislation in this circumstance, the Court responds in the affirmative. Google designated Google Spain as the controller, in Spain, in respect to two legal filings. The EU Directive is to be interpreted as meaning that processing of personal data is carried out in the context of the activities of company of a Member State. Here, Google sets up a Member State subsidiary that it intended to market its activity and promote and sell ads oriented towards inhabitants of that Member State.

Therefore it cannot be accepted that the processing of personal data carried out for the purposes of operating the search engine, should escape the obligations and guarantees of Directive 95/46, which would compromise its effectiveness and complete protection of the fundamental rights and freedoms . . . in particular their right of privacy.

Regarding Question 2, the material scope and whether Google is a data processor, the Court responds in the affirmative. Google locates information, indexes it automatically, stores it temporarily and makes it available to users.

According to Google, the activity of search engines cannot be regarded as processing of data, given that everything is automated, and results are generating, not by actively selecting, this data. Google asserts that results are generated by query relevancy, and so it has no directly knowledge of those data and does not exercise control over that data. Google submits that, by virtue of the principle of proportionality, any request seeking the removal of information, must be addressed to the original publisher because they have ultimate responsibility for making the information public.

Article 2 of Directive 95/46 defines "processing of personal data: as "any operation . . . which is performed upon personal data, whether or not by automatic means, such as collection, recording, organization, storage . . . retrieval . . . use . . . dissemination . . . [etc]." Therefore it must be found that . . . the operator of a search engine 'collects' such data which it subsequently 'retrieves,' [and so forth]. As those operations are referred to expressly and unconditionally in Article 2, they must be classified as 'processing' within the meaning of this provision. Nor is the finding affected by the fact that those data have already been published on the Internet and are not altered by Google.

Google must be regarded as a data controller under EU law. It is the search engine operator which determines the results and plays a decisive role in the overall dissemination of those data in that it renders the latter accessible to any Internet user searching that data subject's name. It should be pointed out that the processing of personal data by a search engine can be distinguished from and is additional to that carried by the initial publishers who load that personal data onto an Internet page. Search engines' activity, in comparison to the initial publishers, significantly impact the fundamental rights to privacy and to the protection of personal data, and the guarantees of Directive 95/46 might never be achieved or have full effect without such a finding that Google is a data processor. Finally, the fact that the initial publishers may exclude content from search engines through coding exclusion protocols, this does not in any way release the search engines from responsibility for the processing of personal data. The activity of search engines must be classified as "processing of personal data," and second the operator of the search engine must be regarded as the 'controller' in respect of that processing.

Based on this finding, the controller has the task of ensuring that personal data are processed "fairly and lawfully" that they are collected for specified explicit and legitimate purposes, and not further processed in a way incompatible with those purposes, and not excessive in relation to the purposes for which they are collected, that they are accurate, and kept in a form which permits access and identification. In this context, the controller must take steps to ensure that data which do not meet the requirements of this provision are erased or rectified.

This provision permits the processing of personal data for the purposes of legitimate interests, except where such interest are overridden by the interest or fundamental rights and freedoms of the data subject in particular their right to privacy with respect to the processing of personal data. Application of this Article thus necessitates a balancing of the opposing rights and interests concerned, in the context of which account must be taken of the significance of that data subject's rights arising from the EU Directive. Where there is a justified objection by a data subject, the processing may no longer involve these data. This is especially significant because information which potentially concerns a vast number of aspects of private life, which without the search engine, could not have been interconnected or could have been only with great difficulty. The effect of this search is heightened on account of the important role the Internet in modern society, which render the information contained in search results ubiquitous. In light of the potential seriousness of such offense, it is clear that it cannot be justified by merely the economic interest of Google. However, the removal of links could, depending on the issue, have effects upon the legitimate interest of the public and access to that information, and so a fair balance should be sought between that and the data subject's fundamental rights.

Regarding Question 3 regarding the scope of data subjects' rights, whether they may require Google to remove from the list of result displayed following a search of their name, links to pages that are published lawfully by third parties, and contain true information on grounds that the information is prejudicial or they wish to be 'forgotten,' and the Court answers this in the affirmative. Even initially lawfully processing of accurate data may, in the course of time, become incompatible with the Directive where those data are no longer necessary in the light of the purposes for which they were originally collected. This is because they may become inadequate, irrelevant, no longer relevant, or excessive in relation to those purposes and in light of the time that has elapsed. Therefore, if the data is so found the information and links concerned in the list of results must be erased. This right overrides, as a rule, not only the economic interest of the search engine, but also the interest of the general public in finding that information upon a name search of that person. However, that would not be the case if the information appeared for particular reasons, such as for public and newsworthy people, since the interference with their fundamental rights is justified by the preponderant interest of the general public in having access to the information in question.

Having regard to the sensitivity for the data subject's private life of the information contained in the link, and to the fact that its initial publication had taken place 16 years earlier, the data subject establishes a right that the information should no longer be linked to his name by means of such a list. Since there do not appear to be particular reasons substantiating a preponderant interest of the public in having access to the information, the data subject may require those links to be removed from the list of results. These rights override not only the economic interest of Google, but also the interest of the general public in having access to the information.

Post-script Google created a page entitled "Search removal request under European Data Protection Law." It asks users what they want removed and why, along with proof of identification. It is up to Google to decide whether to approve the request,This is somewhat in contravention of the company's mission to organize the world's information and make it easily accessible.

Case Questions

1. Change the facts slightly, and describe a fact pattern in which the court would be likely to agree with Google.
2. Is Google to change all EU sites to provide a right of erasure, or just its Google Spain site? Should Google change more sites than it has to?
3. Implementation of this decision will be extremely complex. What are your top two recommendations for Google concerning its EU sites at this time?

Data Privacy in the Era of Big Data

Big data and the **Internet of things** are the top trending issues within the practice area of data privacy. The amount of data generated is nearly beyond conception. This new class of economic asset describes both the data being generated (from devices, sensors, etc.) as well as the sophisticated techniques used to scale the data. Through this we derive more intelligence, new insights that yield competitive advantages, new business models, and more.

Big Data Defined

Data sets so large, diverse, and complex that sophisticated techniques are needed for discovery of insights that were not previously possible to discern. The challenges have to do with data capture, curation, storage, search sharing, analysis, and visualization. This sets that stage for new efficiencies, predictive modeling, new business models, and inventions.

These are among the unique qualities of big data:

- Volume—large and complex data sets;
- Velocity—data captured in real time, so much that has to be received, understood, and processed;
- Variety—increasing variety of disparate data from new sources, from both inside and outside business, creates integration, management, governance, compliance and architectural pressures on businesses;
- Big data is pervasive, passively produced, collection is automatic, constant, geographically or temporally trackable.

Big Data Sources

Sources of big data now include mobile devices, aerial sensory technology, software logs, cameras, microphones, RFID readers, wireless sensor networks (movement, building access, smart power meters, health monitors, surveillance cameras, smart cars, TVs, the Internet of things—even products that measure our pets' activity!).

While the concept of big data sets is not new, there are now staggeringly large data sets and fine, granular measurement tools. Big data is transforming business decision-making, as every aspect of the organization will be able to be measured. The use of big data holds tremendous promise for growth and productivity. In order to capture the full potential of big data, it is necessary for businesses to consider privacy, security, intellectual property, liability, IT and compliance issues.

Managing the Data: Best Practices in an Era of Rapid Changes of Norms

Fair Information Practice Principles (FIPPs) developed by the FTC are a useful reference for businesses and should probably now be considered as a starting point for businesses. The FIPPs are only recommendations, however, and are not law at this time. The FTCs enforcement personnel review companies' policies and compare these to actual consumer experiences. The agency will further scrutinize businesses' manner of collecting and using PII, and whether adequate safeguards exist.

Since big data is a rapidly changing legal environment, this means changes in consumer/user/voter/business norms. Therefore, there is more pressure on businesses to develop management and control systems for the data and lead the way on compliance by practice and in this way, be better able to engage with regulators and courts.

Business best practices will cover a well thought-out data strategy as to collection, storage, contract, licensing, and use, at a minimum. To the extent goods and services are created and built out with these consideration in mind, businesses are engaging in "privacy by design" and "baking it into the process."

- Define what rights users have (notice; consent; access; modify/edit/delete?), and define use limitations;
- Decide which department in organization controls data;
- Anonymize/de-identify data (though studies point to the ability to easily re-identify);
- Know purposes to which data will be put at time of collection;
- Determine how to contact those affected by collection;
- Create policies for use of data within the organization, and by others, including the sale, rental and licensing of data;
- Allowing third parties access to data, but this may then be used to re-identify users, through an unanticipated linkage;
- Consider law at jurisdiction at the point of collection;
- Consider law at jurisdiction of data storage;
- Consider law at jurisdiction of data usage;
- Consider law at jurisdiction of data subject;
- Maintain appropriate security and protection measures for data;
- Create protocols for managing access requests by subjects to edit/delete data;
- Expect more government and agency oversight, both domestically and internationally, especially for businesses in sectors with a more demanding regulatory environment (such as: insurance, tobacco, utilities, consumer protection, financial/securities/banking, medical/pharma, airlines, employment, educational).

Ethical consideration: Say you are a CEO of a small healthcare analytics business. The business receives data from health insurance companies and then figures out the risk of disease for each class of worker in an industry. Say the FDA, a government agency, asks you to turn over your business's data, even the draft work. They assert a warrant is not needed because they don't subscribe to Judge Leon's views in the *Klayman v. Obama* decision. They want to use the data to further their work and advance certain regulatory matters. Should you contest the FDA's request? Should you just hand the data over?

Summary

Data privacy has become an unlikely strategic business imperative in the U.S. and the subject of much regulation at the state and international levels, as well as introspection as businesses see that privacy matters to their customers and international regulators, after years of industry self-regulation. Even U.S. tech companies trade associations and lobbying groups such as Digital Due Process have asked Congress to consider bolstering privacy rules. Data is the new industrial asset, and data management will take priority in businesses as data privacy matures to a point where governance and accountability take a central role.

Key Terms

big data Data sets characterized by volume (vast beyond conception), velocity (increasing speed and masses of data points gathered per swipe/touch/click/step/breath, etc.); variety (data from all manner of connected devices, appliances, clothing, etc.).

Internet of things Every object with a connection and sensor capable of transmitting data.

personally identifiable information (PII) Data that can identify individuals.

data privacy The concept that individuals want to be able to control aspects of their PII.

Fourth Amendment A constitutional protection against unreasonable searches and seizures by the government.

EU Data Protection Directive 95/46/EC The present standard for data processing applicable to all transactions involving an EU citizen, business or country.

third party doctrine Information voluntarily handed over to a third party may not be claimed as privacy, and this information lawfully held by third parties is obtainable with merely a subpoena (rather than the stricter requirements for securing a search warrant).

First Amendment A constitutional protection against unreasonable government intrusions into speech (and other) rights.

Fair Credit Reporting Act Protects the security and confidentiality of consumer data collected or used in decisions concerning eligibility for credit, employment or insurance.

Gramm-Leach-Bliley Act Regulates the sharing personal information by financial services providers.

Health Insurance Portability and Accountability Act Regulates the use and sharing of data provided to and generated by healthcare providers.

Children's Online Privacy Protection Act Provides protections regarding the collection of name, email address and geolocation information so as to safeguard the child's identity and location.

Electronic Communications Privacy Act The law prohibits the interception and disclosure of communications unless an exception applies.

Wiretap Act Requires law enforcement to apply for an order if they want to intercept electronic communications.

Stored Communications Act The provisions covering stored electronic communications and limiting access to these, especially for those older than six months.

Federal Trade Commission Act Establishing the Federal Trade Commission whose mandate is as a consumer protection agency, currently the de facto regulator of consumer data privacy in the U.S. concerning deceptions or violations of written privacy policies.

Drivers Privacy Protection Act Prohibits the use and disclosure of select personal information in states' motor vehicle records.

Family Educational Rights and Privacy Act Governs access to and disclosure of students' educational records. Schools may not release student data or PII other than directory information to third parties without written consent.

Video Privacy Protection Act Prohibits videotape service providers from knowingly disclosing PII concerning rental and sales records, including the videos' title or subject matter, to third parties.

Computer Fraud and Abuse Act In data privacy context, it restricts third parties from collecting PII from sites when the collection violates the sites' TOS.

Telecommunications Act Law requiring telecom companies to protect the PII that they receive or obtain in their provision of services. Known as CPNI (customer proprietary network information), telecoms have a duty to protect the confidentiality of this customer data, as well the CPNI of their customers' contacts, and may not use this CPNI for any marketing purposes.

intrusion upon seclusion Covering claims for intentionally intruding, physically or otherwise, upon the solitude of another or his privacy affairs or concerns, in ways that average persons objectively would find highly offensive and unreasonable.

misappropriation of a person's name or likeness causing injury to reputation Covering claims by living persons that their name or likeness that is appropriated by another for commercial, non-newsworthy purposes, without the person's permission.

publicly placing another in false light Covering claims that involve falsely connecting a person to an immoral, illegal or embarrassing situation resulting in injury to one's reputation.

public disclosure of private facts causing injury to reputation Covering claims that the public disclosure of highly personal facts or information about a person results in injury to reputation.

> **right of publicity** The right of individuals to control their name, image and likeness, and therefore a corresponding right to limit the public use of their name, likeness, and/or identity for commercial purposes.
>
> **Fair Information Practice Principles** FTCs recommendations for businesses on what it considers fair uses of consumer information.

Manager's Checklist

1. Inventory all data generated, including internal operations, and customer engagement;

2. Decide what department within the business entity will manage the data;

3. Create protocols for data retention, access, notice, correction, erasure and transfer (including for transfer, policies these onward parties must comply with);

4. Create data security policies along with provisions for credentials for accessing data, and audits of data;

5. Monitor data privacy legal environments, as this area is rapidly changing.

Questions and Case Problems

1. Zynga, a game developer, offers free social gaming apps through Facebook. Zynga Privacy Policy provided that it did not sell or rent PII to third parties. Zynga programmed its gaming apps to collect information in the http header, and then transmit this information to advertisers and other third parties. This contained the users' Facebook IDs, and the address of the Facebook page users were viewing when they clicked the link to the game. Plaintiffs allege violations of the ECPA based on their disclosure of referrer headers to third parties. Defendants assert that this is not the type of information protected by the ECPA and therefore there is no violation of that statute. What is the outcome?

2. Verizon contracted with Collecto to call Verizon customers and collect debts that they owed to Verizon. Collecto made calls at the direction of Verizon, and under the Verizon name, and recorded these calls. However, the subscribers did not affirmatively consent to the calls being recorded, as is required by state law. Under Verizon's monitoring disclosure policy no disclosure of recording had to be made to subscribers for debt collections. Verizon contends that while Collecto may have violated state law, it did not. Should Verizon be held vicariously liable for violations of state privacy law?

3. A state agency was investigating repeated employee misconduct. The state conducted a further investigation of this employee by placing a GPS device

without a warrant, on his vehicle, and they later extracted 30 days of data for evidence of submitting fraudulent time records. Defendant employee filed a motion to suppress this evidence. What is the outcome?

4. Plaintiff alleges that Interclick, an ad network business, used flash cookies and placed one on his computer. Even though plaintiff attempted to delete this cookie that transmits information back the business so they can create behavioral profiles, he was unsuccessful, because he alleged that Interclick used flash cookies that backed up the browser cookies (according to the complaint, even if users delete browser cookies, flash cookies "respawn" without notice to or consent of the users). Plaintiff filed suit under the Computer Fraud and Abuse Act. What is the result?

5. Plaintiff attended a Lakers game during which the Lakers displayed this statement to fans: "TEXT your message to 525377." After viewing this, plaintiff texted a message for the sole purpose of having the Lakers put this on the scoreboard. Defendants did not inform him that by sending this text message he 'would be consenting to receive future text messages' from the Lakers. Shortly thereafter texting his message, he received an unsolicited message from the Lakers. The Lakers called this a confirmatory reply, though it did not read as such and merely read, "Thnx! Txt as many times as u like . . . " Plaintiff asserts that this violates his privacy. What is the result?

Additional Resources

California's Privacy Enforcement and Protection Unit. http://oag.ca.gov/privacy.

Digital Marketing Association. http://thedma.org.

Electronic Privacy Information Center. http://epic.org.

European Union Commission on Data Protection. http://ec.europa.eu/justice/data-protection/index_en.htm.

Federal Trade Commission. Protecting Consumer Privacy Page. http://ftc.gov.

Google Enterprise. Google's use of students data it collects from its apps for education program. http://googleenterprise.blogspot.com/2014/04/protecting-students-with-google-apps.html.

International Association of Privacy Professionals. http://privacyassociation.org.

The White House. *Consumer Data Privacy in a Networked World: A Framework for Protecting Privacy and Promoting Innovation in the Global Digital Economy.* February 2012.

U.S. computer networks and databases are under daily cyber attack by nation states, international crime organizations, subnational groups, and individual hackers."

—John O. Brennan, Director of the Central Intelligence Agency

Cyber crime is a tax on innovation and slows the pace of global innovation by reducing the rate of return to innovators and investors . . . and has serious implications for employment."

—James Lewis, Director of the Center for Strategic and International Studies

Security and Computer Crime

Learning Objectives

After you have read this chapter, you should be able to:

- Explain how the Internet has impacted the possibilities for and execution of criminal conduct, including how the Internet is being used as a medium for the commission of crimes.
- Differentiate the various means of committing cybercrimes.
- Outline the key elements of various cybercrimes.
- Identify key cybercrimes, including cyberstalking, identity theft, and hacking.
- Discuss laws intended to reduce child pornography and display a working knowledge of agencies carrying out prevention and detection efforts.
- Explain how businesses can play a role in protecting their information resources from cybercrimes.
- Identify the trends in international cybercrime and discuss the role of international treaties and conventions in preventing cybercrime and apprehending cybercriminals.

Overview

Cyberspace is a new landscape for criminal activity that includes longstanding crimes that are now committed in cyberspace (e.g., fraud) along with new crimes born in the information age (e.g., hacking). According to a 2014 study by the Center for Strategic and International Studies (CSIS), computer crime, also called

Chapter Hypothetical: Cyber Hitchhiker

To illustrate the various aspects of criminal activity in cyberspace, consider the hypothetical start up firm Cyber Hitchhiker (CH). The company has two principals who operate a website that facilitates connection between those who want car transportation to a specific geographic location with those who are driving to those locations and wish to share driving costs such as gasoline. CH's initial cybercrime concerns center around security of the data of its customers and protecting its intellectual property. As its operations grow, CH may also become concerned with its liability for cyberstalking and being the target of cyberterrorist and the challenges of enforcing criminal laws in cyberspace.

cybercrime, costs the global economy about $445 billion every year. The same study found that roughly 15 percent of the U.S. population has had personal information stolen by hackers. Media outlets regularly report instances of possible cyber attacks against computer networks used by financial firms, retail chains, health care companies, and government agencies including the Department of Defense. This chapter examines the use of computers by criminals to facilitate crimes, attacks on computer systems, cyberlaw enforcement methods and dilemmas, and international efforts to reduce cybercrime.

Criminal Use of Computers

Cybercrimes are committed either by using the computer as an *instrument* of crime by an individual or when a criminal *targets* a computer or network. Using the Internet for criminal purposes is sometimes referred to as **netcrime**. The legal definition of cybercrime has expanded rapidly over the last decade. Cybercrime is now broadly defined as any use of telecommunication network (e.g., the Internet or cell phones) to cause harm to a victim's computer, network, personal safety, reputation, or mental well-being.

Crimes Related to Fraud: Hacking and Identity Theft

Using a computer to commit fraud comes in a variety of different forms. In a financial context, use of a computer to commit fraud typically involves the alteration of information, data, or software by a criminal to derive an unlawful financial benefit. This is also known as **cyberfraud**, and involves use of the Internet, a computer, or a computer device or network to convey false or fraudulent information, to offer to sell consumer goods or services that do not exist or are different than what is advertised, or to unlawfully transmit another's money, access devices, or other valuables to another's control.

Hacking

Hacking is the exploitation of a weakness in a computer network for nefarious or activist purposes. While there is some quibbling in the cyber community about the definition of a hacker,[1] a generally accepted definition is one who accesses a computer network through unauthorized means. Although some hackers are motivated by profit, other hackers are interested in using hacking as a method of protest or simply for the enjoyment of outsmarting security experts. No matter what their motivation, hackers who engage in cyber attacks are engaging in serious criminal behavior. For example, in 2014, law enforcement officials arrested 20-year-old hacker Timothy Justin French for hacking computers systems of corporations, universities, and governments. The government alleges that French was part of a hacking group called NullCrew that aims to shame targets by disclosing private information to the public. According to the U.S. Department of Justice, NullCrew's cyber attacks have resulted in thousands of private username and password combinations being published on the web.[2]

Computer Fraud and Abuse Act (CFAA)

In the 1970s and early 1980s, a common opinion was that hackers were a minor nuisance affecting a minimal number of people. However, in a 1983 incident that received substantial media attention, a group of young hackers in Milwaukee hacked into a computer at the Sloan-Kettering Cancer Institute in New York City. The medical center's computers stored records of cancer patients' radiation treatment and hackers were able to alter patient files. The incident led to passage of the **Computer Fraud and Abuse Act (CFAA)**[3] and the Sloan-Kettering hacking was cited by Congress in the legislative history of the statute. The CFAA, which was amended in 2001 by the USA PATRIOT Act,[4] prohibits unauthorized use of computers to commit seven different crimes: 1) espionage; 2) accessing unauthorized information; 3) accessing a nonpublic government computer; 4) fraud by computer; 5) damage to computer; 6) trafficking in passwords; and 7) extortionate threats to damage a computer. The CFAA has stiff criminal penalties and also allows civil actions to be brought against an offender to recover damages.

CFAA Controversy

A significant controversy has arisen as to how broadly the CFAA should be applied. The text of the CFAA criminalizes use of a computer without authorization or when a user "exceeds authorized access." Government prosecutors have gradually expanded the use of the CFAA in the context of the employer-employee relationship and in cases that do not center on the hacking but on unrelated criminal behavior. Digital rights activist groups such as the Electronic Frontier Foundation and civil rights groups such as the American Civil Liberties Union

---

1. See, Steele, et al, *The Hacker's Dictionary*, (http://jargon-file.org/archive/jargon-1.5.0.dos.txt) for an interesting discussion of the various types of hackers and the ethics of hacking.
2. "Alleged Associates of 'NullCrew' Arrested on Federal hacking Charge Involving Cyber Attacks on Companies and Universities," U.S. Attorney's Office (N.D. Ill.) *Press Release*, June 16, 2014.
3. 18 USC § 1030. The law amended an existing computer fraud law from the comprehensive Crime Control Act of 1984.
4. 8 USC § 2712.

have called on Congress to amend the law, reduce the harshness of the penalties, and resolve the confusion in the text by amending the CFAA. The proposed amendments are known as "Aaron's Law," named after 26-year-old computer programmer and Internet entrepreneur Aaron Swartz who committed suicide while facing a 35-year prison sentence after being charged with CFAA violations for downloading academic journal articles from his MIT account without payment.[5] The proposed Aaron's Law bill did not receive sufficient support in Congress and must now be re-proposed in a future legislative session.

In *United States v. Nosal,* a federal appeals court analyzes the scope of the CFAA in an employment context.

United States v. Nosal
676 F. 3d 854 (9th Cir. 2012)

FACTS Nosal used to work for Korn/Ferry, an executive search firm. Shortly after he left the company, he convinced some of his former colleagues to help him start a competing business. The employees used their log-in credentials to download source lists, names, and contact information from a confidential database on the company's computer, and then transferred that information to Nosal. The employees were authorized to access the database, but Korn/Ferry had a policy that prohibited disclosing confidential information. The government indicted Nosal on twenty criminal counts, including trade secret theft, mail fraud, conspiracy, and violations of the Computer Fraud and Abuse Act (CFAA). The CFAA counts charged Nosal with aiding and abetting the Korn/Ferry employees in "exceeding their authorized access" with intent to defraud.

Nosal filed a motion to dismiss the CFAA counts, arguing that the statute targets only hackers, not individuals who access a computer with authorization but then misuse information they obtain by means of such access. Following the guidance from the Court of Appeals, the trial court found in favor of Nosal reasoning that there was no way to read the CFAA's definition of "exceeds authorized access" to incorporate corporate policies governing use of information unless the word "alter" is interpreted to mean misappropriate. The government appealed.

Judicial Opinion The CFAA defines "exceeds authorized access" as "to access a computer with authorization and to use such access to obtain or alter information in the computer that the accesser is not entitled so to obtain or alter." 18 U.S.C. § 1030(e)(6). This language can be read either of two ways: First, as Nosal suggests and the district court held, it could refer to someone who's authorized to access only certain data or files but accesses unauthorized data or files—what is colloquially known as "hacking." For example, assume an employee is

---

5. MacFarquhar, Larissa, "Requiem for a dream: The tragedy of Aaron Swartz". *The New Yorker*, March 11, 2013.

permitted to access only product information on the company's computer but accesses customer data. He would "exceed authorized access" if he looks at the customer lists. Second, as the government proposes, the language could refer to someone who has unrestricted physical access to a computer, but is limited in the use to which he can put the information. For example, an employee may be authorized to access customer lists in order to do his job but not to send them to a competitor.

The government argues that the statutory text can support only the latter interpretation of "exceeds authorized access." In its opening brief, it focuses on the word "entitled" in the phrase an "accesser is not entitled so to obtain or alter." Id. § 1030(e)(6) (emphasis added). Pointing to one dictionary definition of "entitle" as "to furnish with a right," Webster's New Riverside University Dictionary 435, the government argues that Korn/Ferry's computer use policy gives employees certain rights, and when the employees violated that policy, they "exceed[ed] authorized access." But "entitled" in the statutory text refers to how an accesser "obtain[s] or alter[s]" the information, whereas the computer use policy uses "entitled" to limit how the information is used after it is obtained. This is a poor fit with the statutory language. An equally or more sensible reading of "entitled" is as a synonym for "authorized." So read, "exceeds authorized access" would refer to data or files on a computer that one is not authorized to access.

. . . .

The government's interpretation would transform the CFAA from an anti-hacking statute into an expansive misappropriation statute. . . . If Congress meant to expand the scope of criminal liability to everyone who uses a computer in violation of computer use restrictions—which may well include everyone who uses a computer—we would expect it to use language better suited to that purpose. . . .

While the CFAA is susceptible to the government's broad interpretation, we find Nosal's narrower one more plausible. Congress enacted the CFAA in 1984 primarily to address the growing problem of computer hacking, recognizing that, "[i]n intentionally trespassing into someone else's computer files, the offender obtains at the very least information as to how to break into that computer system." S.Rep. No. 99-432, at 9 (1986), 1986 U.S.C.C.A.N. 2479, 2487 (Conf. Rep.). The government agrees that the CFAA was concerned with hacking, which is why it also prohibits accessing a computer "without authorization." According to the government, that prohibition applies to hackers, so the "exceeds authorized access" prohibition must apply to people who are authorized to use the computer, but do so for an unauthorized purpose. But it is possible to read both prohibitions as applying to hackers: "[W]ithout authorization" would apply to outside hackers (individuals who have no authorized access to the computer at all) and "exceeds authorized access" would apply to inside hackers (individuals whose initial access to a computer is authorized but who access unauthorized information or files). This is a perfectly plausible construction of the statutory language that maintains the CFAA's focus on hacking rather than turning it into a sweeping Internet-policing mandate.

The government's construction of the statute would expand its scope far beyond computer hacking to criminalize any unauthorized use of information obtained from a computer. This would make criminals of large groups of people who would have little reason to suspect they are committing a federal crime. While ignorance of the law is no excuse, we can properly be skeptical as to whether Congress, in 1984, meant to criminalize conduct beyond that which is inherently wrongful, such as breaking into a computer. . . .

The government argues that our ruling today would construe "exceeds authorized access" only in subsection 1030(a)(4), and we could give the phrase a narrower meaning when we construe other subsections. This is just not so: Once we define the phrase for the purpose of subsection 1030(a)(4), that definition must apply equally to the rest of the statute pursuant to the "standard principle of statutory construction . . . that identical words and phrases within the same statute should normally be given the same meaning." *Powerex Corp. v. Reliant Energy Servs., Inc.*, 551 U.S. 224, 232, 127 S.Ct. 2411, 168 L.Ed.2d 112 (2007). . . .

Minds have wandered since the beginning of time and the computer gives employees new ways to procrastinate, by chatting with friends, playing games, shopping or watching sports highlights. Such activities are routinely prohibited by many computer-use policies, although employees are seldom disciplined for occasional use of work computers for personal purposes. Nevertheless, under the broad interpretation of the CFAA, such minor dalliances would become federal crimes. While it's unlikely that you'll be prosecuted for watching Reason, TV on your work computer, you could be. Employers wanting to rid themselves of troublesome employees without following proper procedures could threaten to report them to the FBI unless they quit. Ubiquitous, seldom-prosecuted crimes invite arbitrary and discriminatory enforcement.

Employer-employee and company-consumer relationships are traditionally governed by tort and contract law; the government's proposed interpretation of the CFAA allows private parties to manipulate their computer-use and personnel policies so as to turn these relationships into ones policed by the criminal law. Significant notice problems arise if we allow criminal liability to turn on the vagaries of private polices that are lengthy, opaque, subject to change and seldom read. Consider the typical corporate policy that computers can be used only for business purposes. What exactly is a "nonbusiness purpose"? If you use the computer to check the weather report for a business trip? For the company softball game? For your vacation to Hawaii? And if minor personal uses are tolerated, how can an employee be on notice of what constitutes a violation sufficient to trigger criminal liability?

Basing criminal liability on violations of private computer use polices can transform whole categories of otherwise innocuous behavior into federal crimes simply because a computer is involved. Employees who call family members from their work phones will become criminals if they send an email instead. Employees can sneak in the sports section of the New York Times to read at work, but they'd better not visit ESPN.com. And Sudoku enthusiasts should stick to the printed puzzles, because visiting www.dailysudoku.com from their work computers might give them more than enough time to hone their Sudoku skills behind bars.

The effect this broad construction of the CFAA has on workplace conduct pales by comparison with its effect on everyone else who uses a computer, smartphone, iPad, Kindle, Nook, X-box, Blu-Ray player or any other Internet-enabled device. The Internet is a means for communicating via computers: Whenever we access a web page, commence a download, post a message on somebody's Facebook wall, shop on Amazon, bid on eBay, publish a blog, rate a movie on IMDb, read www.NYT.com, watch YouTube and do the thousands of other things we routinely do online, we are using one computer to send commands to other computers at remote locations. Our access to those remote computers is governed by a series of private agreements and policies that most people are only dimly aware of and virtually no one reads or understands. . . .

The government assures us that, whatever the scope of the CFAA, it won't prosecute minor violations. But we shouldn't have to live at the mercy of our local prosecutor. Cf. *United States v. Stevens*, 130 S.Ct. 1577 (2010) ("We would not uphold an unconstitutional statute merely because the Government promised to use it responsibly."). And it's not clear we can trust the government when a tempting target comes along. Take the case of the mom who posed as a 17-year-old boy and cyber-bullied her daughter's classmate. The Justice Department prosecuted her under [the CFAA] for violating MySpace's terms of service, which prohibited lying about identifying information, including age. See *United States v. Drew*, 259 F.R.D. 449 (C.D.Cal.2009). Lying on social media websites is common: People shave years off their age, add inches to their height and drop pounds from their weight. The difference between puffery and prosecution may depend on whether you happen to be someone an AUSA has reason to go after. . . .

We remain unpersuaded by the decisions of our sister circuits that interpret the CFAA broadly to cover violations of corporate computer use restrictions or violations of a duty of loyalty. See United States v. Rodriguez, 628 F.3d 1258 (11th Cir.2010); *United States v. John*, 597 F.3d 263 (5th Cir.2010); Int'l Airport Ctrs., LLC v. Citrin, 440 F.3d 418 (7th Cir.2006). These courts looked only at the culpable behavior of the defendants before them, and failed to consider the effect on millions of ordinary citizens caused by the statute's unitary definition of "exceeds authorized access." They therefore failed to apply the long-standing principle that we must construe ambiguous criminal statutes narrowly so as to avoid "making criminal law in Congress's stead." *United States v. Santos*, 553 U.S.507, 514, 128 S.Ct. 2020, 170 L.Ed.2d 912 (2008).

We therefore respectfully decline to follow our sister circuits and urge them to reconsider instead. For our part, we continue to follow in the path blazed by [our previous ruling in *LVRC Holdings v. Brekka*] and the growing number of courts that have reached the same conclusion. These courts recognize that the plain language of the CFAA "target[s] the unauthorized procurement or alteration of information, not its misuse or misappropriation." . . .

CONCLUSION

We need not decide today whether Congress could base criminal liability on violations of a company or website's computer use restrictions. Instead, we hold that the phrase "exceeds authorized access" in the CFAA does not extend to violations of use restrictions. If Congress wants to incorporate misappropriation liability into the CFAA, it must speak more clearly. . . .

This narrower interpretation is also a more sensible reading of the text and legislative history of a statute whose general purpose is to punish hacking—the circumvention of technological access barriers—not misappropriation of trade secrets—a subject Congress has dealt with elsewhere. Therefore, we hold that "exceeds authorized access" in the CFAA is limited to violations of restrictions on access to information, and not restrictions on its use.

Because Nosal's accomplices had permission to access the company database and obtain the information contained within, the government's charges fail to meet the element of "without authorization, or exceeds authorized access" under 18 U.S.C. § 1030(a)(4). Accordingly, we affirm the judgment of the [trial] court dismissing [the CFAA counts] for failure to state an offense. The government may, of course, prosecute Nosal on the remaining counts of the indictment.

AFFIRMED.

Case Questions

1. Compare and contrast the competing theories of the case. In your view, which interpretation (government's versus Nosal's) is more consistent with the purposes of the CFAA?
2. The court points out that the employer-employee relationship is traditionally governed by tort and contract law. How does that impact their analysis of the CFAA in this case?
3. *Ethical Considerations*: Even assuming that Nosal's conduct did not violate the letter of the CFAA, was Nosal's conduct ethical? Doesn't Nosal have a right to compete with his former employer? Should employers address the use of company information in their ethical codes of conduct? Was it ethical to prosecute Nosal?

Identity Theft

A closely related crime that also results from hacking is identity theft through use of a computer. Cybercriminals use tactics such as **pharming, spoofing, phishing,** and **pretexting** to commit identity theft.

Pharming is the term for a perpetrator's redirection of Internet traffic from one website to another. The second website appears to be identical to the legitimate site. The user is tricked into entering his or her username and password into the fake site, setting him or her up for financial or identity theft. The user has no idea that the redirection has occurred and has not consented to visiting the fake site. There are two primary mechanisms for pharming: altering the host file on the victim's computer by use of implanted software or exploiting vulnerability in DNS servers.

Spoofing takes various forms, including email spoofing. Email spoofing, IP spoofing, or IP address spoofing is making an email appear to be sent from one source when it actually was sent from another source—effectively concealing the identity of the sender or impersonating another computing system. The user thinks the email has come from a trusted source. The actual sender falsifies the routing information, making it appear to come from a legitimate, trusted user's account. The user's reply to a spoofed email goes directly to the legitimate email account (not the sender who has spoofed the email). Similarly, forging an email header to make it appear that it came from a legitimate, trusted source.

Phishing, a form of spoofing, occurs when a cybercriminal poses as a financial institution and sends email messages to consumers requesting that they click on a link to "verify" their account. The Internet user receives an email message that appears to be a legitimate message from a reputable company, asking the user to reply with an update of his or her credit card information. The message lures the user to click on a link that actually sends the user to a fake website where the user provides the credit card information, along with other personal information such as date of birth, address, site password, and Social Security number. Provision of such personal information to a bogus site makes the user vulnerable to identity theft. Phishing is also called "brand spoofing." "Puddle phishing" means phishing that specifically targets a small company, such as a local or community bank.

Spear phishing is even more invasive. When spear phishing, the "phisher" poses as someone the email message recipient knows and targets the recipient particularly. Spear phishing is even harder to detect than generalized phishing because the bogus email message and website almost perfectly replicate the legitimate sender and site.

Maladaptive gangs are groups of scammers who pose as legitimate advertisers in order to infiltrate the complex system of nearly 100 ad networks, such as Google's AdSense, that distribute ads to websites all across the Internet.

Pretexting is the crime of obtaining personal information through impersonating someone. In 2007, Congress passed the Telephone Records and Privacy Protection Act or the "Telco Privacy Act." The Act makes it a federal offense to knowingly and intentionally obtain, purchase, sell, transfer, or receive confidential phone records by way of false or fraudulent statements or representations.

Scam Apps

Scam apps is a phrase used to describe the relatively recent phenomena of cyber-criminals who design fake applications that are purchased for use on a computer, tablet, or smart phone. Some scam apps are essentially attempts to fool users by copying famous names and trademarks in order to direct the user to the false app instead of the genuine application. Although apps are difficult to regulate, Microsoft has taken steps to crack down on scam apps and reported that it has removed over 1500 scam apps from its Windows Store and has increased its scrutiny before certifying an application prior to its inclusion in the store.

Cyber Hitchhiker

Consider our hypothetical startup firm Cyber Hitchhiker. The principals would have to have a significant security system in place in order to protect against hacking and identity theft. Their customers would likely be sharing important personal information such as credit card details and addresses and would also be revealing their whereabouts. The management team at Cyber Hitchhiker face the same dilemma as many small business owners: funding. Yet consider the consequences of a hacking incident. For a small business that depends on the cyber community for revenue, even a relatively small breach could create a confidence problem among its consumers and the results might mean a damaged brand or even bankruptcy. It is also likely for Cyber Hitchhiker to develop an app and therefore they must employ means to monitor whether their app is being copied and used as a scam app. The first time that someone fell victim to a scam app, Cyber Hitchhiker would suffer damage to its brand until the scam app was removed.

Counterfeiting and Online Piracy

An increasingly common concern for business owners who rely on intellectual property rights is counterfeiting and online piracy. A report by the Center for Strategic and International Studies estimated that the theft of intellectual property facilitated by computers exceeded $160 billion. Selling counterfeit merchandise is a widespread and global problem. In 2013, an international strike force had their own version of Cyber Monday by seizing and shutting down 706 websites that were selling counterfeit merchandise. According to a U.S. Immigration and Customs Enforcement official, the most popular fake items sold were headphones, sports jerseys, personal care products, shoes, toys, luxury goods, cell phones, and electronic accessories.

Online piracy is typically the term used to describe both the online trafficking of counterfeit goods and online copyright infringement. Digitized works—computer software, music, photographs, writings, and videos—have become increasingly easy to reproduce, causing a rise not only in trafficking but in illegal reproduction as well. Through amending several intellectual property statutes, Congress passed a federal law in 2006 prohibiting trafficking in counterfeit goods or services and included online infringement cases as a defined category of such illegal activity.[6] Online infringement cases are those in which "the infringer (i) advertised or publicized the infringing work on the Internet; or (ii) made the infringing work available on the Internet for download, reproduction, performance, or distribution by other persons."

The Stop Online Piracy Act (SOPA) was a controversial attempt to strengthen the laws preventing copyright infringement and online counterfeit goods trafficking. The bill proposed a law that its proponents claimed would help enforce intellectual property rights in the context of foreign-owned and operated websites and increase criminal penalties for certain violations. However, the bill had significant opposition from the cyberspace community who claimed that

---

6. 18 U.S.C. § 2320(g)(2)(B).

SOPA would chill free speech and discourage innovation. Internet giants Wikipedia and Google coordinated service blackouts to protest the bill and sponsored petition drives that collected over 7 million signatures. The bill did not progress to a vote and has not been reintroduced.

In the United States, the National Intellectual Property Rights Coordination Center is the main federal response to international counterfeiting. The Center brings together major U.S. agencies responsible for enforcing laws related to customs trade fraud and intellectual property crimes, including U.S. Immigration and Customs Enforcement (ICE), U.S. Customs and Border Protection (CBP), the Department of Justice Computer Crimes and Intellectual Property Rights Section (DOJ-CCIPS), the Federal Bureau of Investigation (FBI), the Food and Drug Administration Office of Criminal Investigations (FDA-OCI), the U.S. Postal Inspection Service, and the Department of Commerce.

Warez Sites

Cybercriminals can infringe a copyright directly or vicariously. Although copyright infringement can occur on a small scale, with an individual violating the copyright in a music video, for example, large-scale criminal operations that illegally distribute and trade copyrighted software, music, movies, videos, and games on the Internet have become a major problem for law enforcement worldwide. The illegal online trade in copyrighted material is typically accomplished through **warez** sites. Individuals and organizations that are the first-providers of copyrighted works to the warez underground are called the release groups. These release groups operate as the original sources for most of the pirated works distributed and downloaded by way of the Internet. The fact that the infringement happens online is what makes it so problematic. According to the U.S. Justice Department, once a warez release group prepares a stolen work for distribution, the material is distributed in minutes to secure, top-level warez servers throughout the world. From there, within a matter of hours, the pirated works are distributed globally, filtering down to peer-to-peer and other public file sharing networks accessible to anyone with Internet access.[7]

Paper Counterfeiting

Even the traditional forms of paper counterfeiting crimes have been exacerbated by advancing technology. For example, creating counterfeit currency used to require a significant amount of skill and access to technology that was not typically available to consumers (e.g., engraving plates). However, the digital age has provided low cost alternatives for high-quality color copiers and printers to create a new breed of counterfeiters. Similarly, counterfeiting of other government documents, such as welfare applications, tax returns, identifying cards (e.g., driver license), and immigration documents has increased.

---

7. FBI, Press Release, "Justice Department Announces International Internet Piracy Sweep" (June 30, 2005).

Concept Summary

- Cybercrimes are committed either by using the computer as an instrument of crime by an individual or when a criminal targets a computer or network.
- Using a computer to commit fraud comes in a variety of different forms such as the alteration of information, data, or software by a criminal to derive an unlawful financial benefit.
- Hacking is the exploitation of a weakness in a computer network for nefarious or activist purposes.
- The Computer Fraud and Abuse Act, which was amended in 2001 by the USA PATRIOT Act,[8] prohibits unauthorized use of computers to commit seven different crimes: 1) espionage; 2) accessing unauthorized information; 3) accessing a nonpublic government computer; 4) fraud by computer; 5) damage to a computer; 6) trafficking in passwords; and 7) extortionate threats to damage a computer.
- Cybercriminals use tactics such as pharming, spoofing, phishing, and pretexting to commit identity theft.
- Online piracy is typically the term used to describe both the online trafficking of counterfeit goods and online copyright infringement.

Cyberstalking and Cyberbullying

Cyberstalking is a prime example of the use of computers and the Internet to facilitate a traditional offline crime. Cyberstalking generally refers to the use of the Internet, e-mail, or other electronic communications devices to stalk another person—where stalking in the traditional sense means to engage in repeated harassing or threatening behavior. This includes following a person, appearing at a person's home or work-place, making harassing telephone calls, or leaving written messages or objects that places the victim in reasonable fear of death or bodily injury.[9]

Cyberstalking may involve a spurned or rejected lovers, former or current work colleagues, or classmates. Like offline stalking, cyber stalkers try to control, harass, and intimidate their victims, often out of anger or for revenge. **Cyberbullying** is using "the Internet, cell phones or other devices . . . to send or post text or images intended to hurt or embarrass another person."[10] Those engaged in cyberbullying typically post pornographic, threatening, or harassing information online or send it directly to their victim.

Cyberstalking also occurs outside of personal relationships and inside offices. Cyber harassment, cyberbullying, and cyberstalking "take place in the workplace or on company web sites, blogs or product reviews. Cyber stalkers use posts, forums, journals and other online means to present a victim in false and

---

8. 8 USC § 2712
9. 18 U.S.C. § 2261A
10. Nat'l Crime Prevention Council, "Cyberbullying," available at: www.ncpc.org/cyberbullying.

unflattering light."[11] Just as prudent employers should have antidiscrimination and anti-harassment policies in place in order to encourage a safe workplace and to limit liability, companies also should be aware of, and prohibit, cyber harassment and cyberbullying. Employers should be especially aware of cyberbullying. Malicious, profane, or obscene texts sent via computer or smart phones following work events may amount to bullying and subject an employer to liability based on the work-related nature of the conduct.[12]

Anti-Cyberbullying Laws and the First Amendment

As lawmakers at every level attempt to deal with cyberbullying by passing anti-harassment laws, civil libertarians have become increasingly concerned about government regulation of speech. In the following case, a state appellate court considers whether a local anti-cyberbullying law is consistent with the First Amendment's right to free speech.

People v. Marquan M.
2014 NY Slip Op 4881 - NY: Court of Appeals 2014

Facts In 2010, elected officials in Albany County, N.Y. determined there was a need to criminalize cyberbullying because the state legislature "had failed to address the problem" of non-physical bullying behaviors transmitted by electronic means. The local legislature in Albany county adopted a new crime—the offense of cyberbullying—which was defined as "any act of communicating or causing a communication to be sent by mechanical or electronic means, including posting statements on the Internet or through a computer or email network, disseminating embarrassing or sexually explicit photographs; disseminating private, personal, false or sexual information, or sending hate mail, with no legitimate private, personal, or public purpose, with the intent to harass, annoy, threaten, abuse, taunt, intimidate, torment, humiliate, or otherwise inflict significant emotional harm on another person." The provision outlawed cyberbullying against "any minor or person" situated in the county. Knowingly engaging in this activity was deemed to be a misdemeanor offense punishable by up to one year in jail and a $1,000 fine.

Defendant Marquan M., a 15-year-old student attending Cohoes High School in Albany County, New York, used Facebook to create a page bearing the pseudonym "Cohoes Flame." He anonymously posted photographs of high-school classmates and other adolescents, with detailed descriptions of their alleged sexual practices and predilections, sexual partners and other types of personal

---

11. American Foundation for Suicide Prevention, Public Policy Issue Brief (2010), "Legislation to Reduce Bullying and Cyber-bullying-Federal Initiative."
12. Chartered Institute of Personnel and Development, "Harassment and bullying at work" (rev. Sept. 2009).

information. The descriptive captions, which were vulgar and offensive, prompted responsive electronic messages that threatened the creator of the website with physical harm. A police investigation revealed that the defendant was the author of the Cohoes Flame postings. He admitted his involvement and was charged with cyberbullying under Albany County's local law.

The defendant moved to dismiss the charges, arguing that the statute violated his right to free speech under the First Amendment. After City Court denied the defendant's motion, he pleaded guilty to one count of cyberbullying but reserved his right to raise his constitutional arguments on appeal. County Court affirmed, concluding that the local law was constitutional to the extent it outlawed such activities directed at minors, and held that the application of the provision to defendant's Facebook posts did not contravene his First Amendment rights. The defendant appealed to the New York Court of Appeals.

Judicial Opinion . . .

Challenges to statutes under the Free Speech Clause are usually premised on the over breadth and vagueness doctrines. A regulation of speech is overbroad if constitutionally-protected expression may be "chilled" by the provision because it facially "prohibits a real and substantial amount of" expression guarded by the First Amendment (People v Barton, 8 NY3d 70, 75 [2006]). This type of facial challenge, which is restricted to cases implicating the First Amendment, requires a court to assess the wording of the statute—"without reference to the defendant's conduct" (People v Stuart, 100 NY2d 412, 421 [2003])—to decide whether "a substantial number of its applications are unconstitutional, judged in relation to the statute's plainly legitimate sweep" (United States v Stevens, 559 US at 473[internal quotation marks omitted]). A law that is overbroad cannot be validly applied against any individual. In contrast, a statute is seen by the courts as vague if "it fails to give a citizen adequate notice of the nature of proscribed conduct, and permits arbitrary and discriminatory enforcement" (People v Shack, 86 NY2d 529, 538 [1995]). . . .

A First Amendment analysis begins with an examination of the text of the challenged legislation since "it is impossible to determine whether a statute reaches too far without first knowing what the statute covers" (United States v Williams, 553 US 285, 293 [2008]). In this regard, fundamental principles of statutory interpretation are controlling. Chief among them is the precept that "clear and unequivocal statutory language is presumptively entitled to authoritative effect" (People v Suber, 19 NY3d 247, 252 [2012]; see e.g. People v Williams, 19 NY3d 100, 103 [2012]).

Based on the text of the statute at issue, it is evident that Albany County "create[d] a criminal prohibition of alarming breadth" (United States v Stevens, 559 US at 474). The language of the local law embraces a wide array of applications that prohibit types of protected speech far beyond the cyber bullying of children (see id. at 473-474; People v Barton, 8 NY3d at 75). As written, the Albany County law in its broadest sense criminalizes "any act of communicating . . . by mechanical or electronic means . . . with no legitimate . . . personal . . . purpose, with the intent to harass [or] annoy . . . another person." On its face, the law covers communications aimed at adults, and fictitious or corporate entities, even though the county legislature justified passage of the provision based on the detrimental effects that cyber bullying has on school-aged children. The county law also lists particular examples of covered communications, such as "posting statements on the internet or through a computer or email network, disseminating embarrassing or sexually explicit photographs; disseminating private, personal, false or sexual information, or sending hate mail." But such methods of expression are not limited to instances of cyber bullying—the law includes every conceivable form of electronic communication, such as telephone conversations, a ham radio transmission or even a telegram. In addition, the provision pertains to electronic communications that are meant to "harass, annoy . . . taunt . . . [or] humiliate" any person or entity, not just those that are intended to "threaten, abuse . . . intimidate, torment . . . or otherwise inflict significant emotional harm on" a child. In considering the facial implications, it appears that the provision would criminalize a broad spectrum of speech outside the popular understanding of cyber bullying, including, for example: an email disclosing private information about a corporation or a telephone conversation meant to annoy an adult.

   . . .

There is undoubtedly general consensus that defendant's Facebook communications were repulsive and harmful to the subjects of his rants, and potentially created a risk of physical or emotional injury based on the private nature of the comments. He identified specific adolescents with photographs, described their purported sexual practices and posted the information on a website accessible world-wide. Unlike traditional bullying, which usually takes place by a face-to-face encounter, defendant used the advantages of the internet to attack his victims from a safe distance, twenty-four hours a day, while cloaked in anonymity. Although the First Amendment may not give defendant the right to engage in these activities, the text of Albany County's law envelops far more than acts of cyber bullying against children by criminalizing a variety of constitutionally-protected modes of expression. We therefore hold that Albany County's Local Law No. 11 of 2010—as drafted—is overbroad and facially invalid under the Free Speech Clause of the First Amendment.

Accordingly, the order of County Court should be reversed and the accusatory instrument dismissed.

Case Questions

1. Does the court find that the cyberbullying law was too overbroad or too vague or both? In what way is the law overbroad? What example does the court give?
2. Should crude and demeaning comments of a personal (non-political) nature be protected by the First Amendment? Why or why not?
3. In light of the court's ruling, suggest language that outlaws cyberbullying but would pass constitutional muster.

Twitter and Cyberbullying

In one study on cyberbullying, researchers from the University of Wisconsin-Madison created a computer program to analyze tweets for their content to determine how many of them related to bullying and found that over 15,000 bully-related tweets are sent every day. Despite the fact that Twitter was being criticized over several years in the media for being a cyberbullying playground, Twitter's management was slow to respond. In 2014, after the death of famous actor Robin Williams, his daughter announced that she would be abandoning her Twitter account due to vicious attacks that she called cruel and offensive tweets about her father. Twitter immediately announced that they were disabling accounts involved in the cyberbullying tweets, and would reform its practices in order to better police cyberbullying, and improve support for family members of affected users.

Child Pornography and Exploitation

Exploitation of children in pornography, also called child abuse imagery, is perhaps the most unseemly underside of advances in technology. Law enforcement experts were able to minimize the crime prior to the emergence of the Internet. Now, criminals use the Internet to distribute and trade child pornography through the Web through Internet Relay Chat and via other online sources. Virtually every arrest of an individual for possession of child pornography now involves the use of the Internet.[13] One problem with investigating and enforcement is that there is no single definition of child pornography and state criminals laws can vary greatly. Federal statutes define a minor as anyone under 18 and pornography as photographs or other media that is sexually explicit. Federal law prohibits the production, distribution, reception, and possession of an image of child pornography. It is also illegal to persuade, induce, entice, or coerce a minor to engage in sexually explicit conduct for purposes of creating a visual image of that conduct.[14] Violators of child pornography laws face severe penalties. First time offenders convicted of producing child pornography face 15-30 years in prison. First time offenders for possession or trading child pornography face 5-20 years in prison.[15] All states have similar statutes and "possession" of child pornography typically includes grooming children, or use of the photos for blackmail of victims or offenders.

The United States Department of Justice created a task force called the Internet Crimes Against Children with the goal of coordinating and supporting state law enforcement agencies to detect and prevent children. Their methods include "undercover" assignments whereby police pose as offenders who are trading child pornography and posing in online chat rooms as potential victims. The National Center for Missing and Exploited Children was created by Congress as part of the Missing Children's Act in 2003. The Center operates a CyberTipline

---

13. Wells, et al, "Defining Child Pornography: Law Enforcement Dilemmas", Police Practice and Research, July 2007.
14. 18 U.S.C.§ 2251
15. 18 U.S.C.§ 2252A

to receive reports of suspected child sexual exploitation (including child pornography) and has received over 2.5 million reports since its inception.

Use of the Internet to commit other exploitation crimes against children such as sex trafficking is also a priority for the law enforcement community. The Federal Bureau of Investigation's Innocence Lost Initiative coordinates existing agencies and has developed 68 dedicated task forces and working groups composed of federal, state, and local law enforcement authorities targeting domestic sex trafficking of children in the United States. Most recently, the FBI reported that more than 3,400 children had been rescued and over 1,500 offenders have been convicted.[16]

Companies that offer Internet search engines and online mail, such as Google, have become increasingly aggressive about eliminating child pornography from their systems and reporting offenders. For example, after Google management announced a $5 million initiative to eradicate child abuse imagery online, the company designed and implemented a controversial practice of scanning emails and analyzing content to detect child pornography or exploitation. Recently, this resulted in Google detecting a 41-year old Houston man who allegedly sent explicit images of a "young girl" to his friend. After Google security alerted authorities, police arrested John Henry Skillern, a registered sex offender.

Concept Summary

- Cyberstalking generally refers to the use of the Internet, e-mail, or other electronic communications devices to stalk another person.
- Cyberbullying is using the Internet, cell phones, or other devices to send or post text or images intended to hurt or embarrass another person.
- Malicious, profane, or obscene texts sent via computer or smart phones following work events may amount to bullying and subject an employer to liability based on the work-related nature of the conduct.
- Federal law prohibits the production, distribution, reception, and possession of an image of child pornography. It is also illegal to persuade, induce, entice, or coerce a minor to engage in sexually explicit conduct for purposes of creating a visual image of that conduct.

Crimes Targeting Computer Systems

Crimes that target computers, computer networks, or devices directly in order to harm or infect them are increasingly common. Media reports of criminal syndicates (primarily from Russia) targeting major industries such as retail chains, defense contractors, financial institutions have proliferated in our daily lives. Although some cybercrimes fall into both the "tool" and "target" category, for

---

16. www.fbi.gov/about-us/investigate/vc_majorthefts/cac/innocencelost.

our purposes, crimes that target computers are typically perpetrated through use of malicious software, use of spam, Denial-of-Service attacks, and cyberterrorism.

Malware and Data Breaches

Malware is a shorthand term for malicious software which is used to gain access to information stored on a computer or computer network. This information, such as personal information and credit card data, is then stolen and sold for fraudulent use. Malware is a category of software that is used to describe a broad array of malicious programs including **Trojan horses**, **viruses**, **worms**, ransomware, spyware, adware, and scareware. Media stories of data breaches caused by malware are becoming a relatively common occurrence. In 2014 alone, the Identity Theft Resource Center reported that over 579 data breaches occurred in the banking, retail, education, government, and healthcare industries. These breaches resulted in 76,990,466 records or personal information being breached.[17] Financial institutions are a prime target of cyber criminals and the Federal Financial Institutions Examinations Council, a regulatory body for U.S. banks, recently issued warning against a malware threat called Shellshock which affects a common software tool found in many operating systems used by banks in daily operations. Famous companies who have reported substantial data breaches include Home Depot, Target, AT&T, Bank of America, LinkedIn, eHarmony, Zappos, and Sony.

Trojan horses, Viruses, and Worms

You'll note from Figure 14.1 that according to the Federal Trade Commission, nearly 95 percent of malware is in the form of Trojan horses, viruses, and worms. A Trojan horse is a computer program that appears to be harmless but hides a malicious function. Malicious programs that do not attempt to inject themselves or other replicate themselves are classified as a Trojan horse. Typically, a Trojan is launched when a user is fooled into clicking an innocuous looking e-mail attachment or a providing some routine form for the user to fill out. Trojans are used to either steal or destroy data on a computer or computer network. A computer virus is a program designed to copy itself and spread from one computer to another and throughout a computer or computer system without the computer user's knowledge or permission. Key to a virus is its reproductive ability. The virus infects the computer when the virus' host is taken to the target computer by an email attachment, CD, DVD, or USB device. Many viruses attach to executable files that are part of legitimate software, where they execute code and write to memory. Viruses corrupt or delete data on the infected computer. The deliberate release of a computer virus with the intention of damaging a computer or system is a cybercrime. A worm is like a virus in that it self-replicates, but a worm does not need to attach itself to a system's program like a virus does. Worms can install a backdoor in an infected computer that puts the computer under the control of the worm perpetrator.

---

17. 2014 ITRC Breach Report, http://idtheftcenter.org/ITRC-Surveys-Studies/2014databreaches.html.

Figure 14.1 **PERCENTAGE OF MALWARE IN EACH CATEGORY**

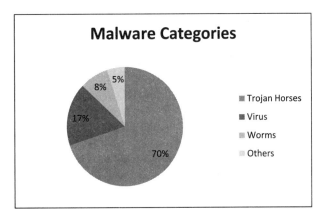

Source: Federal Trade Commission

Other Forms of Malware

Although still a relatively small percentage of all malware, governments, educational institutions, and corporations must be aware of the growing threat from forms of malware that are not classified as a Trojan, a virus, or a worm. Ransomware is malware that restricts access to a computer system and holds it hostage while the cybercriminal demands a ransom to release the computer. Spyware (which can also take the form of a Trojan horse) is used primarily to gather information about a person or organization without the user's knowledge. Adware surreptitiously inserts advertisements that typically result in pop-up advertising when the user is accessing the Internet. Scareware (also called Rogueware) is usually fake anti-virus software used to dupe users into thinking that the software will remove any viruses on their computer.

Business Response to Data Breaches

The Federal Trade Commission (FTC) provides detailed information about the steps a business should take if its information has been compromised. Compromise of personally identifying information necessarily puts individuals at risk for identity theft. First, the business should contact local law enforcement immediately if there is any risk that the information compromise could result in harm to an individual or another business. If the local police are not familiar with addressing this type of cybercrime, the business should contact the local office of the Federal Bureau of Investigation (FBI) or the U.S. Secret Service. Second, if the business has lost account numbers from another business, bank, or credit issuer, the business should contact that other business so that it can monitor account activity. Conversely, if the business monitors account information for other businesses, those other businesses should be notified of an information compromise. Third, if the information loss includes names and Social Security numbers, the business should contact the leading credit bureaus—Equifax, Experian, and

TransUnion—especially if notice to individuals will include a recommendation that they request fraud alerts for their files. Fourth, if someone in the company caused the information compromise by improperly posting personal information on the company's website, the business should immediately remove the information and contact the search engines to ensure that they do not archive personal information that the employee erroneously posted.

Finally, the business must notify, as early as possible, the individuals whose personal information was compromised. Immediate notification allows them to mitigate the misuse of the information. The FTC recommends that when the business makes the determination whether notification is warranted, it should consider the nature of the compromise, the type of information that was lost or taken, the likelihood of misuse of the information, and the potential damage that could arise from misuse. When notifying individuals, the FTC recommends that the business:

- Consult with law enforcement about the timing of the notification so it does not impede the official investigation into the compromise;
- Designate a contact person within the company who will have up-to-date information about the breach, the company's official response, and how individuals should respond, including a website address and/or toll-free number;
- Describe clearly and truthfully what the company knows about the compromise, including how it happened, what information was taken, how the thieves are using the information (if known), and what actions the company has taken already to remedy the situation;
- Explain how to reach the contact person in the company, as well as the law enforcement contact person;
- Provide FTC information that could be useful to individuals;
- Encourage individuals whose information has been misused to file a complaint with the FTC at www.ftc.gov/idtheft or at 1-877-ID-THEFT (877-438-4338).

The FTC also provides businesses with a model letter to send to customers whose information was compromised by an attack on the company.[18]

Cyber Hitchhiker

Consider our hypothetical start-up firm Cyber Hitchhiker. If a data breach occurs, the principals' first response may be to not reveal the breach and hope that it is limited after it has been fixed. But ignoring the breach may trigger a complaint and investigation by the Federal Trade Commission. The management team must design an action plan that includes compliance with FTC guidelines (e.g., notifications) and is consistent with the company's ethical standards.

---

18. *See* FTC, "Facts for Business," http://www.ftc.gov/bcp/edu/pubs/business/idtheft/bus59.shtm.

Spam

Spam, also called unsolicited bulk email or unsolicited commercial email, is the common term for unsolicited email advertisements. Experts who track spam report that the proportion of spam in email was almost 70 percent in 2013 and that the greatest amount of spam, 23 percent, came from China.[19] Although spam has been a problem since email became available to the general public, commercial spam has recently taken on a criminal aspect because current trends of spammers is to offer fake confirmations of airline tickets or hotel reservations in a spam e-mail that includes malware. While several years ago, spam email was used to defraud consumers by inducing people to book a tour package, modern spam induces unsuspecting users to click a link or file containing malware. Notorious spam from Nigerian bankers is declining in favor of other methods of committing fraud.

Halting Spam

Spam became so increasingly problematic that state legislatures took the early lead in regulating spam and even providing tough criminal sanctions for illegal spam suppliers. By 2003, a majority of states passed some form of legislation that attempted to regulate unsolicited emails. California's law was one of the toughest because it required online marketers to obtain a consumer's permission before sending email solicitations. Virginia went a step further and made sending certain unsolicited emails a felony and indicted two men for running a large illegal bulk email operation. Some states, such as New York, passed anti-spam legislation as part of a larger package of identity theft laws. However, state statutes making the transmission of spam unlawful have met with challenges to their constitutionality. Specifically, how can the government make it illegal to send spam without violating the spammer's First Amendment right to freedom of speech? This was the issue in *Jaynes v. Commonwealth of Virginia,* where the Supreme Court of Virginia analyzes the constitutionality of a state anti-spam law.

Jaynes v. Commonwealth of Virginia
666 S.E.2d 303 (Va. 2008)

Facts From his home in Raleigh, North Carolina, Jaynes used several computers, routers and servers to send over 10,000 emails within a 24-hour period in 2003 to subscribers of America Online, Inc. (AOL) on each of three separate occasions. On July 16, Jaynes sent 12,197 pieces of unsolicited email with falsified routing and transmission information onto AOL's proprietary network.

---

19. Kasperersky Security Bulletin, "Spam Evolution 2013", http://securelist/analysis

On July 19, he sent 24,172 emails and on July 26, he sent 19,104. None of the recipients of the emails had requested any communication from Jaynes. He intentionally falsified the header information and sender domain names before transmitting the emails to the recipients. However, investigators used a sophisticated database search to identify Jaynes as the sender of the emails.

The Circuit Court of Loudon County, Virginia, convicted Jaynes of violating Va. Code § 18.2-152.3:1, which is the unsolicited bulk electronic mail provision of the Virginia Computer Crimes Act. The court sentenced him to three years in prison for each of three counts, for a total term of nine years. The Virginia Court of Appeals affirmed, and, in a 4-3 decision, the Supreme Court of Virginia also affirmed the conviction. However, the Virginia Supreme Court granted Jaynes's petition for a rehearing. He argued on rehearing that he should have been allowed to challenge the constitutionality of the statute's anti-spam provision, that the statute violated his First Amendment rights, and that his conviction therefore should be overturned.

Judicial Opinion Jaynes was arrested and charged with violating Code § 18.2-152.3:1, which provides in relevant part:

A. Any person who:
1. Uses a computer or computer network with the intent to falsify or forge electronic mail transmission information or other routing information in any manner in connection with the transmission of unsolicited bulk electronic mail through or into the computer network of an electronic mail service provider or its subscribers . . . is guilty of a Class 1 misdemeanor.

B. A person is guilty of a Class 6 felony if he commits a violation of subsection A and:
1. The volume of UBE transmitted exceeded 10,000 attempted recipients in any 24-hour period, 100,000 attempted recipients in any 30-day time period, or one million attempted recipients in any one-year time period. . . .

. . . Reversing, the Supreme Court of Virginia held that the statute under which Jaynes was convicted, Virginia's Anti-SPAM Act, was unconstitutionally overbroad.

3. Constitutionality of Code § 18.2-152.3:1 We now turn to Jaynes' contention that Code § 18.2-152.3:1 is unconstitutionally overbroad. To address this challenge, we first review certain technical aspects of the transmission of emails. In transmitting and receiving emails, the email servers use a protocol which prescribes what information one computer must send to another. This [Simple Mail Transfer Protocol (SMTP)] requires that the routing information contain an [Internet Provider (IP)] address and a domain name for the sender and recipient of each email. Domain names and IP addresses are assigned to Internet servers by private organizations through a registration process. To obtain an IP address or domain name, the registrant pays a fee and provides identifying contact information to the registering organization. The domain names and IP addresses are contained in a searchable database which can associate the domain name with an IP address and vice versa.

The IP address and domain name do not directly identify the sender, but if the IP address or domain name is acquired from a registering organization, a database search of the address or domain name can eventually lead to the contact information on file with the registration organizations. A sender's IP address or domain name which is not registered will not prevent the transmission of the email; however, the identity of the sender may not be discoverable through a database search and use of registration contact information.

As shown by the record, because email transmission protocol requires entry of an IP address and domain name for the sender, the only way such a speaker can publish an anonymous email is to enter a false IP address or domain name. Therefore, like the registration record on file in the mayor's office identifying persons who chose to canvass private neighborhoods in *Watchtower Bible & Tract Society v. Village of Stratton,* 536 U.S. 150 (2002), registered IP addresses and domain names discoverable through searchable data bases and registration documents "necessarily result in a surrender of [the speaker's] anonymity." 536 U.S. at 166. The right to engage in anonymous speech, particularly anonymous political or religious speech, is "an aspect of the freedom of speech protected by the First Amendment." *McIntyre v. Ohio Elections Comm'n,* 514 U.S. 334, 342 (1995). By prohibiting false routing information in the dissemination of emails, Code § 18.2-152.3:1 infringes on that protected right. The Supreme Court has characterized regulations prohibiting such anonymous speech as "a direct regulation of the content of speech." *Id.* at 345.

State statutes that burden "core political speech," as this statute does, are presumptively invalid and subject to a strict scrutiny test. Under that test a statute will be deemed constitutional only if it is narrowly drawn to further a compelling state interest. *Id.* at 347. In applying this test, we must also consider that state statutes are presumed constitutional, *City Council v. Newsome,* 226 Va. 518, 523, 311 S.E.2d 761, 764 (1984), and any reasonable doubt regarding constitutionality must be resolved in favor of validity. *In re Phillips,* 265 Va. 81, 85-86, 574 S.E.2d 270, 272 (2003).

There is no dispute that Code § 18.2-152.3:1 was enacted to control the transmission of unsolicited commercial bulk email, generally referred to as SPAM. In enacting the federal CAN-SPAM Act, Congress stated that commercial bulk email threatened the efficiency and convenience of email. 15 U.S.C. § 7701(a)(2). Many other states have regulated unsolicited bulk email but, unlike Virginia, have restricted such regulation to commercial emails.

There is nothing in the record or arguments of the parties, however, suggesting that unsolicited non-commercial bulk emails were the target of this legislation, caused increased costs to the Internet service providers, or were otherwise a focus of the problem sought to be addressed by the General Assembly through its enactment of Code § 18.2-152.3:1.

Jaynes does not contest the Commonwealth's interest in controlling unsolicited commercial bulk email as well as fraudulent or otherwise illegal email. Nevertheless, Code § 18.2-152.3:1 is not limited to instances of commercial or fraudulent transmission of email, nor is it restricted to transmission of illegal or otherwise unprotected speech such as pornography or defamation speech. Therefore, viewed under the strict scrutiny standard, Code § 18.2-152.3:1 is not narrowly tailored to protect the compelling interests advanced by the Commonwealth.

4. Substantial Overbreadth   The Commonwealth argues that Code § 18.2-152.3:1 is not substantially overbroad because it does not impose any restrictions on the content of the email and "most" applications of its provisions would be constitutional, citing its application to unsolicited bulk commercial email, unsolicited bulk email that proposes a criminal transaction, and unsolicited bulk email that is defamatory or contains obscene images. According to the Commonwealth an "imagine [d] hypothetical situation where the Act might be unconstitutional as applied does not render the Act substantially overbroad."

The United States Supreme Court recently noted:

> [i]n order to maintain an appropriate balance, we have vigorously enforced the requirement that a statute's overbreadth be *substantial,* not only in an absolute sense, but also relative to the statute's plainly legitimate sweep.
>
> . . . [I]t is impossible to determine whether a statute reaches too far without first knowing what the statute covers.

128 S. Ct. at 1838. Applying that inquiry under *Williams* in this case is relatively straightforward as Code § 18.2-152.3:1 would prohibit all bulk email containing anonymous political, religious, or other expressive speech. For example, were the *Federalist Papers* just being published today via email, that transmission by Publius would violate the statute. Such an expansive scope of unconstitutional coverage is not what the Court in *Williams* referenced "as the tendency of our overbreadth doctrine to summon forth an endless stream of fanciful hypotheticals." 553 U.S. at_____, 128 S. Ct. at 1843. We thus reject the Commonwealth's argument that Jaynes' facial challenge to Code § 18.2-152.3:1 must fail because the statute is not "substantially overbroad."

III. CONCLUSION

For the foregoing reasons, we hold that the circuit court properly had jurisdiction over Jaynes. We also hold that Jaynes has standing to raise a First Amendment overbreadth claim as to Code § 18.2-152.3:1. *That statute is unconstitutionally overbroad on its face because it prohibits the anonymous transmission of all unsolicited bulk emails including those containing political, religious or other speech protected by the First Amendment to the United States Constitution.*

Accordingly, we will reverse the judgment of the Court of Appeals and vacate Jaynes' convictions of violations of Code § 18.2-152.3:l.

Case Questions

1. Would a state anti-spam statute that specifically prohibited pornographic, obscene, terroristic, and fraudulent emailing withstand constitutional scrutiny? Why or why not?
2. What argument did Jaynes make that convinced the Supreme Court of Virginia to reverse itself and the two lower courts?
3. *Ethical Consideration:* Is spam really so bad? Why can a business lawfully send unsolicited traditional mail, or make unsolicited phone calls (as long as there is no violation of a no-call list), but spamming violates the law? Discuss the differences between spamming and traditional forms of unsolicited advertising.

CAN-SPAM Act of 2003

Eventually, Congress took up the issue of spam prevention and passed a federal statute called the Controlling the Assault of Non-Solicited Pornography and Marketing Act of 2003,[20] better known as the CAN-SPAM Act, into law. The new law supplants sometimes-tougher state statutes, but outlaws the shifty techniques used by some spam suppliers, and provides criminal sanctions in severe cases. The statute also prohibits online marketing providers from falsifying the "from" name and information in the subject line designed to fool consumers into opening an unsolicited email message. One controversial provision of the law allows the Federal Trade Commission to start a "do-not-spam" list modeled on the "do-not-call" list to stop telemarketers.

Criminal offenses in the CAN-SPAM Act include: 1) sending multiple spam email with use of a hijacked computer, 2) sending emails through Internet Protocol addresses that the sender represents falsely as being his/her property, 3) trying to disguise the source of an email by routing them through other computers. The government has prosecuted high profile spammers under the CAN-SPAM Act and convictions have resulted in fines in the range of $10,000 and a maximum prison sentence of five years.

Denial-of-Service Attacks

Denial-of-Service (DoS) attacks make a computer resource unavailable to its intended, legitimate user. The attacker targets either: 1) a specific computer and/or its network, or 2) computer servers used to host a website. The attack is typically intended to prevent legitimate users' access to email, websites, online accounts, and services. The most common type denial-of-service attack occurs

---

20. 15 U.S.C. § 103.

when the attacker overloads a network with information, such as numerous requests to access a website, so the computer server cannot process the user's request. A successful attack interferes with a website's proper functioning and eventually halts all access to the site.

Cyberterrorism

The term "cyberterrorism" lacks a precise definition. While some experts believe that any attack on a computer or computer system constitutes cyberterrorism, most insist that the term must be reserved for true acts of terrorism facilitated by computers, computer systems, and/or the Internet. The National Conference of State Legislatures, which provides guidance for policymakers in a variety of areas, provides a useful working definition of cyberterrorism: the use of information technology by terrorist groups and individuals to further their agenda.[21] Cyberterrorism can be accomplished by methods that were discussed previously such as malware, viruses, worms, DoS attacks, and cyberterror threats via electronic means.

In 2014, a federal grand jury indicted five military officers from China on charges of economic espionage and trade secret theft. The U.S. Justice Department alleged that the group had hacked computer systems of American companies such as Alcoa and U.S. Steel Corp. for purposes of taking commercial advantage and private financial gain. Although it is highly unlikely that any of these defendants would ever be brought to trial, the indictments were the first step in the government's campaign to expose cybercrimes committed with the backing of a foreign power.

The FBI takes a more narrow view of cyberterrorism. Recently, their top Cyber Division deputy agreed with the view that true cyberterrorism, while it is a real and increasing threat,[22] has not yet occurred.

> Terrorist groups are increasingly adopting the power of modern communications technology for planning, recruiting, propaganda purposes, enhancing communications, command and control, fundraising and funds transfer, information gathering, and the like. However, mere terrorist use of information technology is not regarded as cyberterrorism. The true threat of "Cyberterrorism" will be realized when all the factors that constitute a terrorist attack, coupled with the use of the Internet, are met.[23]

---

21. NCSL Working paper "Cyberterrorism."
22. Robert S. Mueller, III, Director, FBI, International Conference on Cyber Security 2010 (Aug. 5, 2010)
23. Keith Lourdeau, Deputy Assistant Director, Cyber Division, FBI, *Congressional Testimony Before the Senate Judiciary Subcommittee on Terrorism, Technology, and Homeland Security* (Feb. 24, 2004). See also Mueller, International Conference on Cyber Security 2010. ("To date, terrorists have not used the Internet to launch a full-scale cyber attack. But they have executed numerous denial-of-service attacks and defaced numerous websites.")

Concept Summary

- Crimes that target computers are typically perpetrated through use of malicious software, use of spam, Denial-of-Service attacks, and cyberterrorism.
- Malware is short hand term for malicious software that is used to gain access to information stored on a computer or computer network.
- Malware is a category of software that is used to describe a broad array of malicious programs including Trojan horses, viruses, worms, ransomware, spyware, adware, scareware.
- Criminal offenses in the CAN-SPAM Act include: 1) sending multiple spam email with use of a hijacked computer, 2) sending emails through Internet Protocol addresses that the sender represents falsely as being his/her property, 3) trying to disguise the source of an email by routing them through other computers.
- Denial-of-Service (DoS) attacks make a computer resource unavailable to its intended, legitimate user. The attacker targets a computer and its network connection or the computers and network of the sites a user tries to access, to prevent access to email, websites, online accounts, and services.

Trends and Schemes Identified by the Internet Crime Complaint Center[24]

Internet Crime	Description
Auction Fraud	Fraud attributable to misrepresentation of a product advertised for sale through an Internet auction site or nondelivery of products purchased through an Internet auction site.
Counterfeit Cashier's Check	Targets individuals who use Internet classified advertisements to sell merchandise. Typically, an interested party located outside the United States contacts a seller, who is told the buyer has an associate in the United States who owes the buyer money, and that the associate will send the seller a cashier's check for the amount owed to the buyer.
Credit Card Fraud	Unauthorized use of a credit/debit card, or card number, to fraudulently obtain money or property. Credit/debit card numbers are stolen from unsecured websites or other identity theft scheme.
Debt Elimination	Website advertises a legal way to dispose of mortgage loans and credit card debts. The participant sends $1,500 to $2,000 to the subject, along with all the particulars of the participant's loan information and a special power of attorney authorizing the subject to enter into transactions

---

24. Derived from Internet Crime Complaint Center, Internet Crime Schemes, http://www.ic3.gov/crimeschemes.aspx.

pertaining to title in the participant's homes on his or her behalf. The subject then issues bonds and promissory notes to the lenders that purport to legally satisfy the debts of the participant. In exchange, the participant is then required to pay a certain percentage of the value of the satisfied debts to the subject.

Parcel Courier Email Scheme	Involves the supposed use of various national- and international-level parcel providers such as DHL, UPS, FedEx, and the USPS. Often, the victim is directly emailed by the subject following online bidding on auction sites.
Employment/Business Opportunities	Bogus foreign-based companies ostensibly recruit U.S. citizens through employment-search websites for work-at-home employment opportunities, for positions that involve reselling or reshipping merchandise to destinations outside the United States.
Escrow Services Fraud	Perpetrator proposes the use of a third-party escrow service to facilitate the exchange of money and merchandise. The victim is unaware the perpetrator has actually compromised a true escrow site and, in actuality, created one that closely resembles a legitimate escrow service. The victim sends payment to the phony escrow and receives nothing in return. Or, the victim sends merchandise to the subject and waits for his or her payment through the escrow site, payment is never received because it is not a legitimate service.
Identity Theft	Thief appropriates another's personal information without their knowledge to commit theft or fraud. Identity theft is a vehicle for perpetrating other types of fraud schemes. Typically, the victim is led to believe he or she is divulging sensitive personal information to a legitimate business, sometimes as a response to an email solicitation to update billing or membership information or as an application to a fraudulent Internet job posting.
Internet Extortion	Involves hacking into and controlling various industry databases, promising to release control back to the company if funds are received, or the subjects are given web administrator jobs. Similarly, the subject will threaten to compromise information about consumers in the industry database unless funds are received.
Investment Fraud	An offer using false or fraudulent claims to solicit investments or loans, or providing for the purchase, use, or trade of forged or counterfeit securities.
Lotteries	Persons are randomly contacted by email addresses advising them they have been selected as the winner of an international lottery. An agency name follows the body of text with a point of contact, phone number, fax number, and an email address. An initial fee ranging from $1,000 to $5,000 is often requested to initiate the process and additional fee requests follow after the process has begun. These emails might also list a U.S. point of contact and address while also indicating the point of contact at a foreign address.

Nigerian Letter or "419"	Named for the violation of Section 419 of the Nigerian Criminal Code, the scam combines the threat of impersonation fraud with a variation of an advance fee scheme in which a letter, email, or fax is received by the potential victim. The communication from individuals representing themselves as Nigerian or other foreign government officials offers the recipient the "opportunity" to share in a percentage of millions of dollars, soliciting for help in placing large sums of money in overseas bank accounts.
Phishing/Spoofing	Forged or faked electronic documents. Spoofing generally refers to the dissemination of email that is forged to appear as though it was sent by someone other than the actual source. Phishing, often utilized in conjunction with a spoofed email, is the act of sending an email falsely claiming to be an established legitimate business in an attempt to dupe the unsuspecting recipient into divulging personal, sensitive information, such as passwords, credit card numbers, and bank account information after directing the user to visit a specified website. The website is not genuine and was set up as bait to attempt to steal the user's information.
Ponzi/Pyramid	Investment scams in which investors are promised abnormally high profits on their investments. No investment is actually made. Early investors are paid returns with the investment money received from the later investors. The system usually collapses, and later investors not only do not receive dividends but also lose their initial investments.
Spam	Unsolicited bulk email that can be used as a medium for committing traditional white-collar crimes, such as financial institution fraud, credit card fraud, and identity theft, also can act as the vehicle for accessing computers and servers without authorization and transmitting viruses and botnets. The subjects often provide hosting services and sell open proxy information, credit card information, and email lists illegally.
Third-Party Receiver of Funds	The subjects post work-at-home job offers on popular Internet employment sites, soliciting for assistance from U.S. citizens to act as a third-party receiver of funds from victims who have purchased products from the subject via the Internet. The U.S. citizen receives the funds from the victims, then wires the money to the subject.

Criminal Law and Procedure in Cyberspace

Whether in cyberspace or in a traditional setting a crime has two parts: a physical part whereby the defendant committed an *act* or *omission*, and a mental part focusing on the defendant's subjective *state of mind*. Thus, an analysis of criminal liability involves three fundamental questions. First, did the defendant actually commit the prohibited act (or failure to act, an omission)? Second, did the defendant have a culpable state of mind? Third, does the law give the defendant a palpable defense (such as a self-defense claim to a homicide charge)? While

criminal law defines the boundaries of behavior and sanctions for violating those boundaries, **criminal procedure** refers to legal safeguards afforded to individuals (and in some cases business entities) during criminal investigations, arrest, trials and sentencing.

Cybercrimes present special challenges for law enforcement and courts alike. A committee of the American Bar Association (ABA) studying the growing issue of cybercrime offered three distinct challenges for law enforcement to solve transnational crimes:

- *Technical challenges.* Rapid changes in technology, the inability of law enforcement bodies to stay current in technology, and shortcomings in technology affect and even impair law enforcement's ability to find and prosecute cybercriminals.
- *Legal challenges.* Procedural hurdles or barriers, and the inability with legal systems around the world to keep up with technological changes, and an ever-changing business environment present legal challenges.
- *Operational challenges.* Lack of equipment, lack of training, inadequate organizational structures, and the need to work very quickly despite time zone, cultural, and language differences cause operational challenges.[25]

Technical Challenges in Combating Cybercrime

Computer technology is ever-changing. Many individuals and businesses enjoy the benefits computers bring them but do not keep up with the security measures necessary to continue enjoyment. People try to save costs by using a new laptop without installing antivirus software. Companies similarly try to keep costs down by eliminating their information technology departments. And, even those who try to stay current with computer security measures are challenged to install all the patches needed to correct vulnerabilities in software security. The many computers and networks vulnerable to attack create opportunities for cybercriminals to engage in criminal activities.

Although computer technologies are becoming more sophisticated, the hardware a cybercriminal needs to execute a crime are relatively basic—a computer and an Internet connection. And, although attack software is also becoming increasingly sophisticated, these tools of attack are readily obtainable, often easy to use, and more-and-more automated. Complicating matters further is the fact that anonymity software is also readily available.

Many online crimes are invisible and go undetected. An individual or business might not even know there has been an invasion of a computer or computer system. Even after they are discovered, there is often reluctance to report a cybercrime out of embarrassment, lack of time, ignorance as to which law enforcement body is responsible for fighting what kind of crime, or fear that divulging information about a crime will expose the victim further.

---

25. American Bar Association, Privacy & Computer Crime Committee, Section of Science & Technology Law, *International Guide to Combating Cybercrime,* 83 (Jody R. Westby, ed., 2003).

Legal Challenges

Search and seizure of the evidence of a cybercrime requires highly skilled technicians who are educated in the laws governing constitutional issues related to searching and seizing individually owned properly. Being fully educated in the current state of the law of search and seizure in a given country is challenging itself because the law is constantly refined to keep pace with the technology. One of the most prominent issues facing law enforcement is the extent to which electronic devices, such as cell phones, fit into current law of unlawful search and seizure as defined by the Fourth Amendment. In *Riley v. California*, the U.S. Supreme Court considered whether the police need a search warrant to examine the contents of a suspect's cell phone.

Riley v. California
144 S. Ct. 2473 (2014)

FACTS Riley was stopped for a traffic violation that eventually led to his arrest for concealed possession of two loaded handguns found in his car. An officer searched Riley incident to his arrest and found items consistent with Riley's involvement with a street gang. At the police station about two hours after the arrest, a detective specializing in criminal gangs confiscated and examined the contents of Riley's cell phone. The detective found videos and photographs that connected Riley with a shooting that had occurred a few weeks earlier. Riley was ultimately charged with that earlier shooting and the prosecutor sought an enhanced sentence based upon Riley's membership in a criminal street gang. Riley moved to suppress all evidence that the police had obtained from his cell phone claiming a violation of the Fourth Amendment's warrant requirement. Prosecutors argued that the search of the cell phone was proper because it was incident to a lawful arrest within the guidelines of previous case law. The trial court denied Riley's motion to suppress and the California Court of Appeals affirmed. Riley appealed to the U.S. Supreme Court.[26]

Judicial Opinion Our cases have determined that "[w]here a search is undertaken by law enforcement officials to discover evidence of criminal wrongdoing, . . . reasonableness generally requires the obtaining of a judicial warrant." *Vernonia School Dist. 47J v. Acton,* 515 U.S. 646, 653, 115 S.Ct. 2386, 132 L.Ed.2d 564 (1995). Such a warrant ensures that the inferences to support a search are "drawn by a neutral and detached magistrate instead of being judged by the officer engaged in the often competitive enterprise of ferreting out crime." *Johnson v. United States,* 333 U.S. 10, 14, 68 S.Ct. 367, 92 L.Ed. 436 (1948). In the absence of a warrant, a search is reasonable only if it falls within a

---

26. Note that the Court also considered *U.S. v. Wurie* as a companion case along with the *Riley* case because, although they are factually different, they raise a common question concerning police searches of digital information on a cell phone.

specific exception to the warrant requirement. See *Kentucky v. King,* 563 U.S. _____, _____, 131 S.Ct. 1849, 1856-1857, 179 L.Ed.2d 865 (2011).

The two cases before us concern the reasonableness of a warrantless search incident to a lawful arrest. In 1914, this Court first acknowledged in dictum "the right on the part of the Government, always recognized under English and American law, to search the person of the accused when legally arrested to discover and seize the fruits or evidences of crime." *Weeks v. United States,* 232 U.S. 383, 392, 34 S.Ct. 341, 58 L.Ed. 652. Since that time, it has been well accepted that such a search constitutes an exception to the warrant requirement. Indeed, the label "exception" is something of a misnomer in this context, as warrantless searches incident to arrest occur with far greater frequency than searches conducted pursuant to a warrant. . . .

These cases require us to decide how the search incident to arrest doctrine applies to modern cell phones, which are now such a pervasive and insistent part of daily life that the proverbial visitor from Mars might conclude they were an important feature of human anatomy. A smart phone of the sort taken from Riley was unheard of ten years ago; a significant majority of American adults now own such phones. See A. Smith, Pew Research Center, Smartphone Ownership—2013 Update (June 5, 2013). . . . Absent more precise guidance from the founding era, we generally determine whether to exempt a given type of search from the warrant requirement "by assessing, on the one hand, the degree to which it intrudes upon an individual's privacy and, on the other, the degree to which it is needed for the promotion of legitimate governmental interests." *Wyoming v. Houghton,* 526 U.S. 295, 300, (1999).

But while *[the Court's]* categorical rule strikes the appropriate balance in the context of physical objects, neither of its rationales has much force with respect to digital content on cell phones. On the government interest side, [the Court] concluded that the two risks identified in [previous case law]—harm to officers and destruction of evidence—are present in all custodial arrests. There are no comparable risks when the search is of digital data. In addition, *[previous cases]* regarded any privacy interests retained by an individual after arrest as significantly diminished by the fact of the arrest itself. Cell phones, however, place vast quantities of personal information literally in the hands of individuals. A search of the information on a cell phone bears little resemblance to the type of brief physical search considered in *[previous cases]*.

We therefore decline to extend [the exception] to searches of data on cell phones, and hold instead that officers must generally secure a warrant before conducting such a search. . . .

We cannot deny that our decision today will have an impact on the ability of law enforcement to combat crime. Cell phones have become important tools in facilitating coordination and communication among members of criminal enterprises, and can provide valuable incriminating information about dangerous criminals. Privacy comes at a cost.

Our holding, of course, is not that the information on a cell phone is immune from search; it is instead that a warrant is generally required before such a search, even when a cell phone is seized incident to arrest. Our cases have historically recognized that the warrant requirement is "an important working part of our machinery of government," not merely "an inconvenience to be somehow 'weighed' against the claims of police efficiency." *Coolidge v.New Hampshire,* 403 U.S. 443, 481 (1971). . . .

Moreover, even though the search incident to arrest exception does not apply to cell phones, other case-specific exceptions may still justify a warrantless search of a particular phone. "One well-recognized exception applies when '"the exigencies of the situation" make the needs of law enforcement so compelling that [a] warrantless search is objectively reasonable under the Fourth Amendment.'" *Kentucky v. King,* 563 U.S., at _____, 131 S.Ct., at 1856 (quoting *Mincey v. Arizona,*437 U.S. 385, 394). Such exigencies could include the need to prevent the imminent destruction of evidence in individual cases, to pursue a fleeing suspect, and to assist persons who are seriously injured or are threatened with imminent injury. 563 U.S., at _____, 131 S.Ct. 1849. . . .

In light of the availability of the exigent circumstances exception, there is no reason to believe that law enforcement officers will not be able to address some of the more extreme hypotheticals that have been suggested: a suspect texting an accomplice who, it is feared, is preparing to detonate a bomb, or a child abductor who may have information about the child's location on his cell phone. The defendants here recognize—indeed, they stress—that such fact-specific threats may justify a warrantless search of cell phone data. See Reply Brief in No. 13-132, at 8-9; Brief for Respondent in No. 13-212, at 30, 41. The critical point is that, unlike the search incident to arrest exception, the exigent circumstances exception requires a court to examine whether an emergency justified a warrantless search in each particular case. See *McNeely, supra,* at _____, 133 S.Ct., at 1559.[2]

* * *

. . . Modern cell phones are not just another technological convenience. With all they contain and all they may reveal, they hold for many Americans "the privacies of life," *Boyd, supra,* at 630, 6 S.Ct. 524. The fact that technology now allows an individual to carry such information in his hand does not make the information any less worthy of the protection for which the Founders fought. Our answer to the question of what police must do before searching a cell phone seized incident to an arrest is accordingly simple—get a warrant.

We reverse the judgment of the California Court of Appeal. . . .

Case Questions

1. In what ways does this case illustrate the tension between established precedent and technology?
2. The Court points out that in cases of exigent circumstances, the police may still be able to search a cell phone without a warrant. What types of circumstances might constitute exigent circumstances?
3. The Court has held previously that a search incident to arrest may include the defendant's wallet/purse. Is there really a difference between a wallet and a cell phone? What if Riley's wallet had contained incriminating photographs of him? Would the police be required to get a warrant?

Smartphone Encryption

Although Apple and Google won praise from privacy advocates for using advances in technology to make their smartphones safer from hacking and privacy invasions through encryption, the law enforcement community has publicly criticized the tech giants. FBI Director James Comey held a press conference to announce that the new smartphone encryption methods would prevent law enforcement from accessing certain private data and that the encryption would hinder criminal investigations. Apple announced that the new iOS8 operating system on their smart phones prevents Apple from bypassing smartphone user passwords. This meant that Apple could no longer respond to government warrants for the extraction of this data in their possession running iOS8. Comey accused the companies of marketing something that expressly allowed people to place themselves above the law.

Money Laundering

Money laundering is the process of cleaning "dirty" money by funneling illegal funds (e.g., cash from illicit drug sales) through legitimate sources, such as businesses dealing primarily in cash revenue, in order to avoid attention by government authorities such as law enforcement or the Internal Revenue Service. In 1986, the Money Laundering Control Act[27] was enacted as a comprehensive law designed to institute a reporting system for bank deposits and instituting criminal penalties for middlemen who facilitated the laundering. Efforts by the government to break up organized crime syndicates were often centered on money laundering charges and the crime became increasingly difficult to commit as law enforcement efforts became more sophisticated.

The advent of electronic cash, also called digital money, has created new challenges for law enforcement to detect and prosecute money laundering. Digital cash is a series of numbers that have an intrinsic value in some form of currency even if that currency is not recognized by any government. Bitcoins, which has garnered substantial media attention, has become the digital cash of choice (Bitcoins are discussed in detail in Chapter 12: Government Regulation). One such challenge is applying traditional money laundering statutes to transaction involving digital cash. In *U.S. v. Ulbricht,* a federal trial court determines the applicability of money laundering statutes in the context of an illicit online marketplace.

U.S. v. Ulbricht
31 F. Supp.3d 540 (S.D.N.Y.2014)

Facts Prosecutors charged Ulbricht with a variety of federal crimes alleging that Ulbricht engaged in narcotics trafficking, computer hacking, and money

---

27. 18 U.S.C.§ 1956.

laundering conspiracies by designing, launching, and administering a website called Silk Road as an online marketplace for illicit goods and services.

The government alleged that Silk Road was designed to operate like eBay: a seller would electronically post a good or service for sale; a buyer would electronically purchase the item; the seller would then ship or otherwise provide to the buyer the purchased item; the buyer would provide feedback; and the site operator (i.e., Ulbricht) would receive a portion of the seller's revenue as a commission. Ulbricht, as the site designer, made the site available only to those using Tor, software and a network that allows for anonymous, untraceable Internet browsing; he allowed payment only via Bitcoin, an anonymous and untraceable form of payment.

After he was indicted by a Grand Jury, Ulbricht filed a motion to dismiss the counts. Specifically, Ulbricht sought to have the money laundering count dismissed because the criminal statute requires that the money laundering be part of a "financial transaction" in which proceeds from illegal activity were received by the defendant. Ulbricht argued that the factual allegation that Bitcoins constituted the exclusive payment system that served to facilitate illegal commerce on Silk Road cannot constitute the requisite financial transaction because Bitcoins are not recognized as currency or credit by any government.

Judicial Opinion ...

As an initial matter, an allegation that Bitcoins are used as a payment system is insufficient in and of itself to state a claim for money laundering. The fact that Bitcoins allow for anonymous transactions does not *ipso facto* mean that those transactions relate to unlawful activities. The anonymity by itself is not a crime. Rather, Bitcoins are alleged here to be the medium of exchange—just as dollars or Euros could be—in financial transactions relating to the unlawful activities of narcotics trafficking and computer hacking. It is the system of payment designed specifically to shield the proceeds from third party discovery of their unlawful origin that forms the unlawful basis of the money laundering charge.

The money laundering statute defines a "financial transaction" as involving, inter alia, "the movement of funds by wire or other means, or involving one or more monetary instruments, or involving the transfer of title to any real property, vehicle, vessel, or aircraft." 18 U.S.C. § 1956(c)(4). The term "monetary instrument" is defined as the coin or currency of a country, personal checks, bank checks, and money orders, or investment securities or negotiable instruments. 18 U.S.C. § 1956(c)(5).

The defendant argues that because Bitcoins are not monetary instruments, transactions involving Bitcoins cannot form the basis for a money laundering conspiracy. He notes that the IRS has announced that it treats virtual currency as property and not as currency. The defendant argues that virtual currencies have some but not all of the attributes of currencies of national governments and that virtual currencies do not have legal tender status. In fact, neither the IRS nor FinCEN purport to amend the money laundering statute (nor could they). In any event, neither the IRS nor FinCEN has addressed the question of whether a "financial transaction" can occur with Bitcoins. This Court refers back to the money laundering statute itself and case law interpreting the statute.

It is clear from a plain reading of the statute that "financial transaction" is broadly defined. See *United States v. Blackman,* 904 F.2d 1250, 1257 (8th Cir. 1950)(citation omitted). It captures all movements of "funds" by any means, or monetary instruments. "Funds" is not defined in the statute and is therefore given its ordinary meaning. See *Taniguchi v. Kan Pacific Saipan, Ltd.,* 132 S.Ct. 1997, 2002 (2012) (citation omitted). "Funds" are defined as "money, often money for a specific purpose." See Cambridge Dictionaries Online, http://dictionary.cam bridge.org/us/dictionary/american-english/funds?q=funds (last visited July 3, 2014). "Money" is an object used to buy things.

Put simply, "funds" can be used to pay for things in the colloquial sense. Bitcoins can be either used directly to pay for certain things or can act as a medium of exchange and be converted into a currency which can pay for things. See Bitcoin, https://bitcoin.org/en (last visited July 3, 2014); "8 Things You Can Buy With Bitcoins Right Now," CNN Money, http://money.cnn.com/gallery/technology/2013/ 11/25/ buy-with-bitcoin/ (last visited July 3, 2014). Indeed, the only value for Bitcoin lies in its ability to pay for things—it is digital and has no earthly form; it cannot be put on a shelf and looked at or collected in a nice display case. Its form is digital—bits and bytes that together constitute something of value. And they may be bought and sold using legal tender. See "How to Use Bitcoin," https://bitcoin.org/en/getting-started (last visited July 3, 2014). Sellers using Silk Road are not alleged to have given their narcotics and malicious software away for free—they are alleged to have sold them.

The money laundering statute is broad enough to encompass use of Bitcoins in financial transactions. Any other reading would—in light of Bitcoins' sole raison d'etre—be nonsensical. Congress intended to prevent criminals from finding ways to wash the proceeds of criminal activity by transferring proceeds to other similar or different items that store significant value. With respect to this case, the Government has alleged that Bitcoins have a value which may be expressed in dollars, alleging that Ulbricht "reaped commissions worth tens of millions of dollars, generated from the illicit sales conducted through the site".

There is no doubt that if a narcotics transaction was paid for in cash, which was later exchanged for gold, and then converted back to cash, that would constitute a money laundering transaction.

One can money launder using Bitcoin. The defendant's motion as to [this count] is therefore denied. . . .

Case Questions

1. If the money laundering statutes were passed prior to the advent of digital cash, how can use of digital cash be covered by those same statutes?
2. The defendant pointed out that the IRS treat Bitcoins as property and not as currency. Why did the court reject that argument? Do you agree?
3. In your view, does the defendant's involvement in the Silk Road website have any impact on the court's decision?

Federal Statutes Related to Cybercrime

Law	Coverage	Finding Information
Computer Fraud and Abuse Act	Unauthorized use to commit crimes such as hacking and fraud.	18 USC § 1030
Identity Theft and Assumption Deterrence Act	Identity theft.	18 USC § 1028
Trafficking in Counterfeit Goods or Services	Counterfeiting and online piracy.	18 USC § 2320
Missing Children's Act	Child abuse imagery and exploitation.	18 USC § 1804
CAN-SPAM Act	Misleading and unsolicited emails.	15 USC § 103
Money Laundering Control Act	Laundering electronic cash.	18 USC § 1956
US SAFE WEB Act	International cooperation and information sharing to prevent cybercrime.	15 USC § 44

Concept Summary

- Whether in cyber space or in a traditional setting a crime has two parts: a physical part whereby the defendant committed an act or omission, and a mental part focusing on the defendant's subjective state of mind.
- While criminal law defines the boundaries of behavior and sanctions for violating those boundaries, criminal procedure refers to legal safeguards afforded to individuals (and in some cases business entities) during criminal investigations, arrest, trials, and sentencing.
- One of the most prominent issues facing law enforcement is the extent to which electronic devices, such as cell phones, fit into current law of unlawful search and seizure as defined by the Fourth Amendment.
- The advent of electronic cash such as Bitcoins, also called digital money, has created new challenges for law enforcement to detect and prosecute money laundering.

International Efforts in Reducing Cybercrime

The Undertaking Spam, Spyware, and Fraud Enforcement With Enforcers Beyond Borders Act of 2006 (US SAFE WEB Act) empowered the FTC to share confidential information and investigational assistance with counterpart agencies in foreign countries. Key provisions of the measure are:

● *Expansion of Information Sharing and Investigation:* Allows the FTC to share confidential information regarding consumer protection matters with foreign law enforcers, subject to the receipt of adequate confidentiality assurances. Allows the FTC to share information with foreign agencies to help them halt fraud, deception, spam, spyware, and other consumer protection law violations targeting consumers in the United States.

● *Expanding Investigative Cooperation:* Allows the FTC to conduct and participate in investigations and discovery designed to assist foreign law enforcers in appropriate cases.

● *Obtaining More Information from Foreign Sources:* Allows the FTC to protect information provided by foreign enforcement agencies from public disclosure, when confidentiality protection was imposed as a condition of disclosure of such information by the applicable foreign agency.

● *Protecting the Confidentiality of FTC Investigations:* Safeguards FTC investigations in a defined range of cases; specifically 1) generally protects recipients of FTC Civil Investigation Demand (CID) from possible liability for keeping those CIDs confidential; 2) authorizes the FTC to seek a court order in appropriate cases to preclude notice by the CID recipient to the investigative target for a limited time; and 3) tailors the mechanisms available to the FTC to seek delay of notification currently required by the Right to Financial Privacy Act (RFPA) or the Electronic Communications Privacy Act (ECPA) to better fit FTC cases.

● *Protecting Certain Entities Reporting Suspected Violations of Law:* Protects a limited category of appropriate entities from liability for voluntary disclosures to the FTC about suspected fraud or deception, or about recovery of assets for consumer redress.

● *Allowing Information Sharing with Federal Financial and Market Regulators:* Adds the FTC to RFPA's list of financial and market regulators allowed to readily share appropriate information.

● *Confirming the FTC's Remedial Authority in Cross-Border Cases:* Expressly confirms: 1) the FTC's authority to redress harm in the United States caused by foreign wrongdoers and harm abroad caused by U.S. wrongdoers; and 2) the availability, in cross-border cases, of all remedies available to the FTC, including restitution.

● *Enhancing Cooperation Between the FTC and DOJ in Foreign Litigation:* Permits the FTC to cooperate with the DOJ in connection with foreign litigation of FTC matters.

● *Clarification of FTC Authority to Make Criminal Referrals:* Expressly authorizes the FTC to make criminal referrals for prosecution when violations of FTC law also violate U.S. criminal laws.

● *Providing for Foreign Staff Exchange Programs:* Authorizes foreign staff exchange arrangements between the FTC and associated with foreign government authorities. Also permits the FTC to accept reimbursement for its costs associated with these arrangements.

● *Authorizing Expenditure on Joint Projects:* Authorizes the FTC to expend appropriated funds, not to exceed $100,000 annually, toward operating expenses and other costs of cooperative cross-border law enforcement projects and bilateral and multilateral meetings.

● *Gift Acceptance:* Authorizes the FTC to accept reimbursement for providing assistance to law enforcement agencies in the United States or abroad and to accept gifts and voluntary services in aid of the agency's mission and consistent with ethical constraints.

European Cybercops

The revolution in information technologies that has occurred since the 1990s has changed society in a way that almost nothing has in the past. Today, the information available at the click of a button was, only several years ago, something that could only be dreamed. Of course, this evolution in technology has positive aspects to it as well as negative ones. The fact that anyone with Internet access is able to view, transfer, and communicate videos, audio, and text is certainly an unimaginable improvement for society. However, it does have its downsides. The opportunity that people now have to commit crimes, specifically through technology, is something that was only made possible through the nearly limitless abilities that one has today. For this reason, in 1996 the European Committee on Crime Problems set up a committee to deal with cybercrime. This committee, called the Committee of Experts on Crime in Cyber-space, drafted a convention, the Convention on Cybercrime (the Cybercrime Convention), which took effect in 2001.[28]

The Cybercrime Convention aimed first to harmonize domestic criminal offenses and their elements with cyberlaw crimes. The next step was providing for criminal procedure powers necessary to investigate and prosecute cyberlaw offenses. The third goal of the Cybercrime Convention was to set up a fast and economic regime of international cooperation. Parties that would be bound by the Cybercrime Convention are the member states of the European Council as well as any states that agree to be bound by it.

The Cybercrime Convention deals with different categories of computer crimes in its substantive law section. The first is offenses against the confidentiality, integrity, and availability of computer data systems that includes illegal access of computer systems, illegal interception of data, data interference, system interference, and misuse of devices or data to commit computer crimes. The second category of crimes is computer-related offenses. These include offenses that can be committed even without computers, but today are increasingly being committed through the use of a computer, including computer-related forgery and computer-related fraud. The third category is content-related offenses such as child pornography. The fourth category is offenses related to copyright and related rights. The fifth category is offenses not included in the first four categories, including attempting or aiding and abetting any offenses that are included in the Cybercrime Convention. It also includes corporate liability to impose liability

---

28. European Council, Convention on Cybercrime, ETS 185, available at http://conventions.coe.int/Treaty/Commun/QueVoulezVous.asp?NT=185&CL=ENG.

on corporations that allow their employees or agents to commit crimes in violation of the Cybercrime Convention.

The rest of the Cybercrime Convention deals with a more procedural aspect of the law on cybercrime. It includes the procedural laws set in place for enforcement of the Convention. It also speaks about jurisdictional issues and makes it mandatory for contracting parties to establish jurisdiction over the enumerated offenses. The last issue addressed by the Cybercrime Convention is that of international cooperation. It sets forth procedures and policies regarding extradition, mutual assistance, confidentiality, and other forms of collaboration expected from the contracting parties.

European Commission. The European Union has also taken a leading role in attempting to respond to international cybercrime. In 2001, the European Commission released a Communication on Computer Related Crime.[29] The Communication discussed the importance of a coordinated policy to combat computer-related crime. Several initiatives developed as a result of the Communication.

Additionally, in 2005, the European Union launched the European Network and Information Security Agency (ENISA).[30] The European Union established ENISA "to achieve a high and effective level of Network and Information Security within the European Union . . . ENISA seeks to develop a culture of Network and Information Security for the benefit of citizens, consumers, business as and public sector organizations in the European Union." ENISA is involved in nearly all activities that take place over the Internet.

More recently, the European Union created the European Union Cybercrime Task Force after a two-day meeting at Europol Headquarters. Europol is the E.U. law enforcement agency responsible for handling criminal intelligence.

> Under discussion were operational and strategic issues on cybercrime investigations, prosecutions and cross-border cooperation in the fight against cybercrime. . . . A specific session was dedicated to the establishment of the so-called European Cybercrime Platform that includes the Internet Crime Reporting Online System (ICROS), the Analysis Work File Cyborg, that is actively working to fight criminal groups operating on the internet, and the Internet & Forensic Expert Forum (IFOREX) to host technical data and training for cybercrime law enforcement.[31]

Summary

Although the Internet has had tremendous positive effects on our ability to communicate, learn, conduct business, and handle many aspects of our daily

---

29. See European Commission, "Creating a Safer Information Society by Improving the Security of Information Infrastructures and Combating Computer-related Crime," Jan. 6, 2001, http://www.justice.gov/criminal/ cybercrime/ intl/EUCommunication.0101.pdf.
30. ENISA Online, available at http://www.enisa.europa.eu/about-enisa.
31. Europol, European Union Cybercrime Task Force, http://www.europol.europa.eu/index.asp?page=news& news=prl00622.htm.

lives, it has also made it easier for those with ill intent to engage in various forms of criminal behavior. Around the world, criminals are using computers and the Internet to commit a wide range of crimes, from hacking, to fraud, to espionage and terrorism.

Federal, state and international laws are continually being adopted and/or amended in an effort to keep up with emerging new computer crimes. At the same time, recognizing that many computer crimes are transnational in nature, nations are becoming increasingly cooperative in sharing information and assisting in the prosecution of international cybercrime. Still, despite these various efforts, it is unlikely that the risks of computer crime will go away any time soon. Accordingly, in addition to relying upon the laws that have been implemented to prevent and detect computer-related crimes, businesses and individuals also need to take steps to protect themselves from becoming victims of computer crime.

Key Terms

cybercrime A crime committed in cyberspace or crimes perpetrated using a computer.

netcrime Use of the Internet for criminal purposes.

cyberfraud Use of a computer or the Internet to commit fraud.

Computer Fraud and Abuse Act Federal statute that defines and prohibits cybercrimes.

pharming Malicious redirection of Internet traffic from one website to another.

spoofing Criminal concealment or impersonation of an email sender.

phishing Form of spoofing to obtain banking or personal information from a victim.

spear phishing Invasive form of phishing which targets a specific individual or organization.

maladaptive gang A group of scammers posing as legitimate advertisers.

pretexting Obtaining personal information from a victim through texting impersonation.

warez A website designed to aid in copyright infringement.

cyberstalking Use of Internet or other electronic communications to stalk or harass the victim.

cyberbullying Use of Internet or other electronic communications to hurt or embarrass the victim.

malware Short-hand term for malicious software which is used to gain access to information stored on a computer or computer network.

hacking Unauthorized entry or use of computer or computer network.

Trojan horse Malware that appears harmless but hides a malicious function.

virus A program designed to copy itself and spread from one computer to another without the user's knowledge.

spam Unsolicited bulk email.

denial-of-service attacks A computer crime that renders computer resources unavailable to legitimate users typically by overloading a website server to prevent proper functioning.

criminal law Defines boundaries of behavior and sets out sanctions.

criminal procedure Legal safeguards afforded to individuals during criminal investigations, arrest, trial and sentencing.

Manager's Checklist

1. Business managers should conduct internal and external security audits on a regular basis.

2. Business should develop, implement, and review on a regular basis comprehensive information concerning security policies.

3. Companies of all sizes must be aware that their information systems are vulnerable to cybercrimes, must remain vigilant about new security risks, and must adapt accordingly.

4. Business managers must protect against not only domestic crime, but also international crime as well. Companies concerned about international computer crime should consider becoming more active in developing a dialogue with law enforcement authorities to encourage further international cooperation against cybercrime.

5. Companies must monitor changes in law. This is particularly the case with respect to computer crime, given that laws are changing rapidly and laws from one jurisdiction can have an impact on companies based in other jurisdictions.

Questions and Case Problems

1. Dr. Cyril Wecht is a renowned forensic pathologist and former Coroner of Allegheny County, Pennsylvania. On January 20, 2006, he was indicted on eighty-four counts of theft of honest services, mail fraud, wire fraud, and theft from an organization receiving federal funds in connection with his tenure as Allegheny County Coroner, which commenced in 1996. The indictment alleged that, in each of the calendar years 2001 through 2005, the Defendant, acting in his capacity as Allegheny Coroner, had embezzled, stolen, obtained by fraud and otherwise converted without authority ACCO "property" (i.e., the use of ACCO personnel, vehicles, facilities, resources, equipment and

space) valued at $5,000 or more, in violation of federal law. It appears that much of the evidence utilized by the Government in support of these charges was obtained, either directly or indirectly, through the execution of two separate search warrants, both of which were presented to a United States Magistrate Judge on April 7, 2005. One of the warrants sought the seizure of approximately twenty boxes of private autopsy files from the offices of Wecht Pathology. The other sought the seizure of a laptop computer utilized by the Defendant's executive assistant, Eileen Young, and all of the information and data stored within the laptop. *Should the government be permitted to use the laptop evidence? Is the information sought too overbroad for a warrant search?*

2. Pursuant to several federal acts, the plaintiff in this case, Phillip Becker (Becker), filed suit against his former wife, Mary McIntyre Toca (Toca), for allegedly infiltrating his computers and infecting them with viruses that can steal information from the computers. Becker's suit is based on the Federal Wiretap Act, the Stored Communications Act, the Computer Fraud and Abuse Act, and the Louisiana Surveillance Act. Toca moved to dismiss the case on the grounds that the Acts that were allegedly violated did not apply to this case.

   The Federal Wiretap Act subjects a person to criminal liability when he or she "intentionally intercepts [or] endeavors to intercept . . . any wire, oral or electronic communication." In defining the standard, courts have held that a violation of the Wiretap Act can only be established when the information is intercepted contemporaneously with its transmission. Intercepting information that is stored electronically is not considered in violation of the Wiretap Act.

   The Stored Communications Act subjects a person to liability when he or she "intentionally accesses without authorization a facility through which an electronic communication service is provided [and] thereby obtains, alters, or prevents authorized access to a wire or electronic communication while it is in electronic storage in such system." This statute generally applies to phone companies or ISPs, but it can also apply to information that is held by the ISP for a person. This can be information that is transmitted over email or over the Internet in other ways.

   The Computer Fraud and Abuse Act provides for criminal liability when someone: (i) knowingly causes the transmission of a program, information, code, or command, and as a result of such conduct, intentionally causes damage without authorization, to a protected computer; (ii) intentionally accesses a protected computer without authorization, and as a result of such conduct, recklessly causes damage; or (iii) intentionally accesses a protected computer without authorization, and as a result of such conduct causes damage.

   Toca claimed that Becker did not establish that his computers were considered "protected" and, in addition, argued that Becker failed to show that she intentionally caused "damage" to Becker's computers. One is considered "protected" when the computers are used in interstate commerce or communication. "Damage" is defined as "any impairment to the integrity or availability of data, a program, a system, or information." *Decide what the District Court should conclude on each of the three claims against Toca, and explain?*[32]

3. In this criminal case brought by the United States, Defendant Christopher Andrew Phillips (Phillips) was being prosecuted for breaching an agreement with the university he attended, the University of Texas (UT), and infiltrating thousands of computers and stealing a tremendous amount of information. Despite Phillips' signed agreement not to perform port scans and hack into computers, and despite several warnings Phillips received from UT, he continued to infiltrate the university's computer systems and stole information such as students' Social Security numbers, financial aid documents, and birth records. The jury found Phillips guilty on one count of computer fraud pursuant to the Computer Fraud and Abuse Act (CFAA). He appealed to the United States Court of Appeals for the Fifth Circuit, claiming that the prosecution did not produce sufficient evidence to show that he "intentionally access [ed] a protected computer without authorization," a requirement under the CFAA.

   The Court of Appeals began its analysis with the statute. Because it is very difficult to show that someone intentionally accessed a computer, as opposed to accessing it unintentionally, a violation of the statute can be established by looking at the intended use and nature of the relationship between the owner of the computer and the user. In this case, Phillips infiltrated the entire system that is normally meant for students to access their university information. By doing so, and attacking the system, Phillips was able to obtain a multitude of sensitive and private information about thousands of his fellow students. *Decide and explain why or why not the appellate court should affirm "Phillips" conviction?*[33]

4. Copyright infringement is a major concern in the Internet age. The Internet and related technologies make it much easier for companies and individuals to share pirated movies, television shows, and other works that infringe third-party copyrights. Federal prosecutors brought a legal action against several websites for criminal copyright infringement for showing a number of popular films and television shows without permission. In the case, it was reported that criminal copyright infringement costs the U.S. economy an estimated $25.6 billion. *What remedies should authorities have in these kinds of cases?*[34]

5. Trust is an important part of the continued growth and development of the Internet. This is particularly the case with respect to social networking. Media reports of disturbing stories and case law alike have shown some of the consequences that can arise when individuals create false social networking profiles. In a case in California, an individual established a fake MySpace profile of his former church pastor. On the profile, he posted content that suggested that

---

32. *Becker v. Toca*, No. 07-7202, 2008 WL 4443050 (E.D. La. Sept. 26, 2008).
33. *United States, v. Phillips*, 477 F.3d 215 (5th Cir. 2007).
34. *United States v. TVSHACK.NET*, S.D.N.Y., No. 10 MAG 1421, (warrants unsealed 6/30/10).

the pastor used drugs and was homosexual. *Can criminal charges be brought against the party that created the fake profile?*[35]

6. Online harassment is a problem of increasing concern. Through the Internet, individuals with ill intent are able to send harassing messages to a great number of individuals in virtually no time at all. Consider, for example, a notable case in which a man who previously had a romantic relationship with a woman sent dozens of harassing and threatening emails and faxes to the victim and her coworkers. *Under what laws should this defendant be prosecuted and what penalties should he face?*

Additional Resources

Computer World. Cybercrime and Hacking Topic Center. http://www.computerworld.com/s/topic/82/ Cybercrime+and+Hacking.

Federal Bureau of Investigation. FBI Resource on Cyber Investigations. http://www. fbi.gov/cyberinvest/cyberhome.htm.

Federal Trade Commission. Information on Identity Theft. http://www.ftc. gov/bcp/edu/microsites/idtheft/.

———. Report on the Safe Web Act. http://www.ftc. gov/os/2009/12/P035303safewebact2009.pdf.

National Cyber Security Alliance. Stay Safe Online. http://www.staysafeonline.org/.

The Internet's Own Boy: The Story of Aaron Swartz. (2014) Writer/Director: Bryan Knappenberger (Documentary on events leading to death of Aaron Swartz and resulting legislative efforts).

University of Maryland's Center for the Study of Business Ethics, Regulation, & Crime. www.rhsmith.umd.edu/centers-excellent/cberc.

U.S. Department of Justice. "Appendix A: Unlawful Online Conduct and Applicable Federal Laws, http:// www.justice.gov/criminal/cybercrime/ccmanual/ appxa.pdf.

U.S. Department of Justice Computer Crime & Intellectual Property Section. http:// www.justice. gov/criminal/cybercrime/.

---

35. *Clear v. Superior Court,* 2010 WL 2029016 (Cal. Ct. App. 4 Dist. May 24, 2010).

actual damages Either (1) lost profits the copyright owner would have earned had copyright infringement not occurred or (2) profits of the infringer that are attributable to the infringement.

algorithm A mathematical formula for solving any number of problems.

alternative dispute resolution (ADR) A variety of processes that are alternatives to resolving disputes in court.

The Americans with Disabilities Act (ADA) An act prohibiting employers from discriminating against someone with a disability if they can do the essential functions of the job with a reasonable accommodation.

American Society of Composers, Authors, and Publishers (ASCAP) One of three major performing rights societies in the United States that licenses public performance rights on behalf of the copyright owners of musical works.

angel investor High-net-worth investor who contributes to a start up without further obligation.

Answer The defendant's response to the plaintiff's complaint. In the Answer, the defendant either admits or denies the allegations made in the complaint.

applied research Targeted research to prove feasibility.

anticircumvention provisions Provisions of the DMCA that make it illegal to circumvent (get around) digital rights management systems by hacking or similar means.

antitrafficking provisions Provisions of the DMCA that make it illegal to manufacture or distribute devices that enable the circumvention of digital rights management systems.

antitrust Federal laws that regulate anti-competitive acts.

arbitration A neutral "arbitrator" conducts a hearing taking arguments and evidence from both parties and then, much like a judge, renders a decision in favor of one party or the other.

at-will employee An employee who can be fired at any time, for any reason, unless that reason is illegal or violates public policy.

basic research Creative, theoretical or empirical research and work on fundamental principles to increase knowledge.

Bayh-Dole Act of 1980 A federal law incenting innovation as well as providing the government certain march-in nights.

big data Data sets characterized by volume (vast beyond conception), velocity (increasing speed and masses of data points gathered per swipe/touch/click/step/breath, etc.), and variety (data from all manner of connected devices, appliances, clothing, etc.).

binding arbitration Parties agree beforehand to accept the arbitrator's decision as final and forgo pursuing the matter in court.

bitcoins Most well-known form of digital currency that is based on a de-centralized peer-to-peer network.

blocking patent An improvement patent of a second inventor that blocks a first inventor from making the improved version of the first inventor's own invention.

browsewrap agreement An agreement whereby acceptance of the terms of service is a condition of simply browsing the site.

business method patent Though not statutorily defined, a type of patent that covers methods for processing data or conducting business operations.

business model A series of activities designed to yield a new product or service that will give a company a competitive advantage, as well as a sustainable financial return; a plan that creates value with levers to impact return on equity to shareholders.

caching The intermediate and temporary storage of recently accessed digital content.

cease-and-desist letter A demand letter that directs an individual to cease a stated activity.

Children's Online Privacy Protection Act Provides protections regarding the collection of name, email address and geolocation information so as to safeguard the child's identity and location.

choice-of-law provision A clause in a contract or terms of service that states that the law of a particular jurisdiction will apply.

claims The portion of a patent that states explicitly and distinctly claims the particular subject matter the inventor regards as his or her invention.

Clayton Act Federal law focused on prevention of anticompetitive practices.

click fraud Competitors or others intentionally click on a link for a purpose other than an interest in viewing the result.

clickwrap agreement An agreement whereby visitors to a website click on a box indicating that they agree to the terms of service when they create an account or make a purchase.

collective marks Marks used by members of an association or organization.

commercial speech Speech related solely to the economic rights of the speaker and its audience.

common stock Equity interest that entitles the holder to payments based on profitability of the business based on the discretion of the board of directors.

Communications Decency Act (CDA) Federal law that provides certain immunity to providers of Internet services and website hosts.

Complaint Court filing that starts the litigation process; a short and plain statement of the factual and legal basis of the plaintiff's claim.

composition copyright (music) The copyright covering the musical notes and lyrics created by a composer or songwriter.

Computer Fraud and Abuse Act (CFAA) A federal law that prohibits individuals from accessing a computer without authorization.

concerted activity Action in unison to protest, or protect, their working conditions. Concerted activity can include individual activity where a person seeks to initiate or induce a group to actions as well as an individual bringing group complaints to the attention of management.

consumer report Any communication, whether written or oral, that includes information on a consumer's credit worthiness, credit standing, character, general reputation, personal characteristics, or lifestyle which is used or intended to be used in employment decisions.

contract Contracts create a legal relationship; voluntarily entered into agreements, whereby each party has legal capacity and is bound by obligations in order to pursue lawful objectives.

Contribution Agreement Formal agreement between parties specifying which party is contributing what to a start up.

contributory liability A type of secondary liability that results when a party (1) intentionally induces the primary infringer to commit infringement or (2) continues to provide a product or service to a buyer knowing that the buyer is engaging in infringement.

contract manufacturing/supply chain agreement A series of contracts with different partners throughout the entire creation and deployment process covering design, procurement, manufacturing, quality control, shipping, and retailing.

Copyright Act of 1976 The principal federal enactment of copyright law.

corporation Single or multiple-person entity which exists as an independent "person" separate from its principals.

covenant not to compete A provision in an employment contract in which an employee promises not to compete with the employer should the employment relationship end.

Creative Commons A nonprofit organization that has developed a way for creators to mark their works to let others know what uses are permitted by the copyright owner.

criminal procedure Legal safeguards afforded to individuals during criminal investigations, arrest, trial and sentencing.

cronyism The hiring of friends.

cross-licensing An arrangement whereby two parties authorize each other to make, use, or sell the inventions protected by the other party's patents.

crowdfunding Raising capital through an offering to potential investors using a web-based platform such as Kickstarter.

cyberbullying Use of Internet or other electronic communications to hurt or embarrass the victim.

cybercrime A crime committed in cyberspace or crimes perpetrated using a computer.

cyberfraud Use of a computer or the Internet to commit fraud.

cybersquatting Registering domain names before others appreciate their value to later sell them for a profit.

cyberstalking Use of Internet or other electronic communications to stalk or harass the victim.

damages An award, typically monetary, paid to compensate for loss or injury.

data privacy The concept that individuals want to be able to control aspects of their PII.

debt Money used by a business entity which must be paid back (e.g., a commercial loan).

defamation Legal claim for injury to reputation. To establish a claim the plaintiff must show that 1) a party published a statement, 2) with knowledge that the statement is false and defaming to the other, or 3) with reckless disregard for the truth of the statement or with negligence in failing to ascertain the truth of the statement.

deep linking Linking to a subsidiary page of the trademark owner's site rather than to its homepage.

demonstration Presentation or display to show the knowledge or the product in an operational environment.

denial-of-service attacks A computer crime that renders computer resources unavailable to legitimate users typically by overloading a website server to prevent proper functioning.

derivative works Works of expression derived from other works, such as adaptations or translations.

design patents A type of patent that protects new, original, and ornamental designs on an article of manufacture.

diffusion or adoption of innovation Measure by which new technologies spread among users over time.

digital first sale doctrine A proposed expansion of the first sale doctrine that would allow the doctrine to apply to digital works.

Digital Millennium Copyright Act (DMCA) A 1998 law that created safe harbors from liability for online service providers, while also prohibiting the circumvention of digital rights management systems and also the trafficking in circumvention devices.

Digital Performance Right in Sound Recordings Act (DPRA) A 1995 law that gave sound recording copyright owners the exclusive right to publicly perform the sound recording by means of a digital audio transmission.

digital rights management (DRM) Encryption or other technological means to limit the ability of users to access, copy, or otherwise use a copyrighted work.

digital watermarks A type of standard technical measure that can be embedded in digital works and used to trace the origin of the work.

director Individual elected by shareholders of a company to oversee the overall management of a corporation.

discovery A process, prior to trial, in which litigants engage in the mandatory exchange of documents and other forms of information relevant to the litigation.

distinctive A characteristic by which consumers viewing (or hearing) the trademark are be able to distinguish it from other trademarks.

doctrine of equivalents A doctrine by which an accused device or process may be found to infringe if it performs substantially the same function in substantially the same way to obtain the same result.

Drivers Privacy Protection Act Prohibits the use and disclosure of select personal information in states' motor vehicle records.

due process The entitlement to certain procedures before one is denied life, liberty, or property.

duty of care A duty to act reasonably on the employer's behalf, in accordance with industry standards, free from negligence or recklessness.

duty of loyalty A duty to act solely on behalf of the employer, free from conflicts of interest such as self-dealing.

E-B (1-5) visa Permanent worker visa preference, commonly called the *Green Card*, reserved for workers with "extraordinary ability" and ten years' experience, or those who are investors with at least $1 million of capital to invest in the United States.

economic espionage The deliberate theft of proprietary business information for the benefit of a foreign entity or government.

Economic Espionage Act of 1996 (EEA) An act that criminalizes the theft of trade secrets and provides for penalties of up to $10 million.

Electronic Communications Privacy Act (ECPA) A federal law that prohibits the interception of an electronic communication (such as an email message) while in transit.

Electronically Stored Information (ESI) Documents stored electronically, such as Microsoft Word, Excel, and PowerPoint files, Adobe PDF files, database records, and CAD/CAM files.

employee separation agreement An agreement covering severance pay, if any, along with a host of other clauses, including: a pledge of future cooperation, nondisparagement of the company, confidentiality of company information, noncompetition with the company, and most critically, a release from any present or future claims against the company.

enablement A requirement of patentability that a patent document enable any person skilled in the art to which it pertains to make and use the invention.

enjoin A legal process to prohibit certain conduct.

equity Ownership interest in a business entity.

EU Data Protection Directive 95/46/EC The present standard for data processing applicable to all transactions involving an EU citizen, business or country.

exclusion order An order that bars the importation into the United States of articles that infringe a valid and enforceable U.S. patent (or U.S. copyright or registered trademark).

exemption Carve-outs from the '33 Act registration requirements.

exhaustion doctrine The term used outside the United States to refer to the first sale doctrine.

experimental development Research is translated into practical application and tested for technical limits and commercial potential.

Fair Credit Reporting Act (FCRA) An act, passed in 1970, to protect consumers and their personal financial information by requiring that consumer reporting agencies follow strict accuracy and disclosure procedures.

Fair Information Practice Principles The FTC's recommendations for businesses on what it considers fair use of consumer information.

fair use A provision in the copyright law that permits unauthorized copying when the use is "fair," as determined by a flexible four-factor test.

Family Educational Rights and Privacy Act Governs access to and disclosure of students' educational records. Schools may not release student data or PII other than directory information to third parties without written consent

fanciful mark The word describing a mark that is coined or created and that at the time of creation would not be found in a dictionary.

Federal Circuit The federal court that hears appeals originating both from applications rejected by the USPTO as well as from district court patent decisions throughout the country.

Federal Rules of Civil Procedure (FRCP) Rules which govern the process by which federal civil litigation is conducted.

Federal Trade Commission Act Establishing the Federal Trade Commission whose mandate is as a consumer protection agency, currently the de facto regulator of consumer data privacy in the U.S. concerning deceptions or violations of written privacy policies.

Federal Trademark Dilution Act of 1995 (FTDA) A federal law that provides a right of action for trademark dilution even in the absence of confusion.

fiduciary duty Duty owed by directors and officers to carry out the best interests of the corporation.

First Amendment A constitutional protection of speech.

first-to-file A system by which patents are granted to the first inventor to file a patent application.

first-to-invent A system by which patents are granted to the first inventor to invent an invention.

first sale doctrine An exception to the exclusive rights of a patent or copyright owner, by which the owner of a particular copy of a copyrighted work or patented invention may resell or otherwise dispose of that copy or invention without the permission of the copyright or patent owner.

forfeiture agreement Non-salary compensation (such as bonuses, stock, stock options, and so forth) paid out during a specified period that will be forfeited upon an employee's departure to any company in the same industry.

forum state The state where the court is located.

forum-selection clause   A clause included in a contract or terms of service in which the parties agree that if a dispute arises between the parties, that dispute will be resolved in a particular agreed-upon forum.

Fourth Amendment   A constitutional protection against unreasonable searches and seizures by the government.

framing   Content from a website presented as integrated within the context of another website, violating trademark.

free and open source software agreement (FOSS)   A contract for software rights characterized by more permissive agreements as to ownership and control.

Freedom of Information Act (FOIA)   A federal law under which the public may obtain government documents from federal agencies upon request.

Galapagos syndrome   A phenomenon where goods and services evolve in isolation from world markets and this limits diffusion beyond the original market.

generic   The word used to describe a type of product or service that can never be registered as a trademark.

genericide   Condition of a mark that becomes commonly used to denote a product or service rather than a particular manufacturer or provider of that product or service, causing loss of trademark rights.

grace period   Once a company discloses an invention, it has a one-year grace period to file a patent application or it will lose the right to patent due to lack of novelty.

Gramm-Leach-Bliley Act   Regulates the sharing of personal information by financial services providers.

hacking   Unauthorized entry or use of computer or computer network.

Health Insurance Portability and Accountability Act   Regulates the use and sharing of data provided to and generated by healthcare providers.

H1-B visa   Temporary work permits for high-skilled workers in specialty occupations.

in camera   Out of view of the public.

indemnification clauses   Promises by one party to reimburse another party for liability costs.

independent contractor agreement   An agreement between employer and worker declaring that both parties understand the relationship to be that of independent contractor.

inequitable conduct   Conduct before the USPTO that falls below the standard, such as intentionally failing to disclose relevant prior art to the examiner during prosecution.

inevitable disclosure   A doctrine under which a court may enjoin a departing employee from accepting employment at a competing enterprise if there is a high probability that the employee would inevitably use or disclose the former employer's trade secrets to the benefit of the new employer.

inherently distinctive   The quality of mark that is suggestive, arbitrary, or fanciful and therefore can be registered without the need to show secondary meaning.

initial interest confusion   A "bait and switch" tactic that permits a competitor to lure consumers at an early phase of the decision-making process.

initial public offering   Seeking investment by selling equity on publicly traded markets such as the NYSE.

injunction   An order by a court requiring a party to refrain from certain conduct.

injunction, permanent   An order of a court prohibiting a party from engaging in some action, after a final judgment.

injunction, preliminary   An order of a court prohibiting a party from engaging in some action, prior to a final judgment.

in-license   To receive authorization to utilize intellectual property.

in-line linking   Material from one website appearing within the context of another website.

innovation   A technological, creative breakthrough from conventional procedures or thought, that go beyond marginal improvements in existing products and services that advance the state of the art.

innovators' dilemma   An impediment to innovation when incentives to switch appear to be too low in relation to the assumed risk of a new direction.

intellectual property (IP)   A "negative right" that allows the owner to prevent others from doing something. Intangible work that's given legal protection.

Intellectual Property Clause   The provision within the U.S. Constitution that provides the basis for federal patent and copyright laws.

interlocking directorates Prohibited by the Clayton Act, this is the practice of having the same individuals act as officers/directors in competing corporations.

Internet of things Every object with a connection and sensor capable of transmitting data.

Internet Tax Freedom Act Federal law that bans direct taxation of Internet access by state and local government.

international paradox A phenomenon where diffusion in low-income areas is not occurring and is limited to the extent that revenue does not cover expenses in the least affluent areas.

intrusion upon seclusion Covering claims for intentionally intruding, physically or otherwise, upon the solitude of another or his privacy affairs or concerns, in ways that average persons objectively would find highly offensive and unreasonable.

invention Ingenious ideas that offer a uniquely better solution to a problem; a practical implementation of an idea in the form of a new composition, matter, device, or process that extends the boundaries of knowledge, experience, and culture, that results in something new.

invention assignment agreement (IAA) An agreement to capture and assign to the company all inventions of the employee. The employee agrees to surrender all ownership rights in the invention and assign them to the company (the assignee) who then owns the invention regardless of whether the employee still works there.

issue To grant (a patent).

joint venture agreement A commercial collaboration in which two or more businesses share or integrate some of their resources for a limited purpose while staying independent.

jurisdiction The authority of a court or arbitration panel to hear a case and resolve a dispute.

keyed An advertisement linked to a search term because the search engine has been paid to include it in a pay-per-click advertising agreement.

know-how Information that is not described within a patent and that may instead be kept as a trade secret and separately licensed.

Lanham Act The principal federal trademark law.

license To authorize or allow.

likelihood of confusion The touchstone of a trademark infringement action; exists when consumers are likely to be unsure of the origin, sponsorship, or approval of the defendant's product or services.

literal infringement Where the accused device or process includes every limitation (part or element) of a patent claim.

limitation A part or element of a patent claim.

limited liability company Multiple-person business entity that gives more flexibility than other entities and provides liability protection for its principals.

limited liability partnership Multiple-person business entity that provides the benefits of partnership taxation with more liability protection for the partners.

long-arm statute A law that allows a state to exercise jurisdiction over an out-of-state party.

maintenance fees Periodic fees paid to the USPTO to maintain a patent in force.

malware Short-hand term for malicious software which is used to gain access to information stored on a computer or computer network.

Markman hearings Claim construction proceedings associated with patent disputes.

mediation A form of ADR in which a neutral third party, the mediator, listens to each party separately, and then presents the parties with a resolution that they are free to accept or reject. If the parties reject the resolution, they may still pursue their claim in court.

memorandum of understanding Letter of intent, not as formal as a contract, setting forth the parties' expectations.

metatags Invisible text embedded within websites that can be read by search engines.

minimum contacts test Used to determine what contacts with a forum state can be used to determine jurisdiction.

misappropriation The acquisition of a trade secret by someone who knows or has reason to know that the trade secret was acquired by improper means or disclosure; or the use of a trade secret of another without express or implied consent.

misappropriation of a person's name or likeness causing injury to reputation Covering claims by living persons that their name or likeness that is appropriated by another for commercial, non-newsworthy purposes, without the person's permission.

natural rights The natural rights justification of intellectual property emphasizes a person's inherent connection with the fruits of that person's creative labor and views it as unfair to allow others to copy the creator's works without compensation.

negligent hiring Legal claim made by an injured party against an employer alleging the employer knew or should have known about the independent contractor's background which, if known, indicates a dangerous or untrustworthy character.

negligent supervision Failure to reasonably supervise.

nepotism The hiring of relatives.

netcrime Use of the Internet for criminal purposes.

net neutrality Principle that all movement and content on the Internet should be treated similarly by service providers.

nexus Legal requirement that states justify sales tax based on a connection between the vendor and the taxing state.

No Electronic Theft (NET) Act A federal law that authorizes criminal penalties for willful copyright infringement.

noncompete agreement A contract between employee and employer to prevent employees, upon switching jobs, from using what they have learned to the advantage of a competitor.

nondisclosure agreement (NDA) A contract that requires a party not to disclose certain specified information that a business considers important to its competitive advantage.

nonobvious A requirement that extends the novelty requirement to bar inventions only slightly different from the prior art.

nonrival A quality of the ideas underlying IP that allows multiple individuals to use the IP at the same time without diminishing the ability of others to use those ideas.

nondisclosure agreement (NDA) An agreement used by employers to retain control over the disclosure of any proprietary or sensitive business information that

employees use, learn about, or even help develop during the employment term.

nonsolicitation clause A provision in an agreement (such as an employment agreement) that prohibits a departing employee from attempting to lure away the employee's former colleagues.

notice and takedown Proposed legislation that would require third parties to expeditiously remove (take down) alleged trade secrets from the Internet even without a court order upon notification by the trade secret owner.

novel A requirement of patentability that an invention be new.

officer Individual appointed by the board of directors to manage day-to-day operations of the business.

offshoring The process of locating some function or division of a business in a different country.

online dispute resolution (ODR) A dispute resolution approach including reaching resolution by mediation, arbitration, or neutral evaluation, but which uses Internet technology that may enable communication between the parties and resolution professionals.

organic results Unpaid or "natural" Internet search results.

orphan works Works still under copyright for which the copyright owner cannot be easily identified or located.

out-license To permit others to use intellectual property.

outsourcing The practice of transferring work to a third-party subcontractor.

patent A government-granted, temporary *right to exclude*, awarded in return for an individual's public disclosure of a new and useful invention.

patents, anticipated invention is considered not sufficiently new or novel.

Patent Act of 1952 The principal federal patent law.

patent examiner An employee of the USPTO that ensures that the invention described in a patent application meets the statutorily defined standards of patentability.

patents, hold-up A situation in which a single patent owner prevents third party use of product even though other relevant rights owners have given authorization.

patent landmine   A metaphor used to describe the situation where a businessperson inadvertently infringes the patent of another.

patent pool   An arrangement in which owners of related patents bundle their rights so as to provide "one stop shopping" for those who wish to make or sell a product or service covered by those patents.

patent thicket   Overlapping patent rights that businesses must negotiate in order to conduct business.

patent troll   A pejorative term used to refer to an entity that asserts patents against others without itself practicing the inventions claimed in the patents.

partnership   Multiple-person business entity which uses flow-through taxation and offers limited partners limited liability while holding general partners jointly and severally liable for liabilities of the partnership.

pay secrecy   Rules prohibiting discussion of pay, salaries, or other forms of compensation.

pay-per-click advertising   A tactic in which businesses pay search engines to achieve more prominent placement on certain sections of the search results page.

personal jurisdiction   Authority of a court over a particular individual; a state court has personal jurisdiction over people who are present within the state, live in the state, or have consented to the exercise of the state's jurisdiction over them.

personally identifiable information (PII)   Data that can identify individuals.

pharming   Malicious redirection of Internet traffic from one website to another.

phishing   Form of spoofing to obtain banking or personal information from a victim.

piracy   The act of copying a work with little or no pretense that the copying is lawful.

plant patents   A type of patent that protects new and distinct plant varieties that can be asexually reproduced.

preferred stock   Equity interest that entitles the holder to payments based on profitability and provides for preference rights over common stockholders in recovering their investments in the case of liquidation.

pretexting   Obtaining personal information from a victim through texting impersonation.

price discrimination   Anticompetitive practice of price determination which leads to a monopoly.

prima facie   An initial showing made by one litigant that shifts the burden of moving forward to the other litigant.

principal   Generic term for individual with ownership in a business entity.

prior art   Prior patents, publications, or uses that could negate novelty.

prior-use defense   A provision in the America Invents Act that provides a defense from liability for those who commercially use an invention more than one year before the earlier of the patent application date or the public disclosure date.

private placement   Registration exemption that requires investors to meet certain net worth and income criteria in order to invest.

product design   The design or configuration of the product itself, as distinct from its packaging.

product launch   Actual technology is completed; the model is ready enough for roll-out, with associated manufacturing, marketing, and distribution.

product packaging   The container or packaging within which a product is sold.

proprietary software   Software that is completely owned and whose rights are therefore controlled by the publisher.

public domain   The condition of a creation no longer under patent or copyright and that may thus be used freely by anyone without restriction.

public disclosure of private facts causing injury to reputation   Covering claims that the public disclosure of highly personal facts or information about a person results in injury to reputation.

publicly placing another in false light   Covering claims that involve falsely connecting a person to an immoral, illegal or embarrassing situation resulting in injury to one's reputation.

prosecute   To apply for a patent.

protected activity   Discussion of wages or other terms and conditions of employment with nonemployees.

quash   To declare void.

readily ascertainable   Information is readily ascertainable if it is available in trade journals, reference books, or published materials, or if it can be duplicated quickly and inexpensively or reverse engineered.

Recording Industry Association of America (RIAA) An association of record labels that opposes the unauthorized sharing of its members' music.

redact   To block out or omit a portion of text so that it is not visible.

Regulation D   Section of the '33 Act that provides registration exemptions for relatively small offerings.

remand   To send back a case (to a lower court).

remittitur   Reduction by a judge of an excessive jury award.

research and development   Creative work undertaken on a systematic basis to increase knowledge and devise new applications.

respondeat superior   A legal theory whereby employers are liable for the negligence of employees operating within the scope of their employment.

Reporter's Shield Law   A law stating that a "publisher, editor, reporter . . . shall not be adjudged in contempt . . . for refusing to disclose the sources of any information procured while so connected or employed for publication in a newspaper, magazine or other periodical publication."

reverse engineering   When one starts with a known product and works backward to determine the process which aided in its development or manufacture.

rule of reason test   An evaluation used to determine the validity of the terms of a noncompete agreement. Factors include whether the restraint is designed to protect a legitimate interest of the employer, and whether the restraint is reasonable as to time, place, and scope.

right of first refusal   Restriction on transferring stock that requires the seller to offer the stock to existing shareholders first.

right of publicity   Common law of individuals to control their name, image and likeness, and therefore a corresponding right to limit the public use of their name, likeness, and/or identity for commercial purposes.

royalties   Money paid for the right to use intellectual property.

Safe harbor provision   Part of the SCA that states if a service provider relies in good faith on a court order the service provider has a complete defense to any action brought against it under the SCA.

sales tax   Tax levied by state and local governments on the sale of certain products or services.

shareholders agreement   Agreement among the principals of a corporation with respect to ownership, fundraising, and control.

search engine optimization   Techniques used by website owners to try to ensure that their website appears at the top of Internet search results.

seed round   Preliminary fundraising stage for capitalizing a business venture.

secondary considerations   Objective indicia of nonobviousness, such as the commercial success of an invention.

secondary liability   Liability imposed on third parties who encourage direct infringement or who have an ability to control the primary infringer's activities.

service marks   Marks used to distinguish services rather than products.

Sherman Act   Federal law which is the centerpiece of antitrust regulation.

shop rights   A right permitting employers to claim merely a nonexclusive license with limited rights to use the work, all without ultimate ownership rights.

software licensing agreement (SLA)   Also known as end user license agreements, courts construe these non-negotiated documents as agreements and therefore are governed by contract law)

sole proprietor   Single-person form of business entity in which the principal/proprietor is the alter-ego of the business.

Sonny Bono Copyright Term Extension Act (CTEA) A 1998 law that extended the copyright term by 20 years.

sound recording copyright (music)   The copyright covering the recorded performance of a musical composition (as distinct from the composition itself).

spam Unsolicited bulk e-mail.

spear phishing Invasive form of phishing which targets a specific individual or organization.

specially commissioned work Work undertaken by an independent contractor under a written agreement between the parties stating that the work commissioned is a work for hire.

specification The portion of the patent that describes the invention and the manner and process of making and using it.

spoofing Criminal concealment or impersonation of an e-mail sender.

standard technical measures Technological measures used by copyright owners to identify copyrighted works and protect them from infringement.

statute of limitations A statutory provision providing that suits cannot be brought or damages cannot be recovered after a specified period of time.

statutory damages Damages provided in the copyright act of $750 to not more than $30,000 per infringed work.

Stored Communications Act (SCA) An act prohibiting "intentionally access[ing] without authorization a facility through which an electronic communication service is provided . . . and thereby obtain[ing] . . . access to a wire or electronic communication while it is in electronic storage in such system."

subpoena An order to appear or to produce documents.

subpoena duces tecum A request for the production of documents, materials, or other tangible things served by a party during discovery on other parties or non-parties.

subject matter jurisdiction A court's power to hear certain types of legal claims.

suggestive The word for a mark that hints at the qualities of a product, but does not describe it directly.

tarnishment Use of a famous mark that harms its reputation.

technology transfer/material transfer agreement The process by which a business transfers to another business assets, including facilities, technology, know-how or expertise, in order to commercialize or improve a product or process.

Telecommunications Act Law requiring telecom companies to protect the PII that they receive or obtain in their provision of services. Known as CPNI (customer proprietary network information), telecoms have a duty to protect the confidentiality of this customer data, as well the CPNI of their customers' contacts, and may not use this CPNI for any marketing purposes.

temporary restraining order (TRO) A court order that enjoins certain activities or disclosures without providing the other party a chance to be heard.

temporary workers Contingent workers who typically have specialty credentials and are not employed by the company, but rather by a staffing agency.

third party doctrine Information voluntarily handed over to a third party may not be claimed as privacy, and this information lawfully held by third parties is obtainable with merely a subpoena (rather than the stricter requirements for securing a search warrant).

throttling Practice by broadband providers of slowing down a consumer's Internet speed once they exceeded a certain amount of data.

Title VII of the Civil Rights Act An act prohibiting the use of race, gender, religion, national origin, or color in any employment decision.

top-level domain (TLD) The portion of the domain name furthest to the right (e.g., ".com").

tortious interference with contract rights Tort-based theory providing a cause of action against a defendant for intentionally damaging the plaintiff's contractual relationship with another, for which enhanced damages are available if successfully proven.

trade dress A product's design, packaging, or overall look and feel.

trade secret Information that derives independent economic value from not being generally known by competitors and that is the subject of efforts that are reasonable under the circumstances to maintain its secrecy.

trademark, abandonment Condition of a mark when the owner stops using the mark and does not intend to resume using it.

trademark, arbitrary The word describing a mark used in a way that is unrelated to the product or service represented.

trademark, blurring Use of a famous mark that impairs its distinctiveness.

trademark, certification marks Marks used to certify the quality of third party products or services.

trademark, descriptive The word used to describe the mark for a product or its qualities but is not the generic term for it.

trademark, dilution An extension of the ordinary trademark infringement standard to cases where there is no likelihood of confusion; includes blurring and tarnishment.

trademarks Any word, name, symbol, or device used to distinguish the goods or services of one company from those of another.

translational research Research is translated into practical application and tested for technical limits and commercial potential.

Trojan horse Malware that appears harmless but hides a malicious function.

tying Requiring the buyer to purchase a second product in conjunction with the first product chosen by the buyer.

typosquatting The speculative purchase of an Internet domain name intentionally incorporating a frequently made misspelling ("typo") of a trademark.

United States International Trade Commission (USITC) An administrative agency based in Washington, D.C., that has the authority to issue exclusion orders that bar the importation into the United States of articles that infringe a valid and enforceable U.S. patent (or U.S. copyright or registered trademark).

United States Patent & Trademark Office (USPTO) A government agency located just outside of Washington, D.C., that registers federal trademarks.

Uniform Trade Secrets Act (UTSA) One of more than 300 uniform laws that have been developed by a nonprofit organization known as the Uniform Law Commission.

Unmasking statute A law addressing the identity of persons communicating over the Internet. Specifically, a procedure must be followed when a person files a subpoena seeking to learn the identity of an anonymous Internet speaker.

unpaid internships An arrangement under which individuals work for a company or organization without receiving pay.

user-generated content (UGC) Various types of content created by end-users rather than by the website operator.

utility A requirement of patentability that an invention be useful.

utility patent The most common type of patent; ordinarily referred to simply as a "patent."

utilitarian The utilitarian justification of intellectual property views copyright primarily as a means to promote overall public welfare through the stimulation and dissemination of creative works.

venture capital Money invested in start ups that have no defined business model but have promise.

vesting Minimum time period required to earn ownership interests from a business entity.

vicarious liability A type of secondary liability where a defendant exercises control over the infringing product or service.

Video Privacy Protection Act Prohibits videotape service providers from knowingly disclosing PII concerning rental and sales records, including the videos' title or subject matter, to third parties.

virus A program designed to copy itself and spread from one computer to another without the user's knowledge.

visitor's confidentiality and nondisclosure agreement An agreement by which site visitors promise, in exchange for being admitted to the workplace, to not disclose any information about the company, its employees, or their impressions thereof for a defined period of time.

voting agreement Provision of a shareholders agreement used to ensure that the composition of the board is in accordance with founding shareholder wishes.

warez A website designed to aid in copyright infringement.

Web 2.0 A term used to refer to online activities involving large numbers of users that both produce and consume content.

webcasting The streaming of digital music over the Internet.

wireless spectrum management Managing radio frequency spectrum to maximize use and minimize interference.

Wiretap Act Requires law enforcement to apply for an order if they want to intercept electronic communications.

work made for hire A work prepared by an individual pursuant to their employer or an agreement.

writ of certiorari The Supreme Court may in its discretion review Federal Circuit decisions by granting a party's request for a writ of certiorari.

Table of Cases

Index

609